THE
LESSER EVIL

Victor Klemperer in Berlin, 1946. Photo: Abraham Pisarek

THE
LESSER EVIL

The Diaries of
VICTOR KLEMPERER
1945–1959

Abridged and translated
from the German edition by
MARTIN CHALMERS

Weidenfeld & Nicolson
LONDON

First published in Great Britain in 2003
By Weidenfeld & Nicolson

Originally published as *So sitze ich denn
zwischen allen Stühlen. Tagebücher 1945–1959*

© 1999 Aufbau-Verlag Gmbh, Berlin
Translation copyright © 2003 Martin Chalmers

A CIP catalogue record for this book is
available from the British Library.

ISBN 1 84212 743 8

Typeset by Selwood Systems, Midsomer Norton

Printed in Great Britain by Butler & Tanner Ltd,
Frome & London

Weidenfeld & Nicolson
The Orion Publishing Group Ltd
Orion House
5 Upper Saint Martin's Lane
London WC2H 9EA

CONTENTS

INTRODUCTION

But Job answered and said, 'Hear diligently my speech and let this
be your consolations. Suffer me that I may speak; and after that I
have spoken, mock on.'   BOOK OF JOB, 21: 1–3

Now here comes the next new age.
                                    ERICH KÄSTNER, 15 MAY 1945[1]

In the concluding paragraph of *To the Bitter End*, his diaries of the years 1942–
45, Victor Klemperer writes of the fairy-tale turnabout in his and his wife's
circumstances.[2] It is a phrase varied and repeated in subsequent weeks ('a fairy-
tale world'). The war is over, Hitler is dead and Victor and Eva Klemperer have
survived, their house in Dölzschen, outside Dresden, has been returned to them
and the overgrown garden is full of ripe fruit. Even if otherwise there is little
food, they are constantly afflicted by illnesses and ailments and the future is
quite uncertain, they have come home. The formerly persecuted Jew is now
besieged by neighbours and friends, acquaintances and strangers all wanting,
justifiably or not, attestations confirming their innocence during the Third
Reich. Victor Klemperer is in part repelled by the lack of dignity and mendacity
of some of these requests. At the same time he's flattered, he's somebody again –
'patriarch of Dölzschen' as he, not quite ironically, puts it – he has a provisional
authority while he waits for clarification of his own position, of the future of
the universities, of the Soviet Zone of Occupation – of Germany.

Even when, on 11 July 1945, he writes: 'Yesterday the definitive awakening
from the all-too-beautiful fairy tale', his spirits are only temporarily dampened.
(At one of the first cultural events organised in the ruined city, a performance
of Lessing's play *Nathan the Wise*, he encounters colleagues from the Technical
High School who behave as if nothing has happened since they last spoke ten
years previously, when Klemperer lost his professorship because he was Jewish.)
Summing up at the end of the year he writes: 'Still: this year! After all probably
the most fairy-tale-like of my life.' If anything he is more determined than ever
to catch up on the life and career of which he had been robbed by the twelve
years of Hitler's dictatorship – and before that, when he remembers his disappointments in not being appointed to a chair at a 'proper' university before
1933. He is 'despite nausea and shaky ground under my feet . . . brimful of plans
and a desire to work' and, he continues, 'No 20-year-old can be half as hungry

for life' (23 June 1945). Victor Klemperer is 63 when the war ends. He is an old man in a hurry.

To outward appearances his remaining years are a success. His subsequent ascent has even been described as 'comet-like':[3] restoration of his Romance Languages and Literatures chair at Dresden Technical High School (although he never teaches there again), Director of Adult Education in Dresden, an office-holder, committee member and much-in-demand lecturer for the Kulturbund[4] and other organisations in the Soviet Zone and then East Germany, a professorship at the University of Greifswald, which he soon gives up for more prestigious chairs at Halle and Berlin; *LTI*, his study of Nazi language, is acclaimed and reprinted several times, older books are revised and republished; he produces a stream of academic papers and reviews and articles for the press; he is elected to the Volkskammer, the representative chamber of the young German Democratic Republic, and to the Academy of Sciences; he receives many of the awards the new state has to offer, including the National Prize – Third Class, but that was fairly usual for academics in the humanities – and the Fatherland Order of Merit in Silver; he is honoured with a substantial Festschrift on his 75th birthday. His wife Eva, who has stood by him so loyally during the Nazi years, dies in 1951, but within a year he marries Hadwig Kirchner, one of his students, whom he loves deeply, and is loved in return. In GDR terms he becomes a wealthy man, can afford a 'bourgeois' lifestyle, has a car, a chauffeur, a housekeeper; he travels, usually with his young wife, to Austria, to Poland, Romania, Bulgaria, Italy, France, China, goes on a Black Sea cruise and to West Germany a number of times.

Yet, for Victor Klemperer, these achievements increasingly ring hollow. The life that the 1945–59 diaries reveal is one more of tragi-comedy than of triumph. Nevertheless, the first years after the war are still dominated by elation at a reversal of fortune experienced as little short of miraculous. Recording a trip to Falkenstein and Pirna in southern Saxony, accompanied by his wife Eva, to give lectures and visit friends, he observes: 'With my great success and the completely transformed situation I felt moments of the purest happiness. E. felt the same.' And he quotes her as saying: 'On Sunday morning at the Scherners I lay awake in bed and was happy.'

In counterpoint to that profound feeling of satisfaction, the phrases, the leitmotifs, which will recur in the diaries as a whole are also present. Klemperer repeatedly writes that he finds himself 'falling between stools' – a term which had already often been used in the diaries from 1919–32.[5] He also frequently describes himself as having chosen the lesser, the least evil: in deciding to join the Communist Party, in preferring East to West Germany, in putting up with the restrictions of cultural policy in the East and with its economic shortcomings. It is a phrase whose implicit tone shifts from an expression of necessity, to defiance, resignation, and barely disguised desperation.

Victor and Eva Klemperer joined the KPD, the German Communist Party, one of the parties then licensed in the Soviet Zone, in November 1945. At first sight the decision seems surprising.[6] In earlier life he had not been left-wing, being, rather, fairly consistently liberal and nationalist in his views, and often fiercely critical of more radical friends. Furthermore, during and after the return to Dresden the totalitarian manifestations of Soviet occupation had given rise to unpleasant associations. (A large picture of Stalin in the city centre reminds him of the Nazi leader Hermann Goering – 5 October 1945.) Not only that, within a few weeks of returning home he is beginning to make notes on the language of Communism under the heading LQI (Lingua quarti imperii – language of the Fourth Reich), just as he previously kept notes on Nazi language, which he called LTI (Lingua tertii imperii – Language of the Third Reich), paying attention to continuities and shared features.

So why did he (and Eva) join the Communist Party? On 26 July he had argued:

> I do not want to make a decision according to my – vacillating – emotions, not out of pure idealism, but coolly and calculatedly in accordance with what is best for *my* situation, *my* freedom, *the work I still have to do*, and yet *nevertheless serving my ideal task*, back the right horse. Which is the right horse? [. . .] Russia? USA? Democracy? Communism? [. . .] Unpolitical? Politically committed? Question upon question.

This sounds as if a degree of opportunism was involved. But, then, what apparently purely political decision in Germany in the early postwar months and years might not seem in part and in retrospect opportunist? Every such decision was simultaneously about how and where best to obtain food, to get or keep a roof over one's head, to find some way of earning a living. In a letter accompanying his application for KPD membership, included in the entry of 23 November 1945, Klemperer asserts: 'I believe that we can only get out of the present calamity and prevent its return through a most resolute left-wing movement.' He was by no means trying to ingratiate himself with the Communists. This, too, is a theme varied and repeated during preceding months. On 8 August he writes: 'I want to be on the furthest left wing of the KPD, I want to be for Russia.' Typically such statements are accompanied by doubts and criticisms of the effects of Soviet or Communist policies, sometimes even in the same paragraph, even the same sentence.

Victor Klemperer was never very convincing as a Marxist(–Leninist). When he deploys the names of Lenin and Stalin and refers to their lives or works it is usually to defend a traditional humanist academic or scholarly agenda (although he does, for example, record an adulatory speech to students on Stalin, when the latter dies.) However, because of what he had gone through under Nazism and because of his determination to have those professors, not least certain of his former colleagues, who had collaborated with or accommodated to Nazism, removed from their posts,[7] Klemperer had become something of a Bolshevik. Or, perhaps more accurately and given his lifelong work on the writers of the French Enlightenment, a belated Jacobin.[8]

Seen in this light, it was essentially the absence of a truly radical democratic party that led him to make a commitment to Communism. It should also be borne in mind that in November 1945, not least for someone as politically inexperienced as Klemperer, it was not evident that the Soviet Zone would end up as an oppressive Stalinist or post-Stalinist state sealed off from the West by a fortified internal German frontier. (Klemperer died before the erection of the Berlin Wall in August 1961.) It was not even evident that divisions between the powers which defeated Germany would produce two German states. Victor Klemperer wanted the most decisive break possible with the Nazi past and with those German traditions of thought which, as he saw it, had contributed to the acceptability and popularity of National Socialism, particularly in the 'Bildungs-bürgertum', the educated middle class to which he had belonged.[9] He was hardly the only intellectual at the time to believe in the possibility of a model Socialist alternative to Fascism and capitalism. A considerable number of distinguished German-speaking scholars and artists returned from exile to the Russian-occupied zone or went there from the western zones – even as many 'bourgeois' academics at educational institutions in the East were decamping to the West. It was a project which seemed to hold out some prospect of a realisation of those rational, Enlightenment ideals which Klemperer so much admired.

Many of these writers and scholars were to be disappointed and disillusioned by the shifting restrictions, the censorship, repression and party dictatorship of what, on 7 October 1949, became the German Democratic Republic. Some died before their growing ambivalence became public (the poet and playwright Bertolt Brecht), others suffered harassment and house arrest before being allowed to leave for the West (the poet Peter Huchel), some (the philosopher Ernst Bloch, the critic and literary scholar Hans Mayer) succeeded in maintaining their stature as intellectuals in the West – partly thanks to the revival of Marxist thought associated with the rise of the New Left. Still others (like Victor Klemperer's friend Alfred Kantorowicz, who fled to West Germany to avoid arrest) were marginal figures there, unable to make a new career for themselves.

Victor Klemperer's own disenchantment grew more acute in the course of the 1950s, but he was too old to think of making a new start, was in any case too suspicious of capitalist, Americanised West Germany with its ex-Nazi civil servants and politicians. If the Nazis had failed to force Eva and himself out of Germany and permanently dislodge them from the house they had built after Hitler came to power, then there was little likelihood that anyone else would. He had, in any case, become a big fish, albeit in a small pond, and it was hardly to be expected that he would give up the privileges to which he felt entitled after the persecution and privations suffered under the Third Reich. The diaries, however, reveal a keen awareness of the conditions of his position. As early as 28 August 1947 Klemperer is reminding himself:

> Always remember: 1) You are a war profiteer, you owe your successes solely to the emptiness of the Eastern Zone. 2) These are provisional successes, at no moment are you certain, today powerful, tomorrow impotent. 3) Vanitas vanitatum – one foot in the grave, when will the other follow, and what will survive, and what is the value of this survival?

In his résumé of the year 1949, Klemperer concludes: 'And while I should be indifferent to everything, I was nevertheless tormented by the defeats of the past year: the failure to get the National Prize, to get the seat in the Academy, to get the Berlin chair.' Professional setbacks come on top of the ambivalence – schizophrenia – of his judgement of politics, and if he was in fact to achieve the goals mentioned in the course of the next couple of years, it hardly felt like smooth progress. And in the entry for 16 December 1949, his dissatisfactions with politics merge with a feeling of isolation, even from his wife:

> We are so utterly isolated, the people of our world are dead. [. . .] And sometimes the most tormenting thought of all: What am I still to E., and how far does she share my thoughts? I am often so tired now, physically and mentally. I have a horror of the nothingness and nevertheless wish everything were over. I try to persuade myself to believe in the Soviet cause, and in my heart of hearts I don't believe in anything and everything appears to me equally trivial and equally false. The ghastly similarity to Nazi methods in propaganda [. . .], in the hullabaloo around Stalin's birthday cannot be denied.

Klemperer did indeed become increasingly estranged from his wife Eva. She was disheartened by the loss of her pictures and scores (in her youth she had ambitions both as painter and as musician), by the unpleasantness of the months in Griefswald, and was more and more tied to the house in Dölzschen by ill health. Victor meanwhile was rushing from one meeting to the next, commuting between Berlin, Halle and Dresden. His ambitions, his obsessive drive for recognition, could no longer be shared, when previously they had shared everything good and often bad. There is a telling, almost brusque, aside in an enthusiastic description of a May Day Rally in Halle (7 May 1949): 'Eva at the back in the disabled van – she was unable to see and hear anything.' As Victor Klemperer's absences became more frequent, owing to his academic and political commitments, so he becomes more easily irritated by conditions at home, even as he continues to be concerned about Eva:

> Ever more depressing conditions. I feel I am an intruder here. Eva lives her little woman life here [. . .] with Frau Richter [the housekeeper], the [builders], the tomcat, the flowers. I introduce disturbance, ill humour. I arrive exhausted, dejected, my desk is in a muddle ('tidied up') [. . .]. Then immediately there's an exchange of words, a sharp expression, offence taken, E.'s breathlessness accusing me. [. . .] I feel so bitter. And she feels like a prisoner up here.

When Eva Klemperer died of a heart attack (8 July 1951) her husband inevitably felt guilty. Yet within a year he and his 25-year-old student Hadwig Kirchner had fallen in love with one another, courted (in Klemperer's description, the affair is at once touching and at times farcical) and married (23 May 1952). He was very happy with Hadwig, yet this happiness was overshadowed both by what he felt was his 'betrayal' of Eva and because he fears he is robbing Hadwig of the rights of youth and of the chance to start a family.

Matters are made more complicated still by the fact that Hadwig is a devout, if left-wing Catholic with a much greater sense of distance from the East German state. Klemperer finds himself increasingly unable to answer her criticisms of Communism in action, and so domestic contentment is clouded not only by thoughts of his first wife but by an ever stronger, ultimately unambiguous revulsion towards the GDR regime. The claim of the lesser evil drops away – though Victor and Hadwig Klemperer both continue to dismiss West Germany as a possible alternative.

On 24 May 1950 he could still write: 'Perhaps more bitter than this defeat [failure to be awarded a Communist youth movement honour!] is my great divergence from the SED on all intellectual matters. But I cannot just move over to the West – it is even *more* repugnant to me. In the SED it is only scholarship, only the temporary hysteria, the 150%ers, that I loathe, but over there it is everything.'

By 8 March 1954 he concludes in resignation, 'in the very final analysis people like us are liberal'.[10] And by 19 January 1957, commenting on the contradiction between constitutional form and hard political reality in the GDR, he asks (and the questions are in part a mark of his political naivety):

> if 'the people' themselves really are the rulers, if the Volkskammer really is the supreme authority – what is the Party, what the Central Committee, what the Politburo, what Staliniculus Ulbricht?? And why the game with *parties*, when only *one* rules? I do not understand it, I am an old liberal, and my temporarily suppressed liberalism is showing ever more strongly through the layer of red make-up.

Visiting one of the remaining independent publishers, Klemperer notes that the former is afraid of an open door, in case their conversation may be overheard. 'We sat there over coffee, cakes, whipped cream, and the atmosphere was as if we were threatened by the Gestapo again' (2 August 1958). The final collapse of any kind of belief in Communism comes during a tour of China:

> It became clear to me, that Communism is equally suited to pulling primitive peoples out of the primeval mud and pushing civilised peoples back into the primeval mud. In the second case it sets to work more mendaciously and is not only stultifying, but debasing as well, in that in every way it trains people to be hypocrites. Thanks to my China trip and fully acknowledging the prodigious achievements here I have finally become an anti-Communist. *This* cannot have been Marx's ideal condition.

Klemperer's final years are clouded, too, by his failure to produce (after *LTI* in 1947) any major new book and by criticisms, often political in nature, of new editions of his older work and of shorter pieces he publishes. He had always felt looked down upon by his academic colleagues, the serious philologists of the discipline. In the GDR this sense of inferiority was compounded by his rivalry with the younger, brilliant but unstable scholar Werner Krauss. In his own field, as in politics, Klemperer began to be overcome by a mood of resignation. On seeing the register of his publications, which is to open his Festschrift, he comments: 'It begins with *Aus fremden Zungen* [From Foreign Tongues], 1906, 5 pfennigs a line. I began as a journalist, have been one all my life and have remained between stools' (17 October 1956).[11] And then even more bleakly, after the beginning of his final illness: 'I have lost all belief that I might have an effect. All belief in right or left. I live and die as a lonely literary journalist' (29 April 1959).

Perhaps what gave him the greatest pleasure, professionally, in his last years was his role as a teacher, even if he complained that it took up too much time, did not contribute to his writing, that he was merely tolerated as a harmless old man, even a clown. Nevertheless on 20 February 1952, still gripped by that state of schizophrenia which is so characteristic of his postwar diaries, he writes: 'All my lectures and seminars, in Berlin as in Halle, are a desperate struggle for the freedom of the intellect.' And he must have been a brilliant teacher, plain-speaking, knowledgeable, for all his self-doubt a breath of fresh air from another world. In a travel book on France published in East Germany in 1975, the writer Rolf Schneider devoted a chapter to the influence of Victor Klemperer, from which I shall quote:

If I reflect on where my particular curiosity about France comes from, I immediately find myself thinking about my encounter with a man called Victor Klemperer.

Is he still remembered? I don't know. I only know that I owe him a great deal, that he shaped me in ways which are curious and difficult to explain. They had to do with France, but not only with France. [. . .]

I myself was a student of German [in Halle], of that discipline, therefore, that had produced so many crypto-Fascists and so many bad writers. There came the day, on which I longed for more nourishing academic bread, I went, with many others, who were also not students of Romance languages, to that ground floor lecture theatre, where Professor Victor Klemperer lectured every week on the history of French literature.

The lecture theatre was usually packed. Punctually at quarter past the hour a small elderly gentleman entered and was greeted with lively knocking [a German student custom, desks are tapped at the beginning and end of lectures]. He really was unusually small. His height and features were a little reminiscent of the painter Pablo Picasso. He bowed, a little sideways, rather more with his right shoulder than the left, in acknowledgement of the student applause, smiled and began [. . .] to speak. His voice was very clear and very melodious [. . .].

He spoke in a way which I had not heard an academic teacher speak before. He spoke with considerable digressions, he spoke wittily, entertainingly, but nevertheless always stuck closely to the topic, had titles and dates in his head, some in French, some in German. Only for the exact bibliographical details of secondary literature did he occasionally need [his] matchbox label-sized scraps of paper. In his hands literature, French literature, the literature of the

Romance languages, world literature became a dense and gracefully entwined plant, unceasingly sending out new sprigs like an old ivy.

The longer-serving of his students sometimes made fun of his pronunciation in which there was more than a touch of Paris slang. [...]

Across his figure and his work there lies like a shadow the gentle danger of being forgotten. But anyone who has ever read one of his texts, or even experienced him in person, will find this danger absurd and the shadow barely perceptible.

I know, that I loved him very much.[12]

The picture drawn here may come almost as a surprise to the reader of the diaries, which do not always give a very flattering self-portrait of Klemperer. But then a diarist who was consistently uncritical and uncontradictory in his judgement of himself would not be much worth reading. At the very least, however, Schneider's generous characterisation should remind us that a diary, too, no matter how merciless and seemingly unmediated, is a document among other documents, and has no more claim to ultimate truth.

So, who was Victor Klemperer? Hans-Joachim Petsche has tried to sum up the impossibilities of this life, of Victor Klemperer's twentieth century:

A German nationalist, a liberal, a cosmopolitan, an anti-Bolshevik, an anti-Communist, a Jew, a Communist even?

He was probably first of all a German Jew whom Germans made into a Jew, who never again wanted to be among the losers and nevertheless found himself on the losing side. Is it possible to make oneself more of an unperson than Klemperer? Not a proper German, not a proper Jew, not a proper liberal, not a proper Communist. No representative fate, no typical hero. He was timid and vain, called himself egotistical and unfeeling, had neither the common touch nor was he sympathetic to youth, technologically uneducated and plagued by self-doubts in his own ability as a scholar. With what mischievous and wise good-humour he smiles from his photos, while those who knew him, said how light-hearted he was.[13]

Each opposition in that summation could be the start of a separate essay on Victor Klemperer, which would also be an essay on his times. Here I want to conclude with a few remarks on the shifts in his attitudes to his Jewishness.[14]

Victor Klemperer, son of a very reform-minded rabbi, in the sense of accommodation to German Protestant norms and rituals, had from an early age resisted being defined as Jewish. Like two of his three brothers, he married a gentile wife.[15] His conversion to Protestantism was a mark of adherence to enlightened secularism and a particularly Prussian notion of Germanness rather than a matter of belief. (Much later, to please his second wife, he even goes through with a secret Catholic church wedding, the preparations and event itself rich in comic detail. See diary entries for 20 April, 30 April, 15 May and 30 May 1957.)

Victor Klemperer stuck to his German identity (or it stuck to him) despite what had happened in Germany under the Third Reich and what he himself had experienced. Indeed, his commitment to Communism should also be seen as embodying his hope of working for a renewal of Germany within an untainted German tradition. On 2 January 1953 he notes his negative response to an article about him by his friend and colleague Rita Schober: 'Rita had sent me a eulogy intended for publication, in which there was rather too much talk about the son of the rabbi, Jewish suffering etc. I wrote to her most unequivocally: I found philo-Semitism just as unpleasant as anti-Semitism. I am a German and a Communist, nothing else.' In part this is the official Klemperer speaking, but it also reflects a deeply held view. This continued assertion of himself as German co-exists with the memories and fears of a Jew who narrowly escaped death, which finds expression in a very comprehensible overestimation of Nazism as a political force, whether among the population of East Germany or in West Germany. When he is with other Jews, he records the conversation as always returning to the fate of those who did not return from deportation or who were already murdered in Germany. He remains, however, hostile to Zionism, continuing to equate Nazism and Zionism as racist. The evidence of anti-Semitism in the Eastern bloc, notably when the so-called 'Doctors' Plot' initiates an anti-Jewish campaign in the Soviet Union and the satellite states shortly before Stalin's death, renders him incoherent.[16]

And yet, whether it's old age, regret at missed opportunities, disenchantment with Communism and the GDR – and the interest and influence of his young wife should not be underestimated – Klemperer becomes less intransigent. He expresses a desire to visit Israel to see old friends, he writes sympathetically about the Jewish faith of Albert Konrad, one of his fellow forced labourers during the war. On his sickbed during his final illness Klemperer is several times visited by his nephew Peter (son of his brother Berthold and of Anny Klemperer) and his wife Inge, who is working on a historical dissertation about Jews at the medical faculty of Berlin University. It is a topic with close family associations: Victor's other two brothers, Georg and Felix, had been distinguished doctors, medical researchers and teachers. She tells Victor that she is under pressure to play down the Jewish theme in her work. 'Characteristic of the GDR', he notes. 'And characteristic of me: I would very much like to see the Jewish theme and have it dedicated to *me*.'

That was Victor Klemperer's view more or less on his deathbed. (He did not get the quick end he longed for, the last diary entry is 29 October 1959; he did not die until 11 February the following year.) More typical of the ambivalences that marked Klemperer's life is what he records of an incident during a visit to Prague (where as a young man he had often given lectures to Jewish associations) with Hadwig Klemperer. The couple had made a spring trip to a winter sports resort in Slovakia, Hadwig had skied, he had read. On the journey out they had arranged with a Jewish guide to see the Jewish sights on the return leg. 'I did not tell the guide, at least not for the time being, that I am very closely connected to Prague [he means through his parents and their extended families]; he will in any case have got that from my name in the visitors' book.' Written, I think, not without a touch of pride.

In any case, they stop over in Prague on the way home to Dresden:

> The next morning, Sunday, 7th April, to the Old Synagogue. We found it, but
> not the entrance. A young man, fabulous oriental eyes under the round kippa,
> observed us for a while. Then to me: Are you a Jew. No, but we were looking
> for the entrance. He showed, asked in jargon, naively importunate. Whether
> H. my daughter? No, my wife. 'Such a young woman, such a beautiful young
> woman!' He shook her hand. What beautiful warm hands! I did not know,
> whether to be outraged, or whether I should accept his behaviour as oriental
> courtesy. H. laughed, very amused. Meanwhile the tourist guide came out of
> the synagogue, recognised us immediately – [...] took charge of us, left the
> bocher standing, who looked at us in surprise [diary entry, 10 April 1957].

It is predictable that Klemperer, given what has been said and quoted above,
would deny being Jewish. That is not simply a matter of politics, it also reflects
the sense of superiority of the German Jew over the Eastern ('oriental') Jew,
speaking in 'jargon', that is to say, Yiddish, which Klemperer no doubt regarded
as no more than a debased form of German. (It hardly needs saying that
only two generations back Klemperer's family, too, were 'Eastern' Jews.) But in
introducing the Yiddish word 'bocher' – fellow – he even reinforces that superiority. The 'bocher' is not going to put anything over on him. He, Klemperer,
even understands the 'jargon'.

A reflection on language, one linking language and Jewishness, is perhaps an
appropriate point at which to conclude these notes on the complexities and
contradictions of Victor Klemperer. Acute contradictions had been a part of
Klemperer's whole life, but they became even more intense and difficult in his
final years in East Germany. As Hans-Joachim Petsche remarked, his was not, in
many ways, 'a representative fate',[17] but his life was remarkable nonetheless, for
all that so much of it was lived in the scholar's study, in the seminar room,
behind the lectern. It's a life, too, which would have remained in obscurity but
for the twelve years of the Nazi Reich which dragged him out of the study,
forcing him to turn his academic skills and his literary talents (the despised
fluency of his journalism) to the observation and analysis of the society around
him, which proved so unexpectedly capable of murder on a mass scale. Klemperer's postwar diaries show him still trying to come to terms with that overwhelming fact and trying to catch up on the life and work of which he had
been deprived; still, indeed, trying to make that name in the world which, as
the youngest son of the family, he owed it to his father to achieve. He sometimes
imagines his father looking down on him from above, and maybe there is a
kind of progress in the fact that he no longer fears being overshadowed by his
eldest brother Georg, the fiercely critical dominant family figure of Victor
Klemperer's early years.

A note on the translation

The diaries Victor Klemperer kept from 1945 to 1959 were very detailed. They
were considerably longer than those for the period 1933–45 which, of course,

were kept up under often very adverse conditions. The German editor, Walter Nowojski, made extensive cuts for the German published edition of 1999, on which the present English-language version is based. However, that still produced a two-volume German text of a rather greater length than that for the Nazi years. The English publisher felt, rightly I think, that there was too much material here, on Victor Klemperer's activities in the Communist Party, in Communist Party cultural organisations, as an academic – an avalanche of names, meetings and abbreviations, indeed – to be of interest to the general reader. The decision was taken, therefore, to prepare a one-volume English edition, which, I hope, nevertheless faithfully represents Victor Klemperer's view of his life in post-war East Germany, and of his fears and dilemmas, achievements and disappointments.

Finally, readers may notice that whereas in the earlier volumes the educational institution at which Klemperer taught until 1935, and to which he was re-appointed in 1945, is referred to as Dresden Technical University, here I have used the more literal Dresden Technical High School. Technical University is in fact the standard English translation of the German 'Technische Hochschule'. However, when I was translating the earlier diaries I did not realise that one theme, if a minor one, of the early part of the present diaries would be a debate on the advantages of changing the title 'Dresden Technische Hochschule' to 'Universität'.

Martin Chalmers
London
April 2003

1945

17th June, Sunday. Dölzschen
Time
During every programme, dozens of times a day, Radio Berlin announces the time, and that is a blessing. But when Berlin says 8 p.m., it's 7 p.m. here and 9 p.m. in Bremen: the Russians have Moscow Time in Berlin, Summer Time in Dresden, the English in their section Central European Time.

When I'm on my way somewhere, I'm forever asking: what's the time? Usual answer: I don't have a watch any more either. Once: I'm not going to wear it, am I?

[...]

Wolf relates how Russian soldiers conversed with him as a Communist and liberated prisoner in a really friendly way, but then in just as friendly a way gripped his wrist: Comrade – watch? But he didn't have one any more.

Transport
The isolation of the individual and the group, the lack of means of transport and communication is in literally every respect, physical and mental, the basic problem, which draws all other afflictions in its train. [...] Mail – with Hitler's head blacked out on the stamps! – only within the area of greater Dresden, but even here a letter from Neumark[1] to me, from Reickerstr. to the Kirschberg, took three days, and Wolf thought that was quick ... It is impossible to telephone local government departments because they don't give out their numbers ... Telegraphy appears to be still completely absent ... Trams, as in Munich, only from the outlying districts to the edge of the city [...] The right hand does not know what the left hand is doing, the right middle finger does not know what the left ring finger is doing, etc. etc., in every field. There is now a state of Dresden, a state of Dölzschen [...] etc., each mayor rules, administers, organises, helps, confiscates etc. (so far as the Russians permit, who issue summary orders

and don't bother about details) on his own initiative, without contact with other mayors or knowledge of their instructions.

In many respects I am no less isolated here than I was in Unterbernbach,[2] and here it is more upsetting for me than there. [...] I know nothing at all of many of our friends and acquaintances – there is no possibility whatsoever of making contact or inquiries, only by word of mouth, by chance does something turn up here and there, is a little ray of light cast here and there. [...]

My initial general and political impression.

Almost complete chaos, over which a very thin varnish of comfort is spread by news sheet and wireless. But perhaps that judgement is presumptuous and unjust. To Katz[3] in Borsbergstr., to Neumark in Reickerstr. I walked endlessly along completely destroyed, completely desolate streets, at Plauen Station[4] I saw the refugees with their belongings crouching just as wretchedly as a hundred times on the way here, but I also see really cheerful and calm people of every age, they have almost enough to eat, they do not fear bombs any more, and the looting etc. of the Russians has virtually ceased. The overriding impression is always that of the absolute precariousness and of the absolute isolation of every cell. [...]

A very clever general appeal by the KPD [Communist Party of Germany] has been published in the *Berliner Volkszeitung*, the first newspaper almost worthy of the name, it talks of a democratic bloc of the anti-Fascist parties and bases itself on 'Order no. 2' of the Russian High Command, which permits elections – but what will be the extent of this freedom and what decisions will an elected body be allowed to take?? Non-Socialist parties as far as the [Catholic] Zentrum are supposed to be included in this bloc. Explanatory articles repeatedly and vociferously deny that the aim is a Communist Party dictatorship, pure Bolshevism in Germany. But there is also the repeated warning, that first of all there will have to be a general clean-up, and that the liberation was thanks to Russia, and that the Russians' natural trustee and liaison officer is the KPD. And so everything is uncertain. On the wireless, too, we hear only Russian news or news with a Russian bias [...]. In addition there are constantly appeals and incitements to root out the Nazis, reports about their atrocities, about the capture of hidden Nazi bosses, about interrogations. All of that is undoubtedly right, not exaggerated and necessary – but what will be the long-term effect? And what – this is most on my mind – will be the effect on the future position of the Jews in Germany? Very soon people will be saying: they're jumping the queue, they're taking their revenge, they're the winners: Hitler and Goebbels were right.

19th June, Tuesday. Dölzschen

We got here on Sunday the 10th, the first night we spent with Kalau, a good man, by the second night we were already in *our* house, a still indescribable feeling, still like a waking dream, since then we've been living in a fairy-tale world, a comical, imaginary and yet very real but somewhat uncertain world, a comical, sometimes affecting, sometimes almost contemptible paradise, and still I haven't managed to get any peace to work, I'm making hardly any progress with my diary, the skimpy headings of our days on the road have not yet been filled out, the great wealth of this week has not been set down, I have not yet attended to the fate of my mss in Pirna[5] [...] every errand is a major enterprise taking up a whole day [...]: I am too tired to do anything at all, the day goes by with eating and eating again, with dozing and sleeping, with the numerous visits I receive and make, with chatting, with plans and scepticism, with tiredness, waiting, drifting along and with tiredness again. By turns in a state of astonished bliss and of sceptical amazement I float above this complete fairy-tale reversal of our fortune, and with the ominous fear, it may all have come too late, my heart, my mind growing senile, even the rustiness of my knowledge – I can hardly string ten words together in French any more – may all play an annihilating trick on me. But all of this, hope, dread, scepticism, fear, is deadened by tiredness and a state of sluggish, animal-like well-being: constantly eating, constantly sleeping, from time to time listening to the wireless a little.

Still: on one of the first days here I went to see Neumark, then Katz and yesterday [...] to Melanchthonstr. to see Grohmann.[6]

We had often imagined what it would be like, should we ever really return here. For me it was actually a disagreeable feeling to have anything to do with the people here again. E., whose relationship to the house is different from mine (and whose constant delight from morning to night, whose virtual blossoming gives me the greatest pleasure in this whole business), E. said we would not take the least notice of anyone and live in seclusion in our garden. Instead all this time and from the very first moment we have been a triumphal hub and constantly oscillate between being moved and feeling contempt for mankind. Some are undoubtedly honest, others?? It started just as we had made our way up here a week ago yesterday afternoon. A young woman came running after us: We talked about you so often, in fact only yesterday afternoon! Neither of us knew her, Frau Dr König, wife of a doctor of medicine and dentist. We had to have coffee with her, we were overwhelmed with cigarettes and other attentions, she has meanwhile paid us a visit, has brought us jam and other provisions, we have also got to know her husband. She does not make a bad impression – but, but. The mayor was not to be found, she herself had recommended Kalau to us as a powerful man, the husband of the midwife in Pesterwitzstr. We came upon the man in the field he has rented, ploughing behind two horses. I called to him, that I had come from Dr König, he replied curtly, that he couldn't talk about official business now. But as soon as he heard my name, and what it was about, he not only became very courteous, but displayed a warmth, which has thus far proved to be lasting and genuine. The misunderstanding was cleared up: it is Kalau who allocates labour duty, i.e. navvying, to the [Nazi] Party members and he is inundated with objections and pleas. Everyone claims he was forced to be a pg [i.e. Parteigenosse = Party member]. Among those mustered for the first time that day was also Dr König, of which, naturally, I could have no idea and which, naturally, makes the great friendliness the family has demonstrated since then somewhat questionable.

Yet the man really did give me the impression of someone who was politically uninvolved, who only joined the Party in order to go on practising his profession [...]. (But the millions of Dr Königs – are they not the guilty ones after all??)

20th June, Wednesday

We were exhausted and starved: Kalau immediately said we were now his guests and took us to his home. A small, spotlessly clean and not at all poorly furnished apartment. His wife, with her qualifications as a nurse and midwife, a person of some education as well as perfect manners, moreover no Mistress Midwife, but instead slim and youthful, nice children. We got supper, were forced, really forced to sleep in the couple's bedroom. The next morning the fairy tale began, which still continues, if increasingly in an oppressive way – the inevitably re-awakening anti-Semitism! – and has come to a very awkward climax at this very moment: Kalau has sent us four men, including a former local mayor, to remove the air-raid shelter in the garden, and they must now of course do dishonourable labour for the vengeful Jew.

We went to Mayor Scholz, who, since the day before yesterday, is already out of the post – Dölzschen has been incorporated into an enlarged Dresden district and is being administered from Dresden–Plauen, where Scholz is now an official in the housing office. But during my first week here he was the ruler. He greeted us with a solemn address: the wrong done to us must be made good immediately and in whole, the house was now our property, we alone were free to make decisions concerning it. Berger[7] had fled from the Russians, we should inhabit his confiscated pieces of furniture until others had been procured for us, we should now, in our turn, feel no pity for the man, who had been a crook and had abused us. At the moment, a family, the Wolfs, were in the house, half-Jews, who had already been allocated other accommodation, and perhaps we could get on with them for a few days – but if we insisted on immediate vacation, then it would simply have to be vacated immediately. The decision on the fate of the shop installed by Berger in our music room was also entirely up to us. The local authority wanted to set up a co-operative store there. But naturally: if I insisted, the whole house would be vacated immediately [...]. I just as naturally gave permission for the shop premises to be used by the co-operative free of charge – it was to my benefit, because now my house gets a telephone, which is only permitted 'essential enterprises', to say nothing of the other advantages, to say nothing of the goodwill of the authorities. I have got on with the Wolfs, who will only move out in the course of this week – that was and is very much to my benefit, because we get free board from the Wolfs, they cook for us, keep the house tidy and provide us with many good things, so that we are almost a little afraid of their departure ... We were then taken up to the Begerburg,[8] the former Nazi headquarters, there to be fitted out with confiscated clothing. Very few items could be found for me, but it was touching, how everyone made such an effort to help and please us. We were virtually showered with cigarettes, we were slipped provisions and real coffee. This willingness to help, this desire to give, please, make good, continued and still continues, and much of it really does seem to come from the heart and out of a sense of justice. [...] At the Begerburg I was given a very decent waterproof summer coat, 'to cover your shame'. Meanwhile the moth holes in an otherwise very passable pair of trousers have been mended for me and a jacket is being made out of a frock-coat – [...] for my sore feet (the right one is very swollen) I have been given a pair of very soft, new patent-leather dance shoes as slippers, and by Forbrig, the teacher, a pair of calf-skin boots, which are a perfect fit. I am granted other favours. In accordance with Soviet regulations (very characteristic!) I, as a scholar, get a heavy worker's ration card (4 grades: heavy worker, worker, white-collar worker, non-worker, graduated from 1 lb down to 7 oz of bread, with corresponding amounts of meat and fat). E. has received the same card, because she shared hardships and dangers with me. Then, it is now extremely difficult to get hold of a typewriter [...]: I was given a permanent loan of an immaculate Continental portable from the confiscated property of a district judge.

Of course I am entirely surrounded by things which are borrowed, confiscated, which are not my own: everything, furniture, linen, crockery, every spoon, every glass belongs to Berger. The man must have been making black-market deals, he has nouveau riche furnishings – in quite good taste incidentally. Upholstered easy chairs with a smoking table in the hall, a sideboard of highly polished heavy wood, two couches, one of them a double bed, a good desk in what used to be my room, a (clumsy but genuine) oil painting, a billiard table, a big expensive wireless set, in addition a great deal of tasteful crockery. He came to see me, pleaded with me to let him have the things, he was now without home or work. But at the town hall and elsewhere, I have been told how B. feathered his nest, thanks to connections with the Nazis, how he cheated the populace, and further, what false rumours he spread about us, who were thought to be dead. He claimed to have been our protector, to have provided us with foodstuffs, to have procured a new mortgage for us. In truth, he did everything to get the house into his own hands [...], in truth I didn't even get one cherry from him, instead he made out unverifiable and false bills for the removal of rubble. I have no reason, moreover hardly any possibility, to treat him very considerately. I just don't want to appear the triumphant Jewish spirit of revenge. When he came to me, I told him: everything has been confiscated and I am, at my discretion, only permitted to hand over individual items to you. I shall do that, the rest I shall keep for the time being [...], a part will also serve as my security, since it is likely that I shall have claims to make against you. He departed in a very bitter mood, and I don't feel very happy about the business – but what should I do?

Now the condition of the house. On the whole it is intact. Up here very few houses were hit, and in ours only a very few window panes broken. On the other hand Russian looters badly damaged the door to our former little dining room next to the kitchen, which Berger used as a cellar, and in which they probably expected to find wine. Also a little piece of the chimney is missing, and pointing and the protective coat on house and fence naturally have to be renewed. But as already said: the house as a whole is intact [...]. The blemish of the built-in shop will have to be removed later. Also, and that will be at Berger's expense, there will have to be a flue pipe in the garage again, its ventilation was blocked by the steps Berger had built up to the terrace, i.e. up to the shop entrance. And apart from that the nasty air-raid shelter at the side window of the hall has got to be removed, it's got dry rot, a serious danger to the wooden house! [...] Today four men have been muddling around this shelter fairly listlessly and unsuccessfully. Nevertheless it is yet another sign of what efforts are being made on our behalf, that without further ado I am allocated navvies from labour duty.

The garden affected and affects me more deeply than the house itself. It has become a fertile jungle, what were tiny trees now have big trunks, crowding one another. Chief attraction of the whole place, its finest adornment and our ready exchange, as it were, are nine cherry trees, which are indescribably loaded with fruit. [...] we are all eating cherries almost night and day, our friends have been showered with paper bags and baskets full of cherries (the Königs, Michel, Kalau), and so far only one of the nine has been polished off. Then the big, broad yew [...]. Then the once dainty olive, now a broad powerful tree. The birches, maples, plum trees, chestnuts – everything that was a sapling is now a handsome tree [...]. Redcurrant and gooseberry bushes are thick with green and red fruit, big strawberries growing between them. E. walks around the garden all day, planning, improving, also eating fruit, is beginning to clear the paths, has replanted tobacco and tomato plants, is at last in her element again, also supervises in tolerable harmony the bunker navvies, to whom I do not show my face.

The Wolfs, the family with whom we are sharing the house, are odd, somewhat mysterious people, matching the confusion of the times [...]. The man, early forties, both parents Jewish, nevertheless contrived to get by as a quarter Jew or an Aryan, remarried during the Hitler years, again to an Aryan, was pursued by the Gestapo, eluded them for a long time, but in between was in a labour camp for a while, was a hotel porter in various cities – we always had to *scarper*, says the wife – was in Königsberg, in Bromberg,[9] knows every trick, always bobbed up again and here – how did he get here of all places? how did he come to power? how far did this power extend, how long did it last? puzzling questions all of them – and here, for a moment, when the Russians moved in, he played a dominant role [...] somehow as a negotiator with the Russians and in their good books, without being able to speak Russian, somehow leader of the radicals, house searcher etc. All of it is clear as mud. He talks with some rancour about Mayor Scholz, who is or was not radical enough for him, with some contempt about Bräuer, who is going to manage the co-operative shop, with good-natured condescension about Michel. In fact Scholz is a petrol-pump attendant, Bräuer a joiner, Michel is an invalid from the First World War and works at a knitting machine, Kalau is a precision-tool maker – none of them knows anything about administration and government, are merely decent and convinced KPD men, merely workers and nothing more, and Wolf is of course shrewder than they are. [...] He has a young second wife, a half-grown girl from his first, divorced marriage, an elderly mother-in-law. The wife gets her grammar all mixed up, the mother-in-law [...] makes no secret of the fact, that in her youth she was a maid to 'persons of rank'. But the behaviour of all these people is altogether pleasant, obliging and sensible. Of course, I don't believe that Wolf moved in here *only* to look after the place on my behalf, he undoubtedly also reckoned on my death and that he would be the permanent inheritor, but he immediately acknowledged my claim and made co-habitation so comfortable, that we benefit greatly from it. We are relieved of all the housekeeping, cooking and cleaning, we are excellently fed, and that to a great extent from the W. family's supplies, whose contacts are very good [...]. It is not really clear to me, why the W.'s spoil us so greatly, because I do not know how I could be of help to him and I make no secret of this inability. Is there some calculation involved after all, or a bit of showing-off, or real warm-heartedness? Perhaps a bit of everything. W. says, we are the only Jews up here and should stick together. [...] I do not know on which day the W.'s will really leave us, and what our further relationship will be then, but until now we have fared well with them, and we really have some affection for them. Poor devils, adventurers, declassées, no harmless angels, for sure, but in many respects decent and open-hearted people [...].

21st June, Thursday

One, at most two typewritten pages, that is all I manage in the course of a day. Constant tiredness, but also constant distraction and nothing sorted out yet. The Wolfs still here and the navvies at the shelter and Bräuer in his shop. Yesterday evening young Schmidt from the house behind us called and stayed for a long time. The little boy has turned into a young man with excellent manners, he has just come back from the forces, was a medical orderly in the navy, wants to study medicine. His father, the tax official (compulsorily a pg), learned Russian when he was a POW for years in Siberia [during the First World War] and is now going to organise a Russian course here. (Of course every pg and every pg's son is pleased if, officially or unofficially, I give him a good character reference.) The visit robbed me of at least an hour's typing. [...]

Here in the village I have a somewhat closer relationship, almost of a professional nature, with Forbrig, who was fired and is now once again in his post as headmaster. He has lent me elementary school textbooks of the Third Reich, as well as *Mein Kampf*, but I also owe him pipe and tobacco and boots.

I first made contact with the lost Jewish world at Neumark's. From him I learned, that the people from the Sporergasse [Jews' house],[10] the Riegers and the Feders, are dead (it is sinful, but I don't mourn Feder very much), that from Zeughausstr.[11] the almost crippled Kornblum died, that the rest are probably all alive but have not turned up yet. [...] (In every single respect the lack of contact, the impossibility of finding anything out.) Frau Kornblum and her daughter, very small and not very agreeable people, have meanwhile, likewise time-consuming, been up here. Sitting in Neumark's waiting room was a young gentleman with a neat full beard, whom I did not recognise at first. He introduced himself: Adolf Bauer.[12] He was working with Konrad;[13] although not in the trade, he would like to publish my diaries. Afterwards Neumark firmly warned me against him, the man wasn't serious, furthermore as an SS member rather suspect. Against that, Konrad, who paid us a long visit up here, related this: Bauer had in fact bought his Jews, who had been destined for deportation on 16 February, from the Gestapo for 500 marks each, and now Jewish signatures were being collected on his behalf. On his own account K. is pursuing, thus far without success, the resumption of his activity at the slaughterhouse: for the moment only workers and not businessmen are being approved. He spoke very gloomily about the Russians: they were recklessly slaughtering the farmers' last livestock, our German livestock reserves would be destroyed. The Russians were proceeding just as ruthlessly and only concerned for their own reconstruction [. . .] in other spheres: they are transplanting whole factories with all their machinery ('they don't leave even a screw behind!') to Russia, they also transport the skilled workers there, on important railway lines they tear up the tracks, which are also taken away to Russia and leave only a single line in operation on these stretches, e.g. Dresden–Berlin. When it suits them, e.g. yesterday in town, they fetch people out of the tram, men and women of every age, and set them to work [in the ruins]. They are merciless victors. On the wireless it sounds quite different. [. . .] For sure, everything that is said about the crimes of Hitlerism is absolutely right, and everything that is said about Russian efforts at reconstruction and acts of humanity is 90% right, but the missing 10% and the monotonous and constant repetition – why is all other news, are all other themes absent, why is everything politicised and everything else sunk without trace? – certainly do harm. And because I have observed all this in the Third Reich, and because I must now, whether I like it or not, regard everything with respect to its effect on the Jews, I do not feel very happy about it.

My next call was Katz. He is thin and pale and much more tired than during the Hitler years. He has become 'the slave of his liberators'. He has an assistant physician and a medical student in her third semester [as receptionist] in the place of the dead Ruth Rieger. Blonde middle-class girl, who takes exception to the proletarianisation of all council offices, who was certainly not excessively Nazi, but noticed little of the atrocities of the Third Reich and is very much struck by the unpleasantnesses of Russian and Communist rule. This is where the danger lies, this is the breeding ground of new reactionary, new chauvinist and even Nazi currents . . . Fräulein Mey,[14] who still works at the university and was bombed out, lives with this student. I sent word to her, that she should come up and see me as soon as possible, but have thus far, almost a whole week, waited for her in vain . . . Without having sought it Katz is now medical adviser and senior assessor to all anti-Fascist associations and works from 7 a.m. to 11 p.m., his whole private household is overwhelmed by the excessive amount of work simply in terms of space – I was examined in the bedroom – his lively wife's nerves have suffered just as greatly as his own. [. . .] On the way there, at the sight of the half-ruined new Technical High School, it had suddenly occurred to me: Dresden must become a full university, now or never. Because the Russians, who want to shine culturally, need technology above all, which is established here at the Technical High School, but not in Leipzig and they can make a big impression, if they use the cultural sciences department as a stepping stone to a humanities faculty, set up a proper university [...]. I talked about my plans with confidence and authority, increasingly so as I continued, to Katz, for whom I pictured a future as sport and student doctor and as an academic. *I* would realise this plan. 'Not you alone, but you together with others.' Yes, he was right and I had merely expressed myself clumsily, of course *we* should not elbow our way to the front and give ourselves airs as beneficiaries and victors. Katz, Neumark and I were entirely at one, in being very disapproving of the success of the pushy and overbearing Werner Lang,[15] who has become president of the chamber of commerce (whereas Neumark and Katz remain in the background without big titles).

Soon after my visit to Katz my plans were so extravagantly fulfilled, that I don't quite believe in their fulfilment [...]. I had entrusted Neumark with making contact on my behalf with Lord Mayor Friedrichs,[16] so that I could negotiate with him about my teaching post and my financial claims, without having to wait a long time [...]. I received the reply, that my financial claims should not be addressed to the city, which Friedrichs represented, but to the administration of the state [of Saxony], which was in the process of being set up, I should meanwhile discuss any other matters with Dr Grohmann, head of the department of culture, he would see me at any time, the letter was sufficient legitimation. The journey there was long and exhausting, even though I could use the tram at points. At Melanchthonstr. I was allowed into the building immediately and entered a large school room; men and women were sitting writing at the benches – non-Nazi teachers registering to start work. [...] It was half past eleven, Grohmann had driven off a few minutes earlier and was unlikely to be back before two. The first number of the *Berliner Volkszeitung* [Berlin People's Newspaper] was pushed into my hand and I waited on a school bench. Then suddenly Grohmann was standing in front of me and silently and without introduction shook my hand. My first impression, even before he opened his mouth, was: art, dilettantism, Landauer, Munich 1919.[17] Perhaps, rather, a half-unconscious and ingenuous play-acting. Ingenuous cluelessness, ingenuous confidence in being able to reform, overthrow, idealise. Forty years old, fifty? Thin grey hair above a smooth, well-fed, youthful face. From everything he said by the way and in between, from his first words alone, it appeared that the man had real interest and – perhaps – expertise only in theatre and opera. [...] He told me which singers and actresses he had dismissed, which he had kept for the time being, which were to remain permanently (no individual names, but in groups depending on the date of their Party membership). [...] It was somewhat difficult to get him around to my business and make him stick to it. Naturally I was professor in Dresden again immediately, 'we set great value on your judgement'. I came out with my Dresden University plan, advanced my reasons, said: 'Now or never.' He: 'You want to start a university here? It will be all the easier, as the state of Saxony will now be doubled in size.' And, as if it were a matter of a sandwich: 'Good, then we'll start a university here ... We'll get what can be realised now up and running, the rest will follow. Likewise in Leipzig.' I: let me work in my field and only in my field, give me the double chair of Romance Literature and Intellectual History in Dresden and Leipzig and appoint a linguist along with me, who will relieve me in that area. He: That's exactly what we'll do, and you yourself will pick your colleagues. None of the former professors in your field is there any more ... You must be patient for just another few days, also with respect to your financial claims – I myself have not received a salary for months. The state administration is just being set up [...] Perhaps I myself will move from the city to the state administration. But your business is *one hundred per cent (LTI!)* certain. Very cordial handshake and leave-taking: 'You will have more in writing in the very near future.'

I went, at first somewhat intoxicated and puffed-up, then very deflated and sceptical [...]. But I think, somehow I shall establish myself. Since then, probably already a week ago, I have not been in town again.

22nd June, Friday
In addition to my swollen foot and the general weakness and aimless wasting of time, I am genuinely ill: very badly affected by the stomach and intestinal complaint which has become almost epidemic here, since yesterday I have been helpless on my back, weak and feeling great pain and considerable nausea, I can hardly manage a couple of lines of the diary, a couple of lines of reading, I sleep most of the time. [...]

23rd June, Saturday
Still feeling very nauseous and tired. In addition constant distraction. In the garden they're hard at it removing the wretched shelter, which is full of dry rot. Were it not for the personal friendship with Kalau – for how much longer? he and his factory are supposed to go to Moscow, everything is uncertain – how would we get anything done? Four men on labour duty, at first unwilling, now more tractable, today a mason as well [...], he is also going to attend to the damage the house has, after all, suffered. [...] Danger and blast were closer than we had originally assumed. And in the evening, during a heavy thunderstorm and downpour, the rain came through with a vengeance [...]. In addition to the mason, we now also need cement, but we shall probably obtain that, too, through personal contacts. Then the matter of the shop took up a lot of time. It is to be affiliated to the Dresden Co-operative Society, and the latter wants to have the space fully at its disposal for at least three years. But we would like to be by ourselves again as soon as possible. On the other hand having the co-op in the house has great advantages for us (no tenant, telephone, goods, 'connections'). The issue is still undecided ... Then the affair of Schmidt junior. The well-behaved little boy has turned into a handsome young fellow [...] wants to study medicine and before that prefers to do labour service as a hospital attendant or the like rather than as a navvy ... In fact I myself had to take steps to avoid any kind of navvying duty, since the Russians have extended it to men of 65 years of age (45 for women): I have written to Grohmann for official confirmation that I am appointed professor from the winter semester on, and

that I very much need the time until then for preparation. (Which is absolutely true.) [...]

Every couple of minutes, every couple of lines, no matter where I start I end up with the same sentence: everything is uncertain, everything is in suspense, there is nothing solid under one's feet, in one's hands...

The day before yesterday, when I was feeling worst – I finally had to lie down and leave people to their own devices – there were visitors. Unannounced and driven only by her questing attachment, gentle Maria Kube[18] turned up, whom we had last spoken to when I was already wearing the star [...] and brought her good-looking son. Astonishing how concerned the woman is about the education of both her sons and what trouble she takes. She appears to want them to study. I shall be able to help her. She herself still speaks the somewhat laborious German of a foreigner, but with a great deal of good sense. She was bombed out, her husband is a prisoner of war in Czechoslovakia. She tells us that Agnes[19] lost her house in Piskowitz during the final stages of the fighting [...]. At the same time there arrived, as arranged, Schwarz, one of our fellow-inmates in Zeughausstr. [Schwarz had passed on a message to Klemperer a few days earlier, and Klemperer had gone to pay him a visit.] For all my liking of the man, it was first and foremost the bread connection which made me hobble the considerable distance down to Freital. I was taken up to a gallery, which was where the offices were, overlooking a huge, very warm bakery room. Schwarz was enthroned, cinema-like, in a big private office, looking youthful and used to giving commands, altogether the manager. Lang, the president of the chamber of commerce, had immediately appointed him to his old post, he had also already been allocated a little house, which had formerly belonged to an SS officer, at the other end of the city, however, in Bühlau. We exchanged memories and experiences, Schwarz got an invitation up here and a promise of cherries, I got a loaf under my arm and the promise of further occasional supplies. S. said we were being amply provided with grain by Russia, there was nothing to fear in this respect. [...]

Schwarz is not my first and only extra source of bread. During the very first days there appeared (God knows who had told him about me) a fat elderly gentleman with a touch of Austrian joviality, whom I had difficulty remembering, Herr Steininger. Caspar David Friedrich Str. – Frau Pick[20] – dismissed bank employee – philo-Semite – bookkeeper in a bread factory [...]. And again we immediately got eight pounds of bread coupons as a present and also very interesting news and additional pieces of information. Steininger, in his late 60s, got through the bad years with great shrewdness. At the beginning – he was then already retired – he was sentenced to several months in prison for disparaging the Führer, and his pension was considerably reduced as a result. This and his ('evidence to be provided') active philo-Semitism protects him today. D'altra parte:[21] In the course of 40 years he has built up a collection of several hundred thousand newspaper cuttings about every kind of notable person. He offered the Reich Chamber of Culture material from the archive, and it purchased it from him by giving him a small monthly allowance for several years. That covered him against the Gestapo, before the war he could even take trips and do deals abroad, and in this way get Jewish valuables to safety in England. (He says he was received by the chief rabbi there and got a huge offer for Hitler cuttings – the papers were to be taken over by air plane, but the war intervened.) I don't know, of course, how much of that is really true, but I do know about his loyal friendship to Jews in difficult times, and the blatantly mischievous business pride of the man [...] – he has now sued the Dresdener Bank for back-payment of the share of his pension which was withheld – gave me a great deal of pleasure. Also, he will not only give me more bread coupons, but also bring me from his mostly saved material some things which I myself published.

Towards evening
In the morning Herr Schulz and Herr Neidhardt appeared. S., a pale mechanic specialising in typewriters, has already been here once, he wants to set up an anti-Fascist publishing house with a professional and today he brought along his partner. [...] Youthful giant (42 years old), beard, dark, good-natured and likeable, used to be 20 stone, is now half that. Was a photo-journalist for the Scherl newspaper group, frequently saw the 'Hitler fellow' at close quarters, was in the SPD, nephew of a Reichsbanner[22] leader, is now writing a journalistic book about Hitler [...]. (His thesis: the German people is to blame, not Hitler.) Has Russian permission to start the first new publishing house as an *anti-Fascist publishing house*, already has machines and workers, has Glaser[23] (whom I want to look up tomorrow morning) as legal adviser. Also talks very knowledgeably about literature and is not at all bloodthirstily radical. After sounding each other out for a while I offered: my diary since 1933, precisely the diary of the middling position, the average, the everyday, of lesser events. He was enthusiastic, will come here in the next few days to draw up a final contract, will provide a horse and cart to fetch our things, mss y todo[24] from Pirna – he says there was less damage there and Annemarie's clinic, which he knows, was sure to have been spared. I intend to remain sceptical in everything, but the thing does give me great satisfaction.

[...]

I have now probably put down practically everything that needed to be added from these first two weeks here. [...]

Tomorrow I want to work on the journey back here,[25] which I have only just begun, and then I shall have cleared the decks, no matter whether I plunge into the diary of the Hitler years or my coming French work. Despite nausea and shaky ground under my feet I am brimful of plans and a desire to work. Only, everything is constantly undermined and simultaneously stimulated by the How much longer? (By that alone and not a bit by the so clearly recognised vanitatum vanitas.[26]) Admittedly the desire to work is balanced by a quite vulgar desire for pleasure. To just once eat well again, to drink well, go for a nice drive, to go to the seaside, to sit comfortably in the cinema ... No 20-year-old can be half as hungry for life ... And all the time it makes me happy that E. is working on *her* house, on *her* garden and is coming to life again.

24th June, Sunday

Last night I had a new bout of the unpleasant intestinal business, so bad, that I was unable to get up until late morning and now have difficulty staying on my feet.

Hardly had I sat down in the easy chair, than Steininger came, put 8 pounds of bread coupons on the table and then [...] read out a wild letter of complaint to the lord mayor because of 'Gestapo-like' methods, in which he referred to 'the distinguished Jewish scholar Professor Kl.', and which he has already sent off. His archive has been confiscated as 'state property of the Third Reich'. A highly embarrassing situation for him and for me. Because it is absolutely certain, that the man was playing a clever double game and *also* served the Third Reich. He says, he only sold 'scholarly' material – but he must have known how this material was used by the Nazis.

E. called on Glaser this morning: result, Neidhardt's enterprise is serious, I should work with him.

[...]

25th June, Monday, about 7 p.m.

The same thing for days. I am really and literally completely knocked out by illness. The night is bad, it's late morning before I can get up. After washing and shaving I am so tired that I almost immediately fall asleep in the easy chair. Then at midday I am able to eat something that strengthens me a little, but my eyelids are already drooping again. And then when I can finally think of my typewriter, visitors come and stay until evening. Thus this afternoon Frau Rasch,[27] who was our good angel when E. had pneumonia, turned up with her children [...]. Yesterday evening, after the Forbrigs left, we still had to go over to the Schmidts', where I drank a great amount of rum (which at least tasted good, even if it did me as little good as taking or avoiding anything else). Today has again been completely squandered in the same way. At the moment I feel fresher, but the next attack upsets everything again.

I must slowly begin to pay systematic attention to the language of the *fourth Reich*. It sometimes seems to me, that it is less different from that of the *third* than, say, the Saxon of Dresden from that of Leipzig. When, for example, Marshal Stalin is the greatest living man, the most brilliant strategist etc. Or when in a speech from the beginning of the war Stalin talks of Hitler, very justifiably, as 'Hitler, the cannibal'. At any rate, I want to study our news sheet and the *Deutsche Volkszeitung*, which is now delivered to me, very carefully with respect to the LQI.[28] I want to – but for the moment diarrhoea and lack of time are even more powerful than my will, because all strength and literally any peace and possibility of gathering my thoughts are lacking. (We are still too popular.)

The biggest attraction here remain the cherries, we give away great amounts, much is simply picked from the trees by visitors, there will be very little left for jam-making. In a positive as in a negative sense we live like the lilies of the field.

Since midday yesterday there has been no electricity in the whole of Dresden, Eva used bricks and gridiron to build a temporary hearth in the garden, such as the refugees in Schönheider Hammer had. [. . .]

27th June, Wednesday afternoon
[. . .]

Jung [a neighbour], who has proved to be very solicitous and is now working for a civil-engineering company charged with rebuilding the Pirna Bridge, first wanted to take us to Pirna yesterday and then today. The wood-gas car had a faulty engine: we waited in vain and go on groping in the dark. Fräulein Mey, from whom I hoped to have news about the TH, has sent word – via Schmidt jun., who [. . .] found a place as an operating-theatre attendant in the Friedrichstädter Hospital – that *I* should call on her. [. . .] There's something wrong there, and I'm still tapping in the dark.

The Co-operative Association will not take over the shop after all, since I cannot agree to a contract of three years, such as it requires. Now there is a risk of a tenant being forced on me. We want to guard against that by taking in the Raschs or the Kubes. So here, too: obscurity, nothing decided.

The Wolfs are still not in their new home. Never ending back and forth; the confusion all the greater, as the power cut has continued since midday on Sunday with only brief interruptions – it is said now, because the Russians are dismantling part of the electricity works and transporting it to Russia – and cooking is done in part on the temporary stove, in part in neighbours' homes.

Still visit after visit, each one equally welcome and inconvenient. Yesterday the Glaser ladies, today Konrad: he brought a small sausage (but is still not allowed to work at the slaughterhouse) and got some of Steininger's bread coupons and a couple of cherries in return; I provided a good character reference for Adolf Bauer (see above, the ransomed Jews, exculpating the SS man!); I can, if need be (we still have 280M) borrow 500M from Schlüter.[29] Even at the very end Schlüter still got 38,000M for a truckload of his horrible Schlüter teas! Konrad is working for Bauer and is in close touch with Schlüter.

There is a particular political reason for the fact that Wolf remains unable to move into his new home: it is a confiscated Nazi one. And the KPD here does not support Jews as zealously as, for example, their own party members – in the Jew it evidently suspects the businessman, non-worker, capitalists. Right at the beginning Neumark immediately complained to me, his general requests for the Jews met with resistance from Fischer, the deputy mayor [. . .].

No news from Neidhardt either. At the moment, foolishly, he is of particular importance to me.
[. . .]

29th June, Friday afternoon
So far we have not managed to get into the right mood for our 29 June,[30]

although we have good reason to do so a thousand times over, and the Pirna tragi-comedy is to blame for that.

On Wednesday morning Dr König came to see us: he had written to Annemarie as his colleague and was now bringing her reply, according to which my mss were in good condition. 'Only the mss?' asked Eva mistrustfully, and so we had new cause for worry. But immediately after that Jung arrived: the car of his company, which is restoring the bridge in Pirna, was working and waiting outside with two gentlemen, a bookkeeper and an engineer. A nice big Mercedes with a wood-gas stove mounted on it. We drove off proudly – the first breakdown was by the Bienert mill. Lengthy fiddling around [...] finally a good-natured Russian had to pull us in a circle over the two Weisseritz bridges three times with his lorry, before the engine started again. After that, shaken and anxious, often past rubble and through pot-holes we got as far as Niedersedlitz, there a wheel gave out, and when it had been replaced, the engine wouldn't start again. A break of almost an hour – I collected unripe pears and filled my pockets with them. Nevertheless at half past three, after a good two hours, we were in Pirna, where we were very cordially received by Annemarie, Dressel and his whole family (mother, wife, three children). Very cordially, that is, not with much food, and that did not make Dressel's familiar convenient lukewarmness any more congenial to me. 'Do you really believe that the SS committed *such* acts of cruelty, and why should they have committed so many atrocities?' So once again the convenient: it won't have been quite as bad as that. In addition the bourgeois antipathy to Communism: Natsoc. made things more comfortable for Dr Dressel's social stratum ... [...] But we had not come to talk politics. The main thing, the blessed main thing was, that our things, a still quite inestimable quantity of linen, woollen clothes for E., silver plate, stamp collection were probably just as well preserved as the pile of ms. Probably: the Russians knocked random holes in the suitcases, pulled a lot of things out and – probably, that is, stuffed them all back in again. We didn't have time to check carefully, because we were supposed to drive back at half past four. But the car didn't come, we waited in ever greater despair and finally went to the station to catch the 8 o'clock train to Reick, from where there is a tram. At 8.30 the train had still not arrived, instead we found out, that there is no tram from Reick after 8. Hence we could not reach Dölzschen before the curfew (11 p.m.) and *had* to return to the clinic. [...] Jung had meanwhile been to Annemarie's: the car had broken down completely, he himself had to spend the night in Pirna, he would pick us up at 8 o'clock next morning, that is today, in a lorry, which would take all our baggage. We slept on 2 sofas in our clothes, rather hungry and very disgruntled. Early in the morning I went down to the Elbe, to seek out Jung's company and office. A terrain of dreadful destruction [...], a new wooden bridge over the river, the stone railway bridge completely destroyed exactly in the middle. [...] Not a trace of Jung's company [...]. The lorry came no more than the car had done the day before, exasperated we took the train at 9.50 to Niedersedlitz, from there with trams 19 and 20 through the whole city to Löbtau, we arrived home worn out at half past twelve. Jung himself appeared later: *the Russians had confiscated his lorry*, one of four belonging to the company [...]. The Russians as victors, the uncertainty of the situation: [...] there are power cuts for hours on end, [...] factory upon factory is being taken off to Poland and Russia.

Even the most left-wing are beginning to be anxious.

[...]

And then the Vogel family[31] were here three times, and this afternoon I have already received father Vogel and son. Quite evidently as a result of denunciation and intrigues they have received an order, as Nazi Party members, to give up their shop by Monday morning. At their request I wrote a very warm letter of recommendation to Werner Lang, the president of the chamber of commerce, that he should have the evident mistake of subordinate and local officials checked, the Vogels were *good men*, and many people of the previous regime were still living a life of ease. [...]

With Annemarie and Dressel, with the Schmidts, with the Vogels, recently with Dr Katz's receptionist: I sense everywhere the bourgeois antipathy to the unskilled workers and extremists of the KPD in the various local government offices. And in addition to that, there is now – also among the KPD workers themselves – the fear of complete impoverishment by the Russians, who are dragging off every piece of livestock and machinery. What will be the end of it??

30th June, Saturday, towards evening

Every free minute I have I work on the journey back, which I am fed up to the back teeth with and is becoming ever hazier.

A small satisfaction of vanity: At the town hall a long queue is waiting for food ration cards, I have identification which allows me preferential treatment (as a Jew and because of my advanced years!) and am dealt with immediately. [...] Grohmann sent an attestation of the 'Department of Culture of the City of Dresden', which protects me from all navvying duty as 'one of the most prominent university professors' and for the sake of my work and the prep-aration for it. – But this satisfaction of vanity continues to be balanced by absolute uncertainty. The state government still does not exist. No position, no money.

[...] The Wolfs are finally moving out today – they will go on taking care of our food and cooking [...]. How to repay them? They are poor devils, after all.

Our cherry harvest is gradually turning into a catastrophe: the whole world is pleading and begging for a share, children romp through garden and house, we get no peace, hardly enough will remain for the Wolfs and ourselves to make jam. There's no end to the picking and excessive eating, on my part as well. This abundant cherry harvest – playing on all the senses, optically, acoustically etc. – will govern memories of the first month in Dölzschen.

I don't get around to any reading, hardly even the newspaper, which [...] repeatedly prints the same one-sided Russian-biased reports.

The day slips through my fingers.

I am gaining a little insight into the petty power struggles and tensions of the miniature republic of Dölzschen. Today, Kalau, who is giving up direction of labour duty in disgust, showed me documents about himself, which he had found in police files. He was originally an Independent Social Democrat, was compulsorily taken into the NSDAP and thrown out of it again because of behaviour which was subversive and hostile to the Party, also because he worked for a Jewish company and because he threw his membership card in a Party official's face with the remark: 'Pity it's not a hammer!' He was then under *secret surveillance*, regular reports on him had to be made to the Gestapo. (What organisation!) As a soldier he was declared 'unworthy to bear arms' by a court martial in Cherbourg and sentenced to $2\frac{1}{2}$ years in a camp (which he served) for sabotage and destruction of important documents. Here in Dölzschen he is at odds with Scholz, the Communist pedant and very poor mayor (as Kalau and Wolf say). In particular there is the case of the judge, Richter, whose piano is now standing here and into whose house the Wolfs are moving. Scholz appears not to have acted energetically enough with respect to the confiscation, the judge has fled, but the son-in-law is still in the apartment and making life difficult for the Wolfs. *I* preach: Show no mercy to judges, they are just as guilty as SS and Gestapo.

1st July, Sunday evening. Dölzschen

Finished the journey back at last. Now tomorrow I want to see whether I can find out anything from Grohmann yet – I don't really believe I shall – and want at any rate to get at some library through him and perhaps also make contact with the TH. Also I am waiting day after day for the mss from Pirna. Simply getting to grips with my *18th Century*[32] will also take a great deal of time and will take me a little into my former element again. Apart from that I am all the time waiting for Neidhardt. [. . .]

Cherry picking, cherry eating, making cherry preserve, making cherry jam, baking cherry cake (Frau Wolf of course – the move has still not taken place) continue to be dominant.

[. . .]

2nd July, Monday evening. Dölzschen

In the morning at Melanchthonstr., all the way there on foot, bad heart trouble, once again horrible impression of destruction. [. . .] The Grohmann undertaking presented the same picture as on the first occasion, but the chaos had grown and the mood was much gloomier. I first of all spoke to the same secretary [. . .], then at length to Hirzel [. . .], one of Grohmann's assistants, I could also have talked to Gr. himself, but I'd had enough. Situation: everything is in flux. The state administration has still not been set up, the Russians have not given approval. Perhaps they'll give it tomorrow, perhaps in a few weeks, perhaps never. [. . .] There's a lack of money, a lack of everything, the Russians are not interested in anything here, whatever tempts them, they tear out and transplant to Russia. There is supposed to be a sitting next week, at which the city will concern itself with the TH, meanwhile no one even knows what still remains there, what can be cranked up again, etc. etc. But if a state government of Saxony is set up and if it is the proposed Greater Saxony [. . .] then everything is up in the air again, and hardly very favourable to me. Because then, apart from the Dresden TH, Saxony has the universities of Leipzig, Halle and Jena and will find it impossible to maintain all these high schools and will perhaps have to concentrate on and limit itself to Leipzig. And with what will it then maintain Leipzig? The intelligentsia has skedaddled to the West [. . .]. Nothing at all can be done yet with respect to library matters. There is an administration of the State Library in Blasewitz – I passed close by the horribly burnt out and ruined Japanese Palace – and many of the library's treasures have been saved, but as yet it is impossible to get at the books, nor is any other library operating yet, and of course no one knows anything about the Romance Literatures Department at the TH. I had asked Grohmann for money. I am not a municipal employee, but must wait for the state administration. Meanwhile – curious fact! – two hundred marks from the surplus of an artists' fund, which Grohmann has at his disposal, were assigned to me. I received the money: 5 very new 20M notes, though from 1944 and bearing the swastika, and an ominous one-hundred-mark note of the 'Allied Military Authority'. What value can German money still have?

None of that really depressed me and did not surprise me at all – I am infinitely sceptical and await events with a degree of apathy. I only worry about being able to work. Books are not to be had, and my mss, which could keep me busy for weeks to come, are still in Pirna, for all Jung's promises. If, once again, they do not come tomorrow, I shall have to take the martyrdom of another journey to Pirna upon myself.

3rd July, Tuesday forenoon

On the way back yesterday a slight gentleman with a little grey moustache called out my name very cordially, quite unfamiliar to me. Forgive me – with whom do I have the pleasure? – You don't recognise me? Menke-Glückert[33] – You have become very thin. – I've lost more than 75 pounds ... he began to talk in the middle of the street; he was very bitter and depressed. Three of his sons had fallen, he is almost completely bombed-out, after he was dismissed, the Third Reich saddled him with disciplinary proceedings for giving preferential treatment to Jews, in the final years cut all his pensions, now all his legitimate claims, just like mine, are to the non-existent state administration, he has a large family and no means. In Ebert's time[34] M.-Gl. was counsellor at the ministry, in charge of secondary schools in Saxony, honorary professor at the TH, also, as far as I remember, for some time a deputy of the Democratic Party in the state parliament. Administratively he was my superior, and I received my instructions as a member of the examining board from him. For me he was always the powerful and benevolent 'Herr Geheimrat' [Privy Counsellor]. Yesterday, during our conversation, that had all slipped my mind, perhaps because outwardly and inwardly he had so much dwindled (not shrivelled, his posture was good, like an officer of the Napoleonic army on half-pay [. . .]). I addressed him throughout as Herr Doktor, only afterwards did everything else come to mind and weigh on my conscience. Why had his experience not yet been drawn on, surely he should have a place in a government of reconstruction? 'I've asked myself that, too, but so far no one has shown any interest in me!' This, quite evidently, was at the heart of his bitterness, it seemed to wound him more than the loss of his sons (he is supposed to have had a whole crowd of children) ... Lives somewhere near Wehlen, comes into town only occasionally. I invited him to visit us, and we parted like two friends, suffering more or less the same fate ... From him I also learned, that the Americans had evacuated Leipzig [...]. Yesterday, meanwhile, it was announced on the wireless that the Russians have occupied Leipzig and Weimar. Thus again and again: nothing is certain, no one knows what is happening and what will happen.

But gradually, here and there, little tips of land are emerging from the Flood. Dr Hirzel [Grohmann's assistant] reported on the Windes.[35] They already knew from him, that we are here, they are alive, were bombed out and have suffered, are in Loschwitz (so virtually inaccessible). A Frau Kreisler[36] had also inquired after us at Annemarie's a little while ago, but Annemarie had not yet had any news of us then, and had meanwhile mislaid the woman's address. [...]

The Vogel business is unpleasant and evidently typical. Vogel sen. was up here again for a long time yesterday evening, very agitated and always close to tears. His shop has been taken from him because he was a pg [...]. He was (briefly) protected by a sentry from Russian headquarters. He has taken my advice to do without this arbitrary protection and seek justice from German authorities. It appears, that he has been driven out by local intrigues in favour, not of a concentration-camp man, as is pretended, but of another pg. He had to spend many hours in Lang's waiting room before he could see an assistant or something similar, it looks as if an investigation of the affair will now get under way – but meanwhile Vogel's shop really is in someone else's hands since yesterday ... And as [...] my warm commendation of the Vogels is very much involved, that may have unpleasant consequences for me. E.g. with respect to Frau Kl.'s heavy worker's ration card ... [...]

Since yesterday evening we are without the Wolfs, it is now very hard for us to do the domestic chores, of which they had entirely relieved us, alone. It has been agreed, that we shall eat with them several times a week or that they will cook for us here (for payment 1M per head and lunch – we have now also paid them that for the past weeks). But despite this help, in terms of labour and supplies, we are nevertheless in a fairly difficult position.

4th July, Wednesday forenoon

The LTI lives on [...]. An anti-Fascist language office should be set up. – Analogies between Nazistic and Bolshevistic language: In Stalin's speeches, extracts of which regularly appear, Hitler and Ribbentrop are cannibals and monsters. In the articles about Stalin, the supreme commander of the Soviet Union is the most brilliant general of all times and the most brilliant of all men living.

The surviving things from Pirna came yesterday afternoon. They had their guardian angels: The Russians cut open and hacked at the suitcases, pulled out individual items and stuffed them back in again, nothing appears to be missing, unbelievable treasures, now absolutely priceless, woollen things, underwear, tablecloths, art works of Eva's have come to light. How very rich we were, if this represents only a tiny fraction, hardly one per cent of our former property ... My huge stamp collection is there. We shall try to sell it. To me only land still has value as property, reference works of every kind, a car, a good wireless, these are the only things I would still like to have.

Above all: the mss have been preserved. What an immense amount of work! I shall have to put it in order, I have to think what I shall knuckle down to first – when the universities start up again no longer seems so important to me, I have enough to do. I can now work my way back into the French things again, even if I cannot get hold of any books: there's enough material in the 18ième and lecture notes (and in the work from 34 onwards – the German Image of France[37] – which is entirely finished). But for the moment everything is still restless and topsy-turvy: I pick up this or that, leaf through it, put it aside undecided, am at once depressed and happy – what of any of it shall I still see through to completion?

Before I had finished these lines, the situation changed yet again. An hour ago it was announced on the wireless: The state administration has been appointed. Its seat is Dresden and Lord Mayor Friedrichs is now president of the whole of Saxony. But since, apart from the districts of Berlin and Mecklenburg, only Saxony (and not Thuringia) is mentioned, it follows that it will be a Greater Saxony. Favourable to me?? I almost think, yes. Because after all I am now at the centre and at the source, have already been mentioned to the new master and am one of those, presumably one of the few, who has a claim to a senior university post. At any rate my prospects are much more favourable again today than yesterday. What should I do now? Wait and see? Act?

If only my heart were in better condition, it coped well with the difficult months and now it makes itself felt if I walk ten paces.

The wireless takes up a lot of time, but is very interesting. Although essentially only Berlin can be picked up, and only picked up clearly in the evening, and although sometimes there's only pleasant, often undemanding music. But the news from Berlin reveals in detail the dreadful disorder and the woefully difficult work of reconstruction. Train connections are announced, for example, that one can now already travel as far as Oranienburg twice a day, that on 'even days' a train goes almost as far as Magdeburg, that a goods train is already getting as far as Dresden etc. etc. A talk urgently advises Berliners to plant winter cabbage now, as nothing can be expected from the devastated province of Brandenburg and from further away nothing at all [. . .] etc. . . . The Lord Mayor of the city of Brandenburg is urgently requested (on the wireless, because there is no post) to come to an important conference in Berlin. Every evening long lists are read out: Greetings from ... that is, the name and address of people announcing themselves to family and friends as alive and present again.

[. . .]

9th July, Monday

Hardly anything has changed since the last entry: I read my diaries at random, am very exhausted, walk little, we eat at the Wolfs', are very short of food, Eva does far too much work in the garden, planting vegetables, pulling up bushes (trees really), working with her is excessively exhausting for me.

Yesterday the Jungs invited us for coffee, which was impossible to decline, it was very nice, but I found it a little awkward: the Jungs shower us with this and that, tea, artificial fertiliser etc. What impulse lies behind it, and how long will it last? In the evening Michel and his wife sat here for a long time. They, too, shower us with gifts and attention (tobacco, taking trouble over E.'s footwear – M. is in charge of the store in the Begerburg [...]), but M. invalided out of two world wars, home knitting machine worker, is undoubtedly sincere. [...]

11th July, Wednesday evening

Yesterday the definitive awakening from the all-too-beautiful fairy tale. At first it still seemed to be continuing: 'The Lord Mayor of the City of Dresden requests the pleasure of the company of Herr and Frau Professor Dr Klemperer at the inauguration of the Provisional Stage of the Dresden Theatres on 10 July 1945 in the Concert Hall, Glacisstr. *Nathan the Wise*[38] will be performed. Commencement 6 p.m.' That's delightfully flattering. Admittedly I felt *Nathan* to be presumptuous lack of tact, I would have preferred [Goethe's] *Iphigenia*. Then among the guests – about 600, it was invitation only – I had a really good, though not a VIP seat, E. could not come because of her bad foot, pity, it was a very good performance – to my very great astonishment and greeting me as if we had been sitting together for the last time only yesterday and this meeting was the most natural thing in the world, the Kühn couple.[39] And beside me, completely grey, and taking it even more for granted, Janentzky.[40] And: Why don't you drop by and see us, we (we!) are discussing the re-establishment of the Cultural Sciences Section at a student hostel on Mommsenstr., and the Rüdiger woman[41] was still there, and yesterday Grohmann had wanted to find out what was happening, but he wasn't in charge of course [...] ... Janentzky found it very strange, that I had some objection to these re-establishers. So evidently things are to go on just as they did after 1918: the enemies of the new regime are to be left quietly to continue with their work, which naturally will turn into work of subversion. Without mincing words I told J. my extremely divergent opinion, told him very clearly and frankly, and firmly refused to come before I had received precise information from the government regarding my position. The business made me feel very bitter, and after what I already heard from Grohmann and today have learned in greater detail from Winde, it looks very gloomy for me. Grohmann makes big promises, which he can't keep, has no real power, has no standing, knows nothing about the High School, is essentially limited to *Dresden art* and nothing else. [...] Then today I learned from Winde, that they really do want to leave Kühn and Janentzky in their posts, and that *they* are the Ministry of Economics, to which, at the Russians' request, the TH is being subordinated – separation from the universities therefore. To what insignificance does that reduce me, to what merely tolerated 5th wheel, among what 'colleagues'! Yesterday and today I was at times seized by the desire to insist with all means at my disposal on the purging of the TH (which E. repeatedly encourages me to do), in between I was very much inclined to throw in the towel entirely, to stay in retirement and to complete my books (but how, since *all* resources are lacking?), at times I also told myself, the best thing was to hold on to my post mindlessly and silently for just another year - *if* it is given back to me at all – I constantly vacillate between these possibilities and their opportunities in the financial respect also. Neumark has invited me to consult with him on my monetary claims, I want to do so tomorrow, and that may lead to some clarity on other matters. But the fairy tale is over, and the professional disappointments of the 20s and 30s will be repeated, as if the monstrousness in between had not happened. I have become terribly pessimistic, and Eva too, with regard to alteration of the German morass, to peace, to mankind altogether. All these beautiful phrases and vows from Germany, USA and Russia, I already heard it all in 1918. And then came the Freikorps[42] and everything else at home and abroad, that finally led to catastrophe. And it will be no different this time. And is the language and truthfulness Stalinice so very unlike that Hitlerice? And if I really were able to publish now [...] would I be free to write what I wanted?? My kind of freedom! In short, the fairy tale is completely over and done with, and now I'm only calculating whether they will at least pay me enough for a modest living. Even that does not look likely.

Frau Kreisler accosted me in the entrance-hall, a card was on its way to us, she and Frau Winde would visit us the next day. Immediately afterwards I made the acquaintance of Herr Winde, his wife had not come. The emergence of these people from the buried past – and these people also refers to the TH crowd – was the most important aspect of the afternoon for me. – I had to leave after the ring scene in the play, to catch my three trams before they shut down. [...] As I said, I found the choice of the Jewish play very unfortunate, although I was struck again, as many years ago, that it is not at all about the glorification of Jews or *the* Jew [...].

14th July, Saturday morning

The Berger furniture business takes up too much time. What has been confiscated, what can he reclaim? [...] The claims are in large part blatant lies. I had to go to see Scholz in the overcrowded Housing Office [...]. Lengthy negotiation, Bergers, father and son, also present. Then for a whole morning the two of them fetched things from here. [...] The whole business disagreeable, filling me with very contradictory, extremely mixed feelings. [...]

The whole afternoon yesterday agonisingly taken up with the trip to Neumark in Reickerstr. Discussion of my salary claim on the new state administration. [...] N. holds out very little hope [...]: There's no money and worse absolutely no sympathy for Jewish claims, nor any on the part of the Russians. I also talked to N. about the Kühn affair and about my desires and doubts with respect to my post. He told me the latest news, that since Wednesday Menke-Glückert had been appointed to take charge of universities, I should talk to him. It had been quite a fight to push through M.-G. as a Democrat against a Communist. I: whether at the moment a Communist (clean out!) would not have been better? He: the KPD was doing too little for the universities, they would reject your salary claim as capitalist!

As soon as one has anything to do with politics, one can only chose the lesser evil, it is impossible to make any pure decision. [...]

The food shortage is becoming ever more catastrophic, the only thing we have in abundance is bread [...], but we live almost exclusively on dry bread. Fat and meat are almost entirely lacking, in fact entirely – misery of standing in queues – where to find the time. E. plants, E. has no shoes, E. has a bad foot – I seem to find it impossible to set aside a quiet hour to work in. [...]

My nerves are much weakened, my feeling of happiness has been pushed very, very much into the background.

15th July, Sunday morning
[...]

Since yesterday the 22 – garlanded, red cloth with the words: 'Another step forward!' – has been running again, our best connection to town, as long as there is no 16. On the same day a card from Fräulein Mey: now the 22 is going again, she can visit me 'after High School'; she would come on Wednesday therefore. My relationship to the TH remains inwardly and outwardly unclear. Chorus with respect to everything and from everyone: Uncertainty, opacity of the situation. – Visits I make, and which I receive, eat me up. [...] Glasers here.

16th July, Monday morning
E says: before when a special delivery letter came, it was from the Gestapo. Now: 'The Lord Mayor requests the pleasure ...' He yet again requested 'by hand – urgent' the pleasure of our company the day before yesterday, inviting us in the evening to the first concert of the Staatskapelle in the Bühlau Assembly Rooms. – Very flattering – but the journey there! Then again: one has to show one's face, one has to talk to people, has to become involved or stay involved ... At first it appeared, that it would be just as impossible for E. to come as to the Nathan recently. She literally has no shoes, her only pair has had a broken heel since 13 February, her foot is raw [...]. A cobbler is not to be found. Now yesterday Frau Wolff [sic] found a pair of shoes of her mother-in-law, and Frau Steininger also unearthed a pair – both pairs size 38 instead of 36 – but wearable.

I visited Steininger in Hohe Str. to inspect his biographical archive. A completely bombed-out, but not burnt-out house not far from the Plauenschen Ring. Boxes, folder, envelopes: About $1\frac{1}{2}$ million newspaper cuttings, filed and unfiled, on x topics. Partly in a garage, which rainwater can easily get into, partly crumpled, full of dust and mortar, everything chaotic and in danger, partly in $\frac{3}{4}$ destroyed rooms. Like something from a film. A miracle, that the stuff was saved – but it is only saved, if it can quickly be stored more safely and re-ordered. [...] Request to Scholz, supported by me, for storage and work space for St. At the same time I ask myself [...], whether all of it does have any great scholarly value. On the one hand: yes, very great and especially now. On the other hand, it's all too fragmentary, superficial, jumbled up, and only valuable as a pointer to more substantial material – which is just what's missing.

[...] Now every Nat. Soc. book has to be handed over by today on pain of heavy punishment. A list of the forbidden things – I have not yet seen it – has appeared. I myself collect them for the *LTI*, have already obtained this and that from Forbrig. I shall procure a special permit.

[...]

I am so very tired and so very lazy and so very easily distracted. My inwardly ever-repeated motto: 'I shall make use of it, this brief span.' But I don't make use of it. I lie on the ugly fauteuil in the hall, look out at the greenery, at *my* garden and let the wireless play on. Idiotic music, beautiful music, news characteristic of the times. One box of matches has been distributed to every Berlin household ... [...], every evening (programme: 'Greetings') a list of names and addresses of returnees is broadcast, etc. etc.

17th July, Tuesday morning

Tremendous heat, more than 30 in the shade, so we didn't go to the celebratory concert in more than uncomfortable Bühlau yesterday. See and be seen, be involved?? I am a little apathetic and disgusted. Grohmann is an impotent wind-bag, *my* real post still non-existent.

Glaser, happy to have got a position in the Ministry of Justice (otherwise very decrepit and senile) told me, *all* my claims (notified through Neumark) were up in the air: the new state, which is *no* state at all and [...] does not need to recognise claims on the preceding regime. My objection, that the Allies had declared themselves upholders of Jewish compensation claims, was mockingly rejected as lacking any legal force. I am reading my diaries without making notes, only blue pencil crosses. I cannot get a grip on the difficulties, find a solution to them. What is too intimate, what too general? How should *LTI* and vita be separated? Who should be mentioned by name? How should I comment on what I wrote then? How far diverge from the diary form?? For weeks now I have done nothing else but read the diary. I feel very empty.

[...]

I have to tell myself a little too often: you are in Paradise now, compared to the previous situation. It is so, but I notice it all too rarely – E.'s loss of weight, the never-ending dry bread, the chaos in the house, the uncertainty of my position, my sterility, exhaustion and heart problems: there are a little too many weeds growing in the Paradise Garden. Nevertheless, we are living in it, and there is some hope of weeding it. This spun out metaphor is none at all for E., but reality, she works all day in the garden, mainly planting vegetables, there is *nothing*, literally nothing else she is interested in, except the garden. Pereat mundus, fiat hortus.[43]

18th July, Wednesday morning. Dölzschen

This afternoon at 4 'Installation of the [Saxon] administration' – I am invited (a very inconvenient time, because that's when the Mey woman is supposed to come to see me and it's too late to cancel her) – thus the new life appears to be assuming solid shape, thus the diary can also become a solid book again.[44] – Sounds nice, but isn't true at all. Nothing is solid, everything is in a chaotic fluid state, Germany's, Saxony's, Dölzschen's, my affairs – absolutely *everything*.

Yesterday Scholz [...] was here. I want to get him and through him his KPD to take a keen interest in Kühn, in teachers altogether, since Forbrig complains very bitterly to me about recruitment of pg's. Scholz very insipid: democratic line, don't rush anything, the Party slogan. Then it slips out: People have to starve a little first. First came Kerensky, after that Lenin ... I recently heard something very similar – from whom?? – with reference to the Russians: politically they were not putting any pressure on the Germans, less than the USA at least; they were only removing livestock and factories. First people had to starve in Germany, then it would just go Bolshevik of its own accord.

There's a nice hairdresser running around here, a Hungarian, in the anti-Fascist comité, recently cut Eva's hair, is going to get a tomcat for us. This Hungarian yesterday: the Russians are letting us starve, very pessimistic. He wants to go back to Hungary, the Jews would build things up there. Yes, if the Jews wanted to take a hand here, the Jews knew how to do it, then there would be commerce, wages and life again! [...]

I am so helpless in the face of the immense material of my diaries, that I ask myself, what is the point in piling up more? But it is always foolish to ask what the point is.

19th July, Thursday morning

The tram didn't come – so I decided not to go to the state administration ceremony and came back again. I would anyway have learned only jelly-like things again and heard the usual phrase-mongering.

The Mey woman was here from late afternoon and into the evening. Unchanged, yet almost 60. I was not very warm and spelled out my attitude to my former colleagues. Important points of Mey's report: Holldack dead, Kafka seriously ill, will 'not be involved any more'. Gehrig willing, however.[45] The Romance languages library completely destroyed. [...] No one knows what will become of the TH. At the moment a Lieutenant-Colonel Koslovich was in charge and also had his quarters there. Rubble was being cleared, lists were being drawn up of professorships, lecture courses, dissertations of the last ten years. Sudden commands were received, one knew nada, nada.

[...]

The very poor condition of my heart naturally makes everything seem *even* more gloomy than it already is.

20th July, Friday morning

Yesterday, 19 July, the Hungarian brought the longed-for tomcat which had been promised for some time. I don't need to note all the bitter feelings this arouses in me. The question of feeding is not an atom easier than it was in Mujel's time.[46] The new one, white with grey patches, is unfortunately already a year old and used to complete freedom. He comes from the Moritzburg area, is called Moritz and will probably be called Moische. – I owe Eva the house and the tomcat.

On the wireless yesterday between cabaret turns a bit of live transmission from the first service of the first synagogue [to re-open] in Berlin: a 74-year-old cantor sings the Hebrew blessing of consecration as the eternal lamp is lit. The announcer informs the listeners about it, we hear the singing and the praying congregation. – Frightful, for a start because it is tasteless amidst all the amusements, de- not consecration, and then even more frightful as accentuation of the Jewish victory. It lends support to the assailed Natsoc.

The same is true of a talk about the German General Staff as the brains of German militarism, it is guilty and must be destroyed. There are Russian sentries everywhere, the Russians are driving off the livestock, there is hunger, already one can hear: at least under Hitler everyone got what was promised on the ration coupons [. . .]. The development of a counter-current is inevitable: we are hungry, the Jews are here again, the Russians are here – these are the blessings of pacifism – I also shudder at the military and other triumphalism in Berlin and at the constant kowtowing and confessions of guilt of the Berlin broadcasting station. – And while opinion is virtually being stirred up *for* Natsoc., nothing is being done, at least here in Dresden, to really dislodge it.

I see the situation in a very gloomy light. All the previous mistakes are being repeated and in increased measure. Enemies are reviled and then left in possession of some things. One-sided pacifism is preached at the same time as the enemy expands his power. The title 'Jews' Republic' is virtually invited again. And with all of that there is more hunger every day. Hour by hour the great progress made is praised on the wireless, the benevolence of the Allies is praised and both are only partly true, and each person feels this 'only partly'. – And the populace is so irretrievably stupid and forgetful. Now it thinks only: 'we were not so hungry before', and everything else is forgotten. Very soon it will think: all these Hitler horrors are propaganda inventions.

Admittedly I have no better programme to set against this critique. Hopeless situation.

Childish, but it's true: what affected me most in Mey's reports was the age of my former colleagues: they, too, are now about 60 – I am not the only one who has grown old. (In my memory the others remained young.)

I am so helpless in the face of the great bulk of my diaries, that I cannot make up my mind to continue with the same expansiveness. Also, everything appears to me to be repetition: hunger, the wretchedness of everyday concerns (10 g butter more or less), the errors of the rulers, my heart problems, my most recent and most trivial thoughts on death, my mixed feelings with respect to the tomcat and Eva's love of animals etc. etc. – I have grown too old, and everything has already happened once before.

21st July, Saturday morning
[...]
Very slow and helpless progress in reading the diary. There appears to be no *way* of getting to grips with Curriculum,[47] *LTI* or publication for Neidhardt. Everything is at a standstill, everything is undecided, hic et ubique.[48] Time trickles away in the heat, with heart problems and dry bread – and yet pleasantly drowsy with a lot of wireless.

Berlin Conference of the '*three* great powers'.[49] Always the 'Big Three', always the *three great powers*. France is played out just like Italy. [...]

Jung said: 'The Russians are hauling away our machines, the Americans simply *blow them up*. This blowing up was new to me. So they want to destroy German industry for good. The Russians taking away the railway tracks fits in with that. The result must be *unemployment*. [...] I used to believe there would be no unemployment after this war, after all *everything* would need to be replaced. But if they simply don't allow new production? The present mobilisation of labour is only to clear away rubble and for the harvest – it won't produce anything durable. From day to day I see the future in a gloomier light.

Then in the evening Jung put me on the spot with a request. There was now a 'declaration of nullity' for those who had been forced to join the Party. But this route could only be taken via the KPD. [...] What sort of man was Scholz, could I help? I do not feel very comfortable about the business, neither outwardly nor inwardly. To the outside: I do not want my signature to be devalued, do not want to be seen in general as a friend of Nazis. It may also all too easily be said: he can be bribed. And this is where the inner resistance starts. Do I have a clear conscience with respect to Jung? E. always liked him – I did *not*. He avoided me, was very cautious at least. And now we are very much courted. Trip to Pirna etc., invitation for coffee, and recently even the expensive blue suiting. It was to be 'lent' me for nothing at all, I pressed 100M on the wife – which under today's circumstances, of course, is not a real payment at all. Have I been bribed? Inwardly I do not feel entirely free. I told Jung: Go to Scholz, whom I consider to be a humane man, explain your situation. Refer to me, insofar as I knew you in the years 1934–40 as a friendly and by no means hostile Nazi neighbour, which I can confirm. But the confirmation is only of any value with the double qualification of the date and of knowing you outside professional circumstances. Thus qualified, I can also put it in writing, but perhaps that isn't even necessary...

As I said, I don't feel very happy about it. Vogel, Steininger, perhaps Lehmann[50] at the TH: it adds up.
[...]
I am increasingly strengthened in my own contempt for mankind and my *lack* of vanity. I was treated as lower than a dog, now I am courted by every means – what will tomorrow bring? And contempt and esteem are nothing at

all to do with me as a person, but only with me as an atom or particle or billiard ball – these things are not valuable or valueless in themselves, rather their force is dependent on their particular situation.

23rd July, Monday morning

On Saturday a very cordial letter arrived from Wengler:[51] since April '41 he had been employed in the Wilhelm Nestler[52] Bookshop, Bautzenerstr., and married since June of this year, he would visit us on Sunday with his wife. [...]

Wengler looks considerably aged, with a curiously protruding and twisted lower lip. He already had a stroke a good dozen years ago. – He is very erudite, 1000× more of a philologist than I am, yet without scholarly ambition. He seemed reconciled to his situation, content, although he is only an assistant – the 3rd Reich did not allow him to qualify as a bookseller because of 'unreliability'.

[...]

Yesterday evening [...] I suddenly felt the most thorough-going aversion and absolute saturation with respect to LTI. Decision *not to pursue* any further study of it (as I had originally planned). I shall do the *Notebook of a Philologist*, using the material available, either as a little book on its own or amalgamated with the Curriculum of this period or as the second part of the publication given to Neidhardt. For the time being I must patiently continue skimming through the diaries *for weeks*, with only the blue pencil, and wait for inspiration and also on the development of the general situation and my particular position. – Wengler reported that the Romance languages library at Leipzig had also been completely destroyed by fire, and in his bookshop there were only a very few second-hand items. On the other hand he himself has my works. – Early this morning it occurred to me: obtain a Swiss scholarship, in order to be able to prepare the completion of my 18ième in *Geneva*! At the moment I am very much attracted by everything French, I have had a surfeit of Hitlerism.

24th July, Tuesday evening

Very poor health: serious heart problems on the smallest errand, trouble-someness of the injured foot, which refuses to heal, torment of dental treatment with Dr König, painfully inflamed eyes and neck, but above all and again and again the memento of the angina problems. I dread every errand, at home I fight constant lethargy. [...]

We have had no fat *for weeks* – what good are the heavy workers' cards? I asked the old Vogels – living up at the Pfeifers' – if one was any better off registering at Chemnitzerplatz. – No, there were no deliveries at all to Dresden. Fear of famine, mood towards the Russians very bad. Foolish opinion, things better with the 'Yanks', foolish rumours, the 'Yanks' were going to come here after all. [...]

The food shortage is extreme for us and for everyone – 90% of what we live on is dry bread, which fortunately we have in abundance – and the populace blames the Russians. [...] I no longer wish to write in detail about our own food plight, because as I plough through the diaries, I can see how for years I have been repeatedly writing variations on this theme. What's odd this time, is that we have bread in plenty – but even less of *everything* else, above all of fat, than in the worst times. Poor Eva.

26th July, Thursday morning

If I die now, and my heart is rotten enough for that, I'll get a fine wake. Everyone here knows me, greets me in the street and at home, expresses pleasure at our return. What percentage of that is warmth and what calculation? I shall always be suspicious now. – Yesterday we were visited by Frau Ulbrich, the wife, now widow, of Ulbrich the butcher, whose good customers we were, until he passed on the shop to the young Janiks because of illness. (Frau Janik already spoke to me during the first few days, she is hoping for her husband to return and for her shop to re-open – with her a large percentage of warmth is involved.) Frau U., after many losses very evidently still wealthy, an elderly, good-natured, calm woman, brought flowers and cigarettes, was happy for us, was nothing but an old friend. But then her son did turn up in the conversation, who had survived 6 years in the army, and is a technical school teacher. 'But he is very much needed, he will surely get his post back immediately!' – 'Yes, Professor, but he was *in the club* (sic), he *had* to, after all, and now he's navvying.' There it was. Not a plea to me, but one nevertheless. [...] 'but I have never seen or spoken to your son.' – 'But you know his parents, and we never ...' Etc. etc. [...]

When I fetched E.'s shoes from the cobbler – he had repaired them for the sake of old friendship, E. was for weeks walking around literally in felt slippers without stockings – Schulz, Neidhardt's technical and business partner, jumped from his bicycle at the bottom of the hill; we arranged that he would call in the late afternoon. Afterwards I found the Kornblums, mother and daughter, at home, whom I speedily got rid of [...] Vogel sen. also had to be greeted and thanked: he brought razor blades from his own stock, and potatoes from the Pfeifers, the landowners, with whom he is staying. The late Pfeifer was a farmer, who owned very valuable property up here – we negotiated with him in 1933. His ladies – I don't properly know the family, but there are real ladies there – are friendly to us in a quite disinterested way.

So, later on Schulz came. Some kind of disagreement with the newly appointed department head in the *Land* administration. But the Fackelverlag publishing house, delayed and obstructed, remains. The official wants a sample. *I* am to provide it. [...] For the present: I am working towards an opus, of which I myself do not know *what* shape it is going to take. Diary and *LTI* are *inseparable*, I want to make *one* volume out of them, but how? [...] Schulz makes a good impression, he is evidently really both engineer *and* businessman, was a senior employee or representative of an American typewriter factory, wanted to take a master's exam as a technician and failed because he was 'politically unreliable' [...]. In the course of today I want to force myself to undertake an experiment: I want to write a kind of fair preface to my Diary+*LTI* book; perhaps some possible form of organisation will occur to me as I do so. – Like me, Schulz feels altogether uncertain about the KPD as well as dependent on it. It has to clean out; but it lacks intellectual members, and what will be its attitude to intellectuals and others with an education? The fateful question for *it* and for *us*. I do not want to take a decision in accordance with my – vacillating – emotions, not out of pure idealism, but coolly and calculatingly in accordance with what is best for *my* situation, *my* freedom, *the work I still have to do*, and yet *nevertheless serving my ideal task*, back the right horse. Which is the right horse? The roundabout with the petits chevaux[53] still keeps on turning. Russia? USA? Democracy? Communism? Professor emeritus? Unpolitical? Politically committed? Question mark upon question mark. But perhaps I already took up a position, when I made my opposition to Kühn apparent. [...]

Evening
Professor Winde was here this morning. He, too, bitter at the general lack of thoroughgoing measures. He related: Johst, the very Nazi rector of the TH, good architect (I was acquainted with him 33–35), earned huge sums under the 3rd Reich, was also simultaneously rector of Linz TH, where he was supposed to build a university, and owns a magnificent villa on the Weisser Hirsch. He was supposed to relinquish it and move somewhere more cramped. He managed to keep the villa for himself and get a contract from the city of Dresden to build mini-apartments. The present rector, Hahn, confirmed in office by the Russians, was a battalion commander in the Volkssturm. – Winde said: a general levy was now being demanded of us, a kind of continuation of the Natsoc. Winter Aid programme. From us, who have been bombed out! Why don't they confiscate Nazi assets? – I: We have to join the KPD. – He: Only recently you called yourself a democrat! – I: Yes, but the KPD is needed!

27th July, Friday morning
On the wireless constant appeals to help *bring in the harvest*. In a different tone from the 3rd Reich. Always the dark emphasis on impending starvation. Starvation is not a threat – it is really here. For weeks neither we nor anyone else have had any fat, meat, hardly any food coupons at all redeemed. Always the misery of destruction and plundering [...].

Announced on the wireless: In England (391 out of 640 seats) the Labour Party governing alone for the first time, Attlee Churchill's successor. For the first time 23 women (21 Labour Party) in parliament.

All the strain of these days: the wireless tells us what is happening at every moment in all the world, far away – and there is no postal link with Leipzig.
[...]

30th July, Monday forenoon
I have just corrected the *LTI* introduction, almost 7 closely typed pages, which I have worked on from Thursday until yesterday evening. Beginning and middle are good, the end loses itself in pure philology – *LTI* and diary are simply neither

completely compatible with one another nor can they be cleanly separated. Furthermore, in the final pages, on which I worked hard yesterday, my mood was thoroughly spoilt. This introduction was intended to be the sample piece, for which Schulz had asked, and with which the reluctant government department was to be won over. Schulz and Neidhardt were supposed to come here on Sunday morning for the final discussion of my contract. I had made considerable and successful efforts to finish the piece, as far as was possible, by then, I wanted to read it to the two of them. They did *not* come, and so now the whole business is up in the air again. [...]

In the afternoon we were supposed to be at the Windes'; my foot, on which the minor injury, really only an abrasion, has refused to heal for many weeks now and hurts, was swollen. In a triumphal mood I would nevertheless have gone. In my depression I cried off. Eva went alone, and in the silence of the afternoon I then managed the rest of the introduction. But if the book planned for Neidhardt does not materialise, it's of no use.

On Sunday morning the wireless [...] regularly broadcasts a Protestant church service with ringing of bells, choir, sermon. Yesterday there spoke in a sonorous voice, but quite without affectation and unctuousness, the Protestant bishop of Berlin [...] Dibelius.[54] At first I was very pleasantly enthralled. Paul to the Athenians, that is, as if he were speaking to cultivated people in Weimar today. How can he convey his tidings to the educated, the philosophers? They are not at all intractable atheists, they are *seekers after God*, they know of the *unknown God*. But that is simply not sufficient. One must find HIM, one must come to know him, one must have certainty, one would so like to have it. But how? – And now came the disappointment, which always comes, if one entrusts oneself to pastors. One must just 'change one's ways', one must see Jesus, for Jesus is the side of God turned towards man, the knowable side. So now I know exactly and may believe in the loving kindness of the Heavenly Father despite all the ghastliness of these last years. Every day it becomes more puzzling to me, how people can believe in a kind, loving God etc. I more than ever want to leave the Church, which so shamefully let me down.

Yesterday the Felix Neubert couple came to see us, the people with the butcher's shop in Plauenschen Gasse, whose customers we were when we lived at 8 Hohe Strasse. *Good men*. The wife had already, by chance, spoken to me in the city during the first few days. Bombed out, without their own shop. Now the man has been offered a butcher's in Freital – the trade inspectorate there is causing problems – perhaps Herr Professor can help. (I recently heard from Winde the joke from the end of the Hitler times: Whoever recruits 10 members for the Party, can leave it, whoever recruits 20, gets a J in his identity card! In any case Neubert – always the first question! – was not a pg.) By chance I really was able to help. Frau Wolff's father is an important and influential KPD official in Freital. [...]

Yesterday a little boy, perhaps 12, 14 years old, rang at the door: 'Refugee – have you got something to eat?' I said: 'Unfortunately we have nothing.' My conscience was not quite clear – I should have given the boy a piece of dry bread. I thought of the woman in the Munich old people's home, who systematically sent out her children to beg. But apart from dry bread we ourselves have nothing to spare [. . .].

1st August, Wednesday

A letter from *Leipzig*, dated 3 July, arrived on Monday, 30 July, with a *Dresden* postmark (that is, posted here by a tardy visitor). Trude Öhlmann:[55] hoping that we were still alive, without a clue that for 5 years we had *not* been in our house. She herself is still living at 10 Bussestr., we had believed this house, this street destroyed long ago. She had been through terrible things, she would tell us as soon as she knew whether her letter had reached us. She signed it: 'Your deeply unhappy Trude.' How to send a reply?

[. . .]

Yesterday the widow of Master Haubold was here, a grey-haired woman, careworn, depressed. Her situation: her husband had lost his customers, because the rulers in Dölzschen – Kalix, Sonntag – had called him the 'red plumber' and because he had resisted them. To save him or the business she then joined the Party, and that did help. Of two sons, both plumbers, one (the present master here) remained outside the Party, the other (in the army, somewhere in Bavaria, whereabouts unknown, his wife and child died on 13th February) became a pg. Now the young master was being urged to join the KPD, she, Frau H., was advising him not to – it was impossible to know if everything would stay as it was. After all, it was constantly being said, that the Americans would come here! – Treading warily I said: I myself had never been a Communist, but now a general clean-out was necessary. I, too, would much prefer to stay away from politics, not join a party – but if pressure was being placed on her son, then the Communists were a party and not criminals; and originally SPD – old Haubold was an SPD man – and KPD had been *one* party [. . .] and they must become *one* party again, with a right and a left wing [. . .]. I added: the Americans were no better than the Russians, worse, rather, and they would not come to Dresden and wage war with the Russians and still less would they do so in alliance with Germany.

These rumours America against Russia don't stop. Nazi propaganda still has an effect, is probably still being secretly carried on. Is Dresden especially petit bourgeois, especially Nazi – or is the whole of Germany like this?

I can state to the minute the point at which my bliss turned into the opposite [. . .]: when I saw Kühn at the official performance of *Nathan* and sat next to Janentzky. Since then my depression has got steadily worse, exacerbated by physical things – I am tortured by my teeth, I am hampered by my foot, which refuses to heal, I am worried by my very palpable heart, I am depressed by the chaos in our domestic affairs, to which there is no solution, and which harnesses me to domestic chores, I am tormented by my eternal tiredness. The principal calamity, nevertheless, is that no one is interested in me professionally: I hear nothing from Menke-Glückert, nothing from the TH, nothing from Neidhardt.

[. . .]

Daily questions to myself, no, hourly ones: what is the point of this diary reading? Is the wireless more a stimulus or more a waste of time? Why do German affairs look rosy on the wireless, at least 100 times rosier than in reality? (It doesn't really lie, but it reports *only* and *exclusively* the *snail's* pace progress of reconstruction. And then: I am too old; I have heard all these promises, plans etc. etc. in 1919, and – mutatis mutandis – in 1933 as well.

2nd August, Thursday morning

The Berlin 'Deutsche Volkszeitung' (KPD) [. . .] of 28 July, prints the programme of Wilmersdorf People's High School,[56] and announced there: Dr Linfert: The Style of NS language. My LTI in other words. I should have expected it. [. . .] But this morning I want to go to Nestler-Wengler. Perhaps I, too, shall first present my LTI as lectures at the People's High School here.

Frau Dember,[57] when she was here from Istanbul, stayed in the villa of the wealthy Jew (and Czech) Kussi. We visited her there once and were given a very friendly welcome. Two gentlemen, in their mid-30s, came into the room and exchanged a few words with us. That was all the contact we had. Of faces I vaguely see white-bearded Kussi père, whom I once met at Isakowitz, the dentist. Then we heard: the father had died in a Berlin hospital, the sons, racing to his deathbed, had been involved in a serious car accident, but had escaped with the loss of a few teeth. That is all I know about the Kussi family. The Dembers spoke with the greatest respect of their Rheostat (? electrical instruments of some kind) factory and of their wealth. – Now yesterday a letter signed: '. . . in old friendship your very devoted Dr W. Kussi'[58] on the company notepaper of Rheostat-Habege(??) – an Aryan name in the letterhead has been crossed out and replaced by 'Dr Werner Kussi'. K. writes: '. . . After several years spent in various concentration camps, I have finally returned here from Auschwitz. My family was murdered in Auschwitz . . .' [. . .] He has by chance heard of our return [. . .] the letter is dated 16 July, postmarked the 31st – wants to visit us. Curious the mixture of dubious business German and dreadful private content. Noteworthy the 'in old friendship'. Does he clutch at survivors of those days?

3rd August, Friday morning

[. . .]

Yesterday morning at Nestler's shop on Bautzenerstr. Nestler himself absent. Wengler very helpful. In the shop at the front the scantiest stock, a couple of slim army editions, a couple of music notebooks, stationery. A few second-hand things. Behind the shop a big room as office, a kitchen, in which there was cooking going on. Several women and young people busy. All very, very meagre, the French things I was shown were nothing [. . .]. I borrowed the dictionary I was offered [. . .]. I discussed the LTI possibilities with Wengler. Perhaps *one* lecture or two for the 'preview' of the People's High School. But nothing definite [. . .].

Meanwhile continued very slow reading of diary, everything uncertain, tooth and dentist torment. But basically not despairing. *Everything* is going just as slowly and falteringly for *everyone*: that is the general German condition in the summer of 45. Today the Potsdam communiqué[59] is on the wireless: peace *treaties* with the others, peace *settlement* with us.

At the bookshop I was able to write a couple of lines to Trude Öhlmann: 'The boss' is travelling to L. today and will take it with him for the city post there. [...] The first letter from Leipzig to Dresden has arrived. But on the tram I heard that there is not yet any post from Dresden–Leipzig. [...]

4th August, Saturday forenoon

In the morning the Potsdam communiqué was read out on the wireless. Shattering, quite egoistically shattering. Germany will be so castrated, so poor, such an outcast, that we two will never get on our feet again. The dry bread, no fat, on which we have been living literally for weeks, will accompany us for the rest of our lives. Who is going to pay for my demands, my losses? (Nothing in the communiqué suggests that the Allies want to look after the German Jews.) I shall get a tiny salary or old-age pension, that will be all. Professor at the TH or the university? At most a junior instructor at Dresden Technical School. Publish books and in journals?? Everything will be lacking, publishers, printing presses etc. etc. Shrunken little Germany will be a pitiful agrarian state without independence, without any possibility of recovery.

I continue muddling along with my diary reading. [...]

The dentist continues to torment me, my heart problems continue to torment me, my eye problems too. Despite that: up here there is peace, and between diary, wireless, a nice volume from the library left behind by the Bergers, sleeping, and the most frugal meals, at home and with the Wolffs, together with a few domestic chores, one can doze quite nicely through the evening of one's life.

[...]

6th August, Monday evening

Great heat, great weariness, constant heart problems when walking – I must go to Katz, perhaps iodine will help.

[...]

Today exhausting, not quite unfruitful trip into town. 1) at Nestler's – ('the boss' in Leipzig – the boss is chairman of the new People's High School) – with Wengler, who took notes of what I said and will work it up, agreed the following. a) I shall speak at a 'preview' in September for about 90–120 minutes about the basic outlines of the *LTI* – I found it odd, when Wengler used the term LTI quite as if it were the most natural thing – and will then give a winter course of 8 hours on the details. [...] b) In the winter I shall give 8 one-hour lectures on the German image of France from the beginnings to the present. – Wengler gave me a statement he had composed on the reorganisation of modern language teaching 'in a free, democratic and anti-Fascist Germany'. With extreme agitational brusqueness he demands the combined study of language, literature and culture without 'suicidal arrogance'. 'It is proper for us, above all, to show modesty in the face of the achievement of others and to openly confess our own deficiencies, which is a debt we owe thanks to our own presumption.' He wants compulsory teaching of Russian and *American*; second, more as an optional subject, and only where local conditions make it necessary, the (minor) Slav and the Romance languages. French is not even listed separately. [...]

I then went to Melanchthonstr., arranged [...] an appointment with Grohmann for Wed. The well-informed secretary in response to my questions: Grohmann – 'patrician' Communist [...] was now also involved in the state administration, was to some extent more important than Menke-Glückert, 'could not be pinned down'. But everything was uncertain, and the Russians repeatedly interfered, issued prohibitions, there was no progress. The secondary schools were ready to start, there came a veto from the Russians. Barracks had been made available to some artists: the Russians requisitioned the barracks. Etc. etc. The TH was M.-Gl.'s responsibility, but was ruled by a Russian lieutenant-colonel and Rector Hahn, and Janentzky was doing a lot (with whom??). Fräulein von Rüdiger had been dismissed. (So there my protest to Janentzky was effective.) I set forth the Kühn case. – In Leipzig, at the Americans' suggestion, the majority of professors had gladly departed with the former(!!) – no one had any idea what should happen there. – Now I shall see how things continue on Wednesday. At some point I want to 'join in' myself. It is probably not too late for anything.

8th August, Wednesday morning

Yesterday night and day so wretched (probably influenza? a slight temperature), that I was completely slowed down, slept a lot.

My diary reading shows ever more clearly, that *LTI* is substantially more suitable for publication than the actual diary. It is shapeless, it incriminates the Jews, also it could not be reconciled with the opinions that predominate now, it would also be indiscreet.

[...]

From the Potsdam communiqué, which is still being praised on the wireless as humane beyond all expectation, while the amputation of the eastern German provinces is passed over in silence, it should really be obvious, that not Russia alone, but that all the Allies together are making Germany 'suffer'.

For myself I face a constant dilemma. I want to be on the furthest left wing of the KPD, I want to be for Russia. And on the other hand: My kind of freedom!

Today the wireless is full of the *atom bomb*, which was mentioned for the first time yesterday.[60]

[...]

9th August, Thursday morning

Yesterday forenoon with Grohmann: today forenoon I am to meet him at the state administration building, we will talk with M.-Gl., he wants to introduce me to Friedrichs. M.-Gl. is too reactionary for him, 'wants to open the old TH', has to be pushed, is too old. Gr. wants to influence Friedrichs through me. Gr. is very opposed to Kühn. This 'curious gentleman' gave Nazi lectures. I cautiously said, referring to M.-Gl., he felt bitter. Gr.: 'Not bitter enough.' I: 'a little broken'. – Hardly had I got back in the afternoon, than Anna Mey appeared and stayed until 8. [...] The same conversations as recently. She defended Kühn. He was no Nazi. Just so impulsive. On a questionnaire: 'were relatives members of the NSDAP?' he writes: 'Am I a common informer?' I: 'Do you think he would have dared write that on a questionnaire of the 3rd Reich?' The professoriate is playing the same game as 1919–1933. Fräulein Mey: no one knew how long those ruling now would remain in power. And: the rumour is still going around, that the Americans will come here ... How good Goebbels' propaganda was! How necessary a thorough clean-up would be! – Gr. also objected to the excessively 'petit bourgeois' planning and administration of the People's High School programme. Advised caution. Yesterday meanwhile a letter arrived from Wengler with the formulation of my 'preview', also a card from Riedel, the academic director. I am in a dilemma.

10th August, Friday morning

Yesterday actually entirely taken up with the Saxon state administration. It resides in the magnificent building of the [former] regional air administration and I was there from 12 until 4. One adds to that the difficulty in getting there (dreadful gap with no tram [...] most horribly devastated area), the even greater difficulty of the return journey with constant thundery downpours (without umbrella and coat), after that still a dentist session.

I have often admired the regional air administration with despair and hate, and I never believed that I would one day enter it. A small town embedded in a park [...]. Hundreds of rooms, in the plaster on the walls all kinds of aeronautical symbols. Elegant gatehouse entry at the front; one has to have a pass – I received a permanent one. But upstairs on the second floor lakes in the corridors and rooms, ceilings and walls damp from the previous day's downpour, and water had also come through to the first floor. The roof heavily damaged and still unrepaired, roofers had only just arrived. – Another miserable feature: Grohmann: 'we must go to lunch, we have eaten nothing since early this morning; we cannot invite you, Fischer (the deputy president) recently warned us not to bring a guest again.' [...] So I sat hungry on a bench in the corridor and waited $\frac{3}{4}$ of an hour, reading.

12th August, Sunday afternoon

First of all I met Neumark's very likeable stepson, Dr Kretzschmar, whom I already knew, and who is now working here with Grohmann. Then came Grohmann himself. The same old song: Menke-Glückert needed to be woken up, he wanted to revive the old Technical High School with the old personnel and the old opinions. M.-Gl. received me with uncommon warmth, as if we had been close friends before the 3rd Reich. The Kühn case was discussed, I became very animated (in Grohmann's presence), explained how the state had been sabotaged before, warned against a repetition. M.-Gl. altogether obliging, he also wants to secure a chair for me in Leipzig. But he nevertheless urged me to take an approach, which seemed mistaken to both myself and Grohmann and at which E. was afterwards outraged: 'You write to the TH, you make a request to be re-instated. Half an hour later you have been re-appointed and on top of that have the satisfaction, that your enemies themselves had to propose you. Then you yourself can work to change the spirit of the professoriate ... But by myself I can do nothing; *you* must help me.' – Afterwards, so as to remain on good terms with M.-Gl., I made the application. E. and everything in me protested against it: I do not need to petition the TH to be re-appointed [...]. My financial claims, said M.-Gl., are with the President and they will give rise to a cabinet decision in principle. The government intends – state bankruptcy! – to reject all claims on the Hitler state, mark a new beginning and then give 'assistance' on its own initiative. – Even before we had called on M.-Gl., Gr. had announced my visit to President Friedrichs. So I waited in the corridor, while Gr. and M.-Gl. ate, and then, long after 2 p.m., with Gr. to the First President. Pure cinema. Large room. Right at the back on the far side, many yards from the door, behind a huge desk, the President; intimidating awkwardness of crossing the whole room. But Friedrichs rose immediately [...], came towards me to the middle of the room, where he shook my hand. Imposing figure, thick, completely silver hair down to his ears, face half Friesian farmer, half Field-Marshal Moltke.[61] (It is said, however, he is 25% Semite.) Was a senior civil servant in some pre-Hitler administration, is a legal expert. Very calm, courteously dignified manner. I had to sit in front of his desk. Grohmann sat to one side of me, gave me cues to get me talking, so that Friedrichs was informed about me. In between a telephone call for Fr.; Grohmann whispered to me: 'we'll take our leave shortly.' Fr. asked me: 'You have nothing at all?' I: 'Only the empty house.' For a moment there was talk of my works. [...] Then we shook hands again and left. Grohmann summed up outside: 'He now knows you personally, and that's good when your concerns come to be discussed.' The whole thing a little scene from a play [...] Whether the business was worthwhile remains to be seen.

That together with the subsequent dentist session and the letters to the TH and to M.-Gl., to whom I presented my Leipzig request in writing with a degree of pathos – in the latter I believed 'myself without false modesty capable of making some contribution to the reconstruction of my Fatherland; I emphasise "my", for no matter what has happened to me, I can have no other' – that, therefore, took up the whole of the 9th of August.

On the 10th we both called on the new man in the Begerburg (the clothes store) – he, Seidemann,[62] appears to be simultaneously the leader of the KPD group up here. He made a very good impression on both of us. In his mid-30s, bookkeeper and Communist official, spent years in prisons and concentration camps. A very calm and not uneducated man. The conversation quickly went beyond our clothes etc. requests and on to the political situation. The crux of what we said was: You are too soft! With your kid gloves you will not win over a *single* bourgeois opponent, but put off your own supporters. S. invited us to the first (semi-improvised) anti-Fascist afternoon held today in the Begerburg, the former NSDAP stronghold.

On the afternoon of the 10th Elsa Kreidl[63] turned up unexpectedly; she had learned of our presence here and brought a youthful Fräulein Huhle with her, the niece of Fräulein Ludwig[64]. Elsa Kreidl, become very thin, very ill-looking, was interesting in two respects. First of all because of the terrible abundance of her death notices. According to her information *all* (or almost all) of the Jews who were taken from here to Poland or Theresienstadt are dead: Ida Kreidl, Paul Kreidl (hanged), Kätchen Sara Voss, the Hirschels, the Kahlenbergs ...[65] with them probably also Frau Ziegler, Lissy Meyerhof, Caroli Stern.[66] [...] Frl. Ludwig, the upright aunt of Frl. Huhle, died on 13 February, her body was not found. – After that Elsa Kreidl was important for her bitter fear of the Communists – I think she would still prefer the Nazis to them. That's firmly entrenched in the petits bourgeois. [...] Frl. Huhle is looking for employment – previously a secretary in an industrial company, but that's finished now – I advised provisional teacher training, which is being widely publicised and sent her over to Forbrig to find out about it. (The Russians have recently closed the already 'running' elementary schools again. First the schools are to be 'purged', and provisionally trained lay personnel will simply have to be enlisted to replace the kicked out Nazis.)

I spent the forenoon of yesterday, Saturday the 11th, up in Dölzschen. Registering for coal – for coke I shall have to apply to the highest authority (required for profession) – and trying to get a new umbrella, which Frau Börner, the teller at the giro bank, promised me from her own things. I also received ration coupons, with which (sceptically!) we shall try our luck. The friendliness with which we are treated up there again and again gives me a kind of fairy-tale pleasure. And finally all friendliness is not or at least not only self-interested sail trimming, here and there real sympathy is at work.

Then in the afternoon, as announced, the Schmidts were here for coffee. The coffee was real, but they got only bread and a little jam with it. They themselves brought a large basket of apricots and a little crispbread. Admittedly they turned up four strong. The son, Günther, is now working in a hospital [...]. The daughter, Traute, who is clearing rubble at the moment, I advised, like Frl. Huhle, to take up teaching. Schmidt sen. said very little at all, his good-natured wife talked about her worries. Again the petit bourgeois fear of the KPD. 'If they take the house away from us – if they bring up my husband's enforced membership of the Party ...' Here, too, I tried to set minds at rest.

[...] At 12 we ate at the Wolffs' and then came the event at the Begerburg. And so for days I have not done any of my own work. In the Begerburg from 4.30–6.30 about 80 people. A handsome room (with a view down to the green gorge), a grand piano, benches, a chairman's table. Two girls played the accordion prettily, two others sang simple songs in two-part harmony, a choir of little schoolgirls sang. Seidemann spoke very nicely, only occasionally falling into cliches, the parties, people had to get to know one another. With rather more pathos, with rather more cliches, rather more broadly, but also very passably, Forbrig said the same thing for the SPD side and then read out, as exemplary, a popular pedagogical novella, *Fraternal Strife*. With a rather Saxon-accented pathos, another man read political verses by Heine, to which Seidemann gave a short literary history introduction – saying nothing about the Jew Heine. (Heine and Mendelssohn are now the most frequently mentioned Germans.) More interesting than the harmless afternoon was the epilogue in the office, where I got two neckties and a pair of underpants. Again I preached to Seidemann: Your gentleness is futile, the petit bourgeois fears you and thinks you are being hypocritical. S. invited me to give a lecture as rectification. I declined for the time being. E. said: otherwise people will just say: 'The Jew wants to take his revenge.' [...]

Dominating wireless broadcasts and interest is *Japan*.[67] It is, though, being treated a little better than Germany.

Seidemann said it was so very bad for the KPD that the Russians were such a disappointment to us. In point of fact, the starvation, the dismantling of machinery and no doubt the looting just goes on and on.

14th August, Tuesday forenoon
Visitors all the time, occasionally (yesterday) trip into town necessary; apart from that the wireless, everything else has come to a standstill, and beyond and above that the need to sleep.

Yesterday forenoon to Nestler-Wengler; more fiddling around with the announcement of the LTI lectures. (Made W.'s draft a little less radical and cliched.) [...]

[...] Forbrig complained [...] bitterly about the Russians [...]. The occupiers received far too much meat, the population for weeks neither meat nor fat, there was a shortage of potatoes and the Russians requisitioned potatoes for distilleries, looting and outrages occurred repeatedly, and the German police was not allowed to do anything about it, trains of refugees from Silesia were being robbed by Poles every day and the Russians permitted it. [...]

16th August, Thursday morning
The Hungarian barber, who brought us the little tomcat, came yesterday evening and we both had our hair cut. He is a Communist. He complained almost despairingly about the Russians: they let us starve, they take away the last potatoes even from the factory workers' canteens, prevent *any* reconstruction, bring even the most peaceable small companies to a halt through looting, there are frequent robberies by the soldiers. And all that is laid at the door of the KPD and benefits Nazism and stands in the most harmful contrast to what wireless and newspapers preach. *They* lie, just as they lied under Hitler ... Now the barber really is vox populi, really does express the communis opinio [...]

Otherwise monotony; very wearisome reading in the closely written diary. Much tiredness, frequent heart problems, very gloomy mood.

The principal political events: Japan capitulation and Pétain[68] sentenced to death (not carried out, because he is 89 years of age). A real newspaper is lacking, the Communist newssheet, which is delivered daily for 20 pfennigs, contains nothing more than the same news and dubious phrases which are broadcast at least three times a day. My kind of freedom – I see no difference [...] between LTI and LQI.

17th August, Friday morning

Yesterday evening something blew up in the wireless. The house feels as deserted as after the murder of a child. It is hardly any different for E.; we laugh about it, but it's true. That's how used to the wireless we have become; there is something opium-like, numbing about it, we doze with the wireless on, sleep, get through the day without thinking and without boredom. It is or was especially important to me now, when everything is stagnating.

[...]

I have to go to see Nestler again, I am to be introduced to Dr Riedel, the director of the People's High School. I fear the trip into town. I do not have a Russian identity card, and there are said to be checks, arrests, also robberies. No one who is not a resident here or has work here is allowed to stay in Dresden. Same measures and prohibition in Berlin. – Misery of the refugees driven out of Poland and the Czech Republic. They beg their way [and] are to be crammed into overcrowded Mecklenburg.

We live *literally* on dry bread. Without the heavy workers' cards, without Steininger and Schwarz-Braune, without the Wolffs we would be starving. Yesterday Dr König, who pesters me a lot, said: 'Good thing, that we don't have any gas yet; otherwise there would be plenty of suicides.' [...] I told him about the Gestapo words: 'Go and buy yourself 10 pfennigs worth of gas!' For all that: we, too, suffer very greatly from the food shortage. But even more depressing is the overall situation.

18th August, Saturday morning

Yesterday forenoon very long session at Nestler's. N. himself, back from Leipzig, calm, congenial grey-haired man. Riedel, somewhat pinched, clean-shaven, mid-forties, a little school masterly [...] but very reasonable, level-headed, polite. I was able to considerably simplify and de-politicise the announcement. [...]

In the wireless it was only a fuse that had gone, Wolff patched it, and it is going again without a care.

19th August, Sunday towards evening

Yesterday morning, on 18 August 45, at the registry office on Chemnitzer Platz (town hall) we both – a dry formality – left the Lutheran Protestant Church. It let us down too badly in the Nazi times. A great deal could be said about it – emotionally the business is very complicated. Time is lacking.

In the afternoon we had to obtain our new residence cards at an office in Westendstr. An extremely bothersome and wearisome business, one had to go to several tables, was showered with questions – on the one hand they want to replace files that have been destroyed, on the other they want to trace Nazis [...], thirdly, only those who were already resident here on 1 September 39 are to be allowed to stay in Dresden and receive food ration cards. People stood in line and, as I heard, had to sacrifice almost three hours. I was helped by my priority certificate, which I had from Scholz – because of my sufferings as a Jew and because of my ripe old age! I was treated very courteously, hardly any documents were required as proof, and was dealt with in about half an hour. But the cards for E. and myself now also have to be 'registered' at the town hall on Chemnitzer Platz, and later they have to get a Russian stamp as well, because without it one risks being picked up on the street by Russian soldiers and pressed into clearing rubble. I found the town hall closed. – Driven by lack of coffee substitute, I now walked the long, beautiful and memory-laden stretch to Caspar David Friedrich Strasse down Nöthnitzer and Moreau Str. by way of Zschertnitz. The military hospital, in front of which I shovelled snow with Dr Magnus,[69] while inside there were not enough doctors to carry out amputations, is in ruins, the Berghof inn next to it intact and open for custom. The beautiful vista.

I found Elsa Kreidl at home, here, too, memories in garden and apartment.[70] Nothing changed, only the bench, on which Friedheim[71] and Kreidl were in the habit of sitting, was gone. Elsa K. gave me a friendly welcome, she gave me ersatz coffee, a hat belonging to her husband, fragments of shoe laces and French books. I then walked to Wasaplatz, to our old grocer Hähnel. I had to go into their sitting room as a guest, I was presented with a cigar, I got Rispa coffee and Maggi cubes without coupons – the people want to visit us.

I then took the tram back and was not home until 6.30. Hardly had we eaten, than Seidemann (the new KPD group leader) appeared with his wife and stayed until midnight. In the end E. put tea and dry bread on the table. S. is 37, dull eyes and blond hair, calm resolute character, a certain hardness and abruptness in manner – then one realises that there is feeling, reflection, idealism, experience, self-education, also unsureness behind it, his wife reddish pale, hollow-cheeked, very quiet. They have a six-year-old daughter. S. had to get to know the child again, with interruptions he was in prison and concentration camps before and during the war. [...] I asked him about his profession, his schooling. Elementary education, autodidact, idealist, seeker, visionary – not a fanatic, hungry for education [...]. He was a bookkeeper for his brother, he tried this and that, has now registered for teacher training. What he has lived on until now and how he has supported his marriage is obscure to me. No doubt she worked. [...] I already noticed recently during his introductory words on Heine, how he seeks and turns things over in his mind. At the same time all woolliness, narrowness, also all show is absent. The man is unpretentious and, I believe, genuine. – From the library of Kluge – the Nazi judge, in whose confiscated apartment the Wolffs are living – I had taken for my permanent use a Schiller, a Nietzsche, a tiny English dictionary and a couple of school textbooks:

Seidemann looked longingly at the Nietzsche and I gave him both volumes. [...] The concept of property is becoming completely lost: I do not mourn my own stolen and burned things, with just as little emotion I make use of the 'confiscated' furniture and books of others, I also calmly hold on to the rings of the late Kätchen Sara, I worry very little about my debts and my lack of income. I live like the lily of the field.

20th August, Monday forenoon
Curious how people gradually emerge from the chaos and the ruins. Yesterday afternoon Frau Jährig, formerly Neumarks' secretary [...].

22nd August, Wednesday forenoon
Most wearisome progress in the diary with constant distraction, inflamed eyes, tiredness etc.

On Monday forenoon I was at the State Library. The big, well-preserved Scharnhorst School on Eisenacherstr. (22 tram as far as Schandauerstr., Zeiss-Ikon factory – the ruins of the inner city stand out all the more horribly, the more clearing up that is done.) [...] Dr Neubert, whom I remember as young, looks very much aged given his thin grey hair and general undernourishment and speaks with great resignation. (Become director and Party member in 39, his position is of course very shaky.) 'We are in suspense here, from day to day I do not know what is going to happen.' I related it to his own person, which he denied. 'If I go, there'll be someone else; but we are beginning to get settled here and now State Secretary Menke-Glückert plans to move the college of education here.' About 200,000 volumes had been burned, much was still in store in the cellar of the Japanese Palace, a large proportion had been removed to the Bautzen area and had been looted – it was as yet impossible to determine what had been saved there and when what had been saved could be transported back. And that is precisely where the Romance literatures things are likely to be. But he would write to me, if some of my needs (French literary history and bibliography, my own works) turned up again; and as long as no reading room had been opened I could also have books at home. He was very accommodating, simultaneously, as already mentioned, very resigned and sceptical. Complaints about the Russians here, too. [...]

At the Wolffs the talk was and is only of the forfeiture of all deposits at present held by banks,[72] her mother, typical of very small savers, loses 7,000M, all her fortune. (We ourselves must still have 150 marks in the blocked account in the Deutsche Bank – no great loss) [...].

On Tuesday forenoon (yesterday) up to the Begerburg to see Seidemann. E. will (as agreed recently) play and accompany on a Sunday. A few weeks later I will give a lecture there, which is supposed to draw the middle classes. I want to show how each nation contributes to culture as a whole, each in its own way is chosen, each has its own special hour. [...] From the stores E. got a raincoat, I a shirt, a pair of braces was also found. [...]

At around coffee time Hilde Rasch, quite grown up, appeared. We want to take in the Raschs as soon as possible: 1) there are already admonitory letters coming from the housing office, 2) we need help with domestic chores. Yesterday an investigator from the housing office took up a lot of our time. (When he heard that I was Jewish and a friend of Scholz, he became *very* affable.) 1) the shop fittings have to go; the ground for that has now been prepared, a very talkative Frau Müller will get them for her new haberdashery shop – the braces already mentioned above come from her. 2) the shop has to be turned back into a proper room and 3) coke delivery has to be approved by the coal office.

[...]

Letter from 'State Secretary Menke-Glückert' (official letterhead), he would issue instructions for my teaching appointment at the University of Leipzig, as soon as I had been re-appointed professor here. And what if the TH does not propose me again?

[...]

Letter from Trude Öhlmann. Her son Claus has been missing since December 42, he came down with his plane over Murmansk. During an air raid in Dec. 43 she herself suffered concussion and her arm was broken in two places – 'arm not much use' – in the Deutsche Bücherei in Leipzig. In December 44 – supposedly after-effects of the fall – she had a major operation: tumour (cancer?), her right breast, a muscle in the upper arm removed, 4 months in hospital. Her clothed weight (and she was a very fat woman), less than eight stone, her apartment damaged. The Deutsche Bücherei is also badly damaged, 220,000 volumes and the publishers' catalogue destroyed by fire, $2\frac{1}{2}$ million volumes evacuated. Bitter complaints also about hunger.

Towards evening

Old Testament-like: when I went up to Haubold at the village square – a drainpipe running from the eaves gutter has come loose and there are rain and thunderstorms every day – I met Frau Dr Eichler [a neighbour] and her boy. They were going to *glean*, acquaintances were doing it as well, they could manage to collect at least a little bit of grain. The shortage is simply tremendous. Yesterday our baker up here issued a $4\frac{1}{2}$ pound coupon to me, in addition there are Steininger's and Schwarz's gifts (for how much longer with the ever-greater shortage?), and Eva's heavy worker's card (for how much longer??), and with all of that we shall only barely make it to the next ration. [...]

24th August, Friday forenoon

Invitation from the *Democratic Cultural Union* [Kulturbund][73] to sign its appeal, to participate in its scholars' group. Analogous to the Berlin and Leipzig undertakings, association of all Dresden 'notables' (nebbich,[74] with the exception of the actor Ponto really very paltry). This is no secret little clique, however, and I must join in. And once again Herr Kühn is there, I also find the name Felix Zimmermann suspect, he is chairman of the Literary Association and I think he has an unpleasant article on Gerhart Hauptmann's[75] 80th birthday on his conscience. I shall talk to Grohmann, he and Kretzschmar are naturally also present.

[...]

Visits are killing me. Yesterday the beautiful Maria Kube, who is living in Räckelwitz – her husband is still a prisoner of war, the boys are supposed to go to grammar school here – and the Steiningers, who brought us a bread coupon, but also see the bread future as gloomy. In addition still the dentist torment. He said the terrible drilling literally took twice as long as it did before, because there was no hard steel to be had.

[...]

25th August, Saturday forenoon

Very little time for working through the diary.

Yesterday afternoon, a brother of Seidemann (commercial artist) here with a woman singer, who is to give a concert with E. in the Begerburg. [...] At all events E. [...] and myself in despair, despite all the stimulation, at the loss of time.

Today a large part of the morning was taken by the letter, which I *had* to write to Trude Öhlmann. Someone is just travelling to Leipzig and will take it along, that's still quicker than the regular post.

[...]

My efforts to read something after supper repeatedly come to nought because of utter tiredness. [...]

27th August, Monday forenoon

On Sunday we eat with the Wolffs at 12 instead of 1 (infinitely wretched and hungry, a most scanty plate of soup). As we were about to go over, Elsa Kreidl appeared [...] Elsa Kreidl, absolutely good and generous, nevertheless once again showed herself a narrow-minded petite bourgeoise with a tendency to Natsoc. Everything inside her is fear and antipathy towards the Communists and the Russians. But, with respect to the Russians, I shall soon be the only person in all of Dresden who will half or quarter way defend them: the want is too great and everyone feels robbed and unsparingly subject to hunger.

Back late from the miniature lunch, we very soon had to leave for the Windes, who are occupying the apartment of a painter on Calberlastr., off Pillnitzer Landstr. The moment we were leaving, Lewinsky[76] appeared unannounced, become very much thinner, but utterly unchanged in character. Still armed with freshly bought books of every kind, even though all his earlier ones were burnt, even though there is hardly anything to buy, but someone who grabs indiscriminately will always find something, still the old mixture of great modesty and great thespian affectedness. Since we were already taken today, he simply set off to see his woman friend – it turned out she lives around the corner from Calberlastr. and so we had to make the long journey on no. 22 and no. 18 together (and we met again on the return journey!).

The route took us past the Jacoby Villa,[77] the only ruin in a well-preserved part of town.

The view from the Windes' apartment across the Elbe to the hills [. . .]. Inside, much modesty and much art – a large, brightly coloured Central Asian painting dominated. He was very lively and youthful in a close-fitting, very short and very worn leather jacket, she looking much aged, very thin, a very little bit slovenly. Tea and jam at a tiny table – we had brought bread. For hours he showed us his work (one of the three rooms serves as a studio). Turned bowls and beakers and little boxes in different kinds of wood [. . .]. On the whole I was of course very quiet and very aware of my lack of competence and response.

28th August, Tuesday forenoon

Before midday yesterday I was able to work through a couple of pages of diary [. . .]. Then came the Krömer letter from Falkenstein, the first post from there! and the reply took a long time. I once chatted to the Krömer couple for half an hour in Scherner's private office,[78] without them making any very strong impression on me. He, a doctor who fled from Oppeln, was employed by the pension office in F. and has now lost his job. His wife turns to me 'in despair', could I somehow help him obtain a post, in Dresden they had been 'downright negative'. Although he had never been a pg. He does not know how he will survive. – I asked for further details, at the same time included greetings to the Scherners. – I felt very flattered. Deplorably human, all too human: for some people here I am now a bigwig. How small I would be, if the musician Otto Klemperer[79] were still alive! That often goes through my head, when the wireless praises the returning Jewish conductors etc. What a fuss there would have been for Otto Kl.! Now he means nothing to the public. – Yesterday the news of Werfel's[80] death was broadcast. He was only 54. What right have I, with my almost 64 years, to want to go on living any longer?

Just as the letter to Krömer was finished, Seidemann appeared with his wife and little daughter. [. . .] Again talk turned to the excessively hesitant and timid activity of the KPD. Once again I found it embarrassing, how little the Communist officials know about bureaucracy, about administrative and academic matters. [. . .] Seidemann is more educated than Scholz, but likewise 'untrained'. – It is very greatly to my advantage, that here in Dölzschen I am a kind of honourable grey-beard and, so to speak, intermediary between Communists and bourgeois. Now, for example, I am enlisting Housing Office and KPD (Scholz and Seidemann) in order to obtain coke instead of the briquettes allocated to private household by the Coal Office.

[. . .] After supper I then fell asleep listening to the wireless. Eva too.

30th August, Thursday forenoon

[. . .] Meanwhile I heard yesterday at the Kulturbund, that the People's High School is changing hands, that its first 'preview announcement' was banned by the government after it had been displayed as a public poster for one day. The new man is called, I think, Professor Wachs. – I [then] went to Scharnhorst School and was again given a friendly welcome by Neubert. A big Sachs-Vilatte, the bibliography and the lit. history by Lanson [. . .], as well as a briefer survey of French lit. history, dating from the early 30s were waiting for me there. I took half of this very weighty blessing home with me, will fetch the rest in the next few days. [. . .] I also talked about Kühn to Neubert. He said: 'Even though Kühn is on such friendly terms with the very democratic Scheffler.' I: 'The lead article writer of *Das Reich*.' N: 'He only wrote about English humour. Grohmann also published in *Das Reich*.'!

The afternoon was swamped by visits. First Konrad came. We had to invite him for coffee, although we were already very short of bread. The forfeiture of bank accounts is costing him the last of his wealth, 20,000M. He complains that the Russians prevent any kind of wholesale business. He would like a united campaign by the Jews here: they were *not*, as was *explicitly* happening in the Anglo-American zone, being given preference over the rest of the population. Also the Entente must commit itself to compensation for Jews. [. . .]

After Konrad, Steininger came, truly a good angel, because he brought a 4-pound bread coupon. But even that does not get us through to the end of the extended ration period. And another but: from 1 September the stocks of the bread factories will be reduced by more stringent accounting – and so Steininger will no longer be able to help us. Apart from that the talk was again of placing the Steininger archive.

Last to come was Forbrig. He brought me (with the picture of the head of a repulsive Jew) the list of Jewish shops, which was distributed in schools for boycott purposes during the early Nazi days. [. . .]

Early yesterday morning I caught an already broadcast talk about Johannes Becher, who is now constantly being excessively celebrated by the Communist side as the greatest German poet. I have already frequently heard as a list of the greats: Goethe, Heine, Thomas Mann, Becher.[81] Yesterday the superlativising went even further, the list of the greats was: Dante, Goethe, Heine, Becher. I gathered from the pompous blather that Becher (presumably born at the beginning of the 90s) began as an Expressionist during the Great War. I heard two rather good sonnets by him, the first a spiritualised description of Tübingen, the other (which the speaker compares to the Inferno) about General Mola, the initial leader of the Right-wing revolution in Spain, who was killed in a plane crash early on.

Yesterday afternoon at 4 (29 Aug.) first session of the Kulturbund, Scholarship and Research Working Group. Well preserved rooms in a villa at 28 Leubnitzerstr., corner of Liebigstr. Way there, through much destruction, accompanied by bad heart complaints [. . .]. Memento. A writer, Herr von Hanstein,[82] dark, middling height and age, took the chair, apart from myself 9 people, of whom I knew Gehrig (become very thin, otherwise unchanged) and Janentzky. Kühn not present. [. . .]. A little man, sleek, agile, somewhat precious and pedantic in speech: Prof. Wachs – Prof. where? and of what? Hanstein opened with the usual thanks; spoke about the tasks of the coming broadcasting station, the coming People's High School. Here Prof. Wachs spoke. The first People's

High School announcement had been banned, he himself had been appointed to re-organise and direct it, asked for our co-operation, 'ultimate goal' was university entrance. At that I spoke; I had already offered my services, university as goal was out of the question, but there also had to be clarification as to who belonged to us, both there and here in the Kulturbund – the case of Kühn. Brusque protest from Janentzky [...] and unfortunately, apparently out of a misconceived spirit of democratic broad-mindedness, also from Gehrig, who called me subjective and schoolmasterly. I argued heatedly and quite evidently met with the approval of several there, but no one dared pick up the hot potato. After that, as belated straggler, Undersecretary Menke-Glückert, now altogether accustomed to his power, appeared, and it was taken for granted that the chair passed from von Hanstein to him. He was sceptical of the whole Kulturbund enterprise and its subsidiary working groups. What should be the task of the Kulturbund, how far should its authority and power extend, who should belong to it? All that was unclear and remained unclear, although there had been hours of talking. [...] I said, the Kulturbund must act with a degree of authority as a democratic guide to conscience – M.-Gl. thought that amounted to a 'censorship board'. I: rather to Académie Française. [...] The whole endless blather ran its course as futilely as all the discussions in which I have taken part in countless faculty and senate meetings. More important was the post festum: Janentzky told me, he had immediately passed on my petition, the 're-establishment of the Romance Languages and Literatures chair' had been proposed; M.-Gl.: he would attend to it 'first thing tomorrow'; Gehrig: it had taken 8 weeks before he was re-appointed. The same old red tape. [...] Afterwards I asked myself, why have I saddled myself with this affair? What good is it to the general public, if I bring down Kühn? And what good is it to me? Defeat as much as victory will have unpleasant consequences for me ... Hanstein also asked me about Janentzky. I said: dubious, his background was Romanticism, which could mean one thing or another, there was German and Teutonic Romanticism. The phrase made a great impression, I should not be surprised, if I received an invitation to talk about *G.* and *T.* Romanticism on the wireless.

31st August, Friday

[...]

The forenoon today, Friday, was largely taken up by an obligatory visit to Steininger. I looked through his motley collection of books and took a few with me. Gradually some things worth reading are accumulating here, but I don't get around to anything. A couple of pages of diary every day, and in the evening I fall asleep to the wireless. I also got a piece of bread as a present [...]. People are queuing at the bakers' shops and buying as much as they can. The new coupons were issued yesterday, they are not actually valid until tomorrow – but everyone is starving ... Famine and *typhoid*, general vaccination has been ordered first for Berlin, now also for Dresden. [...]

Again and again the rumour: the Russians are exchanging Dresden for Hamburg, and the English or the Americans are coming here, and then everything will be better. It is as impossible to argue against this rumour as against the rumours of new weapons in the final stage of the war and of Germans and Americans joining up against the Russians.

2nd September, midday Sunday

Did not get down to any work all day yesterday. In the morning the Begerburg. E.'s music-making is to take place in two weeks, my lecture ('Chosen Peoples') already this Wednesday. I have just been sketching it out. [...] Bread sold out everywhere, not to be had again until midday tomorrow. So today we are in dire straits – I am eating masses of unripe tomatoes from Wolff's abundant planting.

3rd September, Monday morning

[...]

Trude Öhlmann told us, in a long letter, that she has a holiday this month. I wrote, she should equip herself with provisions and come to us.

[...] During the day I devote the few hours in which I feel fresh, and am not distracted, to my diaries. I must manage the 'Notebook of a Philologist'. Nothing will come of the Curriculum part for the time being.

5th September, Wednesday afternoon

The days are frittered away, they are full, without my getting down to actual work. – Just now two hundredweight of coal had to be hand-carted here in two trips, only downhill, and only the few yards from Marienburger Str. to here: but heart and hands rebelled and by now it's 6.45 and at 7.30 I'm supposed to talk for an hour at the Begerburg on 'Chosen Peoples'. I ran over the topic once again in my head this morning – without making any notes. – E's approaching music evening with the singer Luise Ulrich took up the greater part of yesterday afternoon: they rehearsed here, the brothers and Frau Seidemann listened, afterwards we talked about politics and people. [...] futile errands to buy bread. Constantly sold out, queues and despair up here and down in Plauen. Once a still warm four-pounder, once potatoes from the Wolffs, once from the Jungs. Misery from day to day.

But the principal loss of time arises from the constant demands placed on the influential Jew. The whole world wants my help – and I myself am still without position and money.

6th September, Thursday forenoon

[...]

There is more trouble for the Vogels. They had been allocated a shop, it was due to open on 15 September close by Plauen station. Objection by the mayor or district chief officer: as Nazis the Vogels will not get any merchandise – they are checkmated once again, therefore. Yesterday Father V. burst into tears here; 40 years work, money and house lost, the poor children and grandchildren – what crime had he committed? I shall talk to the mayor in person. – Complaints of my neighbour Jung, who is unceasingly really helpful, and for whom I already wrote a testimonial a little while ago. His Party membership is to be 'annulled'. But now he is being pressed to join the 'Free Trade Union' and (truly!) the KPD. 'I'm an engineer, I'm not a politician, I was forced to join the Nazi Party, I'm sick of it all, I don't ever want . . .' I shall speak to Seidemann about Jung. – The Wolff–Kluge affair. Wolff has a very bad press up here; it's not only Scholz, the all-powerful man at the housing office, who is his enemy. Through his initial arrogance W. has forfeited *every* sympathy, he cannot manage to obtain sole use of the apartment in Marienburgstr. This is now to the advantage of old Wittig, the co-occupant, who is trying to protect the apartment and property of his son-in-law Kluge. Meanwhile Kluge, the harmless young man, whom Forbrig spoke up for at first, is so incriminated that even F. has to abandon him: 1934 junior lawyer, 1943 or 44 already district judge and as such transferred to Danzig, important post in the Party organisation. He won't dare show his face here any more. But the Wolffs will not benefit even from this state of affairs . . . For me all this results in errands, writing, bothersome visitors.

[. . .]

Yesterday evening, Wednesday 5 September, therefore, I gave my first lecture up in the Begerburg, in the very place where the Nazis had their seat, my first lecture after more than ten years. An emotional reflection could be written on the reversal in my situation, about the ups and downs of my life. Here only the plain facts. The room is supposed to accommodate 130 people, extra chairs had to be put in, crowded, oppressive heat, audience quiet as mice. To what extent they could follow me I have no idea. I had no notes, had written down only a series of keywords beforehand – I spoke completely extempore for $1\frac{1}{4}$ hours: [. . .] Everyone considers the other nation inferior, his own chosen. General human weakness. But thanks to German thoroughness it has become a crime. [. . .] The deviation into arrogant zoology, into falsification and suppression of information, into isolation and adulation of the *only* chosen Nordic or Germanic spirit. – I had asked Seidemann *not* to introduce me, as he had intended, as a 'victim of Fascism'. There was no discussion. But afterwards on the way home: Forbrig and E., there had been too little on modernity. A representative of the Democratic Party: he would like to have heard something about China. A Catholic: he was a Catholic and had *nevertheless* liked it very much, I was so unbiased (I had said many good things about the Catholic Church). A dark little man with a pinched face: he had found my 'historical retrospective' interesting, but as a convinced Marxist he was a follower of the materialist conception of history. I had set forth how material and mental interact, but had then concluded with the 'spirit, which builds the body'. – Without exaggerating: I can still talk.

[. . .]

7th September, Friday morning

Coal question: If we get coke, we can heat the whole house and take in the Raschs. The coal office has to be influenced via the Housing Office, the latter (Scholz) spurred on by Seidemann (KPD). Yesterday evening I went across to the Seidemanns about it – we chatted for a long time. How difficult it is, coming from two different social strata, to find common ground. One feels one's way, one is uncertain, one never knows whether the other is really behaving naturally, whether he is not self-conscious, mistrustful, is playing a role. Seidemann himself is no longer 'people', no longer a KPD man plain and simple, is already above it, is already sceptically outside the stratum and party into which he is born. [...]

With respect to coal, thanks to Jung's intercession, we have now got a small slow-burning stove which eats briquettes. Except, unfortunately, it costs 64M and a big electricity bill is imminent and a big dentist's bill, and I still haven't received any money from the state – yes! 200M once from Grohmann's artists' fund! – and I have still not been confirmed in my post. But in principle and in fact I no longer worry about money matters, truly they no longer weigh on me, they have become unimportant. Things will work out somehow.

A few weeks ago Theodor Plievier[83] was the most topical name. His novel *Stalingrad* was serialised in the *Berliner Volkszeitung*, he read chapters from it on the wireless, in a curiously inhibited, somewhat foreign-sounding – E. said: boozy voice. I racked my brains, trying to remember where I knew the name from, although I have never read anything by the man. Yesterday, deliverance, a short article about him and a brief sketch by him, sailors' revolt Kiel 1918. *The Emperor Went, the Generals Remained* this book title is a catchphrase reminiscence of the time. The man is a German Barbusse,[84] he lived in Russia, has now risen again. He has led, says the article, the life of a worker and an adventurer, has also been a sailor. That's where the 'boozy voice' could come from.

[...]

10th September, Monday forenoon

The uncertain situation, the activity and emptiness of the days, the brooding over *LTI* and diary, the stimulation and distraction of the wireless – all unchanged. Recently inconvenienced again by interruptions to electricity supply. Just now E. is building a stove again in the garden, we are without breakfast at 10 a.m. Our tomcat is a worry. He is not very likely to survive, and has recently been dirtying the house (particularly unpleasant today).

[...]

What disturbs me most each time about the anti-Fascism meetings of the KPD (which at least here in Saxony are not followed by any deeds), is the identification of 'Prussian spirit' and National Socialist mentality. That is not true.

Yesterday afternoon invited to the Steiningers, the Windes also there and common friends of the Steiningers and the Windes: Prof. Hanusch and his wife.

He is 65, very grey and shaky, painter, professor at Plauen art school until 33, then dismissed because too modern. His wife bent by age, but her wrinkled face very finely cut, big blue-grey eyes, imposing forehead, Jewish. Was staying with relatives in Bohemia when the Heydrich murder took place and despite her mixed marriage and her husband's every effort was taken to Theresienstadt for 40 months. She says that, apart from hunger and work (in a painter's studio), things were not too bad for her, but countless people, particularly the elderly and children, everyone who was not able to work, were taken to Auschwitz to be gassed, very many had also died of starvation. On 8 May the Russians came as liberators and were greeted enthusiastically. They immediately threw cigarettes, chocolate, tea etc. to those still waiting behind the barriers, then made sure there was better food. The SS had already handed over the running of the camp to the Red Cross a few days earlier – out of fear and to save themselves. – The Hanuschs are the first people for a long time from whom we hear anything good about the Russians [. . .]

The Vogel case causes me a lot of bother. On Saturday afternoon Deputy Mayor Witecki at the town hall on Chemnitzer Platz let me know, he would be available for me to talk to him on Monday morning – today. It occurred to me that the man might already know me as his enemy from the files. I shall therefore be cautious [. . .] I myself may be dependent, as far as E.'s heavy worker's card is concerned, on Witecki. As I was returning from this errand, at Plauen station I met Aris,[85] the ambitious Jewish foreman at Schlüter; he now has a temporary post in charge of the dismantling of a metal and armaments factory; after 13 February he hid in the neighbourhood of Dresden, using false papers which were obtained for him by a pg and policeman. – On the same errand, a beaming, tall, blond man, whom I could not place, addressed me. 'But I was your foreman (shovelling snow)!' He inquired about Magnus.

Seidemann sent us oatmeal, flour and fruit conserves from confiscated stocks. As fee for the lecture!

14th September, Friday forenoon

On Tuesday morning, 11 Sept., I got the Russian stamp on my resident's permit, without which one can be arrested on the street or in the tram by military patrols. In Coschützer Str. [. . .], at a little table four Russian army clerks, in front of them a queue. Since they could not read my priority certificate, I had to queue, too. But people were dealt with at lightning speed. By contrast across the road in Schopenhauerstr. there was a crowd of people waiting in front of the headquarters building. The pg's had to register individually there, whereas we of unblemished character were allowed to present the permits of our dependents.

[. . .]

I spent all of Wednesday morning (12 Sept.) at the State Administration. [. . .] I let M.-Gl. know that I would like to see him and was received immediately with a quite touching and disarming warmth, I had the definite impression, that M.-Gl., who on this occasion appeared even older than before, nourishes an almost comradely goodwill towards me. That was such a comfort, that the continuing uncertainty of my situation weighs on me less than before. M.-Gl. spoke with a certain degree of despair about his helplessness. The Russians' never-ending new directions, inquiries, prohibitions, changes, made work almost impossible and repeatedly Sisyphus-like. The secondary schools *should* start on 1 October and the intention was – but it could hardly be said there was any hope of it – that the TH could somehow begin on 1 November. [. . .] Anyone who was working at the TH at the moment was doing no more than clearing away rubble . . . My own case [. . .]: the chair would be re-established as soon as another one was cut – but others were being cut, and mine was a priority . . . The People's High School: 'the Russians came to him with the poster of the first "preview"; political topics were announced on it without their approval. Ban, and I should be shot!' [. . .] But, as already said, he would do everything humanly possible for me. And also with the financial matter; there was constant discussion of my case, President Friedrichs must finally make the decision; it was obviously difficult for him, because in principle he wanted to refuse all demands on the Hitler state, and so he could not create a precedent by recognising my demands – on the other hand I was to be compensated somehow . . . I therefore had the general impression, that they want to set me on solid ground and assist me, but when and how?? [. . .]

15th September, Saturday forenoon

A concert general rehearsal was arranged for Thursday afternoon in the Begerburg. I let E. go alone and worked at my diary for as long as my constantly inflamed eyes allowed. Then towards evening I went up. I encountered [. . .] a new situation: the KPD, in the name of the anti-Fascist bloc has decreed an educational or commemorative week with regard to concentration-camp people. Consequently the concert programme was much reduced, a political core – poems and songs from the camps – inserted. Seidemann asked me to visit him on Friday evening at a KPD meeting in the Party office on Coschützer Str. [. . .]

16th September, Sunday forenoon

On Friday evening I went down to the KPD meeting with Seidemann. There's a little KPD book and newspaper shop in Coschützer Str., the meeting room is behind it. Since some repair work had to be done there, we moved the few steps across to Plauen town hall, to the chamber on the first floor [. . .]. The chamber contains a long table, a few chairs and a number of rough, stool-like benches. Everything about this town hall is bomb-damaged. – Seidemann [. . .] had carefully prepared me as we were on our way: I would meet only workers and 'Party men', the chairman, his concentration camp comrade, Glöckner, was a rigid Communist. S. then introduced me to Gl., a younger, very slight man. Not quite appropriately, but he probably meant it as a joke, S. said: 'You should be very nice to the professor, his brother was Lenin's doctor.'[86] I immediately cut in: 'that's no recommendation, someone can have a very good brother and be good for nothing himself.' Whereupon Glöckner with deep seriousness and in a loud oratorical voice: 'Yes, for us it's only the man himself who counts and his class-conscious revolutionary character.' With that I'd already had enough, and also, I cannot deny it, the fact that the little group consisted only of evident workers, alienated me. So we moved across to the town hall chamber, I sat there with 8 or 10 people, among them an old and a younger woman – 'Frau Eva Schulze, her husband was beheaded, Planettastr. is now named Fritz Schulzestr. after him,'[87] Seidemann said, who sat down almost protectively beside me – so I was sitting in a row with the others at the long table, opposite us there was only Glöckner as chairman and at his side an elderly gentleman who looked more as if he came from an intelligentsia stratum – the former publisher Rudolf, presently employed at an information office, as I learned yesterday ... I now have to say, that, despite a few class-conscious cliche phrases, I was thoroughly impressed by Glöckner as 'functionary'. He spoke quite matter-of-factly and instructively, we were swiftly in the picture. The Antifa Bloc was holding 'question-and-answer meetings' throughout a propaganda week. No speeches are to be given, rather the public – it is to be hoped also the pg's themselves, because they will be invited to come – is supposed to find out through its own questions, how matters stood with the law in the 3rd Reich, and what the prisoner in the concentration camp suffered. At each meeting 1–3 victims of Fascism will allow themselves to be questioned. There will be detectives in the audience, who will start the ball rolling. Beforehand the concentration-camp inmate will get a sheet of paper with questions. (Why and how arrested? – Treatment in camp? – Attitude of the doctors? etc. etc. eleven points, some with subsidiary questions.) No one needs to be a public speaker, each should simply remember and really answer what he experienced. The last point on the questionnaire is: 'What depressed and tormented you most as a prisoner?' After the exposition, Glöckner asked whether all those present were willing to participate. I said, I had not been in a concentration camp and would not want to make a boast of my almost everyday misfortunes. This was indignantly overruled. No one would boast, each person would simply state his experience, and mine was also important. Public meetings have been arranged for this district [. . .] between 19–22 Sept. In addition a general rehearsal in front of an invited audience (100 people; teachers, doctors, lawyers, many pg's among them). At this general rehearsal, which was supposed to take place at 7 p.m. yesterday evening in the town hall chamber at Chemnitzer Platz, those to be questioned were Seidemann and myself. [There ...] it turned out: the invitations were posted too late and will not be delivered until Sunday or Monday. – Yet this hour in the town hall was not quite wasted. There were only a few people invited by word of mouth sitting in faraway corners, and the comité chatted at the table. E. had come with me and Kovacs, the Hungarian barber, who really did not want to take any money from us the day before yesterday for cutting our hair, because I am still not receiving a salary. This time the chair was to be taken by a certain Vogel, a no longer young, no longer so very working class functionary. He told me what battles had been necessary to carry the expropriation of land[88] and the closure of banks [in the Soviet zone], 'particularly against the Christian Democratic Union' [...]. I repeated my usual dictum: You are not proceeding determinedly enough in civil service and school posts! At which he, and this did give me a poke in the stomach: 'For the time being we have to play along with the democratic state; later ...' he stopped meaningfully. The KPD'ers have therefore been promised, that the Party will behave towards the other Bloc parties just as the Nazis behaved towards their Conservative allies etc.

18th September, Tuesday forenoon

Berlin wireless talk: Reconstruction of the Junkers air plane plant, democratic-peaceful-denazified. Among other things there are 45 apprentices, who on two afternoons a week get *'ideological instruction'*. It is impossible to say just how often I hear 'orientation', 'action', 'militant'. All that's missing now is 'fanatical'. – When Dr König told me gloomily yesterday: 'They have "taken away" my cousin and handed him over to the Russians, even though they said they were not going to arrest anyone who was just a pg, and wasn't active – we don't know what the charge is and what has happened to him': then here the survival of the ignominious LTI expression is doubly comprehensible, 1) in the mouth of a former pg and 2) because the thing itself has remained the same. (König related that his cousin had been in the Party since 1929, he had been 'taken away' with 6 other doctors and dentists, presumably the founders and progenitors of the local Party medical group.)

Moscow announces Kutusov celebrations.[89] Certainly, K. will be celebrated as liberator of Russia – yet also as Tsarist general and commander. One can add to that – [...] Stalin's picture in uniform with medals, as it is displayed in gigantic size at Albertplatz, further the constant parades and the rest of the military fuss of the Allies in the newspapers and on the wireless: that's how anti-militarism is demonstrated to the Germans, that's how their 're-education' (LQI) is brought about.

[...]

Recently our tolerable neighbour Frau Charles stopped me in the street: could I do something for a pg teacher, a certain Anders, who had tutored Victor or Ralph von Klemperer's[90] children and had shown himself to be altogether philo-Semetic? I replied, that I had had little contact with the emigrated Kl.'s, knew nothing of their children and their tutors, could therefore give no testimonial of any kind. – But I had the same name! – I explained to Frau Ch. very firmly, that it was a matter of a serious testimonial and not a favour; she exculpated herself, she had thought we were intimate with the bank Klemperers. The embarrassing matter appeared to be disposed of, but then yesterday Frau Ch. brought the man here, a pinched elderly face, and the request was repeated. I said *No* extremely clearly; perhaps for all the clarity it was still much too polite.

Meanwhile I have had to give two new testimonials and did so gladly: for Frau Paul,[91] who is looking for Jewish contacts in Switzerland [...], and for the decent pharmacist Weisbach [...], who was once recommended to us by the Dembers because of his philo-Semitism. – This whining after testimonials is disgusting. And some time or other the Jews will get the bill for it; I see a new Hitlerism coming, I do not feel at all safe. [...]

The concert in the Begerburg on Sunday came off very well, but unfortunately it was neither fish nor fowl, also the audience was small, about 60–70 people. Seidemann had tried to find a middle way. He wanted a purely artistic afternoon and his party wanted a propagandistic commemoration of the concentration-camp victims. Seidemann abridged Frau Ulrich's programme [...] and in the middle placed a little talk, delivered by himself, about life in the camp, more amusing than tragic [...] as well as a few partly folk song-like, partly unpoetical bad poems from the camps, above all the 'Moor Soldiers'.[92] [...] Eva played the Beethoven funeral march as introduction and then accompanied Frau Ulrich in a number of Schubert and Mendelssohn lieder.

[...]

20th September, Thursday morning

[...]

Vogel plagues me, gives me a lot of bother [...], and I cannot help him. Vogel, Weisbach (the pharmacist), Jung, Schnauder (the Schlüter clerk), Bauer, Frau Paul: I have already had to give testimonials of philo-Semitism for all of them. And twice already I have had to refuse such a testimonial. And now Scherner, too, in his short letter, which crossed my letter to him, writes: if the Ministry asks you for information about me ... [...]

A first bit of *LTI* has been typed: 'Poverty of the LTI'. But now I want to go through the mass of my diary once again with the typewriter beside me and first of all excerpt and put together everything that belongs with the *LTI*. It's possible, probable even, that in doing so one or other article will emerge already halfway finished – so now I want right away to type the Rousseau beginning of the fanaticism section – but there must everywhere remain room for additions, and there is no question of an immediate completion of the manuscript.

[...]

24th September, Monday, morning and later

[...]

... meanwhile the ground beneath my feet is *doubly* shaky.

a) the Kühn case, ever more poisonous – only chance saved me yesterday. Ceremony (23 Sept.) in the Faunpalast, big cinema, Leipzigerstr., to inaugurate the Kulturbund, the announcement had been in the previous day's newspaper, Kühn's name immediately after mine. Accompanied by Seidemann I got there late – it had been unclear whether summer time was still in force in Dresden or winter time as already in Berlin. Hall only $\frac{2}{3}$ full, Menke-Glückert's speech the usual worthy lemonade ('Noble is man, helpful and good'[93] and similar quotations), [...] – the whole thing shabby. On leaving I bumped into Nestler. He had written to ask for the title of the France lectures to be changed, I wanted to call on him today, Monday. He: my lectures had been cancelled, there had been discussion of the Kühn case, it was to be 'clarified' first. I said that was a piece of 'boundless effrontery' and insisted on immediate clarification. Prof. Wachs., who was present, was fetched, and in the middle of the foyer, while loads of acquaintances were streaming past and shaking hands [...] I indignantly explained the issue to him. He immediately took my side, we were companions in adversity ... This morning [...] I spoke to him once again at Nestler's. Mutual ingratiation. [...] At the People's High School I shall now provisionally give a seminar course of five one-hour sessions: How language went astray in the Hitler Reich (idiotic botch of the *LTI* title!).

b) the one cause of the ground shaking is the hostility of the Kühn supporters, therefore, for Wachs said quite openly, the 'polemic' against Kühn had had such an effect on him, he could not understand why Janentzky had defended him so forcefully. [...] The other cause of the ground shaking: yesterday afternoon we had invited the Windes and the Kreisler-Weidlich couple for tea and had a cake ready for these 4 people, which the Wolffs had baked here from our supplies. Instead of 4 people, seven appeared – pauvre gateau!:[94] Elsa Kreidl, one of the Winde twins, who has come back,[95] and Dr Kussi. Winde said: 'The prospects for you are not very favourable. The Russians only want to open 3 technical departments at the TH and *nothing else at all*.' What will become of my abolished chair? Winde related that he is already receiving a civil-service salary. Everyone is finding a place, except me. Kussi related ghastly things about Auschwitz. A selection was made on arrival of every transport: all people under 16 and over 45, all mothers of small children, all those wearing spectacles, all those evidently sickly were picked out. These were gassed immediately. Dr Kussi, mid-30s, very obliging, is a Czech citizen, often travels to Prague, from there he can forward post abroad, but *not* if it is written in German. I gave him a few lines in French for Hilde Jonson.[96] I found it terribly hard to form the French sentences. – Kussi said that the Hirschel family, taken from Theresienstadt to Auschwitz, had undoubtedly been completely exterminated, husband, wife, 2 boys.

[...]

The Allied law 'for the purpose of the ending and prevention of military training in any form on the territory of Germany' is as harsh as it is terribly elastic. One paragraph states, that the following are forbidden: 'Lectures, films, plays and wireless broadcasts about military actions, which glorify the warlike and similar characteristics of the German nation, individual units or individual persons (sic).' *Anything* can be done with that. And the crime 'is subject to any sentence, including the death sentence, at the discretion of the court' (of an Allied military court).

28th September, Friday forenoon
[...]

Now I have to attend to the lecture for the 'Teachers' Union'. A curious story. About two weeks ago, I received a communication from Schools Inspector Sachse, as chairman of the teachers' section within the general 'Free Trade

Union', asking whether I was willing to tackle the subject of which branch of scholarship had suffered most under Nazism, as part of a big political instruction course (the words themselves to be avoided) for Dresden teachers. A series of speakers on this and that subject, a couple of respected people, Menke-Glückert among them, I think, were mentioned. I talked to Forbrig, now my constant adviser. I said the subject was impossible, a) because I cannot talk about *all* branches of scholarship as an expert, b) because in principle *all* branches of scholarship have been robbed of their scholarly character by Nazi doctrine. Forbrig retorted: it was a very good cause, I should definitely speak. The audience was the whole of the teaching profession, elementary, lower and higher schools. Each lecture would be given 3×, each time to around 300 people. The proposal was clumsily put, Sachse would be just as satisfied with a different formulation of the subject, I should talk to him. He, Forbrig, would arrange for us to meet on Monday morning at 10 in Melanchthonstr. I got there, found a little band of besiegers outside S.'s office, who were being intimidated by a coarse doorman. I announced myself with authority, the doorman was recalcitrant, I snapped at him, he would be called to account, he roared, he had been in a concentration camp and did not let anyone order him around – I went away having achieved nothing and feeling very depressed. (Embarrassing scene in front of the audience of teachers, some of whom knew me. At his: he had been in a concentration camp, I burst out with the only half true: 'I too!' At which he: 'Tell me, which camp!' Whereupon I gave up the struggle.) Forbrig pacified me. He brought me Sachse's heartfelt apologies. There had been repeated unpleasant scenes with this attendant. The man really had been a concentration-camp inmate, was disturbed, bullied the public, was quite unsuitable for his post. But the KPD insisted on him keeping it, there was nothing else for him at the moment, and the non-party Sachse was powerless against the KPD. (Forbrig added mysteriously, this man was needed for 'shots in the back of the head'. I: is this to be taken literally? And who here is ordering shots in the back of the head? And don't the Russians have their own men for that? Forbrig: it was to be taken literally, and he could not say any more about it! F., an old SPD man, on the whole temperate and not a wind-bag, certainly no Commie basher!) He, Forbrig, could conduct the negotiations with Sachse. My suggestion 'National Socialism and Scholarship' was definitely right, Sachse would write to me with further details. Now I am going over in my mind, how to fill an hour on the subject, because in the end the whole business can be dealt with in two sentences. Either one is objective or 'fanatical'. Forbrig's 'one cannot be objective' must be cordoned off by: one must have the ideal of objectivity.

[...]

In the last few years there was often talk of a colour film which displayed great technical progress: *'The Woman of My Dreams'*.[97] Eva very much wanted to see it, but she never wanted to go alone, because I was not admitted. Now this film has again been around for a while, but we never have the time. Something like that takes up a whole afternoon nowadays. Finally E. said with some emotion, since the celebrations for the 'victims of Fascism' were in full swing, to see this film would be our own private celebration: for the first time together again in a Dresden cinema. So on Wednesday we went to the Capitol in Freiberg [...]. The colours really were very nice and discreet. But the film itself was a disappointment. An empty and outmoded costume revue and operetta. [...] The high mountain sets obviously cardboard. Dances in the style of the Monopol Theatre before 1914 (cancan), circus and USA style adventure. No progress. No content, no acting proficiency.

[...]

We are shivering terribly and without hope in very autumnal weather: the Coal Office has still not responded to our coke application, and the little iron stove bought for emergencies has still not been connected.

Everything is at a standstill, is in doubt, chaotic – in the house, in my profession, in every respect.

30th September, Sunday morning

Yesterday evening from 7–9.30 there was no electricity for $2\frac{1}{2}$ hours, whereas usually the misfortune lasts for $1\frac{1}{2}$ hours. We had not got the gipsy stove in the garden working in time, gas was naturally off as well. We sat in the dark, starved and waited. *This* loss of working time, as I said, we have almost daily.

Yesterday at 12.30 p.m. the Dölzschen group moved off in a column with a red flag from the public house up in the village. A ceremony for the 'victims of fascism' on Karl Marxplatz (formerly Wilhelmplatz; on the tram I heard a young woman say indignantly: 'if it had been called Hitlerplatz! But what did Wilhelm[98] do to them?' Vox populi – voces populi). The two of us went as far as the Plauenschen Ring, where a couple of hundred people from other groups were already drawn up. *I* (not E.) was on such a demonstration for the *first time* in my life. Beside me engineer Schlegel, elderly gentleman who represents the Liberal Democrats here [...]. I said, in my thinking I was a Democrat, but first of all there had to be a clean-up. [...] In the column of demonstrators, they had to walk the whole way, the pg couple Dr König. [...]

The Food Office has rejected the heavy worker's card for E. Now Seidemann, whom I called on the day before yesterday during the usual evening interruption in electricity, has written me a couple of lines for the office at which the 'victims of Fascism' are registered. If we are accepted, and Seidemann says that will be a formality, then we will get privileges. Besides, the broadcasts from Berlin are full of fine words advocating compensation for the small saved remnant of Jews (they say 5% saved out of half a million). Perhaps that will help me. [...]

Schlegel reported: in factory council elections at the Leuna chemical plant, the SPD got 23 seats, the Democrats 3 and the KPD *1* seat. (But the KPD is not to blame for that, the Russians are!)

[...]

5th October, Friday forenoon

Yesterday at last an undisturbed (or disturbed only by the terrible cold of the unheated house) day of typing. I am now excerpting the LTI from the diaries;

perhaps that will be a help – at least it provides me with material for talks and trifles. The whole of the rest of the week from Monday on was completely occupied.

It began on Monday the 1st with the municipal relief office for victims of Fascism (at Albertplatz [...]). Seidemann had given me a note for the head of the office, who is a close friend of his. I was to be 'registered', that would ensure me E.'s withdrawn heavy workers' card and all kinds of privileges besides. Typical: the management had changed; the new boss [...] did not even deign to receive me, had a secretary tell me, *only* political concentration camp inmates and activists are 'victims', I should apply to 'social welfare' or wait for the still to be established Jewish Relief Office. (Seidemann has meanwhile obtained a worker's card for E.) [...]

From the [KPD] district headquarters I went to the State Library on Eisenacherstr. Neubert had offered me the supplementary volume of my *Modern French Prose*[99] of 1926 from his private library. I found him in a fairly depressed state, he more or less made me promise to use a little of my influence on his behalf. [...] perhaps they would allow him to remain a librarian; the Allies were merely demanding that no *executive posts* remain in the hands of pg's. [...] (with $\frac{1}{2}$ and $\frac{3}{4}$ words I promised help I cannot give. [...] Who helps me, me?!)

Finally – all this in one morning! – to nearby Pohlandstr. where Fräulein Papesch,[100] not bombed-out and hardly changed, only even more shrunken, is still in her old apartment. Petit bourgeois elegance, all carefully dusted. My collected works are preserved there. Fräulein P. who now lives on private lessons – forbidden! The Russians allow only teaching of Russian and even that must be approved by them – lent me the 4 vols. Literary History, Modern Prose, Modern Poetry and 3 cultural sciences lectures of 1925.[101] Now I could start again, if, *if* I had my chair. It seems ever more threatened: no English and French teaching is permitted at the People's High Schools [...]. Personally the Papesch woman was very obliging, but, in accordance with her character, a little cool.

In the late afternoon of this same Monday, I then also called on Neumark. Getting there was a penance. Unceasing heavy rain, and when I wanted to come back at 7.30, the electricity was cut, I had to go from Reickerstr. almost to Bürgerwiese on foot. Then a tram came; but walking through Bienert Park in complete darkness was an assault on my repeatedly rebelling heart. Neumark, with whose wife I became acquainted, and to whom for a while I talked by candlelight, sees the situation in general, that of the Jews in Saxony in particular and my own quite particular case in a very pessimistic light. Claims on the Hitler state are not being acknowledged. The Russians don't take any notice of Allied decisions to help the Jews, and our Saxon administration is downright anti-Semitic; Neumark has had the most unpleasant experiences. In his case there is also an element of personal embitterment. A [Communist] town councillor, Fenske, told him he had been 'middleman between Jews and Gestapo', such a middleman between Jews and administration was no longer needed. (There must be a Jewish denunciation or grudge at the bottom of it.) On my behalf N. intends once again to call personally on Menke-Gl. and Friedrichs.

The Russians! The picture of Stalin on Albertplatz could be of 'Hermann'.

Uniform with medals! What Neumark, via his stepson, relates fits with that: Zuckmayer's 'Captain of Köpenick' was forbidden after rehearsals and passed again only one day before the premiére. Reason for the ban: the play ridiculed the military!

Meanwhile at the London Conference[102] there has been open disagreement between the Russians and the Western powers. We shall be all the more cut off here from the rest of the Allies. Gradually no one has doubts any more about Russian despotism. A great misfortune, because there are those who view it as a belated justification of Hitler.

[...]

And someone else has emerged: Frau Streller has just written to us. Helmut Richter,[103] the honest trustee of my house, who did not return from Buchenwald and was missing, died in the hospital at Weimar. The man, barely forty, never saw his youngest child. I shall erect a beautiful memorial to him in my Curriculum. Which will not feed his widow and his four children.

[...]

Günther Schmidt, who is matriculating in medicine at Jena, paid me a farewell visit. There and in Halle the semester really is supposed to be beginning now. What will happen here, to my chair? The uncertainty plagues me terribly.

A card from Katz, he was in Kreischa Sanatorium for two weeks to rest, still has excessive demands placed on him...

[...]

One evening I went to see Seidemann. He is already employed as an auxiliary teacher – in Forbrig's school. Sitting in on classes for 10 hours a week, already teaching 10 hours himself after instruction. Practical months are to be followed by provisional courses – dependent on suitability, proper teacher training comes later. I am convinced, that S. will make his way here. I told him: 'You surely want to write at some point.' He: he was searching, one day he would like to set forth a Communism *without* the Marxist dogma. Once I would have called Seidemann a typical German idealist and seeker.

[...]

8th October, Monday morning

Yesterday another nice cultural afternoon in the Begerburg. Ulrich and Eva. – A music group of mandolin, guitar, accordion. [...] In the evening, when electricity was cut off again, Dr König here. We had – sadly – to share our meagre soup with him. He wanted to discuss with me, whether he should join the Christian Union [...]. I advised joining. He complained because allotment gardeners up here had been pushed out by Communists, although they were innocent pg's. He emphasised: Forgive us our trespasses ... but he also talked about his fierce struggle against a senior cleric still in office, who had persecuted his, Dr König's, brother as a Confessing Christian and driven him to his death. So there!

Afternoon
At the Coal Office on Karl Marxplatz, formerly Kaiser Wilhelmplatz, they were very friendly and quite helpless: there is absolutely no coke. Thus the Raschs will not move here, which is not really a misfortune. E. has already drawn up her plan for the winter: the bedroom will become the kitchen, we shall live entirely in the music room, which at the moment is still a shop.

10th October, Wednesday morning
I made every effort to celebrate my birthday yesterday with a cheerful heart. I did not quite manage it – my situation looks far too much like that of a has-been and my heart is far too rebellious. Nevertheless, it was different from the last 12 years.

The Wolffs and Trude Öhlmann behaved very touchingly. They belong together insofar as the W.'s (both) have made contact with Trude Öhl. on one of their mysterious business trips to Leipzig and Thuringia. Trude overwhelmed me, partly by post and partly via the Wolffs, who just came back from Leipzig yesterday, with letters, congratulations, presents from her boy's things; she is still hoping for his return – she also sent me his picture in flying suit and with parachute in front of his 'plane. [...] She sent shirts, pyjamas etc. She sent 100M, which will be returned. She appears to be clinging to us with some desperation. – The Wolffs brought back a goose from their trip, which we ate with them as my birthday dinner, they gave me confectionery, two tins of fatty Russian liver sausage, a pair of gloves. They donated the cake to go with the coffee, which they drank here in the afternoon. An embarrassing offset, however: later in the evening a delivery van drove up here, 3 sacks of sugar – black market stuff – were hauled up to our loft. In the next few days they are to be partly exchanged for flour, we are to have a share in everything – but we undoubtedly also have a share in the risk of this trade.
[...]

12th October, Friday morning
Semper idem:[104] everything is in suspense. In every free minute I excerpt from *LTI*. But there's no more than an essay in it. Otherwise I would have to read for a year and a day – and that would not be worth the effort.
[...]
Scherner is sending me my Montesquieu and my Corneille[105] from his library, Papesch sent me a couple of off-prints. (How distant it is!)

I do not manage any reading – I do not quite want to give up LTI and yet no longer see any benefit in it, the topic is chewed over and thin. Every day I observe anew the perpetuation of LTI in LQI.

The wireless allows me to indulge.

The little tomcat Moritz does not look likely to survive.

Constant struggles for bread. In particular the baker on Grenzstr. here is completely unreliable, again and again there are unpleasant scenes. Just now it was only with very firm words that I was able to obtain a loaf, which I then had to share. [. . .] Yesterday evening we did not have a single piece of bread.

13th October, Saturday morning
Yesterday Neubert, the library director, came to me. A very pitiful impression. Thin, with thin grey hair, one arm, very depressed – it was twilight, suddenly, without ringing, he was standing in front of me in the hall, humbly, hunched. He has already been dismissed as director, it appears he will also have to go as librarian, without a pension. He is 53, looks older than I. I promised to plead on his behalf when I see Menke-Gl. – Am I doing right, am I sentimental?

Evening
In the afternoon first Nestler called. Wachs as director of the People's Evening School suddenly became impossible. He has been denounced as a pg and having been close to the SS. Even if this is not true, his shattered mental state was 'insupportable'. Did I want to be his successor? I was Nestler's candidate. It is a matter of academic respectability. There were also other candidates. The whole thing of 'major importance'. Position of a city secondary school headmaster. Flattered, I agreed, but do not believe I shall be the one chosen.
   [. . .]

15th October, Monday morning
Wonderful autumn colours in the garden, especially the delicate Japanese maple in rich rose-red – a place of absolute peace here, when one comes from the ruined city and the overcrowded tram. The house, admittedly, cold and chaotic – the shop still not cleared out.
   [. . .]

17th October, Wednesday morning (and later)
Very depressed. My heart gives way so frequently, that I see death very close. Next to zero work. I listen to the wireless for hours and fall asleep over it; I read nothing any more, I merely note a couple of LTI excerpts and the material shrinks ever more. And finally: my professional position becomes ever more hopeless.

   Yesterday the actual work part of the day – because afterwards I was completely washed-out and was not revived until about midnight by wonderful wireless music and that lasted until one and I'm suffering for it today – consisted of an hour spent in the State Administration (and the ghastly journey there and back, squashed and unpaid). I started in the cellar of G block with Kretzschmar. [. . .]

   Kretzschmar talked indignantly about the ruling Communists; they were shameless in displaying their new riches, cars, villas food . . . On top of that their lack of education. It was repellent and very depressing. He himself had now – a risk, taken with a heavy heart – signed up with the Liberal Democrats. It is very possible that I shall follow his example. – I then went to M.-Gl.'s secretary, asked for an appointment and shall be given a time in writing. Then to Principal Secretary Wetschke, a swarthy civil servant, whom I had already seen once together with Menke-Glückert. Here I met His Magnificence Heidebroek [rector of the TH],[106] gallant appearance, sort of French grand seigneur, languidly courteously offhand. He said, we must know each other from before, he had come here in 31 – but the distance between the two parts of the High School. I emphasised to the gentlemen with some vigour, that I considered my request for reinstatement mistaken, because legally I remained a professor of the TH. Both said I was taking a formality too seriously, no one doubted etc. etc. Only: first of all the Finance Ministry had to re-establish my chair in the budget. Heidebroek, in his fifties,[107] reported that they wanted to or should start on 1 Nov. He added nonchalantly, there was no hurry with me, there was a lack of rooms and coal. – I reported the People's High School offer, and that I would *only* do it as a subsidiary appointment. Both thought that self-evident, Heidebroek talked fairly arrogantly about the whole institution. The People's High Schools were shooting up 'like mushrooms' [...]. I presented my [arguments] pro Neubert and also, very vigorously, contra Kühn. Point two was received silently and courteously, point one with lively sympathy. Wetschke immediately took me to a colleague, who was in charge of the relevant section, and whose name I have unfortunately forgotten. A sprightly grey-haired, typically hearty Saxon [...] old civil servant – he said he remembered me from Herr von Seydewitz's time. In his room there was an at first unfamiliar, likewise grey-haired gentleman [...]. The gentleman greeted me with enthusiastic cordiality: 'we all thought you were dead, it was said, you had hanged yourself in prison.' Gradually I made sense of it all. He was the librarian, Dr Assmann, just appointed Neubert's successor. [...] Assmann was there to plead for Neubert, who was now also dismissed as librarian from 1 Nov. The principal secretary was sympathetic but considered the case a hopeless one. Trade union people had demanded N.'s summary complete dismissal, N. was personally disliked. Assmann defended him as merely clumsy and stiff, but 'very upright'. [...]

Thus I am still dangling, and even more awkwardly than before. [...] And since bank accounts were forfeit, there are no more offers from publishing houses.

[...]

6 p.m.

The whole afternoon today crowded with visitors. (And – lamentably! – each must have 'just a slice of bread' with his coffee, and we miss each slice, especially as E. now only has a worker's card and Steininger and Schwarz are failing us. Seidemann came for a piano lesson, just as we were about to drink coffee. In between there was engineer Schlegel [wanting] vocational guidance for his son, who has just returned from captivity. Then little Hilde Rasch. Then Peter Kalau.

[...]

19th October, Friday morning

Menke-Glückert informed me by messenger, he would be available for me on Thursday (yesterday) afternoon (outside his office hour). He received me very cordially; mixed result. In the presence of Wetschke and after telephone conversation with Heidebroek: I am now a professor once again, replacing an economist in the budget [...] like all civil servants I receive for the time being a monthly part payment of 200M, perhaps of 400M in October, like the other professors I can probably start in November. With that I now have firm ground under my feet. Against that: M.-Gl. has no powers regarding other compensation. I remain indebted, therefore, and financially as immobilised as before. And the Leipzig dream has evaporated. Above all because Jan is present. [...] But after that because M.-Gl. is very much a weak reed. 'I shall immediately appoint you honorary professor, if there's a proposal from Leipzig, but I can't interfere with the university's autonomy! Go to Leipzig, talk to Jan and the rector, arrange matters yourself!' (That would lead to humiliation for me!)

M.-Gl. likewise weak-kneed with respect to Kühn. '*I cannot undertake anything.*' It will not be easy for me to maintain my position. Nevertheless: the really essential thing has now been secured, I am no longer altogether on the scrap heap.

Earlier I had been to see Nestler. The People's High School kettle is still on the boil, but there are problems. Also a candidate, not very flattering for me, is a writer, Dr Seber, who had an embarrassing article in the *Volkszeitung* yesterday: the People's High School must encourage 'the value of experience', not scholarly knowledge, in addition invective against specialist knowledge, the arrogance of university teachers and similar woolly-minded nonsense [...]. It would probably be a very good thing, if I were blessed with failure in this business. [...]

22nd October, Monday morning

[...] even without visitors I don't achieve anything; too much tiredness, too much wireless. I don't read anything any more; slowly excerpting *LTI* is all I manage. In the evening (usually electricity cuts) I sleep and doze to music.

[...]

Late in the evening, while I was copying excerpts, my attention was caught by the Europe verses of the Nazi Bade.[108] 'All is simple in the gleam of swords'. And on Albertplatz the picture of 'Marshal Stalin' – it could just as well be Hermann Goering. And the Europe poet was no doubt just as much a believer and just as sincerely enthusiastic as some anti-Fascists are today. And 65 out of 70 million believe exactly what they're told, and another $4\frac{1}{2}$ million are indifferent, sceptical, resigned, and acquiesce in everything, today in this and tomorrow in that. And who the half million are, from whom a dozen come to power and who that dozen are – who, who knows that? All the talk about re-education, reform, democracy etc. etc. is a fraud, at best self-deception.

Seidemann had written a letter of complaint on my behalf to the relief office of 'Victims of Fascism'. I have now been courteously invited to go there again. 'J'y vais[109] this aft. without illusions.

Without illusions, yet not really discontented, that is more or less my basic attitude in every respect.

Evening

The 'Victims of Fascism' business went hardly any differently from the first time. A Herr Loewenkopf[110] received me very politely and essentially turned me down. I had neither been in a concentration camp nor had I been a political activist. The Jewish question had not yet been sorted out. Nevertheless: I am to be 'borne in mind' – presumably with a Christmas food packet. But the heavy worker's card for E. was again refused. And our bread is almost finished.

Trude Öhlmann writes, the Romance Languages and Literatures chair in Halle is vacant, Mulert deceased, I should apply. I replied: I would like an honorary professorship in Romance Lit. hist. there, but could not make an application myself.

26th October, Friday morning

Aggravation, distraction, stagnation, depression.

Re-organisation of food ration cards places us in an essentially worse position. Thus far, as professor, heavy worker, that is first category. From now on there is very heavy worker, heavy worker and worker, and the professor is placed in category three as a worker. – Aggravation also over coal with an official up here, whose goodwill, furthermore, determines whether Eva receives a higher category card.

More generally it can be said, and Neumark has repeatedly been outraged by this, that the Saxon state government's behaviour is virtually anti-Semitic.

Most recent aggravation: the Vogels' lawyer has brought the 'Jewish professor Klemperer' into play to such a degree, that I appear in a most embarrassing light and had to demand a disclaimer. [...] This odious business is upsetting and time-consuming.

Loss of time almost daily due to 2–3 hours electricity cut between 6.30 and 8.30 p.m. Interruption of electricity also often in the morning. Always unpredictably and without advance warning.

The excerpting crawls hopelessly on, my heart fails me daily while walking.

[...]

In a broadcast from Berlin the day before yesterday a *most embittered* talk against German desires for separatism, against Bavaria. I do not know, to what it was referring – but it was such a passionate German-patriotic outcry, such an independent effort, that we both sat up and took notice in considerable surprise. Because usually it's forever the same old song on the wireless: they say how the Allies are helping us, how much we have all become Anti-Fascists and democrats, how much is being 'purged', overturned, made better. They preach against every kind of militarism – and with all of it they fly precisely, so very precisely, so blatantly in the face of all truth and reality, as, the other way around, but with the same, the very same words – LTI = LQI!! align, militant, true democracy etc. etc. – as did the Nazis. Is it the pessimism of old age, which judges thus?

But, whether I am old or young – that is how matters really stand.

Yesterday while copying excerpts I was struck by the truth, the real truth of a Goebbels sentence, which now of course cannot go into the *LTI* book – inasmuch as its publication is conceivable. I mean Diary 4/3/44 [The relevant passage was not included in the printed German edition of the Klemperer *Diaries 1933–45*, which was the basis of the English translation, see notes.] conclusion: Russian policy of imperialism, abolition of the Comintern, acquisition of a Russian national anthem.[111] O Marshal Stalin! I remember his speech at the end of the war against Japan: we have avenged 1904![112] Heir of the Tsar and of Tsarist policy. I feel more divided than ever. If I were not a Jew, I would put myself in Freikorps souls.

29th October, Monday

[...]

The suspension of postal services between the zones of occupation has now been lifted, so the way to Bavaria is open. Hence, and this is all the work I have managed in two days, I have written two long letters to Vossler and to Leo Ritter.[113]

[...]

31st October, Wednesday morning

[...]

Fräulein Papesch and a certain Freya (Freya!) Strunz, sister of a classmate of Günther Schmidt, have begged me, in the name of other pupils, [to intervene] on behalf of my former student, Fräulein Berndt, teacher of music and French, who has just been dismissed as a pg. The helpless mother, the usual. Berndt then came herself, a good person, and I can help her. But it's all pitiful. [...] Amusing is a mitigating circumstance, which Berndt advances in her exculpatory letter to the ministry: she had always done Mendelssohn with her pupils.

Afternoon

In the morning I was at the State Library, Eisenacherstr., to ensure the extension of the loan of the Sachs-Vilatte and the Lanson. The whole of literature is lying in huge boxes in Bautzen and cannot be conveyed here. The library is supposed to be moved from Eisenacherstr. to one of the North barracks. Assmann [...] as new director received me warmly. Despite Assmann's and my own intercession Neubert has now been completely dismissed and without a pension. Politically he was far too incriminated. [...]

1st November, Thursday evening

Schwarz [...] called on us this morning, very bitter. The Communist works council had sided with a pg whom he, Schwarz had opposed, he himself had been dismissed as temporary manager, the owner, Frau Braune, with whom he had a private contract, had also been rebuffed. Matters did not seem to be quite like that to me: nevertheless the arbitrariness, power and unpredictability of the KPD appears to be fact. And at all events one of our bread sources is stopped up. Schwarz says, the Russians are not capable of administering us well, they are culturally far too backward – the territory occupied by them and fallen to communist dictatorship was going to rack and ruin. One had to get oneself over to the West. [. . .]

4th November, Sunday forenoon

[. . .]

On Friday I at last went to the TH. For the first time in the buildings of the new high school on Georg Bährstr. Huge edifices, huge area, a whole town – but badly damaged. Heidebroek received me cordially and again made a good impression on me, he is matter-of-factly dispassionate. [. . .] When lectures will begin, whether tomorrow, whether in 4 weeks, is quite uncertain. The rector of Leipzig University has somehow offended the Russians. Too few people appear to have been dismissed there at first, and when the Russians sent a committee to purge it, the rector seems to have raised a lament. At any rate the notified inauguration was cancelled again, and since Leipzig remains closed, the 'little sister' in Dresden is not allowed to start either. That more or less was Heidebroek's account. [. . .] So everything remains up in the air.

[. . .]

6th November, Tuesday forenoon

On Sunday afternoon Frau Cohn and her sister came unexpectedly, we pleaded an invitation of our own and so they left after 'only' an hour. To make up for that later there was Kussi with his nephew, who is 19, was in Auschwitz for two years and is now being prepared privately for the school-leaving certificate.

The Kussis must have oodles of money; he bought himself a furnished and intact house in Hellerau.

K. gave (advance) notice of a letter from Hilde Jonson, which had come via Prague. I received it yesterday. In English, very cordial. Georg alive, or was still alive on his 80th birthday. She knows nothing of Marta.[114] The Jonsons themselves are not doing well – their business was oriented to Germany.

[. . .]

8th November, Thursday forenoon

E. has got a spreading rash (lichen?) in her face; my sore foot, daily bandaged by her, sore since arrival, will not heal; my heart bothers me greatly, any walking, any kind of physical effort causes pain. Conclusion: we want to go to Katz today, although it will cost us the whole afternoon.

[. . .]

Seidemann requested a lecture in the Begerburg on 18 Nov. on the language of the 3rd Reich; so that will be the première, as it were, of the *LTI*.

Principal content of the day apart from the slow-moving excerpts from the *LTI* and apart from the many visitors, domestic errands etc. is the wireless, time-wasting, a fairy tale repeatedly marvelled at – now Zürich, now Vienna, now Hamburg, now English, now French etc. etc. Omnipresent, godlike – greatest and real enrichment.

Most important in the last few days. Radio Beromünster: Reddar (that's what the magic word sounded like), the English ray invention, which allowed them to see U-boats and guide air planes by wireless, and gave them victory at sea and in the air. Inserted in the talk a piece of a Hitler speech, the very piece I once myself heard standing outside the offices of the *Freiheitskampf*.[115] And if the war lasts 3 years – we'll still have our say! – and if it lasts 4 years ... and if 5, and if 6 ... we will not capitulate! It was his voice! It was his voice, his agitated and inflammatory furious shouting, I clearly recognised it again ... And with it applause and Nazi songs. A shatteringly present past. And sirens over London and the noise of the squadrons. A tremendously varied impression. [To think] that this is past, and that its presence can be restored to the present, always and at every moment!

The Russian commemoration of the Revolution, 7 October 1917, filled the Berlin–Leipzig station. The Germans are crawling right up the Russian a. Many, perhaps most of the good things said about the Russians may be true: the humanity, the justice, the success of the Bolshevik fundamental spirit. But here it is constantly being demonstrated to us through shortages, administrative chaos, daily outrages, arbitrary acts by individual commanders, officially sanctioned looting, that matters are in fact quite different from how they are on the wireless. Which gives rise to great bitterness and danger for the future. The equivalence of LTI and LQI, of Soviet and Nazi, of the new democratic and of the Hitlerite tune is horrifying! That fact obtrudes and intrudes everywhere from morning to night! In every word, every sentence, every idea ... Utterly naked Russian imperialism!

Cauchemar de devoir répondre à Hilde en français.[116]

Evening or night, 12.30
Katz expedition; getting there the fight for the tram in wind and rain, getting back wind and darkness. But successful. E. and I, she in her face, I on my foot, have the same non-virulent eczema, she probably infected by me; my heart is unchanged since the last time, not worse. I had not been to Katz since June, E. not at all since our return. He welcomed us with great warmth. His apartment on Borsbergstr. is now entirely devoted to the medical practice – the family has been given a separate private apartment. He has a medical assistant and three receptionists; he is the real medical adviser to the Russian and the State Administration, will probably become a department head in the ministry and have a big title. He has aged a lot, looks pale and unwell, but is obviously happy. At the same time unchanged in his whole way of thinking and speaking. His wife has reopened her fashion shop, we talked to her for a moment. He told us, that

one of our two Gestapo bloodhounds, Weser, the small one with the dark, spiteful eyes, the spitter, had taken poison. There is still no news of Clemens, the boxer, and of Köhler, the Jews' pope.[117]

11th November, Sunday night

E. is sleeping after a lengthy washing-up. – Cold slushy weather – fragmented days – always new visitors, mostly seeking help.

The enclosed letter, written after long reflection, replies very firmly to a touchingly clumsy, offensively fawning missive from Frau Hirche in Ober-lössnitz in the Erzgebirge.[118] They had read my name in the Kulturbund list and had been *so* pleased and had thought of us *so* often, and after all I was the guarantor of her Hans, who was still in English captivity. If I had not known by chance that he was a major on the general staff, and if it had not very recently been announced on the wireless, that the members of the general staff are counted as war criminals, I might have halfway fallen for the ingratiation. The reply is certainly firm, but it is also self-defence on my part. If young Hirche got to the rank of major on the general staff, then politically he *must* also have known to whom he was selling his soul.

[...]

Much time was finally also taken up by a double errand to the pharmacy. People were queuing in the little temporary shop on Nöthnitzer, corner of Hohe Str. The eczema ointment, contrary to the prescription, had to be made up *without* alcohol; 'we have not had spirit for a long time.'

For all that the *LTI* excerpts are gradually creeping toward their end. I am afraid of this end, because then it must finally become evident, whether I can do anything with them. I am not afraid, of course, of the lecture in the Begerburg; there's certainly sufficient *for that*.

[...]

13th November, Tuesday forenoon

[...]

Then to the TH, to Heidebroek, telephoned Menke-Glückert in person. Chaos – the TH has still not had any instructions. Nor does anyone know when the semester is to begin. [...] I received an advance of 400M and the most definite assurance, that everything will now be regulated in a few days. Meanwhile – very welcome! – on Russian orders full peacetime salary will be paid backdated to 1 Nov. It is, admittedly, not yet certain how much that will mean for me – but thus far it was always said, that the highest salary must not exceed 450M.

At 12 in the evening, we were about to go to bed, a play by 'Dr Friedrich Wolf' began on the wireless: *Professor Mamlock*[119]. Very interesting and we were not in bed until about half past [1?].

After that we were late getting up today, and before I could even get to the bathroom, there was a man here putting down rat poison, and when he had gone Vogel sen. appeared, and now it's after half past nine and I'm still unshaved and without breakfast.

I heard Friedrich Wolf's name for the first time in my life from Grohmann; he told me in June, Wolf was expected back from Moscow and was to become education minister in Saxony. Yesterday on the wireless, we were told that *Professor Mamlock* had already been performed on x European stages. A play with a political point, the usual recipe and without particular depth to the characters, but very decent and done without being excessively black and white. [...]

Afternoon

The whole day is dwindling away again. Immediately after Vogel sen. Fräulein Berndt appeared and stayed for breakfast and until 12. She is now finally, but 'until further notice' finally dismissed; i.e. all pg teachers have now been discharged – Jung jun. tells me: at his Plauen grammar school 26 out of 42, so that the place is at a standstill – but there is to be another review after the radical action has been completed. [...]

After lunch I had to fetch coal slack here in the handcart [...]. After coffee, Weisbach, the pharmacist, came: his shop is being closed down now after all. I cannot help him. And then came the wife of an engine driver and pg from 1942, a woman and her 2 children were being quartered in her kitchen, and her husband needs peace and quiet. Of course I cannot help, but I always have to advise, comfort, and the time is always lost. And now it is half past five and dark, and I have to fetch bread from down the hill.

17th November, Saturday evening

Seidemann, here for a while the evening before last, strongly urged me to join the KPD. My situation has changed fundamentally insofar as I *must* join one of the four parties,[120] if I am to be accepted as a victim of Fascism because racially persecuted. Schwarz had informed me of this new regulation the day before. For that we still need 3 attestations that we wore the star. Schwarz and I are vouching for each other. Our other witnesses are to be Neumark and Katz. Schwarz [...] is a fierce opponent of the Russians, he always hopes that the Americans will march in, and has joined the Christian Union.

18th November, Sunday evening

This afternoon in the Begerburg from 5.15–6.30 in front of about 100 people I gave the première lecture on 'The Language of the 3rd Reich', which has cost me all my (actually rather few) free hours since Friday. Before the lecture we were visited by the Cohn sisters, at the last moment Martha Wiechmann's[121] sister also turned up; I did not recognise her, she was an unpleasant reminder of a world that once was. After that, weary and depressed, I had bad heart problems walking up to the Begerburg. Nevertheless, the lecture was a success – I got two invitations to repeat it to a larger audience: by Forbrig to the teachers' union, by a gentleman I did not know to the KPD of a Dresden district; I begged to discuss the matter at a later point in time, at the moment I would be too tired. That was true, I was and am completely drained. I set down only a bare written outline on one side of paper. Of importance for my *LTI* [. . .] the sentence: it [i.e. Nazism] is not, after all, as I had formerly assumed, something un-German, but essentially a cancerous tumour in German flesh, the final degeneration of *Teutonic* Romanticism. – After the lecture Seidemann gave me the forms for joining the KPD.

[. . .]

20th November, Tuesday evening

I am plagued by a terrible head cold.

My working day yesterday completely taken up with the two letters in French to Hilde Jonson and Georg (via Kussi – Prague). Depressing how completely I lack linguistic proficiency. Today went back to *LTI* excerpts. Again and again distraction through tiredness and constant visits.

Steininger calls repeatedly, he brings bread and robs me of time. [. . .] At the moment he is more concerned with cataloguing his library than with his newspaper collection. I have to advise him. In him idealism is paired with the sharpest business sense, that in turn with a very genuine good nature. [. . .]

Then beautiful Maria, Maria Kube was here; delighted at the return of her husband, who has turned from a harp builder into a postman, delighted that they have a small apartment of their own. She related, that her husband, radicalised by terrible war experiences, now wants to join the Communists, despite his Catholicism, and she was very glad, when I declared the same thing. She brought us home-made cake and invited us to visit them.

The pharmacist Mayer, recommended to me by Glaser, and who would like to be an assistant at the TH. He, too, leaning towards Communism. I think that my joining is encouraging some others. [. . .] M. said that Glaser has become a senior provincial court judge (and that he had suffered a Russian assault or robbery in the street). Apart from a few remnants the Jews have been exterminated, but these few now occupy 'key positions'. Victory – but at what price! Oh Yahweh![122]

[. . .]

Since yesterday my mind has been occupied with Trude Öhlmann's letter, the Halle business. What is more comical, Trude Ö's action or my response to it? She writes: 'You are on the list of those proposed for the chair at the Martin Luther University, Halle. Don't be cross, dear V., in accordance with your own words, I have personally whispered diplomatically in the ear of Eissfeldt, the rector.' Background: she wrote to me about the vacant Romance Languages and Literatures chair at Halle – I should display an interest. To that I replied, a personal display of interest was not in my line, she could ... 'whisper'. Now Trude has got down to business. It is very comical. But even more comical is my inner attitude. What should I do with a chair which I would not at all be equal to, and which would deprive me of the possibility of writing my books?

And yet I know, that I fervently want it, and that the certain appointment of another will wound me badly. [. . .]

The wireless, substitute for cinema, car, reading, has recently given me a great deal. [. . .]

The deepest impression was made on me by a report on the resistance against Hitler at Munich University during the Stalingrad days of 1943. The appeals on the walls of houses, the leaflets; the circle around the philosophy professor, Huber; the beadle as spy and informer. Huber and Sophie Scholl executed. (Her last words: trust in God.) Basest tortures of her [sister] Inge Scholl; her steadfastness and survival.

The application forms for admission to the KPD are lying on the desk. Am I a coward, if I do *not* join – (Seidemann says so); am I a coward, if I do join? Are my reasons for joining solely egoistical? No! If I have to join a party, then this one is a lesser evil. For the present at least. It alone is really pressing for radical exclusion of the Nazis. But it replaces the old lack of freedom with a new one! But at the moment that is not to be avoided. But perhaps I myself am backing the wrong horse? [. . .] But I think I must now show my colours. – E. is leaning towards joining, and I have really decided in favour. But it feels like a comedy: Comrade Kl.! Whose comrade?

23rd November, Friday morning
In a letter dated 16 Nov. (but which did not arrive here until the day before yesterday), Heidebroek writes: 'the document confirming your appointment has been accepted here. I request you to receive the same from me, so that I may admit you to the professoriate and instal you in your post.'

I am going there today. I shall also today hand in my application to join the KPD. The very brief curriculum vitae concludes after a few dates with these sentences: 'I have never belonged to a party, but in my opinions and as a voter have stood by the Liberals; that can also be gathered from my publications. If, without any alteration to this inclination, as far as my fundamental view of philosophy and especially the philosophy of history is concerned, I nevertheless request to be admitted to the Communist Party, then for the following reasons: I believe, that to remain unattached to a party today is a luxury, which with some justice could be interpreted as cowardice or at least as excessive indolence. And I believe that only a very resolute left-wing movement can get us out of the present calamity and prevent its return. As a university teacher I was forced to watch at close quarters, as reactionary ideas made ever greater inroads. We must seek to remove them effectively and from the bottom up. And only in the KPD do I see the unambiguous will to do so.'

I formulated and typed that until 12.30 yesterday evening. And with it I could be drawing my black and my white ball. It will certainly soon be in the newspaper. [. . .]

[. . .] Seidemann came uninvited and soon Forbrig as well. F. brought me commissions for the coming Tuesday [to speak[on the language of the 3rd Reich in the teacher-training hostel in Wachwitz and to the teachers' trade union on National Socialism and scholarship in Trachenberge and Altgruna elementary schools on the 5th and 7th of December. It gives me great pleasure. [...]

My fingers are so stiff, that I cannot go on writing.

26th November, Monday night

On Friday morning Heidebroek received me very cordially. The whole administration had just been moved to the Mommsenstr. student house, the whole administrative staff had just been '100%' purged (reduced by 124 people, I think) – there was even greater chaos than usual. There was no coal at all, and H. does not expect lectures to begin until spring. I asked him about the meaning of the sentence: '... so that I may admit you to the professoriate and instal you in your post.' – 'Well, I greet you and hand you the document.' Did I have any kind of duty to attend before lectures began? '*No.*' The document (identical for all professors) abolishes all civil service rights: one is appointed *provisionally* and until revocation by immediate dismissal; for the present, pension and widow's pension do not exist, salary still to be settled. Nevertheless my appointment runs from 1 September, so I got another payment of 800M and am to get the remainder of the full salary (which has not yet been fixed) in the near future. Curiously ambiguous financial situation. I now have sufficient and more than sufficient money to live; but if I wanted to pay my accumulated debts – Scherner, Schlüter, Annemarie, ground rent and mortgage, I would not remotely manage with it ... Next door to the student house is the Eratonen House,[123] where the General Section [of the TH] has been accommodated. [...] In a wretched and primitive library room – all the rooms there are furnished in a primitive and rough and ready manner – I came upon the dwarfish Kühn, who stared at me without greeting, and I responded in kind. It was an awkward situation, since others standing around introduced us or said 'You know each other, don't you!?' Afterwards I met Janentzky, who was unable to contain his informal cordiality and inquired after my wife. I responded in kind, while inwardly completely retaining my reservations, said I would put my cards on the table, I did not want to deprive Kühn of his livelihood, but certainly of his chair, I was determined to go to the extreme left. [...]

[...]

Ulrich, the singer, relates that the words '*Down with the KPD*' were on walls in Dresden-Neustadt. I shall be isolated among my colleagues and perhaps some day a student will shoot me down from the lectern.

[...]

27th November, Tuesday forenoon

[...]

Just now, this morning at about 9, a letter (*the first*) arrived from Munich, having taken a whole 9 days, half-puzzling, half-welcome, very brief. *Süddeutsche Zeitung* [newspaper],[124] signed Dr Kleinmayer. Greetings from Vossler, and the undersigned had a 'publisher's interest' in my 'work on language', requested 'communication by return of post' – 'the necessary conditions exist'. That makes me very happy. (The publisher here has evidently foundered on the confiscation of bank accounts [. . .].) That gives my *LTI* fresh impetus.

[. . .]

30th November, Friday morning

Too much shivering, too many colds (E. and myself) too much distraction, constant doubt, as to whether something can be wrung from the *LTI* and how it is to be shaped. I have almost finished working through the material. [. . .]

Official and officially cordial letter of welcome from the 'Dean of the General Faculty of the TH' [. . .] and from the section head, Janentzky. Simon [the dean][125] does not appear to know that I already occupied my chair 15 years ago; Janentzky, as already recently in conversation, acts comme si de rien n'était.[126] [. . .] I have the most bitter feeling in my heart, when I think of my 'colleagues'. [. . .] Today I have to go to the TH again, to hand over a declaration about my party membership as required(!) by the government, the KPD will very much separate me from the rest of the professors. [. . .]

The day before yesterday, when I gave Seidemann our applications to join the KPD, he said, more in earnest than jokingly: 'Would you not rather leave your wife outside, as insurance in case things go wrong again?' It is almost a relief, that no one can accuse me of going over to the victors; because the mood continues to be anti-Communist, and in Austria the Communists have just suffered the most astonishing failure (only 4 seats in parliament). Apart from that it is completely uncertain what this step will mean for us. And both egotistically and in terms of ideas, it is questionable whether I have made the right decision. E. for her part definitely believes, that today the KPD is the lesser evil and a *necessity*.

Seidemann wanted to give me a 50M fee for the lecture. I refused, promised my services gratis for the Begerburg, merely asked for help with respect to coal and food. Which will do me 1000× more good. My now dominant and patriarchal position up here is very very comical: Shining light of the KPD and refuge of all hard pressed pg's! [. . .]

From Pfeifer up in the village we were able to buy (quite above board) 10 kilos of rye grain. The Hainsberg Mill, a long way out, almost at the terminus of the 22 tram, accepts such small quantities as barter. As result of the arduous journey I got 7 kilos of flour and 2 kilos bread. The ride through industrial and hardly damaged Freital was interesting. Big Bolshevik decorations on many factories. Red bunting and flags, pictures of Lenin, Stalin, Marx etc., banners. Up here in the petit bourgeois garden suburb there is no sign of Soviet Russia.

Yesterday morning, therefore, to the mill; in the aft. to the Kubes, to the family of our good Maria. Long way out on Kesselsdorferstr. Wretched house, but the apartment not so terribly cramped. [. . .] For the time being her husband is a postman until he can take up his harp-building again. A mountain of cake, we even received left-overs and two eggs as a gift. But nothing ostentatious, nothing crude, also nothing obsequious; they speak ungrammatical German, but with excellent content and complete tact – we felt animated and very much at ease. The husband was an infantryman and with technical support troops in Russia and Czechoslovakia, finally a prisoner of war in Romania. He told us of dreadful shootings of young soldiers, eighteen-year-olds, who had refused to advance, he told us of ghastly mass shootings of natives. He, *too*, despite his Catholicism, is drawn towards the KPD.

1st December, Saturday night (actually already 12.30, 2nd Dec.)

Yesterday handed in my party declaration at the TH. [...] In Fräulein Mey's office I met Janentzky and explained to both, what had driven me to the KPD. Janentzky literally turned green, when I related details of the house searches. [...] Unfortunately the errand once again brought frequent chest pains in its train. How much longer? And I would so much like to go on living!

At the TH there was a second letter from Kleinmayer. Here he is called Weinmayer, and his letterhead bore the company name Knorr & Hirth, and in between an explanatory letter had arrived from Vossler. (It took 2 weeks!) K. and H. are planning a series 'On the Psychology of National Socialism', and that is where my *LTI* is to go – Vossler praised me as a 'psychologist and sociologist of language'. There is another sentence in his very warm and some-what doddery and emotional letter which arouses childish hopes in me. 'I hope and believe, that your aspirations, as far as your studies and your teaching activities are concerned, will soon be fulfilled.' Could he have remembered me for a university chair? After all, for want of better, old materials are everywhere being used for reconstruction. But how do all these hopes and plans match my heart? [...] Vossler had a serious attack of heart trouble in June and was laid up for three months. He cannot 'manage much even now'. The unfamiliar gen-tleness and friendliness of his tone is presumably related to that. One passage sounds almost like a testament. [...]

[...]

7th December, Friday forenoon

In anticipation, as an autobiographical date: yesterday, 6 Dec., the city of Dresden offered me the academic directorship of the People's High School. Voir ci-dessous.[127] – In anticipation: there will be another anti-Semitic wave, even bigger than the first, and this time coming really spontaneously from the people as a whole. Because here in Dresden before 33 there was a Jewish community numbering thousands, it has been exterminated, there must be less than 100 Jews living here. But how many of these few occupy leading positions! Lang is a minister,[128] Katz senior medical adviser, Glaser senior provincial judge, Neumark on the committee of lawyers advising on new legislation, the trades-man Berger is head of the plain-clothes police in Heidenau, and now I have two important offices simultaneously!

8th December, Saturday forenoon

Lack of time and much has happened, very numb fingers – today it is 10 below zero and our coal is running out.

[...]

On Sunday, 2 Dec., we, together with the Steiningers, were at the Hanuschs' in Freital-Niederhäslich. An expedition, at 1 we met the Steiningers at the no 22 tramstop, from Freital station it was then a half-hour walk through straggling industrial village suburbs, which are now part of the town of Freital, with views of the wooded hills. Steininger related: Frau Hanusch, the Theresienstadt survivor, was the daughter of a Bohemian–Jewish 'florin millionaire' and cousin of the late Frau Pick (from Caspar David Friedrich Strasse). Hanusch was the talented son of a peasant and she was his patron, making possible his art studies. The two did not marry until very late, she was probably already in her forties. She was in applied arts (embroidery); he was professor at the applied arts academy in Plauen, paints portraits and landscapes, is an engraver [...]. A large, well-preserved, but essentially unaltered half-timbered village house, which H. inherited from his parents. [...] Over coffee I talked seriously about my attitude to politics. Afterwards Hanusch showed us a large number of his etchings of dunes – I quickly wearied of them, E. was *enthused* – and photographs of his paintings, among them the humorous *Porter with Blue Parcel*, a fateful picture for him: the Führer bought it at the Munich exhibition – inquiries were then made, with the result that the husband was dismissed from his post, and the wife, who was staying with relatives in Bohemia, was sent to Theresienstadt. At 6, when we wanted to leave, a proper large supper appeared, a big meat dish, which derived from Swiss donations. That was normal for the Hanuschs, said the Steiningers, who are old friends of theirs.

9th December, Sunday afternoon

Curious, how we now find ourselves in artistic circles. On Monday morning, the day after our visit to the Hanuschs, Winde called. From Hanusch we had already heard the rumour, that Grohmann had been toppled as department head [...]. Now Winde reported: G. really had been forced to resign and would now become director of the Dresden High School of Applied Arts, which would remain independent of the Fine Art Academy.[129] There had been lengthy discussion of a fusion of the two institutions. He, Winde, was very satisfied with this solution. He was hoping for a chair under his friend Grohmann [...]. Winde did not view my joining the KPD with particular sympathy. They were too barbaric, they were lining their own pockets; the SPD, whose views were close to his own, was more civilised ... We charged W., to ask his friend Hanusch, for what price he would sell us 2 etchings. Then on Wed. Winde came to my lecture in Trachenberge and was very approving. I had looked 'so young' at the lectern and was a born speaker, and the time, a whole $1\frac{1}{4}$ hours, had flown by for him.

[...]

On Monday aft. (3 Dec.) a meeting of the Kulturbund took place at Leubnitzerstr. [...]. When I arrived, late, having lost my way in the ruins of the Swiss

Quarter, I found about 50 people, among them the immovable Kühn, Menke-Glückert, Nestler, Frau Kreisler. Two overlapping things. What attitude should be taken towards the Berlin Kulturbund, which was demanding strong centralisation and firm leadership for the whole of Germany. And what should the Dresden management and organisation be. In Berlin it was emphatically solely the association of artists and scholars; in Dresden 'the four political parties' were in charge, nominally at least – in fact Herr von Manstein was absolute ruler, thus far he had never convened the 'Initiative Committee' and entirely of his own accord given lectures on Christianity in the name of the Kulturbund [...]. The politicians [present] attacked Hanstein fairly brutally [...]. At the close of the meeting it was about 6 o'clock and completely dark outside. During the break Nestler had already informed me, that I had now been unanimously proposed to the city council by all 4 parties (by the KPD last!) [...]. Nestler and I left together. It was utterly dark and deserted. The ruined quarter lay quite deserted. It is considered very unsafe because of riff-raff in hiding there, the Glasers are said to have been *repeatedly* attacked. We walked to the station arm in arm and then along Ammonstr. as far as Postplatz. We stumbled frequently, once we encountered two policemen, otherwise not a soul. It was gloomily Romantic.

[...]

On Wed., 5 Dec., I gave my lecture on Nat. Socialism and scholarship for the first time. I noted down an outline and examples on a sheet of paper; it turned out well. Fatiguing journey to the 38th Elementary School on Marienhofstr. Vast building, in the yard a large gymnasium transformed into an auditorium: $\frac{2}{3}$ of the room filled with benches, a very high platform with a wide red cloth hanging down, a long table [...]. I made the acquaintance of the somewhat crumpled, but friendly town councillor Sachse. $1\frac{1}{4}$ hour talk, considerable success. [...] Afterwards a young lady came up to me, to ask whether I could give her my ms for an article. [...] Since I had no ms, I asked her to call on me on Thurs. aft. Yes, gladly, then it will turn into an 'interview'.

It was after 7 p.m., when I got back to Dölzschen; that evening there was some kind of early Christmas party taking place in the Begerburg, E. was to accompany Ulrich again. [...] When we got there, things were already under way. The hall full, long table festive with fir twigs. Forbrig on a low platform, partly reciting, partly reading a prepared text, somewhat poetically cliched, but quite nice. The history of Christmas. [...] Altogether anti-religious in tone – Christ can no longer be our ideal, he has no job, has no relationship to women, none to the family – F. read out astonishing non-Christian analogies to the Jesus legend. Some of it was absolutely new to me. Whenever F. concluded a section, Frau Ulrich, accompanied by E., had to sing an old Christmas carol. But only ones which did not contain anything really Christian were chosen. [...] This celebration was not organised by the Antifa as a whole, only by SPD and KPD. A KPD member [...], a young man, then reported what had been prepared for the distribution of children's presents and for the adults' party on 16 Dec. The children will receive toys and biscuits [...] the adults in the evening likewise biscuits and 'ample potato salad'. In order to be able to join in, we had to contribute 10 grams of fat coupons and a tablespoon of sugar each.

On the morning of Thursday, 6 Dec., there was a meeting of the committee of the academics' section of the Kulturbund in the engineering building of the TH. The convenor was an engineer, Reingruber, a young man[130] I did not know at all; present were Simon, the faculty dean, probably in his early 50s, fat, well-groomed, calm, not unpleasant [...] finally Janentzky, very aged, very anaemic looking, very sunken around the mouth. Everyone was very polite, I evidently appeared to them to be almost romantically dangerous. I was invited to sit near the stove, my particular agreement was asked on everything. I said, I agreed with them entirely if they wanted to keep our scholarly contributions absolutely unpolitical – only, the professors could no longer be allowed, as in the Weimar years, to sabotage the policies of their state. [...] Reingruber said, it was a mistake on the Allies' part, to spin out the Nürnberg trial[131] so far and so long on the wireless. It made people numb and indifferent. That was also my opinion exactly. Then there was discussion of our contributions to the Kulturbund, of popular talks. [...] I: it would be necessary to come to an understanding with the People's High School, in which I myself had a strong interest. At that moment, on cue and as if pre-arranged, a beadle entered, Prof. Klemperer called to the telephone. Fräulein Mey outside: Schools Councillor Dölitzsch wanted to know, when he could meet me at the TH. A moment later I was speaking to him on the telephone. He wished to inform me, that the town council had ... etc. He had wanted to come to the TH, we could save time, if I would come to the Saturday meeting at 2 p.m. at the Education Office on Melanchthonstr. I agreed immediately and particularly emphasised my great pleasure at the new task. I then informed my colleagues at the TH of my appointment. All that I required now was the formal consent of the rector and of the State Secretary. Indignation! We had every right to take on part-time appointments. Only notification (not, for example, a request for approval) of the rector, who passes it on to the minister.

Then at 4 in the afternoon the journalist from the *Sächsische Volkszeitung* came; when she left it was 9 in the evening. Frau Dr Gerlandt, earthy blonde, quite a strange life, still in her 20s, divorced, 4-year-old daughter – proper Germanist and Romanist, student of Gamillscheg and Winkler – we gossiped shop. She did not know what had become of Neubert[132] – he had not been in Berlin for a long time. She had wanted to become a journalist, but had been rejected as 'politically unreliable' – as a schoolgirl she had been a member of the 'Red Falcons'. She had been a film extra in Paris for 2 years, had married, had lived in Romania for a while, had her child looked after here ... Fairly confused and mysterious. She was in the KPD, was an editor with a monthly salary of 800M – but there was something not quite right about her Communism. She always felt a pang at the word 'comrade' [...]. She had no idea what the future would bring, she did not believe in the fusion of the Social Democrats and the Communists, after the huge defeat of the Austrian Communists, the Social Democrats here were also on their high horse ... What did she want to write about my lecture? [...] What did I have to say about school reform, how did I imagine the comprehensive school? – surely there must be sections for the different educational backgrounds! I: certainly! Only the primary school comprehensive, and selection from this basic pot made without regard for parents' social and financial circumstances. I am now curious how this interview will turn out.

The second lecture was on Friday, 7 Dec. This time in the more easily reached 31st Elementary School; Altgruna, Junghansstr. Seidemann called for me, we got there so quickly, that we found the hall still quite empty. But then it filled up completely, I certainly had the anticipated 3–400 listeners. [. . .] In the lecture I drew on the experiences of Wednesday and said immediately, that freedom to teach was not freedom to sabotage the state. Nevertheless a radical spoke up afterwards. Scholarship was not objective, but tied to the subject. I banged him on the head with the ideal of objectivity and the approximateness of everything earthly. The man [. . .] got no applause, I very loud applause.

Then on Saturday, 8 Dec., I was at Melanchthonstr. at 2 p.m. for the meeting of the 'People's High School advisory committee'. I met Nestler, Frau Hoppe, the secretary, Krebs, a retired primary school teacher, as well as a slim grey-haired man called Kissling, an engineer, I think, and a somewhat stern and distant Frau Schwarz. Then Councillor Dölitzsch ushered us into his large, nicely heated room. Likeable, fairly hard man, about 50, dark-eyed, leaning heavily on a crutch. He told me afterwards: Had been a teacher and SPD official, concentration camp, ill-treated, close to death, bleeding heavily, saved by a transfusion. Simple and friendly natural language. I gave a short address: Thanks, pleasure, and now I wanted to speak quite plainly. Political confession, intention to tackle the evening school seriously, serious and popular, strict separation of lectures of a general educational nature and genuine university preparatory courses. [. . .] After that I had personal requests. [. . .] I explained my financial situation and asked for 'decent pay'. Referring to a list Dölitzsch established: [. . .] a headmaster [Klemperer's equivalent rank] receives a maximum salary of 9,000M. The payment of two salaries is not permitted, you will, therefore, get very little from us. I was silent. Then Frau Schwarz – representative of the KPD, as I had heard a couple of minutes earlier – said that, after all, the 9,000M were allocated in the budget, anyone else would have got them. If I could not have them as a second salary, one could get round that with a private contract; it would be justified as reparation to a victim of Fascism; also I had to look dignified and could not – glance at my shabby trousers with their moth holes – run around in patched things! Dölitzsch: if that was the consensus, he would propose it to the council. [. . .] It was then further decided to request a secretary's salary for Frau Hoppe. I said a few words of particular thanks to Hoppe and Nestler.
[. . .]

10th December, Monday afternoon

[. . .]

On Saturday, at the Dölitzsch session I also requested a telephone and a car.

They will assist me with the telephone; as for the car I was told: 'Be glad that you don't have one yet. Only old cars are allocated, they constantly break down, and there are no spare parts. Also, on the road the Russians frequently confiscate a car. In the last few days someone who refused was shot out of hand.'
[...]

14th December, Friday morning (and later)

I am brooding over and feeling my way with the programmatic lecture: 'Dresden People's High School 1946', the main points are clear in my mind. [...] I am especially pleased with my plan for the programmatic talk insofar as this work on the one hand benefits the *LTI* (youth movement!), on the other leads me back to the 18th century, thirdly really adds to my knowledge. In a textbook on educational theory, borrowed from Forbrig, I for the first time read something about Pestalozzi.[133] His 200th birthday on 12/1/46 is to be commemorated in the Dresden Kulturbund [...] and *I* – this was my suggestion gladly accepted by the advisory board – in my inaugural lecture [...] will go to the root of the Pestalozzi business, more precisely to the *Encyclopaedia* and Rousseau.
[...]

I spent one afternoon this week at Nestler's [...]. I sat in the kitchen with Frau Hoppe and she informed me about people and things. Of course for me everything depends on diplomacy. I want to make it clear to the KPD, that it is in *its* interest that I want to place humanism and *non-politics* at the centre. I want to bring *Antigone* to the workers, I *want* to be *impractical* at the centre. In sharpest contrast to the principles of my predecessor, Riedel, probably also of the majority of the KPD.
[...]

Möbius, my boss in the envelope factory, visited me; at first I didn't even recognise him, as he was wearing corduroy work clothes. His father will be able to carry on the factory in another location – he himself, as Party and SS member, is impossible. He wanted a testimony from me against the foreman Bergmann, who was hated by Jew and Christian alike – but in fact he did not do anything bad to me. Instead of this attestation against B. I gave a testimony in favour of Möbius and so he was delighted.
[...]

Would I accept a professorship? I am very much taken with this new municipal post. On the other hand the Kühn affair is ever more awkwardly coming to a climax. I was at the TH today (dreadful heart trouble in an icy contrary wind). Rector Heidebroek, very courteous and pleasantly natural as always, reported that some panel of professors is to decide the business between K. and myself(!), it was not right that I talked about the matter in public lectures, something like that must be kept among colleagues! I: Kühn was not my colleague, I had not mentioned his name in the lecture, I expected nothing at all of any consultation.
[...]

15th December, Saturday morning

Yesterday towards evening, Winde, who regards me as something like a government undersecretary, was here. He brought etchings from Hanusch, which E. liked so very much and about which I had inquired via Winde. As friends we got two of them – dunes – for the price of 30M each. Winde himself will have them framed. My first art purchase, and my first Christmas present for E. for many years. [...]

17th December, Monday forenoon

[...]

Yesterday aft. from 5–8 [...] the Christmas party of Dölzschen SPD and KPD. A big room, too hot and too full, we sat at long tables, in one corner there was a decorated Christmas tree, without lights – though single candles were burning on the tables.

Speeches by the SPD man and Seidemann [...]. A youth group performed various modest and harmless 'sketches' [...] a choir sang Christmas carols (with Christian texts despite Forbrig!). The main thing was the quite excellent food [...]. There had obviously been donations, in particular from the Braune bread factory. With a little pot of coffee, each person got a full-grown stollen cake and all kinds of biscuits, so that we even took a lot home, and then later came the advertised potato salad, for which we had to provide our own plate and cutlery. All very nice, but a little dreary nonetheless and very exhausting. We sat close to the platform, with us the Forbrigs, the Seidemanns, Frau Ulrich.

Very depressed once more. My heart is packing up. Our heating situation is catastrophic. The Kühn affair weighs me down.

[...]

22nd December, midday Saturday

Out and about for days at a time. Catastrophe of recent days: the heating. The coke Berger left behind is finally running out. Now a cooking stove really *has* to be installed in the kitchen, and from there a pipe laid up to the hall. Wollenschläger wanted to do it, passed it on to Haubold, mentioned a Bastian company on Markgraf Heinrichstr. as supplier of materials. Yesterday and the day before yesterday I was down there with the most questionable success. This business has cost me literally two whole days.

On top of that there was the sorting out of my salary at the State Administration. [...] Neumark writes to me, that Friedrichs rejects every claim for compensation. On the other hand Assistant Secretary Weschke, with whom I was 'sorting out my salary', said that, with respect to compensation I would have to sue the state. He offered a higher salary, on condition I waived any claim. I refused to do so. I think that at some point the Allies will intervene on behalf of Jewish claims. [...]

I have now received my pass as a 'recognised and registered victim of Fascism' and on the strength of it a huge stollen cake and a tin of fatty meat as Christmas gift. [...]

The fine blue material, which I bought from Jung in the summer for 100M, is now going to be made into a suit by young Anders, the Seidemanns' neighbour and a tailor – for 75M. It will be the most expensive suit in my life.

[...]

23rd December, Sunday morning

I take note of the name Herbert Gute.[134] First Hanusch mentioned him as Grohmann's successor and permanent secretary in the state government. Then I came across his name in the programme of the PHS [People's High School], giving a lecture on 'Imperialism'. Yesterday a certain Liebmann[135] called on me, recommended by his friend and fellow party member, Gute (KPD), to teach at the PHS. We sounded one another out [...]. Liebmann, writer and dramatist (he as ignorant of me, as I of him), would like to lecture on Nietzsche. I set forth my PHS plan, we talked about university professorships, the Kühn case, the KPD and the intelligentsia ... Liebmann is going to arrange a meeting between Gute, Liebmann, Frau Schwarz, myself. My egoistical ulterior motive is always the university chair. [...]

26th December, Wednesday morning

I thought Christmas would give me a special thrill this time – the tremendous contrast to Christmas 1944! At the last moment my mood was considerably soured. Fräulein Weidel, the librarian at the Leipzig Deutsche Bücherei, who lives here and is Trude Öhlmann's messenger, brought me [...] the bad news. 'You wrote the article in the *Volkszeitung*, didn't you, professor? My father immediately said it could only be you.' The Christmas number came later, and then I saw the fine mess for myself, 'Leap over the Abyss'.[136] The Gerlandt woman writes about a well-known academic, dismissed because of his race, who is now working on the French 18th century and on the *LTI*, all in the first person of the man thus characterised. 'I was in a prison cellar. Again and again my hand chased woodlice and spiders from my face ...' a whole paragraph like this, undoubtedly copied from a trashy novel! There must be at least 100 people in Dresden who, although I am not mentioned by name, nevertheless identify me with the narrator. To them I have not only been held up to ridicule, but made to look impossible. How do I face the hostile professors at the TH, how, as director of the People's High School, fight against hollow phrases? But if I demand a public denial, I make the matter even worse. I am at a loss. I want to talk about it to everyone I meet. Thus far I have discussed it only with Seidemann. He had read the thing, recognised me immediately and really believed that I myself had written it and expressed my own experience 'a little oddly'.

But subsequently Christmas Eve turned out very nice after all. For the first time in years I was able to give E. something. The two engravings by Hanusch, two heavy hammers, a painfully heavy crowbar (carried down from the village smithy with some difficulty – my heart provides a very doleful accompaniment to all my pleasures). On top of that there are the rhododendrons. Then we were guests of the Wolffs for a late supper. A little tree without candles in our home, a tree with candles and decorations in theirs. [. . .] In the course of the evening I drank eleven schnapps and held them remarkably well and without after-effects. (The things one can be proud of!) The W's are poor devils. He *has* to belong to a party, otherwise he can neither be registered as a victim of Fascism, nor buy a hotel, nor lease a cinema. He wants to do that in any event, in order to get his fortune, which is quite unsafe as cash, out from under the mattress and into safely. Where did he get this fortune, what does he live on? 'On the Russians,' he says. But what business does he do with them? a mystery! In May he played a leading role in the KPD up here, at the same time, with the aid of the Russians, treated the comrades, in particular Scholz, roughly. Now they are presenting the reckoning, refusing to admit him to the Party, refusing him sole ownership of the disputed apartment. [. . .] The Dölzschen KPD has refused to admit Wolff, and we made ourselves at home with the Wolffs on Christmas Eve and yet again for lunch yesterday *and* for the afternoon. And now (in his and my interest) Wolff wants to take over the mortgage on our house at $3\frac{1}{2}$%. Hence this whole story is in some degree embarrassing and depressing [. . .].

Compensation for the abyss article was a letter from Knorr & Hirth: agreement to my *LTI* plan ('Between Scholarship and Life'), 300 pp at my disposal. Now I am constantly turning over in my mind: to what extent pure LTI, to what extent expand into Curriculum? [. . .] But first the lecture for the PHS has to be done. [. . .]

The wireless is broadcasting a great quantity of religious Christmas music and Protestant and Catholic services. Russia evidently cannot do enough to emphasise its religious tolerance. On the other hand, morning gymnastics have been dropped for weeks now. And recently, when I wanted to have Dr Katz for sport hygiene at the PHS, Dölitzsch told me, *all* sport had recently been forbidden by the Allies. I repeatedly ask myself whether this is the right way, at the same time as their own militarism is being intensified, to achieve the true, spiritual disarmament of Germany.

Because of this and because of the systematic brutality of the 'purging' I feel the ground shaking beneath my feet. One day we shall have revolt against the outside [world] and civil war at home.

[. . .]

27th December, Thursday evening

At the Steiningers' yesterday afternoon. Together with the Hanuschs and the Windes. Each party received a loaf as a Christmas present. Overheated room, somewhat scanty hospitality with tea, a little boring. I beseeched them to tell others I was not responsible for the newspaper article.

This aft. the Windes and Frau Kriesler here. Boring and tiring, the same conversations as the day before. Except that I raged at Kreisler, when she mentioned my 'fine article' in the newspaper. [. . .]

In the morning Dr Dressel here by bike. 'Wave of arrests' in Pirna. Dressel belonged to the SA (*not* the Party) until 43. [...] I gave him an attestation, like the one I had drawn up for Scherner: at considerable risk to himself he had sheltered me during my flight. That should help. – I heard what the other side had to say. Annemarie Köhler's brother is among those expropriated by the land reform, is in a camp (was a Stahlhelm[137] man and against Hitler). [...]

29th December, Saturday morning
Yesterday lunchtime Nestler sent Comrade Naundorf along with me to the district headquarters of the KPD at Albertplatz, and Naundorf got me Comrade Leitner,[138] chief editor of the *Sächsische Volkszeitung* on the telephone. I made my complaint indignantly and emphatically. Leitner was very polite and promised redress, but not much dismayed, a little lukewarm and not very specific. [...] All the same I have now, in front of witnesses, lodged the most brusque protest and will so inform the rector's office at the TH and other official bodies.
  [...]

31st December, 7 p.m. Monday
Liebmann (cf. 23rd Dec.) sent a telegram on Saturday, he was coming out with Gute on Sunday morning. We really did have this conference yesterday. Liebmann hardly opened his mouth; Seidemann, who came up on his own accord as a personal friend of Gute, likewise. It was a very lengthy discussion, between two powers, as it were, between G. and myself. G. represents the Party and the ministry. He is in Grohmann's place, believes he is able to hold his own and foil the 'dirty dog' (sic) Menke-Glückert. It was repeatedly emphasised on both sides: 'You need *us*' – 'You need *me*'. Position of the intelligentsia in the KPD. My PHS plan met with complete approval. In place of Krebs I get a KPD man as manager. That doesn't bother me. But I do not have any real confidence in Gute, although he makes a more energetic and concentrated impression than Grohmann. These unskilled workers do not see the difficulties on which they later founder. To me, Gute, too, spoke all too frivolously of a Dresden University to be built from scratch. And equally frivolously of a Leipzig professorship for me. [...] I should first of all put the PHS here on its feet, then I would be sent to a university. He, Gute, had long voted against me as the choice for the PHS, I had been the Soc. Dems. choice; he had wanted to save me for the university.
  Also, my plan of turning Kühn into a librarian met with his approval ... I was no longer quite as swell-headed as after my first conversation with Grohmann. Nevertheless, the permanent secretary had come by car to confer with me ... Wait and see how long he stays at the helm. I was also asked my advice about the Kulturbund. Today I am working out a programme of lectures over 8–10 evenings on the 'Italian Renaissance'.
  Then yesterday afternoon 4 strong comrades effected our internal removal: we are now domiciled in the music room and the study has become a bedroom.
  Today, while I was giving Fräulein Berndt an audience, Alfred Seidemann

drew my portrait. I was aghast: a *Stürmer*[139] caricature, drooping lips and cheeks, Jew's nose like a trunk...

My vanity was deflated by a letter from Trude Öhlmann: my PHS post did not impress her at all, my place was in a university. Very interesting in her letter her attitude to the KPD. She is a passionate anti-Fascist – but the KPD repels her. The workers are so hostile to her, 'a woman who wears a hat', there was nothing in common between her and them. And then: she would immediately be excluded from her circle, if she went over to the 'cloth caps'. I must show that to Seidemann. [...]

Today I said to Fräulein Berndt, *today* I had some power, but whether I would still have it tomorrow, was doubtful, I felt the ground beneath my feet all too shaky. And that ultimately is my fundamental New Year's Eve mood.

Still: this year! After all probably the most fairy-tale-like of my life.

We shall bring in the New Year at the Wolffs.

1946

1st January, 8.30 Thursday evening

E. has gone to bed, after already sleeping for a long time in the afternoon, and I, too, shall soon call it a day. The New Year's party at the Wolffs yesterday lasted until 3 a.m. after all and was very alcoholic, at once neither so very boring, nor especially interesting. E., already fatigued beforehand, recently suffering greatly from her dropped stomach, had a brief fit of fainting or weakness.

From early yesterday there was snow and frost, which is continuing now. It does not chime well with our lack of coal and space. With somewhat of an effort we are getting used to the one room, the little iron stove consumes a great deal and yet only occasionally prevails against the size of the space and the frost. My desk stands against the terrace window and the out-of-action central heating. The kitchen downstairs is icy cold, and God knows when the planned cooking stove will be put in.

[...]

4th January, Friday morning

Astonishing how emphatically KPD and SPD put the Germans, German unity, nationalism almost, at the centre of things. Yesterday in Berlin a meeting in honour of the 70-year-old Wilhelm Pieck (freeman of Berlin – founding member of Spartacus League!!).[1] All, including him, spoke as national patriots, Dahrendorf,[2] the SPD man, even – a faux pas! – of the 'blood bond', the late Adolf Hitler would have been satisfied.

For *LTI* there comes to light after the event: A witness at Nürnberg repeatedly talks of the *FINAL SOLUTION*, to which the Jews were transported, and means by that the gas ovens. Along the lines of human material, items. The commentator says, 'the terrible words' are constantly used. One of those ordered to put it into effect, so runs the statement, had been horrified. 'Don't get sentimental!' was the rejoinder. The basic attitude here: 'become hard!' and that out of racial principle, that is, out of Nordic morality. LTI.

Terrible tiredness, endless distractions, no progress in the PHS lecture. Very cramped in the *one* room.

Mood once again depressed by the tomcat. He appears to be blind – excessively large pupils, extremely unsteady movements. Soils the room, pity and despair. We are unable to decide on the 'final solution'.

[...]

One morning (2 Jan.) was taken up with a meeting in the TH to which I was invited by telegram. Heidebroek informed us that the TH, i.e. the General Section, must participate in the training of lay teachers. [...] For the present only this: the Russians *forbid* history as a subject in lay-teacher training! Kühn was not present, our business was not mentioned. Heidebroek related: it was due to the Russians' antipathy towards officer students (and to demonstrations by the latter in Leipzig and Jena) that no university had yet started on Soviet [-controlled] territory. Moreover matters were no further advanced in the west; the shortage of coal made everything illusory.

20th January, Sunday afternoon

The diary has lived on notes for 16 days; there was too much to attend to and I very much wanted to get the 'Dresden People's High School 1946' lecture out of the way. I had finally managed that the day before yesterday, and then *Waldenburg* came along, i.e. the task of inaugurating a local branch of the Kulturbund there. I worked out a speech yesterday. The Begerburg lecture 'Chosen Peoples' got a preface, 'Culture and Civilisation', which is to become a jewel of the *LTI*. [...]

Now, in order, the 16 days.

Throughout this time a battle with frost, snow, ice, heart trouble in the biting wind, craftsmen, haulage companies, lack of coal. The work on the kitchen stove is almost complete, that on the heating system is now to begin. [...] The 6 cwt of coal have at last been got here. [...] I also got 6 cwt of briquettes from the coal merchant in the village. Despite all that the reserve is barely sufficient, the feeling of cold and the related worry great. All of that [arrangement of transport] also involved considerable loss of time.

Master tailor Anders, a Party member, with whom, therefore, I am on first-name terms, delivered the suit. My first new suit since 1935 or 36 [...] the first suit which I have had made to measure on my own account. In 1912, when I was equipping myself for my studies in Munich I had frock coat and tails made to measure at Berthold's expense.[3] Since then off the peg. [...]

But in the last few days Alfred Seidemann drew me: I sit hunched up like an 80-year-old dodderer, tired, shaky, wasted away. A profile drawing looks a bit younger but like a *Stürmer* caricature. These were by now Seidemann's second and third drawings – all three dismayed me. [...]

Further business of these past weeks, still not quite out of the way the compulsory inoculation against typhus, a little post festum,[4] since the disease is fading. We first made an appointment with a woman doctor up here, there was a crush. So I telephoned Katz and then called on him at his apartment – Lipsiusstr., the only intact house; the two large rooms of his not very likeable wife's fashion shop – behind them K.'s simple bed and living room in one. He himself in his dressing gown, very thin, very tired, almost apathetic. He had a pneumonia relapse behind him, was to go that same afternoon to Warnekross sanatorium at Kreischa to recuperate for two weeks. I wanted to cheer him up, tried to recruit him for the People's High School, for the KPD, showed him in every way my feeling for him and my effort on his behalf. He appeared to me fairly moribund: he had no strength any more, wanted only to see his son again (from his first marriage, married in England years ago). It affected me. The man has waited as I have; now he has the chance of his life and has no more strength. Because of angina I received an inoculation exemption certificate. E. is to be inoculated or exempted tomorrow, I think: likewise exempted. That will happen in K.'s old apartment in Borsbergstr., which is now entirely a kind of clinic, and very busy: medical assistant, receptionists, office. The assistant will 'attend to' E.

All this in addition to profession or the actual vita activa, to which I reckon: TH, PHS, KB (Kulturbund), KPD, school and writing.

I like least being in the TH. Like in a cage of wild beasts. I know they are all my enemies.

On 8 Jan. there was the [. . .] meeting in the teacher-training college hostel in Wachwitz. [. . .] Janentzky spoke on behalf of the TH. [. . .] Of the TH people I saw and spoke to the very emaciated and much aged Spamer,[5] who showed me such warmth, that I invited him to visit us.

He came, too, and we became friends. He was professor in Berlin and as a folklorist aroused the hostility of the Rosenberg[6] and the SS people. Completely bombed out he then returned to Dresden seriously ill – it must be sclerosis – and is now to be rehabilitated here. He said he had always, without belonging to any party, voted Communist and was not at all shocked at me. – After that Tobler.[7] Small, nimble, very obliging, curiously enough already 66. He was in the Stahlhelm, his wife is Jewish. With some difficulty he had kept his post, had suffered much. [. . .] He makes a good impression on me. But Wildführ[8] (the great surprise of 10 Jan.) very much warned me against him. Tobler had concealed his wife's Jewishness, denied it, he had ingratiated himself with the Nazis, affirmed their race theory etc.

A session of the KB academic committee had been fixed for the 10th in the TH. There were more people present than at the first sessions. Heidebroek chaired. [. . .] Beside me sat a young man, resemblance to Lerch,[9] he could have been an SA man: the hygienist Wildführ. – As I was about to go home W. was standing in a window recess by the exit, and we got into conversation. Which led to an alliance, which then, on the 14th, turned to friendship. I shall sum up. W., 41, 3 children, his career impeded under the Nazis, took his post-doctoral here nevertheless, KPD member, is provisionally administrator of the Municipal Hygiene Institute and professor of hygiene at the TH. Like conspirators we resolved [. . .] to do away with the forces of reaction at the Technical

High School. W. said, that of the three pillars of reaction, the Junkers,[10] the army and the university, the first two had fallen, the third, the university, not yet. We agreed to telephone to arrange a discussion with Gute ... In this way I found myself at a meeting as to the purpose of which I had not received any information. That was on Monday, 14 January. It was about the KB Hanstein business. [...] Hanstein had behaved almost criminally, squandered funds, virtually embezzled them, got himself validated in Berlin for the Dresden and the Saxon chairmanship by providing false information. The Berlin general secretary, Willmann,[11] had come down, and Hanstein had been forced to abdicate immediately and completely; [...] a general meeting was to elect the new KB managing committee. – First of all a small circle met in Gute's room. Gute, Hennig and his secretary Dr. rer. pol. Blank and Grüttner, secretary of the KB and a Party official. Later Willmann. Berlin's view, and Gute's, was that the management had to be unpolitical, placing 'culture', scholarship, literature exclusively at the centre. [...] Hennig strongly objected; politics must remain the key. It was decided to let the general meeting decide. A large room, probably 80–90 notables and would-be notables. I knew Janentzky, Wildführ, Kreisler, Kretzschmar, Mauthner, Wolfgang Schumann, had Balzer[12] pointed out to me, saw Frau Hoppe and Nestler. Menke-Glückert presided. On his left Gute, on his right Willmann. Central to W.'s lengthy report: No imitation of the parties – only culture and the arts. But he made a psychological error. Instead of saying, people didn't just and always want to do and hear about politics (which would *also* have been true), he explained: people did not want to join any party, 'falling for it once was enough' and now they wanted to wait and see. That was of course accurate, but was splendid material for the opposition. Those brave democrats Menke-Gl. and Kastner immediately protested, the KB was no bolt-hole for shirkers etc., here colours had to be nailed to the mast. Now Hennig was in his element, there was applause, and in a trice political *and* cultural people were elected, eleven in all, among them Gute, Wildführ, myself from the KPD, Hanusch also. The first sitting of this far too large committee is to take place on Wed. 23 Jan.

For Wed. I'm also hoping for a preceding special discussion among us KPD people on the subject of TH and university. The TH is plotting something. On Sunday, 13 Jan., the teachers held a Pestalozzi commemoration. (Scala, Grossenhainerstr., a hall with a stage among the buildings of the Göhle plant – so this is where the bulk of the Jews did labour duty for the 3rd Reich. Beautiful Beethoven and Brahms music by the Staatskapelle. The much talked-about new conductor, Keilberth.[13] Pg – but since Berlin wanted to buy him up – he was kept here with a professorship. New and sweet to my ears during Sachse's words of welcome was the mention of my name. 'I welcome as representative of the TH Prof. Janentzky, I welcome the Director of the People's High School Prof. Klemperer ...' [...]

So before the beginning of the ceremony Janentzky told me: the Russians were now demanding a reduction in the number of our professors – and French was not even taught in secondary schools any more. I brooded over this during the ceremony and at the end said nothing more to J. than: he should not misjudge the situation. As I did so, I thought of Baeumler's words of 1933:[14] 'You misjudge the situation, gentlemen!' J. replied immediately, that it was of course the bad engineers, who were jealous of the General Section. But the warning probably did some good. The following day during the KB session, Janentzky, glowing with friendship, gave me the copy of a letter, which he had handed to the rector's office. List of the professorships in our section. They had been cut to such an extent, that there was nothing more that could be cut. But I am extremely mistrustful of J. He covers himself with the letter and secretly tries to get rid of me. I would very much like to 'liquidate' both him and Kühn. [...]

Neubert, the one-armed dismissed director of the State Library, also visited me in recent days; he must 'earn a few pennies', did I have or know of 'any kind of subordinate work' for him. I cannot help. Yet my feelings are mixed. Kussi, who lost his relatives in Auschwitz, was here at the same time as Neubert. Kussi introduced his wife, a Dutch woman just arrived, to whom, on the day of her arrival, he was married in a registry office ceremony and an ecclesiastical Catholic one. A very refined, slim, bespectacled intellectual with [...] 'fluent' (so she says) strongly accented German.

PHS: Grützner. [...] Brisk, somewhat squirrel-like man in his late forties, KPD official, in prison with Gute [...]. So far everything is going well. [...] Grützner wants quickly to get off to a strong start, then wait until Easter and expand the timetable by then. He has already got hold of 2 rooms in Melanchthonstr. as an office. There I shall have a consultation hour twice a week and have Hoppe at my disposal for two 3-hour sessions. She wants to do only intellectual work, have only press and co-ordination work. Co-ordination is her ever-repeated favourite word, by which she means finding out about the activities of other People's High Schools. Of course Grützner demands more work and real office work from her. I played the wise Solomon. [...] Also, Grützner was going to put pressure on Weidauer[15] so that I at last get a telephone. I really need it, and an application by the Schools Department on my behalf has been refused. Running to the usually shut post office is nerve-racking. – On the 18th I held the decreed lecturers' meeting in Melanchthonstr. A large school room. About 20 of about 50 lecturers appeared. I brought Hoppe to take minutes; I summed up my principles. Grützner on expansion of the programme. [...]

Last Wednesday evening – frost, big moon, glittering snowy landscape, fantastic view down into the valley and to the hills – political meeting in the Begerburg. Comrade Liebermann from the information office. Against the rumour mongers, who gave the Russians a bad name, expect better things from the West, talk drivel about war between USA and the Russians. (That same day I heard from Frau Schmidt: 'Is it true – I am so afraid for our boy in Jena! – that there's rioting in Jena and the Americans are already in the town?') In the discussion afterwards, repeated questions about war (the people speak incorrect German, but they all speak without inhibition – 'all', that was at most 30 people in a circle around the speaker, shivering in the unheated room) [...]. Liebermann went on to talk in favour of a united workers' party, as on the same day Matern and [Buchwitz[16]] had demanded at a mass meeting here. [...] Liebermann, a calm, likeable (younger) man said very calmly and as a matter of course: if over there [in the west . . .] they do not join in, then *'we'* might have to do more than just pay our dues and hold meetings. The very gentleness of his voice made the threat of civil war sound especially disquieting.

Meanwhile elections in Hesse (only 3% for KPD) have also shown, that they want something different there than here. [. . .]

A couple of days ago, on the wireless, Johannes R. Becher attacked Thomas Mann respectfully but seriously; he could not understand that Mann was not returning to Germany. [. . .]

27th January, Saturday afternoon

Sometimes very down: tiredness, my heart, uncertainty of the situation, very strong feeling of vanitas vanitatum. Then again great uplift and happy feeling of having an effect, of being recognised. One rendezvous was on Wednesday the 23rd. KB session in the meeting chamber of the State Administration [. . .]. As recently, preliminary discussion in Gute's room. Wildführ had fetched me in the car [. . .]. There were 'introductory talks' and similar speeches to be allocated. [. . .] In addition, it was suggested the PHS could be inaugurated during the planned 'Culture Week'. But the Culture Week has been postponed from mid-February to March [. . .]. I could not [. . .] find the nimble Grützner [. . .] anywhere. I did and do suspect Grützner of proceeding on his own account and neglecting me. [. . .] thus I felt myself very much pushed aside.

Furthermore there was and is the recurring uncertainty about the *LTI* book. I cannot find the right order, the right tone. [. . .] Another friendly prodding letter from Weinmayer (Knorr & Hirth) has arrived.

If that improved my mood, then it reached a peak at the State Administration yesterday. [. . .] I got into conversation (and use of the Du![17]) with Gute, and he handed me an invitation to the 'Central Cultural Congress of the KPD in Berlin' from 4–6 Feb. I am to travel with him, will be accommodated and fed there by the Party; all schools issues will be discussed before the Central Committee at least of the KPD of the Soviet territory. This could be *my* hour in every respect, and at all events it will be interesting in many ways. Yet what already weighs on me: everything that tied me to Berlin is gone or dead, mostly dead. [. . .]

That morning the *'Du'* made further progress. Apart from Gute, his no-longer-young secretary, Mattauch, was included and Frau Blank, whom I met on the way there. She is in the SPD, Hennig's right hand, a student of Gehrig, half Jewish. We became chummy. She is also new to a workers' party and has [. . .] like us, Du inhibitions, she found it easier with the KPD people than within her own party. She was very relieved, when I made a start . . . I feel again and again that there is something a little comedy-like about this spreading of the Du. [. . .] And again and again I repeat: the *Du* of the workers cheered me up, that of the Gestapo enraged me.

[. . .]

Once, after a great deal of waiting and explaining and identifying, one has secured an individual entry permit at the gate house of the State Administration, then it still has to be stamped at a special police counter. Recently a pert, curly-haired policewoman was sitting there. 'Don't you recognise me, Professor?' It was young Ilse Frischmann from Zeughausstr., who [...] ended up in prison, her parents were also arrested.[18] The girl and her Aryan mother survived; the Jewish father is missing, undoubtedly dead.

A nice Du incident: I telephoned Frau Schwarz at KPD district headquarters, who supported me in the PHS salary business [...]. I addressed her as Sie. Reply: 'For me you [Du] are Comrade Klemperer, even if you [Du] are a professor!' I: 'That is what I prefer.'

[...]

The cooking stove and the heating pipe up to the hall are now finished at last, but there is not the fuel to make proper use of them, and cold and lack of space are still a torment. The bill for mason and fitter will be large, every single bit (old, naturally) of the piping had to be 'organised', and the most expensive thing will in every case be the transport here.

Haubold, very enlightened and altogether anti-Nazi, asked me: 'The Saxon State Bank, Arnhold owns it doesn't he? He's supposed to be here and to have bought the Prager Str. *They* say, it's all done with Jewish capital.' I talked it out of him. The Arnhold rumour has been around for six months now. Vox populi. What would happen to us few Jews, if the Allies withdrew?!

On the wireless the evening of the day before yesterday: the Americans have permitted the setting-up of a Bavarian Royalist Party, which wants a Bavarian kingdom on the English model. This party will become the most powerful in Bavaria together with the Bav. Zentrum.[19] And that will mean an end to the unity of the Reich. Strange, that no one here has so far expressed an opinion about it. Except that SPD and KPD constantly emphasise patriotism and unity of the Reich. [...]

29th January, Tuesday morning

[...]

Rasch,[20] the smith, who had returned from American captivity the day before, visited us after dark. I tried to win him for the KPD. He was wearing bits of blue American navy uniform with shiny metal buttons. He had been held by the Americans, French, Belgians, often under very bad conditions, and fallen ill with hunger. He praises the Russians. Transport was working much better than in the West. [...] He had no contact with his family for a year [i.e. since before the Dresden raids], then yesterday stood in front of the ruined villa on Lothringer Weg and not known whether his wife and children were lying under the rubble.

3rd February, Sunday forenoon

[...] At every step my heart troubles me: vanitas! – Thus the initial great and hopeful pleasure about Berlin has also completely faded, and I would, best of all, like to back out. [...] Apart from Gute and myself, 4 people I do not know are going [to the Congress]; the car will pick me up tomorrow morning before 6.

I have managed to write very little in recent days. [. . .] The long forenoon journeys – the torment of the trams, then worn out in the afternoons. Turnabout PHS and State Administration, Melanchthonstr. and Bebelstr. [. . .]

Once in Vogels' wretched cellar dwelling – I accepted a pound of salt. These people are having an undeservedly bad time. Next Friday I shall seek out the new mayor in Plauen about their hopeless situation. [. . .]

I am at last to get a new permanent pass for the State Administration; the old one had been declared invalid, getting a temporary pass at the always crowded control point is very time-consuming. Photos were necessary which I can also use for a new driving licence. (I have become *so* old. Everything preaches my age et finem to me.)

Through the Kulturbund came an invitation to the Dresden première, on the afternoon of 1 Feb., of a German version of the Soviet film *Merry Lads* in the Faun Palast. Most arduous journey there [. . .] great disappointment. A washed-out, completely witless over-American slapstick film from 1933, in Russian, with a few strips of German words stuck at the bottom. [. . .] We have had no luck with the cinema so far – and I so often longed for the cinema![21] Instead the wireless is now our great passion.

[. . .]

Politically everything on the Soviet side is now dominated by the idea of German unity, anti-Fascist bloc unity and SPD–KPD union. [. . .] But it does not look to me as if anything of these three unities will be at all permanent or even come to pass. Via Hoppe I got to look at a newspaper from the American zone. There the SPD wants in part to de-marxify itself, and in very great part have nothing to do with the KPD. [. . .] And the CDU may serve as Zentrum Party in the West – *here* it is cloaca maxima, refugium nazisticum and will one day be exposed.[22]

The transformation in me! A while ago when Wollschläger told me, he would like us to become a state of the Soviet Federation, I was shocked. Now I would like it myself. I no longer believe in the united German patria. I believe, we could very well cultivate German culture as a Soviet state under Russian leadership.

4th–6th February, Berlin trip to the KPD Congress (noted 7th–10th Feb.)

The five destinies in the car: The driver very young, very cautious, circumspect in every way (at the same time constantly smoking) shot down as a pilot over Sicily, bullet in the head (visible hole in his temple). Beside him Gute, early 40s. Originally commercial artist, essentially probably an autodidact. Very cultured, very energetic. 'Taken away' three times and given and served sentences for 'Intent to commit High Treason'. Now permanent secretary, in fact after the re-organisation that has just taken place in many respects more powerful than Menke-Glückert, as many decisions go via Fischer, (Deputy President, KPD) and by-pass M.-Gl. (who, however, still has higher education in Saxony in his hands). Squeezed into the back of the car: Klemperer, Grundig, Laux.[23] Gr. as late addition wedged in the middle. My fate familiar. Grundig: 45, silver hair. KPD veteran, prison, concentration camp. His wife, Lea Langner-Grundig, likewise painter, Jewish. Allowed to emigrate, after already in prison, if they divorce. Do so, she to Tel-a-Vif.[24] He reads in a German news sheet, which appeared in London in July, that Lea Grundig had a successful show. He is waiting for her, and the marriage will be valid again – divorced under pressure! – but she does not yet know that he is alive. He was in a concentration camp. At the end of 44 a battalion is formed from camp inmates, given a few weeks of military training and commanded by demoted army officers. It is to be deployed against partisans [...] but is suddenly rushed to the Eastern Front near Budapest and immediately deserts to the enemy with all its weapons. ('A couple of officers decamped.') Grundig is taken to Moscow, to a clubhouse – freedom, the best food, best impressions, is allowed to paint. Now designated rector of the Academy. [...] Laux's fate is the simplest. About 50. Music journalist in Darmstadt, is conspicuous as anti-Nazi because far too modern, Hindemith follower,[25] comes to Dresden, employed by the Dresden Neueste Nachrichten, gets by all those years at the paper without becoming a pg. On 13 Feb. he and his wife were so badly burned, that both were in hospital until June. Now responsible for music and theatre under Gute, similar position to Kretzschmar.

Together for a long time, and at such close quarters, I made friends with these people; the Communist Du – with which I inadvertently addressed Laux, because he is not *yet* in the Party, because he fears the accusation of opportunism – played its part. Gute and Grundig had friendly relations with Gusti Wieghardt,[26] hostile ones with the Gestapo (Clemens, Weser, Köhler etc.). What an interlocking of biographies, how strangely Gusti is now rehabilitated! Her Communist, somewhat primitive, children's play, passed on to Moscow by Gute, is supposed to have been a gigantic success there and *in many languages* ... Will Gusti rejoice and be happy, or will she scorn me, when she hears of my present position? I said immediately, that we had many political differences in those days, I had only become a convert much later. [...] Grundig talked about Villon drawings he had made. I suggested an illustrated parallel edition, to which I would write the introduction. I am to give individual lectures at his Academy ... [...] Laux very important for E. How curious that now – an entirely new phase in our lives – we have contact with art and music ... [...]

On Mon. 4 Feb., Mühlberg, the driver, was already here shortly after 5.30, I was just shaving. Hurriedly finished, criss-cross journey through the dark city with its rubble and disfigurement. Gute lives in Laubegast, Laux near Karcher Allee, Grundig in Neugruna. I did not know where we were, everything was eerie. [...] We halted at the district headquarters on Albertplatz as it was dawning. Of the people who joined us there, I knew Sigrid Schwarz and Glöckner. Glöckner is the absolute proletarian, who repelled me down in Plauen months ago, and who is now in the Agitprop(!) Section at District Headquarters. He will certainly not understand anything of the intellectual questions ... There was a column of 4 cars, so presumably 16 participants altogether, not counting the drivers, among them a couple from outside Dresden. [...] We went on the autobahn. 'With four cars one can risk it, otherwise not, too many robberies and shootings take place.' The motorway itself unlovely and in tolerably good condition. Now only occasional destroyed vehicles, civilian and military, at the side. Just as we saw it in Bavaria. The landscape very bare, we did not touch on any town. I do not know what route we took. A couple of times a car behind us had a damaged wheel, then we had to go back to help out. On such occasions unembarrassed 'stop for a pee'. Only close to Berlin a bit of variety and settlements. [...] I did not notice any very great destruction [in Berlin] on this first day. Certainly: destruction. More like the picture presented by Munich. But hardly comparable to Dresden. I still maintained that on Wednesday, after we had seen much of the city centre. Gute and Grundig contradicted: it is worse than Dresden. Matter of taste: Berlin lives, Dresden is dead. – In the KPD building in Pankow each of us got a billeting slip and a big food packet (two big portions of bread, some butter, sausage, cheese and *20* cigarettes, which I brought back for E.), in addition two lunch coupons. Then we immediately drove to the conference location: the assembly hall of the List School in Niederschönhausen [in NE Berlin]. A very large hall, at least 300 people sitting on chairs and benches. In front of them, on a stage, at two long – red covered! – tables, sat the praesidium, in the middle the bulky figure of Wilhelm Pieck. It was about 11.30, the talking was in full swing – it was already the second day, the conference had begun the day before with the inevitable *Nathan the Wise* and a speech by Pieck, but this was the actual working day. I had lost the others and sat down at the very rear of the hall. Then Pieck said: 'we welcome our guests from Mecklenburg, Thuringia and Saxony who have just arrived. We would ask to take their seat up here with us in the praesidium for Thuringia Herr ... for Mecklenburg ... for Saxony' – as a government man Gute was presumably up there already: 'Comrade Klemperer, Professor of Romance Cultures (sic), Dr Laux ...' I said to my neighbour: 'What are those called out supposed to do? Because I'm one of them.' – 'You have to go up there.' So I went. Pieck met me on the steps. No bigger than I – but built like a house, not fat, but altogether solid, Hindenburg-like. My hand disappeared into his paw. The following day I exchanged another few words with him. A massive, impressive head, grey hair brushed straight back. He looks 60 at most, not at all 70. I now sat until about 5 o'clock in my place of honour in the second row, with a heavy cold, my head splitting, much pain and misery. 3 speeches [...] went past me fairly dully: words and content basically the same as what one has already heard too often. The KPD wants to be tolerant, and it wants to be the party of the intelligentsia, [...] and it is national and anti-separatist. New to me, and here I intervened the next day, was that they want to treat the university professors mildly and 'the old intelligentsia' with consideration. Interesting for me was what happened by the way and in between. But that only really developed the next day. On Monday when the programme of speeches had been exhausted, those from outside Berlin got their dinner in a little room behind the stage. Semi-military and quite good: a full bowl of plain and star-shaped noodles with little scraps of meat among them. We, Laux and I, then went by tram to our not very distant quarters. [...]

[... On Tuesday] a neighbour [of the Neuberts, with whom Klemperer was accommodated] found out for me, that Anny Klemperer[27] was still living in the same place. But I did not find the time to look her up. – Tuesday 5 Feb. was the day for 'discussion'. One caught the chairman's eye and had the floor for 15 minutes. People talked back and forth about this and that. Many had composed entire speeches, cliched, with the usual phrases, were unable to finish in time. [...] I seldom followed a whole speech. [...] Well after 3 p.m. after perhaps 20 speakers there was the closing speech, I think given by Ackermann:[28] enlistment of the intelligentsia, unity of the workers' parties, one German nation(!), no separatism. – I was among the first speakers on Tuesday. I [spoke] about university professors, university self-administration and People's High School [...]. Applause. Later I was criticised by a speaker, I wanted 'a red university', on the contrary the 'old intelligentsia' had to be treated considerately, the question had to be addressed 'not morally but politically'. – Some time later this speaker came up to me, and there was a short conversation and very friendly contact. He was Herr Wandel,[29] a still young man, President of the Central Administration of the Sciences in the Soviet Zone. I had already got to know his head of personnel, a Professor Rompel[30] (or something like it) earlier. And with that I have come to the most important part, for me, of these days in Berlin. I have come into contact with several important people, and a great number of things have been initiated, of which perhaps a fraction will materialise. Above all I emphasised again and again, that I would like to have a university chair.

Results: Wandel and the personnel man (Rompe) want to have me in Halle. (With home in Dresden and a car.)

[...]

A Berlin publisher [...] wants to bring out compendia of the kind world of nature and world of the intellect for a general public, high schools and People's High Schools 'by the top people in every field'. Would I ... on France ... I: 'if you make it possible for me and my wife, as my secretary, to stay in *Geneva* for 8 weeks. The teacher responsible: that could be done, I would be hearing from them.

Willmann, general secretary of the KB fetched over the editor of Aufbau, who seems to be subordinate to him. I am to publish my speech with Aufbau, I also suggested: comparison Plievier's *Stalingrad* – Barbusse's *Under Fire*. Agreed, I immediately received a review copy of *Stalingrad*.

I add the plans floating between Grundig and myself: lecture at the academy and Villon edition.

What will become of all of that. Halle? But if they say there I'm a 'journalist'? Geneva?? I fear for my heart, I am sceptical of everything. But for the moment it is encouraging nevertheless.

On Tue. 6 Feb. the conference finished at about 4 p.m. Once again those of us from outside Berlin were fed, this time with a very thin soup. [...]

Picked up early next morning by Gute's car. For a discussion with Willmann

(KB). I owe my view of Berlin to this discussion (and a subsequent business trip by Gute). Saw much or little? Both. We covered a lot of ground, but the car roof was inconvenient, I got only fleeting and partial images. Nevertheless, I did get a picture. [. . .] For sure, the 'Lindens' and Wilhelmstr. and the big squares look very bad, certainly whole street fronts are partly burnt-out, partly collapsed – but on the whole, it's as I said: more Munich than Dresden, not total destruction. Dresden is more cleared up and so brighter – like a well-kept cemetery; in Berlin much rubble in streets which are lived in and where there is traffic, a sombre life, but life nevertheless. [. . .] The office of the KB, also Aufbau publishing house and probably some other things besides, Charlottenburg, Schlüterstr., well-preserved building. Willmann is going to send us [in Saxony] a Sudeten German chief secretary, who is to take care of all the administration, clear up the chaos and get things moving. [. . .]

We then drove to a workshop at Halensee station; a tyre was vulcanised. (British sector) Then for lunch to the KPD Central Committee building in Wallstr. Big offices and a restaurant [. . .]. After that Gute still had business in Wilhelmstr. We had to wait and got out for a moment. The destroyed building, outside which we stopped, was the Adlon Hotel,[31] a big sign announced '5 o'clock Tea'. The building was a completely burned-out ruin. Through a court-yard and past another ruined building a surviving block visible. (Main entrance presumably from Unter den Linden. Grundig said, a few rooms, half-damaged, were still going; a crowd of waiters and some cutlery provided an eery reminiscence of the Adlon's great days.) Opposite the Adlon, on Wilhelmstr., a much boarded-up building: the Central Administration for the Sciences. [. . .] The very strongest impression of destruction was actually made on me by the deforested waste [of the Tiergarten Park] in front of the Brandenburg Gate, where remains of statues stand amidst tree trunks and single trees, and a rostrum is a reminder of the Allies' victory parade. [. . .]

We did not drive out of Berlin until about 4 p.m. As a single car we did not risk going on the autobahn. The driver hoped to pass the forests around Elsterwerda before dark. (Sicily a 100 years ago!) But [. . .] a tyre burst. The spare tyre was weak too. Lack of material. In Jüterbog to another vulcanising shop. [. . .] Apart from that the journey disappeared in chatting, darkness and tiredness. In the end we probably deviated from the route I knew. [. . .] I saw nothing. In Dresden to all the same places again, this time to set the travellers down. Finally I was alone in the car with the driver. Here at about 9 p.m.

10th February, Sunday afternoon
[. . .]

On 9 Feb. to Katz because of mange. His very young assistant, Dr Vetter, prescribed me a salve, immediately had it made up in the pharmacy opposite – great favour, there was alcohol in it! He told me that Katz is dangerously ill with heart trouble and probably (at 67) close to the end. It upsets me.
[. . .]

In the evening, meeting of KPD + SPD in Dölzschen inn. A Social Democrat

I already knew, and a great doctrinaire, gave a historical overview, passionately advocated the unity of both parties and the national unity of Germany. Bitterness against Bavaria and the West. This is now the general mood. I myself tend ever more to Germany (East Germany) as a federal state of Soviet Russia. What is the point of the link with Bavaria, which inwardly never existed?! *That* is how much I have changed!

12th February, Tuesday forenoon

12 Feb. 1912, father died 34 years ago,[32] with what right am I still living?

On Sunday evening after x distractions and repeatedly falling asleep, when E. was already in bed, I woke up and wrote the article for Aufbau [...].

I did not go to bed until 2.30.

Yesterday only business. In the morning went to see the new district mayor, Dobberke, about the endless Vogel affair. A reasonable and moderate KPD man, we got on very well. – Bank and after that correspondence. [...] This afternoon was then taken up with a more than 3 hour session of the advisory council of the PHS [...] In fact nothing new came up. [...]

Grumpy letter from Heidebroek, why wasn't I attending the regular 'staff meetings' Tue. 11 a.m. (I knew nothing about it.) [...] At the same time request to give notice of lectures: I have given notice of 5 classes. 1 hr. on Petrarch, 4 hrs. 18ième, 2 of them seminars – although it is still unclear what texts can be dug up.

It becomes ever more questionable, how I am going to find time for all of that. I could, if I had a car; but I cannot manage it with the terrible trams. I am fatalistic, my hopes are on Halle.

[...]

2 p.m.

Session in the Student House. More a large room than a small hall. Horseshoe table, settee. Perhaps 40 people present. Heidebroek reported. *I* always have an impression of hostility, particularly on the part of my former colleagues. Only Spamer is cordial, Gehrig ignores me, Janentzky is very cool. – Very interesting: the Russians have conceded the opening of an education faculty; after pleas they also permitted forestry and structural engineering – but not mechanical and electrical engineering. I.e. they fear a revival of armaments manufacture. [...] Gehrig asked: will the Pedagogical Institute be affiliated to us or *inc*orporated? *I* said, misjudgement of the situation: *We* were being affiliated, the education section is central and dominant. The rector: It was not *quite* like that, but there was something to it. He had introduced me to the meeting as a returnee, who was now working 'especially intensively' for the PHS. – I invited the gentlemen (not 'colleagues') [...] to collaborate with the PHS. The rector responded, that all the PHS plans had already 'flown past' them, they would like more details in writing. [...]

21st February, Thursday evening

I just now put a sample [of *LTI*] in an envelope for Knorr & Hirth [...].

Now I shall probably need a whole day for the diary. A week in the clutches of politics.

22nd February, Friday evening

On Saturday 16 February I was overtaken by the new political wave. I called on Gute, so as to show my face again and to find out more about the TH. G. was alone and he immediately revealed: Menke-Glückert was ripe for a fall, after he had been already more or less checkmated by Fischer, the deputy president, KPD man and, it is said, the real wielder of power [...] After that, on Tue., Wildführ, turned up here. Car waiting, terrifically excited, already perorating in the hall, waking E. (2 p.m.), taking caffeine and handing it out (it had no effect on us!), master of the higher education world. [...] He would fetch me in his car the next day, Wednesday, at 1.30, for the decisive meeting. [...] The Wednesday disgusted me. Wildführ picked me up. First of all an ante-room. Some Party secretary, Locherer, south German, about 40, expressionless. A young woman with a pince-nez. Lotte Gühne, evidently just promoted from minor functionary to senior civil servant or departmental secretary [...]. More people came, we went into the adjacent main room. We now sat, 10 of us, at a round table, a Party and conspirators' conference. Fischer was not present. Locherer chaired with the authority of a sergeant-major, but held the debate together not unskilfully. It was astonishing with what ease he required and got obedience. From Gute as well. A tapping of the pencil was sufficient to end a dialogue or a digression. He had set himself the goal of discussing the TH, of drawing up a new curriculum, and he managed it, too. [...] So first of all the 'Education Faculty'. Everyone the TH had wanted to save from the shut-down departments had been installed here. But naturally the technical and scientific departments there require a much smaller staff than the proper departments of the TH. First, I spoke at length. Naturally I was only interested in the humanities section. [...] The following list of the building, forestry and wood departments was dealt with more quickly [...]. Here there was a practical problem: to what extent could, to what extent did engineers have to be appointed (telegraphy, railways, agricultural machinery etc.), without the Russians believing that their ban on the engineering departments was being circumvented. [...] The selection was made on political grounds, many professors will lose their jobs. There are to be new political appointments to the posts of rector and of dean of education. For my part I declined the rectorship. There should be a new broom, without encumbrances of tradition ... All of it was discussed conspiratorially, yet with great certainty. [...] I came home feeling very detached and disgusted. [...] Very small and very ignorant people are sitting on shaky little chairs, have big titles and don't know whether they will still have chair and title tomorrow. To whom have I committed myself? What will become of me? If I stumble over the politics, I can lose my professorship. [...]

[...]

My disgust at the pitifulness of these people had already begun a couple of days before with Gladewitz.[33] Newly fledged [government] department head, in charge of the information section, to which the PHS has now been attached. Grützner had urged me to plead with Gladewitz to allow us to open on 3 March. Gladewitz wanted to go to the SMA [Soviet Military Administration] immediately. He didn't get anywhere: the Russians want the People's High Schools to begin on 1 April throughout the Soviet territory. So Gladewitz received me with extraordinary friendliness; he then had me taken home in his very elegant 'big guzzler' Horch car. (This is my latest way of living: I beg car rides from the city and state administrations and at the same time constantly press for my own ... I seem everywhere to be regarded as a coming man, but at the moment I am nothing.) [...]

Melanchthonstr. with its Wednesday and Friday consulting hours takes up quite as much time as the State Administration. X people want posts or information, which I cannot provide. One wants to teach stenography courses, another graphology. I reject both. An engineer wants to teach structural engineering. The Russians forbid it. People want to give language teaching without having sufficient qualifications. I am oversubscribed for speech training. [...] Constant bickering between Hoppe and Grützner – I have to meditate. Grützner is in charge of the office and a KPD official, well aware of his power, and friend of Gute. Hoppe [...] 'intellectual' in quotation marks, wallowing in fine words like 'co-ordinating' [...] does not want to be any old 'office worker', and Grützner needs office workers (plural). [...] Spamer called on me at the PHS. He wants to contribute. [...]

Private experience of the past week: again and again I fall asleep at my desk from exhaustion; I got the parcel for Munich ready [*LTI* sample], I read a couple of pages of Plievier.

[...]

I don't care for our neighbour Schmidt. He was a pg from 1933, has lost his post as tax inspector since the 15 Feb., will only be re-appointed with a much reduced salary and thus be unable to support his son Günther, who has just begun studying medicine at Jena. He experiences that as a great injustice, feels himself to be a martyr and repeatedly begs me to help him. He has given me a diary he kept in Russia, which demonstrates his anti-Fascist attitude. I have not got around to reading it. I could not quite conceal the fact from him, that *I* and millions of others suffered far worse things.

23rd February, Saturday afternoon

I spent the greater part of the working day on the above entry which I began yesterday. Then [...] I revised the Culture–Civilisation lecture, which I sketched out on 18 Jan., at the time for Waldenburg, and which was given neither there nor in various other places, because each time there was no car. Now a car is supposed – supposed! – to be here at 7, to [take] me to the 'Recruitment party of the Gross-Weinböhla group of the KB', [which] takes place at 8. This time the invitation came the day before yesterday from the Plauen KPD group.

Yesterday morning I agreed on condition of a car. A tram does go there, but it would take hours and I would be unable to get one back in the evening. Janny, the youthful political officer down in Plauen, agreed without further ado and will fetch me himself at 7. Vedremo.[34] [...]

Nasty cold snowstorm weather. The wireless warns of ruins collapsing in the wind.

26th February, Tuesday morning

The lecture almost came to nothing once again. The propaganda man in Weinböhla unhappy – all efforts in vain, only two dozen people in the large hall, which holds hundreds. [...] I placed my chair in front of the few people (without climbing up on stage) and spoke for about $\frac{3}{4}$ of an hour. – A very large restaurant, before the event I got a supper [...]. Janny and his young wife came with me in the car. Janny not so 'youthful', man of 47, businessman with some education, passionate left-wing politician. [...] Janny said, that *language* stands between the workers and the educated. 'The workers say shit and arse at every turn.' I: 'and if we do the same, it sounds false and affected and only increases the distrust.'

[...]

28th February, Thursday afternoon

For 2, 3 days my heart has been in a worse state than ever before. Very severe pains while walking, I have to halt every couple of steps. Slow easing off only when I come into the warmth; yesterday after dinner severe pains at home also.

[...]

On the morning of Tue. 26 [...] a telegram arrived from the Central Administration for Popular Education, Berlin: 'Please immediately contact Rector Jena and Lindemann State Office Popular Education Weimar with regard to chair at Jena University. Professor Rompe.' (I got to know Rompe in Berlin.) Then towards evening another corresponding Weimar telegram reached me by way of the People's High School. I always think of the officer whom Napoleon promoted on the battlefield of Waterloo. The officer says: Il est tard.[35] – I made my way to the State Administration. Gute, still ailing, was there, Wildführ attached himself to me, the three of us wanted to go to Fischer. But in the end only Wildführ and myself had the audience. Fischer, grey en brosse hair, large grey eyes, determined appearance. He is said to be anti-Semitic and vain. To me he was enchantingly pleasant. 'You have no idea, how often your candidature is mentioned; one would have to cut a man like you into six parts, you are so much in demand. Wait a couple of weeks – do you have enough to live on? – *I* take the decisions, only a little bit longer, than Menke-Glückert will be gone. You will carry out the reforms for us here, and will then be dean of the education faculty in Leipzig, you will get the professorship there, and we will propose Herr Jan for Jena ...' – 'Will it happen just like that, Herr President?' Laughter: 'But I alone take the decisions. I shall have a telegram sent to Berlin: "Kl. in Saxony committed to Leipzig and Dresden. Propose Eduard von Jan for Jena ..." There is no need for you to do anything more with regard to this matter.' I thanked him warmly. He, beaming courteously as he gripped my hand: 'It is we who should be thanking you.' I was given a whole packet of cigarettes as a present. [...] To *il est tard* was added a second permanent keynote: *Maître Corbeau* ... I have let the Jena crumb fall; will I receive the more important Leipzig?[36] Fischer vouches for it – but who vouches for Fischer? But 1) I had to risk playing the game, and 2) vanitas vanitatum, when death is so close at my heels. [...]

2nd March, Saturday forenoon

[...]

A young, likeable, good-looking man came to me, greying hair, one-armed, very humble, although his bearing was good: Gerhard Christmann, formerly Nazi mayor, now without employment, is to lose his apartment (wife and small child). I attested, that in 1942 he had accepted my refusal to sell the house and *not* turned me over to the Gestapo.

[...]

To be added is the reception by the new Lord Mayor, Leissner,[37] on Wed., 27th Feb. Leissner, SPD, lawyer, coming from Breslau, recently installed, very emaciatedly thin, fair-haired, mid-50s, very courteous, cautious but relaxed and likeable. *We*: Dölitzsch, Hoppe, Kiessig and Nestler as 'advisory committee' [PHS] and 'supporters'; purpose: introduction for our part, sizing up on the part of the new lord mayor, who wants to familiarise himself. Individual higher education questions: [...]. Everything jelly-like, undecided. Crucial point of the whole very long palaver (cigarettes, fauteuil and sofa): The KPD has appointed a still young man, Egon Rentzsch,[38] whom I do not know, as salaried councillor and head of the Culture *and* Schools Department and thus superior to the unsalaried town councillor and director of the Schools Department, Dölitzsch; he is in the SPD, should actually be in charge of schools, is a veteran teacher and party member and in very poor health having been in a concentration camp. Dölitzsch sees in this development an encroachment on his position and wants to go. The lord mayor, himself SPD, sympathises with D., but is faced with established facts and is first of all feeling his way. Dölitzsch says: the Communists are completely violating parity, they want to get a firm grip of as many posts as possible, before [party] unification has been accomplished. I cannot contradict, am in the KPD, preach my scholarly viewpoint, my [liberal] origins, my desire for the united party. Leissner smiles benevolently at me; I was an idealist, scholar, did not yet know the conditions in a 'mass party'. I: I was not quite so childish, but I should be granted my real or apparent naivety, perhaps I could carry my line; if not I would go ... Nothing positive came of the long conversation – but I did nevertheless see the shakiness and difficulty of all these political lives [...]. Why should not Fischer sacrifice me tomorrow morning for a different combination? [...] After that I was brought home in D.'s car and introduced D. to E. At the moment I am the more important man and am more firmly in the saddle than Dölitzsch. But for how long? ... [...]

Afternoon

All of the foregoing will be of no account if, entirely without ceremony, death grips my heart. And this morning he did so again plainly and remorselessly.

As I was not down in town yesterday Hoppe sent post by a messenger. Inter alia: tomorrow morning at 11 [...] I am to speak in Gute's place on the setting up of the local, Dresden, group of the KB [...]. I went to the post office, to send a telegram: the Russians have more less uncabled Dölzschen. I went down to the KPD office in Plauen, to Janny. [...] I called the PHS in vain, no one in the office. Then district headquarters. There I got hold of Grüttner. Result: *if* tomorrow he is up here by 10.30 with a car, then I shall speak, otherwise not. I shall give a slightly altered version of the Weinböhla lecture, *if* I speak.

Today we had an invitation. Eva went alone. If I sit here quietly in the warmth, the pain is very slight; but the memento is always there, and if, as just now, I carry up coal, it makes itself very perceptible. What will become of all my plans and possibilities. Probably nothing any more. What will become of E.? There are no widows' pensions any more. What will become of me? [...] Has generous nature saved me, only to let me die now, to leave LTI and Curriculum and 18ième[39] and Leipzig chair y todo, todo[40] unfulfilled? [...] I want to work to the last. [...]

4th March, Monday forenoon

The car really did come yesterday. I spoke – but, hampered by my miserable condition, very badly – I found it embarrassing. Large hall, half-full, unheated. I spoke, as also recently in Weinböhla, as is altogether common [...] in my coat. A pianist [...] played boringly on a tiny grand piano. Then Menke-Glückert. (Is he so unsuspecting, or only pretending?) First simply information on establishment, fees, a provisional committee, 10 people, including myself [...].

After the lecture yesterday, Dobberke came up to me (cf 12th Feb.). The Vogel business was now being taken care of. Today an ecstatic Vogel sen. was here: he has finally been allocated a new shop. He wanted to give me a packet of tea and a bottle of schnapps. I took the tea, I paid 42M for the schnapps, the regular price, in order to slip it to the Wolffs for 49.

5th March, Tuesday forenoon

'To the Director of the People's High School, Herr Klemberer [*sic*], Dresden. The Central Administration for Popular Education in Berlin informs us, that you are interested in finding employment at the University of Jena or in the sphere of Popular Education in general. Could you please send us a curriculum vitae, the form enclosed here and a list of any publications. On behalf of etc.: Lindemann.'

This letter arrived yesterday and the telegram from this Lindemann to Herr Klemberer, PHS, Dresden was already an indication of what was to follow. Evidently a civil servant like Gühne here or Scholz, the petrol-pump attendant mayor. The Berlin telegram was undoubtedly a call to a chair and Fischer understood, appraised and replied to it as such. Nevertheless: I feel very deflated and inwardly something of a fool. On E.'s advice I replied: After consultation with the Government of Saxony, I have decided to decline the honourable call to the University of Jena conveyed to me by the Central Administration, Berlin, and the State Administration has already wired that to Berlin. In accordance with the request from Berlin I am informing you of this fact. With the greatest respect Dr V. Klemperer, Professor at the Technical High School, Dresden, Director of the People's High School, Dresden.

But it is foolish to allow this affair to irritate me so greatly. Because I am completely checked and crippled by my condition. Severe pains again and again. I do not see how I will be able to meet all my obligations, I do not think that much time is left to me. – At all events, today I must get down to the dermatologist in Westendstr., because my head is becoming ever more leprous.
[...]

6th March, Wednesday morning
[...] Since Sunday, no more lunch at the Wolffs. The Raschs, who are to move in here in April and are just now felling and sawing up a couple of surplus trees in the garden, brought a bagful of potatoes, which he had bought in the country.
[...]
Very awkward my position between coming or perhaps not coming power and present rumour-enveloped lack of power or possible power. That's what I infer from the Hoppe woman's reports, who listens and whispers to everyone, and whose soft-soap I do not trust, but from whom a great deal can nevertheless be learned (although it must be weighed with the greatest caution). [...]. Hoppe is not well-disposed to the KPD, no one in my orbit and in my stratum is sympathetic to the KPD. I am constantly aware that I am walking a tightrope.

Slow and disappointed reading of *Under Fire*. Sooo faded, so empty! And the frightful translation [...].

9th March, Saturday evening
In the morning I wanted to go into town: Summoned to the CID in Bernhardstr. about the Kluge–Wolff business. The pains became so dreadful that I dragged myself back from Residenzstr. with great difficulty. Then at midday Frau Dr Frenzel, who lives nearby, came; likeable person, looks more like a housewife – and has 3 children – than a modern doctor. Her judgement after examining me: my heart was not in an especially bad state, only there was some muscle weakness; it was probably a mixture of neuritis and a strained heart. She prescribed a heart drug and 8 days at home. (That will then make a second holiday week). In the afternoon, despite warmth and sitting still, I had a renewed bout of pain and this time with a quite distinct heart spasm. I do believe, that my angina has entered the final stage. It is very sad. Now that I am becoming a success, now that there is no pension or other security for E. The whole burden of my illness rests on her. Today she was constantly on the go: to the Police, in the pharmacy (so far without success), hunting for food (in vain; we do without

lunch, have the thinnest soup for supper and use up our bread reserve too quickly).

This morning E. came back with the CID man to whom she had made my excuses: Comrade Wiczorek – 'I am a skilled moulder and now I'm supposed to be a detective!' – very honest man, concentration-camp friend of Seidemann. Kluge, fighting for his apartment, is suing Wolff for slander, for calling him a Gestapo agent. [...] At issue is a document, which Frau Wolff gave to me, and I gave to Seidemann, who has mislaid it. This document does *not* show that Kluge was in the service of the Gestapo, but that he certainly had something to do with a Gestapo matter (confiscated Jewish property). I argued from the beginning, as I still do today: in the 3rd Reich the man became provincial court judge with uncommon rapidity. He claims he was *only* a magistrate, when he was a provincial judge. And it is clear from this document, that he knew about nasty things. Ergo he deserves to lose his apartment and his furniture. This was the substance of the statement I recorded here today. I wrote, inter alia: 'I do not know Kluge, but I make no secret of the fact that, as a victim of Fascism, I have a very great aversion to active National Socialists, among whom I most certainly include judges.'

[...]

10th March, Sunday evening
[...]

E. was away for many hours, searching for food. At our Maria Kube's she got lunch, and tomorrow Maria is going to bring us a pailful of potatoes. Meanwhile Seidemann sent his little daughter to us with some bread and cereal flakes [...]. Thus far today my food has consisted of dry bread with my coffee [...].

Also I ran around the whole day with my head covered in ointment and bandaged and my face thickly smeared with sulphur, of course tormented by itching. But I would make light of this misfortune and the lack of food, were it not for my failing heart.

[...]

12th March, Tuesday evening
At home all day. As soon as I leave the warm room, I get bouts of pain. Heart or rheumatism? And when will I be fit for action again?

Worked on Barbusse–Plievier. In part warming over old things, in part more. [...]

Weidhaas writes (very politely), could I speak for 300M in the Plauen theatre[41] on 31 March at the Culture and Recruitment Week, the PHS had not yet been given permission to open. But he says nothing about a car.

15th March, Friday evening

In the night from Tue. to Wed. I had the first really serious attack of angina, not just very bad pain, but such terrible difficulty in breathing and shortage of breath and anxiety for such a long time, that I woke E. The next day I was completely washed out. In the evening Dr Frenzel came. Recently she had still found my heart passable; now she found it weak and very fast and was certain that all my complaints were the result of angina. She prescribed me all kinds of things (of which most were not to be had today); she wanted to put me to bed for 4 days. She said I was allowed to do intellectual work and give lectures. But not take a single step. I could only leave the house, if a well-sprung car took me from door to door. She thought that, if I rested, my health could be restored 'in six months'. – [...]

My existence now literally depends on this ... Without a car I can go neither to the TH, nor to the PHS, nor to the State Administration. I shall lose *everything*, if I have to own up to being a cardiac invalid. For the time being I still have 'neuritis'.

[Then] Hoppe appeared. She brought a request to speak next Thursday at the KPD training course for intellectuals. – Yes, *if* I get a car. [...] Apart from various bits of paperwork, she had brought a very courteous letter from the *Volksstimme* [Voice of the people]. Could I contribute my talk from the Kulturbund celebration on 3 March for 'Unity'. – Gladly – but it was not formulated as a printed article. Hoppe had her cutlery and lunch with her. The three of us ate together, I dictated; we drank coffee, I dictated. When she left with the finished article it was half past seven. I impressed on her once again: *without a car* I was helpless. We avoided talking to her and others about my heart problem. [...]

I forgot: yesterday evening a young man from the Middle German Broadcasting Station, Hahnewald, came to see me. Could I please give a 10 minute talk at the end of next week on anything to do with PHS, culture and the like. A car was promised in this case. But the ms had to be provided in advance. The Russian censors (2 officers) were very strict and did not, inter alia, like the word 'fatherland'. [...] I am sure I can cobble something together. I want to do that tomorrow, before I complete the Plievier.

[...]

17th March, Sunday evening

[...]

Gute came to see me yesterday afternoon. Two urgent matters, cars were promised for both: today I was to speak to the Meissen KB (for this he left behind a canister of petrol) and next Sunday in Jena. I accepted both, the culture lecture was designated for Meissen, a shortened version of which is to appear in 'Unity', and for Jena: Barbusse/Plievier, which will have its première on Thursday in Melanchthonstr.

Meissen dealt with very agreeably today, back after 4 p.m., then too tired for further work. [...] It will all have to be noted at greater length. [...]

[...]

[22nd March], Catching up, addendum for the last week (notes)

[Talk in Meissen, Sunday, 16 March] I had spoken in the cinema. There I met again – 'Don't we know one other?' – 'Of course, from the times we were shaved in Zeughausstr!' – Kociollek,[42] the singer and charge hand of the Jewish workers for the feared Schwarz. He ended up in Auschwitz, was saved, is now theatre director in Meissen. [. . .]

Christmann, the one-armed, now grey-haired former mayor, sought my protection once again, to avoid his apartment being taken away from him. But Janny had told me, Ch. had wanted to turn in 20 KPD members, a list had been found in his home. And E. had by chance heard someone complaining about Nazi doings in Dölzschen: 'And Comrade Prof. Klemperer is sticking up for the Nazi swine Christmann!' So I held back, even though Ch. swears, with every appearance of telling the truth, that he never drew up such a list. [. . .] But I cannot expose and incriminate myself any further; the man has a friendly attestation from me, I cannot do anything more. [. . .]

Meanwhile our Wolffs, who since 1 or 2 of March can no longer cook for us, are furious, because Kluge, the Nazi district judge, has been allowed to move back into his apartment and furniture – for the time being this large family is stuck in *one* room and the shared kitchen. There is no clear line at all in dealing with the Nazi cases. Now blowing cold, now hot – all in all an ever greater strengthening of reaction.

25th March, Dresden

[. . .]

On the forenoon of Thurs. 21 March, young Hahnewald picked me up for the wireless recording. Villa in Tiergartenstr. Building and equipping going on, a large studio is just being completed, there's already a grand piano. A room with all kinds of lead wires, a microphone in front of the reader, who is given a silent signal to begin and to stop. Once a worker came in, the tape had run out, a new one had to be put on. (I still understand nothing of the technical side; Hahnewald told me: You are recorded on a tape, in which cuts can be made, and that is submitted to the censors. [. . .]) I read from a copy of my manuscript [. . .] which had not yet been submitted to the Russians. They were very strict and suspicious, unpredictable and incomprehensible. Particularly since Churchill's anti-Russian speech in the USA.[43] [. . .]

[. . .]

Then finally I took a few hours to complete my crib for the Barbusse–Plievier lecture, which was due at 6 p.m. at Melanchthonstr. as part of the KPD training course for intellectuals. [. . .] I addressed about 150–200 people in the hall which holds 400, really spoke very well and got considerable applause. The subsequent 'discussion' was amusing. The chairman, an all too gently enthusiastic teacher, said one did not pick such a 'flower' to pieces, he advised against any discussion. At that a forceful man spoke up: he insisted on the right to make criticisms, that's why we had democracy! That was all he wanted to say – and sat down again. [. . .] Frau Hoppe introduced a very slim, blonde young woman to me:

Frau Knabe-Schulze, a painter, widow of the executed Fritz Schulze [...]: she wants to paint me. (I was wearing a bandage around my ointment covered head!) [...]

25th March, evening, 11 p.m.
A messenger came from the State Administration: tomorrow I am to take part in negotiations in Berlin about the education faculty. [...]

26th March, Berlin trip
The car for the Berlin trip was here at 5.30 a.m. on 26 March. A Mercedes 6 cylinder, which covered long stretches on the autobahn at more than 60 m.p.h. ... The Hentschke couple. Not particularly likeable. He 42, in charge of the teacher courses in Wachwitz, immatriculation supervisor in Leipzig, assistant to Schneller. Most radical representative of the teachers' point of view. Repeatedly emphasised goal: to smash the grammar schools, break the arrogance of the grammar-school teachers, create the comprehensive teacher for the com- prehensive school. The educational standard will naturally suffer as a result: this was the lesser evil *for the moment*.

Discussed, futilely, in Berlin-Karlshorst[44] were only schools (on which there was agreement) and the course of study for teachers (on which there was no agreement). [...] the Russians appear to firmly differentiate: elementary-school teachers to training colleges, secondary-school teachers to the universities. The Russians simply have no political misgivings any more and are concerned *solely* with the scholarly goal. Here [in the Soviet Zone], therefore, they to some extent go along with those on the Right, with the 'reactionaries'.

The return journey, finally in complete darkness, went well. I was up here before 9 p.m. and immediately drove to the Grubes, where we had been invited for Tuesday evening. While I was still looking for the entrance, Grube himself appeared in his own car and brought me in. Warm welcome. Except first of all there was a musical evening. Frieser, my colleague from the TH, played cello, an elderly woman musician and friend of the family played piano, one of the two young daughters of the house played violin. Grube is probably in his mid to late 40s, his wife (dark speckled hair, otherwise very youthful) a few years younger. It turned out: in 1919 he was a student in Munich (born there) and went through the whole business on the revolutionary side. [...] He is on the point of defecting from the SPD to the KPD. He is a city councillor and in charge of hygienics, which has always been his specialism. [...]

29th March, midday Friday
[...]
Tomorrow after a month's gap, we are to eat at the Wolffs again.
On Monday the Raschs move in here.
And now the question is, whether I get the promised car for Plauen tomorrow.

2nd April, Tuesday afternoon

The bitter and depressing experience of recent days was the foundering of the Plauen lecture. The State Administration had twice promised me with the greatest certainty a car for 2 p.m. on Saturday; in Plauen Weidhaas, the mayor, had arranged a hotel room for me, I was invited for Saturday evening and Sunday midday, I was to speak in the theatre, which has 900 seats, I had been promised a fee of 300M, the prospect of foodstuffs had also been held out to me; the Scherners were also expected to come to Plauen ... On Saturday at 2 there was no car here. At 3p.m. I called the State Admin.: no one there any more. I was put through to the motor pool: abruptly altered instructions, no car free, etc. etc. I shouted, it did no good.

[...]

I then wrote a courteous and exasperated letter to Weidhaas.

What hurts me more than the business itself: my helplessness, my being left in the lurch, pushed aside. No one cares about me, my imaginary importance caves in. If I cannot pursue my profession, then simply not, then I am dropped and replaced. I no longer believe in my post in the ministry, no longer in my Leipzig professorship; I ask myself how I shall be able to retain my posts here. I *must* go into town again, even if the pains return. I must go on, for as long as I can. How long? And what will then become of E.? Welfare, 26M a month.

Very bitter days.

At the same time industrious. Barbusse–Plievier completely corrected. [...] My wireless speech has *not* been broadcast, and now the Culture Week is over, and so it is not going to be broadcast. That, too, a hurt.

[...]

Since Saturday we have been eating with the Wolffs again. Honest Michel sent a couple of potatoes. But otherwise things look very bad with food. Terribly poor bread, it is said to contain acorns and chestnuts.

Shortages everywhere. Today Fräulein Berndt wrote to me: Irene Papesch is lying in hospital with a serious oedema, could I use my influence with Frau Fenske, the city councillor, so that P. gets to a rest home, 'otherwise she will go out like a light'.

The Raschs have been living with us since yesterday. 4 strong. But Frau R. looks after the household, the children are quiet and well-behaved, I have not yet seen the husband in person. If it stays like this ... if ... if...

Our neighbours, the Jungs, invited us for coffee. They want me to use my influence again to have him rehabilitated, he has been drafted into a lower post. When I saw how his children were starving and mourned each little piece of cake that was forced on us, I felt horrid. I can do nothing about the matter itself; all rehabilitations are blocked for the time being; also everyone wants to be rehabilitated; also in the eyes of the Party I cannot be the advocate of all pg's.

[...]

After an interval of some weeks, I am now in a position to resume work on the *LTI*. But how? The old inhibitions are coming to the fore again. Also, I am anxious because Munich has not yet responded to the sample sent off on 22 Feb.

The green outside is getting ever brighter. A French phrase haunts me, by some Catholic: le leurre éternel [du printemps].[45]

[...]

6th April, Saturday evening

Out of the house yesterday before 9. Still tremblingly painful at every step. It cannot be helped. To the KPD at Albertplatz, to see Schwarz and Grüttner. Cigarettes? No. Trousers on a ration coupon? No. Lunch? Yes, at 1. To the PHS. A series of acceptances and rejections of applications by teachers. Otherwise little correspondence. However, I stayed until after 12. I proofread my article '10 Years of Fascism'. At 1 back to the Party. Disappointment: No lunch. I had a couple of slices of dry bread with me, that had to suffice. [...] In the *Tägliche Rundschau* [newspaper] a very good picture of *Vossler, Rector of Munich University.* He wrote to me in the autumn, he had been on his back for 3 months with a weak heart. [...] And now active again. Today I wrote to him at *great* length and very frankly. About the KPD, about Jan, about my aspirations. Could he help me to give lectures, in Munich, in Switzerland? Could he help me obtain modern French literature ... I seriously declared my commitment to the KPD and to sitting between stools.

At $\frac{1}{4}$ to 4 back to the Mordgrundbrücke with the no. 11 tram. There, at 41 Schillerstr., a villa belonging to the Kulturbund. Kneschke, from Bohemia, old-looking, but a briskly skilful secretary[46] had convened the managing committee of the Dresden group. I was now pronounced 1st chairman, Tobler the 2nd, Balzer the 3rd, Eva Blanke, an economist, becomes secretary. There was talk of working groups, of the April programme. Much talk, nothing of substance. Tobler and Heidebroek have a Science and Research Working Group, Balzer and the sculptor Volwahsen: Art, myself with Eva Blank: Literature ... [...]

7th April, Sunday after midnight

The section 'Blurring boundaries' completed for *LTI*. – After lunch to the Markgraf-Heinrichstr. Hospital where, according to Marta Berndt, Irene Papesch, on whose behalf I wrote to Fenske, was supposed to be. She was *not* there.

Apparently it is possible to send post abroad again; I wrote to Hilde Jonson.
[...]

10th April, Wednesday forenoon

[...]

At the moment despite constant weariness and distraction I am making good progress with the *LTI*; yesterday 'The first three words of the Nazi language' completed. But the proofreading of the typed pages is not going well. And there is still no reply from Knorr & Hirth, whom I sent the first mss at the end of February.

Yesterday morning, I risked going to the TH on foot once again. Still pain and discomfort, but my heart is fitter. (Only neuritis and scabies plague me. That my feet are swollen appears to be normal for the times.) The meeting was cancelled, since the Russians were just taking away epidiascopes; but I showed my face and talked to various people, and so the purpose of the excursion was fulfilled. I got the cash payments for first book purchases by the Romance Languages department going; a new catalogue has to be set up, starting from the very beginning. Everything is gone, not even a list of accessions could be found. [...] I am now ploughing through Kühn's *Sinn des Krieges* [Meaning of the War].[47] The man *must* lose his chair; I told Mey and Spamer so. [...] People undoubtedly respect, probably also fear me. Apart from that, no one knows what will happen. At the moment the education faculty appears to have been dropped – here and elsewhere [...] and the Russians appear to want the old teacher-training college. Heidebroek says, they are now expecting to open the TH on 15 May. But which sections of the TH? And for which students? And with how many professors?? Everything, everything is undecided. [...]

15th April, Monday afternoon

Work in recent days: Reading Kühn [...] article about him for *LTI*. [...] The whole thing: *LTI and the history of scholarship*. A lot of work on that, especially as there were many matters which had to be dealt with away from home.

On Thursday evening the PHS got under way with a shallow lecture by Weidauer [Dresden's mayor] on Nazism and Scholarship – pure propaganda speech – in the hall at Melanchthonstr. I made a few introductory remarks, the celebration is delayed until 28 April, praised Weidauer as the rebuilder of Dresden. The lecture was poorly attended. It has meanwhile turned out, that interest in the PHS is altogether very slight. (Likewise for the Culture Week!) A number of lectures have been cancelled because of lack of students, among them my LTI with three (!) enrolments. What goes down well, is language teaching, English above all, then Russian. Not French. Second, wireless engineering. Third: Goethe. [...] We are expecting the celebration on 28 April to have a very positive effect. The 'Friends and Patrons of the PHS', i.e. the active Kiessig and decent Nestler now want to print my speech. [...] For the second time I had the help of the KPD car to get home. I now have a most zealous new friend down there at Albertplatz: Gertrud Keller, with whom I became acquainted on the trip to the Culture Congress of the KPD in Berlin, and who has now taken charge of the Party's cultural office. [...] I got a loaf, and a cwt. of potatoes is supposed to arrive at 6. [...] Further with respect to food. The shortage of recent days was extreme, especially as lunch with the Wolffs has been terminated again. Nothing but dry bread and the thinnest potato-water soup. – I also got 12 cigarettes from the good Frau Keller. – Then today I also made friends with Loewenkopf, the previously tight-fisted manager of the Victims of Fascism office on Albertplatz. He is head of the Jewish Community here, he praised my Party activities, we have now got to 'Comrade' and 'Du'. That produced more than 30 lbs of potatoes.

After lunch yesterday to the Johannstädter Hospital [...] to Irene Papesch, who looks terrible, and on whose behalf I approached city councillor Fenske. Hunger oedema, blood poisoning. [...]

To my very amused surprise a book has appeared: *For the Renewal of German Culture*. It is the record of the KPD Cultural Congress in February, and my speech is printed there, exactly as I delivered it (in full swing – 'For God's sake!'). Some sentences incomprehensible due to mishearing, the whole thing peculiarly lively.

17th April, Wednesday morning

Spring. Very beautiful. But ... my neck, my eyes, my shoulder, the agony of walking, the memento. – Yesterday the Tuesday meeting at the TH. I counted 24 colleagues. Old, old, old. Tobler, 66, is trying, via Klemperer–Vossler, to obtain a professorship in Munich. Heidebroek says: The separation from the German West is becoming ever more marked. We cannot appoint anyone from there, over there he has a pension etc., here he is taken on at one day's notice. – Main theme: our attitude to the new Berlin title 'Technical University'.[48] Heid. angrily quoted a crude article in the *Tägliche Rundschau* [newspaper]: The significance of the new title is, that now *people* are to be educated, whereas previously, in the Technical High Schools, the seat of military technology, 'criminals' were trained. [...] The most profound reason for the dismantling and remodelling of our TH's is that abroad they are feared for their *'military potential'* ... [...] And the majority, myself included, in favour of the new designation, because one could not play second fiddle to Berlin, because other countries misunderstood 'High School', because England says technical university.

After that there was lamentation and uncertainty about the state of our TH here. Its centrepiece paralysed. And we need engineers, there is already a shortage of new recruits to the profession. We must have industry – our agriculture can feed at most $\frac{2}{3}$ of the population. Apart from that the Russians make us build the forbidden heavy machinery (forbidden to *us*) using pg engineers; 100 pg engineers are working in Berlin, Junkers is building air plane engines 'like crazy!' according to the rector.

[...]

18th April, Thursday morning

PHS office hour yesterday, because tomorrow Good Friday. The twin patrons Kiessig and Nestler: my lecture is to be printed immediately [...] run of 5000 copies. So last night I was up until 1 making one of the two versions ready for press. Doubly sceptical: it is far too long, and in *this* form I cannot give it, and will it be printed in *this* form? [...]

At 11 today there is a meeting with Becher [...] at the State Administration. (Becher will recite in the evening) [...]

I am a kind of Dölzschen patriarch. Yesterday, as I am completing 'The People's High School 1946', Werner, a young enthusiastic KPD official calls: I must help him. – ? – For a couple of weeks he has been teacher at the training establishment for police dogs and police-dog handlers; things are not going well, there have been complaints about the head of the establishment; he, Werner, has the task of observing, [...]: the man in charge is good, but too good-natured; the teachers, however, lack discipline and respect etc., even set the students against the chief trainer. And now he must write a report about this state of affairs, and that he finds difficult. Thus I dictated the report to him, word for word, in accordance with his account. (In the last Russian film I saw, people come to the village scribe: write me a letter!). Because of that, it was 1 a.m. before the lecture ms was finished.

Just now at 7.30 Nestler had it picked up and let me know: Wengler died in hospital yesterday. He already told me yesterday: 'Losing strength, dying.' An unhappy man. My feelings: Relief, because his case was weighing on my mind; also: hurrah, I'm alive!

20th April, Saturday forenoon
[...]

Thursday entirely taken up with Becher, in three parts so to speak.

In the morning the meeting at the State Administration; he arrived late [...]. Then in the evening officially at the Ernemann Plant. Then 12 of the Chosen in the Guest House of the City of Dresden.

Becher, thickset, chubby, round head, grey and bald, grey eyes behind spectacles, by no means like a poet, still less an Expressionist, revolutionary poet, completely the bourgeois, good-natured, concerned paterfamilias, civil servant or businessman of a senior, but not too high rank, not at all a 'captain of industry'. Agreeably simple in his speech, in his conversation, in the simultaneously heartfelt and unsentimental delivery of his poems [...]

I shall sum up what he said, half-chatting at the meeting, just chatting at table. Tremendous strength of reactionary forces, shallowness of the so-called change. No one did it, everyone was an anti-Fascist, had Jewish relatives etc. The Allies scoff. They are suspicious, one cannot blame the French if they want to hold onto the Ruhr: Jünger[49] [...] is publishing again, comme si de rien n'était, now with a democratic tinge, but basically the same, Gottfried Benn[50] writes to me, as if we have always been friends ... But from this [spirit] of reaction Becher does not, for example, draw the conclusion of a certain intransigence – on the contrary! [...] He spoke a great deal in favour of canvassing in private conversation 'with 1, with 2, with 3 persons'; that was the only thing that worked with intellectuals. He strongly supported Menke-Gl.'s constant pleas for a clubhouse. In place of the unjustly mocked literary café. (With reading matter – difficulties of the zonal division, of importing newspapers and books.) Lord Mayor Leissner was present at the State Administration session. [...] He was directly addressed because of the clubhouse. In the evening in the Ernemann Hall, we were informed by Menke-Gl., that on the telephone Leissner had made the villa at 37 Emser Allee available. [...]

[...]

My personal affairs. 1) Agreed with Becher and the Aufbau editor. I shall speak in Berlin in the near future on something French. Hope through that for French books and a stipendium for a stay in Geneva. (I would like to produce a new *'Modern French Prose'* and give it to the Aufbau Publishing House!) 2) Menke-Gl. asked me if I really wanted to become 'director of the Education Institute in Leipzig', as Fischer had told him. I responded: Mistake! I could explain how it had come about. I need to be professor of Romance Literature there, I had assumed the philosophical faculty will be replaced by an educational one – I fit into both. M.Gl. in the old manner: Don't you want to speak to the colleagues there? I, calmly and matter-of-factly: no, that wouldn't lead anywhere, I must have a chair, the somewhat colourless von Jan should be shoved off to Jena or to the free chair of Romance languages. [. . .] M.Gl. was not in the least shocked, seemed relieved, rather, merely admonished me in a friendly way, he knew from his own experience, Leipzig *and* Dresden was too much, I should give one of them up. I: with my own car both could be managed. [. . .]

In the Ernemann Hall – several hundred guests; I sat right at the front in the row of honour – a quartet played a long piece by Hindemith, who is so acclaimed now. I do not understand him, but this time I did not find it quite so dismal as what I had heard before. Then B. read, with his head down and somewhat hunched over in an easy chair in front of a little table, that was far too low. Fatherland – Fatherland – Fatherland: next we shall have a pacifist National Socialism.

Afterwards, at about 9.30 to the Weisser Hirsch in several cars. The Guest House appeared to me to be a villa on a lower terrace somewhere near Luisenhof. Anteroom, cloakroom, dining room, elegantly laid table, waiter service. The food very much in keeping with the times: a soup, carrots, noodles, potatoes, meat sauce, a sweet blancmange. *Nothing* to smoke. But very good red wine and then very good sparkling wine. An altogether uncommon pleasure. [. . .]

At the end, when I wanted to climb the long flight of steps up to the car, my heart failed me painfully. The memento. – Back at midnight.

[. . .]

24th April, Wednesday morning

Worked quietly on *LTI* [. . .] over Easter, but various people here nevertheless. The Dr Neumark household on a long Easter walk [. . .] from Reick. Very friendly. N. very disgusted by politics in general and by the KPD in particular and very much by its behaviour to Menke-Glückert [. . .]. I could naturally only half or quarter contradict. [. . .] I wish I had the chair in Leipzig. [. . .]

Out today immediately after breakfast. [. . .] To Nestler, meeting with the very active Frau N. in the small, crowded backroom, where half a dozen people are working and there's a constant coming and going of people delivering and picking up periodicals etc. etc. Wengler was buried this afternoon at 3; I could not go. I only found out towards 12 and at 4 I had to be at the Kulturbund in Schillerstr. and in between eat at home. [. . .] At home at about 1, out again before 3. Heart failing me, bad memento. Meeting of the Dresden branch at

Schillerstr. We set up the 'Literature' work group. Myself: chairman. Will speak in June: 'What we knew about France'. Back in the KB car. [...]

[...]

25th April, Thursday morning

I dealt with the following correspondence:

1) Proposal to Becher, Kulturbund Berlin: 'What we knew about France'. Title is essentially Eva Blank's (instead of 'Image of France').

2) Letter to the Stühlers[51] in Munich, who wrote. Bernhard's letter in the most ghastly Latin – but Latin nevertheless! They want to go to the USA.

3) 'Dr Dr Weidhaas', Plauen.

4) The Scherners.

[...]

7) Dr Mannhart, Hamburg, secondary-school teacher, Adviser for Language Teaching in Hamburg. They want to publish a modern languages periodical, he requests my participation. M. has my name from a Dresden newspaper, which a friend gave him in hospital. He asks about various Romance teachers, inter alia as to who holds the chair in Leipzig! With the barriers between the zones, one lives 'as if behind a Chinese wall'. [...] In my reply I mentioned my '$\frac{2}{3}$ complete' 18ième, parts of it were very suitable for publication in a periodical. [...]

Evening

The whole day ruined by a stream of visitors. 1. Wunderwald, Dember's technician at the TH wants to be rehabilitated. 2. Öhmichen, a secondary-school teacher, wants to be rehabilitated and teach at the PHS. Don't know him at all. 3. Martha Wiechmann from Meissen. Very meek and small. Very awkward for me. Emphasises, she wants nothing, but does nevertheless also want to be rehabilitated. 4. The Komanns.[52] Simply called by + requests a card for Sunday, PHS. 5) Glaser's ladies. 'Out for a walk.' 6) Wolffs, dispute with Kluge over the furniture. Hateful! He has called up Russian help. 7) A school leaver from the Wettin Grammar School for academic advice. 8) Schmidt jun. Where could one borrow medical textbooks?

[...]

28th April, Sunday forenoon

Today at 2 p.m. the PHS is to be officially inaugurated in the Tonhalle. Hundreds of invitations have been sent out, but there has been no announcement in the press or on the wireless. My study is good – but will I be able to deliver it without getting muddled? The brochure is to be printed – but paper has not yet been allocated. I have a sinking feeling about the whole affair. I also tell myself, any call to Leipzig depends in great measure on my performance today.

I heard parts of Grotewohl's speech to the SED Party Congress of Unification.

In it word for word: 'The planned direction of labour deployment' corresponds to ... complete identity of LTI and LQI.[53]

29th April, Monday forenoon
I very much have the feeling: *this* at least has been achieved. All in all it can probably be registered as the desired success: the minor individual glory of having put *my* stamp on the new People's High School. The brochure (*if* it appears) will occupy a lasting and much-noted place in People's High School literature. The break with 1919, with Rousseau, the Enlightenment as watchword! I spoke well, very well in fact and very calmly and confidently. But beforehand I suffered from anxiety and heart trouble, and afterwards I was very exhausted. I do not have much time left. The applause was *very* considerable, clapping for a *very* long time. I then got (Seidemann, Frau Höhndorf, Grützner) as criticisms: a little too long (55 minutes). But two preceding welcoming speeches were to blame for their weariness [...]. I had to wait over an hour before it was my turn. – There had been no announcement in the paper, there was beautiful weather and the trees were in bloom, 2 p.m. was a most inconvenient time! Nevertheless the house was half-full, about 400 people I'm told. – Menke-Gl. shook my hand, I had 'expressed his feelings exactly'(!), Rentzsch and Dölitzsch agreed with me. Gertrud Keller, too [...]. Against that. a city and schools councillor, Roenisch, KPD, is supposed to have grumbled on political grounds. But it was very good politics on my part to emphasise freedom of thought within the Bloc. – On the whole, as already mentioned, a success. Whether and how it will have an effect, remains to be seen. [...]
On Saturday I completed the article 'Autochthonous writing' for the *LTI*. [...]

4th May, Saturday forenoon
Managed the chapter, 'Names', yesterday after all. [...] At 1.30 p.m. Gladewitz will pick us up for the Falkenstein–Plauen trip. Scherner sent word (an excessively long telegram!), I should come via Plauen. At that I asked Gladewitz to take E. as well.
On Mond. evening, 29 April, with E. to a Kulturbund concert in the hall of the Versöhnungskirche [Atonement Church], Schandauerstr. Lecture by Laux on the unity of German music, political inflection, a pianist with stamina, Eiben. It was awkward, when Blank somewhat presumptuously congratulated her in the name of the Kulturbund, while I as first chairman stood next to her. Later I gently pointed out the faux pas to the good 'secretary' and graduate economist. Locherer was there and afterwards sent me his car for the journey home – a good thing because of thundery showers.
[...] In the [...] afternoon Laue came up. I crossed off 8 'rehabilitated' pg's from the list of teachers for the Evening Grammar School.[54] He is willing, but thanks to his stone deafness communicating with him drives me to despair. We sat in the hall. When I went into the room, to fetch a document, I heard familiar

sentences. Parts of my speech were just being broadcast: 'A lesson well learned', the conclusion, the loud applause. I did not recognise my voice, I felt embarrassed by pauses, real breaks within sentences – yet I am always being told, I speak too fast with excessively brief pauses ... [...]

Wednesday, 1 May, was the May Day celebration. The local council had sent a couple of little red paper flags; in the garage E. found an old piece of ticking of Berger's and made three big flags out of it. Thus our house was magnificently adorned. At 8 a.m. we went up to the village and then with the column of demonstrators from the inn to Plauen Town Hall. Then back to us, looking at the march-past of other groups. It was wonderful spring weather, E. expressed herself very happy at the turn of events both in itself and for our sakes. – Then in the afternoon up to the inn once again: concert, speech – quite nice.

Thurs., 2 May, at the State Administration for an excessively long time, cultivating old contacts, fingering this and that. Most important the lengthy meeting with Gute, for which, admittedly, I had to wait endlessly. He declared repeatedly, that I would definitely get the Leipzig professorship. [...] I also spoke to Gladewitz. I once characterised him, the man in charge of the Information Section, to which the People's High School is attached, and the man with the fine Horch car (which was supposed, *supposed!*, to leave the repair shop yesterday evening), I once described Gladewitz here as a very small man, probably an insignificant reporter. I did him an injustice. He is at least a brave man. He fought in the Spanish Civil War, then in the French resistance, his family were meanwhile in Russia. His 17-year-old Sonja educated entirely in a Russian institution. He spoke affectionately of her. At the same time very cordial to me. I asked for a place for E. in the car, he had intended to take his wife and daughter, since he was district secretary in Plauen for a while. He talked to his daughter on the telephone, she wanted to go only as far as Chemnitz. Another car can take her there, said Gladewitz, and so there will be room for E. As already mentioned, I had the most friendly impression of the small, thickset, dark man – I estimate in his late forties. I am now curious to see, whether things work out with Plauen this time.

[...]

After that a brief letter from Scherner. His condition had worsened, he was dependent on a wheelchair. A second stroke therefore? Will then our mass visit, announced by telegram, be all right with him, and E. staying over night??

[...]

7th May, Tuesday morning and probably later in the day

How can I separate private and official business on the Plauen trip? The friendship with Gladewitz – it really did become a friendship – is of course of the greatest professional value. The man, 48, originally a waiter, a weaver's son, a dozen or more siblings, not all of whom he knew, a KPD official at an early age, evidently best Party training and good self-education; outstanding, passionate, simultaneously direct and hearty political speaker, ready at a moment's notice and immediately up and running. Happy, that in summer 45, in Plauen, within a few months, he made friends and encouraged the dejected. [...] The fine Horch came at about 3 and first drove us to Leuteritz Park, where the Gladewitzes have been given a little house with a huge kitchen garden. [...] Beside the driver, who is treated as one of the family, Gladewitz, his daughter on his knee, in the back Frau Gl., E., myself, squeezed but pleasant. The top up because of the draught. Again a most beautiful spring day; now and then I caught something of the familiar beautiful landscape. [...] With my great success and the completely transformed situation I felt moments of the purest happiness. E. felt the same. ('On Sunday morning at the Scherners I lay awake in bed and was happy.' And then she repeated one of the walks from our time on the run. – It would be nice to be naive and sometimes thank one's maker and become pious. But the fate of the millions stamped out??) Drive *not* on the autobahn, but through villages. In Chemnitz parents and other relatives of Frau Gl. Drove around for a long time, the daughter was set down in Dittersdorf. We were in Falkenstein at about 7. [...] Scherner not, as I had feared, badly crippled, only rheumatic and rather more awkward than before. I.e. agile in his pharmacy, simply has to be brought there in his wheelchair. Otherwise both Scherners unchanged and unchanged in their warmth. Immediate mutual concord between the Gl.'s and the Sch.'s. Hospitality with real coffee and little cakes, showered with good things such as soap, sweetener etc. etc. The following day *I* also got pens, ointment, etc., in addition my Montesquieu and Hettner's volumes on France and England. – We left E. in Falkenstein, departed after a good hour and were in Plauen as darkness was falling. I only knew: Weidhaas, Schlossstr. Not the number. While we were still looking, Gladewitz by chance met Hengst, his successor in Plauen, and now everything went smoothly. I only fleetingly made the acquaintance of 'Dr Dr Weidhaas' (engineering and phil. and town councillor) that evening, also saw him only a little the next day [...]. A beardless man, reddish-blond, somewhat sectarian-looking, malcontent, about 40. Gl. told me he was a 'religious Social-ist', reactionary in church matters, not much liked. Weidhaas himself com-plained to me on Sunday morning, he was in the wrong place, was wearing himself out on petty tasks, had personal enemies who were plotting against him – the SPD had sold no tickets for the forthcoming occasion – he wanted to leave. He is an architect, specialist in the history of Oriental architecture, would very much like to have an appointment teaching it, a lectureship, some kind of post at Dresden TH. It was now agreed, that I should right away drive with the Gladewitzes to have supper at a co-operative society celebration; the Gladewitzes would stay overnight with their friend Hengst, I would be dropped at my hotel ... The car drove somewhere far out in the countryside. An inn, a place for outings, a very hot dancing room, tables along the sides, oompah band, beer and schnapps on every table, the evening well advanced. Gladewitz was welcomed literally with embraces and cheering. Was himself loud and emotional. (As to his character: on the drive there, the car suddenly stopped 'a hare!' Gl. snatches a pistol from his back pocket, 8 rounds in the magazine, jumps out with the driver, they kneel down, but Gl. does not fire. He had too much 'discipline', to fire when there was no certainty of success ... 'Have you had military training?' 'Of course! I was political commissar, after all.[55] He is senior to the battalion

commander and must be able to judge the combat situation.') I became
acquainted with [...] various Party figures. We received a meagre portion of
potato salad, but beer and even more, much more, schnapps [...]. I was very
careful with the alcohol, Gladewitz drank copiously. He also danced frequently
and well. And in between he gave an address, political and private, emotional
and manly, cliche and yet not cliche, because quite evidently everything came
from the heart. He was then royally pleased at his success, beamed at me again
and again: have I not conquered these people, are they not devoted to me?! It
went on like that until midnight. And then: we have to show our faces at
another party, which the district administrator is holding tonight!

Now we, a group of three cars, drove back into town, out at the opposite end,
again far into the countryside, into a forest, probably to a lodge. There the same
scene as in the previous place. Ordinary people, noisy and in high spirits, hall,
band, dancing, schnapps. A grey-haired female district administrator dances
tirelessly. Gladewitz dances, drinks, delivers short speeches, is ever more animated, strokes my head, demands we address each other with 'du', wants to
force me to dance. We finally leave long after 1. The Hotel Deil, near the station,
formerly the most elegant of the wealthy industrial town. Side entrance over
debris and rubble. We ring and knock for a long time, before a woman appears
high up at a window, throws down a packet with keys. We descend to a cellar
on a firm ramp (not stairs). Chaos, devastation. Up through a chute. Then above
there's a magnificent room, except the ceiling is crumbling, scaffolding in front
of the window (without glass, with wood or cardboard), no running water. But
electric light and a good bed. – I slept late. [...] Various committee members in
front of the theatre. Gladewitz appeared at the last moment. Fresh. But during
the night he had fallen asleep in the bathtub, his wife had to wash and wake
him. – Director's box, myself at the front in the middle. On stage a men's choir.
Then Weidhaas read a fairly long official welcome. [...] Then Gladewitz. Again
without notes, lively, encouraging, without cliches. Conclusion: now the concrete instruction could begin. Then it was my turn. Until the last without a
definite plan. But curiously calm. I simply conversed about this and that from
my LTI. I had a dazzling chandelier in front of me and had to shield my eyes
with my hand the whole time. But I spoke altogether fluently and freely and
had (after about an hour) very good applause. Gladewitz could not stop singing
my praises. Then there were two Russian gentlemen outside. A heavy dark
civilian, lieutenant and local boss, and a young captain in uniform, Bernstein,
evidently a Jew, speaking fluent German, in Plauen by chance, political editor
of the *Tägliche Rundschau*. He asked for an article about my lecture [...]

Departure at 4 p.m. A good hour later back at the Falkenstein pharmacy.
Hearty reunion, many presents. Left at 6.30. [...] Detours and stop in Chemnitz-
Dittersdorf. Home at 10.

[...]

This morning we received the first card from Gusti Weighardt in London. In
the evening I attended – the back of beyond, Marienhofstr. Elementary School –
the first political course held by Gute for the Dresden PHS. It was very nice.
About 30 people of a very proletarian character. Gute spoke and taught without

notes and in very lively fashion, asked questions, got answers about the foundations of Socialism. [...] I had earlier shown him Gusti's card; he wanted to add something to our reply. On the way home there was talk of Gute now becoming minister of culture, of my being appointed at Leipzig. I said, then I would give up the PHS. He: then Gusti could be my successor in this post. We agreed that I would immediately write to her to this effect.

10th May, Friday evening

LTI has come to a standstill once again. Recent days were taken up with the article for the *Tägliche Rundschau*, which only recapitulates the Plauen lecture, which itself was only an imitatio of my first lecture at the Begerburg, merely an overview, marking no progress. I ask myself once again, whether I shall manage to draw it [*LTI*] all together. I am unable to master all my scattered notes. Nevertheless: 14 sections are already written, some 50 or 60 printed pages.

I was much distracted, had many errands and visitors.

Everyone wants to be rehabilitated, in writing and orally, everyone rehabilitated wants an evening teaching post, everyone showed a Jew kindness, expects my help. It is sickening. And there is no end to it.

[...]

11th May, Saturday morning

[...] The driver of the PHS car told me recently: 'Why do the Russians dismantle everything? They rip out every switch, every door handle. Why don't they just let us make 1 million new door handles instead? Why do they pull up railway tracks? Why do they allow factories to be rebuilt and then dismantle them again? [...] Everywhere among the workers the fear of unemployment, the disappointment by the Russians. Things are not going well with the KPD, it gets blamed for the Russians' mistakes. And the upshot will be a new NSDAP and a new agitation against the Jews.

On Wed. 8 May [...] to police headquarters [...] for restitution of the old driving licence. When I at last found the room, it was closed. But in the meantime I bumped into Kussi, back from a trip to the western territory. His judgement: in the English zone the food situation is no better than here, in the American zone truly better. Intellectual separation of the zones is increasing, prospects of a united German state slim. Christian Union and Schumacher tendency [of SPD] in most absolute majority over there.[56] Aversion to Russia (which 'is not as bad as it is painted'), rejection of Communism and of 'Berlin'. Then again many want a united Reich.

On Thurs. afternoon, 9 May, a Kulturbund meeting, literature section, at Schillerstr. (The beauties of spring – afterwards we went down to Körnerplatz, the road cut into the hillside, a high wall on one side, blossom hanging over it – quite Italian!) I am the chairman both of the city branch and of this section. As at the recent Laux–Eibentraut musical evening, the secretary, Eva Blank, was again somewhat presumptuous. I warned her quite clearly to toe the line. I then welcomed Spamer, whom I have won over from the 'Research and Scholarship' section. He is now a member of the Berlin Academy of Sciences, has simultaneously been offered a professorship at Berlin and at Munich. I would like him to talk about the creation of legends. And distinguish between legend and non-legend (Nürnberg trial!). – Then an evening of readings from Wiechert was discussed with the grey-haired actress Crusius. [...] The *Totenwald* [Forest of the Dead] concentration camp book too shocking?[57] We cannot only spare people's feelings, where would that leave democratic renewal?! So Decarli will be asked to read the *Forest of the Dead*. [...]

Yesterday summoned to Gladewitz with Grützner. The SMA is raising problems for the PHS. We are to be a *school*, hold *courses* exactly on the Berlin model. Objections to lectures, to titles. A great deal is due to linguistic misunderstanding. [...] I would be overjoyed, if Leipzig worked out and Auguste Wieghardt were appointed my successor at the Dresden PHS.

14th May, Tuesday afternoon

On Sun. morning with E. – resolution! – to the exhibition of graphics in the Arts and Crafts Museum, Dürerstr. Balzer guided and talked, it was a Kulturbund event. [...] Interesting to me, was what Balzer said about contemporary painting of ruins. He compared it with the 18th century's cult of ruins. But the essential difference is this: the people of the 18th century did not sing the praises of their own ruins. To make ruins look melancholy may be very nice, if they became ruins 1500 years ago. But if my, my house is destroyed ... The brutality of the destruction and the brutality of the new spring should be highlighted.

In the afternoon Spamer called on us. I read to him at length from the *LTI* and he seemed truly and sincerely taken by it. E. again emphasised, that she found my approach between confession and scholarship quite new. [...] On Monday 13 May I tried in vain to get help with food at the KPD and 'Victims of Fascism'. Once again things looked bleak. [...] There was unpleasantness at the 'Victims of Fascism'. [...] Loewenkopf had assigned me a food parcel, which another official refused me.

[...]

16th May, Thursday evening

No special party, no special presents,[58] no possibility of better food: but yet an awareness of the degree to which the great question mark chose us above a million others. Sometimes one feels like turning pious, but I consider that immodest and impertinent. Today Eva planted 7 cucumbers, 50 tomatoes and some 80 heads of lettuce. In the afternoon I had a Kulturbund meeting (Literature) in Schillerstr., the KB car did not bring me back until almost 8.

Yesterday evening, in the very overcrowded lecture theatre of the dermatology department of the Friedrichstädter Hospital, a very long and very boring hygienics lecture by Dr Grube. But various things by the way were important. [...] For the first time since the catastrophe of 13 Feb. 45 I spoke to the much-younger-looking Dr Magnus. He believes, that both Steinitzes were killed. They had run towards Sachsenplatz, which was a sea of flames. Missing since then. [...]

LTI yield of recent days: 'On a single working day' completed. ' "System" and "Organisation"' begun.

19th May, Sunday towards evening

[...]

On Sat. morning (18 May) to the district headquarters of the KPD – no, SED! [...] Long talk with Gertrud K.; Staffel, whom I met with her, is her SPD deputy. She said: 'We have to educate the SPD to be a Marxist party.' She said, the forthcoming plebiscite on the expropriation of the factories[59] would demand tremendous work from each official. Every worker was personally attached to his boss – 'he's all right', 'I've been there for 30 years' ... 'my father was already' ... 'decent' ... 'Christmas present' ... etc. etc. In opposition to that the Party official must go from house to house, work on the people with precise statistical material and enlighten them about every industry, every industrialist having an interest in war and having funded the Hitler war, and if he remained owner, causing the next war – and inevitably so! [...]

[...]

25th May, Saturday forenoon

Rather unproductive week with many calamities.

[...]

Rehabilitation questions occupy, torment me daily. I feel mistrust and contempt for everyone. Recently a woman here, blonde, stupid-looking, poorly educated. It turns out, her husband was *the* medical examiner at Sternplatz, who was friendly in his treatment of me despite my Jews' star and was taken aback, when I told him my profession. I am now supposed to confirm that for him – perhaps it will get him his post back, although a pg since 33. I provide the testimonial, and the woman pulls out her purse: 'what do I owe you?' I: 'Really I should now take the paper back from you and tear it up.' She begged my pardon, she had meant no harm and departed. [...] Minor pg case, joined late, no position. Why did he not pursue rehabilitation. 'I cannot say, like all the others, that I was an anti-Fascist and only went along with it because I was forced to. I believed in the Führer, even in 1945 I believed in him. I knew nothing about the atrocities, about the murders and concentration camps, I really knew nothing about it!' It is unbelievable – and it is undoubtedly expressed with a subjectively genuine sincerity.

This scene on the 10th on the tram between Postplatz and Albertplatz also somehow belongs here. On the front platform a young man fairly wretched-looking, not at all Jewish in appearance, only his eyes were dark. He has – a rarity! – a real cigar, not a stub, in his mouth, although not smoking it. Two voices behind me. – 'A Jew ... of course. Well, if they come back now. Then business is going to boom!' I saw the two of them as I got off. Young, very blond, brutal, very Nazi types.

Among our visitors in recent days, Kussi and his Dutch wife. He: young people were thoroughly Nazi, thoroughly against the Communists and the Russians. – A letter from Lisl Stühler in Munich: more Nazism and more anti-Semitism than ever. Bernhard St.: 'If my classmates knew that I'm Jewish, none of them would have anything to do with me!' In autumn they want to go to San Francisco. – Kussi said, that as a Jew one immediately got an entry permit.

[...]

[...] Vossler wrote yesterday – the letter, opened by the American censors, took a month to get here. V. is a member of the 'Union of Cultural Producers', but as a scholar does not wish to join any party. He reads *nothing*. Only administers the rectorship. [...]

On the evening of the Tue. and Fri. I again taught German at Herbertstr. [i.e. Evening School] Almost entirely lecturing. Students rarely speak. I am still dealing with individual concepts: Classicism, Romanticism, tragedy, comedy, catharsis etc. etc. It goes smoothly and effortlessly, but afterwards I am totally worn-out and shattered. Beforehand I sit in a little on other teachers. [...]

26th May, Sunday evening

The last three weekdays were taken up with the fight with the SMA over the PHS. The headquarters here is causing tremendous difficulties through arbitrary interpretation of instructions from Berlin-Karlshorst. The former wants us to be a school with a fixed number of pupils, a small number of teachers with fixed salaries – the Kulturbund can take over everything university-like, fluctuating, lecture-like.

28th May, Tuesday night

Letter from Northampton, England, from Max Sebba. He heard my name on the wireless. Jule Sebba is still living, likewise Frau Schaps after a stroke; Gerstle[60]†

29th May, early Wednesday

[...] It was decided to start the Whitsun holiday now [PHS and Evening Grammar School] and to extend it 'until further notice'; further: to travel to Berlin as soon as possible. Present state of affairs: Gladewitz, myself and Staffel (for the Saxon SED) are to go to Berlin, probably on Friday. [...]

So yesterday evening I gave the last German lesson for the time being at the Evening Grammar School. Great alarm among students and teachers at the provisional closure. I defended Russian mistrust and chaotic governing. Afterwards a young man and a girl poured out their hearts to me: Absolutely reactionary mood. The Communists, the police, those in power have plenty to eat, confiscate, do everything 'just like' the previous regime, etc. etc. .... I spoke optimistically. I am convinced, that the Hitler way of thinking is stronger in Dresden today than the Communist one.

Worry about the plebiscite also comes under the heading of Reaction. It is *only* about expropriating the industry responsible for the war (but where is the boundary? Elastic!). But the petty bourgeoisie (and who here does not belong to the petty bourgeoisie??) fears for its property, fears for private property, fears the Communists per se. And the KPD is undoubtedly behaving in a two-faced and clumsy and unconfident manner. In the newspaper, it preaches that no one wants to touch private property, it emphasises the same in its meetings. But at the same time [...] it nevertheless emphasises, that *we* want a socialist state, that *we* only put up with the democratic state for the time being. [...] The outcome of the plebiscite is quite uncertain.

[...]

Yesterday morning, no TH session. Instead a long chat in Fräulein Mey's office with Janentzky, Spamer and the very likeable Straub,[61] who has re-surfaced. [...] I chat pleasantly, even warmly with Janentzky, he likewise with me. And yet we do not trust one another in the slightest. Whom do I still trust in Germany? No one!

Deeply depressed by my skin complaint. Pain and disfigurement for months now. Again and again scabby, again and again my head bandaged. Now my ear is in a ghastly state, tomorrow it will be both ears.

Evening, 11.30.

[...]

Visitors: Steininger, Berndt. In between the much-lamenting Frau Schmidt: Her dismissed husband is threatening suicide. I am trying to make the boy's studies easier for him. (2nd semester in natural sciences at Jena; would like to get into the overcrowded medical faculty.)

[...]

4th June, Tuesday evening

Latest misfortune: a few days ago at the Party office I bumped against a bucket and hurt my shinbone. It has turned into an alarming inflammation, today I had to see Dr Frenzel, she is worried, ordered me to keep the leg up, poultices and rest. All of it lacking. Pain, handicap, serious worry.

In addition extreme food shortage, literal lack. For 3 days now, morning and evening, barley soup, which ran out today. What is to be done?

In the afternoon – wearisome journey there – long session with Dölitzsch about the People's High School. But tomorrow at least a KPD car will pick me up. Incidentally I bought a season ticket for the tram for June; dodging the fare was getting on my nerves.

[...]

A letter from Dr Mannhart in Hamburg: collaboration on the soon-to-be-revived *Neuere Sprachen* [Modern Languages]. Lerch is professor in Münster again.

For the *LTI* I wrote: 'What remains?' (Coventrise)
[...]

6th June, Thursday night
[...]
The first letter from Georg, dated 9 April 46. Youthful flawless handwriting, flawless English. He enlightens me as to the two types of angina, the nervous and the *pernicious form* with the *quick end*. He advises rest etc. Doctor, your advice is wonderful! – He has 11 grandchildren and is expecting the 12th. Otto Klemperer's eldest is just beginning his medical studies at Oxford.[62] The Jelskis are living '*in difficult circumstances*' in Montevideo.
[...]

9th June, Whit Sunday morning
Holiday mood? Yes and no. The *quick end*, the torment of the scabies, the food shortage, the uncertainty about the Leipzig chair. D'altra parte:[63] a garden in bloom, myself a kind of little big shot.

On Friday afternoon I was sound-filmed. It was tragicomically awful. Publicity film for the plebiscite. Closing scene of a Kulturbund meeting. I spoke the words (formulated by myself): 'So, ladies and gentlemen, we are agreed on that, we shall set everything else aside for the moment. The most important thing now is the plebiscite. Because the future of democracy depends on the result and with it the future of every one us.' When I repeated this *speech* for the fourth time, I began to trip over my tongue, and I had to recite it at least 8 times. Now the sound engineer didn't like a pause – 'more quickly please – more slowly please'; now a fuse blew, now Eva Blank cast a shadow over me ... My fellow actors – only extras, but they were shown in close-up as I spoke – were E. Blank, Kneschke, Tobler, Wildführ. In addition to the ordeal of speaking, the dazzling light and the heat. Incomprehensible to me how actors produce great performances under these conditions. [...]

In the Party House – now SED! – I was entirely surrounded by SPD people: G. Glöckner, Staffel, Dölitzsch. Of course there was angry, almost bitter talk about the KPD. And *my* people (Gertrud Keller!) say: we want to turn the SPD into a Marxist party! [...]

10th June, Whit Monday night
Yesterday two very long letters to Georg and Marta,

Today worked through the whole ms of my *Deutsches Frankreichbild 1914– 1933* [The German Image of France], sixty pages, serious pain in my face and eyes the whole time (usual inflammation due to sunlight + boils forming on my nose).
[...]
The day before yesterday in the course of a conversation about concentrated

food Dölitzsch told me with mild matter-of-factness, without any sense of outrage: 'Around Sachsenhausen concentration camp there was a track with a number of different sections (swamp, water, sand, asphalt etc.). Prisoners had to run ... climb ... wade etc. along it. As they did so, they received only pills as nourishment. Some died very quickly, others took longer to die.' [...]

16th June, Sunday evening

[...] On Friday I had to cry off a session at the State Administration, very unwise, since I am already more or less sidelined there. (Although Gute repeatedly promises me Leipzig.)

All day yesterday it was doubtful, whether I would be able to speak in Weixdorf-Lausa. Nevertheless I had more or less prepared the lecture 'French Writers as Politicians'. Towards evening the stormy and rainy weather of recent days had improved, E. had bandaged me up, had a mind to come along herself, and so I went ahead. It turned into a nice family party, an oasis in the quite desolate sequence of recent days. The drive out was already pleasant, past Klotzsche air base in a comfortable car. After that the place itself; Weixdorf-Lausa Inn and the house and garden opposite. In the little house, Dr Lange and family, grammar-school teacher, not *yet* rehabilitated, harmless, in charge of culture and the local (camouflaged) PHS, favourite of the KPD mayor, teacher of modern languages, my student in 1928, very pleasant and likeable. The mayor, Krause, middle-aged, widely travelled oil engineer, calm good man, had provided L. with foodstuffs and so there was a wonderful supper, mashed potatoes and tinned meat. [...] Then in good spirits over to the inn. Large room, somewhat funereally decorated stage, orchestra, small grand piano, about 200 people, perhaps more [...]. Music, speech of welcome by Krause, the mayor, then my speech, drawn from the wealth of material; Chénier, Corneille, Racine, Voltaire, Montesquieu, Rousseau, Chateaubriand, Lamartine, Hugo, Claudel – all in an hour. Hugo's exile and his return on 4 Sept. 1870[64] – polemically, here Gerhart Hauptmann had *not* gone into exile, Th. Mann *not* come back. Much applause of course. Then 'informal evening' with dancing. A good sweet wine, something to smoke – and once again one saw oneself Calvinistically confirmed in grace. [...] And around midnight the drive home, the driver a friendly policeman, formerly driving instructor. And we also got a little packet: a bit of beef suet, 6 eggs, white flour and sugar. That is the only important thing now, I would have refused a fee. At about 1 content to bed, and the next day as depressed as ever. – Dreadful always the matter-of-factness and the agreement in the stories of SS bestiality. Krause, who himself did labour in a camp, talks of the shooting of a long row of Jewish children. They were brought out of a truck in nightshirts. The troops had got schnapps and now shot the children in the back of the head. One child turned round; at that one man went off his head and fired in all directions. – A Jew's eye was knocked out, they stuffed cotton wool in the socket and made him fall in for work...

Always the two-edged topic of rehabilitation. As already mentioned, Dr Lange is a *good man*: they should finally stop all this rooting around in what's past and the retribution. Well and good – but then when I see the mass of those who have been rehabilitated and their shamelessness, et le reste … It is very sickening.

[…]

23rd June, Sunday forenoon

[…] We, Lachmann, Dölitzsch, Grützner, myself have been trying for days to have a meeting with the SMA. Now there's no interpreter, now the officers are not there, now the two sides miss one another. This whole week, by car and by tram, I have been quite futilely chasing around because of this business. Yesterday finally a conference with a young Russian major, who spoke broken German and was very friendly. It was agreed, that we offer only courses and not individual lectures, with fewer teachers than before and with precise adherence to the generally permitted syllabuses. […] So the courses start again on Monday, and on Tue. therefore I shall again be standing behind the lectern at the Evening Grammar School, and even merely teaching German there causes me problems and distracts me from my real tasks – and with every painful step, I realise how short my time is.

[…]

On 28 and 29 June there is a conference on teacher training at Berlin University, Gadamer and Litt[65] are speaking; the TH wanted to send Janentzky (the dean) and Straub – the Central Administration, effectively the State Administration here, has delegated *me* instead of Janentzky … […] My colleague Arthur Franz from Königsberg,[66] now here without a job, tells me, that I would be held to be exploiting the political situation, if I pushed my way into Leipzig – on all sides I feel the hostility of my peers, and I shall certainly encounter the Leipzigers in Berlin: I must at long last have the call to Leipzig as backing, as it is I am falling between every conceivable stool. […]

My work this week with its innumerable expeditions and frittering away of time consisted of […] 3 long letters. […inter alia] long letter to Hilde Sussmann […] an even longer one to Berthold Meyerhof,[67] who had sent a letter to Prof. Kl. 'Rector of the TH Dresden'. He, too, had somehow had word of the broadcast announcement of my appointment as director of the Dresden PHS, and had construed it just as mistakenly as Blumenfeld in Lima, from whom, via Wilhelm Jelski,[68] oboist at the Lima Opera House, it reached Georg.

I had to spend more time on the talk for the Kulturbund, 'What do we know about France?', which I crudely cobbled into shape from my 1933 text 'The German Image of France'. I gave it on Friday evening in the small but very crowded hall of the Academy (to around 175 listeners) with apparently very great success: they clapped until I stepped forward once again and said that I was not a tenor. But afterwards Gute explained: he would have to discuss it with me, I had not spoken 'dialectically' enough. With that the evening was spoiled for me, because I am dependent on the Party, at least as long as I am not certain of Leipzig.

[…]

Mannhart, Hamburg, writes to me frequently, with respect to the modern

languages journal planned by the publisher Westermann. He wants my France lecture for it. Lerch, at Münster again, is to edit the Romance Languages and Literatures section. I have not yet had any personal contact with Lerch. [...]
[...]

27th June, Thursday forenoon
Card from Lerch. His son fallen, Anna Lahmann gassed in Poland. He will 'not stay much longer' in Münster.
[...]
The plebiscite is in full swing. Posters, wireless etc. Not altogether skilfully. Dr König, the dentist: Since seeing the list of those to be expropriated – so many! *so* many! – I have become uncertain after all. To the Saxon or Dresden petit bourgeois it does indeed smack of Communism. (And they are not so far wrong!) – People were driven out in a 100 cars to Zeithain, to see the mass graves of the Russian prisoners there. But their number has grown all too rapidly in the newspaper. From about 80,000 to 140,000 dead. And Dölitzsch says, the business was organised as propaganda. The individual got to see only a pit with a few bones in it. (From someone else, admittedly: there were several such holes. In any case, no overall impression.) [...]
Nestler, the bookseller, has been arrested [...] he is said to have been denounced. He was – I learned of it only yesterday! – a pg, but by arrangement with the KPD and active illegally; but he was also proprietor of a 'Wehrmacht' [army] bookshop. I only learned of the affair from Balzer, who is doing what he can for Nestler. After that, very curiously, from our hairdresser Gustl Kowacz. G., who was very welcome when he came yesterday evening, is now permanently employed as barber in the police prison – oh my memories! – and shaved Nestler.
[...]
Announced on the wireless yesterday: the conductor Otto Klemperer is returning to Germany and conducting in Baden-Baden. Strange. Why has he not long ago been named along with the other émigré musicians? I believed him dead. [...] What was my first thought? That my name, which is just beginning to become known, will now be drowned out again.
Dölitzsch and Grützner accuse me of grabbing at too many posts. They are not altogether wrong. And yet I would so like to be – the [local] elections have just been announced for 1 September – city councillor, one of 80.

30th June, Sunday afternoon
Very hot, very worn out by the two days in Berlin. Puffed up and inwardly torn: Leipzig? – Greifswald? – nada?[69] – mors?[70] Overwhelmed with work and incapable of it. Read correspondence, ordered papers a little. Sent my excuses to Munich [i.e. to the publishers in Munich, Klemperer now intended to publish his *LTI* with the Communist house Aufbau, see below]. Morning: election,

plebiscite, up at the inn. Great crush. But the final outcome is doubtful never-theless.[71] [...]

Now the trip to Berlin 28 and 29 June, Frid. and Sat. Invitation by the Central Administration for Popular Education to a conference on 'Philosophy, Educational Theory and Psychology in the University Studies of Teachers'. Sessions in the Senate Chamber of the University, 43 Charlottenstr. (Corner Dorotheenstr., opposite the red ruined wing of the Friedrich Werdersche Grammar School, which I attended exactly 50 years before.)

The principal event is still Greifswald and, therefore, crumpled Herr Jacoby[72] in front of the lectern, with his ear trumpet, professor of philosophy and dean, very conservative, it seemed to me, very forceful during the discussion – and courting me as if I were a diva. 'If you give me just some grounds for hope, if you allow me to propose you ... We need an important man. You must be our prorector. You do not need to lecture on Old French, you'll have someone to do it for you. You will have a house and garden. You will have peace and quiet to write your books. As a Victim of Fascism your salary can be higher. The only thing we cannot give you is a car. But you don't need one. We are a small town (50,000 inhabitants) and 3 miles from the sea. From here I am going to Schwerin.[73] To propose you to the government [of Mecklenburg-Vorpommern]. If you give me even the least grounds for hope ...' Thus, tempestuously, on Friday. Then on the Saturday a fraction cooler, but very earnest and definite. [...] I emphasised that there was nothing binding between us, I considered that I had given my word to the Saxon government. – Of course it raised my self-confidence, and since then my thoughts have been regularly drifting off in the same direction: sea, quiet, king of the village, being able to write books, not being pulled in different directions. And E., too, has to some extent been drawn into this fantasy.

At the same time I let the cat out of the bag as far as the Leipzigers were concerned. Gadamer, man in his early 40s, slightly paralysed (infantile paralysis), ignored me on the first day, but on Saturday came up to me very respectfully and courteously, was entirely in the know. Yes, but if von Jan did not *want* to go to Jena, my view of self-administration was not shared in Leipzig, further compulsory measures on the government's part would cause another mass exodus of colleagues to the West. I said [...] Jan could be given the language chair. Gadamer relented: did I want to take all of Lit. Hist. away from Jan? I: Not at all, there were so many topics after all! 'But I must have the chair of Literary History [...] – that is my area, that is where I have proved myself, there he is colourless, that is what I must teach the students.' We parted very amicably. [...] Litt, grown grey, but little changed, brave, stubborn and eloquent, greeted me most warmly on the first day, was honestly and of his own accord shocked at the Nazi horrors, but was astonished, when he heard of my assault on Leipzig. [...] If I am really appointed to Leipzig, I will have a fight on my hands. And again and again I hear, as now from Hentschke: 'Will Leipzig *and* Dresden not be too much for you?' All of that speaks in favour of Greifswald. [...]

And my agreement with the Aufbau publishing house points to Greifswald, very much so. Hentschke had given me the car for Saturday morning, I cut the psychologist's lecture and went to Schlüterstr. in Charlottenburg. Result: I promised *Scholarship Renewed* by 1 Jan. 47, the *LTI* by 1 Oct. 46. I took on a Becher study. It will of course be impossible for me to keep to those dates. But the Aufbau head insisted, he was not making any contracts for any longer period of time – di doman non c'è certezza.[74]

In Berlin I got least out of the proceedings themselves. That is only to a very minor extent due to tiredness and heat. I have absolutely no understanding of and no ability to take in pure philosophy. It causes me a great deal of effort to uphold the fiction that I understand something of it. Gadamer's 'The Importance of the Philosophical Conception of the World for Teacher Training' was completely obscure to me, I had difficulty fighting off sleep. I picked up this and that from Litt's 'Importance of Educational Theory for Teacher Training', but was infinitely bored, I couldn't follow it. [...] There were 60, 70 people from the universities of the Soviet Zone, from the Central Administration and another couple of the elect sitting there, listening to lectures and then endlessly talking around and missing the point of the topic. [...]

More important, although also confused and on the whole fruitless, was the committee meeting on Saturday afternoon, in the Central Administration itself, on curricula. 16 participants, 3 of them Russians. [...] Afterwards I shook hands with Brugsch.[75] He had known Georg and Felix[76] well. – I made friends with the people from the Central Administration: Rompe, Deiters.[77] D. is a scholar and has completed the ms of a Sainte-Beuve study.[78] (So naturally very friendly to me!)

For me, therefore, the actual core of this Berlin trip was the least important thing about it. But now everything else.

[...]

On Friday evening I wanted to seek out Anny Klemperer, from whom I have heard nothing more, since, at the beginning of the war, I gave the necessary answer to her remark about German culture saved from the Russians. I went through the Brandenburg Gate on foot – 2 of the horses on the quadriga are missing! – Ebertstr., Potsdamerstr. dreadful devastation, in places nothingness. [...] If I ever write the final volume of my Curriculum, then I would have to describe this walk. How many memories, how many dead! I went on this walk on 29 June,[79] it took me past the house in which I visited E. in summer 1904. As I walked I told myself, Berlin was after all no better off than Dresden. On Privatstr., which is now called Bissingzeile, one tiny house has not been destroyed, no. 11. Through an open window an old woman told me: 'Klemperer? Yes, they were bombed out in no. 7, the caretakers are still there.' No. 7 was a ruin; behind an elegant cast-iron railing a young couple was working in an overgrown garden. I worked my way through the rubble to the railing and started a conversation. Yes, the old lady was very hard of hearing, but otherwise she was well; Georg was an engineer, Peter was studying, she had moved to Grunewald, 15 Falterstr., with an elderly cook. I would easily get there with the underground from Kurfürstenstr. So I walked to Kurfürstenstr. Here Potsdamerstr. is not quite so destroyed. Again memories! When I reached

Wittenbergplatz on the underground, it was about 8.30, the last train in the opposite direction from Dahlem to Berlin was due to leave at 9.30. At that I gave up the
journey. [...]. Terrible crush in the train, even worse than in Dresden. [...]
   [...]
   At the Kulturbund a great deal was discussed in half an hour. 1) My speech
ms had arrived. We agreed that I will come to Berlin with E. and by car for
Sunday. *Perhaps* there will also be a car going to Ahrenshoop. [Through the
Kulturbund the Klemperers had the privilege of a seaside holiday beginning on
8 July.] If not, then God will have to lend a hand. 2) They wanted *Scholarship
Renewed* in 8 weeks! The young man in charge of this section said quite scorn-
fully: a contract for next Easter? Who knows, which of us will still be here by
then?! We agreed on the 1 of January. 3) They want to take on my *LTI*. For 1
October. I prefer Aufbau to the Süddeutsche Publishing House. Here the *Süddeutsche Zeitung* [newspaper] is constantly attacked as reactionary and Bavaria
is for us and the Russians increasingly a hostile foreign land. [...]

5th July, Friday forenoon

Sweltering tormenting heat for days, always errands, meetings, time-wasting,
bother, not a moment for the *LTI*, yearning for Greifswald. [...]
   [...]

Evening

[...]
   E.'s lymphatic inflammation has subsided. So tomorrow the trip to Berlin and
Ahrenshoop, more difficult and more of an expedition than the journey to Rio
and Buenos Aires once was.

Ahrenshoop, 8–17 July + Berlin trip, 6–7 July

12 July 1946, Saturday morning. E.'s birthday

E.'s first words, at about 5 a.m. – we don't have a clock: 'What I want as a
birthday present, is that we go home a week early!' My feelings exactly and we
will manage it somehow, even though 2 weeks have already been paid for [...].
We are suffering far too greatly here. Above all: we are starving, starving as in
the worst days in Falkenstein. And we are bored. Noisy, overcrowded recreation
rooms, staying on the beach made impossible by a strong, cold, unremitting
wind, we are too tired to go for long walks, and the district has nothing to offer
which could not be seen in two circuits. And at home things are all right – why
be worse off here? Food shortage here as there, and at home we can perhaps
buy something on the black market, here there's not even that ... The sea is
beautiful as always, there is even a strong surge, but everything else – Irun n'est
plus Irun.[80] Perhaps also: we have grown old. [...]
   The days creep by. Our spirits are very low. Everything that formerly made a

stay on the Baltic coast pleasant: seafood, the cafés everywhere on one's way, the trips by boat and on land, even the sociability is absent. We are alone, not very mobile and always hungry.

[...]

Before dinner today we went to Michaelsen and said, because of our poor health we had to depart early. He was very accommodating, a surplus amount of money and coupons which had already been provided for 14 days would be given back to us, we shall travel back on Mon. via Rostock – *without* Berlin. We both heaved a sigh of relief [...] And as far as the Kulturbund is concerned – je m'en fous.[81] [...] Most of the visitors appear to be Kulturbund connected, i.e. actors, literary people, musicians and the like. – I suspect Ahrenshoop, like this whole coast, was *judenrein* [free of Jews] and Nazi a più non posso during the Weimar years. [...]

I shall now catch up on the two days in Berlin, the Kulturbund anniversary and the mishap. This then was the programme for the evening of 7 July at 7 p.m., as it appeared on big posters on the advertising pillars. 'Meeting in the Large Studio of the Broadcasting House, Masurenallee. The speakers: Jonannes R. Becher, Ricarda Huch, Prof. Stroux, Wolfgang Langhoff (Düsseldorf), Prof. Bennedik, Prof. Krauss (Marburg University), Horst Lange (Munich), Prof. Pechstein, District President Dr Friedensburg, Prof. Klemperer (Dresden), Klaus Gysi, Cathedral Preacher Kleinschmidt (Schwerin).[82] Music by the Berlin Radio Symphony Orchestra.' In fact, Werner, the limping lord mayor,[83] was first to speak, roaring banalities and Becher was already very long. After that Rector Stroux long, boring and sticking to his ms as did everyone with the exception of Bennedik, brown, intelligent eyes, the director of the Berlin Academy of Music. Huch had excused herself by telegram, in her place Plievier, a grey-haired scraggy little man with a minor speech impediment, read something from a sheet of paper. But much too long and hackneyed. The well-behaved public clapped. And when Bennedik talked with great liveliness about Nazism's concepts of honour the audience was enthusiastic. But then came the catastrophe: Krauss, the teacher of Romance languages and literatures and KPD veteran, student of Vossler and Spitzer,[84] mid-40s, we had made friends, I expected and still expect a great deal of him. His subject: The situation of the universities. He said he wanted to annoy people, and I was expecting fierce words against reactionary forces. Instead he whispered (in substance no doubt very solid) endless statistics from a sheet of paper, barely audible even in the front row in which I was sitting. The audience became restless. Heckling: Louder! – Time! – We want to hear the others – Louder ... I do not at all think this was because of the content. One gentleman (from the Kulturbund) indignantly told the innocent audience, if one was a genuine democrat, one also had to listen to the other side. Krauss, too, appeared to think he was being opposed and felt duty bound to go on reading. People clapped in time, to get him to stop, he waited patiently and went on reading. Yet it was already late, after 9, and very many people were dependent on the underground, which did not run very late. Irritated, Willmann came up to me. 'He's mucking up our whole evening – but

I can't tell him to stop. Would you be cross with me, if I took you off the speakers' list?' I said: yes, I would be *very* cross. [...] Krauss finally called it a day, there was provocative frenetic applause. Pechstein spoke against kitsch. There was applause, more and more people left, it was getting on for 10 o'clock. I went out into the corridor. There was a despairing debate going on. I resisted being dropped. I said, it would be an insult to the Dresden KB. – 'But you'll be talking to empty benches!' Inside meanwhile the economist Friedensburg had begun to speak. Finally it was announced: We are now going to break off and the remaining speakers (Klemperer, Kleinschmidt, Gysi [...]) will take the floor at a later date. Willmann placated me, there would be a special meeting on my return from Ahrenshoop – I did not believe him, but had to acquiesce [...]. Everyone then shot off without taking leave, I did not catch sight of Willmann or Krauss or Kleinschmidt again. We drove back with Kneschke and he resolved to clearly voice the necessary criticism in the next day's secretarial and business meeting. [...] Thus the Berlin trip completely failed its purpose.

13th July, early Saturday

But otherwise there were a number of interesting and also worthwhile things.

First of all, to stay with the evening in the broadcasting studio. [...] At the end while I was conferring with my people, a blond boy I did not know spoke to me: 'Uncle Victor!' I immediately put two and two together: my nephew Peter, whom I had *never*, literally never seen before. They had moved again, from Grunewald to nearby Heinrich Stefanstr. (we were at the radio tower, far out in Westend), his mother was passably well, his brother Georg, 'exactly 10 years older, I'm 17 now, about to take my leaving certificate', in Hof [in Bavaria] at the moment, looking for a job – he is a high-frequency engineer. I promised [...] to visit Anny Klemperer on the return journey. [...]

Peter Kl. must have taken me for a tenor or a boxer. Because when I stepped out into the anteroom, in which the discussions were taking place, two photographers dragged me into a brightly lit corner with a chair and a folding screen, sat me down and snapped me repeatedly. I asked: why, what for? – I had not even been allowed to speak. – That didn't matter, I was after all 'at the centre of cultural life', so they had to have my picture for the Russian news agency. (But [...] it is no longer any kind of distinction, to have one's picture in the newspaper. Tom, Dick and Harry are in it by the dozen every day.)

On Saturday 6 July Kneschke picked us up at 10 a.m. [...]. Shortly before that the Zabel twin sisters from the Evening Grammar School, who recently presented me with a basket of fruit, had sent two little baskets for the journey, plums, apples, peaches. The woman who brought them said: the twins' parents had more than 60 acres of orchards in Weinböhla, they were doing very well, I could easily accept the fruit.

We drove leisurely, ate fruit, rested once in woodland by the motorway. In Berlin, Schumann, the driver, [...] did not know the way, *I* guided him [...] to Schlüterstr. Everywhere memories for E. and myself, everywhere destruction. E. was seeing Berlin for the first time, I for the fourth time. Chaos at Schlüterstr.

Meeting with Becker did not take place, he barely saw me. We received the programme, were assigned to the Adlon Hotel [...]. In a canteen of the large building [...] we were able to get the most meagre leftovers of a lunch for cash payment: cold fruit soup and potato salad. – Here Werner Krauss introduced himself to me, the most important acquaintanceship, actually the only new one of this trip. Mid-40s, slim, tall, boldly swept back dark blond mane of hair, more artistic than scholarly type. From his whole manner, he is the last person whom I would have expected to fail as a speaker. KPD member and cultural revolutionary. Talks with great contempt of Jan, who wrote a wretched covert and grovelling anti-Semitic Lit. Hist. [...]. Calls himself 'primo loco His-panicist'.[85] Strongly advised me against Greifswald, thinks Leipzig is my due. We talked at length at the club the following day, then in the evening sat together in the front row of speakers. [...] I have not seen him since.

From the KB we drove to the Adlon, whose ruinous condition and surrounding ruins I was already used to, but which made a very fresh and strong impression on Eva. I was greeted as an old acquaintance [...] I had [...] with me a letter from Loewenkopf to Nelhans, head of the Jewish Community, Oranienburgerstr. [...]. It turned out that instead of the man's private address Loewenkopf had given the office in the hardly damaged synagogue, and there no one opened up for us. So we made use of the late afternoon for a little walk through the immediate neighbourhood: Ziegelstr. (where Berthold tutored me in his student lodging), the River Spree, the Museum Island in the distance. Above all, the most moving impression of this trip: the *Jewish Reform Synagogue in Johannisstr.*[86] It stood – *stood* – at the back of a large courtyard. I had religious instruction in the house to the side. The house in ruins, the synagogue itself: its frontage a heap of rubble. Behind that a nothing, no roof, no wall, a surface of rubble. Beyond this nothing, there was the rear wall and a suggestion of the vaulted cupola preserved like a stage flat. In the wall the altar niche and above it two tables of the law with Hebrew lettering. I thought, how often did I see father standing there ... There was a rattling and scraping from the rubble-filled rooms beside us. After a while a man came scrambling out, an enamel sign in his hand, which he rubbed enthusiastically. Evidently a looter. He said quite unselfconsciously to us: 'You can't get something like that at all now, and it's really needed!' On the sign were the words: 'Please adjust your dress before leaving.'

[...]

On Sunday morning we stayed late at the hotel, then with Knescheke to the Komödie, a little theatre a long way down the Kurfürstendamm. Box; I dozed off and really slept. Recitations, again and again Goethe, Schiller, Hölderlin. [...] Admittedly I was very tired and pre-occupied. – We drove back to the hotel, rested a little while and then went to the club, a few yards away in Jägerstr. My knowledge of it is derived in part from stories, in part from the report in the *Tägliche Rundschau* [...]. An imposing palais-like building dating from 1892, first the club of an association of big landowners and industrialists, then (under Hitler? already before Hitler?[87] The article mentioned Papen[88] and the year 1939) the Gentlemen's Club [Herrenklub]. The hardly damaged building has been repaired. The parquet of the huge dining room – several hundred of us sat at long tables – comes from the Reichskanzlei,[89] it was said: from Ad. Hitler's rooms. The feed at 2 was substantial, but proceeded fairly stiffly. [...] Krauss sat beside me. After the dinner we sat and stood around in other rooms. ('Dinner' of course in keeping with the times: a soup, a plate of vegetables and a decent piece of meat, a little bit of jelly, a glass of schnapps and a beer. (A meal like that used to cost 60 pfennigs at the station, said E.) We went for a short walk in the neighbouring streets, we got tea and cakes at the club, later a soup for supper. Chatted to Krauss [...]

I am writing on the verandah, it is 10.30 in the morning, Saturday 13 July. E. is sleeping, *I* went for a swim early in the morning.
   [...]
Here we are *abroad*. What do *we* know about Mecklenburg-Vorpommern, about Schwerin? What do they know here about Saxony and about Dresden? And yet we are both in the Soviet Zone. What must it feel like, when one goes to the West? There is no Germany any more, only individual districts, petty states or colonies of various countries.
   Now it is certain that we are going home on Monday, our mood has improved, and we are enjoying, what there is to be enjoyed here.
   [...]

(20 July Dres.) The day [Monday 15 July] was frittered away in preparations and waiting, we did not make any more excursions. We drove off in the late afternoon – in the luxurious car of the Rostock Police Chief, Scholz, a young man, who to his driver's concern took the wheel himself and wanted to show us how well he could drive, and how fast – because who would book the chief of police? At times he went over 55 miles an hour before braking abruptly. It was not altogether safe and to the driver's sorrow wore away the most irreplaceable rubber. It had taken months of work to assemble and 'organise' the vehicle. Howitzer covers had been used for the splendid leather seats. [...]
   For the first time we had bad luck with the weather: it rained heavily. In Rostock we would have got neither lodging nor food without the Police Chief's help. Even with his help we were still in difficulties. Hotel and restaurants were allocated to us in different places and with the luggage and in the pouring rain we were dependent on ourselves and on the tram. [...] The fast train, coming from Warnemünde, left Rostock at 6.30 a.m., was due in Leipzig at about 5.30 p.m. [...]. I had sent a telegram to Trude Ö [in Leipzig] on Sunday, it was not forwarded until early on Monday, would it have reached Trude in time? [...] Trude Öhlmann was not at the station and we went off to Bussestr. feeling somewhat worried. We found her, however, well prepared. She is (at 55) more lively and youthful than I had supposed, has to her advantage become slimmer, but not skinny. She welcomed us enthusiastically, but without the anticipated hysteria. She is still hoping for the return of her [son] Claus, who was shot down and reported missing in 43 as an aircraft radio operator in the far north of Russia. – We were touchingly fed, slept on the same landing in the bedroom

of her recently widowed sister. Husband died in a POW camp. The next day, Wed. 17 July, with Trude to the Deutsche Bücherei [library], where she has now been a middle-ranking employee for exactly 25 years. The building battered, under repair, but the thing as a whole is standing nevertheless. Round about it everything is used for vegetable patches – one of them in Trude's charge. [...] Appointment by telephone with Fräulein Triepel at Teubner [publisher]. – Ate with Eva in the ratskeller. Large, well-run restaurant. This is the trade-fair town after all! [...] While E. went home, I called on Triepel at 1. The badly wrecked Teubner building in Poststr. Triepel a refined lady in her late 50s [...]. We chatted for almost 2 hours [...]. I expounded very generally my long-term plans. 1) New edition of *History of French Literature in the 19th and 20th Centuries*[90] in *one* simple volume, extended to 1945, text German and French, French quotes in the appendix: 1,000 printed pages. 2) *The 18th Century* 2 vols of 600 pp each, in German – French originals in the appendix.[91] 3) *Modern French Prose* extended to 45. [...] No binding commitment was made on either side. [...] I said, at the moment I was working with the Aufbau publishing house; but to me for my life's work Teubner was ultimately the most appropriate publishing house. – We were due to leave at 5.30, the train did not pull out until 6.30 and came to a halt x times afterwards; it was due at Neustädter station at 8.30, it arrived towards 10, then there was a fight at the left luggage office [...]. Finally we did manage to catch the last tram. We arrived up here exhausted and woke up Frau Rasch with our knocking. And so that was on the evening of 17 July.

20th July 1946, Saturday afternoon. Dresden

The lines about the return journey and *one* letter of the many to be written, is all that I have been able to manage thus far. Constantly on the go in extreme mugginess, heart problems yet again. The day slips by arduously and emptily.

[...] On the 31st I am to chair a youth debate: *What is humanity?* I have been searching for suitable quotes from the classics. I have only Schiller to hand – useless. [...] Eva Blank told me, that today, 20 July, there is a big ceremony 'The new Dresden'. I did not get an invitation.

Chasing after one took up most of Friday. [...] I only had one ticket for the preceding *Magic Flute* in the Tonhalle; I gave it to Eva, whom I shall pick up there. [...]

21st July, Sunday forenoon

I got to the Tonhalle at 8.30 yesterday, to meet Eva. I was allowed into the boiling hot theatre, and from a seat at the very back saw and heard more or less the final act of the *Magic Flute* [...] Without pleasure. I find the plot, which as a whole I do not know, the mummery *and* also the music half-childish, half-childlike! Apart from that everything was all too squashed and basic, taking place on a bare stage and without the usual props and too often in darkness or gloom. Perhaps it should have been sung entirely in modern dress and without any production at all. [...]

At about 9.30 we drove with the Grubes, in the Grubes' car, to the Luisenhof. Little tables laid in several rooms for a large crowd of people [...]; only in one room a large horseshoe probably for the very top of the official tree (but Gladewitz was sitting at a little table beside us). Two official toasts then emanated from the official horseshoe, which no one in our room understood. [...] We sat with the Grubes. I made the desired contacts with many people, against all expectation I pulled some strings here and there. At our table Frau Fenske. She spent 10 years in prison, was given the death sentence, then commuted to life imprisonment, she still has a voice impairment. At the next table the Glade-witzes. Renewal of friendship, reminder of the promised suiting from Elsterberg, of the print permit. [...] Very animated, we stayed until after 3. The Grubes drove us home. To bed at 4.15 in high spirits. Thus do my moods change. Today somewhat washed out, but the high spirits remain.

28th July, Sunday morning
[...]

Session at the TH. Nothing has changed. Gehrig and Janentzky are tame and courteous to me. Gehrig desires to give a lecture in the Kulturbund. Janentzky is dropping Kühn, 'realises' ... Lends me Jan's Literature Manual, the lack of equivocation in it will finish him. [...]

I come home late and exhausted from such forenoon errands; then fall asleep over eating, then there's some visitor or some kind of distraction, and then the day is over – without *LTI*.

[...] Directly before going to the State Admin. on Wed. morning I met Dr Kretzschmar. Very agitated: his stepfather, Neumark, arrested 2 days ago – Jewish denunciation. [...] I offered my testimony. Cohn, the investigating public prosecutor, a returned émigré, had been cold and hostile. [...] I literally bumped into [Chief Public Prosecutor] Schröder. [...] He made it possible for me to meet Public Prosecutor Cohn immediately. Eloquent Jew with foreign accent (Hungarian?) suspicious, cold, guarded. About 38–40. Became more friendly, as he gradually understood my position. I explained to him psychologically, how such denunciations came to pass, how exposed the clover leaf, Katz–Neumark–Lang, was. I [...] said of Neumark: 'I vouch for him with everything, that I am and have.' Twice Cohn expressed something characteristic. Once I said: 'On my word of honour.' He: 'Also on your honour as a Communist?' – Then: I said I had formerly known no one from the Jewish community. 'You are not affiliated to any faith? – Neither am I!' (He became friendlier.) Evidently a fanatical Communist and nothing but. I to him, as already earlier to Kretzschmar: one could easily have become an anti-Semite in the Jews' House. He: one has to see it in terms of the Jews' situation. [...] During the next few days Kretzschmar came to my PHS consulting hour, and his mother called on us up here in the evening. The family is trying to find character witnesses. Nothing appears to have been achieved thus far. N. has been inside for a whole week. Frau K. is terrified (and not without reason) that he could be hanged without being guilty. President Friedrichs has refused to receive Kretzschmar, even though he knows

N. well. And Gute, when he heard of my intervention, blurted out in alarm: 'Look, be careful!' It can cost me dear.

30th July, Tuesday morning
Awkward as the Neumark affair is also that of his stepson, whom from now on I shall call New Kretzschmar, since the painter Kretzschmar has just turned up. Laux tells me that New Kretzschmar had put his foot in it with his boss Gute and so had to go. [...]
  [...]
On the forenoon of Sunday the 28th, in the hall of the Academy, a discussion on the 'Realist Conception of Art'. Frightful cliched babble of a number of speakers, obscure muddle of some replies. I sat in the front row and repeatedly nodded off, was annoyed at the waste of time and my inability to understand. [...] Then something very funny: the painter Bernhard Kretzschmar, mid-50s, pale, slim, bit mad pale blue eyes. In the discussion he had spoken passionately against 'reportage' and against 'isms'. Coming up to me: he would like to draw me, I had sat there with such 'concentration', as if the embodiment of pure intellectuality. (Comedy! *I* play the part, others fall for it: because I now have an important name, I must also be important.) Vanitas! He came to us at about 5 in the afternoon and began drawing, talking all the while about art, his unfortunate lot, his deceased wife, many pictures burnt, conflicts with colleagues. At the same time a great deal of ethics and mysticism, almost, no, truly, spiritualism. The drawing turned out very well, except I have the stooped posture of great age – he said, no, that was concentration. He now began a second drawing [...]. Meanwhile a never-ending thunderstorm with ceaseless downpours began. Of necessity Kretzschmar remained for – a very scanty – supper; he had a couple of potatoes in his bag with the painting things, he gave those to us. He spent the night in his clothes on the sofa in the lobby – we did not get to bed until 1. Next morning breakfast together – despair at every slice of bread – then Kretzschmar went off to Hanusch in Freital and I to the teachers' congress.
  [...]

5th August, Monday morning
For the first time in weeks free of the pressure of the unfinished 'German roots'; the first new part of the *LTI* since 8 June. There are so many things pulling at me, the conflict grows ever greater, the uncertainty of my position also.
  The Kulturbund evening on Wednesday 31 July turned out a great success for me. My formulation: 'Young people ask questions – young people reply in the House of the Kulturbund'. Certainly more than a 100 present. Impassioned debate. [...] Distrust of *all* contemporary solicitations and theories, of the governing party, of the Russians. ('There's a film running called *Victory over Japan*, in which it says: "now we have avenged 1905!" How is that compatible with humanitarianism, pacifism etc.??') I did not find it easy to be the diplomat.

But everything went *very* well and then when I asked, who should chair the next evening – on the theme 'culture' [...] the whole auditorium roared: 'You, you, you!' – E. was in the audience and confirmed the grand succès. The newspaper also wrote kindly about it. [...]

6th August, Tuesday

[...]

The remainder of the week aside from the two congress days was taken up with two long, well-attended and hectic consulting days at the PHS. X applicants for teaching posts. [...]

[...]

Then [yesterday evening, 5 August] Frau Jährig, formerly Neumark's secretary with whom I discussed the case. The day before, Frau Neumark had been here, very desperate and in tears, they wanted to destroy her husband. [...] Gustl Kowacz, the prison barber, brought me Neumark's greetings. N., now in solitary confinement for two weeks, had been very calm, but said to warn me to be extremely cautious.

At the congress I spoke to Donath who, if the occasion arose, would be my young man, head of department and Grützner no. 2. My programme: professor at the TH, which I shall open as a technical university, honorary professor in Leipzig, Jan ousted, temporary replacement for 6 months, then myself to Leipzig. The department responsible for the PHS, which has just passed from Gladewitz to Schneller, affiliated to me ... As I set it forth to Donath, it all looked very nice, and I felt very good about it. Later, under the impression of the thwarted Dresden candidature, I thought it all trifling and built on sand.

[...]

Frau Jährig related: her daughter, recommended by me to Sigrid Schwarz to study teaching, passed through a Russian language course of 3 or 6 months, and on the strength of that is now supposed to start teaching Russian in the autumn. It's sheer nonsense. Heinsch gave me an article from the anti-Russian and anti-Communist *Tagesspiegel* [newspaper in – West – Berlin]: mocking triumph at the failure of the schools reform in Berlin, written by a grammar-school teacher ... I preach repeatedly, we can only choose the least evil. But it is certain that matters will go wrong time after time if they are rushed or approached only from purely political perspectives.

[...]

8th August, Thursday morning

Late yesterday afternoon Eva Schulze-Knabe, the widow of the executed painter, was here. She wanted to paint me (with the bandage) after the Plievier lecture, and I have bumped into her frequently since then. She brought a request from the SED to be present during a wireless report (intellectuals – election propaganda) today. Very likeable woman, in her early forties, tall, thin, blonde, [...] absolutely natural, warm-hearted, simple. Was sentenced to life, was in

Waldheim prison for five years, [...] also knows Gusti Wieghardt. [...] E. Schulze-Knabe has long scars on her right arm and the joint is stiff, which interferes with her work. Competently operated but then brutally massaged septicaemia in the prison hospital. In general, however, she said, it had not been bad for her in prison, at any rate incomparably better (and safer) than in a camp ... work at a sewing machine ... they had always had news about the situation, newspapers from the warders, reports from prisoners working outside.

During the day yesterday read through what I've managed so far of the *LTI*, i.e. 10 out of 23 sections. Frequently tired and Eva Schulze from 6 p.m. until almost 9 (in between Kretzschmar-Neumark, whose stepfather is still inside. He talked of a rabbi [...], back from Theresienstadt in Berlin and there just sentenced to 8 years in prison, because he had assisted the Gestapo – the man was *legitimately* sentenced.) I can by no means finish the *LTI* quickly. Sometimes I believe I am completely incapable of real production. And my heart...

[...]

10th August, Saturday morning

Eva Schulze-Knabe said recently: actually she found Dresden more beautiful now than before. 'If I think of all the tenement blocks and the kitsch buildings. Now by comparison: the beautiful pink of the ruins and then the blue sky above – when I saw it for the first time, I was quite enchanted. And I like it every time I see it again.' Yet she is a warm-hearted person, a victim of Fascism, widow of an executed man...

Yesterday at the Evening Grammar School [...] After the lesson people stand around my desk for a long time, until it gets dark. I am surrounded by a cluster as far as the tram, I have to eat some of the fruit, which the Zabel orchard sisters [...] always have with them. They complain about some teachers [...], they pour out their worries to me in other respects, too. I really do believe, that the young people have taken me to their hearts. Why, only God knows. After all, I am unsystematic, assume too much knowledge, feel my way. I even tell them so, try to excuse the other teachers, try to ignore political difficulties etc. etc. They take it all in – yes, but with you it's interesting, with you we learn ... In short, just as at the Kulturbund discussion recently ... [...]

11th August, Sunday morning

Yesterday forenoon faculty meeting in the Inorganic Chemistry Institute [...] The chemist Simon is dean, Janentzky is section head. I was present for the first time. [...] It was not nice; on the one hand the uncertainty of my position, the awareness of being among enemies or at least among the distrustful [...] on the other the awareness of my perhaps-power and of my political duty. And behind all that the bitter awareness of my failing heart. I do indeed now live in a tragic state of suspense: great potential influence, satisfied vanity as to 'historic' achievement – both only perhaps, my heart is decisive and the political constellation. – Everything went well. Simon said courteously, we were entirely in agreement, the motion just passed merely stated that the Simon–Janentzky management would remain for the time being, but a Russian order had come in, requiring a steering committee to be named. [...]

Curious makeup of this faculty: Simon, a fat, jovial, *diplomatic* dean, about 50. Janentzky. Straub. Beside Straub on the settee in a white suit: Kühn. I shook hands with everyone. Only K. and I ignored one another. [...] After the meeting long conversation with Woldt.[92] Bond of friendship and party. I told him, that *I* had been proposed to head the ministerial department. That I wanted him to be dean. Already at the meeting I launched the question of the name 'Technical University'. I am obsessed by the passionate desire of myself delivering the Tech. Univ. address on the 1st of October.

12th August, early Monday
[...]

Evening
Dies ater.[93] Wildführ telephoned me at the PHS in Melanchthonstr.: the TH was plotting, Simon had told him, he [Simon] was going to be department head. We had to go to the State Administration immediately, he would pick me up in his car. [...] Saw Gute and Donath and was faced with the fait accompli that Simon had been appointed. No one had promised me anything, it was also incomprehensible, that I as an academic could have taken Fischer's 'I'll make you dean' seriously. I said: Breach of promise ... I was not going to be anyone's clown, and as soon as the pensions law was passed [...] I would retire. Gute: he could understand that. Gute and Donath cool, Wildführ, since his call to Leipzig assured, indifferent. Finally: one would see to it, that I obtained the Leipzig chair. One would see to it ... I came home feeling very bitter. [...]

Thus have I sunk back completely into nothingness.

13th August, Tuesday afternoon
In the morning the TH rector reported. The TH will be formally opened on 14 Sept. Gute is Undersecretary, quasi minister of education, culture and church affairs, Donath assistant secretary, between the two of them – not yet officially appointed, Simon. I said to Woldt: they think they have him in a pincers; he will bend the pincers. He will outmanoeuvre them. I said: everything is going the same way as 1919, they are thwarted by the high schools, by their spirit (the 3rd pillar of reaction). – The TH will train only technical-college teachers and teachers of the natural sciences. That means my chair is pointless. And I think it out of the question, that I shall receive a call from Leipzig. – All my plans and hopes shattered in a single day. I see from today's newspaper, that I am not on the list of candidates for the city council.
[...]

14th August, Wednesday morning

Woldt is a pale, slight, very old and austere-looking little man, 4 years my senior, irregular career, from the trades union movement, SPD veteran, originally appointed to the government, here he has a professorship in Gehrig's field. We got to know each other better only very recently, before yesterday's session I told him with bitterness about my defeat, he then invited me to his out-of-the-way room. (In Mommsenstr., in the former student hostel [...].) W. preached to me in cordial and paternal fashion: steer clear of all day-to-day politics. People like Schneller and the rest [...] 'red today, dead tomorrow', and none of it has any lasting value. Work in *the* field, of which one is master, write one's books in that field – only that has lasting value. He himself had started as a junior technician, then he had drawn the attention of Kautsky,[94] who had introduced him to all the important people in the [SPD] party. [...] He had spent 12 years as a very autonomous assistant secretary under the free and fine Democrat Becker[95] in the Prussian Ministry of Culture and Education. He appeared to be proudest of this period.

Very depressed all day yesterday. Teaching at the Evening Grammar School later was almost refreshing. No matter how much of my time it takes up – I again and again hesitate to finally resign from it. But perhaps because of the money, or because I am afraid of concentrated proper work? Keeping oneself busy is so much easier than work.

[...]

16th August, Friday morning

[...]

At last a letter from Gusti Wieghardt – one letter appears to have gone missing or is still en route. Very cordial, but she cannot come, she wants to visit her very sick sister, Maria Strindberg,[96] in Stockholm, she has to see to her son Karl,[97] who is without a post [...].

18th August, Sunday forenoon

Yesterday or rather today I got to bed at 2: Humanism and Kulturbund article for the *Tägliche Rundschau* newspaper finished. In the morning and into the afternoon, I was with Kneschke in Schillerstr. (Kulturbund) where we dealt with quite a lot. [...] As I was on my way out I bumped into a fat, grey-haired lady – Eva Büttner,[98] cf of the diary of the time of trouble, the death by cancer of her husband, her feigned suicide, which we believed. Very tumultuous greeting, soon the familiar 'Du'. She is in charge of culture in Kamenz district, came to ask me for 2 lectures, in Kamenz and Grossröhrsdorf. Immediately there was also contact with Piskowitz (Agnes), promise of help with potatoes. Then we drove up here in her tiny car. Greeting with Eva. Everything full of enthusiasm and emotion and promises and shared politics – she, too, is for a radical course in the universities and is taken aback by Gute's giving way. [...]

21st August, minuit Wednesday

I worked all day on the 'Literature and Politics' lecture, which I then gave for the Intellectuals' Evening of the SED in the Luisenhof. Car with nice comrades picked me up, E. came with me. The elegant restaurant by the cable railway with the wonderful view of the Elbe and the city. The sun was just setting and the destruction was not particularly noticeable. [...] The lecture, swiftly put together from the most modest materials, was good.

But unfortunately a whole day and probably several days to come soured by a long letter from Georg. I should immediately refrain from all public appearances, restrict myself to the TH chair, rest a great deal, walk and climb stairs very little or I was a goner. So says Georg, the specialist in angina. Furthermore no Kulturbund and no appearances by a Semite were of any use. Germany could only be saved by a statesman, otherwise it would be completely destroyed in the '3rd Punic War'.[99] What was the point of G. writing me that? I already have one foot in the grave anyway.

[...]

22nd August, Thursday morning

[...]

In recent days I was so overwhelmed with work, that I am hardly able to reconstruct them.

The Sunday with the anticipated visit by Frau Jährig was very boring. After Frau Neumark was also here on Monday, I have a very gloomy view of the N. affair. Russian viewpoint: the law 'Crimes against humanity' also applies to *him*, who acted under orders, he should have refused to carry out inhuman orders. In Neumark's case: on Gestapo orders he had drawn up lists of 'isolated privileged' Jews to be deported. (I.e. of Jews protected by Aryan marriages, but recently widowed or living separately, or who enjoyed protection because of Aryan children *under* 16 years of age and living in the family home, and now the children were over 16 or no longer at home.) Without Neumark's help the Gestapo *might* have overlooked this or that person. Ergo he was a guilty accomplice. In Berlin a number of Jews had already 'disappeared' months ago because of similar accusations. Among them admittedly '*bloodhounds*', i.e. Jews who had to cordon off streets during raids. [...]

28th August, Wednesday afternoon

[...]

The Sunday (25 Aug.) was interesting. Although I once again felt ashamed at the narrowness of my own field, that I understand nothing at all of art and music. Very solemn inauguration of the First General German Art Exhibition.[100] 5th Symphony by Shostakovich. Again and again I sensed great beauty – but to follow the whole thing, to grasp its coherence? Impossible! Dejected boredom, thoughts wandering. Afterwards many speeches. [...] Going round later was no pleasure. A lot of Expressionism and Cubism of the 20s. I get nothing from it.

[...] Then bumped into Eva Büttner and again warmest greeting. At the last moment I learned of a Russian invitation for the VIPs and got hold of a second card for E. – Schloss Wachwitz, a princely villa built in 1938 for a Prince Heinrich. The 18 to Calberlastr., then up the hill on foot. My poor heart, constant memento. Together with a number of painters – while big guzzling government cars rolled past. Finally a Russian car stopped for us. The guests stood on the terrace behind the house for a long time and had a splendid view of the Elbe and the city and the chain of hills beyond [...]. Finally, it was probably already 9, called in to dinner. Large table in a main room, small tables in an impressive side room. We sat in the sideroom with a couple of painters; which was no bad thing. Great elegance. The table covered with hors d'oeuvres – caviar, small fishes, eggs, sausage, tomatoes, plenty of butter, unlimited white bread. A paradise. (Povera Germania.[101]) A Russian maître d'hôtel or Armenian headwaiter, fat, in uniform, a slim Russian Armenian lady, black dress, oldish, dignified, expensive bracelets, demonic, theatrical; German waiters, no wine, no beer – only large quantities of schnapps: vodka bottles, liqueur bottles. Heidebroek had warned me: strict custom to empty a full glass at each toast. One had to secretly pour some of it into a vase under the table ... The toasts, Russian and German, resounded incomprehensibly from the next room, at our table we were entirely German [...]. After the meal, informal socialising. I made contact with various people. [...] I would say: the external mechanism of my existence was lubricated a little again ... After 12 Gute made sure, that a car took us home. Naturally I slept badly and my heart was again overtaxed.

Since yesterday I have a telephone.

[...]

1st September, Sunday evening

Trip to Kamenz, 3 p.m. Saturday–6 p.m. Sunday.

Very exhausted at the moment and that casts a shadow over everything. In fact this trip was very nice and very successful – only at the very end there were two annoyances, whose effects continue to be felt.

2nd September, Monday

The lecture itself, in the hall of the Lessing School, about one third full, 120 people I was told – Kamenz has 13,000 inhabitants and there were political meetings at the same time. Posters had been put up for me as for a circus: 'Meeting. Subject: The Kulturbund and the Local Elections. Speaker Herr Professor Dr Klemperer of Dresden TH and the University of Leipzig, Director of the People's High Schools (plural! and Leipzig as well!) Followed by Discussion! Organisers Hermann Grafe, chairman of the Kamenz Group, District Administrator, Eva Büttner, Department of Culture.' I spoke about culture and humanism. – [...] Discussion immediately turned not to me but to the local election campaign. A youthful lady accused the 'only true church', the SED, of unfair personal attacks, Eva Büttner replied sharply, and so it went back and forth for a while. A gentleman at the very rear stood up: the speaker knew him and would confirm his humaneness, he simply wanted to plead for fairness all round. I asked who he was, I could not make out his face – Schlüter, tea manufacturer, now settled here. I expressed my warm gratitude to him, spoke appeasingly to the embittered lady, poured oil on the waves. The evening ended well. The lady and Schlüter came up to me and were very friendly. She a student of Romance languages, wife of a pastor [...]. Earlier at Eva Büttner's. An old, chaotically built house near the market; both Kulturbund office and E.B.'s private apartment. Beautiful rooms with many art objects, pieces of furniture, paintings. Most inherited [...]. Very great warmth, obligingness, flattery, even more so after the success of the evening: I should be in charge of the Saxon KB, should be in the Saxon parliament etc. etc. ... What is left of all of that today, after the election defeat, was left of it yesterday, when I asked for help for Agnes against the mayor of Piskowitz? Oh politics! – [...] Not back until 2. The market floodlit, big red banners everywhere, instead of the swastika a white 1 (list 1, SED!) in the middle. The police station open. They had the front-door key for our hotel, and a policeman – a comrade – took us across to the hotel and opened up for us. The next morning our first pleasure was the red banner without, *without* a swastika. A brass band began to play in front of the town hall, it was followed by agreeable choral singing, the election began solemnly. – We breakfasted with Eva B., she then had us driven to Piskowitz. We found our Agnes very wretchedly accommodated in the wooden huts of the former girls' land-labour camp. But the food was as abundant as in 45 during our flight, rabbit and cakes – we were also able to hoard all kinds of foodstuffs, even butter. Jurik and Marka and Agnes herself had changed little. Their farmstead was shot to pieces and is not one of those, which is being rebuilt. She complained that she was a poor widow, Hanski, the new mayor, didn't help her, only people with connections or who could grease hands counted – apart from rebuilding the house there is also a cow and a cart at issue. Krahl, the former mayor, who as a pg spent 13 weeks in a Russian camp, is back on his farm, was well-disposed to her, but unable to help. I talked to Krahl, I called on the mayor. His attitude was quite negative. I turned bloody rude, threatened to call District Administrator and government down on him, it was his duty to see first of all to those who had helped anti-Fascists. – Afterwards Eva B., with a laugh at once irritated and pitying, told me that I did not have a clue about local politics, the mayor, no doubt elected and confirmed on the ticket of the non-partisan Association for Farmers' Mutual Aid,[102] was master of the situation, the District Administrator would not lift a finger against him, it was natural that the mayor would first of all help his supporters ... The business rankles very greatly in me and is a personal defeat. – Agnes also related very matter-of-factly and without making a fuss of it – she did not mention the word 'rape' – [that the women] had to sleep with the first Russians to arrive, she too -'what could one do, he put down his rifle, the children were there, I had to go outside with him, the only good thing is that nothing came of it!' – later, however, the Russians had been very friendly and helpful. [...]

At 5 p.m. we were back in Dresden.

[...]

2nd September, Monday evening

Today has been overshadowed by the election result, which only leaked out very late and slowly.[103] (Yesterday evening and this morning I waited in vain at the wireless), I also asked and puzzled over it down at the newspaper kiosk at 8, there was nothing more than a printed note from Freital. That, of course, is red, 15,000 votes out 25,000 for the SED, but there was already talk of results in Dresden which were the opposite. After that I heard at the broadcasting building, that overall in Saxony the SED had barely managed 50%, therefore is everywhere dependent on coalitions with the bloc parties. That means my Leipzig plans will come to nothing. Now the SED will be *even more* timid and do nothing, absolutely nothing about the arrogance of the academy.

[...]

A great deal of correspondence is piling up, which I shall have to answer at some point. Today there arrived letters from: Frau Vossler [...]. He, Vossler, has already resigned from the rectorship again – too much trouble.

[...]

From Frau Dember, whom Wunderwald wrote that we are here again. She is living happily in New York, has 3 grandsons, two by Emita, 1 by her son.

A touching little packet from Frau Stühler in Munich.

6th September, Friday

[...]

At the TH session on Tue. 3 Aug. I moved that Vossler's 'honorary doctorate be revived'. I dictated an appropriate letter of proposal for Simon and Janentzky to Mey over the telephone. – I discussed my intention of standing for the Saxon parliament with Woldt. [...]

[...] What is the point of it all? My life is draining away ... And even these notes here – who will make use of them? Eva says, *she* is not capable of it. [...]

Most interesting recent letters: from Berthold Meyerhof (in most straitened circumstances in New York; brewery employee, his wife works at home as a seamstress. Hans Meyerhof lives in Palermo); from Doris Machol, daughter of Heinz († in a concentration camp) and his first wife, the Austrian Communist,[104] who visited us in Holbeinstr. in the 20s. There will no doubt be more to be said about that. I answered the girl's letter at length, since it sounds very likeable. Painting student, returning from French emigration, resident in Berlin, mother † January 46 in Nice. D. asks about her grandmother Hedwig, whose picture had 'impressed' her; she had heard vague things about us from her mother; now she asks whether the author of 'Plievier–Barbusse' is the Klemperer who is one of her relatives. The letter sounds honestly interested. Or is it merely looking for a contact? I am so mistrustful. But I replied very warmly.

[...]

7th September, Saturday morning

Two young Party officials, with some such post as youth leader, complained to Eva Blank and myself at a long meeting (in Melanchthonstr.), that our discussions with the youth organisation had been too bourgeois, too historical, *too unpolitical*, too unsocialist. We tried to convince them, how *unpolitical* any other approach would be in the Kulturbund. We advised them: send us people from *your* workers' and elementary school circles. There was talk of 'young people' joining the LDP en masse, which acts as if it is the inheritor of and has the monopoly on the German Classical tradition. I talked about my experiences at the Evening Grammar School. One person has been through the Hitler schools, another comes back from the war and now feels himself disregarded and devalued.

10th September, Tuesday afternoon

[...]

Evening, 11 p.m.

[...] On Mon. morning I took part in a section meeting for the first time in 10 years. Janentzky chaired, present were the completely bent, apathetically quiet Hassert, old Woldt, the dwarf Kühn and Straub, who as dean of the coming Education Faculty, dominated. Janentzky depressed – checkmated like the whole Cultural Sciences Section. Since only vocational-school teachers are to be taught here, we, the pure humanities men, are unnecessary. [...] I requested very forcefully, that my motion for the renewal of Vossler's honorary doctorate be speedily approved by the Senate. No one could very well oppose me. Woldt to me after the meeting: why was I pursuing Kühn; his fall would harm me and it did seem a case of a personal feud with a harmless man! I responded simply: 'and *you*, a fellow party member, say that to me!' ... Besides Kühn will keep his post just like von Jan.

Yesterday the section 'If two people do the same thing' finally completed, no not until today.

12th September, Thursday afternoon

Yesterday devoted essentially to preparation of the evening lecture to the Free Youth: 'Youth and Scholarship'. Half of it was the talk National Socialism and Scholarship, half really new. Appeal to youth: You have the opportunity presented by new conditions, the adventure of creating something new! Cautiously against sport. [...] A success nevertheless [although] there were far too few people in the large hall, perhaps a 100. But they really were young people, and I spoke to them as a fatherly teacher. [...]

15th September, Sunday
[...]

After minuit[105]

I lost the whole afternoon sitting for an oil painting by the crumpled Arthur Rudolph;[106] the painting was less than half finished, but it will be good. He himself talks very disparagingly about all his colleagues; his fat wife, who feeds him, makes a very good-natured and robust impression and speaks of him with the most tender respect. During the war she was a waitress, she has now leased land and grows vegetables. Lewinsky was there at the same time, unchanged. I had to translate a registry office attestation into French for him, which proves that his son, held in France as a prisoner of war, is of Jewish descent. This task, with its specialist terms has kept me busy just now from about 10 p.m. until almost midnight. Awful, my linguistic ignorance.

[...]

27th September, Friday
[...]

The *Bohème* evening as conclusion of the Technical High School festival was very fine. Mimi rather too large and robustly healthy in appearance. Astonishing what can be done with the small stage. The action spills down the side stairs into the auditorium itself. Melancholy memories: I saw *La Bohème* in 1902 and 1903 in Geneva and Paris. Gehrig sat behind me, old, shaky, still the same old 'sly dog' – Christmas Eve in French was not called réveillon, he was very sure of that – what he did not know, is that his chair is threatened. What I did not know, is that mine is threatened also. (Donath yesterday: the three chairs: Janentzky, Gehrig, yours are superfluous, you have not been incorporated in the Education Faculty, are just being carried by the Russians ... But you have been taken care of, we have secured your position, you will get your money, even if you do nothing at all ... etc. etc.) ...

On the morning of this High School festival, Kretzschmar-Neumark, whom I had telephoned the evening before, called. N. had passed a message on to me through barber Gustl: he asked for bread and a winter coat, he was so hungry and cold. He had now received the indictment – crime against humanity, by drawing up a deportation list – he believes conviction is certain ... Nothing more is known; help impossible. – Altogether similar the case of Schmidt, our neighbour, who was a tax inspector in the Ukraine. He has been inside for a month. The family in deep distress. Traute S., who is about to take her school-leaving certificate, is painting lampshades. Günther S. sees his 3rd semester as a medical student in Jena at risk, because the most recent questionnaire includes the question: 'Is any member of your family in prison?' Yesterday Günther came to see me before leaving for Jena. I could *not* advise him to answer the question in the negative.

[...]

On Sunday 22, the *Day of Commemoration for the Victims of Fascism* I had been due to speak about 'Heroism' in Kamenz. We were both invited, were looking forward to it, were looking forward to prospects of potatoes. At the last moment Eva Büttner telephoned to cancel, the meeting had fallen through. – Instead we took part in commemorations here. [...] Then in the evening, it was a great rush and a bravura feat for us, we got back from the Tonhalle at 6, ate quickly and departed again – big celebration in the Constantia, a huge suburban ballroom in Cotta [...]. A poor concert, a wildly shouted, very revolutionary speech by Gladewitz – the people of the Spanish International Brigades, the people from the concentration camps should determine the politics of Germany – conclusion [...] To the dead the laurels etc.[107] After that a one-act play by Bert Brecht, with whose work I had thus far been unfamiliar: *Senora Carrar's Rifles.*[108] [...] The woman has lost her husband through politics. She does not want to give up her two sons, nor her husband's weapons, which are still in the house. Outside there is the battle against Franco's troops, who are breaking through. Neither the woman's brother, nor the one son who is present are able to persuade her. [...] Then, despite his non-involvement one of the sons is shot. And now the mother not only hands over the rifles, but arms herself and goes to the front as well ... Was it my tiredness? I found the play sluggish and monotonous, nodded off a couple of times and on waking did not feel that I had missed anything. [...]

Today, it is now almost 8 p.m., I have devoted all my free time to the diary – one should never ask, what the point of it is. In the morning in a conversation with E. resolved on a stubborn course and a provisional resignation – is there a 'later' for me? [...]

The Soviet News Agency asked me by telephone for a statement on Stalin's Peace Declaration. I said the usual approving words.

[...]

There are letters to be answered from: Georg, Martha, Walter Jelski,[109] Doris Machol, Anny Klemperer, Hilde Jonson, Berthold Meyerhof, Schaps, Gusti, Helene Ahrens[110] (turned up in Quakenbrück). In addition letter to Vossler. That makes a dozen. And Stühlers, Munich, as nr 13.

29th September, Sunday evening

[...]

After one and half days of despair and inability to progress I finally got into my stride again with the *LTI* article 'Europa', which I have already twice interrupted. It is now called 'Cafe Europe', and I immediately want to follow it with the Jewish theme as a whole.

[...]

1st October, Tuesday night

Two days of meetings. Yesterday morning to Party headquarters in considerable suspense. Invited by telephone, taken there by car. Disappointment on arriving.

Meeting of the culture section, chaired, however, by Koenen[111] and Buchwitz, whom I saw for the first time, and with the participation of prominent Party figures. Koenen, seen only from afar, tall, thin, dark full beard, somewhat fanatical schoolmaster's face; Buchwitz grey-haired, likeable. Everyone, especially Comrade *Undersecretary* Gute (promoted a few days ago) spoke about the necessity of carrying on cultural propaganda, of winning the intelligentsia for the Party and of bringing the workers to the intelligentsia. I learned immediately, however, that I was not on the Party list [i.e. for the election to the parliament of Saxony]. Afterwards I approached Buchwitz and requested not to be separated from the Party. He said, he was pleased at my wish, I was valued, and shook my hand; he would take a look at the list. However, I remained stuck on the Kulturbund list, and the SED list does not have a single intellectual in the first 50 places, some technical professor from Freiberg excepted [. . .] Becher and Gysi and Gute turned up for [the meeting], in addition, as chairman, Menke-Glückert, who has been isolated, behind whom there is now only the LDP, and against whom there is involvement in some Nazi publication or other. [A decision was made in favour of a separate Kulturbund list, the SED having outvoted the other parties. A second meeting was agreed for the afternoon.] This morning at the TH nothing particularly new; Kühn, who was not invited to the gala dinner and was thought to be finished, was again sitting with the professors comme si de rien n'était. [. . .] Finally a list was ready. 1. Prof. Menz, independent, journalism, Leipzig. 2. myself. A dozen further names – I am not yet convinced that this will be the end of the matter.

[. . .]

2nd October, midday Wednesday
Yesterday evening Gustl, the prison barber, was here for a while – Neumark needs his spectacles repaired and food. [. . .]

Today Mannhart, Hamburg, sent back my article 'What do we know about France?' It was too negative and 'too journalistic' for the publishing house's scholarly referees. I shall give the messieurs the necessary reply. [. . .]

3rd October, Thursday evening
Yesterday afternoon long People's High School session: Dölitzsch, advisory board, Wolfgang Schumann. Old stories. The final resignation was not easy for me. Schumann will probably be my successor.

This morning excitement on the telephone with Kneschke, at home with Eva Blank, who was rushing from one place to the next. After Menz was moved down the list for some reason, my non-Party technician colleague, Reingruber, who has already been elected to the city council as an independent, but is 'close' to the SED, has been placed at the top of the Kulturbund list. I felt that was a demotion and threatened to resign. But of course myself took the threat only a quarter seriously and still felt flattered by my place second from the top ... I think it almost impossible for the Kulturbund to really get two candidates through (for which it needs 50–60,000 votes!). Nevertheless the next 3 weeks will flatter my vanity. In the afternoon to Arthur Rudolph in Krenkelstr. He had turned his apartment into an art exhibition; masses of pictures everywhere, also stacks of water colours and drawings. Every kind of motif: Portraits, landscapes, compositions [...] every style, Symbolism, Expressionism, Naturalism.I understand nothing, let E. do the talking. [...] I liked a very large not yet completely finished still life: *Blue Jug with Sunflowers*. Its colours magnificent beside the inconspicuous model. It is supposed to cost 6,000M. Then a very bright water colour: *Sea and Sky in Sweden*. Perhaps I shall give it to E. as a present (400–600M). I myself shall never understand why one puts up pictures. – Two drawings of me, done at the beginning of the 20s. Soft, smooth, chubby, smiling good-humouredly, black hair! [...]

7th October, Monday forenoon

On Friday 4 Oct. there was a long faculty meeting at the TH [...] The Cultural Sciences Section (or 'Group') under Janentzky is suspended in mid-air without any purpose whatsoever. [...] officially [...] we are not on the timetable and therefore non-existent ... Kühn was present. Likewise Simon, who has been appointed an undersecretary, but remains professor. He to me: 'Will you authorise me, to say to Gute and Donath, that you would be willing to see Kühn employed as a librarian or at an academy?' I: 'I have requested that a 100×. K. is neither a Nazi nor a bad man – only he must not be allowed to instruct teachers.' [...] The Saturday turns out to be the worst black day for me since the beginning of the new age. I already had a foreboding of calamity, when E. Blank telephoned me on Friday, Comrade Koenen wanted to speak to me. Then on Saturday morning I heard from Kneschke, the list had been altered again, I would get 'an equivalent'. I was with Koenen at 1.30 [...]. Very friendly reception, cigar, man-of-the-world – yet altogether negative. [...] It had been necessary to take the Leipzig people into consideration, hence give precisely my place to someone else, because after all I was a fellow party member, and the interests of the Party required ... I: I felt offended by the Kulturbund, and would resign my chairmanship. K: he could not understand that, it was a question of a very natural acceptance of a Party instruction, it was nothing to do with the KB. Apart from that, I was to be professor in Leipzig and probably also dean – Fischer had told him, Koenen, so 'only the day before yesterday and with the greatest certainty'. I (with some bitterness), that was presumably intended to sugar the pill, but it had been promised me too often and for too long, for me still to believe in it, I thought very highly of Comrade Vice-President Fischer, who was a very well-meaning gentleman, but he did not quite understand how universities worked. We went on talking back and forth in friendly fashion, it did not lead anywhere. Koenen graciously: I must keep on giving talks, the workers enjoyed listening to me. [...] All day Saturday I suffered increasingly from serious heart problems. [...] Then at about 2 the Rudolphs appeared, the painting began [...]. The afternoon was quite nice, but nevertheless time-consuming and tiring. The portrait, head almost finished, will be very good.

Since R. presented me with a water colour (marine view) and the two drawings of me (from the 20s), I felt bound to buy something from him: another water colour (*Saxon Switzerland*) for 300M. No doubt it had to be (and the *Tägliche Rundschau* recently sent me 250 for the *LTI* article).

[...]

9th October, Wednesday evening

In Naples in 1914–15 I often heard: each person says of his giornale 'è pagato',[112] and yet the press has an effect. Thus I tell myself: I know how these ovations happen, how little sincerity there is behind them, how brief the fame they provide. And yet the comically conventional business of this 65th birthday did me a great deal of good. – Baskets of flowers, official congratulations in the shape of speeches, printed addresses from the State Administration, signed by Gute, from the SED, signed by Grotewohl, Buchwitz, Koenen, from the Schools and Culture Department and from the People's High School, signed by Döl-itzsch; little article and photo in the *Sächsische Zeitung* newspaper. I am 'the great scholar', the 'authoritative Romance scholar and teacher famous beyond the borders of Germany' (State Administration), the fighter for ... etc. etc. It goes down smoothly yet tastes bitter-sweet after the failures with respect to the Saxon Parliament and Leipzig and with the angina death sentence in my pocket. – The congratulations of the SMA, conveyed by First Lieutenant Kochi-kov (or something like it), were very nice. He was already here yesterday evening with his Major Ausländer – while we were in the Academy. He came again this morning. Pale, blond, very tubercular looking man, is said to be a professor of music. Broken but educated German. I talked to him about the Nazism which persisted among young people. He: Here in Germany old age appeared to be more progressive than youth. I: there were very good reasons for that. At the beginning of the conversation he had conveyed the congratulations of the SMA. At the end I solemnly said to him: I stand with all my heart and with gratitude by Soviet Russia. – Then he had his chauffeur carry in: 3 bottles of spirit, a $2\frac{1}{2}$ lb lump of beef, a month's ration – (povera Germania!), a large bag of sugar, 2 lbs of butter and something like 10 lbs of white flour. – That is the most significant yield of the day, and there were also 240 cigarettes in the Soviet gift. – And visits and telephone calls all day long. Eva Blank with magnificent, most sumptuous roses from the Kulturbund. She organised the visit and the presents from the Russians. She also brought the agenda for tomorrow: the greeting by the Russian State Choir. [...]

14th October, Monday forenoon

Terribly worn out, terrible chaos with a constantly changing programme – there will be no improvement before the 20th (the election). Standing out from the chaos: the two Russian addresses, foolishly enough accompanied by pal-pitations, the Russian choir and – above all – brother and sister Doris and Ernst

Machol, a human find and an addition to the family. I must try to turn headings into entries.

[...]

15th October, Tuesday

[...]

At 2 in the afternoon in the Tonhalle a concert by the Kreuzchor [choir] under Prof. Mauersberger (looks like a schoolmaster), I did not quite understand the enthusiasm of the audience. Droll, when during the applause, at a nod from the professor, two little fellows stepped forward martially and bowed like synchronised automatons. After that the addresses with interpreters. The audience was on its feet, the film camera whirred, the light was blinding. First Gute, who presented a picture, Dresden in days gone by, then Weidauer, who read a long ms, then myself with palpitating heart [...]. In the evening in the Nordhalle the [Russian] choir. Wonderful. Tremendously theatrical. At times literally scenes of dispute, real drama. Then again the choir treated like an instrument. The rasping of the basses. The grotesquely rounded mouth, the mask-like face of the deepest bass. 120 singers. Two rows of women, 2 rows of men. A kind of uniform. The women in long white gowns with identical embroidery strips in tomato-red and gold. The men in Russian blouses with corresponding stripes and edging at the neck ... We sat in the places of honour of the notables, and everyone important, Friedrichs the president included, shook my hand. But afterwards great and small drove home in their cars – and we walked to the tram and I was deflated. [...]

16th October, Wednesday

[...] From Saturday evening until Monday morning the 14th – they telephoned at 11 a.m., I brought them up here from the no. 22 tram stop at midnight – we were occupied in an exhausting but most delightful way (see below) with brother and sister Ernst and Doris Machol. On Monday evening, in Freital, I spoke after Becher. (Lecture on Personality with Montesquieu at the centre.) That day E. was already ill in bed. She feels better today, but far from recovered. In Freital audience of more than 200. Despite Becher and despite philosophical difficulty of my thing *very* loud applause. – On the afternoon of Tue. 15 Becher read exactly the same piece about idealism, Kulturbund etc. in the wonderful huge Chemistry lecture theatre of the TH. His key sentence: '*We do not write anyone off.*' Mushy conciliatoriness towards the West, towards the pg's, towards Gerhart Hauptmann, towards everyone. Tepidness as principle. I got more from private conversation with him – in the car (he picked me up 2×), while eating potato salad with him afterwards – than from the piece [...]. I had to open the meeting in the [TH] amphitheatre, because – Tobler, together with Kühn has been abruptly dismissed. In some palace or other, Gute told me brusquely, a letter had been found in which he prostitutes himself to the NSDAP. Tobler was in fact present and I had a friendly conversation with him about his prospects in Munich, and I recommended him to Vossler ... After Heidebroek's greeting as host, my 10 words and Becher's lecture [...]. After we had got the lecture behind us – it was wretchedly cold – I loitered in the corridor with Becher. Simon, now department head in the ministry, came up to us, we should discuss things in his room and warm ourselves. A wonderful warm office and living room [...] a schnapps, a cigar. It was very interesting for me. In 2 respects. a) Becher. our list should have been: Gadamer, Litt, Ramin.[113] The Kulturbund must not be politically radical. He, Becher, had joined the Party, when it had great personalities, Liebknecht, Luxemburg etc., he was staying in it 'despite Koenen'. [...] I told Simon [...] how matters stand in the Jan affair. He is cautious and appears to be a little afraid of me. He is tremendously nice and is in many respects essentially closer to me than 'my' party. But he and Becher always have an eye to the West. 'Gadamer has threatened to go to Heidelberg!' says Becher. Awkward situation for me, and I shall end up falling between all stools.

[...]

Doris and Ernst Machol 26 and 25 years of age. The boy grew up with his father. [...] Then to his mother. Doris with her. Into exile at 13 years of age. Spain. Doris a good friend of Richard Gladewitz [...]. Spoke to him on the telephone ... France. Knowledge of French, Spanish, English. The boy in a hotel school, then sometimes a page, sometimes a cook, sometimes what do I know. In French-German camps and prisons. Now she had just been licensed by the ADN News Agency. In this position she attended the whole of the Nürnberg trial. (Just now on the wireless: sentences carried out at 2 a.m. this morning; Goering committed suicide beforehand – cyanide.) Doris says: Goering's defence of himself had been more than a match for the court, he had completely crushed Jackson, the American prosecutor. An aura of independence, ability, adventurousness around both Machols. Certainly also idealism. Especially around Doris. Curious figure. Small lively indefinable half-dark eyes, huge fuzzy head of hair. She lives with 'Mackie' – Max – Kahane,[114] 35, chief editor of the same agency, fought in Spain and France, separated but not divorced from his wife who has disappeared to Palestine, child of petty bourgeois Jewish parents from Kiev. – Ernst M. Jewish-looking, somewhat thick lips and hair, spectacles, both brother and sister have very protruding upper teeth. I thought I could recognise a picture of the late mother taken in Nice at the beginning of this year. She was in fact of North German peasant origin, but, as Doris said, not quite as Nordic as was claimed. The pretty story about the 'rabbit'. Doris related: Once in the camp she had a fit of weeping, and an otherwise brutal SS doctor had given her medicine and spoken words of encouragement: 'You are a white rabbit with black patches, your children will only have little black spots, and your grandchildren's fur will be completely white!'

[...]

23rd October, Wednesday morning

On Monday 21 there was a meeting of faculty [. . .] at which the rector reported. [. . .] Outcome: there is absolutely no place for me in the present Education Faculty. The Russians are turning the TH more or less into a *school* (not *high* school) as with the People's High School.

24th October, Thursday evening

Light cut off for hours at a time (today from 5.30–9.45 p.m.), plus frost and lack of heating are the latest misfortune.

Slow progress on the 'Juda' chapter.

[. . .] Frau Neumark and Kretzschmar called on me in utter despair: N. has been transferred to a camp, no one knows why and where. I am supposed to help find out, have no possibility of doing so and am now held to be cowardly and disloyal.

My colleague Frieser, successor of photography-Luther at the TH, music-making friend of Grube – forever owing us a visit, otherwise courteous – has been shipped without warning – the order came in the morning, departure took place at 5 p.m. – to Russia for 5 years with his family and all his household effects.[115]

No progress in the Leipzig affair. Yesterday to see Donath. Now Gute-Donath think the Berlin Central Administration, Rompe above all, must press Leipzig, because Leipzig's independence must not be infringed upon. Not even after our election victory on Sunday. (Of 120 seats: 59 SED, 2 Farmers' Aid, 1 Kulturbund, Reingruber = 62 SED seats.)

[. . .]

27th October, Sunday morning

What happened on Thurs. Fri. and Saturday morning? I do not know. A sign that I have at last plunged into the *LTI* once again. Naturally there is no shortage of errands, correspondence, impediments of every kind – but none of it sticks in my mind. I am breaking the big chapter 'Juda' into smaller parts. [. . .]

Yesterday afternoon tea reception as prelude to the Artists' Congress.

Evening

The reception yesterday, of the kind I am by now familiar with. In the Nordhalle long tables, two little pieces of cake at each place, tea is served with them, this time even real and sweetened tea. A band plays. Then one wanders around, shows one's face, chats, talks *business*. [. . .]

Two forenoon hours, from 9.30–11.30, in the Nordhalle again. Fischer spoke first, the usual stuff about German unity. Then a Russian colonel from Berlin, Tulpanov or something like it.[116] In very broken German, but good content. Very sharp against reactionary forces (Berlin election![117]), almost threatening, very emphatically praising *free* Soviet democracy and its attitude to culture. Then a representative from the Department of Popular Education [. . .]. Finally as the actual main speaker Gute on the 'Conditions and Experiences of the

General German Art Exhibition'. (Of which I now possess a fine catalogue, and which I have never really seen, because each time I went I had to talk to x people. And I also felt, as so often, incapable of absorbing such a collection.) Gute reported the very interesting statistical result of a questionnaire. Of 73,000 visitors, 65% disapproved of the exhibition, apart from 2% who were rude about it. The greatest approval was on the part of housewives and young girls. Expressionism and abstract painting are without exception disliked. Gute did *not* come out in favour of them, but on the one hand of the absolute freedom of art, on the other of its closeness to the people. Used the phrase 'art a social function' and the like a great deal. [. . .] Once again I was together with all kinds of people: Grundig, Winde, Grohmann etc. Trifles, but I pick up this and that . . .

At home, as arranged, I found the Neumarks and Gustl, the prison barber. He was to confirm to them, that there really is no way of getting through to the Russian Military Court and to the Russian police. (They always think I could help them in some way, and everyone advises me to be careful.) Gustl has meanwhile heard that N. has not been put in a camp at all, but in the gaol at Münchener Platz. That means that he is still subject to legal proceedings, and that again, that he will probably be released.

Then again, for the fourth time! Arthur Rudolph and wife, tormenting sitting until about 5.30. The picture will be very good, but it takes up far too much time.

Hardly had the Rudolphs gone, than the light was once again taken away for an hour. [. . .]

Now I am relieved of the PHS and yet the LTI is still not making any headway. And the mountain of arrears of correspondence is piling up instead of diminishing. It is about 11 p.m., I want at least to knock off a little correspondence now.

31st October, 1 a.m. Thursday night

[. . .]

Heart problems, rheumatism, inoculation against the everlasting furuncular leprosy. Relaxation and falling asleep while sitting. Correspondence and the usual tangle of distractions. For all that immersed in the *LTI*. 'The Jewish war' has just been completed. – Dost, at whose Blasewitz secondary school I bought books for the Romance department, told me yesterday articles on the 'Language of the Beast'[118] were appearing regularly in a Western newspaper. [. . .] That worries me. I know that my *LTI* will be like nothing else; but I fear, that it will no longer be topical and perhaps even not be published. Progress is too slow.

[. . .]

4th November, Monday evening

Friday, as far as I remember, was for once entirely devoted to the *LTI*. 'The Jewish spectacles'. I have meanwhile received the contract and have undertaken to deliver the remainder in 4–5 weeks.

[...] At about 5 p.m. agitated telephone call from Eva Blank and Egon Rentzsch: in the evening Kneschke was due to speak to the Aue KB on 'Tasks and Goals of the Kulturbund': I must go and speak in his place. In fact, I did do so. The car left here at 5.30 – 72 miles to Aue by way of Chemnitz. There at 7.45.

6th November, midday Wednesday

[...] Our life has meanwhile taken a serious new turn; it is as if E. begrudged me my angina and my expectancy of death; since Monday I know that she herself is threatened by cancer. That in her stoicism she has known it since the summer, without telling me, without doing anything about it. Recently her dropped stomach has been bothering her again, she wanted to be examined in Pirna, the Wolffs drove us there on the afternoon of the day before yesterday [...] and the outcome of the examination there was an urgent recommendation to Dr Fritz, senior physician in the surgery and x-ray department of the Johannstädter Hospital. His decision this morning: radiation treatment 4× a week for 4 weeks, then operation to remove possibly only the small tumour on the right breast, possibly the whole breast. It is not one of the fatal spots – we know of women who have had such an operation and lived for many years or are still alive – Trude Scherk died in Theresienstadt in her seventies, Trude Öhlmann is still alive; but it is a memento nevertheless, at least as dreadful as the angina and at all events E. faces some difficult weeks. [...]

The mood in Pirna was not good. Annemarie's face is very puffed-up, subordinated to Dr Dressel in altogether voluntary bondage, depressed by the expropriation and imprisonment of her brother. Dressel still not rehabilitated [...]. Annemarie to me: 'Now *you are the pg*.' Behind it is the usual: 'You behave just like the Nazis!' But 1) we do not behave like them, 2) perhaps we should behave like them, at least we should learn from them. [...] And 3) whose fault would it be if we had to do it? The curse of an evil deed! ...[119] At any rate: In Pirna we are politically among enemies. [...]

We did not see Frau Dressel; she was just giving a Bible class, she comes from a very Christian home. Dressel also inclines to the CDU. Annemarie not in any party: she had taken such a decided position against the Fascists, now she did not want to join anything at all any more.

8th November, Friday evening

Cancer weighing on my mind. In addition rheumatic pains and forever shivering with cold. In addition *LTI* at a standstill for 48 hours yet again.

Yesterday Gladewitz summoned me to the State Administration: the cloth promised months ago. Something of a Greek gift: too heavy for a suit, too light for a coat – and boringly grey. Price not yet settled and ominous. But straightaway gave it to the tailor nevertheless. It is too much needed. Gladewitz said: 'impossible for a professor to run around as you do.' – Doris Machol, who knows 'Richard' from the International Brigades, is probably behind it. And who has sent us a couple of American tins. And who has already telephoned us 2×. And who has talked to Ufermann of the press association. As a result of which I received a telegram yesterday, to speak at a matinee on 1 December. But thoughts of E. force their way into all feelings of pleasure.

This afternoon was once again messed up by sitting for Rudolph. But now he has almost finished the picture. Almost.

[...]

14th November, Thursday evening

After many inner and gloomy impediments my most difficult *LTI* chapter 'Zion' is at last finished. The whole book must now be finished in the coming weeks. Better to abridge than to let it drag on any longer. [...] I have had enough of the subject, also it is less and less topical.

Yesterday, 13 Nov., I spoke at a district meeting of the SED, Plauen, in the elementary school next to the town hall to 90 intellectuals on 'Who Makes History?' [...] Place intellectual history above the history of battles. Role of the individual and of the generality ... My lectures this year, all set down in headwords on long strips of paper, present in ever new combinations and variations always the same 3, 4 themes 'Cultural interdependence', 'Humanism', Montesquieu (personality, state principles), 'heroism'. Somewhat sterile with the passage of time.

I read the proofs of 'People's High School 1946', which *Paedagogik* [Education] has now given the title 'Encyclopaedia and People's High School'.

[...]

Among my themes I forgot 'High School and Democracy'. That is really what made my name in February in Berlin. – In the audience yesterday Barkhausen[120] and Reingruber, *the* Kulturbund MP, the only one in the whole of Soviet Germany. I so much wanted to sit on the city council, so much in the Saxon parliament. Nothing came of either. Now I am fighting for the Reichstag.[121] – Vanitas. And always suppressing the thought of death. Lately E. troubles me more than myself. What would become of me, if I were to outlive her? I would not have the courage to put an end to things and yet I would be completely empty. Her condition is not good. [...]

At the moment between all stools. Completely out of the PHS, no one thinks of somehow making me honorary director. Without employment at the TH, and Leipzig unattainable.

23rd November, 11 p.m. Saturday evening

Of the greatest importance is the unexpectedly revived Greifswald question (see 28–29 June). I had thought the business over and done with long ago. Now there arrived a canvassing letter from Dr Dr Weidhaas, who provisionally holds the chair of art history there and one from Jacoby, the dean. [...] We are very seriously considering an acceptance; I feel to some extent let down by Dresden, by government, city and Party equally. I wrote *very* 'fundamentally ready' to both the people in G. [...]

[...] My days are entirely taken up with the *LTI* – everything else has been pushed to the margin, must wait, is only distraction. And E. is entirely occupied with the radiation treatment in the Johannstädter Hospital. Thus despite all the incidentals a consistently full life.

Slow progress. Jewish suite completely finished, likewise 'Dedication' + 'Heroism' and 'Superlative'. – Distressing lighting cuts.

[...]

My visitors: Mother and daughter Jährig (Neumark's secretary). Tragicomedy of the 18-year-old daughter: trained as a Russian teacher in crash courses, would like to take the general teaching course, *must* stick with Russian alone, because has shown particular talent for it. Overburdened – has to simultaneously already teach and continue studying [...]. She talks about the serious resistance of parents to the Russian lessons of their children. 'If I come home with a 5, my parents are pleased' ... [...]

One evening recently a wireless adaptation of Jean Anouilh's *Eurydice*.[122] Very well acted and it moved me greatly. So very French – Antiquity, Manon[123] and set in an express train; tradition, classicism with neo-Romanticism and eroticism, very modern and carefree. After an infinitely long time an augmentation of French material for me. But first the *LTI* must be completed. It *must* be brought to a conclusion before the end of the year.

25th November, Monday afternoon
[...]

Yesterday, Sunday, the good Frida Dittrich,[124] my instructor at Thimig & Möbius, was here in the morning, together with the Wolffs we ate at the Rudolphs. Success: R. is to paint Frau W., but is disappointed that the Wolffs did not buy any finished work.

Work on the *LTI* crawls along. 'From the great movement forward.'

28th November, Thursday morning
The second roast rabbit at the Rudolphs together with the Wolffs of last Sunday will be paid for like this: Frau Wolff will be painted for 4,000M + taxes.

The good Dittrich wrote me a letter. I should help her pg brother. The usual.

[...]

8th December, Sunday towards evening
This morning in the Academy hall. Trinks spoke on the cultural consequences of the Dresden exhibition. I chaired and slept. Afterwards the usual discussion. The public does not want to know anything about Expressionism, Volwahsen[125] etc. defend it passionately. New was Erich Seidemann turning up. He would have been unable to bring his class, they would have laughed. He quoted Andersen's fairy tale of the King's new clothes [...]. It seems to me a political tragicomedy, the way 'abstract art' is now being brought into play against the

SED and is alienating the workers. The SED only believes it has to support the abstract artists, because Goebbels suppressed these people as 'degenerate' and turned them into martyrs.

Berlin trip for the lecture to the German Press Association Central Office [. . .]. That's already long past, and I shall be brief.

Constant battle, constant telephoning and new arrangements for the car. At midday on Saturday a heavy French car with a very brisk driver arrived from the local FDGB [Freier Deutscher Gewerkschaftsbund – Free German Trades Union Federation]. With me Frau Freese and a female secretary from the FDGB. Terrifically fast journey, 70 miles an hour [. . .] in Berlin in $2\frac{1}{2}$ hours, shortly after 4. – Adlon. Standing behind me in the office, a complete surprise for both parties, Weidhaas. On Sunday morning I breakfasted with him alone. [. . .]

I had the big car at my disposal for the afternoon and drove first to Anny Klemperer, 11 Heinrich Stephanstr., near the Radio Tower. I visited her again on Sunday afternoon. Bombed out, a summer house, evidently only 3 rooms of a much-divided apartment. A handsome room, which contains her bed, as living room. There must also be space for 18-year-old Peter and for the white-haired, stooped, but vigorous maid, who was already part of the household before Peter's birth. Anny youthful looking, but almost deaf, 61, very cordial to me, I had to drink cocoa, eat white bread, I got cigarettes and unroasted coffee as presents – she receives packets from the USA and Switzerland, but complains greatly about confined and difficult life. Her finances are unclear to me. ('The property has been confiscated – if only I had not had *those* houses!') Her son Georg wants to marry a Swiss woman and go abroad, at present looking for work somewhere in Bavaria. Peter, about to take his school-leaving certificate, wants to be a doctor, politically interested in the SPD (Schumacher), against SED. Came to my lecture, is solicitous of me [. . .] – but obviously does not have a good relationship with his mother, talks very quietly to her, although one has to shout at her, in order to be understood. [. . .] Anny, too, astonishingly modern. If Berthold had heard her talking about the rape of an elderly aunt. 'He threw her on the bed – she didn't even know what he wanted.' (Without particular disgust and agitation!)

So on Saturday afternoon I drove off from Anny in the car; on Sunday, after the car had let me down, I took the Circle Railway from Witzleben to Prenzlauer Allee to Doris Machol. She lives with her Mackie (Max Kahane) in Gudvangerstr. [. . .]. The third person there is a vigorous 81-year-old, Doris's grandmother, a calm easy-going old woman, who is treated very affectionately. Bohemian household. A kitchen-living room and a large room with few but elegant and tasteful pieces of furniture. Two couches placed at right angles, a table in front of them, a bookcase, in the middle of the room a desk. Whether the granny lives next to or in the kitchen I do not know. Kahane, mid-30s, speaks very calmly and openly about their relationship. He knows nothing of his wife in Palestine, has become estranged from her. Both names, Doris Machol and M. Kahane, are on the lobby door. 'No one is interested in that now. If there are children, we'll see what we do then.' Calm happiness of both without affected emotion. He was well advanced in his studies when Hitlerism brought them to an end. Slim man, sharp-featured Jewish face, very slightly the same type as the musician Otto Klemperer – but without any fanaticism whatsoever, without any affectation whatsoever. He fought at Teruel,[126] was the German head [of the prisoners] of a camp in the south of France,[127] Gladewitz was an orderly there [...]. I must get Doris to tell her story in greater detail. She paints, showed me a picture she had done of her mother, who died of breast cancer, gave me a water-colour landscape for E., who for her part has given Doris a little golden ring from Kätchen Sara's estate ... Both evenings with K. and D. passed very pleasantly and nourishingly. I soon found it easy to be on close terms with him and have a calm objective conversation. [...]

The stay at the Adlon was woeful. Horrible damp cold; I froze and had bad pains on the first night; on the second I slept in pullover and underpants, the new coat over the quilt. In the morning the electricity was cut off and no substitute light to shave by. At breakfast: 'Please wrap the bread and meat up for me. – Does Sir have paper? ... No? ... I shall see what I can do.' Then the elegant stuff is packed in newspaper for me. An apartment in the Adlon, the most elegant hotel! But of course no warm water. I breakfasted up against the iron stove.

On Sunday morning, therefore, I first of all conferred with Weidhaas and told him all my demands. Then Julius Mossner[128] picked me up. A large handsome hall on Leipziger Strasse, but hardly $\frac{1}{3}$ full, there are supposed to have been 150 people there, exclusively journalists. Doris and Mackie among them – I had palpitations, but then spoke well, and it is supposed to have been a success. [...].

On Monday morning to the Central Administration. Rompe sick, his department head, a grey-haired Dr Böhme[129] was in the picture. A sort of colleague, Romanist/Hispanicist. [...] He acted as if I were an applicant and should jump at the opportunity, as if I were obliged to accept quite vague promises, as if I were making exorbitant demands. At that I became very forceful. Weidhaas was present at the meeting. I said, if they wanted to have me, they should come to me, I would not lift a finger, I did not need Greifswald. Böhme was shocked, and matters concluded fairly hopelessly. (Meanwhile a fairly flattering letter has arrived today, 11 Dec., from Jacoby, he will do his best. Meanwhile I had a bad argument on the telephone with Donath, who would like to have me away from here, in which I slammed down the receiver. Meanwhile I am so worried about Eva, who is becoming ever more frail, very worn out by the radiation treatment and the terrible shortage of food – no fats, no meat, no tea, nothing! – and who is very evidently facing a serious breast operation, that the Greifswald question no longer seems very important to me.) In the middle of the negotiations, there came a telephone call from the Press Association: there was no car for me, force majeure. Mollification: I should contact Willmann (Kulturbund), something would happen. I arranged to meet W. Rendezvous and meal in the 'Club of Cultural Workers', the house in Jägerstr., whose opening we had celebrated in the summer. It was very nice and elegant there, and I was Willmann's guest. With him came Klaus Gysi, a gentleman from the drama publishing section of Aufbau and Dr Friedrich Wolf, who had been due to speak to our Dresden KB on Sunday and had not been picked up, who was supposed to attend his Tuesday première [in Dresden] and did not know how. He did not make any very overwhelming impression on me, just as I do not think very highly of his plays. Rather loud man, forced heartiness, roughly in his early 50s. While we were eating, Ufermann appeared, a car was waiting for me downstairs. It was a very little car with a very weak engine and a driver, pure Berliner, nevertheless tremendously calm and slow. Stage comedy character and complete opposite of the 70 mile an hour guzzler on Sunday. [There were] strict instructions not to continue driving after nightfall, there were too many armed holdups precisely on the Berlin–Dresden stretch. (I had recently even been told, I would be assigned a Russian officer as escort – which of course did *not* happen …) It was almost 2 p.m., the car would take 5 hours – how then could the darkness be avoided? And Wolf even wanted to go to his apartment in Pankow, change his clothes and, as he hinted to me, fetch a nicer set of dentures. There was a lengthy discussion and finally, in annoyance, Wolf slammed the car door shut from the outside and we drove off. Wolf then attended his première here after all, but did not get in touch. Pity.

[…]

11th December, Wednesday evening

[…]

Characteristic features of recent days: the increasing concern about E., the ever greater food shortage, the many aches while walking. The walk to the Büttner concert[130] in Weintraubenstr. yesterday was desperate. I understood next to nothing of the music; but it was good that we talked to Eva Büttner; she is going to try to obtain foodstuffs for us from Piskowitz. But it will be Christmas before it gets to us. And meanwhile E. goes on starving.

[…]

16th December, Monday morning

It has turned terribly cold, our little stove is not enough, we suffer greatly, I am writing in my winter coat.

Today, for the first time in $11\frac{1}{2}$ years, I shall speak in the TH. For the Kulturbund about the *LTI* in the large Chemistry lecture theatre. I am now talking about it for the third time (Dölzschen, Plauen, TH). […] Fräulein Mey just told me on the telephone, I had already also spoken to the teachers at the Junghansschule about the *LTI*. So today is the 4th time. – 'Running hot and cold' is finished and 'Putting the theory to the test' begun. This week *must* see the end of it. My hands are too stiff to write. So type *LTI*.

17th December, Tuesday night

Tonight for the second night I shall sleep on the sofa in the front here by the stove under two coats in all my clothes. *All* available blankets have been piled on top of Eva. In this cold our bedding is not enough for the two of us.

Yesterday for one and a half hours I dragged myself step by step in great pain in the cold wind to the TH. I did not think I would make it any more. Once there I recovered immediately and then spoke well – to 50 people at most in the large Chemistry lecture theatre. [...]

On Friday, the 13th, we were invited to the Steiningers. Coffee and cake, later a plate of potato soup as well and two slices of bread as a little supper, on top of that a warm room – under present circumstances it was splendid. The Hanuschs were there and a married couple, the man, seemingly a dismissed pg grammar-school teacher, now in business, often in the English zone. He talked about the liveliness and harmlessness of the illegal passage between zones. Sometimes it cost a small fine and confiscated foodstuffs, but in the southern Harz hills hundreds were managing it every day. The tanks on either side of the Russian–English border were a legend. – Today Frau Rasch burst out bitterly: The Russians take everything away from us, in their headquarters there is an abundance of light and food – and here? The workers were incensed. The Americans and the English would drive the Russians out ... Then again: the war would have come anyway even without German responsibility. Capitalism was to blame for everything! ... It won't take long, then we'll have a new Hitlerism. Frau Rasch: the Nazis were doing all right again, the workers badly. In short complete confusion. As I said, in the end we'll get a new Hitlerism.

Still to be added is the Dölzschen Christmas party on Saturday 14 Dec. Crowded but warm room with potato salad and coffee and cakes from 7 until about midnight. Eva accompanied two pupils, a boy and a girl, of Lotte Kreisler, who was there with her husband. Quite a nice evening – only the pain while walking!

Saxon government: Hartsch, an unknown schools inspector,[131] SPD man, has become education minister. What will become of Gute?

20th December, Friday evening

E. has a second suspicious lump on her breast. Very depressing. I myself am greatly tormented and impeded by rheumatism + heart + cold. Bad pains when walking.

We are both now sleeping here in the study; E. on the couch, the mattress is got in for me every night. Battle with the lighting cuts. Yesterday in the dark until 10, then wrote until 2. The *LTI* is approaching its conclusion. [...]

Today futile running around for coal. [...] Frau Rasch in an outburst against the Russians, whom the popular mood now blames for everything, said with Nazi quotation marks '*Soviet paradise*'[132]. Counterpart: the SED announcer of the Leipzig broadcasting station says: by recruiting worker-students etc. we must get rid of the '*so-called objectivity*' of scholarship! It could drive one to despair.

25th December, 10 p.m. Christmas Day evening

On Saturday 21 Dec. I wrote the last part of *LTI*; since then winding it up: making a copy of one part, reading the whole thing through, looking for repetitions, ordering the pieces ... I began writing on 25 July 45; I studied my diary for it almost from the day we arrived. Frequent interruptions – People's High School and many lectures. Always, even now, vacillation: how far a study, how far a diary? The most difficult book of my life. And even now I do not know, how I should judge it. Some things very good, others doubtful. Perhaps the book will sink among a 1000 similar ones, perhaps it will be a success. Possible that I shall be completely finished by New Year's Eve.

Recently very bad rheumatic-heart problems; walking is torture. Most excruciating the walk on Saturday 21 Dec. to the Christmas party of the Victims of Fascism in Kaitz Inn. [...] I did not think I would manage it. Head wind, dreadful pain. I recovered at the inn, and we got a car back (crammed full). Once there it was very nice, even though the heating was hardly adequate. We each received a little bag with gingerbread, 5 cigarettes, a piece of soap. We got a schnapps, potato salad and a meatball, coffee and four(!) pieces of cake, very nice cabaret turns. There was dancing. Next to us the Glasers. The Erich Seidemanns, Eva Schulze-Knabe. Hilse, the head of the VoF. office,[133] Bautzenerstr. gave an address, will try to help me get coal.

On Sunday morning to the Christmas Fair in the Nordhalle. Ordeal of getting there. Bad rheumatic or heart pains or both together. Alleviated as soon as I sit down and do not have to breathe the cold air ... We needed presents. There are only toys [...] and pictures. The Kulturbund stand we looked for was closed, a young man who knew me buttonholed us: Kneschke's nephew, employed in a second-hand art shop. We bought a few sheets for around 100M for the Wolffs and other obligations. E. very charmed by a framed oil painting of a gently foggy winter landscape *Our Garden* by a woman painter unknown to us from 1901. Since she wanted the picture, I bought it for 300M. The first time in my life, after we recently bought a water colour from Rudolph for 300M. Aside from that I have called in the mortgage on our house. Of the 12,000M I shall have 11,000 on my account by the beginning of January, the sum in full before the end of January. In order to pay it off immediately I am making a short term borrowing from Wolff. Just avoid having any cash! – Insane conditions. I have saved that up in the course of $1\frac{1}{2}$ years, and we're starving. One can't spend anything in the normal way, and it's not enough for black market prices. And now we shall have the house unencumbered and nothing in it belongs to us, except a piano stool (present from Wolffs) and a couple of paintings.

[...]

29th December, 11.30 Sunday evening

After a week of very intense correction work I have just packed up the *LTI* and will send it off tomorrow. I was at home the whole time – as soon as I go outside, the pain is too great. [...]

For all that I worry more about E's health than about my own. The distressing radiation treatment – interrupted in the last few days by skin inflammation – is drawing to an end, and the operation is to take place then. God knows, how big and with what result. E. lies down a lot, is alarmingly thin and very pale. On top of that the lack of food. The expected packages don't come at all.

[...]

31st December, Tuesday, New Year's Eve 11 p.m.

E. is already asleep, next to her the Raschs are making up my bed which has to be brought in every day.

Very gloomy New Year's Eve mood. E.'s prophylactic radiation treatment ended today, after an interval of four weeks, she will be referred to Dressel for the operation. Finding on the right side: undoubtedly 'malignant' lump; the knot on the left is 'cause for concern'. [...]

I myself: at home I have no problems, out walking I am brought up short after a few steps by serious pain. Merely neuritis or also heart?

On Thursday Wolff, who is being very obliging, will drive us to Pirna, where Dressel will also examine me.

[...]

Since sending off the *LTI* I have continuously dealt with accumulated private correspondence, long letters to the Jelskis, Agnes Dember, Hans Meyerhof, Berta Meyerhof.[134]

Résumé of work – I shall cover the period June 45–31 Dec. 46, because last New Year's Eve I did not yet make any proper summing-up. It's not much. The *LTI*, the study 'People's High School 1946', the Barbusse–Plievier study, a couple of short things for *Aufbau* [periodical] and newspapers; very many (how many?) lectures, all variations on the same theme 'Cultural interdependence'. The two great successes: Central conference of the KPD in February, and the matinee of the Press Association on 1 Dec. 46, both in Berlin. – My work at the People's High School, essentially at the Evening Grammar School, until the 1st of Nov. A couple of lectures on the LTI [...]. Spoke frequently in small places and suburbs.

The question of my actual professional employment remains open. As long as it trains only vocational teachers I am superfluous at the TH. Leipzig appears finally closed to me, Griefswald in the balance. Since Eva's condition has been added to my angina, I no longer attach so much importance to the academic question. My salary here will not be taken away from me and everything else is vanitatum vanitas.

In these one and a half years I have earned so much, that I am redeeming the 12,000M mortgage.

[...]

Today a very extensive catalogue arrived from the Aufbau publishing house; my *LTI* is already announced in it – also the Romance Philology, on which not an atom of preparatory work has yet been done.

[...]

Eva is asleep, on the wireless a New Year's party from the Leipzig 'Oper-ettenhaus' – what kind of place is that – is in full swing.

It is only another 10 minutes to 12. And where shall we be next New Year's Eve? Father always said 'on Sirius'. – Keep on working, everything else is nonsense and a waste of time. And when at last some foreign package reaches us and the grub gets a little better, then perhaps my mood will also improve.

1947

2nd January, Thursday evening
[...]

In Pirna today in Wolff's car at about 12, back from there at about 4. E.'s radiation treatment over for the time being, will only have a sample taken at the end of January. Question whether the tumour is malignant. On the same day I myself am to have a small wart on my chest removed, which I have had for many years and has now become painful. Dressel thinks my terrible pains while walking are caused by spondylitis. He urged me to place myself under observation by a heart specialist, and to give fewer lectures out of town. He appears to take my condition more seriously than Eva's. – We had brought potatoes and ate lunch with the Dressels–Annemarie. The Dressel family, himself, wife, 3 children, old mother, dominate, Annemarie is a kind of tolerated, incorporated aunt. Her face puffed up with illness, her mood bitter – her brother missing in Mühlberg [Soviet] camp. Under the wife's influence the Dressel family emphatically Protestant. Grace said by a child: 'Come Lord Jesus ...' [...] They are anti-Russian, anti-SED. I feel as if in a hostile foreign land.

I consider the situation here in general, mine in particular, to be altogether critical, the Russians are hated by everyone, the ruling SED likewise, and one day it will be taken out on the couple of Jews.

[...]

Dressel asked: The TH has been closed, hasn't it? – 'Why?' – 'The professors are all said to have been sent to Russia!'

5th January, 3 p.m. Sunday afternoon
[...] At home Agnes from Piskowitz had unexpectedly turned up with her brother-in-law Rothe, the man from the Wendish spinning room. He left in the afternoon, she remained until the following midday; it was something of a

strain, but a little bit nourishing. (A small amount of butter, some flour, a loaf.) We are due to be in Kamenz on the 8th and then get some potatoes from Piskowitz – they are sorely needed. [...]

As a Christmas present Aufbauverlag sent several books and calendars, Willmann telegraphed New Year's greetings, Gysi sent his by post.

An altogether fine, humanly deeply moving letter from Major Hans-Joachim Hirche in Munsterlager [camp]. Lüneburg district. A long time ago [...] I wrote a curt letter of refusal to his mother; I intend to give this letter a serious reply.

[...]

10th January, Friday forenoon

Frost moderated, but the resulting misfortunes, especially the frozen water pipe, still unchanged.

[...]

Loewenkopf warned me in the strongest terms against doing anything in the Neumark case. He himself had just had 9 days under house arrest and under guard because of some business, young Pionkowski (see my diary of the Hitler years) had been inside for 3 months[1] – 'what are 3 months to the Russians?!' – Acquainted with Eva Büttner from earlier days, he broke out in enthusiastic memories of her – he was inordinately jargon-ridden and inordinately Zionist. (How will these people receive my *LTI*?) He read from a letter from Palestine – 'Criminals, who are now leading the English nation!' (At the moment the Zionists are conducting a real war against the English.)

11th January, Saturday forenoon

8th–9th January, Kamenz-Piskowitz

Eva Büttner arrived here at 5 p.m., we drove very packed in and infinitely slowly to K. Ice, fog [...]. – Hotel Blauer Stern on the market place, where we stayed on the day of the plebiscite. Russian quarters, therefore well heated, we got a warm room, a splendid supper with meat, the next morning butter with syrup with breakfast. The lecture, set for 7 p.m. in the 'Stadt Dresden', was given at 8 to about 40 people. Great success, all very nice, but the couple of steps between the hotels were agony and I also felt extremely ill before going to sleep. [...] So I spoke about the LTI. [...] Then we sat with Eva Büttner for a while drinking grog. [...]

Then, at about 12, E. and I were driven to Agnes. She lives in the former girls' land-labour service hut, very cramped, but very warm (wood and hearth) [...]. We were splendidly [...] fed: rabbit, sauerkraut, cake, pancakes – we were able to hoard a great deal from Dresden: cake, 2 eggs, a loaf, a cwt. of potatoes. I obtained a second cwt. from Krahl, the Nazi mayor in February 45. He says, and I believe him, because he knew our and the Blumenfelds' maids, courted our Anna Dürrlich,[2] he says, at the time he had known very well, whom he was dealing with. (Naturally he also knew, that the Nazi regime was close to collapse.) He is now very decently looking after Agnes, who speaks highly of him. [...] From Agnes we also got a feather bed. We gave her 100M for everything, we paid Krahl 10M for his cwt. – all most reasonable purchases, the price for a cwt. of potatoes alone is already 50–100M. We commissioned Agnes, for good money, to get whatever she could spare us to Eva Büttner. Very loaded down and squashed, we drove slowly back to Dresden with Eva Büttner. [...] I did not feel at ease until we had all our booty in the house, unconfiscated. It was about 5.30. There was no light; we sat in darkness until 10 p.m. [...]

The Wolffs, arriving from Berlin, said it was forbidden to import the newspapers of the other [Berlin] sectors – *Kurier, Telegraf, Tagesspiegel* – into our zone. The *Tagesspiegel* wrote about my speech of 1 Dec., it had been one-sidedly pro-Russian for political ends.

13th January, Monday night

Yesterday telegram from Anny Kl. 'Georg passed away peacefully in his sleep.'[3] It did after all touch me with a shudder and a sense of isolation.
[...]
I corresponded a great deal. Vossler, Hilde Jonson, Marta, Anny Kl. etc. etc.

15th January, Wednesday morning

Dr Willy Katz 13 Jan. 47 † [...]. Strange how it coincides with Georg's death for me. I had given Katz Georg's last two letters to read – about the ineradicableness of German anti-Semitism and with the warning against a political career – and he was delighted and flattered. I had not seen him for months, had spoken to him on the telephone less than 2 weeks ago. He had for a long time been a lost and broken man, a sanatorium stay [...] did not help him any more. He had been elected an LDP city councillor, he was supposed to get a post in the city administration and had to turn everything down. When I last spoke to him – I had the ambition of promoting him – he was already tired to death. He wrote to me, we were now 'companions in suffering' – he meant the angina.

Despite much pain I had to risk going into town yesterday: Victims of Fascism, SED, Food Office – as I was beseeching Hilse for tea at the Victims of Fascism, a comrade came in: 'we need 2 wreathes, for X and for Dr Katz.' Later Frau Heidenberger telephoned me on behalf of Katz's widow, whether I would speak a few words at the coffin. [...] Katz was only two years older than myself.
[...]

19th January, Sunday morning

Frau Rasch has been in bed for several days and will stay there for a long time yet: heart. Her husband, here at the moment (because he has no boots in which he can work outside!) helps a little with the heaviest work, but otherwise: stress for E. and chaos. – As in earlier days, Rasch encompasses voces populi (plural) in himself. Constant within them the contempt for the Russians. The others are hated and respected, the Russians hated and despised. They are supposed to be just as much to blame for our misery as the others, and '*they* did not defeat us'. And: it will turn out like after 1918, and we shall help ourselves [...]. Etc. etc. It is the return of Hitlerism and the workers agree with it. One thing he said shook me: 'Already today there are families, who are burning their wardrobe [for fuel], their table, their chairs, are sitting on *one* chair, they don't care about anything.' I add here, what Wildführ recently told us when he visited: '40 people a day are dying in the Friedrichstädter Hospital; every morning the corpses are taken to the crematorium in a tramcar – the plague cart!' ... My purely personal feeling: I wish I could leave Germany, before the next Nazi wave kills me...

About contempt for the Russians: [...] at a Dölzschen meeting a little while ago the warning complaint from Russian headquarters, the public was behaving disrespectfully to the troops.

[...]

[...] On the evening of the same day [15th] meeting of the Victims of Fascism in the Münchner Krug tavern. My first walk for a long time. Pain, managed it nevertheless. A national association of the VoF, all-party and radical, is to be set up. Hilse had talked to me about it the day before, I would probably be elected a delegate. Which is what happened. One of four, as representative of the 'racially persecuted'. I was not very pleased by this designation. Earlier a Jew I do not know had spoken in favour of 'equal representation for Jews' and got an almost anti-Semitic brush-off as a result. *I* had intervened and emphasised, that I rejected all differentiations between Jew and Christian and acknowledged only Fascists and anti-Fascists. There was also an embarrassing point. The chairman of the meeting (Körner) inveighed fiercely against testimonies of friendship for pg's, it was unworthy of a Victim of Fascism. From those present, perhaps 60 or 80 people, one heard: some do it 'for a packet of cigarettes'. I unfortunately said, I had written only 2 testimonies, for people who had saved my life (but Vogel and Weisbach, E. objected later. Utinam si tacuisses![4]). The Dresden delegates are to meet soon, and then representatives for a central Berlin meeting will be elected. – I do not feel very comfortable with all of that. Anti-Semitism everywhere. And my position between *all* stools. [...]

The day after, Frau Hamann here to make music. She too one of the little pg's on whose behalf I would gladly intercede. She brought E. a silk slip, for which E has long been looking. We forced a tablecloth on her in return. But is it not nevertheless the 'packet of cigarettes'? At least it *can* be construed as that.

[...]

Letter from Helmut Hatzfeld, the 25% [Jewish] man.[5] Fled 38, lecturer under good conditions at the Catholic University of America, Washington D.C. He 'would never want to return to Germany'. In addition he writes, 'that Friedmann[6] lost his nerve attempting to cross the Pyrenees and committed suicide. A collection is being made here for his wife and child.' [...]

Under the pressure of the current personal and general situation I see things particularly gloomily today and envy Hatzfeld greatly.

A few months ago I felt sorry for Kafka, who without a post, ailing, having fallen out with everyone, is living in poor conditions. Now he has been called to a chair in Würzburg.

22nd January, Wednesday morning

Cold, hunger, Frau Räsch's illness, approach of the day of the knife in Pirna, at a standstill professionally, both in connection with the outside world and my work, deep pessimism as regards politics, the Allies, Germany, the SED – for all that more dullness than depression: mostly I sit at home, work my way through the volumes of *Neuere Sprachen* [Modern Languages], doze off, listen to the wireless, turn lively late in the evening, read until about 1, lie down freezing - all in this one room, hope from post to post for something encouraging, improving – in vain.

On the forenoon of Monday the 20th funeral of Willy Katz († 13/1/47). A cab (something new) picked us up, then the widow [...]. Many mourners, the hall at the crematorium fairly full – 80–100? Chaotic arrangements, the Jewish cleric from Freiberg *not* present. Deliberation. A middle-aged Catholic priest, Father Hartmann, who lived in the same house and was a friend of the deceased, with him in mortis hora,[7] asks: 'did he believe in eternal life?' Lewinsky categorically: 'Not a bit, I knew him for 35 years, he thought, when you're dead, you're dead!' The priest: 'Then I can do nothing.' I: 'You cannot know that, Lewinsky, I had a different impression of him.' (Of course I made it up.) The priest: 'Then *I* shall speak – he may have changed his mind.' Then Lewinsky, in the shabbiest coat, his back to the mourners, spoke, at his own request, Schiller's (absurdly inappropriate) 'Nänie' [Lament].[8] Then, from the small lectern, speaking extempore without embarrassing pathos, the priest. He was speaking as a Catholic for the Jew, who in life had been a doctor of the body and who in his calm dying had been an example to the soul. Eternal life – without belief in it, life here would be 'a bad joke' Tolstoy had said; also we have an inborn longing, a natural instinct for it and such instincts never deceived ... Everything about this little sermon was good and tactful – only the man said a dozen times: Katz's 'brothers in race', where once he would have said 'brothers in faith', and that was yet again a victory for the LTI. [...] Then as representative of the Jewish community Pionkowski read a few simple words. (Cf my diary 1942 or 43. P. was secretary of the community [...]. His mother was allowed to remain with him, when others were transported from Dresden. Later mother and son were evacuated together. A while ago I heard he was back, recently Loewenkopf, who was also present, said that P. had been detained for weeks by the Russians on suspicion of something or other.) After the ceremony P. told me, he and his mother had been deported to Riga – she had later been taken away – not heard of again. How he himself was saved, I do not know. – I spoke after P. [...] E. told me, what I said was very suited to Katz the officer. Afterwards at the coffin some representative of the medical profession shouted a few pathos-laden words, a wreath swinging on his arm. Introductory and concluding music much too long. Before the end, the Kaddish spoken by Lewinsky. Ghastly. We stood with our hats on our heads. The responses sounded very faint. How many understood??

[...]

Yesterday (21 Jan.) Kretzschmar-Neumark was here. He now wants to approach Buchwitz on behalf of the missing Neumark. To this end I had to repeat in writing (more or less) my statement to Cohn, the public prosecutor. I did it perforce and not without a quiet shudder, mindful of Loewenkopf's recent warning ... [...]

Literally my whole working day – it is now almost 6 p.m. – has been lost due to two visits. First Frau Cohn, then the wife of the carpenter Lange.[9] What the latter had to say was interesting enough: her husband is working for the 'Yanks' over in Bavaria, Lechfeld air field, near Augsburg. She was with him for a couple of months, 'made herself healthy' with respect to food and clothing. But what was most interesting about her story, its tragic aspect, are the adventures, the hardships for days on end, losses and deadly dangers of illegally crossing the zonal boundaries: Yanks, English, Russians, German police: all hunt, arrest, confiscate, the Russians also shoot. She told of a mountain pack march through deep snow, pursuers behind them – one of the three was caught, completely stripped, beaten ... Poor Germany!

In the evening we are with the Raschs for a quarter of an hour, seeing how the patient is. The only warm room in the house. The whole family is in our small bedroom, which always seemed like a hatbox to me. A little iron stove with thick pipe spreads great warmth ... We want to get rid of our tiled stove again and go back to the round iron stove, but now we lack the necessary pipe. [...]

26th January, Sunday forenoon

Yesterday evening excessively weary, cold, worn out from lack of sleep, depressed. On the morning of the 23rd spoke on a refresher course for new teachers, 160 people, Erich Seidemann spokesman. [...] In addition to the regular courses there are individual lectures, 3 speakers from the parties, 1 from the Kulturbund. I chatted about the LTI, probably with some effect. – Then over breakfast in the canteen an older man came up to me, former worker, good-looking, later Seidemann spoke well of him: 'A question of conscience, Herr Professor. Sitting beside me is a woman teacher, 20, from a civil service family, LDP. She is writing an essay, instead of listening to you. I said to her, she should pay attention to the lecture. Reply: "No – I don't like the man." She wants to have nothing to do with Jews, that has been impressed on her, they are dirty, inferior etc. ... Should I report her, should she be struck from the teaching profession??' I referred the man to Erich S., spoke to S. about it for some time – we were both shocked and uncertain. Today I shall hear from S., how the matter turned out. But whatever happens: the fact is there. One out of 160 new teachers gave herself away. How many do not give themselves away, how many are really genuine?? And above all:

Georg with his last warning: the Germans want to have nothing to do with the Jews, is 100% right. I am deeply depressed.

[...]

Yesterday afternoon at 1.30 the delegates' meeting to set up the Victims of Fascism association. Assembly hall of the Lande cigarette factory, Junghansstr., near the Ernemann works. More than 100 participants. Hilse as chairman. I saw, in part spoke to, Gladewitz, Gute, Erik Mauthner, Eva Schulze-Knabe, public prosecutor Cohn, Koenen [...]. Many unknown to me, little people, workers. After the first few words with Hilse, I knew that I would *not* be among the eight to be sent to Berlin. I regretted that I had offered my services, and again felt that I count for nothing in the Party: I was not an activist, did not join until after the victory, am an intellectual and hanger-on. Max Opitz, a middle-aged man, spoke generally but not badly: the charitable society must be turned into a politically active organisation, radical and above party. Only later did I learn, that Opitz is the Dresden chief of police.[10] Very long debate on individual points, e.g. may a VoF exonerate Nazis? Above all: did we have a *resistance movement*? One side: No, merely resistance groups. To be called a movement, there would have had to be an effect, action by masses of people, [army] divisions defecting, not just individual deserters. The others: We had a resistance movement, had a 'scaffold front'. The first side: Abroad they think us presumptuous, if we talk about a German movement, even compare it with the partisans, the maquis etc. [...] I said, the French would misunderstand our reservations, and also we should simply say resistance, and completely discard the ghastly LTI word 'movement'. That pleased Opitz, who himself had spoken against the word movement ... Koenen passionately preached unity and pacifism, again and again pacifism, that alone can help us gain fairer peace conditions. (The Germany negotiations are to begin in Moscow on 10 March.[11]) ... But how can one preach pacifism here, when all around each country is outdoing the other in armaments? [...]

A great many letters read and answered. [...] The unfulfilled longing for packets from abroad. The Russian zone has been open since 15 Jan. Berthold Meyerhof, New Jork and Sebi Sebba, Northampton, have given notice of parcels, the Care packet was ordered on 1 Nov. and nothing has come. An American newspaper cutting was enclosed with Berthold M.'s letter: 'Private Rites for Dr Klemperer', brief biographical words of praise (*'noted in Germany for his research in cancer and metabolism'*, his *book*, *'his well-known standard textbook on medical diagnosis'*).

The little bit of correspondence and diary writing fills my days. I am very worn-out. I stand by the stove and drop off to sleep. My feet are constantly freezing. I always wear my old winter coat. The windows are thick with ice.

[...]

31st January, 4 p.m. Friday afternoon

[...]

The car should be here in half an hour. Then at 6.30, Wolff, true friend in difficult moments! will take E. to Pirna. She will spend the night there and will be operated on tomorrow under a light anaesthetic. It is tentatively supposed to be a minor matter, two tiny tumours – the tissue must then be examined for cancer. I am not thinking any further, am apathetic. – Then at midday tomorrow Wolff will drive me to Pirna, a very old danger spot, the wart on my chest will also go under the knife. And in the evening we both hope to be here again.

2nd February, Sunday forenoon

Yesterday after our return from Pirna at 4 p.m., utterly exhausted and unable to take anything in hand. E. suffering great pain, I a little also. I stood by the stove, E. lay and groaned, I brought her this and that. To bed at 10.30, got up at 8. Still not washed and changed, still the terrible cold, 7° in the room.

In Meissen therefore [31 Jan.–1 Feb.] from dinner over to the theatre. I did not see it from the outside; inside miniature and comfortable, 450 seats distributed between stalls, boxes and circle. I was in the office, then came from the back past the stage to the director's box. Onstage behind the curtain was the scenery for the ballet from the 'Land of Smiles',[12] of which I saw the last two acts. [...]

Intimate and very pleasant contact with Kociollek in his theatre office before and between the acts [...], during the meeting itself and finally and principally in his apartment on Friday evening and Saturday morning. Born 1893 in Lodz, father a tailor with many children, poverty, learns tailoring himself. Then autodidact, tenor and stage performer for many years. [...] But he is genuinely educated, thinks calmly and dispassionately, speaks with particular fondness of Spinoza, has good people (classics, philosophers) in his library. As charge hand of the Jewish workers at the Schwarze factory he was arrested because he had not reported wireless listeners. [...] Auschwitz, 'Going to sleep one put one's two daily slices of bread under one's neck. One's life depended on it. If one prisoner stole these pieces of bread from another, he was beaten to death by the camp inmates themselves' ... [...]

At about 11 p.m., after the performance, I spoke in a hotel – the way there was torture! – to about 40 SED members, most of them theatre people. They were very satisfied. Then a dozen people, the actual core of the future theatre employees' group, remained behind around a table in the next room. General discussion, jumping from one thing to the next, on the party and cultural questions, attitude towards intelligentsia and working class, the West etc. etc. What had already been achieved, whether the situation of 1918/19 was being repeated. I brought up my Wachwitz case, the new teacher, who did not want to listen to the Jew. Education or dismissal, leniency or harshness – which causes more harm? I said, I myself was undecided, also felt myself to be partial. Opinions were divided ... I was entreated to speak to them again soon. (In the SED naturally gratis!) ... Meanwhile Erich Seidemann was here today: he reasoned with the girl and quashed the matter. To him I voiced all the pessimism that haunts me on this point and on the others ... [...] Back here at 10, washed, ate breakfast, and at 12 Wolff kindly brought me to Pirna. I found Eva very poorly after the ether anaesthetic in bed in a cold room. I had to go to the operating table and was stabbed with an injection. The operation did not hurt, but made me terribly nervous, especially the shaving beforehand. The journey home not very pleasant for E., past the Friedrichstädter Hospital, where I right away handed in our 3 suspicious objects at the Pathology Institute. The rest of the day very unpleasant for E., but also for me. To bed at 10.30 and slept until 8.15. Eva better today, but still very much in pain, and myself: tired, usque ad mortem.

[. . .]

In letters which crossed one another Marta had asked me, I had asked Marta, what had become of the Frankes.[13] Anny Kl. knew nothing of them. Yesterday a letter arrived from Else Franke, she had belatedly discovered my picture in the *Illustrierte Zeitung* and asked the editors for my address.

[. . .]

3rd February, Monday forenoon
The first *LTI* galley proofs arrived by the morning post.

8th February, Saturday evening
Eva is still in bed feeling a great deal of pain. Yesterday morning we both had the stitches taken out in Pirna. We only managed to get a car to take us there – the promised KB car was on strike again – after dramatic toing and froing. [. . .] My health is very poor, the terrible freezing from morning to night is finishing me off. By turns I look after E. – we have not yet got the [histological] result – and myself. Mostly I do not even look after myself, but am merely apathetic and – to quote father – 'I would it were bed-time, Hal, and all well' [*Henry IV*, Act V, Sc. 1]. To add the final straw to our misery, the Raschs have managed to get an apartment, today they moved out without warning, and now we are without help. A replacement is supposed – supposed . . . – to come on Tuesday, but not right away, and until then . . . The cold is not letting up, the kitchen is freezing, just before he left Rasch heaved aside the tile stove, bought a few months ago and completely useless, and in its place re-connected the small old iron stove; it provides a little warmth at least, and one can cook on it. But this one room which is now everything – sick room, bedroom, study, parlour, everything – looks terrible. [. . .]

Reingruber reported from the Saxon parliament; he sits with the SED but does not have to vote with them. On Wednesday in the car he said: the cold had achieved a 'biological selection', the old and the weak had died. [. . .] And later once again: a friend had told him, there was no need to make too much provision for the future, nature itself would make the necessary corrections. Many of the desolate ruins would simply collapse in the next few years without anyone doing anything, and the surplus of people now crowded together in Germany would also diminish of its accord – biological selection!

[. . .]

Yesterday the official call to Greifswald arrived from Schwerin. Very courteous, but they can make me no special promises of any kind. But I am recommended to travel to Greifswald and confer in person, especially with the lord mayor there. I think it out of the question, that anything will come of the matter, also it tempts me only to a limited degree; but I will no doubt undertake the journey to Greifswald (when I go to Berlin).

[...]

Vossler [...] sent me his latest things: the *Luis de León*, which I already have, 'The World in a Dream', and the *Wesenszüge romanischer Sprache und Dichtung* [Characteristics of Romance Language and Literature].[14]

A nice letter from Peter Kl., who is taking his school-leaving certificate, he has gone over from the SPD to the SED, a youth discussion had convinced him that I was right, the SPD had a one-sided Western orientation, what counted now was the right foreign policy, and a Socialist could not be against the Soviet Union. He asked for a testimonial as to his anti-Fascist attitude; he needs it in order to be matriculated in Berlin.

11th February, Tuesday evening

Very difficult days. Continuing tormenting cold and walking anywhere tortures me with pain. On Sunday to my half-hour introductory lecture (Contemporary Writing) at the Academy, which in fact went down well. [...]

Aside from that proof reading, proof reading. The publishers are printing at a breakneck pace, the galley proofs will soon all be here. [...]

Letter from Sebi Sebba: obituary for Georg in a German, evidently Jewish–German New York newspaper. Very accurate: father rabbi, brothers Felix and Victor, who 'made outstanding contributions' as a Romanist.

[...] Sebi, who again also enclosed sweetener, thread etc., writes, from 1 April he will be dismissed in favour of a British subject,[15] and thus without an income. – Letter from Willy Jelski: he is no longer an opera oboist, but in a freight company; he wants to return to Germany.

Letter from Vossler: he advises against Greifswald, my place was Leipzig.

[...]

12th February, Wednesday after minuit

Today Dressel telephoned with the histological result: Eva quite unexpectedly completely harmless, no trace of cancer; my wart in the process of transition to malignancy, but everything probably removed, and Dressel thinks we can afford to wait and see whether anything else appears. – Almost comical. And with respect to E. a deliverance. Removal of the principal worry. Except there still remain so many smaller miseries, that the appropriate joy does not really make itself felt.

Today father has been dead for 35, thirty-five! years. What right do I have to still be alive?

Frost, pain, lack of food, proof reading.

At 11 p.m. telephone call from Doris Machol in Berlin. Simply out of affection.

18th February, Thursday evening

Yesterday eventful. Call from Hilse: I am now after all going – one 'delegate' has resigned – to Berlin as a delegate to the foundation of the Victims of Fascism association. (Friday–Monday). In the afternoon it turned out that I may perhaps travel to Berlin one day earlier and take Kneschke's place at an Executive Committee meeting of the Kulturbund. [...]

On the telephone in the afternoon there was an impassioned exchange with the KB. They had arranged as programme of the celebration of the first anniversary of the Dresden group: gala concert by the Staatskapelle (cond. Keilberth) and address by Prof. Klemperer. Concert programme: Prokofiev, Debussy, Hindemith. I protested: Berlin fashions, affair of cliques and aesthetes, we shall have opposition just as against the Expressionism in the art exhibition. After a fierce argument I succeeded in having a change made: instead of Hindemith, Beethoven's 7th Symphony.

[...]

The post brought two packages from the excellent Stühlers in Munich: full of bacon, cheese, coffee, it was a blessing and immediate help and improved our mood. At the same time a letter from Toni Gerstle and Jenny Schaps, who announced a London packet. But the shortage of potatoes remained. And the still-continuing frost extends it indefinitely. So today I went to the Grubes and offered sugar in exchange. As a result, Frau Grube came to us, brought 20 lbs and stayed for hours.

[...]

19th February, Wednesday night after 12

Kneschke telephoned after our meal, there was no car to be had for Berlin, we would have to forego the Executive Committee meeting. Since walking and breathing in the icy air are bad for me, I was not especially offended at being unable to drive until Friday. – The light was cut off all day until after 10 p.m. [...] Until then read proofs. [...] Then Wolff drove his car into the garage and told me that early tomorrow he would drive (slowly with a new machine to be run in at a snail's pace) to Berlin. I vacillated greatly as to whether I should go. Fear about my health, fear of the agony of walking. Eva advised me to go. I would in any case set out on the journey a day later, only to do it in a greater rush. – As far as lodging and board are concerned things are uncertain. The Kulturbund will have to help out until Friday. My professional and private programme is long: Doris, Anny, the Frankes, Kulturbund and Aufbau, Central Administration, *Paedagogik* [periodical], Neues Leben publishing house and the Victims of Fascism business.

I am leaving E. here without any help, I am travelling with great handicaps and in a very light coat, I do not feel good about it all, and yet I must no doubt do it.

27th February, Thursday afternoon

I have not caught my breath since the extremely successful Berlin trip Thurs. 20–Sunday 23 Feb. On Tuesday I spoke on the wireless about the VVN [Vereinigung der Verfolgten des Naziregimes – Association of the Victims of the Nazi Regime], then until this afternoon I wrote the short VVN essay[16] – publication date still uncertain. Almost daily electricity cuts, frost, tiredness and poor health are a great hindrance.

[...]

The light was gone until 10 p.m. Now it's after midnight. I wrote letters.

28th February, Friday afternoon

[...]

Will I go to Greifswald, will I stay here? Today I heard: retirement already in force there, but coming here, too. No widow's pension, either here or there – for women over 65 dependent's pension, at most 90M a month. New worry. – From October we shall train elementary and grammar-school teachers here, so I would have nothing to fear. Stay? Go?

Thurs. 20th–Sun. 23rd February, Berlin trip.

Supplement in abbreviated form

Results

1) *Negotiations and conclusions*

a) KB, Abusch,[17] Wilhelm, Gysi. Contract promised for French Lit. Hist.. [...] I shall perhaps get to Paris for a few weeks. Contract also for the 18ième. Poss. [...] a monograph in addition. 4 broadcasts for the KB.

[...]

A young publisher, Henschel[18] (at the club) is bringing out 'Dramaturgische Blätter' [a drama periodical], has connections with France, wants to send me things, wants my collaboration. Also, cars from the VVN were travelling to France.

b) At the club spoke to Leuteritz[19] of the *Tägliche Rundschau*. Advance extracts from *LTI* and articles: French lit. and Russian lit.

c) At the Central Administration made the acquaintance of Dr Lange[20] of *Paedagogik*. My lecture at the Dresden People's High School inauguration will bring in 800–1000M. I am to write an essay of the same length on Kulturkunde [i.e. an approach integrating language, literature and culture of a country etc.].

2) *Executive Committee meeting of the KB*

Friedensburg chaired. Bennedik gave the main paper. Theme Kulturbund and

Moscow.[21] Voice of the KB. Can we make demands? Long discussion of the word 'demands'. The Left rejects it as presumptuous. But nevertheless calls for German unity, export and industrial opportunities. [...] The session in the 'Red Salon' on Frid. 21, began at about 11 a.m. At 1 dinner was served at the same horseshoe table, then the talking went on until 4.

3) *The VVN Congress Saturday and Sunday, 22nd 23rd February*
    [...] I did not hear Dahlem's paper;[22] I was at the Frankes' then. – Awkward was the Jewish question. Julius Meyer[23] spoke of the 'Jewish people' as one speaks of Poles and Russians, and isolated himself amidst animosity, not from the Nazis, but from Germany altogether. 'We shall never forget, not *Crystal Night*, not the 6 million dead' etc. Loewenkopf was more adroit. He roared with terrible fierceness what he once read to Eva Büttner and myself (as we were coming from Kamenz) from the letter of an émigré friend: 'they should wash themselves with soap, made from the fat of Jewish bodies; they should sleep on mattresses, stuffed with the hair of Jewish women – then perhaps they would not forget!' But he did not separate the German Jews from Germany. But in the canteen, when we were eating, he complained vehemently about new anti-Semitism, even in the SED [...].

4) On Saturday from 5.30 until about 9 there was a performance of *Pastor Hall* by Ernst Toller[24] in the Deutsches Theater. The most curious thing about it: the set for the first act: Realistic: the Hall family dining room. Expressionist: behind it a nightmare, anticipatory backdrop; the concentration camp, the masts of the live wire fences, the wooden watchtower. At first I did not understand it, because I had never seen such a camp. [...] Content of the piece worthy, but not overwhelming. Perhaps also because what was new for Toller in 1938 or 39 is now old hat. [...]

1st March, private matters
Journey there with Wolff and a young black marketeer. [...]
    I was set down at the KB building on Schlüterstr., got a frugal meal there, spent hours with Willmann, Gysi, Abusch (the new man and 'ideological director' of the publishing house – Wilhelm is business manager, but does not much like to be reminded of this restriction), during intervals – as during the rest of these days – read my *LTI* proofs. [...] I then drove to the club – I had telephoned Doris earlier, without catching her, only leaving her a message ... When I had finished supper – the food in the club is very good [...] Doris appeared. She is 'announced', I had difficulties getting her in. She complained the club was on the one hand very exclusive, on the other many insignificant journalists frequented it, and she herself was now chief editor of a section of the Soviet news agency. [...]
    Once in touch with Doris and Mackie, I had no more worries. I have become very attached to both of them and not just via my stomach. They are people of intellect and somehow congenial to me. During these days they really filled me

with warmth, gave me a kind of home. I lived in their kitchen, they themselves slept in *the* big room with the two couches at right angles [...]. Doris is more at home in French than in German. She has told me a great deal about her disrupted childhood. Heinz evidently treated the children of the first marriage lovelessly and brutally. With Mackie ('uncle', he says to me, as if it were the most natural thing [...]) talked about the Jewish theme. He is a little bit – pas trop[25] – more well disposed to the Zionists than I am, belongs to the Jewish community, without believing, has a completely German education (36 years old), parents Eastern Jews, is 'very mad' at the Germans. [...]

On Saturday afternoon I skipped Dahlem's paper and went to visit the Frankes: the tram set me down where Grossbeerenstr. begins at an oblique angle to Königgrätzerstr. (vieux nom),[25a] but 55 Grossbeerenstr. lies almost at the foot of Kreuzberg hill [...]. Old Berlin, when I crossed Yorckstr., memories of Loewenstein & Hecht[26] came to mind. In places great destruction, some corners unrecognisable. The Frankes in an old undamaged building. Large apartment, nicely furnished, but only one (large and gloomy) room very feebly heated. I only gradually recognised the three sisters again – not shabby, but sooo old and grey. Else at 71 the least changed. Stone deaf despite ear-trumpet, interrupting conversations with something unrelated. Great affection for me. They made me ghastly coffee, gave me 3 spread slices of bread, a gift. [...]

Those are probably the essentials of the Berlin trip.

In the catchwords of the Berlin notes I also find:

From the Frankes' I took the underground to Oranienburger Tor, went from there along Karl and Albrechtstr. to the Deutsches Theater. The house from 1890 with Denks, the tailor, is no longer standing.[27] The barracks square opposite is still empty! On the corner of Karlstr. and deep into Albrechtstr. a mysterious palace prison, a huge block with the tiniest window slits. Monumental decorative statuary on the Karlstr. side. Inscription 'Mother and Child'. I do not know what the thing was. At Doris's I heard: a bunker. So solid that it withstands attempts to blow it up.[28]

[...]

2nd March, Sunday morning

Every second day now the same thing: waiting and counting flower petals – will the car come, will it not? Has it been 'organised', will it get up the hill in snow and ice? – Particularly awful weather since yesterday. [...] Now at 9.10 I am waiting for the car, that is to pick me up at 9 for Bischofswerda. Presumably it is not managing the hill; the car from Dresden broadcasting station recently turned back at the beginning of the incline, and I had to go up on foot. [...]

Yesterday afternoon at 4, therefore, to the huge hall of the Sachsenverlag [Saxony publishing house], Riesaerstr., for the VVN founding meeting for Dresden district. At least 1500 people, perhaps more, there are more than 3,000 Victims of Fascism in Dresden. The already familiar presentation of such meetings. We were guided right to the front. It was horribly cold, there was a draught from the stage with the chairman's table. I was called onto the platform.

Grosse[29] and Hilse the managers, Loewenkopf, Eva Schulze-Knabe, another couple of people. Very fine introductory music, Schubert's 'Unfinished', as in Berlin very fine homage to the dead – Egon Rentzsch spoke to the accompaniment of quiet music, addresses by Kastner, now deputy prime minister, embarrassing pathos [...]; Koenen very interesting, comparing the Saxon constitution adopted yesterday to the tame Weimar one; Weimar was democratic; we are 'militantly democratic', guarding against the forces of reaction. No freedom for enemies of democracy! – Then it went wrong: E. Rentzsch's paper about Berlin became so unreasonably long, that the shivering audience began to leave. Finally someone shouted: 'Make it shorter, or the hall will be empty!' At that he finished. Now a management committee of 15 people was proposed, *I* was one of them. Usual unanimous adoption. Finally a choir sang 'The Moor Soldiers'. Via Loewenkopf who spoke briefly and again very well on behalf of the Jews – Grosse and Rentzsch had also stood up against anti-Semitism – once again desecration of graves at Weissensee![30] – via Loewenkopf I put my France plan into circulation here, also made an effort to be a participant at the forthcoming VVN conferences in Frankfurt and Munich. Still uncertain. – 9.30 the car for Bischofswerda has not appeared.

4 p.m.
Then it came after all. [...] In Bischofswerda – little town of 10,000 (now 12,000) inhabitants, 2 large rectangular squares otherwise rows of houses on long bare streets – in a huge room in the House of the People a book exhibition, in a well-heated restaurant 47 people sitting at tables. I placed myself close to the stove and recited my *LTI*. 100M, a poor dinner, the definite promise to send me potatoes again at the end of the week, finally a swede and a couple of handfuls of potatoes – 'a dinner' – cadged from the hotelier and received as a present.
[...]

11th March, Tuesday morning
[...]
Steininger visited us and showed me a printed (therefore sent to very many people) letter from a Hamburg carrier. Principal content: We regret that your Stockholm packet No 6 ... has been stolen. Our storeroom is guarded, but 'we are powerless against large gangs armed with pistols'. Another carrier, Grünhut, Bremen, writes to me, that he has our Stockholm packet (of 31 October!) in store and it will go on to Berlin, 'as soon as the weather permits an escort of reliable customs officers'. I must indicate, how it should reach us from Berlin.
Cold, pain, hunger, frost – that fills 95% of my thoughts and of the day. The inner vacillation between journalism and scholarship the remaining 5%.

13th March, Thursday evening
Here this afternoon from Falkenstein a pharmacist, Kizio, employed by Scherner. Scherner died on 7 March of pneumonia. [...] It weighs heavily on me. In a

very egoistical, otherwise unfeeling way: When will it be my turn? And what will become of Eva? [...]

After the unprecedented famine of recent days, and after I had spent literally hours on the repeatedly failing telephone making SOS calls, there was a dramatic morning yesterday. First Frau Steininger brought a small portion of potatoes, then one of the Zabel twins appeared with 2 heavy bags; contents: a loaf, a larger quantity of potatoes and turnips, several tins of vegetables, plum spread, syrup, some sugar. Last came Frau Heinsch (her nails and lips thickly painted) on behalf of the Neuers – acquaintances and neighbours – with potatoes and some flour. In addition the Zabels and Neuer donated a couple of bottles of fruit drink. With that the most extreme shortage has been removed for a few days. But if the frost holds – it thaws during the day – at night the frost is still very hard – the shortage will return. [...]

Yesterday and today I wrote 'French Poetry' for the Kulturbund broadcast. [...]

23rd March, Sunday forenoon etc.
Berlin trip 19 and 20 March 47

Kneschke telephoned on Monday, the journey to Berlin to negotiate a compromise with refractory Leipzig would already take place on Wednesday. Departure 6.30 in the morning, return journey Thurs. afternoon [...] I spent the two days until departure working intensely on the broadcast topics, which I wanted to speak on tape in Berlin, and indeed managed them all by Tuesday night. (These 4 variations and compressions of earlier work: *The Marriage of Figaro*; *French Poetry*; *Politics and Writing*; *Humanism, Humanity and Humanism Again* have taken up the whole week.)

Meanwhile the weather had changed quite programmatically from the most typical winter with snow and ice to early spring, again typical. Melting snow, rain, ice, mud, flood, fog.

On Tues. evening the whole trip was thrown into doubt: a permit now necessary to enter Berlin had not yet been obtained. Wed. morning (the 19th) passed with waiting in filthy weather. [...] We (Kneschke, myself, Schumann, the Kulturbund driver) did not get away from Dresden until after 12. [...] We were in Schlüterstr. at about 5. A car from the Berlin Kulturbund was waiting for us in Potsdam, the Leipzigers had been waiting at Jägerstr. since forenoon. – We drove there and met Becher, Willmann, Gadamer and Engewald, a bookseller in his early 50s. Everything [...] had already been settled amicably: henceforth the Leipzigers will pay dues to Berlin like every other local group, they will have a place on and recognise the management committee for Saxony in Dresden. [...] There really only remained – but this was important – a discussion, a kind of reconciliation of a personal kind. I said: we Dresdeners were a little sensitive, I recalled the tension between Leipzig University and the Cultural Sciences Department [at Dresden TH].[31] Gadamer was friendly as shit, I was, too – outwardly and for the moment there was friendship. During the negotiation there was a good meal, with the addition of a bowl of soup for us famished Dresdeners. [...]

On Friday 22, proper early spring day with rain and wind and snowdrops and first tinge of green on the trees, at the TH in the morning. Walk there not quite as tiring as usual, but still painful, came back very slowly but without pain. In the autumn the Educ. Faculty is to start working normally, and I am to start training teachers *normally*. Recently a warning shot: the Russians are demanding a teaching plan according to which I have to give 8 lectures a semester on Lit. Hist. *and* prosody *and* historical grammar. I said to myself: if I must, then rather in Greifswald. Now I have heard from Straub: it's not as bad as that. I can leave historical grammar to a teacher, who will be specially engaged for 'Methodology of Teaching French'. Nevertheless [...] from the winter semester on my complete freedom to write and to give talks is over and from Whitsun I already have to give 4 lectures on the 18ième. Once again: if I am to be restricted by academic tasks, then perhaps rather in Greifswald.

[...]

On Saturday I prepared my 'address' for the first anniversary celebration of the Kulturbund. I kept closely to the concert programme. 1) Prokofiev, 2) Debussy, *L'après-midi d'un faune*, 3) Beethoven's 7th Symphony. I was to speak between 2 and 3. I started from Mallarmé's poem ['Prélude a l'après-midi d'un faune']. Parallels to the situation of the KB and model. Intellectual ascent, link to other countries. Link to Germany's true friend, to the true torch-bearer of culture: Russia, Prokofiev. Appeal to Moscow for German unity, Germany whole: Beethoven! The sketch was really good – and the evening turned out a very serious failure. Kurhaus Bühlau, 22 March, 6 p.m. Most dreadful rainy weather, the huge shed $\frac{3}{4}$ full. Ministry, authorities not represented, front rows almost empty. When I come to the Russian passage, demonstration. Coughing, scraping, laughing, noises. Shouts: Cheek! Don't interrupt! I talked over it all, loudly, calmly, for about 15 minutes. At the Germany conclusion it grew quiet, applause at the end. I noticed no agitation. But I developed pains, and when I walked back to my seat, I had a proper attack of angina for several minutes, a serious memento. Then Keilberth conducted the symphony, it was played with passion, and it got thunderous repeated applause, which was an unmistakable continuation of the demonstration. It meant: No Kulturbund policies, no Jewish Bolshevism, but Beethoven and our [...] Keilberth! What riled me most, was that in the discussion of the situation Kneschke and Eva Blank did say, that perhaps I had been too radical. Always the fear of showing one's colours. Always the democratic meekness of 1919. [...]

28th March, Friday evening

On Mond. afternoon meeting of the regional committee of the Kulturbund at Emser Allee. Menke-Glückert chaired. So thin and pale, after a recent illness, that I felt sorry for him. Kneschke reported on Berlin. [...] On every side some firm voices against the demonstration during the anniversary celebration. Egon Rentzsch had telephoned me about it the day before, definitely adopting a more drastic tone. – All of today taken up with the KB. 'Area Conference' in the Academy from 9.30–4 p.m., with a (meagre) dinner together in the refectory. [...] I [...] spoke about the work of the Literature Section. 'De-Nazification of German Literature. They have appropriated Schiller, Herder etc. Even Nietzsche belongs to them only in part ...' I was elected onto the area committee. I am to give lectures in various places again. On the whole the day passed with empty talk. [...]

Work: I began the 'Culture' pamphlet on 25 March.[32] On 2–3 printed sheets it must condense and formulate the various themes I have talked about dozens of times since summer 45. I have run my legs off with these things, I am fed up to the back teeth with them, and yet I find the task so very hard.

In addition France reading: Salacrou:[33] [...] Saint-Exupéry: the flying book.[34] At length a little too refined for me. I want to start a special folder for all of that.

[...]

29th March, Saturday evening

After lunch today I spoke from about 3–4.15 in Görlitz, in the assembly hall of the former classical grammar school on culture ('democratic cultural policy') [...]. About 150 present, teachers – an outstanding success. I had to say, whether I had published or would publish any of it, referred to the forthcoming pamphlet and to the *LTI*. [...] I should speak there again as soon as possible ... The success and the 120M were not the important thing about this trip. Nor that I saw the German border – we drove to the Neisse. The silent (abandoned) row of houses on the river bank of this insignificant river already belongs to Poland. Over the bridge, upriver, there is a tall shed, painted like a sentry box, Russian sentries in front of it [...]. Important was the provisioning in Piskowitz. Hahnewald drove with us, FDGB [Free German Trades Union Alliance] official, 49-year-old, originally a draughtsman, manner of a primary school teacher. He came punctually at 9 and at 11 we dropped off E. at the land girls' camp in Piskowitz. [...] Back in Piskowitz [from Görlitz] shortly after 6. Coffee and pancakes for everyone. And E. had amassed a cwt of potatoes, a little sack of swedes, a round $8\frac{1}{2}$ lb loaf, some curd, butter, syrup, a couple of pancakes. But now the driver declared, his tyres would not take the weight. I decided [...] to leave E. in Piskowitz. She likes to be there and can rest a little. There is no train on Sunday. Perhaps Eva Büttner will drive to Dresden at the beginning of the week. I advised E. to take her time. – At the last moment I came within an inch of losing the loot. I had fallen asleep. We stop just before Bühlau. A policewoman, coming up to the car: 'You can drive on, you've just been inspected haven't you?' – Yes, says the driver and continues. – 'Did I sleep through a checkpoint?' – 'A minute ago a policeman shouted "halt", but I was already past him and accelerated. It would have been a waste of the potatoes. They confiscate everything.' By then we were already in Dresden. Home at 10 p.m.

[...]

Everywhere on the road carts: handcarts, horse-drawn carts, whole convoys of carts drawn by heavy tractors. Everywhere in the woods the felling of trees. On all sides complaints about woodland being laid waste. [...]

30th March, Sunday midnight

A day without Eva is a long one.

I managed more than 2 pages of 'Culture' even though there were visitors both morning and afternoon. [...]

In the afternoon Lotte Kreisler and her elderly husband. They brought their own bread, we gossiped cheerfully over coffee. She showed me a printed concert programme from 1940 in which Laux, comrade and Assistant Secretary Laux writes quite repulsively about the half-Jew Hanslick,[35] 'the evil spirit of negation', the 'fierce enemy of Richard Wagner', and who had vituperated against Bruckner. And now, 'in June 37 in the presence of the Führer the Bruckner bust had been unveiled in the Valhalla'.[36] Embarrassing. They are none of them innocent. [...]

31st March, Monday evening

Unexpectedly E. already came back this evening. On foot from Piskowitz to Kamenz, to Eva Büttner, from whom she received an official rail pass.

In the morning at the TH a very drastic change in my situation. I brought the required completed timetable for 6+2 teacher-training lectures per session and the request for the re-appointment of Irene Papesch. That is what had been agreed. From October we were to be fully responsible for the training of all teachers, from Whitsun I was to lecture, optionally at first, on my 18ième. – Yesterday a supreme decision overturning everything came from Russian head-quarters in Karlshorst: sharpest possible separation of TH and university. Here *only* technicians, vocational teachers and natural scientists will be trained, all educational-historical chairs (German excepted) wound up. Thus I am left hanging in the air. Greifswald possibly essential.

[...]

In the afternoon visit by Frau Hoppe-Freund (after having long borne a grudge). Loewenkopf sent word, I can come to the Dachau meeting on 8 May.

2nd April, Wednesday evening

Telegram from Greifswald. Rector 'appoints me professor', requests me to go there – 'official trip' – for discussion.

[...]

In the afternoon at Melanchthonstr. Long SED session. Should the opera house be blown up or renovated or how should it be replaced?[37] Passionate discussion. Gute gave a paper about opera and opera houses, in which in his usual way he emphasised exclusively the political-social element. (New to me: boxes point to courtly coterie diplomacy.) Several architects for a radical demolition of the ruin; Gute wants to have a palace for people's opera and people's cinema there. The conservative opposition wants to preserve 'the townscape': the loss of the opera would destroy the whole square. Dölitzsch in a passionate speech: 'Don't say, one is a bad Socialist, if one has conservative views on this subject. And show consideration for the people of Dresden, who are 95% in favour of preservation.' Interruption: '95% also voted for Hitler!' Mayor Wagner, who is in charge of food: defer the question for a few months! We're starving, there's no time for art. – Comrade Schön: we have to clarify it; in the city council the LDP is moving that 250,000M be set aside to 'safeguard the structure'.

[...]

3rd April, Thursday evening
[...]
Highlight of the day: Late in the evening, quite unexpectedly a Russian Easter packet brought by a chauffeur. Plenty of butter, white flour, herrings, potatoes, tinned meat, sugar, jam, brawn, 100 cigarettes. – We were as happy as children.

6th April, Easter Sunday evening
[...]
On Friday 4 April at Melanchthonstr. in the morning. Victims of Nazism meeting: Buchenwald. Statements by individuals with ghastly details. Then Mauthner: precise details. Such and such facts suitable as propaganda. Slipped in as unannounced surprise broadcasts – that way the public is forced to listen. [...]
Second proofs of *LTI* arrived at last. I am working on them – the pamphlet is at a standstill.

[...]

12th April, Saturday evening
Yesterday long session at the Kulturbund. From 10.30 a.m. until almost 6 p.m. Preparing the regional conference in Chemnitz, where the regional management committee is to be elected. By arguing for Renn,[38] I avoided Gadamer, who nevertheless cannot be neutralised. [...]
Lotte Sussman – with us until Monday – then starts at Löbtau Hospital – a firm believer. [...] Apart from that she is sensible, unaffected and educated. [...]

14th April, Monday evening
In the afternoon in the broadcasting studio of the Hygiene Museum an SED recruitment event, works committee of the Saxon administration. About 500 people, concert by Keilberth, readings, address Prof Dr Klemperer. Some variation on the usual, applause. It does not satisfy me at all any more. Yet it gave me palpitations and aches. [...]

Then taken by car to the Saxon administration. Talk with Gute and Simon. New situation, like a blow to my head: Jan goes to Jena, Werner Krauss *already* appointed in his place. That is what the Central Administration in Berlin had wanted. Krauss was a gain from the West, the first one, and was younger than I, who was of retirement age. I am being allowed a free choice between retirement here (which Gute advises) and acceptance in Greifswald. One other person has been called to a chair in Leipzig: Kühn. What a farce! There wasn't anyone else, he had retracted his pamphlet, was 'not really Nazi' – a few real Nazis had also had to be put up with. We were depopulated, half of Leipzig was threatening to go off to the West.

16th April, Wednesday evening
The serious ill-humour at Leipzig almost overcome. But in the afternoon on the wireless a big rigmarole about the de-Nazification and democratisation of the universities, and just now in the news, Leipzig Univ. has gained scholars with international reputations. Among them: Professor Johannes Kühn from Dresden. It did after all upset me badly again.
[...]
Continuing vacillation with respect to Greifswald.
[...]

17th April, Thursday evening
In the morning at the Tonhalle from 11–1 opening of the Art Academy and of the High School for Arts and Crafts (Grundig and Grohmann). The usual. Keilberth rampaged again with the orchestra. Hindemith, Maler Mathis. [...] Speeches. Gute, Buchwitz etc. I showed my face and shook hands with prominent persons. Donath beside me. He said, the Kühn affair had been settled between Gute and Simon alone and would cause a scandal yet. I gave notice that I would protest to the Party.

In the evening Wolff drove me to a district meeting of the Victims of Nazism on Hohe Stein. Beautiful spring evening and a grand sunset. Excellent robust provocative talk by the comrade on the district committee: Grundt. He several times pointed to the recent demonstration against me in Bühlau. [...] At my table the Steiningers. I also spoke to Werner Lang, who looks in the best of spirits and (as once before) was sitting beside a wild red-haired Jew. Edmund Müller. Suddenly it dawned on me: he must be the brother of the tragic Stephan – Gestapomüller.[39] 8 people had to be elected for the local groups as a management committee; there were 10 names on the ballot paper. I did not put a cross at the names of Werner Lang and Edmund Müller. On the last lap of the Culture pamphlet.
[...]

21st April, 11 p.m. Monday evening

Back from Meissen. Very nice springtime drive there at 6.30. Kulturbund lecture Zola–Barbusse prepared yesterday. From my own Lit. Hist. with remarks from my present position. (Taine[40]– Marx: Socialism and Materialism. Marx the idealist!) Much applause. [. . .]

Today, during the day, the culture pamphlet.

Letter from Frank Forbrig in Greifswald. Jacoby says, he will satisfy me domestically, but expects the scholar and teacher – the politician 'only fifth'.

[. . .]

29th April, Tuesday after supper

[. . .]

So Chemnitz [KB regional conference]. Saturday and Sunday, 26 and 27 April. About 200 people there, about 190 were eligible to vote, 188 did so. I am in 4th place with 172 votes. Ahead of me, apart from Renn (elected by acclamation), Gadamer and Grüss, the rector of Freiberg Mining Academy, and quite unknown to me, CDU. Gadamer 180, Grüss 174, myself 172 votes. I must, perhaps I should, be pleased. The Leipzigers no doubt voted against me. [. . .]

(2 May) Most interesting about the whole thing was the journey there and back with Renn, who picked me up here. Thin blond man, fairly bald, decent, unaffected appearance and manner, 58. A little amusing, the way they turned him into a very big shot here (counterpart to Becher), and how he gets the regional chairmanship as 'above party' (after the ousting of Menke-Glückert.) Confidently talkative. Less a writer than a semi-scholar. He talked about his autobiography *Aristocracy in Decline* [. . .] about a book on primitive cults (*Vom Affen zum Menschen* – From Ape to Man) [. . .]. Something else affected me more. He says it is vouched for and very well known abroad, that Dresden was destroyed by the English and Americans against Russian objections, and only because they did not want the Russians to have the city.[41] [. . .]

The Chemnitz meeting took place in the hall of an insurance company. [. . .] Boring. Debates as usual without content, [people talking] past one another. Longest, far too long speech by Abusch. Semper idem ... Over lunch in the ratskeller discussion with Abusch and Gysi. They attacked my traits éternels[42] in 'German Roots' [in LTI]. That will possibly turn into a 'debate' for the Berlin Broadcasting Station. On 12 May I am to speak on the LTI in Jägerstr [in Berlin]. For the night to the Chemnitzer Hof, elegant, well-preserved hotel at the main railway station (hot water!) Russian billet and its function rooms out of bounds to the conquered. A number of us stood around thirsty in the lobby. Völske, the Chemnitz Kulturbund director with the strong Berlin accent, invited us to his apartment, in which the Kneschkes and little Arnold were quartered. The man has several elegantly furnished rooms in the house of a furniture dealer. Up there we chatted over tea and cognac. As already over the meal Gadamer and I talked informally, innocuously and both as friendly as shit, I chatted with Volwahsen [. . .] etc. [. . .] To bed at 12, up early on Sunday. Unpleasant start to the day: I met Eva Blank, and we went, as we had been directed, to the canteen next to the hotel. There the German waiters, not brutally but nevertheless firmly showed us the door – the premises were *only* for Russian officers, it would be awkward for us if we stayed. It then turned out, that we got our breakfast in another hotel. After that another trying session, in the morning and in the afternoon the election. [...]

2nd May, towards evening

At last made the final correction to the 'culture pamphlet'. I have been working on it since 25 March, and I am not quite satisfied with it. But how many distractions!

[...]

Then yesterday 1 May something completely new. Popular orator! Drive [...] through half of Saxony: Meissen–Döbeln–Hartha–Mittweida–*Burgstädt*. [...] A wild driver, carpenter from Dölzschen, who knew all the circumstances up here and our own story. [...] When we arrived at 10, zealous welcomes were already being spoken. Or rather shouted. Beside the orator a loudspeaker. Announcement: Now we have the principal speaker Professor Kemperer (sic) from Dresden. A moment of emptiness in me, then I started shouting. Beside me IT, the megaphone, roared and reverberated. [...] A primitive business, this speaking in the open air.

Now I am to speak on the 'Day of the Book Burning' a week on Sunday.[43] Twice. In the museum, Dürerstr., and in the evening in Freital. A version of the speech is to be broadcast in advance.

I am squandering myself, I think: I must go to Greifswald. We talk about the pros and cons of it x times a day; my heart is very heavy. Eva is clearly for staying, only does not want to inhibit me. I am attracted by the new, I am haunted by the thought of being laid up here as a pensioner.

Now for days I have to dispose of the private and official arrears of correspondence that have been piling up. Today decent Flamensbeck from Unterbernsbach asked me for an exonerating testimonial for the de-Nazification tribunal.[44] I can commend him, cf *LTI*, penultimate page – but I cannot 'exonerate' him.

[...]

Mimesis by Erich Auerbach,[45] which on Vossler's recommendation I requested from Francke [publishers] in Bern, arrived by way of a private person in Konstanz. [...]

[...]

Better diet with a constant stream of packets.

4th May, Sunday forenoon

My self-confidence badly shaken by Auerbach's overpoweringly good *Mimesis*. (Read the first 50 pages yesterday between deadly private letters.) He knows Latin, Mediaeval Latin, Old French, Hebrew – he is a philologist. What would I have been able to achieve, if I possessed such resources. Suddenly I am shaken by fear that I could disgrace myself in Greifswald. Veteres angustiae redivivae.[45a] Should I allow myself to be pensioned off after all? But then here I am a clown of all trades, a soon-used-up locally important person and always overshadowed and disdained by Leipzig.

[...]

Very depressed.

7th May, Wednesday towards evening

Yesterday E. made a public appearance, accompanied the tall Stephan-Hamann in a Schubert evening in Freital, then herself played the *Wanderer Fantasie*. It gave her evident pleasure. She is at once far more talented and far less vain than I.

For my part I cannot get over the defeat with respect to Leipzig. On top of that the terrible uncertainty of my financial situation here. It will no doubt be Greifswald – I am now considering leaving E. here and living there alone. It will only be for a few semesters.

[...]

Reading *Mimesis*.

11th May, Sunday

The Day of the Burning of Books, 10 May 33. Big propaganda affair. I spoke 3×. Yesterday afternoon at the Dresden Broadcasting Station [...] – during the actual broadcast my part was read. This afternoon to a good 90 people at the Arts and Crafts Museum, this evening to about 60 in Freital. Very great success.

[...]

Yesterday afternoon from the broadcasting station to Loschwitz – spring, suspension railway, Hermann Prellstr. There in a villa with a most beautiful distant view [...] the cultural research institute of the TH was officially opened. Directors: *Professor* Ludwig Renn and Spamer. I suggested, that I might have something to fall back on there. Renn, who is on first name terms with me, enthused, Gute in favour of course – but would that be security? [...]

15th May, Thursday forenoon
Berlin trip 12th–14th May 1947

The book [a ringbinder VK now used for his diary] is a present from Doris and Mackie. And the beginning is perhaps really a 'historic moment' for me, a caesura. If the Berlin guest professorship comes to pass, if...

[...]

On Sunday all hopes of a journey by car came to nothing. Left early on Monday morning at 6.15, difficult upsetting fight for the overcrowded tram, my heart affected. On the train I found a seat and quiet. A couple of pages Werner Krauss *PLN*.[46] What duplication: *PLN–LTI*. [...] At Aufbauverlag, Französische Strasse at 3. Wilhelm's successor Wendt,[47] no longer young man, very nice. He was not entirely in the picture, I once again summarised my plan for the Lit. Hist. He will give me a definite decision in two weeks; I really do believe that my 19th and 20th Century will be to his liking. He wants 'humanism' at a high level, but not philology. As a present I received 1,000 sheets of typing paper (a blessing!) and a packet of cigarettes. – *LTI* will come out at the end of June, 1,000 copies, price 5M [...]; a second edition in winter. No cause for vanity in that; 'the booksellers buy any rubbish and pay in advance, just to have something at all'.

By the time I got to Wendt I was exhausted and had very bad pains – the short stretch from Jägerstr., but immediately after eating, and I was worn out already – he gave me a car, which took me to *Neues Leben* [New Life], Kronenstr., and from there back to the club. *Neues Leben*, i.e. the periodical of the FDJ, the Communist Youth organisation and its pamphlet publishing arm. Schlesinger, a friendly man, mid-40s, its head – an intellectual, presumably Jewish. [...]

(24 May. Now everything has been overlaid by what came later, I am reconstructing with difficulty.) From Schlesinger I presumably drove to the club, where my LTI lecture was set for 6 p.m. Brugsch, the good-looking and engaging, somewhat garrulous old gentleman, doctor, wanted to have particulars for the introduction. Which he then delivered fairly feebly. The Klemperers Georg and Felix with their hospitals and their literary talent. Now Victor, admittedly not a doctor, but also with literary talent(!). A book on Montesquieu, a history of French literature. Now *LTI* ... There were less than 75 people there, and I rattled off my piece. Much applause. The discussion consisted of additional examples, was in no way hostile. Schottländer[48] (who is getting the Dresden chair) asked, to what extent the LTI expressions were invented by the Nazis and used by them alone. I gave a detailed answer to that and several other questions. [...] At Kahane's prompting I was driven to Niederschönhausen after the lecture. Mackie [...] was on night duty and did not come until almost 1. So it grew late. But on Tue. the 13th I woke up very early, felt fresh and, sitting on the bed, noted down a few points for the Becher wireless birthday congratulations. In the morning the news agency car brought me to the broadcasting building. Made the acquaintance of Dr Deml and Frau Jung [...].

I spoke the Becher congratulation haltingly. For a moment I wanted to abandon it; but Deml whispered to me, it would turn out well, it could be touched up on tape. I then listened to what I had said; despite or because of the pauses it really was good. Afterwards I agreed 4 pieces of work with Deml: two of 14 minutes for 200M each about the People's High School and about France and two 9 minute ones for 150 each about Petrarch and about Voltaire.

It was now almost 1 p.m.; I skipped dinner and went (by underground) to the Central Administration in Wilhelmstr. I finally met Rompe, also spoke to Böhm, Heise (and last I met Lange in the Adlon). [...]

To Anny Kl. Warm welcome. Peter present. Today, the Saturday before Whitsun, he has gone to the FDJ meeting in Meissen. [...] Finally back to the Kahanes (underground). – All day they had been trying to arrange my return journey. [... But] Schlesinger had offered me a seat in his car [...]. I chose the car. It fetched me punctually at 6.15 a.m., was supposed to be in Dresden at about 11 a.m. ... At 5 p.m. it had its 5th and final tube problem. Until then repeated rests at the forest edge of the motorway. Now tube gum and good cheer were at an end. We spent about a quarter of an hour outside Ortrand, less than 20 miles from Dresden. We hoped for galvanisation in the village. Impossible. There was no train until 8 the next morning. A coal convoy came up, tractor and 3 waggons with briquettes. Potato-foraging women were taken along. They were standing waiting in little groups all along the road. I climbed up, sat on the cardboard box with potatoes, which the Kahanes had given me. It rained, thundered, poured. The convoy went about as far as the terminus of the 19 tram. Afterwards I had to get up the hill with the heavy baggage. Home at 11 p.m. very exhausted, very wet, with many pains.

The next day very wretched and depressed, very unwisely on the trip to Dachau.

15th–19th May, VVN [Victims of Nazi Persecution] Trip Dresden–Munich/Dachau
Actual congress 17th, 18th May 47

We met at 3 p.m. at Bautzenerstr. 23 delegates from Saxony. Hilse and Loewenkopf as leaders of the delegation, Schrecker as journalist. – Left Neustädter station at 5 p.m. Fast train, 2nd class, very comfortable and restful. At 10 p.m. in Plauen. Waiting room. A meat broth. Waited until 1. Then a coal train. Baggage van. Stops after a short time; stops again and again. The fuel is supposed to be to blame. Everybody out! Burning coals are dropping under the engine. La Lison![49] Wait for a later goods train! It comes at about 2.30, and at 4.30 it reaches Gutenfürst, the Soviet border station given on our zonal pass. Check without any bother. A tiny strip of no man's land. Then Feilitzsch the USA border point. The confiscated bottle of wine, the impounded Gorky.[50] This part we travelled on the once-more-functioning coal train. Then we found a goods train, which for an extra charge got us to Hof at 8.50. On from here at 9.15 in a goods train which took us towards Munich by way of a long detour. At 11 in Lichtenfels. 4 hour break. Two plates of soup to be had in a restaurant. At last a limited stop train: Donauwörth, Nürnberg, Augsburg. In Munich at 10 in the evening, i.e. after 30 hours. It could have been worse, we had to reckon on not arriving in Munich until the following morning. A few minutes made all the difference. (The incalculability of the border stops and therefore of connections.) – On the way friendly impassioned arguments with Schrecker; I gave him my VVN article in the *Sonntag* newspaper to read; he was furious at me, because I had spoken of a German anti-Fascist 'movement' and of the 'other Germany'. (Which then at the congress everyone did.) [...] In Munich from the station to the VVN office in Goethestr. Very bad pains. There they (and Schrecker) took care of me. Car to the Hotel Burghof on Marienplatz. Choice accommodation. Schrecker (moved out the next day) in the room next to me. He had real coffee with him, had it made for us. Restorative night. – This day of rest, 16 May, had been our wedding day. I only remembered on Saturday, the 17th, when I hoped to lay hands on E.'s compositions and experienced such a

severe disappointment. I already had the telegram in my head [...] On Schrecker's advice I presented myself autocratically at the Goethestr. office as a
person of importance, whereupon one of the still-very-elegant Munich taxis
was put at my disposal. We first drove to the Stühlers. A long way out, near
Nymphenburg Palace, Carl Schurzstr., very warm welcome. (I helped them get
an attestation that Bernhard had worn the Jew's star. The Americans had not
believed them, which is why the planned emigration had thus far come to
nothing.) They had collected the things deposited with Landsdorfer, the baker,
and will send them to Berlin. (It is still not possible to do so to Dresden.) They
had not yet received the packet of sheet music from R[...] and feared it had
been sold off illicitly. I packed in the Stühlers, and we drove to R[...]. Another
suburb (where?) [...]. I did not know the man, had only seen him once beside
cemetery-Jacobi in Dresden. His landlady said he was out, but mentioned a
restaurant in town, where he usually eats. We really did find him there, an
altogether likeable-looking man, blond, slim, calm, almost distinguished. No –
he had never fetched the things from the hostel – Yes, he had received the letter
from me back then. He would come with us. We drove to St Martin's Hostel.[51]
There everything as it was 2 years ago. Statement: the packet had been handed
over, since the person – unknown – calling for it had presented my handwritten
letter, there was no receipt, R. himself had not fetched it. – I took R. aside, told
him: I was not out for revenge, if he *only* got the sheet music back to me, I
would leave him in peace, give away nothing, but otherwise I would report him
to the police. He insisted, that he had not fetched the packet, nor had it fetched.
I let him go and with the Stühlers drove to police headquarters, where I laid a
charge against R. for misappropriation. The police officer shrugged his shoulders,
evidently considered it a hopeless case. – Since then I have not had a peaceful
day. I felt every success to be an injustice to E., who has now lost everything,
the compositions after the pictures and the architectural drawings. She is so
infinitely more talented, and nothing of her remains. I feel somehow guilty ...
At her request I sent an urgent telegram from here promising a 'large reward'
for R [...], if he procures the sheet music. E. says, I should have done it
immediately; now under the pressure of the criminal charge, he has certainly
burned the sheets. Also in the packet were two woollen dresses and underwear
... From then on the whole trip was soured for me.

[...]

From police headquarters I had myself driven to the 'big canteen', a food
shed, not far from the Ostbahnhof station, where the general feedings took
place in a fairly charmless Bavarian barracks manner. [...] From there (by
bus? details are already becoming blurred) to the Prinzregententheater, whose
impressive auditorium I remembered, and which did not disappoint me. The
State Commissioner for the Racially Persecuted, Dr Philipp Auerbach, huge
man, very fat, his neck unduly swollen (somehow sickly), little piggy eyes in a
plump, bulky head, very forceful on his frequent appearances, altogether fiercely
anti-Nazi and fierce in his opposition to Bavarian domestic politics – but exceed-
ingly nervous at mention of Russia and the SED. He was the only government
man to appear, the prime minister sent his apologies. The whole congress was

ignored as far as possible – one did not want to be reminded. So Auerbach delivered the words of welcome.[52] Afterwards Verdi's Requiem was played by a large orchestra (conductor Georg Solti).[53] Some of it I immediately found beautiful – but on the whole my mind wandered.

Now the majority of the 1000 participants moved off to the big canteen again, to which I also had my invitation. But I was passed word: the delegates were eating in the Spatenbräu, and I was taken there. There and then Auerbach wrote a special instruction for myself and x others on some bit of paper. Perhaps 100 of the 1000 participants were present here. Chosen according to what principle? Who was a celebrity here? Indecent gluttony. [...]

Sunday the 18th. Breakfast in the hotel, Loewenkopf picked me up by car, then to the Deutsches Museum, where from 8 a.m. the actual congress itself got into its swing. [...] Semper idem – it's easy for politicians, they repeat themselves x times over. Except that here everything sounded angrier and more bitter than in Berlin. To be remembered: Bishop Kaes with the black ear muffs on his plump grey head, with his 'Rhenish heart' and prayer to God for the soul of the Communist friend who saved his life; the strong Berlin accent of the quite unsanctimonious Provost Grüber[54] ('We are here!' – 'Whoever abuses a Jew, abuses us all'), Jeanette Schulz, the LDP city councillor from Berlin: 'The foreign diplomats who negotiated with Hitler are *also* guilty' – characteristic that this got the loudest applause – but was that not in the afternoon in Dachau??

[...]

Demands: [...] Away with Nazi lawyers. Schools! [...] No posts to be held for persons still to be de-Nazified. Take the offensive!

I want to incorporate the afternoon in Dachau town hall here. First there was a press conference. The press people sat round a long table and were supposed to ask questions, but asked very little. We stood and crowded round them. Interesting was only a report on the Siemens company. The management was guilty, it had requested people from the camps, it had handed over worn-out people to the death camps, it had wanted to move parts of its plants into the camps themselves ... Immediately following that the 'Parliament of Resistance' itself. Large hall, packed. Auerbach opened. Indignation, that the town of Dachau had not put out the flags, that they *wanted* to be indifferent. But then when Dr Katholitzky, of the Sachsenverlag publishing house in Dippoldiswalde, editor or the like, spoke about working-class unity and no more than hinted at the SED, Auerbach became nervous, interrupted, that was not allowed, we were above party ... And when Cohn, the public prosecutor, came back to it, saying it was part of VVN business, he was literally silenced by A. Very restless divided mood. A wordy, excessively long and unclear resolution, finally as reconciliation the common [Socialist] song: 'Brüder zur Sonne' – Brothers to the Sun.

So from the Deutsches Museum I drove with Loewenkopf and Jolles to the Jewish restaurant in Baader Str. Banner on the wall with Hebrew words (meaning: Welcome to Children of Israel), pictures of Herzl, Buber[55] etc. Good meal without coupons for 50M. I was a guest therefore. Then, after 1 they drove me to the Maximilianeum, but unfortunately stopped on the ramp side. I should have had half an hour for Vossler, wandered, with extremely severe pains – heart and spine, right round the walled building one and a half times, before I found the entrance beyond the police guard. Thus I had only 9 minutes left for the visit. The Vossler household. She warm and almost youthful. He considerably aged, incomparably more senile than in 1945. Pathologically thin, indistinct hissing voice, damaged dentures. Yet displaying the greatest warmth and evident pleasure at my visit. [...] He insisted on accompanying me downstairs and around the outer wall to the car – very slowly.

That made me late, Jolles was evidently offended and asserted that he had to get back to town earlier in the afternoon than I did. I felt embarrassed. But in the evening we ran into one another in front of the porter's lodge of our hotel, chatted amicably and parted as good friends. – The car then took us to Dachau, the ceremony at the cemetery had already begun. A field with a company of identical crosses in ranks. On a higher piece of ground, a circle of people around it, there was a flame in a candelabrum holder, and a preaching voice. Individual customary words. 'The prayers for the dead will be spoken by clergymen of the 3 denominations,' stated the programme. Few people, little interest, very matter-of-fact mood. Then we were told we could either visit the camp or go to the press conference. Unfortunately I chose the town hall. I saw just as little of the actual camp as in 1945 ... [...]

20–23 May, National Congress and Election of the Executive Committee [of the Kulturbund] in Berlin

[...] About 175 people, of these, 153 delegates voted. Klaus Gysi got the largest number of votes 140, myself with 106 was 24th out of 30 [committee members] [...] Gadamer with 53 votes has *not* been elected. What made me even more cheerful, was the fact that he was on the executive committee of this congress. Among those elected are Stroux, Meusel[56] (whom I still do not know personally), Paul Wandel, Wiegler, Anna Seghers,[57] grey-haired somewhat Chinese-looking, of course Abusch, Willmann, Friedensburg ... [...]

The main feature of the forenoon of Tuesday the 20th was a long and clear speech by Becher. He summed up everything he had often already said about the character and task and position of the KB. Excessively conciliatory and soft towards pgs, above all very emphatically for the Russians. Here he said exactly, point for point and almost word for word, what I had said on the Dresden anniversary of the KB in Bühlau and paid for with an anti-Russian demonstration. And finally he spoke for innocent youth. He got tremendous applause and was elected president by a show of hands. After lunch I asked leave to speak and underlined the 'patience with young people', underlined how necessary it is to refute Nazism to them [...].

Now when was that during these two days Tue. and Wed.? [...] And at some point I dictated an article about Munich to a typist at the ADN [news agency] who took it down in shorthand. ADN wanted it as material, it was supposed to serve me as an aide-memoire – later Kahane found that it was a fully formed article, and at the broadcasting station they thought it was exactly the right length to be broadcast.

[. . .] On Wednesday – report on activities by Willmann, a speech by Tulpanov – I was not much in the hall. I sought out the publishers Volk und Welt in a very badly damaged building on Taubenstr. Tschesno,[58] a blond young man, Frau Graf his colleague or senior employee. I elaborated my plan: 10 weeks with E. in France. History of the Resistance, lectures, my Lit. Hist. up to 45. He says: it would be no problem for him to obtain the money (the foreign currency) and an official invitation for me – he feared only friction with the Aufbau publishing house. On Eva's behalf I agreed translation of a French novel. At the club I first of all ran into Abusch. He grumbled, Tschesno lived from poaching Aufbau authors, I should speak to Wendt. He, too, was rather displeased, wanted to publish the Resistance himself, feared only the difficulty of procuring the foreign currency. He had my French Lit. Hist. on his desk, wanted to give me an 'I believe: positive reply' in 10 days time; with respect to Resistance he would give me an answer in the evening at the opera. There he told me, he had exhausted his possibilities and could obtain no foreign currency. If Tschesno could arrange it, he would let him have the book; but I should be careful, Tschesno's publishing house was young and all too active, perhaps T. was promising more than he could fulfil, it was a mystery where T. wanted to get the money from. At that I telephoned Volk and Welt once again on Thurs. morning. Frau Graf told me, I could rely on it, the necessary 40,000 francs were available. I emphasised once more, that the period from 1 July until after the beginning of September was suitable for us. [. . .]

On the Thurs. I was due to travel home with our group. Becher's secretary brought me a semi-confidential invitation for a birthday celebration for Becher: Thurs, the 22nd, 4 p.m. (Second telegram to E.)

[. . .]

On the morning of Thurs. 22, the ADN car took me to the broadcasting centre in Charlottenburg. There, against all expectation, I remained from 11 a.m.–3 p.m. The longest time with Frau Jung and Deml, as whose guest I got a meal in the large canteen of the house. They made a great deal of my article 'Congress of Bitter Words'. It was suitable for the political comment of the evening just as it was. Girnus,[59] the deputy director, had already decided that, G. also wanted to talk to me about the Becher congratulations: it should be brought up to date – his election as [Kulturbund] president and a response to a poisonous attack in the *Telegraf* had to be included. – The hour with Girnus himself, well-fed, neat, black-haired man in his forties was then more interesting than pleasant. He could not broadcast the Dachau report: a) too Russophile in 'anti-Bolshevik Berlin', b) disunity in the VVN must not be made public, c) Kulturbund must not be given priority over VVN, d) USA too heavily attacked. He also advised against press publication. I said: his confidential views were more important to me than publication, we parted on the most friendly terms. [. . .]

[. . .] I reached the club house by underground. In the 'Red Salon' a long horseshoe table and small birthday table for Becher with books, wine, liqueurs. Becher moved that there should be no speech-making, we had all heard enough. And indeed everything remained very informal. We got the usual (not bad but also not especially festive) food. [...] I almost had the impression of a certain coolness on the part of Gysi, Willmann, Becher, but probably everyone was worn-out and tired. [...]

The next morning, Friday the 23rd, car to the Anhalter Bahnhof [station] without any adventures, journey 7.30–12.30 to the Dresden Neustadt station. Here deep depression over the lost sheet music. [...]

26th May, Whit Monday
[...]

Many distractions. – On Saturday evening haircut by Gustl, the prison barber. He came (shaken) from his own imprisonment. Like all his predecessors he had succumbed to temptation and passed on a secret message in return for 3 lbs of peas. He was put inside for 10 days and then simultaneously released from the cell and his post. [...]

28th May, Wednesday morning
E. is more than ever attached to her garden and her little tomcat. It is already settled [...] that she does not want to come to Paris with me – and also that it would be better for me, if she did not come. And I also have the impression, that she should not accompany me to Greifswald. The loss of the compositions was a heavy blow to her soul and nerves. It is painful to me, upsets me greatly – but I am dissipating myself completely here, I must do serious work.

Yesterday: a couple of newspaper cuttings: Sartre (THE fashionable name, haunting me) translation of an anti-Semitism essay which Schottländer gave me in Berlin.[60] Esprit + French sexuality, not original. – A chapter of *Mimesis*. To be able to work again, without doing too many things! But on 5 June I have to say something about Thomas Mann in Grossenhain, on 31 May again go to the Executive Committee in Berlin, on 7 June speak on Rolland[61] in Freital. [...]

2nd June, Monday forenoon.
Berlin trip Executive Committee 31st May, 1st June Saturday, Sunday
I forced President Wandel, His Magnificence Stroux, Meusel, the dean [...] to declare themselves. Meusel stayed anxiously in the background; Stroux said: '*I* have always heard good things about you, but Wartburg is against you and says, Vossler only praises you, because you are his student'; Meusel said: 'I am only an unimportant dean, and if I speak up for you, then they immediately say: "It's because they're both in the Party!" ' Stroux said, a Frenchman had just been appointed to lecture on recent French Literature. All said: things 'looked bad', at best I could get an invitation to give a guest lecture. I wanted a definite invitation before 20 June,[62] the negotiation date in Greifswald. That was rejected. Thereupon I thanked them for being so friendly as to give me the information and went.

That was in the 'Red Salon' after the Executive Committee meeting, which *also* upset me. Willmann reported, that the American sector was making things difficult for the Kulturbund – Kneschke just told me on the telephone, that the KB will probably have to vacate the office in Schlüterstr. [...] A press conference has been called for 27 June. There everything is to be done to defend the KB against the accusation of being a camouflaged SED organisation, and all meetings of local groups are once more to emphasise non-partisanship [...].

5th June, midnight Thursday

Back from Grossenhain to which a car took me at 5: the lecture, the drive, the conversation with the chairman took their course as they usually do in small towns. Hall of a secondary school, probably 150–200 very attentive and generously applauding people. I spoke well [...] – but it was shamelessly superficial, even though I had been working on it since Monday. Thomas Mann (born 6 June 75) and the modern novel. [...] Tomorrow I must finish off the Rolland lecture for the day after in Freital. [...] New in it is the question: why is the novel the dominant genre today, and why the novelist the representative spokesman of his nation?

The Schmidt affair took up a lot of my time in recent days. The man appears to be sentenced as a war criminal[63] – it's always the smallest fish who get it in the neck – now his property has been confiscated, the house is being cleared and the family is desperately clinging on to me. Medical student Günther Schmidt, who is now – at my recommendation! – in his 4th semester at Jena, is very much at risk. He did *not* declare in the questionnaire, that his father was under arrest.

8th June, Sunday forenoon

[...]

My Munich–Dachau report was broadcast by the Dresden station yesterday. After the neutral introduction it broke off: the 'Congress of Bitter Words' etc. etc. was missing. They are afraid just as in Berlin [...]. I was paid 50M for the speech, I am sure I shall have the whole thing printed, I think in the next issue of *Neues Leben* (Schlesinger, FDJ) – nevertheless: pinprick! I am so sensitive, because I am without security in my profession, my essence. My chair at the TH, my Romance literature studies, what are they now in truth? There is an inner, psychological significance to that – but also a powerful economic one. What am I in the Kulturbund, what in the Party, what as speaker and journalist? An elderly not very useful man, sometimes too radical and undiplomatic sometimes too much a mere decorative object and as such of the second rank. [...]

Whom can one trust? [...] Whom in Germany should one believe? Quagmire everywhere. And everywhere here the most narrow-minded hostility to the Russians. Everyone hopes for the Americans, even for war against Russia. It is enough to drive one to despair.

10th June, Tuesday forenoon

Considerable annoyance at *Neues Leben* publishers. In the Culture pamphlet they have 'smoothed out minor stylistic infelicities', i.e. some presumptuous schoolmaster has been 'smoothing out' in every second sentence of the galley proofs. [...] Completely senseless. I have forbidden publication and threatened proceedings, if text changes are made. I have withdrawn the promised pamphlets 'From My School and University Years' and 'Speeches on Cultural Policy since 1945', unless I am given an assurance, that my mss will be printed verbatim. 'Culture' (for which a fee of 2000M has already been paid) lies uncorrected in my desk and weighs on my mind.

[...]

Reading: Anna Seghers *The Seventh Cross*[64]. Not quite as enthusiastic as Eva. A bad conscience, whenever I read a novel 'just for the sake of it'. But after all I must look at one thing and another.

[...]

12th June, Thursday afternoon

[...] The new suit was finished yesterday [...] and Frau Richter[65] picked it up in the afternoon. Brown, cotton and creased, but new and only 178M. – Apart from that yesterday morning I dictated a 'nine-Minute Voltaire', the 4th piece for the Berlin broadcasting station. – Apart from that at 5 in the afternoon in a splendid villa, 24 Emser Allee, the 'Society for the Study of the Culture of the Soviet Union' was launched. Some 40 guests, ministry, art academy, Kulturbund – Renn (main speaker), Heidebroek and Gute the initiators. Gute took charge of a conducted tour through the mostly still empty house, which with Russian money is to become an important, elegant and *nutritious* club. As one of the couple of approving speakers I said: as already in Berlin I wanted to emphasise here also, we had need of real instruction in Russian literature, everything came to us second or third hand, knowledge of the language was lacking. – Richard Gladewitz took me home in his car. On the way he told me: Doris Machol had once come under suspicion in Paris, Kahane had been ordered to separate from her. But then Doris had been rehabilitated, and Kahane himself was 'completely all right'.

[...]

15th June, Sunday forenoon

The Falkenstein, Plauen programme was concluded. In F. I spoke indifferently to about 70 people, in P. to 200 people very well and for at least $\frac{3}{4}$ of an hour – just whatever occurred to me and my mood allowed. Always the same thing, now one way, now mixed another way, now long, now short. In F. a hotel restaurant (the Adler, across from the Scherners), people sitting at tables, in P. a full hall. [...] At Trude Scherner's. She does not show her 62 years, nor the great loss. [...] We were very warmly received. [...] The following afternoon at 6 p.m. to Plauen, nice drive, 15 miles. After the lecture we sat a little over a glass of beer – here, too, the lecture took place in a restaurant room [...] but the people sat as if in a hall [...]. More important to me was the talk with the [...] secretary of the Kulturbund [...]. Member of the SED, newly qualified teacher, suddenly dismissed. Her father unacceptable. Public prosecutor, de-Nazified, member of the SED ('no objections') from summer 46. [...] The daughter was at first accepted as a teacher, then dropped after all. She would like to study – has her school-leaving certificate, wants to take history as her main subject, is getting nowhere – I promised her Greifswald. But all of that is nothing new to me. New to me was this: 'I [I said] do not like it, if children have to suffer for their fathers, but it can be assumed, that children's minds are influenced by the parental home. Tell me honestly, what you thought.' She had believed in victory. And all the atrocities? 'We were taught a physical aversion to Jews. There was a class text: an Aryan girl marries a Jew; her horror as the racial characteristics became evident in their child: black curly hair, crooked nose ... I thought, it may be hard for the individual, but they must be got rid of, they are a contamination, this race ... with dogs, too, we try to keep a pure pedigree ...' 'Did you never think, that with human beings it's not the physical, the dog-breeding that counts, but the mind?' 'But we were taught that everything is derived from race ... It made such an impression on me, Professor, when I heard you speaking in the theatre ... I was very shaken, when I was told you were a Jew. I would never have believed it ...' I told her: 'Just as you shrank back from a Jew, so do people like us sense the smell of blood, when we hear of a man, he was a public prosecutor in the Third Reich. One then asks oneself: what has the child of such a man absorbed in murderous character?' ... The girl made a good impression on me. But I regard the father as vermin, even were he not to have demanded a single criminal sentence in a political trial. He nevertheless served a criminal state as a lawyer. And he nevertheless did nothing to interfere with the Nazi education of his daughter ... It is the first time, that I have heard a girl speak so openly about her Nazi education ... The Glaser case is closely related to that. He recently defended [in court] Nazi judges and passionately demanded their acquittal; as a result he has been (according to whose decision?) struck from the Victims of Fascism list. I received a copy of his letter of protest: he had been an assigned counsel, and the judges had acted as prescribed by law. Furthermore no evidence had been submitted, that they had participated in bloodstained trials ... [...]

At last finished reading Seghers, *The Seventh Cross*. [...] I did not often really warm to it. Very many excellent sketches around the theme – but the theme itself narrow and partial. Excellent the technique of the detective story.

[When I returned] I found a telegram from the *Neues Leben* publishing house: 'Manuscripts will as a matter of course appear word for word and without any change. Letter follows'. Is that a complete kowtow?

18th June, Wednesday evening

It was reported [...], Friedrich's successor [as Saxon prime minister] is likely to be Zeigner. We heard of Friedrich's death – angina, at 55, the bulletin an awful memento for me – on the way back from Falkenstein.[66] The flags there were just being lowered to half-mast. Schumann heard in a shop: 'What are the flags at half-mast for? – Well, the Russians are doing that, because they're leaving – the Americans are coming.'

[...]

23rd June, Monday evening
Greifswald trip Thurs 19th–Saturday 21st June

[...] The journey was harrowing. 2nd class as far as Berlin, but shoved up against an upright arm rest between people in proper seats. [...] tram to Stettiner station, there at about 1. [...] Opposite the station a cellar restaurant, well fitted-out. However, I got only undefinable broth of pine needles or something. My dry bread with it. The train was due to depart at 6 p.m., until 4 I sat on a baggage counter in a large no longer roofed hall and read the 'Culture' proofs. Then I thought the train might now be standing ready, went up and found it packed. Several carriages taken by the Red Army. For a good hour I stood squeezed in on a corridor. Then this part of the train was also claimed by Russian soldiers and the German public (myself included) driven out fairly forcefully. So I had to let myself be squeezed into an even fuller carriage. It was oppressively hot. When the journey eventually began the situation improved somewhat. Air came in, and from time to time I could sit for a while. Sometimes on a proper seat, sometimes on a nurse's rucksack. I dosed a little. In Greifswald at 11.30. I had sent Weidhaas a telegram, he was not at the station, but there I was given the address of a hotel, the Preussische Hof.

An elderly man took me most of the way, there was a more direct route, but it went through the park past too many Russians. The town was not safe, there were wild sailors among the occupiers. A beautiful large market square with very well-preserved imposing old houses, baroque gables, Baltic gables, everything here freshly whitewashed. The Preussische Hof on a narrow street, pretty room with a raised bay. In the morning nothing but black ersatz coffee and the dry bread I had brought with me. Then to the university. A row of whitewashed tall old houses. Opposite, surrounded by greenery, the magnificent massive red-brick cathedral with an almost clumsy big spire. At the univ. at first no one knew anything about me. An elderly minor official or senior beadle, was full of pitying surprise when he heard that I was a proper full professor. 'And you want to come here?!' (As if I were an idiot.) [...] Little food, much Russian uncertainty, houses were requisitioned. He unlocked the Romance Languages and Literatures department for me: in terms of literary history and the 19th century it was remarkably well stocked, apart from other large rooms it had a magnificent director's room, which I looked at longingly: to be alone here with typewriter and secretary! But the department (and that only as space) was the only plus. There appeared a pale and puny-looking lecturer from Schwerin, at the moment provisionally maid of all work, spoke of 30 students, of a secret Dante lecture – because Italian and Spanish lecture courses were still forbidden – of a desire and intention to return to Schwerin. A small younger man turned up, formerly lecturer, now a budding professor of Slavonic languages and literature, already courted inter alia by Dresden. There appeared a young man walking with a stick, the student representative of the department. All pleasant, all surprised that I wanted to come here. The student promised to cycle to Jacoby, who was in the habit of arriving at 11 – but it was not certain. [...] finally Jacoby appeared. Even more hard of hearing than in Berlin, excessively polite – but evidently completely surprised and put out by my presence. A conference of university rectors in Halle, exceptionally the registrar also there – the lord mayor on holiday, his deputy an opponent of the university – why had I not written again? ... what a 'run of bad luck', the phrase came repeatedly. He had evidently forgotten everything, he was dismayed, and I did not have any travel coupons with me? ... Weidhaas appeared, and I clung to him as to an old friend. Now there was an emergency organisation of a few things, above all my return journey the next morning was to be taken care of ... I was to lunch with Jacoby. Torment, walking with him: he considered he was innocent, I should have written again, reminded ... Something between parlour and old-fashioned living room, little too much upholstery, on the wall picture of the fallen son, Frau J. younger than he, livelier simply through not being deaf, energetic, dissatisfied with him. She 'had already eaten' (really?) – we got tiny jacket potatoes, which she peeled for us, a fish sauce with hardly discernible little atoms of fish, and lettuce, it was very difficult for me to even halfway eat my fill after the previous one and a half days of starvation. Following the meal he retired for a little while, he had a lecture at 4, and I told the good-looking woman of my anger and that I had little intention of accepting. She also advised me fairly openly to refuse: they would be unable to give me a house. After that he called, she went to him, and he immediately came in showing his irritation. He had to go to the lecture now, his wife said I was intending to refuse: if that were the case he did not want to pursue the matter any further, there was after all also a very young man, who ... but if I were nevertheless able to make up my mind, I should call on him at 6 at the dean's office. I gave him an open answer, and we shook hands ... Then Frau J. took me the few steps across to Weidhaas. [...] The return journey was organised, the Food Office and my hotel informed, a coffee ordered in the university hospital. The coffee was the best thing about this completely abortive day. The red-brick buildings of the hospital are crowded together beside the city wall. [...] A hospital supervisor gave us a friendly reception: room next to the kitchens, ersatz coffee but with sugar, jam, good bread and butter. And afterwards I even got an egg sandwich to see me on my way! – We sat there blissfully [...]. I then met J. in his office at about 5: he was evidently pleased that I had come after all, emphatically promised me house and garden, demanded: stay past the age of 68! asked after my health ('angina!'), again encouraged me very strongly to come.

He then accompanied me back to the hotel, we parted amicably ... I got a tiny supper and a couple of slices of bread for the return journey; then, as arranged, Weidhaas called for me. We had a beer in a restaurant and went for a long walk which curiously agreed very well with me and caused me no pain. [...] On the way Weidhaas told me a great deal about the university conditions.

The natural science sections appear to be in a good state, the humanities in a miserable one. For English there are only two lecturers, for French only 1. Of 3 history chairs only one is occupied. [...] The whole Education Faculty evidently consists of newly qualified SED elementary school teachers. Jacoby [...] was born April 81, suspended during the Nazi period, because not indubitably Aryan, politically evident fairly far right (his wife, from Königsberg, even further right), as a scholar presumably no leading light, as dean (according to Weidhaas) not only deaf but altogether detached from the world. W., together with the Socialist group of professors now wanted to attend to my house and my other requests. [...] On Saturday I was then woken at 3.30 and took, travelling somewhat more comfortably than on the journey out, from 4.50 to about 10 to get to Berlin. Home at about 10 p.m., two days before my telegram. – On the way every so often I read some proofs, so that I was able to finish them and the postscript to Thomas Mann's *Thoughts in Wartime*[67] [...] on Sunday and Monday. [...] On the way out I talked to a middle-aged theologian. He had been in Russia for years. His tune: The Russians are lovable, but Bolshevism is un-Russian, inhuman ... Everywhere else complaints about the barbarism, poverty, tyranny, Nazi system of the Russians of all people ... On the way back the strange second-class compartment. [...] A man in his mid-40s, educated speech, and a young fellow. The man: the disgraceful trial of the poor nurses, who obeying orders to put a few incurables out of their misery gave the fatal injection. The lack of justice altogether, of course, in our zone. The young fellow: justice? Because I was a lieutenant – everyone who had a school-leaving certificate was made a lieutenant – I'm not allowed to study ... and men who got the Knight's Cross used to be thought the best ... and now ... At the glorification of the nurses I saw red, I said very loudly: I'm warning you – I'm not denouncing anyone, but I'm warning you! – Awkward silence. The young fellow: I can say what I think. I: I'm not giving you any private lectures ... Proofs, the other talked about the weather ... An hour later, the young fellow had got out, a more or less friendly conversation developed. It turned out that there were another two SED people in the compartment, a senior railway official, member of Victims of Nazi Persecution, and a woman official. [...] The conversation ended peacefully once more on pro and contra with the respect to the Russians.

25th June, Wednesday evening

After rejecting Greifswald I must find my feet here again. Thus yesterday despite the exhausting and feared walk to the TH: meeting of the SED works group. [...] Again and again I am struck by how well the workers speak and discuss in their bad German.

[...]

Hardly any work done except business correspondence dealt with: people comment on work or lectures by me and must get a word of thanks. [...] A certain F. C. Weiskopf, émigré journalist in New York has asked me via Steininger for my co-operation on an émigré lexicon.[68] I promised articles on Plievier,

Bredel, Friedrich Wolf in return for payment in Care Packets ... I read a little bit of *Mimesis*.

[...]

29th June 1947, Sunday evening. Together for 43 years!
Berlin trip Thurs. 26th June 7.30–Saturday 28th June 9 p.m.

It went really badly, I'm fed up to the back teeth with it all, and I do not want show my face there again for a while. In terrible heat – up to 40° – extremely exhausting, two short but unpleasant bouts of palpitations, the first during the fight for the tram on Thurs. morning, the second on Friday afternoon, as I was walking in blazing heat from Jägerstr. to Aufbau in Französische Str. (Wendt gave me a car to take me back.) Personal frictions, in particular with Abusch, a little also with Gysi (Willmann not present, Becher remote and cold). [...] I did not feel myself sufficiently respected and there was a slightly strained atmosphere between myself and the Kulturbund. Worse, and that especially irritated me, my Lit. Hist. has not been accepted yet, a yes is being made dependent on editors' judgements and – since Abusch is 'ideological director' – this will now presumably not be forthcoming. I cast doubt on the authority of the editors; I was told they are not judging my academic competence, but whether the book fits without the framework of the 'material humanism' (what's that?!) which the Aufbau publishing house has knocked together. Abusch declared, he had immediately been dismayed, when he heard of an unscrutinised acceptance by the meanwhile sacked Wilhelm.

[...] I also found little favour with Wandel, who was aggrieved by my rejection of Greifswald. G. would become a major university, he claimed. Then they should have treated me better, if they wanted and needed me, I said. He, very bitterly: that is what the universities were doing all the time and sabotaging him or the Berlin Central Administration; Leipzig was not doing enough for Werner Krauss, whom he, Wandel, would so much like to have there ... I said, I would not get involved again, unless I were treated with dignity. [...] Professionally I enjoyed only the call on, the discussion with Schlesinger – He apologised once more for the faux pas with the Culture proofs. [...]

The session itself on the Friday was completely insignificant. [...]

The one thing: journey there: on the train police check at Grossenhain. In our compartment a painting was taken from a young man, because he did not have a receipt with him. Confiscated goods can be reclaimed in Dresden after 2 weeks, if a receipt or documentary evidence is produced. In order to prevent racketeering. (But 1. where can one always find documentary evidence? And 2. the little fish are caught, the big ones ...) Indignation in the compartment, and the man with the picture – his appearance did not inspire confidence: 'They harass us. And the UNRRA Jews bring lorry loads of stockings out of Chemnitz.[69] Buy them at 60M a pair, sell them in Berlin for 120M.' (The UNRRA Jews [...] and the cemetery desecrations in Chemnitz and Zittau. Desperate.) And always hostility to the Russians. [...]

[...]

[...]To the club, where I was picked up by Mackie Kahane, and where there was the unfortunate quarrel with Abusch. What nonsense to tell Mackie this was a club for cultural workers and not for journalists! I rubbed Abusch's face in it the next day. Of course he denied having put it 'like that' and meant it 'like that', and of course it will be taken out on my Lit. Hist. – We then drove out to Niederschönhausen, where we spent rather more agreeable hours. [...]

Towards evening on Friday Mackie called for me at Schlesinger's and made friends with him. Both were in France with the Resistance, and both Jews. Schlesinger displays a calm cordiality towards me, which does me good. [...]

30th June, midday Monday

Until now in suffocating heat the above diary entries. In addition business correspondence and at last completed *Mimesis*. (Is to become an article for *Aufbau*.) From time to time pleasant remembrance of our wedding day. [...]
[...]

6th July, Sunday morning

Yesterday morning faculty meeting about the university statute. Simon told me during the meeting, afterwards in a long evidently sincerely friendly conversation: in Karlshorst my chair was cut for the moment; if the SMA did not after all leave teacher training to the TH, I would have to go. It is very bitter ... Faculty and government are in conflict with Rector Heidebroek: he holds on to his executive power and to his exclusively technical establishment (in which the Russians support him, in *both!*) while we want democracy. At the same time Trinks and Woldt, the SED people, then uphold the rights of academic autonomy against the rector and against the government, whereby they in turn lend help to the cronyism of the reactionary professors. And the government (Simon) is paralysed, because it does not want to detach itself from the West. Thus I am between all stools. It is impossible for me to be more between stools.
[...]

9th July, Wednesday night

[...]
On the afternoon of the same day [the 7th] district committee meeting of the VVN in Bautzenerstr., there were 14 of us. Discussion of the Glaser case. [...] Everyone condemned him. Long debate, to what extent it was permissible for us to intercede for a Nazi. (Never in general and absolutely!) [...] Cohn, public prosecutor, in the shortest trousers, almost swimming trunks, naked thighs, naked legs and feet, sandals) reported on the trial of the injection [euthanasia] doctors.[70] 4 death sentences demanded, out of 11 accused.
[...]

14th July, Monday afternoon

[...] (NB What has happened to Kretzschmar-Neumark [...]? It is as if he had vanished from the face of the earth. I last heard from him in June, he wrote a bitter letter to me, a plea for help for his stepfather; I thereupon tried to reach him by telephone, later in writing. Not a word. Have the Russians arrested him, has he fled to the West?)

[...]

Visit by the twin Hiltrut Zabel; she asked for a recommendation for admission to study medicine. I gave her the requested reference, but was very pessimistic. Overcrowded faculties! There were tears: we're fighting so hard for it and now we may get nowhere! [...] The people from the Evening Grammar School still place their hopes in me and do not know how powerless I am.

17th July, Thursday evening

[...] After I had at last finished reading *Mimesis*, I squeezed out a review of it; then I prepared the lecture on the Realist Novel, which I gave as normal in Blasewitz Secondary School [...] to 75 *mostly* youthful listeners. That is now to become a study for the *Aufbau*. – Today meanwhile I dictated without a break two recently commissioned wireless things to Frau Stephan [...]. Apart from the journalism the only work I managed in recent days was a little modern reading: Plievier: *Im letzten Winkel der Erde* and – begun – Ostrovsky *How the Steel Was Tempered* .[71]

18th July, Friday morning

From day to day this waiting which wears one down: will the Aufbau publishing house take on my Lit. Hist.? Will the Paris trip ... will Greifswald ...?? And lately also the pitiful waiting for 'packets' and for the pajok allocation.[72] [...]

The SED requested an opinion from me on Heinsch, who has applied for the 'Diplomatic Service'. I wrote an emphatic and detailed pro.

[...] Long private letter to the faithful Berthold Meyerhof, the most recent packet sender.

20th July, Sunday forenoon

On Friday afternoon I recorded the two pieces at the studio, after I had revised them again in the morning: 'The London Conference'[73] and 'On the Inner Reconstruction of Dresden' (Cultural Sciences Institute etc.). Subsequently I sat by myself for an hour in a conference room and read Ostrovsky, after that from 7 until almost 9 in the big broadcasting studio the Spain rally of the VVN (11th anniversary of the beginning of the Civil War). All too soon after the Poland meeting, all too great saturation of the all too hungry population with useless political talk. Very dull. The 200 or so people were hardly noticeable in the huge hall. [...] Richard Gladewitz, who took his place in giving the address of welcome and as manager, recognised the mood, Hilse did not. I myself see everywhere in the SED, Kulturbund etc. the same thing: retreat, accommodation ... Very long speech by a Spaniard, Lorenzo, of which I and probably most people did not understand a single sentence: because he read very quickly with very incorrect emphasis in very broken German and the acoustics were very poor. It was amusing how he and Gladewitz embraced and kissed one another. After that Hentschke, a German combatant [...] delivered a few political-historical generalities, but did not touch the sole essential question: why did Russia withdraw then and sacrifice the Spaniards? Cf. on this score: why did it sign a treaty with Germany, why did *all* the Allies not lift a finger as long as the Nazis unleashed their fury *only* in Germany and *only* against the Jews? What happened to humanism? [...] The actor Lewitt and his wife (Küter) declaimed, the ceremony passed sluggishly. Who is the Pasionaria,[74] whose picture hung in front of the lectern and whose speech to the International Brigades was spoken by Frau Küter?

On Saturday [...] afternoon with E. and Frau Kreisler visited Kussi in Hellerau. I always like talking to him, he is educated, sees the larger picture, is considered in his judgements. [...] About the Russians, with whom he has considerable and amicable dealings (Rheostat is a reparations company): Obliging and good-natured, but industrially and organisationally unable to cope. Chaos ... Their mistakes: why the secretiveness, the spiriting people away instead of public trials? (The Neumark case – Kretzschmar is said to have gone to the West, after he was arrested once or in danger of arrest ... Mysterious business. His mother still here. [...] Going through my own mind: I was always too much harnessed to one thing. For many years my world was *only* that of Romance language and literature, not even the general philosophical milieu. Now the danger is of becoming so one-sidedly SED man and Soviet citizen. I am beginning to see beyond this milieu. But I am tied, I am tied to it.

The primitive Ostrovsky.

[...]

25th July, Friday forenoon

On Mon. 21 there was a not especially well-attended meeting of the Bloc Parties in Dölzschen Inn on the subject of securing the harvest – protecting the fields. All speakers very depressed. The sheer starvation, the excessive mortality everywhere. The thefts, the senseless pulling out and trampling down while gleaning and during the too early invasion of harvested fields, 'before the last waggon has rolled out'. This mediaeval image is altogether familiar to me. People of 'the better classes' join in. Dölzschen needs 200 volunteers for night patrols. They are promised definite supply of their potato ration and two pounds of root vegetables as compensation for each nocturnal patrol. A whole crowd of people put their names down afterwards. [...]

Tuesday to Thursday (22nd–24th) was taken up with the visit by the Kahanes announced by telegram at the last minute. They come depressed: their little house was suddenly to be vacated for the Russian army. They were then informed of a postponement [. . .] but also simultaneously, that there had been a burglary and curtains and blankets stolen. Their arrival here at first meant we did not have enough food. Immediately afterwards, however, I received news from the Kulturbund, that the pajok voucher had arrived after all. There had been talk of cancellation this month. Frau Richter was put in the news agency car, which Mackie had at his disposal, and in an hour brought up not only the voucher, but also the wonderful things themselves. (Shop in the Antonstr.) We then lived sumptuously. [. . .]

This evening Eva is speaking (maiden speech!), as newly elected Dölzschen 'women's officer' in Cafe Dölzschen, on women in the Western European countries. A pity, that I'm not allowed to be present. 'A harem matter,' says E. Also addressed to Eva is the translation proposal from Volk and Welt. The book, Jacques Roumain's *Gouverneurs de la rosée*,[75] arrived the day before yesterday; but no word of how matters stand with my planned trip to France.

[. . .]

I read to the Kahanes from my Talmud sayings.[76] 1910! To be so ancient and still not satisfied and as unready for death as ever!

[. . .]

31st July, Thursday forenoon

[. . .] Then in the evening Gottfried Heinsch was here [. . .].

Then Heinsch spoke very pessimistically about the Party: Very great tension between KPD and SPD, a lot of 'Schuhmacherism' even among our people, very many nasty goings-on [. . .] . . . But the most interesting thing about Heinsch was this: it turned out, that he is absolutely convinced of the world domination of the Jews organised through Freemasonry. The headquarters was in Jerusalem, the 'higher degrees' (from the 33rd degree) were in the USA, his uncle wore a diamond pin, which supposedly represents a G = Goodman, but in reality represents a J = Jehovah, and before which everyone trembled. His uncle was not a Jew, but all instructions, all orders concerning America and the world came from powerful Jewish bankers and the leadership was to be found in Jerusalem. The enthronement of the Pope also took place in such a way that 'the Grand Rabbi' blessed him. I drew Heinsch's attention to the fact, that much or all of the ceremonial and the ritual of the Church was derived from Old Testament examples – he himself, however, evidently believed literally in the domination of the Lodge Jew or of Jewry concealed in Masonry. That means, therefore, that this decent Marxist and philo-Semite, whom I had recommended for a diplomatic career, is completely convinced of Nazi theory and legend. Probably he also believes in *The Elders of Zion*.[77] E. just said, perhaps he is a Freemason himself ... So how far have we got in the de-Nazification of Germany? And what does it say about enlightenment and rationalism in our Party? Que sais-je?[78]

3rd August, Sunday morning

[...]

Yesterday forenoon the [...] meeting of the regional steering committee of the Kulturbund. [...] Eva Blank had urged and pestered me, I *had* to speak for an hour. Subject: the last Executive Committee meeting. But there was nothing at all to say about it. Grüss, CDU, Rector of Freiberg Mining Academy, [...] attacked the Russians (justified unpopularity! – people disappearing, mining ...) [...] A great deal to no effect was said about uniform guidelines for denazification and appointment of civil servants. One speaker demanded denazification tribunals for the Eastern Zone. Willmann, just back from a trip to the West, was very interesting at this point: denazifications by these courts were 'the most popular article on the black market'. Complete fiasco of the institution, extremely corrupt nonsense. – The 'curtain' between West and East had become ever thicker in the last year. The people in the West did not ask, how things were with us in the East, but 'how is it in Russia?' People believed, inter alia, that in Berlin the interzonal pass was needed to go from one street to the next. [...] Grüss pointed out, that Bloc parity did not in fact exist. He mentioned figures: in the district there were about 70 villages in which *only* the SED was organised and recognised, the CDU was unable to hold meetings, put up candidates etc. ... I am convinced, that in a truly free election today the SED would become a tiny minority party.

4th August, Monday forenoon

Yesterday, Sunday 3 Aug., forenoon, opening of an exhibition of Dresden artists at Emser Allee (Kulturbund). Renn opened, Kröner[79] read meaningless familiar phrases from a sheet of paper, Helene somebody a pretentious letter by Rilke about Rodin. An inordinately overcrowded hall, terrifically close, from outside the racket of the crowd of those who had been unable to find a place. Proceedings were shortened as much as possible. [...]

[...] The article on the realist novel for *Aufbau* is still in abeyance. And absolute uncertainty, what to undertake after that. Everything in the balance and undecided. [...]

Yesterday at the exhibition I met, among others, the Glasers. I gave him my hand, which he took, and afterwards had a brief conversation with Frau Gl. She told me, I should not take the matter to heart, she agreed with *me* – he was simply 'so unpolitical'.

5th August, Tuesday morning

Yesterday Heidebroek told me in open session: it was final, the decision had come from Karlshorst, my chair was cut, the TH was paying me on instruction of the ministry, which would now, however, have to give me notice. [...] But my role is now presumably really at an end: Johannes Kühn is professor in Leipzig, Wildführ, who sat coolly and mockingly beside me, is professor in

Leipzig, and I am nothing at all any more. Neither in the university nor in politics.

8th August, Friday evening

Professionally I live from hand to mouth. I stuck an ending onto the failed study of the 'Realist Novel' and sent it to *Aufbau*. Very possible that I get it back, as I got the *'Mimesis'* article back from the *Tägl. Rundschau*. – I wrote, tiresomely slowly but with a good outcome the article 'For and Against Romanticism', a review [for *Neues Deutschland*] of the jelly-like Lion book *Romanticism as German Fate*, which Rowohlt sent me some time ago. [...] I now want to undertake a review of Küchler's Rimbaud [translations], I have avoided it for a long time. From one small job to the next I hope, always in vain, for something that will focus me on one of my bigger plans. There's no word from anyone and I'm left in a vacuum – Aufbau, the Beltz publishing house – only Volk and Welt has written to me, the Paris plan has fallen through. [...]

12th August, Tuesday forenoon

[...]

Since being elected to the Executive Committee of the Kulturbund, I regularly receive *Sonntag* [weekly] and *Aufbau* [monthly], I buy *Einheit* [Unity – an SED theoretical monthly] and *Neue Welt* [fortnightly] from a hawker, the Kahanes in Berlin send *Bam* [Berlin am Mittag – a daily, pub. Feb. 47–Feb. 48] and *Les lettres Françaises* [French weekly for art and literature, which emerged from the Resistance], *Lancelot* [a German monthly on French culture] often reaches me – but I *read* hardly any of it, I consider *the book* more nutritious. Thus I am now in the middle of Becher's ghastly *Abschied*[80]. On the other hand: I can only become up to date through the periodicals. Those mentioned gave me two things – it cost me the late evening yesterday: a) a supplement to my Rimbaud article; I am sending the addition, really only a single sentence, to the *Sonntag* today, to which I have also sent a Küchler article I wrote during the last few days; b) an initial very vague idea about Sartre. Yesterday I read [the article]: A. Leutis: 'Die Philosophie auf Vieren' [Philosophy on all fours].[81] Cardinal question: d'où cette haine impitoyable des Bolchévistes?[82] [...] I am straying through the topical matter like this, because I am all the time sitting in uncertainty between stools, because there's still not a word from anyone – Aufbau publishing house, Beltz, Greifswald. [...]

14th August, Thursday afternoon

[...]

Wed. forenoon. Assmann, the director [...] had asked me to view the State Library, which is about to open. It has been transferred from Eisenacherstr. to the north of the city, according to Assmann due to spite on the part of the city of Dresden, because this new and very difficult move was not necessary. Barracks quarter [...] a hike. A huge building partly rebuilt inside, partly still being rebuilt. Shortage of workers and librarians, of materials, of machines. [...] A long flight (doors broken through) of shelved books, a reference library of some 120,000 volumes, acquisitions since 1927, completed catalogue rooms, an issuing desk, a huge half-finished reading room, lending service will begin in the next few days. Then there is an enormous heap of books: German History already classified. A periodicals room is extant: [Some] Western journals [...] available. But: everything else, more than a half a million volumes, all the treasures of the 18ième, exactly what I need for my Lit. Hist., lies in the cellars firmly stowed away and piled like bricks up to the ceiling. This is now to be sifted into groups. 'In about six months' the Romance literatures could probably be ready for use. 'Director, you are an optimist!' It could also take a whole year or even much longer than that ... The hopelessness of the situation speaks for Greifswald. Assmann talked about the new problems cropping up all the time. Only *one* academic librarian, no trained library attendants etc. Shortage of transport. Of 1 million volumes, 200,000 are gone. The Russians removed crate-loads of 'treasures' including valuable periodicals. On 13 Feb. 45 the Japanese Palais only contained 'whatever was hardly worth evacuating' ... [...]. Assmann also related how he had dug up his own daughter, an academic librarian [...] and removed her 'completely crushed body' on a handcart. He himself is now in his mid-50s ... I resolved to read for a couple of hours every 10–14 days in the periodical rooms – an excursion!

Back very exhausted at 3 p.m. I found as house-guests Trude Öhlmann and her nephew Werner Fischer, a modest, educated, calm fair-haired man of 36, a commercial clerk here. The nephew left today, Trude will remain until Sunday. Features of this visit: the infinite hostility of the population to the Russians and the SED, especially on the part of the petty bourgeoisie, very especially that of Leipzig. There the shortages seem *even greater* than here. The viewpoint of the 'salaried employees': the workers hate us, the workers get more to eat (higher ration cards), the injustice of the Russian [food] packets, (the Leipzig people say 'Stalin packets'), the workers, the 'Communists' insult the middle classes, the Russians take 'everything' from us. Most of all I was shaken by something the very calm and altogether anti-Nazi Werner Fischer said, who had served at the front as an infantryman, and had seen great destruction but no atrocities in the East: 'Do you believe that there were mass gassings?' ... The doubt that it happened is being fostered, is widespread. What good is all the educational work? ... Immediately after that the question: 'Is it true that Pieck and Grotewohl live in Karinhall?'[83] ... The SED behaved in every respect just like the Nazis. And again and again: people say that under Hitler they got their butter. And again and again: robberies by Russians! And: when a German paediatrician told a commandant 30% of infants in Leipzig were dying, the latter had replied: 'Far too few!' – Thanks to the trade fair hypocrisy there appears to be particular wretchedness in Leipzig ... But nevertheless the worst thing is the radical doubt: there was no gassing! – I spoke in favour of the Russians and the SED to the best of my ability, probably in vain ... [...]

16th August, Saturday forenoon

Leipzig, 16 Ritterstr. (town centre) Faculty of Philosophy. The old cleaning woman: 'Which committee? Romance [Languages and Literatures]! This room please.' It was 12.30, they had begun at 10.30. They: a distinguished, not very intelligent-looking slim old gentleman, clipped grey moustache, pale blue eyes, everything pale and distinguished [...]. I immediately thought: Eduard von Jan, was quite unembarrassed: 'Klemperer – the usual breakdown – pardon me ...' stuck out my hand, it was taken with sourire figé.[84] On the other side of the table, out of the glare, little changed apart from the greyness of his short hair, Neubert. With perhaps well-acted casual heartiness: 'Still the old Neubert!' And beside him, keeping the minutes, Brummer,[85] modest man of 40, in poor health, Neubert's student from Breslau, he once had a friendly exchange with me in the Kulturbund here, just called to the chair in Rostock. Apart from that three taciturn Slavists whom I did not know – the Anglists were meeting somewhere else. They had already discussed the French curricula, had just come to the appointment rules, everything was evidently settled by Neubert and Jan. I immediately cut in: the curricula were intended for the average teacher and not for the researcher. I won another hour for the 20th century in French literature, it was cut from the fat of Old French, I won an internal essay test in *German*. Neubert and Jan, half-approving, conducted rearguard actions. At 1.15 Jan said: 'We are finished, therefore, and I am closing the meeting' and hurriedly left the room, without taking leave of anyone. During the discussion he had not once looked at or addressed me, but matter-of-factly given way to me in everything [...]. What will he have been thinking? He knows that I have driven him out of Leipzig to Jena, yet myself have not gained Leipzig ... Now, engaged in friendly-unaffected conversation(!) with Neubert and Brummer, I walked over to the guest house of the city of Leipzig, a villa converted into a club, behind the Reich court building. (Oppressive heat and bad pains.) At dinner there were Böhme from the Central Administration, Steinitz from the Univ. of Berlin[86] and some Americanists and Slavists likewise from there. I said to Böhme, I would like to inform him to the effect, that I was now after all prepared to accept Greifswald, since retirement did not greatly appeal to me ... Inwardly I am very much *against* Greifswald since yesterday: 1) Wretchedness of a small university [...]. 2) It now looks as if I were running after the people. [...]

So for once at least I sat down officially with the Leipzig Philosophical Faculty and even had a decisive influence on curricula. [...]

18th August, Monday morning

The dreadful famine now also weighs on private feelings. One can really see catastrophe approaching. One *sees* the famine, one hears the weather report, 'no change' as something inexorable.

[...] It was impossible to think of work in recent days. But on *what* should I have been working? I am so empty. I cannot make up my mind to undertake any major enterprise. And *how* should I carry out a major enterprise without books – condition of the State Library!

[...] Brummer, Neubert, von Jan – [...] this narrow-minded stuffiness of the clique! And *that's* where I long to be, and their disparagement – Neubert laughed derisively: *'LTI*! yes, I've heard of it,' the way one says: piece of journalism, muck! – their disparagement wounds me! Stupid, of course – but it wounds me nevertheless...

20th August, midday Wednesday

At midday on Monday came the humorous kowtow from Greifswald,[87] an infinite comfort to me, because it puts solid ground under my feet, and it flatters my self-confidence. I telegrammed Jacoby: 'Very moved. Delighted. Looking forward to our next meeting. Your Kl.' [...]

Then at 5 in the afternoon there was a VVN session at Bautzenerstr. to discuss the programme for 14 Sept. Two tendencies: Hilse wanted all kinds of events and demonstrations in the open air. Others feared empty halls, fiasco as with the Poland and Spain meetings, demanded restriction to the essentials. I belonged very vigorously to the latter, repeatedly emphasised how unloved *we* were – we, i.e. the VVN, the OdF [Victims of Fascism], the SED, the 'stooges of the Russians'. [...] I met with understanding, the limitation of the ceremonies was also accepted – no street demonstration. I am one of the delegates to the VVN ceremonies in Berlin (12–14 September).

[...]

21st August, Thursday forenoon

[...]

On [Tuesday] evening – E. was about to go to bed – the Seidemanns arrived after 10. Erich back from his holiday–black market trip to the English West. Very shaken: over there enough to eat, at cheap black market prices even abundance. Complaints about Russian tyranny. Especially in the mines. The Party here gave in too much to the Russians. It sounded rather Schuhmacher-like and rather like the popular tune here. [...] We already knew that Seidemann would not be re-elected Dölzschen chairman of the SED. – Now yesterday in Dölzschen Inn, *from 6 until midnight!!*, big meeting: new management committee elected, delegates to the Party conference elected, talk by a man from the district committee, Gabriel, on the Party line and intentions for the Party conference. Central: see it through, go hungry, must not sell ourselves to the Americans! Passionate discussion. One comrade: we *are* starving, we are collapsing at our machines, it cannot go on! Into the middle of this now came Seidemann's hardly moderated Schuhmacherism of the previous evening. Extremely fierce attack on him by a radical foreman at Braune's bread factory. Attacks on Seidemann and on Schubert the always somewhat embittered 1st chairman, a dark obstinate little man [...]. Waist, the paper-hanger, who would so much have liked to have gone to the [Art?] Academy, became chairman, Schubert and Seidemann got other posts – shout from the audience: 'Party discipline!' Eva, only recently become women's leader of the neighbourhood group [...] advanced to women's adviser for the whole Dölzschen group. [...] It makes me very happy to see with what enthusiasm she is getting involved. She wears the SED badge as a brooch. – At the same time she has signed the contract with Volk and Welt for the Roumain translation and has already buckled down to it. [...] It seems to me the beginning of a renaissance after the terrible blow of the theft of the sheet music.

This morning telegram from Teubner: licence [to publish] granted – whether I can deliver the ms of Mod. French Prose by the end of September. I replied 'in principle *yes.*' (I think I shall give notice of a supplement for Easter 48 – for the moment a great deal would already be gained by a reprint of the 2nd edition + my foreword.) My mood very much improved!

Perhaps Greifswald will be our salvation, Eva's and mine, academically, musically (organ playing!), politically. Perhaps – an hour later I am down again.

[...]

28th August, Thursday towards evening

Always remember: 1) You are a war profiteer, you owe your successes solely to the emptiness of the Eastern Zone. 2) these are provisional successes, at no moment are you certain, today powerful, tomorrow impotent. 3) vanitas vanitatum – one foot in the grave, when will the other follow, and what will survive, and what is the value of this survival? – Nevertheless: the last few days have once again given nourishment to my wounded vanity and, beyond all the aches in my bones and thoughts of death, have given me all kinds of pleasure. [...]

30th August, Saturday forenoon

Telegram from Jacoby in Greifswald: 'Villa definitely bought. Department moving. Letter follows' ... God wills it. Does he, or just my childish vanity, and against E.'s interests?

Yesterday afternoon, at the Dresden broadcasting station, I spoke my 5 minute congratulation for Vossler in shortened and improved form. I read, only half understanding, Brecht (*St Joan of the Stockyards*);[88] I read – from the State Library – Julius Wilhelm: *Nietzsche und der französische Geist [N. and the French mind].*[89] Very flat. And *I* don't exist in it. But now I'm on way back!

[...]

High spirits above the constant substratum of the vanitatum-vanitas. I talked about it over breakfast to E., who is now also making her first appearances: yesterday evening she accepted her first resolution as head of women's affairs for the district [Dölzschen]: joint meetings of the neighbourhood-group women; this morning there was a telephone call about her choir for 14 Sept. E. is much more indifferent towards age, death and the awareness of nullity than I. She also has much less retrospective erotic longing than I. For myself I formulated: dulcis gloria, dulcior juventus.[90]

[...]

2nd September, early Tuesday. Görlitz

[. . .]

After the lecture for a beer with the grey-haired, gentle, careworn Riepke and a like-minded fellow and friend of his, a welfare official. Two complaints the subject [of our conversation]: a) *the Russians*. They have forfeited every sympathy. People are 'taken away', 'disappear' (to Bautzen[91] [prison]), are bullied, spied on ... There is greater freedom in the West; we are not allowed our Germanness: Riepke's daughter has gone to the West, because, not guilty of anything, she was picked up by the Russians and kept in custody for weeks ... Why is Silesia, the *German province*, under Polish control? Because the Russians have stolen eastern Poland and are compensating the Poles with German territory ... The *pajok* is unfair and a Russian form of bribery ... These are all complaints of *our comrades*! b) *complaint no. 2*. Why is there still a rift in the SED? Why are 'we SPD'ers' oppressed, discriminated against, muzzled? Treated as heretics if we are not the most hidebound materialists, do not completely ignore personalities, ideas in our view of history?? – Both complaints shake me equally. But I believe I *must* stick with the radical and Russophile line, it is not nice, but probably necessary nonetheless.

[. . .]

12th September, 9 p.m. Friday evening

Completely exhausted. The Land [Saxon] conference has been in full swing since yesterday afternoon in oppressive numbing heat. [. . .] with all the repetitions in the discussions I fall asleep, wake up again, suffer ... it is all so empty and monotonous, I only endure it because I am on the list for the Party Congress. [. . .]

Very questionable is the semi-hypocrisy, the half-measure of our SED position: We are sincerely pursuing bloc politics, we want real democracy, for we are not *yet* ripe for a Socialist republic, we must prepare for it, in fact through real democracy! [. . .] Schrecker came up to me, I gave the most wrong-headed speeches, was impossible, would not be re-elected. I laughed at him and felt annoyed. Others told me that Minister Hartsch, whom I missed this morning, had said something very similar to myself on the universities issue. [. . .]

When I speak in Berlin at the Party Congress, I shall seriously quote, what one of the educationalists in Leipzig recently said to me in all seriousness: 'You still here? Anyone who has a good opinion of himself goes to the West.' (He was thinking of Gadamer and Litt.)[92]

[. . .]

28th September, Sunday evening. Dresden

[... Here the dating of the entries is inconsistent because Klemperer did not get around to writing them up immediately.]

On Friday and Saturday (27 Sept.) I strove in vain with the *Mod. French Prose*. The 1926 study emphasises the 'national religion' so strongly and the typically French humanism of the French and their occasional cruelty, that I can hardly get away with it all ('we are incapable of it') today. Should I moderate by making changes, leave it out completely, neutralise it with a foreword? [...] ... I am sure I will not get down to proper scholarly work until Greifswald; here I am too tired and my attention too divided.

[...]

22nd September 1947, 6.45 Monday morning.
Niederschönhausen/Berlin at Mackie's

[...]

(On the same Sunday [VK was attending a VVN congress in Berlin] E. was accompanist at the event in the Apollo Theatre – Lewitt, Küter, Löwen; broadcast of her composition had taken place on the Saturday.) We drove to the Gendarmenmarkt [square in Berlin]. There columns were assembling with flags and placards: 'Veterans of Spain', 'Buchenwald', 'Auschwitz', 'Emigrés', 'Mauthausen' etc. etc. [...]

On Mon., the 15th [...], we picked up E. from Friedrichstr. station at midday and Mackie drove us to Anny Kl. in Charlottenburg. E. was very exhausted, physically and mentally throughout these days. Heat, train, preceding exertions and – Greifswald. Caught Anny in the middle of her meal. She had some cousin by marriage with her, told me afterwards the lady was a strict Catholic and came from Cologne. When I talked about my call to Greifswald, the cousin cried out in genuine horror: *'My God – then you might as well be in Russia!'* [...] - and when we both laughed and tried to enlighten her, she quickly took her leave.

[...]

On Tue. forenoon (16 Sept.) with E. to Volk und Welt, where she delivered a quarter of her Roumain translation and made a big impression when she introduced herself. [...] 10,000 copies of *LTI* have been printed (price 8.50M, royalties presumably 12,500M, but the taxes!), next year a further 10,000 are planned. [...] At the Stettin Station at 5 p.m., palpitations, when our legitimate claim to seats was not at first recognised. [...]

But then – just before midnight – the welcome in Greifswald! [...] An elegant car, the registrar, Jacoby the dean. Jacoby merely greeted us, E. with a kiss on the hand, requested that I call on him the next day, disappeared. [...] Wohlgemuth, the registrar,[93] slim man of indefinable age with almost grey hair en brosse, charming, firm, immediately a comrade. We were at once on first-name terms, and really everything was decided from the first moment – but always the weight on my mind because of E. We were driven to the Ear Hospital, and we had a nice meal – cold hospital ersatz coffee and sandwiches we had brought, got to bed late.

Then Wednesday, 17 Sept., brought the decision. The offer we were made was such, that I could not refuse it. The villa with a front garden, a plot of land nearby, furniture and kitchen appliances etc. which will become my property, in part [other] newly made furniture at a reasonable price, pajok *and* potato deliveries, appreciably more money than Dresden [...]. Only literary history lecture courses, no more than six hours a week. I am to be appointed to the chair of 'Romance Literatures'. E. seemed by turns pleased and very depressed. My conscience is not clear, but again and again I think that I have made the right decision. [...] We called on Jacoby, with whom I talked over my appointment. Wohlgemuth had told me he was altogether deutschnational [i.e. an old-fashioned nationalist], and his wife was from an East Prussian noble family, a Countess Kalckreuth or something. So Jacoby said to me: 'My dear colleague, we want to win you back to the side of scholarship!' [...]

Early on Friday the 19th to Anhalter Station [in Berlin]. At first seats only in the corridor, afterwards comfortably in a carriage for travellers going on to the Balkans. Home at 1.30. A stack of post. Requests for lectures from every direction. [...]

24th September, Wednesday morning. At the Kahanes', Berlin

Since Sunday I have been completely encapsulated in the [Party] congress, which closes this evening, and leading a monotonous, very taxing life. [...] It remains deadly enough [...]. Five days are hard, especially after preceding local and district and Saxon conferences.

[...]

The themes: Two points are crucial. 1) Tulpanov's speech, behind which is Vyshinsky's UN speech.[94] This is the beginning of the war against the USA, this removes the muzzle from us. I remember how I was not allowed to give my Dachau report in May. And now! The talk is of the two Americas – les deux Frances – les deux Allemagnes. The term 'monopoly capitalism' is from now on a pillar of the *LQI*, as a specialist term it has of course been around for a long time. [...] The theme of the West [i.e. of delegates from the Western zones], also that of the East, of course, was: SED in all zones, a free Ruhr, a united Germany. *Theme 1* therefore, against the USA, for Russia, against Soviet-baiting. *Theme 2*: Inner unity. *Theme 3*: Against Schuhmacher. He was repeatedly represented as seducer, seducee, traitor, also as an ignoramus [e.g. with respect to Lenin]. [...] *Theme 4*: Mobilisation of women for all political posts. Many women were allowed to speak, in part they spoke in cliches, but some also very well on more general (West) topics. *Theme 5*: Winning over the peasantry. Strongly emphasised. *Th. 6*: Youth, only touched on. *Th. 7*: Culture, schools, universities. All only touched on, all good intentions expressed, also self-criticism. [...]

1st October, Wednesday forenoon. Dresden

I only just now completed my notes on the Party Congress, I am far too worn-out, swamped, tired and restless, doing too many things at once – at the same time happy and always imbued with only the one prayer, may heaven grant me another couple of years – because the possibilities of making an impact are great and varied, and I place many hopes in Greifswald. I shall certainly not get down to concentrated deskwork before that – lecture after lecture, conference after conference, visit after visit. [...]

Afternoon about 6 p.m. (1st Oct.)

From 12 until about 5 Dr Weise was here, he had come over on my account. Romanist, interpreter, before the 2nd World War language assistant at Bordeaux Univ., student of Vossler, Hatzfeld, took his doctorate with Gelzer, now senior figure at Teubner. The timetable for *Mod. French Prose* is clear – by 15 Nov. I shall deliver the old 2nd edition almost unchanged with a foreword. We are still fighting over the Literary History; for the 18th Century I have allowed myself to be pushed back to 800 pp, for the 19th and 20th centuries I am sticking to 1000 pp and am rejecting any abridgement of the extant text. – The planned periodical became more tangible. I suggested Humanism in its double meaning as a title[95] – what has just occurred to me, since Teubner are holding on to the *Neue Jahrbücher* [New Yearbooks] is *Humanistische Jahrbücher* [Humanist Yearbooks] with an introductory study on 'Humanism' by me.

[...]

6th October, Monday evening. Dresden

Towards evening yesterday I was also called over to Frau Schmidt. [Her daughter] Traute Schmidt, recommended by me to Greifswald as a student of dentistry, had been refused by the [state] government in Schwerin, but the rector wanted to propose her once again. [...] I dictated a letter of recommendation to the rector. Today one of the Zabel twins came to see me: the girls have been refused by Leipzig. I promised to get them into Greifswald as medical students; she pressed my hands to her face and wept. [...] then Frau Ahrens and her daughter from Quackenbrück turned up and cost me the whole long afternoon [...]. Awkward and interesting about this visit was their absolute support of the West, of England and Schuhmacher, their conviction of the pure Hitlerism of the Russians, of the 'coolie' situation of the East Germans dependent on them, of the mendacity of Soviet propaganda, of the well-meaning democratism of Truman and the English, of Russian blame for the blocking of the zonal boundaries and the difficulties at the UN. In every respect the Ahrenses thought us as ill-informed and as pig-headed as we them, it was utterly impossible to find something to agree about, to come to any understanding. At the same time personally we remained very friendly. [...] East and West Germany have become not so much hostile brothers as strangers to one another.

9th October, Thursday afternoon

We are both rushed off our feet, by turns happy and downcast. Greifswald should help. [...] 'We want to win you back to the side of scholarship,' Jacoby said. He is not entirely wrong, and I hope he will not be entirely wrong in the end. – 66 years old today. How much longer? What will be completed? – Most courteous congratulatory telegram from the Aufbau publishing house. Most charming letter from Weise at Teubner (*not* for my birthday, just like that). My Lit. Hist. has not yet been fitted in. But everyone is exerting themselves on my behalf. [...] Very curious birthday mood in me: 66, frequent bad pains [...] tiredness – and yet more activity than ever and flattered vanity and plans and fulfilment, very strange. And all this extra life is a pure gift, because really I should have been dead long ago ... And what is this gift worth? What will its worth be to me a second after my end?? [...]

[...] On Wed. at 2 p.m. meeting of the district committee and of the delegates at Albertplatz: evaluation of the Party congress. Length 6 hours. 2 – until almost 8. At first I slept a lot, then became more lively. [...] The most interesting thing: at the close of the meeting the list of some 20 to be expelled. The commission has resolved, the meeting has to decide. Where the charge was theft and the like, it was over in a second. But there were a couple of unclear, at least unclearly formulated cases, accusations of Nazi attitude, few and far from unprejudiced witnesses. Here there were repeated objections by conscientious people, which were usually granted. (Investigate once again, formulate, submit!) To me that *very* much spoke for the assembly as a whole. [...]

15th October, Wednesday forenoon
Evening 10 p.m.

On the regional broadcasting station I heard that Plievier really has gone to Munich. In an interview there he said that he had been forced to remain silent for 11 years and now wanted to live in a country in which he was allowed to say everything. At the same time I learned that Erik Mauthner has been in the West since 18 September [...]. It is very upsetting for me that the whole of the intelligentsia is going over to the other side like this. But we must, we must hold on to our position and I still believe – not in the pure idealism and the blamelessness of the Russians, but that their cause, regarded ideally, is the better one, and regarded practically, is, in the long term the winning one.

[...]

21st October, Tuesday forenoon. (–4°, since yesterday late autumn in earnest)
[...]

Eva has completed her Jacques Roumain and is just now sending the ms to the Sachsenverlag publishing house, which as early as tomorrow will have it passed on to Volk and Welt by courier. Teubner has also proposed I send my *Mod. French Prose* there 'by courier'. Back to the Middle Ages ... [...]

23rd October, Thursday forenoon
[...]

Yesterday morning – a hike and an expedition for me – at the TH. [...]

Curious, how I never, never in all of these 2 years, went into action again at the TH. – Vanitas vanitatum: I can hardly bear to admit to myself, what a relief it is to me, that now at the end of my life I have after all obtained a university chair. Even if only in the Eastern Zone and there at the smallest university.

[...]

I began the excruciating job of mending the *Modern Prose*. [...]

25th October, midday Saturday

Yesterday morning I wrote at length to Teubner, that it was impossible for me to leave the 'Introduction' to the *Modern Prose* unchanged or to re-edit it with only a few corrections. Instead an open avowal of the changed objective and subjective situation! I wonder whether they will agree.

The rest of the day was completely lost. Eva Schulze came and drew me until 3 and of course prohibited me – after saying something else beforehand! – from wearing glasses and from moving, and the torture is to be repeated on Tuesday. She turned me not only into a sleepy old man but also into the most hopeless pessimist. [...]

Then [...] I exerted myself almost entirely in vain with a volume of essays borrowed from Buttig 'Ärgernis und Zuversicht' [Scandal and Trust] which circles with pompous words around Existentialism. *Existentialism* and *genuine* are *the* fashionable words [...]. Again and again: everything philosophical and everything mystical simply does not go into my head, I am quite helpless in this respect. How often it made me anxious in the last few years before my dismissal: [...]. During the Hitler years it was sometimes almost a comfort that I had come to the end after all ... And now, with the increased demands of the university chair and after I have learned nothing new and forgotten so much, I am going to take up the game again! I am sometimes shaken by fear. On the other hand: I would have very quickly used myself up here. [...]

29th October, Wednesday evening

4 or 5 times a week we have a power cut from 5–8 p.m. I am already quite used to dosing or sleeping through this time in an easy chair. That makes about 75 hours a month to be deducted from the remainder of my life. [...]

30th October, Thursday forenoon

[...] What is happening with Greifswald? What with trip to the West? What will happen to the Modern Prose? In addition domestic hardships: no packet for months (plural), shortage of coal, lighting cuts. Health problems: E. very pale, very thin, very exhausted – I: [...] My heart, my neck and recently worry again about the place where the suspected cancer was operated. [...]

Gladewitz said yesterday: 'Why is it? The shabbiest atrocity tales of the Nazis were believed. And now? 100 witnesses, the firmest proof of the awfulness of the concentration camps etc. To no avail! None of it is supposed to be true, is at least thought to be "exaggerated", we are not getting through!' – That is the hopelessness of our situation. No VVN can help there.

31st October, Friday towards evening

[...] Yesterday evening '30 Years Soviet Union' in the Vier Jahreszeiten [Four Seasons] Inn, Radebeul. Small unpleasant adventure on the way there. On Grossenhainer Str. two Russians want to halt the car, are already about to open the door. The driver accelerates. Immediately the comrade travelling with me: 'Bend down! He's going for his revolver!' But nothing more happened ... 'Why did you drive on?' – 'They might have thrown us out and then we would perhaps have been without a car!' – I spoke to SED officials and their families. Music before and after, passages from Mayakovsky's October poem – a very young man read amateurishly and pronounced 'oranges' with a hard g. I spoke in between, was rather more radical than planned [...]. But passable on the whole. One worker said to me: 'I could have listened to you for hours,' my companion from the car: 'it was something different for once from the same old stuff the Party secretaries give us' ... But nevertheless I feel how with this constant talking I am going to waste intellectually. It really *must* be reduced, I want 'to win myself back to the side of scholarship'.

I consider the many Soviet Union celebrations altogether inopportune. They make the mood worse. Or at least they blunt people.

I now have to go to the Hygiene Museum, where a Col. Dymshits (SMA)[96] is speaking. The meeting is organised jointly by the Kulturbund and the Society for Soviet Culture.

[...]

1st November, Saturday morning

[Dymshits meeting] [...] The place was full, all the VIPs there. I had to talk to a great number of people. Made the acquaintance of Comrade Dr Lobe, somewhat self-confident younger lady, as a city departmental head she is Lotte's superior and recently came into conflict with her a little, on which occasion Lotte seems to have waved her big uncle's wooden slippers ... Our conversation was very friendly, I repeatedly said 'Comrade Lobe', she said she had been sitting very close to me at the Party Congress in Berlin; with respect to Lotte: she is *already* a senior physician, definitely listed and paid as such [...] Lotte was present at the meeting, but afterwards I did not manage to catch her and later telephoned her with news of the success. I am now consciously pursuing family politics: Lotte Sussmann-Klemperer, Doris Machol-Klemperer. Vanitas vanitatum of the first order. If I could imagine that father and my brothers were watching through a hole in the sky, it would be even more pleasant. The difficulties of the way home – no car, my heart, my spine – deflated me.

[...]

2nd November, Sunday evening

In the morning Schottländer, our tenant, was here to dig the garden and play piano. Made a lengthy and withering critique of my lecture in the student house [...]. The historical part shallow and without sociological, economic etc. knowledge, the directly political part – 'I would not have opened the university yet' – offensive and 'naive'; I should stay away from politics, which I did not understand and return to scholarship. My LTI lecture in Berlin had been very good, this one here very bad. – I was very depressed, especially as there are so many hitches at the moment. – In the afternoon visit by Lotte Sussmann. Told me good things about my *LTI* book, about the Zion chapter, and thus consoled me. [...]

3rd November, 1 a.m. Monday night

[...] Everything is all right, we can come [to Greifswald] on 1 Dec. – Load off my chest. But not for long. Then the weight of worries again. Recently above all: that I cannot speak French.

Letter from Teubner. Want the *Modern Prose* as unchanged as possible, want if possible no declaration of principle, since 'the transformation of a view of history is self-evident'. I wrote back: it is not self-evident, on the contrary, nationalist sentiments were smouldering among the students again. Either I would have to nail my colours to the mast, and explicitly distance myself from the 1926 edition, or leave the book buried. [...] I was very afraid, that will break my connection with Teubner, also with respect to the Literary History. But I *had* to write uncompromisingly.

[...]

8th November, Saturday forenoon and later

[Trip to Berlin on Kulturbund business: the KB had been banned in the American sector of Berlin from 5 Nov.]

Just now on the wireless – it is 10 o'clock Saturday evening – the KB has also been banned in the English sector of Berlin. Perhaps it's a good thing. It will now become even more emphatically pro-Russian.

[...]

Early this morning [in Dresden again] call from Leipzig, Dr Weise at Teubner (cf 3 Nov.). He's eating humble pie, our conceptions can be combined, and he has really given me a free hand. I triumph and am up to my neck in work.

[...]

10th November, Monday evening

Yesterday [...] afternoon commemoration of 'Crystal Night' (*who* invented the phrase?[97]) organised by the VVN in the Hygiene Museum. There by car with the Wolffs. The place packed. All the VIPs: Koenen, His Excellency Fischer, etc. – I was among them. Vanitas. Loewenkopf and Geschke spoke – the usual. Lewinsky and Löwen, the actress, recited [...].

After that I went to the ministry to initiate the interzonal pass from Frankfurt. This gave rise to such a deal of bother, there turned out to be such a number of travel difficulties – it's an expedition, not a trip – that the effort expended would be quite disproportionate to this *one* lecture. [...]

For a moment we had considered whether I should travel back via Munich and finally fetch the baggage, that is still stored there. This very morning a letter arrived from the Stühlers, sent from Bremen on 24 Oct: by now they are probably already in the USA, want to go to San Francisco, write very bitterly about Catholic anti-Semitic Bavaria. Our baggage is now in the attic of Lisl's sister, Frau Fuchs [...]. It then occurred to me that there was a very great risk of losing the baggage again when crossing the border. How should I prove, that it is property for personal use. Expensive ladies' woollen things in my masculine hands! A pitiful piece of cultural history, this abandoned trip, this untransportable baggage in Bavaria, lying there for $2\frac{1}{2}$ years now!

[...]

12th November, Wednesday evening

Violent storm, for the second day now. *Storm warning* because of the toppling ruins.

[...]

Yesterday from 6–9 p.m. Party officials' meeting at the Bienertmühle. Insight into day-to-day work. [...] Against the slanders on the Russians. (I spoke). About the wood campaign. Swindles of the small wood merchants ... Edmund Müller, the red Jew [...], trustee of a factory takes deliveries of agricultural produce from peasants out of their family use allocations [...]. I was asked privately as to my opinion. I advocated especially harsh action, because as a Jew he has special responsibilities. The barter deals here were already being called 'Jewish deals'; in Lisl Stühler's farewell letter of 10 Nov. she says she heard on a Munich tram 'dirty Jew!' What use are all the Crystal Night commemorations against that?

[...]

29th November, Saturday. Dresden

The day before yesterday, 27 Nov., I made the packet of *Modern French Prose* ready for Teubner, it is to be picked up by a courier. In the accompanying letter I wrote: definitive version, I shall change *nothing* more. [...]

[...]

On Mon. morning, 24 Nov., to the TH (my last appearance) rectorial election dramatically protracted in the 4th act. Heidebroek's event. I hate him, because HE is definitively to blame for the elimination of my chair. HE insinuated to Soviet Headquarters in Karlshorst, that we do not need a linguistic etc. philosophical faculty, a technical *university*. He wants to be sole ruler of the plumbers. [...] Aside from that LDP and chairman of the House of Technology and very smart. Thanks to his autocratic fiddling around he had made an enemy of the whole Education Faculty. He evidently did not want the election. [...] Set for 10 o'clock in the morning. All the professors, student representatives and assistants present, about 50 people in all. Rector announces: an objection had come from the SMA, request for details from Karlshorst under way, new time 12.30. Everyone suspects some plot. I spent the intervening time in a seminar room of our faculty, partly reading, partly chatting to Schottländer. [...] After that the election. A huge 'urn', in fact a monstrous box borrowed from the city, which can hold several 1000 ballots. [...] Result: 49 valid votes, 40 for Straub, the Education dean [...], CDU; 6 for Heidebroek [...]. Now the battle is about whether Heidebroek automatically becomes Prorector. If there is an election, he will lose this position also.

[...]

In the evening there was a big Bloc meeting for 'Unity'. [...] The big broadcasting studio was packed, there were knots of people along the sides and in the corners. In complete contrast to the usual emptiness and indifference. Afterwards Hose[98] told me in all innocence, gentle pressure had been used to get people here from all the factories. Exactly the Nazi method, therefore. Whom is one deceiving? Oneself. Autosuggestion.

On the evening of Thurs., the 27th, my farewell party in the elegant house of the Soviet Society. I was present at the setting up of the society, later I somehow lost touch, I received no invitations, was out of the picture ... Reingruber, our Kulturbund deputy and simultaneously Prorector of the TH picked us up in his car. The affair was poorly organised and rather measly. Some 30 people had been invited, a number sent excuses, others stayed away without excuse; the little band of about 15 people was lost in the big dining room, the huge horseshoe table had been laid for about 30 [...] Renn welcomed me, Kneschke gave a lengthy speech, likewise Reingruber, Frau Heidenberger, the town clerk, gave a shorter speech on behalf of the city. I received an address signed by Weidauer and Rentzsch and a basket of flowers with it, another basket of flowers from the Kulturbund, a packet of cigarettes from the Soviet Society, a portfolio of art by the painter Bodenthal whom I do not know and to whom I am completely indifferent. I gave a speech. [...] I came home fairly depressed. (I also said [in the speech]: at such a jubilee one was like a corpse which was allowed to express its feelings. But there was nothing to fear [...].)

During the day I had worked on a speech for the Dresden–Leipzig broadcasting station about the 'People's Congress' [for Unity and Just Peace, called for 6 Dec. 1947] – I read it to Kneschke over the telephone, he found it too harsh towards Jacob Kaiser,[99] I toned down. [...] At 3, as had been agreed, the broadcasting station car picked us both up, I spoke my thing in a few minutes, and now the car was supposed to take us to Elsa Kreidl at 15b Caspar David Friedrichstr. The car had meanwhile 'gone just to the parliament'. We waited in vain for $\frac{3}{4}$ of an hour, then walked all the way to the tramcar, and again from Wasaplatz to Elsa K. A walk and visit full of memories – what a turn of events. I thought of the dead. [...] We sat by the light of a candle, got good tea and little cakes, chatted pleasantly and recovered. Home towards 8, immediately out again to the neighbourhood group meeting in Cafe Dölzschen. [...] Forbrig gave a short farewell speech for me.

LQI words: Frankfurt the German Vichy or the Vichy government. – Monopoly rulers. – Bizonesia, more mildly Bizonia.[100] [...]

On Saturday 29 Nov. at 2 p.m. there was a VVN session in its new home on the Wilder Mann.. There were ten of us present, and surprisingly it was here that I was given a particularly cordial send off. Egon Rentzsch gave a very warm speech, presented me with a nice address and, with dedications, the two art books published by the Sachsenverlag: the Daumier and the concentration-camp pictures of Leah Grundig. – Afterwards during the actual meeting I spoke very pessimistically about the mood of young people and met with complete agreement, and Clemens Dölitzsch, with whom I have not always seen eye to eye, added remarks. Afterwards there was a car to take me home [...].

3rd December, Wednesday evening about 11 p.m. Dresden.
Berlin KB trip (2nd/3rd Dec.)
[...]

It was also emphasised on all sides, that everyone knew the formal reason [for the American prohibition of the Kulturbund] was a pretext, the Americans simply did not like 'the SED orientation'. [...] I said: it was not that *we* were pro-Russian in our attitude, rather the Russians were the only ones who were pro-German and pro-Kulturbund. [...] Then the People's Congress was also discussed. His Magnificence Stroux, looks like three philistines gone mouldy, spoke warmly in favour, 'although that, too, could be reckoned against us as SED partiality'. Ackermann on behalf of the Party: it was only issuing the invitations, was only the initiator, was keeping in the background. The KB – incidentally less than half the committee was there, I have the impression, that everything is fixed within a small circle, 35 of 40 Executive Committee members are supernumerary, Becher, Willmann, Gysi, Kleinschmidt do everything, even Friedensburg [CDU mayor of Berlin] and Stroux are only objects, admittedly ones that have to be taken account of. [...]

Thurs. aft. 4 Dec
On the morning of 2 Dec. I travelled to Berlin by train. [...] At Potsdamer Station at midday, by foot to the KB. After ejection from the British Sector the offices now at 1 Jägerstr. My room, apartment in the expensive and inhospitable Adlon – a chambermaid found a thick eiderdown for me, so at least I did not freeze for all that money. From there to *Neues Leben* [periodical of the youth organisation, FDJ]. Schlesinger, whom I like very much. We chatted for a long time. The Culture booklet is to cost 2.50. Since I get a share of 10% and 30,000 copies have been printed, I'm rich. [...]

Schlesinger gave me a car out to Anny Kl's. I came upon her and Peter over a late lunch, got a splendid pea soup and real coffee, was able to buy a kilo of peas for 50M. We both had to laugh at the turn of events when Anny explained she had only 10M in the house and would not receive a rent payment until the

7th and I, on my side, offered her money – ('what would Beo [Berthold] say?!' –
'He would have learned to think differently too!'). Peter accompanied me to the
station of the elevated railway, we agreed he would call for me at the club to go
to the cinema [...]. Shrouded in swathes of fog and drizzling rain we walked
along Friedrichstr. as far as Oranienburger Tor. Darkness, destruction [...] but
in between also inhabited houses, traffic, not the complete deadness of central
Dresden ... A small cinema. [...] Peter, very long-haired, good-looking boy,
something artistic about his whole appearance, 2nd semester, wants to be a
psychiatrist – I also saw a pretty picture of his brother's, Georg's, fiancée, Jewish,
organist, at present a correspondence clerk in Zürich, where he has become –
presumably unpaid – an assistant at the TH. Peter asked me what it had been
like in my parents' home, how I had got on with my brothers and sisters. I
briefly pointed to the tensions, in addition the tremendous change in notions
of propriety and in the position of women since the beginning of the century.

[...] At midnight Peter accompanied me to the door of the Adlon ruin. (All
these walks without pain, the next day also, but then around 3 p.m. on the few
steps to Unter den Linden all hell was let loose and I felt again, how much of
my time has run out.) ... The next morning [...] to Volk and Welt on Taubenstr.
There Frau Herrmann and Tschesno himself were most profuse in their praise
of E.'s Roumain translation. So sensitive and 'musical'. An actress is soon to give
a reading of passages from V & W books. E.'s translation is to take its proper
place there, precisely the translation itself. E. was very pleased by this professional praise. I emphasise everywhere (that is, to Schlesinger, to Tschesno,
recently to Henschel), that is her widow's pension, they should give her commissions.

[...]

5th December 1947, Friday evening towards midnight. Dresden

Yesterday evening E. got the shakes out of exhaustion and aversion. In the
middle of the night at 4 o'clock she told me bitterly, once she had been chased
out of her home by the Gestapo and had lost everything because of the air raid,
now she was being chased out again, and what was left and what had been
newly accumulated would be stolen from her. It was very painful for me. Have
I sacrificed her contentment to my vanity? Perhaps yes – but perhaps I have
nevertheless acted rightly and also to E.'s advantage. [...]

7th December, Sunday afternoon. Dresden

The hateful and truly nerve-racking peripeteias of the business of moving. The
railways failed us: we should hire a remover tomorrow, but really tomorrow,
then the things could go express and be insured. But where to get a remover so
quickly? And where is the security? The higher the insurance, the greater the
incentive to theft ... 'Yes, Professor, the best thing is for the Party to supply a
truck!' Sheer mockery; the Party will not give me any petrol whatsoever. Then
this morning came deliverance. On the steps of the Hygiene Museum Egon

Rentzsch gave me his word, he will have the chests, which we can leave here, brought to Greifswald, right to our new address, by a municipal truck which has to fetch potatoes from Mecklenburg. Hopefully – I consider Rentzsch to be particularly conscientious – that will work out well. [...] Now after the transport of the chests has been halfway assured, Wolff, who is supposed to drive us, who was supposed to be back from Berlin yesterday evening, has not (4 p.m.) turned up yet. [...]

8th December, Monday [...]
[...] Chaos. We shall hardly get to bed. – 2 packets even arrived, one from Denmark, 22 lbs, one the mysterious dried fruits from Australia – from the editor whom we do not know, to whom Blumenfeld sent one of our letters, and whom Lore Petzal-Isakowitz[101] mentioned as her friend. Piccolo mondo moderno.[102] We are taking both packets with us unopened ... The car will be overloaded. [...]
The beginning of a completely new period of our life therefore

Greifswald 9th December 1947–23 August 1948
IF ONLY!

[The months in Greifswald were not happy ones for the Klemperers; nevertheless, at the age of 66 Victor Klemperer had at last achieved his goal of a chair at a proper university, and Greifswald was to prove only a brief intermezzo in his Indian summer of an academic career, though there were to be disappointments and losses enough – academically and otherwise.]

I have always told myself: one day after the wedding you know it all! I know today, I've known it since 9 Dec., the first day here: it was the worst mistake, I have gambled away the evening of both our lives.

14/12/47.
That's what things looked like in the morning. And now in the aft. it is a little bit warm here in the bedroom and the real coffee has warmed us, and the tomcat is purring, and so one tells oneself – as long as the coffee effect lasts – 'perhaps ad astra[103] after all!' But then, when the effect of the coffee has worn off and the stove has grown cold: see above di nuovo.

Sunday 14/12/47

14th December 1947, Sunday afternoon. 8 Pommerndamm, Greifswald
From the very first moment things went badly. The packing took the whole night, we did not get to bed at all. Wolff appeared shortly after 5. Since his wife was coming along – an act of reconciliation, which I myself had encouraged – it was impossible to take all the hand luggage. E., embittered and harassed, repacked some things. It then turned out, that some of the most important items, stockings for E., my shaving stuff, underwear for both of us, had been left behind. We have now been suffering because of that for almost a week, and an end to the suffering is not in sight. A suitcase and a kind of seabag, both unlocked, are lying in Dresden – we do not know to whom to entrust them. In addition, with the constant robberies, constant anxiety about all the chests . . . We were very cramped in the car, in a very depressed mood as we drove through ice and fog. [. . .] At the registry at around 5 p.m.: Franz Wohlgemuth, Otto Jürgens – to the Ear Clinic, Erich Kaiser, Isolde Meinhardt (Dr Dr). Supper, room like the first time, the Wolffs as well. During the night E.'s bitterness, the next morning the beginning of the disappointments, which have not ceased since.

Wolff charged me 559.50M for the 'friendship trip'. Here at Pommerndamm the new brick stoves (one plastered, 2 not) sweated water; it was beastly cold and completely inhospitable; the first pieces of furniture have just arrived, all old and chipped, from the estate of an anatomy professor arrested by the Russians, not one piece new, although I had been promised new furniture which could be purchased, utterly inadequate tableware, a single huge cooking pot . . . Chaos, dreariness, damp discomfort everywhere. And that is how it has remained. Not until yesterday evening did we move over here from the clinic, are still living, and presumably will do so for months to come, in chaos and cold and *one* room, are still, and that for almost a week now, not properly washed, shaved, have not brushed our teeth, are still in the grubby conditions of refugee life, are most deeply disappointed. The days run into one another, we are kept busy and do nothing. Until yesterday, as I said, we were accommodated entirely in the clinic, last night here for the first time under many blankets, but for lunch and through the afternoon over there again with Kaiser-Meinhardt for hours.

Apart from the desperations and exhaustions – both Eva's and my health is suffering badly, many pains, also E.'s heart is giving way, and in my case excruciating lumbago has been added to neck and angina – also more agreeable things. The Kaisers feed us very well, help in every possible way, likewise Wohlgemuth (although it is really he who has let us down with respect to housing, but he says it was impossible to do more!), Jürgens and Roethe, the head of personnel, Frau Dunkel, the university's household superintendent.

On Wednesday evening, before the elections to the student council, there was a meeting of the SED students in the refectory. Struck, the dean of the education faculty, spoke about the People's Congress. I spoke after him. Poche ma sentite parole. 'You must learn more than the others!'

University politics conversations with Franz [Wohlgemuth]. 'Conspiratorial group' – sworn society: A very full discussion with Franz and Dr Müller, the assistant secretary and department head in Schwerin [administrative capital of the *Land* of Mecklenburg-Vorpommern] responsible for the university. He offered me his post, I turned it down. At issue is, whether I become dean or rector or nothing at all. At issue, as in Saxony, as since May 45, is the breaking of the both secret and noisy obstruction and opposition [in the universities], which relies on the democratic principle of self-government. I always preach the same thing. Will I have more success in Mecklenburg than in Saxony? I doubt it. But the attempt must be made. On Tuesday I am to go to Schwerin with Franz and set forth my views to the minister. Jacoby has a bad reputation as being sly and obstinate, he takes cover behind his deafness; the rector, Seeliger,[104] whose acquaintance I have made, has the reputation of a 'nitwit'. He had not sent down a first lieutenant who had lied about his rank [. . .], merely giving him a severe reprimand. And similar cases. – Weidhaas, appointment as lecturer, member of the senate as representative of the non-professorial teaching staff, reports strong reactionary tendencies – Jacoby called on me at the clinic, tried to bring me round. Dornseif[105] should be his successor, I was still too new here, with respect to the rector he would give me a tip. I pretended innocence, let myself be advised. We sat in the stairwell of the clinic, doors opened because of our bellowing, even though they are used to quite a lot in the ear clinic after all. Franz said: 'They are afraid of you and are trying to take precautions.' His opinion: I should not immediately be put in an exposed position as rector, but appointed dean. Müller asked me, whether I would risk functioning as imposed rector. I: without drastic measures we would never reach our goal. [. . .]

The department looks as elegant and comfortable as our apartment looks bare and impossible. I have not yet managed to look around at leisure.

This the real university news of the first week in Greifswald. The semester is ending now, and I shall start in April.

[...]

16th December, Tuesday forenoon. Greifswald

Hopeless: damp walls and floorboards, damp wood, damp stoves – everything is lacking. Yesterday terrifically tormented by lumbago (or kidneys?). Today a little better in *this* respect. Damp sleety weather, very wet feet. Everything is lacking. E. ever paler. Because of her I reproach myself most desperately.

Eating at the clinic – preliminary talks with the Party. [...]

Empty days, full of despair.

I look around the icy department, am provided with information [...] Everything appears wretched to me. I should have remained outsider, journalist, politician, myself. I have sacrificed everything to the damned, so very stupid vanity of being a university professor. And now I am nothing, just an 'SED prof.' And every student who knows Old French and Provençal looks down his nose at me.

17th December, Wednesday forenoon

[...]

And constantly the terrible feeling of guilt towards E.

[...]

My reading for days: *Georg Büchner*, monograph by Hans Mayer[106] from the book packet from Volk and Welt.

Since 8 Dec. without newspaper, without wireless – nothing but hearsay. The London Conference [of the 4 powers on the future of Germany] is supposed to have collapsed.[107] Now I suddenly learn about the Mecklenburg People's Congress[108] and that I have been delegated to it. What is the Mecklenburg Congress supposed to do? [...]

Snow, freezing rain, storm, slush, ghastliness of the weather.

19th December, Friday. Greifswald

Yesterday Schwerin–Mecklenburg Congress [...]

Journey by car with Wohlgemuth and Kaiser [...]. Departure at about 6 a.m., 140 miles, route Stralsund, Rostock, Doberan, Wismar. I saw next to nothing, journey there half in darkness, return journey completely so. On the way out, until about Stralsund snow-covered road, then dry, on the way back snow flurries, ice, slow and dangerous driving. There 6–10.30, back 8–1. [...] In Doberan we were told, that the sea was just over a mile away – Heiligendamm. That provoked childhood memories, mother's golden watch lost in the fallen leaves of the wood, a boy found it and was allowed to go on the carousel. In

Schwerin the beautiful pond, our hotel on the motoring holiday with Grete![109]
The very elegant theatre and museum square, the little ducal capital. [...]

This time the pre-arranged demonstration game [i.e. the congress] was especially empty and pointless, first of all as a warmed-up version of Berlin, after
that as especially worn-out, and further and above all: completely without
purpose after the failure of the London conference. Everything was built up on a
mood of irredenta[110] and defiance. The Berlin delegation remains as [permanent]
promoter of unity and peace, corresponding committees are being formed in
every region, in every district, and are supposed to keep alive the demand for
unity. How that can happen, is not said. [...]

[...] Wohlgemuth said, I should speak for the university. I did not feel
myself legitimated to do that. I said therefore: coming from the University of
Greifswald, I was speaking as an old university teacher for old and young at the
univ, and delivered a couple of sentences entirely about culture, for the re-
establishment of which we, above all, were responsible, and about *our one
fatherland*. There was a little applause [...] Then an already printed resolution
was read out and accepted unanimously, then a list of 30 permanent committee
people for unity and peace treaty – and once again I am also on this regional
committee. – At 2.30 the awful shivering was over. [...]

20th December, late afternoon, Saturday. Greifswald

[...] Errands and repeatedly pointless errands. Begging for every little thing, for
deep plates, shoe brushes, etc. etc. [...] Each blames the other, grumbles about
the other, nothing is right; damp, smoking stoves, blizzards, cold – now almost
two weeks in this state. – Yesterday aft. in the dean's office 'meeting of the
faculty proper', 'introduction of Prof. Kl.' as first point. Only half a dozen people
present, all of them natural scientists. Weidhaas, as representative of the non-
professorial teaching staff, kept the minutes. Jacoby goes up to each speaker
and holds up his ear trumpet, then one has to shout into it. The ear trumpet is
his visor, he lowers it – then he's inaccessible, then one is at his mercy. [...]

25th December, Thursday morning. Greifswald

Christmas began terribly. In the morning on the way to the clinic – I was
fetching my typewriter, had myself shaved, was given some fir branches – the
worst pains I have had at any time recently. Then at home constantly the feeling
of absolute isolation and the burden of the guilt towards E. ... Then in the late
afternoon Franz Wohlgemuth called. A real comfort to both of us, everything
turns livelier and more hopeful again. [...] He invited us for New Year's Eve. He
brought us the ms of his novella (only excerpts have appeared thus far) *Pitiless*. –
Once he was gone, E. made a little Christmas tree out of wastepaper basket,
stand, the fir twigs and three candles – one for each of us, little Moritz [the
tomcat] as well. It stood on the desk in the study, which immediately no longer
appeared so gloomily damp [...]. After the nice evening meal with meat I read
Pitiless aloud in one go: the first time I have read aloud since the reading in the

wood in Unterbernbach.[111] (with the air planes above us). [...]

26th December, Friday midday. Greifswald
[After noting a dull Christmas dinner invitation] Picture postcards with New Year's greetings to Dölzschen etc.

I am reading along with the Roumain proofreading, and thus for the first time E.'s opus; it truly is a work of literary adaptation.

27th December, Saturday afternoon. Greifswald
[To add to the Klemperers' sufferings Eva K. is suffering from both a skin complaint and boils exacerbated by inadequate washing facilities and poor diet.]
[...]
Letter from Teubner today, very happy with my *Modern Prose*. The letter is dated the 17th, a duplicate of the study [...] will be with the Culture Advisory Board[112] 'even before the holiday'. A ray of hope – but the rays of hope no longer last very long.

31st December, Wednesday morning, New Year's Eve. Greifswald
Unchanged gloominess and tedium of outer and inner life. Quite tiny walks, a couple of times in the evening, to get a breath of air – E. complains about stomach pains, I about bones and heart – walks to get shaved, be alone. No relationship to any living soul in Greifswald, beached, beyond saving. Food packets have not come [...].

Wildly indiscriminate reading. [...] For the present my browsing and dipping into books is going in the *3 directions Revolution–18ième, recent French prose and the image of France* all at the same time; only groping and sniffing at everything while feeling completely empty. At first I had been so tempted by 'scholarly' work again, and now this footnote and specialism business seems so musty and trivial.

The *Aufbau* publishing house sent me, presumably as a Christmas present, without an accompanying letter a very fine bound copy of my *LTI* which is in paperback only for the general public. But in this fine volume the wretchedness of the paper and of the print is even more blatant than before. Apart from that one hears nothing of the *LTI*. Where are the 10,000 copies? In no bookshop, with no editors. No newspaper has taken any notice of it.

What is my résumé of 1947? *LTI* appeared and 'Culture' appeared (and both have *not* appeared, i.e. appear nowhere) and *Modern Prose* has been revised, and [there was] a mass of lectures, wireless broadcasts. And smashing of my position in Dresden and also in the Kulturbund. And Greifswald, which is making us both unhappy, Greifswald for which I am to blame. Because I wanted to be a university professor.

Youth: You have everything before you. Age: it's all behind you. Youth: It does not ask about the value of actions and events. Age: You ask about everything, and everything is without value. I think that even during the Nazi years I did not feel a New Year's Eve to be as dismal as this time. Because this time I bear the blame for the misery, and because I have dragged E. into this mess, and because I see no way out.

1948

1st January, Thursday evening. Greifswald

We are living in exactly the same chaos and pigsty as yesterday – study, bedroom, dining room in one, ordures de matou[1] in front of the stove under my nose, when I lie in bed, because our little cat is without his box (where to get one? there are no cartons, never mind small boxes) – and yet we are both, really both of us in an altogether different mood since yesterday and now after all almost certain, that with Greifswald we made the right choice and have a future before us. – The evening with Franz Wohlgemuth, him, the lord mayor, Max Burwitz,[2] the professor of the Education Faculty, Schmidt-Walter,[3] the young professor of chemistry whose name I have forgotten. In addition the wives of Wohlgemuth and Schmidt-Walter; less important but not a nuisance the refectory manageress. The tremendously warm, amusing, but altogether intellectual tone of the company. The greatest efforts on behalf of both of us. On behalf of E. as musician and comrade, on behalf of myself; the most definite assurance, that we are to have a position here, that we are being counted on. The first time that we sat in a little group, hatched plans … Most definite assurance, that there will now be progress with our apartment. In the near future a musical circle is to be formed around E. I myself am to get the post of dean – am in the meantime to play the gentle nothing-but-a-scholar until the election is over. Am already supposed to have done that successfully at the first faculty meeting. Jacoby, the reactionary old fox, had declared to Franz that he was very satisfied with my attitude and begged him to leave me to the world of scholarship. He would also thereby be doing the SED the best service, 'I had a European reputation'. On the other hand I heard again, my appearance in front of the Socialist students on the last evening of the semester had won their hearts. The Comrade Lord Mayor – 'Max' – paid me compliments, Schmidt-Walter likewise, E. was not neglected for a moment, we were both very content and our hopes have now held up for the whole day. […] there was a great deal of liqueur, there was potato salad with a little dumpling, there was punch and coffee, a proper warm pancake each and biscuits, there were cheese sandwiches, there were solemn little speeches – I had to start – gossip, conspiracies and memories of Russian and English captivity, there were many insights into the conditions and balance of forces here [...] finally E. tried out the piano, and well past 4 a.m. the whole company brought us home, Wohlgemuth was rather merry and very loudly declaimed Goethe's 'Prometheus' [...]. Firm snow has been lying on the streets since the start of New Year's Eve – literally overnight the damp weather has turned into a proper fine winter. I did not get away quite without pain, but on the whole even the march back was almost bearable. Almost at least – I just cannot get away without a memento any more. [...] Two telegrams had arrived in the late afternoon. One for E. – had the Roumain proofs been sent off [...]. One for me, signed Prime Minister [of Mecklenburg-Vorpommern] Höcker: Constituent meeting of the Committee 'for Unity and a Just Peace' (Mecklenburg) 11 a.m. Saturday 3 January Schwerin. Of course between me and Schwerin there is again the question of a car ... [...]

Stopped work very late today, during the day got to grips with Sartre's *Nausée*[4] [...].

In every other respect relieved – but the worry about our baggage is becoming never-ending. Thus far Dresden has not sent its potato truck, because export from here was banned – and now, with the cold, it will not be possible to send it either. [...]

10th January, Saturday forenoon. Greifswald

Worse than the apartment, underwear etc. calamity is the dullness. There is no life in Greifswald, we are buried alive. We were far too used to the Dresden bustle. E., too, says: 'Meetings give me pleasure.' Here there are none: SED, VVN, FDGB etc. etc., nothing is in evidence, no one takes any notice of us. We are cut off from the world. 'The peace and quiet for scholarly work.' But that is so musty. And who will read my 'rigorously scholarly works'?? 2 dozen people, of whom 22 think them too journalistic. Whatever I want I fall between stools. [...]

A large packet from Berthold Meyerhof; a small one from Otto Klemperer. Both of recent date. All the parcels between July and October appear to be lost. [...]

18th January, Sunday evening. Greifswald

[...]

I will shortly put together the list of my reading; all this reading is not useless, but it depresses me, appears to me narrow and trifling, does not help me get over the feeling of emptiness and deadness. On top of that E's complete misery. Sometimes she urges me: 'go to Dresden, see if you can get some kind of post there, perhaps you can take charge of the People's High School!' – But I consider that quite futile. And it would mean breaking my contract with the government here; which will always shield its own failure behind higher authority.

Nice here is only the department library. But it de- and oppresses me, I shall never manage to write anything here. [...]

21st January, Wednesday forenoon. Greifswald (Berlin trip 19–20th. Mon. Tues.)

Monday

1) Volk und Welt – Tschesno. Enthusiasm for E.'s Roumain. [...]

2) Aufbau publishing house. a) *Sonntag* [periodical]. New editor, Hilprich or something like it. Does not know where my Rimbaud ms has got to [...] wants to turn the periodical into a newspaper [...] and short articles instead of essays. b) Gysi [for Aufbau, the principal periodical of the Kulturbund]: accepted the abridged Auerbach review to be printed very quickly; we agreed 3 pages on Deiters' Sainte-Beuve [...] which has just been published [...]. c) Wendt. *LTI* still at the binders, not on sale, not with the review editors. [...] At all KB offices, as well as at the Jägerstr. club, I complained about Greifswald, about my being neglected both with respect to housing and professionally. People will try to help in various ways [...].

3) Neues Leben publishing house. – Mystery of the Culture pamphlet. Objection. By the Russians? By the 'Cultural Advisory Board'? For what reason? Schlesinger on leave, nervous collapse. [...] I resolved to call on the Cultural Advisory Board, both name and institution itself I know thanks to my *Modern Prose*.

4) Anny Klemperer. Wolff has *not* taken the hand luggage there. [...] Peter absent. Is supposed to be more passionately devoted to politics than to medicine, of which only psychoanalysis interests him. Anny very warm as always, very confiding, frank on money matters. [...] To Kahane, ADN [news agency] to whom I had earlier spoken on the telephone.

5) [...] Mackie has been in London. [...] Doris has been in bed for 3 weeks. She is in her 7th month, a growth, worries about the child, yet fair state of health ... Evening and Tue. morning in Niederschönhausen. [...]

Tuesday

6) Jägerstr. i.e. office and club of the KB. a) Cordial meeting with Heinz Willmann. [...] I also communicated what Mackie had told me: that Arnold Zweig[5] feels very uncomfortable in Palestine, as well as in a bad financial situation and is offended not to have received any invitation to Germany. Willmann: they had already tried to get in touch with him, they wanted to re-publish his books. It was impossible to make contact with Palestine. (I know that from my own experience with Walter Jelski and with Sebba.) b) At 11 there was a meeting of Kulturbund secretaries. Before that I had breakfast with Karl Kneschke [...] Very cordial. I told him how much I would like to return to Dresden as soon as possible, and how I would accept any post in the government, the city, the Party, unless or until my Dresden professorship were re-activated.

He showed a great deal of sympathy and will use his influence to that end ...
[...]

7) Cultural Advisory Board, Unter den Linden, House of the 'International Book Shop' (Russian). [Here Klemperer learns that there are no problems concerning his *Modern Prose* or any supplementary volume, but he emerges none the wiser as to what the objections to his 'Culture' pamphlet might be.]

8) Central Administration Wilhelmstr. No luck. [...] I went on foot along Leipzigerstr. to Spittelmarkt. Shaken to see, on a ruined building, the new gold letters *Conditorei Hillbrich*. As a student how many bittersweet hours of drinking coffee with Berthold, who had his office nearby.

9) 11 Oberwasserstr., Volk und Wissen [People and Knowledge] publishing house [responsible for school and other educational books. [...]

10) Yet another important result: the Kahanes have lent me a couple of examples of very recent French literature (Editions de Minuit: Vercors[6] etc.), know a bookshop in Berlin, which could make my department regular comprehensive offers. Prices are supposed to be high (but not quite prohibitive), a lot can be done with a couple of hundred marks, and for that I have Wohlgemuth's assent.

[...] On the return journey at the train at 3.30, which left at 5 – yet no seat left. Only from Prenzlau. Impossible to read. Every woman, young and old, smokes. A young one opposite me with a little boy was rolling herself cigarettes: 'My husband, if he comes back after all – missing – will complain: I'm smoking 20 a day.' [...] All these women without men, on their own feet, morally quite free, with their trousers, their cigarettes, their children ... if I could write novels! – The train was already in G. at 10.15. Walk home troublesome again. Then chatted until 3 in the morning.

23rd January, Friday forenoon. Greifswald

The department received two numbers of *Romanische Forschungen* [Romance Researches]. Lerch on *aveugle* and *avec*,[7] Curtius[8] (Curtius as well!) on grammar in mediaeval education, a dozen *Miscellanies* by Philipp A. Becker[9] (86!) etc. etc. I could do that too, and it tempts me – and it repels me. [...] 'Between stools' will be the subtitle of my Curriculum vitae. [...]

25th January, Sunday evening

The 'Trade' at the market square. Shocking. A queue through a house entry to a little back room. Long and never growing shorter. Ordinary people, women, children, men, evidently the poor, needy. And they all buy cigarettes, 1.80 each: one, 10, 20, 100 mark notes, the saleswoman throws them carelessly onto a pile, at the front the barter shop itself is empty, I saw only a Russian officer in it ... The whole louche enterprise is of course 'Jew business'. I bought E. 25 cig. for 45M.

This morning Jacoby and wife *finally* called [...]. Bellowing with him – while the ladies sat in the bedroom – was no pleasure. He spoke disparagingly of the Education Faculty, which he does not acknowledge to be scholarly and wants to be set only practical tasks. [...]

28th January, midday Wednesday and Wednesday evening. Greifswald

[...] On the whole we are both very depressed; I for my part am burdened by my conscience, but as soon as I am immersed in work, feel a little more hopeful. But a) are there not also possibilities for E. to make an impression? b) is there any point to my work, does it have a purpose? I read, read, read – make notes, prepare – essentially the Image of France, in addition the very modern writers. For the university I should be drawing up in detail the programme for my summer seminar. How shall I sustain it? I do not know any of the recent specialist literature on the 19th century in France. [...] will I rely on my old (outdated) stuff? What will my seminar look like? I still do not know on which texts it can be based. [...]

31st January, Saturday forenoon. Greifswald

On Thurs. E. returned in despair from a walk; G. was so very ugly, from now on she would only walk round 'in a circle' [...], in a circle round our block of houses. – Yesterday she was elected first chair of the DFD [Women's League] here. That gives her a daily goal, and her mood improved. That was yesterday afternoon; in the evening I spoke to a small grateful bunch in the refectory, the SED group of the University Preparatory Institute. In addition a couple of guests: Markowski, Szolbe, *Frau Jacoby*(!). The individual in history and in Marxism. It was a pure Montesquieu lecture, thorough, conversational, intelligible to all. All my old chestnuts [...]

Constant reading on the Image of France. Reading aloud. At the moment Maurois.[10] [...]

3rd February, Tuesday forenoon. Greifswald

[...]

On the afternoon of the same Sunday to tea with the Jacobys. I had very much feared it, and it was indeed very trying, since I am involved in a ceaseless bellowing dialogue with him, while E. converses with her. [...] I actually felt sorry for the Jacobys. They live in cramped conditions, they have a single room overladen with plush, and a bedroom – the remainder has been given up to refugees. Everything about them leaves an impression of shabbiness, confinement. (Why exactly? He cannot be paid less than I. A son fell in action, a daughter is self-supporting in the West.) One perhaps does his wife an injustice. Eva says she is quite tolerable. From aristocratic old times. [...] He: a captain in the reserves, in his youth professor in Japan for a year, lectured in English. [...] Jacoby is neither intellectually nor morally inferior or hidebound – but he is not on the side of the SED and is sly and tenacious. I am just as little honest with him as he is with me. I pass on everything, which should be confidential faculty business, to Wohlgemuth – my oath! – and he pushes me away from any power within the faculty. [...]

Every other word everywhere: the currency reform, just don't accumulate any money, just don't give away any material assets!

[...]

Unceasing reading, reading aloud, collecting, making notes – but when shall I get down to writing again? ... At a standstill since 9 November.

[...]

Monday 9th February. Greifswald: Trip to Berlin, University Conference of the SED, 7th and 8th February

To put the overwhelming fact of these two days right at the beginning: On Sunday came deliverance from Greifswald [...]. Downright dramatic: the chair in Romance Languages and Literature at Halle has been quite categorically offered to me and in Leipzig a chair in the sociology faculty can be arranged for me. Freedom! E. in bliss. Re-entry into life.

In order:

At the station far too early at 4.20 a.m. because of unreliable clock. Pain on the way there. After a while Wohlgemuth appeared with [...] Schmidt-Walter and Beyer. [...] First talk turned to university politics. [...] The fearful professors were left with the choice [in the rectorial election] between the SED professor Schmidt-Walter and myself; they appear to be able to swallow S.-W. more easily, he has been designated at any rate. Then we got around to my personal affairs. [...] From there the story shifted to our difficulties and to the governing body's unfulfilled promises. There were several reproaches from Wohlgemuth [...], as if I were immodest in my demands and had no appreciation of the situation, more was being done for me than for any other professor, I evidently lacked the proper idealism. I for my part told him with some passion and very bluntly, that I felt myself deceived, that promises made to me were not being kept; that they were cowering behind the 'as far as possible' of the contract, that they were very well aware of the helplessness of my position, that I was filled with deep bitterness and would leave Greifswald at a day's notice, if I had the opportunity to do so. Both sides then gave way and a rupture was avoided, but the feeling of bitterness remained. [...]

Conference in the huge less elegant room on the second floor [at Jägerstrasse]. I estimate 200–250 people at two endlessly long tables. Very many acquaintances. [...] Meusel had just begun his paper on 1848. Extremely instructive from the Marxist standpoint. Dry humour. I learnt a great deal for my own lecture, which I am supposed to give to the students here at the start of the summer semester. [The paper] was expanded by the additions and the critical remarks of the discussion. [...] The starting point was always: what should we, the SED, as official speakers and writers of articles say about it all? a) *not* talk about Greater Germany – inopportune![11] b) place 18 March [the outbreak of the

Revolution in Berlin] at the centre and not the Frankfurt Parliament, because Berlin is our capital and not Frankfurt!! c) main thing Marx and the Communist Manifesto [...] It was very instructive but after the preceding night and journey also very exhausting. The common lunch in the same room was no relaxation. [...]

I spent almost the whole morning [of the second day] in conversation with Krauss in a corner of the empty breakfast room. From the start I was surprised by his great warmth. His offer: in the first instance *Halle*. It must be occupied. In Greifswald I was in the wrong place. [...] He would obtain testimonials supporting me (from Auerbach in the USA), so that I would get the guest professorship in Berlin. Did I want to be in charge of the Kulturbund in Leipzig? I should give a lecture there. He fetched Rocholl, the Saxon Undersecretary, also the Halle registrar, they would write to me forthwith. [...] On the other hand: in the new Leipzig sociology faculty, Behrens the dean[12] – I spoke to [the latter ...] chairs were still unoccupied there – I could have a professorship under some title, without any conflict with the overburdened Krauss, who himself gives lectures in this faculty and would like to have time for his Hispanic studies. Thus the result of these discussions is one certain and one $\frac{3}{4}$ certain offer of a chair, the open window, as E. says, which we can jump out of, away from hated Greifswald. And that, one day after the rancour of the clash with Wohlgemuth! – About himself Krauss related: he and his wife are being divorced, she has remained in the West ... The KB has been boycotting him since his fiasco at the first anniversary [...], his PLN novel was getting no reviews. I consoled him and promised him a notice. [...] Krauss said: everywhere there was a clique of émigrés, in order to thrive in Germany today, one had to have been an émigré or a Nazi, best of all both.

[...]

E. very happy, would best of all like to pay a forfeit and go to Halle immediately; but we shall presumably have to get through the summer semester here ... Nevertheless: the feeling of still counting for something and of escaping the chains!

[...]

Today worn-out, depressed, self-doubting – since arriving in G. I have only been groping around and not yet got anything down in writing. How much time is left to me?

The Volk and Welt publishing house has today sent E. a second book to translate; she must first of all send back a blurb and suitable passage from it as a sample. I immediately began to read the book out: Jean Cassou *Les massacres de Paris*.[13]
[...]

12th February, Thursday evening. The day of Father's death. Greifswald

[...]

Towards evening yesterday E. returned from one of her visits: Comrade Pfeiffer had tickets for his people and for us for the première of *Madame Butterfly*. So quite unexpectedly we found ourselves in the (always sold out) theatre. For the second time. Good seats in the fourth row of the orchestra stalls, only cold. The natives bring blankets and wrap themselves up, of course everyone wears a coat. We saw *Butterfly* in 1926(?) in Genoa [...], I enjoyed the music very much. [...] The tragedy a bit crude, naive and kitschy. The performers [...] had to take curtain calls again and again [...].

16th February, Monday forenoon – and later. Greifswald
[...]

Towards evening Schmidt-Walter, just appointed provisional Prorector, called. The senate, placed under heavy pressure and threatened with my even more unpleasant person, had to consent. [...]

At the Pfeiffers', Sepke, supported by Pf., had quite a go at me: more had been expected after the 'revolutionary reputation' which preceded me. I should not be giving talks, not be distracted by the Soviet Society,[14] the Kulturbund etc., but 'organise' the university for the Party, keep an eye on Schmidt-Walter, mobilise, use all my energy to activate the jaded Wohlgemuth, the pro-Schuhmacher Jürgens, the sluggish SED group of lecturers and students ... How I am supposed to manage this quite privately, without any official or Party authority, was not revealed by these wise people. [...] The business weighs heavily on my mind. Nowhere any support, let down by all sides ... I wish I could get away from here – Party and scholarship give me equal cause for concern.
[...]

17th February, Tuesday evening
Jacoby called yesterday [evening ...]. [...] There was an interesting discussion with Jacoby. He wants to divert me from politics with the clumsiest flattery: my books would still be read in 100 years (but nothing small, only a thick book lasts!), I should found a 'Klemperer School', that was my gift, my duty [...]. I said, duty was a mysterious business, it was perhaps precisely my duty now, to set youth on the right path.
[...]

20th February, midday Friday. Greifswald
[...]

On Wed. aft. there was a meeting of the SED University Committee in Franz's office. Franz chaired, Prorector Schmidt-Walter, Sielaff, myself. Also two from the student council and an elderly lady, lecturer at the Preparatory Studies Institute. Main question: how to get control of the student council, we have only 7 of 16 votes. Eternal question: how to break the power of the reactionary professors? I said: I advocated a harder line in every respect, but was not yet fully in the picture. Franz – evidently given a nudge by the Party – I should take over the chair [of the committee]. He and the Prorector would advise me, the students would call on me next Wednesday to be briefed. I accepted. Like *this* I really get significant possibilities.

22nd February, Sunday evening. Greifswald. Stopover. Political training conference Schwerin

[...]

Yesterday morning up at 3 after $2\frac{1}{2}$ hours sleep, in icy wind to the Party office, bus journey 4–10. Set off today at 12 midday in the car with Franz, back at the university at 5, here a quarter of an hour later.

[...]

[Overnight in Schwerin Klemperer was quartered with the family of a postal official.] I myself was in bed before 9, enjoyed the warmth and the quiet until almost 7.30. The wife [...] then said in all innocence about the *Trades* [see above, p. 240] which have been closed down: *Jews*. People had taken 'the last things they had' there, gold, silver, crystal. She had seen a woman who had to have shoes for her child. She imitated (without mocking, without malice) the accent of the man at the scales. 'Not a German Jew, a Polish one probably' – 'more, much more!' – spoons in this case. There had been tears in the woman's eyes. I: so people generally talk of Jews. She: there were no doubt also 'white Jews' among them. I: ? She: that's what Germans who carried on this trade were called ... [...]

Bredel[15] had spoken in resounding words of the intellectuals we have won over and could easily continue winning over at the universities, these young people were open-minded and not at all hidebound. Franz and Reinhard urged me to make a sharp reply. I spoke without sharpness, but clearly enough. Comrade Bredel's high-flown words did not take us anywhere. When *I* took my school-leaving certificate at the beginning of the century, I had never heard the name Karl Marx. For some old teachers it was no different now, nor in the parental homes of the bourgeois students. On top of that the 12 years of Hitler education, the foolish hostility to the Russians – how then could things be easy for us?! Many were indifferent, some full of ill-will, all ignorant – and the students from workers' homes often traitors to their class. We had very simply to teach with infinite patience and from the very beginning. Start with Acker-mann's: Marx does not attack property, only *bourgeois property*. Property gained through one's own labour was protected by Marxism. And [...] proceed step by step, show them the compatibility [of Socialism and human rights], then: that without Socialism there are no human rights, that the individual personality can be successfully asserted *only* within Socialism. Finally I said: be under no illusions about the difficulty of winning the students. [...] New to me in Ackermann's speech: in its desperate struggle against Socialism, the USA was becoming ever more Fascist, racial ideology, persecution of Negroes was becom-ing ever stronger ... [...] Very important for me was the instruction on the route from Marx to Lenin, on the new monopoly capitalism; on the neo-Revisionist deployment of 'people's community' and abolition of classes [as against] the Marxist theory of class struggle; on the new oligarchy of 'managers', who in big companies dominate the small shareholders. [...] I am pleased at having something altogether new to think about. Extension or diversion? What will I be able to use, how much time is left me?

In between I composed a more concise version of a motion which E. will propose at a meeting of the DFD in Berlin tomorrow on behalf of her group and on *her* initiative: that the independent income of a wife should be taxed separately and not together with that of the husband. Because otherwise the higher bracket neutralises the gain.

On Saturday E. had half the theatre here for discussions and rehearsals: all women, singer, actress, dancer. For Women's Day on 3rd March. E. presides, speaks, listens to her own songs. What has become of the two of us!

[...]

25th February, Wednesday forenoon. Greifswald: Berlin trip 23rd–24th Feb. after Schwerin trip 21st–22nd Feb.

Really the main person this time was E. All of Monday and Tuesday she sat and spoke in the DFD at the Jägerstr. club. She called on Tschesno (Volk und Welt): her new job (Cassou), enthusiastic compliments, a pajok card via Colonel Dymshits. Pressure on Greifswald by the SMA to make better provision for us.

I: as purchaser via Gerd Rosen's bookshop to the Internationale Buchhandlung [bookshop] in Albert Achillesstr. ... To Wendt and the *Sonntag* [periodical], to the Neues Leben publishing house. Amusing solution to the 'Culture' mystery: the brochure is 'too tame' for the Russians. (I: 'That had to happen to *me*! When I thought I had to approach the thing with kid gloves!') All 30,000 copies are now to be sent to the West, where they would find a ready market – all that remained (why?) was to obtain Ackermann's certain agreement; after that produce a new edition for our zone with certain passages stiffened [...]! Schlesinger has left: health reasons, business failure – too much sketched out, too little carried out, nervous breakdown, the Party will appoint him to another post, which he can cope with more adequately. [...] In the front office another young man, heard my name, pressed the first edition of *Forum* into my hand: on the front page in big letters statements by 4 professors about the People's Congress. Among them Victor Klemperer and Karl Vossler. (Two sentences from my Dresden wireless speech). In particular to find VK–KV together pleased me greatly [...].

These therefore the results of the trip. – Private matters:

[...] At the Stettin Station before 12 (instead of 10.30). Overnight there had been an enormous snowfall in Berlin, deep snow still on the streets. [...] We left [the ADN news agency], relieved but in a rush, to Anny. From Witzleben station to Dernburgstr. it was a long and arduous way through the snow. [...] Anny took us to the nearer Charlottenburg station. I left E. at Zoo station, went to Rosen's bookshop, got a good impression of the new Kurfürstendamm. The big city above and amidst all destruction, one place of amusement after another: cinemas, restaurants, elegant shops, thronging people. Yet every building somehow more or less heavily damaged and the Gedächtniskirche [Memorial Church] at the dominating point, the most characteristic building of the whole area: [...] Imperial-era church, half a spire knocked off, every side a yawning ruin. Everything cleanly covered in snow. [...] Underground to Jägerstr. I had E. called out of her meeting room, was able to revive her with a good dinner, then Mackie arrived and we went out to Niederschönhausen. Snow and moonlight, Russian barrier. Doris monstrously deformed by advanced pregnancy. Warmest welcome and hospitality. [...]

[...]

6th March, Saturday forenoon

Greifswald has turned from a calamity into really serious misfortune. E. for many days contending with coughing, bronchitis etc. was overtaken by the ominous shortage of breath of 1943; I had Dr Gülzow, assistant director of the university hospital, come, younger, very pleasant man. Mild pneumonia, a couple of days in bed. The same bedclothes for three months now, they're torn, bloody (because of E's dermatosis, which has now improved – whereas mine is worsening). Last night E. literally in a frenzy, one of the worst eruptions I have experienced in almost 44 years. We are both exhausted and ill. – For days now the thick fog, which we can both no longer breathe, for weeks the frost, the frozen pipes, the filthiness of the closet, unbathed since 9 December – I am so infinitely tired of all of it, at the same time I reproach myself for regarding E.'s desperation with egoistical despair. [...]

The only good thing about E.'s (in fact probably mild) illness. As far as the big DFD meeting on 8 March is concerned, which gave her so much trouble and annoyance and where her address turned into such a contested matter of prestige – was it or was it not worth fighting that battle?? – she is now out of the game thanks to vis major. A women's committee meeting was held at her bedside – I meanwhile shivered in the unheated study. [...]

12th March, Friday afternoon. Greifswald. (Berlin trip 8th–9th March)

[...]

The Greifswald People's Congress on Sunday was altogether pitiful: the theatre, the balconies at least, quite empty, the public apathetic [...] Everything was reeled off in one and a half hours, as unceremoniously as possible. [...]

The morning train on Monday and reached Berlin punctually – filthy thaw weather. Tried in vain to telephone Rompe from Mackie's office, nevertheless went there. Novelistic good luck: the usually absent Rompe was in the building [...] and by chance the registrar of the University of Halle and a government man from Saxony-Anhalt were there at the same time. [...] The Halle people: 'You would have been appointed long ago, if we had a house and garden for you.' – I: I was worn out and would do without them. Result [...]: immediate call to Halle, we are to get a decent $4\frac{1}{2}$ room apartment, all kinds of furniture will also be made available for us to purchase. [...] (I had had enough of all the big promises in Greifswald and now appreciated the caution of the two men; I thought to myself: we'll get hold of something in G. and something in Halle, it will mount up.) There was also immediately talk of giving me leave to teach in Leipzig one day a week [...]. Since then we are both as if delivered. [...] Tremendous sphere of activity and new link with Saxony and closeness to Dresden. I dream of a combination: government man in Dresden with backing from Leipzig. E., too, is full of hope. [...]

Then I travelled out to Anny. Very necessary coffee break. Peter there with a school and university friend. Both completed their first semester in medicine. [...] Desire to work for the press. Peter wanted to be advised by Kahane. We went to ADN, where there was a car waiting for me. Very warmly received – Peter made an excellent impression, stayed to eat with us, had to be smuggled out of the Russian kraal.[16] [...]

16th March, Tuesday evening. Greifswald

Torment of the eczema intensified to the extreme. To Braun at the skin clinic. Result: not like E., but vulgar scabies. Peacetime treatment impossible. Precondition a warm bath – not to be had at home, nor in the skin clinic itself(!!!). I went to the public bath, way out at the older clinics. There was a crowd waiting. And a sign: 'Persons with infectious and disfiguring illnesses prohibited.' I did not have the nerve ... Further: You should rub in the sulphur ointment in warm surroundings. But I cannot spatter the warm room and must treat my unbathed body (unbathed since the beginning of December!) in the cold bathroom. And afterwards where will I get fresh bedclothes? And how is E. to be protected? – A dreadful state of affairs, and at the same time I am suffering ever more, and what I have is ever more evident on my wrists and hands. Braun laughed: 'we've all been through it, the hotels no longer wash the bedclothes, so infection is unavoidable.' [...] And now I am travelling to Berlin tomorrow. To whom shall I pass it on – the Kahanes or a hotel?
   [...]

19th March, Friday afternoon. Greifswald. People's Congress (The Second – 1848[17]) Berlin 17th–18th March

With such a congress [in Berlin] it is much as with the circus: it's fun perhaps at most every couple of years. This time I felt everything to be worn out and chewed over, and everything external exactly as before. [...] The sight of the State Opera, the public, the newspaper sellers, the presiding committee, the photographers ... I already know it so well. And is there anything new that anyone can say about 1848 from an SED standpoint? I sat inside as little as possible, and did not hear the whole of single speech, what I need to know for my address, I shall read in the newspaper. But I shook hands x times, have been seen by x people, and that is the important thing and enough. [... heard] some bits of Ulbricht[18] on the economic situation. He let the cat out of the bag and drew an optimistic picture of a separate East Germany and its economic plan.[19]

[...] I soon left to visit Anny. The usual: good coffee, warm friendship and matter of course anti-Russianism and anti-Sovietism. People 'disappear', safes are looted, friends of Peter did not have good manners and had not gone to grammar school ... [...]

The demonstration started at 10.30 [the next day]; I would gladly have gone along, particularly as I have never seen the Cemetery of the Fallen of March 1848.[20] But it was pouring down [...].

Back in the Opera again towards 2. [...] then Mackie Kahane appeared and reproached me for not having joined them. He said the demonstration, which he had watched from the car at various points – pity! I could have had that with him! – had been impressive. Despite the downpours and a competing enterprise by the SPD, the police estimated 80,000 participants. (Later a higher figure was given: 100,000, 120,000 ...) – I was annoyed about the prepared ballot paper [with the list of names] for the Volksrat [People's Council]. [...] Who put it together, why am I not among these 300? From Mecklenburg there are only Party people: no farmer, no university or literary man. In addition to these named 300 there are 100 people from the West, who have to be swallowed [their names] unprinted. This secrecy is the most interesting feature of the whole business.

[...]

22nd March, Monday forenoon

On Saturday aft. from 5–8 at Wohlgemuth's, in his magnificent apartment (he has influenza), Schmidt-Walter, the prorector, present. Fight about my staying or leaving. Always just avoiding personal argument. They want to keep me, feel deceived, say: I am leaving for personal, not substantial reasons, try to present me as immodest, as without idealism. I gave Franz a very serious and very clear reply. [...]

Aside from that [...]: Cold and scabies.

[...]

29th March, Easter Monday forenoon. Greifswald

Wretched Easter. Once again nothing at all to eat, only dry bread, no packet, everything used up. – Scabies ever more excruciating. Yesterday in fine weather – the days warm, hoar at night – crawled with E. through the quite dreary landscape for less than a mile; E.'s strength already failed her on the way back, she looks very wretched and very much aged. [...] yet we are industrious and E.'s work, at least, is going with a swing: the typewriter is always clattering away and the first 50 pages of her Cassou have already been sent off. I myself completed my speech 'Arbeiterblut, Studentenblut' [Workers' Blood, Students' Blood] the day before yesterday and will type it up [...]. Much of it is copied and compiled; but composition and application appear good nevertheless and my own property. But I cannot publish any of it, because the material '1848' is completely worn out and the whole world glutted with it. By and large the work has not been worthwhile for me. [...] Since yesterday I have been trying to prepare for the *De l'Allemagne* seminar[21] [...] How frivolously my Literary History was written! But without this frivolity it would never have come to be. It's good, but a student or a teacher cannot live off it, it is sauce for the roast which has to be got somewhere else.

[Jacoby calls to try to persuade VK to remain in Greifswald] But 77 horses cannot keep us here ... My plan and inner tranquilliser is now: I work up the lecture courses here, with which I shall fill the first winter semester in Halle/Leipzig, entrenched behind my double appointment I ignore all politics and thus find time, at least for my 'German Image of France'.

The department library overwhelms me [...] after having existed far from any Romance language and literature studies for 13 years.

[...]

I wrote to Vossler, to Lerch [...], to Kneschke (I would like to remain in the Saxon Kulturbund) [...], to the Gerstles, to Max Sebba. The arrears of correspondence weigh on me. Constant fatigue. After our meal, I fall asleep over my book for one or two hours, after that, after tea and a snack, I work until at least 1.30 often until 2.30. Start early at 7, dropping off in the morning. E. sleeps after our main meal and in the evening in bed after eating, but then also translates until 1 or later.

[...]

9th April, 12.30 a.m. Friday

On Wed. aft. in the department 'preparatory conversation', giving out seminar papers, today from 5–7 first lecture: Romanticism, Definition. First lecture in 13 years, first university lecture in 28 years![22] Once again my reputation at stake! I can still do it, I think I found the right tone. But in the last few days I have prepared myself intensively and this preparation, as far as the main lecture went, was no more than repetition and recollection, not a gain in knowledge. With *De l'Allemagne* it is a bit different.

I struggled with [Krauss's] *PLN* for a couple of days. The review is $\frac{2}{3}$ written – but I understand *one* third of the book at most.

[...]

11th April, Sunday evening

My first Voltaire lecture yesterday at the university [...] was a small triumph. We had to move from the designated lecture theatre into the main lecture hall. It admittedly is a main hall with about 160 seats, of which perhaps 100 were occupied.

PLN study 'Philologie unterm Fallbeil' [Philology beneath the guillotine] finished at last and good. I want to give it to *Forum* and make a shorter version for *Heute und Morgen*.

[...]

16th April, Friday afternoon

Lectures and seminars claim much of my time, but also give me pleasure. Much work, little sleep, even less to eat. In this respect the nadir of nadirs, no parcels at all.

[...]

18th April, Sunday evening

Since 2 o'clock this morning: summer time. And proper spring. Even here there are a couple flowering trees. [...] Spring: for the first time since the beginning of December(!!) water touched my poor body, I splashed it on myself. Perhaps it will do my body, bitten and flayed and martyred and mottled by 'post-scabious eczema', good. My body, unbathed for 5 months...

Telegram from the Halle registrar: apartment with garden ready for me in a semi-detached house, furniture was being procured. That [...] gave me a sense of security.

[...]

I had written to Vossler for the first time since Dresden. About the call to Halle and Leipzig and a request for suggestions as to a successor [in Greifswald]. The reply deviates alarmingly from the usual warmth and liveliness. A little d'outre-tombe,[23] failing interest. Briefly dictated and signed with a scrawl: he has been suffering from leukaemia for a year, he was in bed, he was so weak, that he could not walk down the stairs of his house, he could not work, only read. Very cool in tone. I very much had the impression this was his *last letter* to me.

19th April, Monday evening. 'Academic Festival Day'

Great success. I spoke – a gown, which was pinned at the top, so that the absent foundation of the white shirtfront was not evident – in great form. My address is to be published immediately as a pamphlet. Fritz Müller, representing the government here, offered me the rectorship if I stayed, also offered me his post in Schwerin, because he himself would like a university position. *I walk on air.* Wohlgemuth just rang: Russian permission to print 1400 copies as university offprint already granted. [...]

29th April, Thursday forenoon

[...]

There are now some 20 people enrolled in my seminar, about half the number attending my main lecture. The papers are weak. Few questions are asked – it always comes down to a lecture, to my *speech* holding it together.

[...]

9th May, Sunday afternoon
[...]

Urgent worry now: the appointment trip. I sent telegrams to Halle and Dresden to fix appointment times. Halle replied immediately: Quarters on 18 May for 2 persons in the surgical clinic, meeting on 19 May. Dresden has not replied. [...] Meanwhile a letter from Kneschke: whether I want to speak on Barbusse at the Dresden Kulturbund ... They have bought Rudolph's Klemperer portrait and hung it up in the Emser Allee office. Curious how that flatters my inner self.

[...]

[16th May] Sunday evening – Whit Sunday and wedding anniversary
We did not celebrate at all – little to eat and little time. But our mood was relatively good, it still is, although the few steps of an evening walk just now, made us both ache. – Hallelujah!

[...]

18th–26th May, trip: Halle–Leipzig–Berlin. Dresden at Heinsch's, 55 Plauensche Ring (West End view) 11.30 p.m. Friday evening, 21st May
Whit Monday: To the Schmidts [in Dölzschen] in the forenoon. Tragedy of Günther Schmidt in Jena: The GPU is forcing him to spy on fellow students. Threatens to arrest him otherwise. He signs, asks the rector for advice, who recommends flight to the West. What is my opinion? Our advice: wait and see! Very awkward. [...]

[Victor and Eva Klemperer take a full day on 18 May to reach Halle from Greifswald, and spend the night in the surgical clinic. The city makes a good impression on them [...] They are shown their promised house and garden which also make a good impression. Inspection of future department. Begins to make dispositions, establishes good relations with Frau Dr Hetzer (later Schober) teacher of Provençal.] Comrade Dr Hetzer[24] [...]. Just turned 30. Curiously delicate, energetic, at the same time feminine face. Characteristic: 'my fiancé and I, we live together' (cf Georg Klemperer, Berthold's son!, Doris ... that's the way it is now. Her husband missing at Stalingrad, not yet declared dead. [...]).

During the course of the day I repeatedly told both of them [Hetzer and Joachim Storost,[25] professor of Old French, subsequently at Greifswald University]: you have a free hand, I am not jealous, I want *only* to pursue my literary and intellectual history, and be relieved of everything else. – For the rest, I am now the master of a proper institute [...] What a comedy ... [...] To the clinic, supper in the matron's room. [...] 'The fiancé' called for us, she was meanwhile to speak on the People's Petition.

23rd May, Sunday afternoon, at Kahanes', Berlin

Comrade Schober,[26] a Sudeten German like Frau Hetzer, a joiner, his Communist father died in a concentration camp, he himself in a camp, in a punishment battalion, went over to the Russians, functionary, now at administration school, soon in the government. – By the romantic Saale. Rowing boats. Raft in the river decorated with greenery, loudspeaker vans on the bank. People's Petition. Hetzer among the speakers from the raft. [...] Pretty, lively scene. – To the couple's apartment. Us and the Storosts. Frau Storost [...] friendly soul. A librarian at the university. Coffee. Accompanied us a fairly long way to the tram [...] From Hetzer's apartment I wrote Vahlen a letter of thanks and acceptance. Very pleased, very tired out. – So now the director of an institute, under me an associate professor for language, a lecturer for Provençal, two assistants.

On Thurs. 20 May early train to Leipzig. Stood for an hour. Very exhausted. At the tidied-up and still very elegant station an indefinable bouillon and radishes. Then on foot – memories, the dead around us, where was Platen, the coffeehouse? where the Merkur Café, where is Harms, where Scherner, where Kopke?!?[27] – to the publisher Teubner [... more good news here for Klemperer, proofs of his *Modern French Prose* have arrived and further academic publications are requested and promised ...]

[...] At about 1 over to Krauss at his Romance Languages and Literatures Department. He looks very worn out, complains about circulation problems, heart, lack of medicines, reactionary elements in the philosophical faculty, Kühn...

Situation in my affair. Great hostility [to me] in the philosophical faculty, while in the social science faculty he taught French intellectual history and they did not want to have two chairs. But there was the alternative of giving me a post in comparative literary history. Also he, Krauss, was so overworked, that he was soon going to give up his teaching in the social science faculty.

24th May, Monday, at Kahanes'

At the moment Krauss was evidently more interested in *Bloch*,[28] over whom he was involved in a fierce fight with the faculty, than in me. I pretended I was completely in the know. [...]

[The Klemperers travel on to Dresden, another exhausting if relatively short journey. On the 22nd Klemperer attended the Saxon regional congress of the Kulturbund. He gives a well-received talk on Barbusse, signs copies of *LTI*. A young man came up to me: after reading *LTI*, he wanted to study philology. That was the best compliment for me. [Klemperer is nevertheless 'replaced' on the regional committee.]

30th May, Greifswald

[Calling at the Education Ministry in Dresden the next morning] the man at the barrier addressed me as a KPD comrade and pointed to the two flagpoles on the big square outside. On one hung the red flag, on the other – for the first time, after a Zone decision of the previous day, the flag of the Democratic Republic [of Germany – as opposed to the Federal Republic in the western zones]: Black–red–gold. (Extremely unfortunate choice! Reminds one of Greater Germany and of the Weimar Republic.)[29] [...]

[On Sunday morning the Klemperers travel on to Berlin. They arrive at the Schlesische Station at 1 p.m., eat some] indefinable vegetable stew. I phoned Niederschönhausen, half an hour later Mackie picked us up in the car. (On leaving I wrote down the following for him: Je le dirai sans trêve, / Je le dirai sans peur: / Tu es le neveu de mes rêves, / Tu es le neveu de mon cœur. // Moi je suis faible poète, / C'était toujours mon malheur; / Donc, bégayant, je répète: / Tu es le neveu de mon cœur![30]) The home is ruled by Dominique, born 30 April [...] and regarded as beautiful by everyone, and Mackie philosophies about the sudden display of paternal feeling which only recently he had still smiled at ... [...] We were kindly given the bedroom of the couple, for whom we brought the heavy silver and gilded ladle of the child's great grandmother (my mother) as godparents' present.

On Monday 24 May [...] Forenoon Aufbau Publishing House, Wendt. [...] *LTI* sold out, 11–20 thousand is to come in the autumn [...].

30th May, Sunday afternoon. Greifswald
[...] For days on end now we have been living on dry bread and watery soups. Yet *one* pajok parcel is waiting in Berlin, and this time two are supposed to be coming from Schwerin, apparently an advance delivery. [...]

Evening
On Friday evening we entered our names on the People's Petition. No crowd. Still only about 30% on the lists. Towards evening visited the Pfeiffers. There are always young people swarming around there. Fellow students of the two daughters? Youth movement?? Wonderful gramophone-record music: Spanish War songs by Ernst Busch.[31] I myself heard him sing 'Freiheit' [Freedom] in Berlin. International etc.

8th June, Thursday forenoon. Greifswald
Concern about Eva. On Wed. evening, 2 June, loss of consciousness at Judith Kwiet's. Not a faint. It was humid, stuffy – I've know her to faint in such conditions before. But this ... She played piano beautifully, she took out money for a big purchase of fat and bacon. Afterwards she remembered nothing of it at all. She went in the wrong direction to come back here. Later at home she repeatedly asked the same thing, the next moment had forgotten her question. Better the next day, but very exhausted. Now halfway well again. Judith wants to consult Katsch, who is away. Cerebral haemorrhage? Senile decay? Simply overtired and undernourished?? I feel as afraid again as when she was suspected of having cancer. Afraid and with a guilty conscience. [...]

On the afternoon of 1 June in the great hall, student assembly convened by the student council. There had been an attack on the People's Petition on the notice board, at the SED meeting of our university committee we were told: in the houses where even *one* student is lodged, *no one* enters their name, they are agitating against us! Arrests, expulsions. A vigorous speech by Schmidt-Walter, a very good, very serious speech by the representative of the union or the factories, the scientific manager of the gas or waterworks here, Erdmann (?): the workers are *paying* for the students and are less well-off than the students – the workers could lose patience one day. A very poor speech by Wohlgemuth; he talked about the expulsion of a few criminals – theft from institutes – not about political expulsions. A student council resolution for the People's Petition and against the reactionary students. A third, at most, of those present, raised their hands. (The great hall crowded, included the gallery.) When contributions were asked for, there was naturally silence, at the questions 'Who is against?', 'Who abstains?' not a hand was raised. What is gained by this resolution? Nothing at all. [...]
[...]

20th June, Sunday afternoon

The never-ending rush, the pointless activity. Sat. 12th–Mon. evening 14th, Hakeburg, Berlin; Tue. 15th, Stralsund, Kulturbund LTI; Wed. 16th, Staël seminar; Thurs. 17th, lectured SED students on the socialist novel in France (without depth, purely compilation of what I already knew); Frid. 18th, lecture–Vigny[32]; Sat. 19th, double seminar Voltaire. All of it repetition, mosaic, barren memory work – no PROGRESS, and at the same time *so* wearisome, strenuous. Rarely more than 5, often only 4 hours sleep, falling asleep over work. [...] The nightmare of the inner conflict: exhaust myself in public dissipation of my strength and influence (if I have any – constantly growing despair about politics, mire everywhere) or write fine books?? So much *has* to be done, has been promised – and I need all my strength to attend to my daily duties.

[...] Early yesterday, 19 June, the siren sounded for several minutes, we thought the control button at some factory had got stuck. (Our wireless still in Dresden!) But it was a call to a protest meeting on the market place. The West's currency reform.[33] In the afternoon I saw a queue outside the bank on the market place. People were taking their money there [...]. The black marketeers are not parting with anything until the new Soviet regulation is out. I have about 720M in the house, are they lost? [...] Today, Sunday, the currency situation has still not been clarified. The newspaper reports are quite idiotic: everything is calm, business transactions continue. Everyone knows, everything is at a standstill.

[...]

My afterword to the *Salammbô* edition in Reutlingen[34] has just been printed; in it I already figure as professor in Halle.

22nd June, Tuesday forenoon. Greifswald. To Klein Machnow, Hakeburg, 12th–14th June

[The SED Party High School had been set up in the Hakeburg, a nineteenth-century mock castle just outside Berlin. Here Klemperer attended a conference-cum-training session on philosophical problems with reference to Marxism. After summarising points from a number of lectures and reflecting on his comprehension or lack of it, he notes:] [. . .] about 300 comrades attended this 'Conference of the Central High School Committee', the whole intelligentsia of the party. In the throng I spoke fleetingly and by turns to: Otto Halle and Rocholl (the ministry people from Saxony and Saxony-Anhalt), Rita Hetzer and her carpenter [. . .], Such from Leipzig University, Deiters, Gysi, Abusch from the (unpleasant) Berlin Kulturbund, acquaintances from the Saxon culture departments, whose names and exact position I never know. In short, the whole cultural circle of the SED. [. . .]

The guest professorship at Leipzig was now finally promised to me by Krauss, Rocholl, Behrens [. . .]. Naturally I do not yet have the formal appointment, neither from Halle nor from Dresden. The usual state of affairs.

[. . .]

23rd June, Wednesday afternoon

Very depressed and weary of life – hunger and poor physical state may play a part in that. I find the political situation bleak and all our doings a waste of time. A few days ago a meeting at which we, the university committee of the SED, called on a number of invited students to either work with the Party or be prepared to be thrown out. I had to appeal to their consciences with reference to the general situation. Yesterday a somewhat similar meeting of the SED university teachers' group. I spoke again. Reactionary currents in the West *and* here, position of the university, of the lecturers. My speech was pretty radical. But again it emerged that government, Central Administration etc. do not at all proceed radically, anzi.[35] [. . .] The wretchedness of making appointments . . . Pg's the lot of them.

[. . .]

26th June, Friday morning

Revulsion. Pointless activity. Repetition. Dissipation of energies. – I read Rolland's play *Danton*, the only new reading in months. In order to produce something new, I would have to be able to study, what good to me are all the topics and commissions, if I have not got the time for them?

Food shortage, hunger, lack of everything that could be a stimulus: tea, coffee, sausage, even sugar. There have been no packets for months [. . .].

Chaos of currency reform.[36] We have been badly caught out, are losing a good 5,000M. To blame is the perfidy which prevented us buying furniture. [. . .]

Exasperated also with the Neues Leben publishing house: my 'Culture' booklet is not selling – where was it publicised, what was done for it?? My 1848 speech cannot now be published after all. In my vita nova since 1945 this is more or less my first publishing defeat. Against that there is the big essay on my *LTI* (27 columns!) in *Sowjetliteratur* 1948, number 3/4, by Igor Saz (who?) and the short but extremely positive notice by Weiskopf in the *German-American*, New York.

[...]

What else is to be added? A film evening? *Irgenwa in Berlin* [Somewhere in Berlin].[37] Irun n'est plus Irun. I no longer get the old pleasure from film. (It is just the same with driving.) The poor sound reproduction probably contributed. I was unable to really understand how the action hung together. Brutalised lads in Berlin, playing at war in the ruins with hand grenades, thieving, the returning soldier, optimistic conclusion: the lads clearing rubble, joining in the rebuilding, in between there was tragedy, sentiment – very pretty individual scenes, but one recognises the intention from the start – and I don't really believe in anything any more.

[...]

27th June, Saturday night after 2 a.m.

[...]

[Klemperer notes the pleasant evenings with the Kwiets as one of the few bright spots of this period, partly thanks to the real coffee, the radio, the conversation ...] In such conversations reports on Judith's lectures for the FDGB [trades union federation] on venereal diseases mingle with ones on her dissertation etc. An unthinkable mixture, in which there is much gossip, but never, no matter how plain the words, any smuttiness, in which neither mother nor daughter blush – and now if I reflect on what was considered proper and improper in my parents' home, in Georg's! It is not only a curious bohemian degeneration that gives rise to that, but an unbelievable change in sensibility and change in the conception of propriety in the times that I have lived through ... if only I had enough time for my Curriculum! I shall die like a hen with a dozen half-finished eggs in its stomach.

11th July, Sunday [...]

On Thurs., 1 July, [in Berlin ...] The chaos of the currency reform. With great difficulty I got 100M each from Volk and from Aufbau; it appears, however, that old debts are, without exception, being paid 1 to 1, and financially that relieves us of worry – although of course the tax question continues to weigh on us. At Aufbau I made the acquaintance of a new senior editor (name?), who was very polite. Curious how friendly the publishing house, how cool the Kulturbund (Becher, Gysi, Abusch) is to me. At Neues Leben Hartwig was friendlier than I had expected; the publication of my 1848 speech had not at all been definitively rejected – only postponed until the university turmoil had died down; the issue there is the competition of the Westerners, the planned American counter-university [in Berlin].[38] Interesting was the constant drone of the big air planes, with which the Americans are provisioning their blockaded sector.[39] [...] In the morning Mackie had straight away driven me to Dernburgstr., where I found Anny and Peter. Anny very bitter, naive and exclusively on the American side: the Russians left the children of the Western sector without milk, cut off electricity etc. The vexation of the triple currencies: West Mark, new East Mark, old East Mark, everywhere a different reckoning-up and a different attitude on the part of the shopkeepers – one doesn't accept this money, the other not that, goods are being held back, prices fluctuate. [...] Povera Germania. [...]

12th July, Monday morning

E.'s birthday: we are sitting here with dry bread just as on 29 June. E. looks very pale and scrawny, often complains about aches, about feeling weak, recently lost consciousness, is 66 today. Sometimes I worry more about her, sometimes more about myself. We are both close to the end, and I am altogether sick of vita et mors.[40] The point of the whole thing?

I am often envious of E. She was always a 100 times more talented than I. I had only the one domain of writing and speaking. Now she has even broken into this domain and is outstripping me. Her latest plan: to write a novel herself. Why does fame (since *LTI* truly gloria) go to me?

[...]

15th July, Thursday. The Berlin day

[Session of the Kulturbund Executive Committee. Klemperer finds the meeting quite sickening (a) because he feels himself ignored by the dominant figures – Becher, Gysi, Abusch, (b) because of what he regards as excessive caution to placate non-SED participants and to avoid appearing as an extension of the SED.] Willmann gave a paper [...] on the development of the Kulturbund during the last year. [...] always the same dilemma: are we only an association of intellectuals, or do we draw in the workers as well? To what extent should we win people through 'entertainment', through dancing, philately, chess etc.? To what extent should we be politically active? [...] The best thing was the plentiful food during the meeting.

[...]

22nd July, Thursday forenoon. Greifswald

[...]

Eva better, but still confined to bed. [She had been suffering from a boil on her upper thigh.] – Sultriness, rain, thunderstorms day after day for weeks. – Barbusse. – Correspondence, again and again on *LTI*. Everybody finds something else interesting about it, everybody has some piece of advice, in addition, a correction. Some are self-important, some are moved.

[...]

24th July, Saturday afternoon. Greifswald

[...] The nights feel cold and damp, the days tropically hot with thunderstorms that never come to anything. Eva still laid up – great problems with food, *one* pajok arrived and was less than a drop on a very hot stone.

[...]

The GSS car has just arrived. My Stralsund–Rostock–Schwerin–(Wismar) lecture tour is due to begin at 3 p.m.

24th–27th July. GSS [Society for the Study of Soviet Culture] tour 'Barbusse and Moscow', Stralsund, Rostock, Schwerin, Wismar

25th July, Sunday afternoon. Gorky House, Rostock

[...]

Here [Rostock] a very large, elegantly furnished Gorky House with a restaurant. The most elegant and plentiful lunch, soup, schnitzel, asparagus, two helpings of mashed potatoes – a feast. [...]. Then drive (fairly bleak 9 miles) to War-nemünde, on the beach there for a good hour and more. The eternally unchanging picture, 55 or 56 years ago, when I first saw the Baltic here, it was the same. Crowds in between the wicker beach chairs, heaps of children. More exactly the picture as in the Weimar years or 46 in Ahrenshoop. The bathers higgledy-piggledy. No: the women wear pants and breast bib, naked in between. Mostly unsightly figures. Big Sunday crowd, as if there had been no annihilation of millions. They go on living, they multiply. What do I have in common with these people? The people of my generation are dead. All these Baltic resorts look the same. Hotels and promenade, somewhere a bit of coast rising up and woods around. [...]

[...]

27th July, Tuesday forenoon. GSS library room, Schwerin

SMA yesterday not altogether pleasant. [Klemperer had been requested to call on [...] the Popular Education section of the regional Soviet Military Administration.] First the battle with stubborn guards, telephone calls back and forth, no getting through – 'go home!' – until Lieutenant Raissin (in civilian clothes) fetched me. Up many flights of stairs, a captain who spoke only Russian and had Raissin interpret. First of all: why was I leaving Greifswald? I had to convince him ... Then: I should give him in writing what I thought necessary to reform Greifswald University. I: were I to give that directly to the Russians I would be considered dependent, in their pay etc ... Then I should send an appropriate farewell letter to Minister Grünberg. I promised to do so, but that, too, is very awkward for me [...].

[...]

1st–8th August, The Göhren week. Wilhelm Pieck Trade Union Home
[The Klemperers spend a week's holiday in Göhren on the Baltic island of Rügen.]

3rd August, Tuesday morning. Verandah
[...] But my landlord [the Klemperers' room is actually in a house a little away from the holiday home proper], master locksmith Marzahl is vox populi: Against the SED, of which he himself is a member, against the Russians. Accusations of bossdom, of corruption, of 'submissiveness to the Russians', police bribed by racketeers, the bosses keep quiet and guzzle, the refugees starve, anyone who opens his mouth 'disappears', the Russians take everything away etc. etc. etc. – It's just like the Weimar years. On our sea cruises of those days Eva often formulated it like this: *'Where is the Republic?'* It is exactly the same today. Where is democracy? I do not believe in its durability, we sit – what is this WE? a hated minority, a very small one – we merely sit on Russian bayonets. The day the Russians withdraw we – i.e. Eva and myself – are dead people. *I* have no confidence in the situation. Worse: I do not believe in the worth of the things I espouse. To be sure, the idea of Marxism is pure. But are the Russians any less imperialistic etc. than the others? And why have we lost Stettin, do we have the Poles on purely German land? Because the Poles are being compensated in the west, for what the Russians took from them in the east ... There are so many individual questions on which theory and practice are not at all in accord. And over and above all these political doubts: what is humanity to me, what is humanity? There is always only the individual, the self in its own little circle. And here everything is founded on murder – the countless sweet little chickens here, the handsome rabbits in Marzahl's cages – do they have immortal souls – why do we have to eat them, and what do the worms think, when the hen ... and etc. etc. The worn-out banality of all these questions as to the meaning of it all will no longer let me go – a seaside holiday with time to reflect is not the thing for 66-year-olds with angina and without religion. [...]

I now only note down whatever is of human and cultural-historical value, but in such a way, *as if* I were certain my Curricula were going to be continued, as if I were certain of the next few years. I hold to Marxism and Russia, *as if* I believed in them (in a double sense a) *believed* in them, b) were confident in *backing* them. And yet I do not know whether they possess the ultimate truth, and I certainly do not know whether they will win. But I shall not change horses. And it makes no difference at all, whether I am finished off by angina or a bullet.
[...]

7th August, Saturday forenoon. Göhren
Countless chickens everywhere, countless chicken. The chickens will be slaughtered, the children will shout heil Hitler and be killed in the next war.
[...]

... I must get down to work again, here I feel like a wandering ghost ... Back at about 7, very early to bed.

[...]

8th August, Sunday forenoon. Göhren

[...]

[... From his table companions] I for the first time heard the new National Democratic and Peasant parties mentioned.[41] They were emergency valves and concessions by the SMA. Now I am paying for not having had a wireless in Greifswald; there was never enough time for the newspaper.

Today we want to take [...] the afternoon steamer to Sellin; our luggage is to be brought on board at Baabe. I hope everything goes smoothly.

[...]

Work yield: a couple of sea novels by Peisson,[42] the whole of the Vogüé dissertation[43] read, the Tolstoy in France dissertation begun. No notes made so far.

At the moment rain has set in, bad for the afternoon walk.

[...]

10th August, Tuesday evening. Greifswald

Proofs of *Modern Prose*, desperate efforts to arrange furniture removal.

Offer from Volk and Welt to E. to translate an American and a Spaniard.

Dr Schon in Mainz, the manager of the Lerch Festschrift, has accepted my 1934 Delille in its entirety.[44]But who will copy the study for me. And a Delille dissertation was published in Geneva in 1936 – where am I to get it?

12th August, Thursday evening. Greifswald

[...] All efforts to arrange furniture removal have failed. [...] Now we must somehow entrust the things to the railway after all ... And our hand luggage, and the tomcat and changing trains in Berlin – the Kahanes are on summer holiday – and what awaits us in Halle? At some later point in time it may sound funny, at the moment it is truly tragic. [...]

15th August, Sunday morning. Greifswald

[Attempts to have the furniture transported by road or rail having come to nothing, they are now to be conveyed by canal taking about 2 weeks.]

Torture of the Barbusse paper. I cannot let it go nor get on top of it. Alternation of repulsion and attraction. On the whole I find him narrow, uncongenial, obscurely pompous. [...] I still lack scattered material and I have to excerpt the material I have so far assembled here and return it as soon as possible, *before* I get down to writing. [...] I am so tired, I sometimes really wish, it were 'time to sleep'. And always the inner uncertainty. How long will I be included among the 'VIPs'? Am I still today? When will I finally make a fool of myself?

I am even more tormented by another series of questions, the very banal ones as to the point or lack of it of one's life, as to the splendid bon Dieu. Barbusse's atheism is shallow. – I read (and make notes), in order not to think.

19th August, Thursday forenoon. Greifswald

Days monotonously filled up: every free minute devoted to preliminary work on Barbusse [. . .].

These free minutes are not many: the move is taking up an excessive amount of time. Everything has to be arranged x times over, endless telephone calls, running about by both of us. Latest, presumably definitive state of things: the furniture by boat, ourselves on the 23rd to Halle via Berlin by service train. [. . .] the apartment is supposedly ready for occupation, the chests have arrived from Dresden, there is no crockery yet.

[. . .]

22nd August, Sunday. Greifswald

Two pleasant mitigations of the bitterness: I am in the end not leaving here with an all-too-terrible rupture nor as a vanquished party. First, Friday evening. Ruth Sepke telephoned, could I attend a GSS meeting before leaving? To my embarrassment and surprise I found Schmidt-Walter, whom I had put out of sight and mind, as deputy chairman. At the end of the session he dedicated profuse valedictory words to me, liqueur was brought in, I was feted. Afterwards I said to Sch., actually I had 'written him off', but now I wanted to voice my bitterness to him. He accompanied me home. I should bear in mind how much he, as prorector, was 'ground down' [. . .]. Furthermore, he, too, was dissatisfied, and on the brink of leaving ... [. . .] He then helped me pack downstairs in the department for a while, we parted in friendship. – Then yesterday leave-taking at the Party. Sepke especially warm, first in his room, then downstairs in the canteen, again with liqueurs. [. . .] S. apologised after a fashion and sang my praises. He was forced to admit that to a great extent I was right, he had not sufficiently appreciated my 'outstanding intellectuality', we had not got to know one another well enough [. . .]. It was all pure cordiality, and we parted the best of friends ... I realised on this occasion, that it was not such a minor post that S. occupied. My insight into the Party hierarchy, which began in Dresden and continued here, is very important to me. Soviet Germany is now a closed piccolo mondo of its own, the SED the central point within it, a domicile not without risk, but the most important one. And the same people constantly rushing back and forth within it.

[. . .]

[. . .] What impressions does Greifswald leave? The bare room, in which every sneeze and clearing of the throat rolled like thunder, the bare windows with their eternal glare, the unusable bathroom, never-ending bohemian conditions, the permanent state of being in the middle of a move, the feeling of homelessness. [...] More pleasant only the two poplars to the left out of the bedroom window, and behind to the right the stork's nest on the tall chimney – now and then the couple stood side by side – but I never saw the beasts approach or fly off.

We were here for exactly 256 days: from 9 Dec. 1947–23 Aug. 1948.

23rd August, 10 Kiefernweg, Halle

27th August, Friday morning

On the extreme NW boundary of the town, in the midst of heath and woodland [...] E. is again and again entranced by this landscape, she also very much approves of the pleasant big city of Halle – over 300,000 inhabitants – and just as her constant gloominess and bitterness about Greifswald paralysed me, so does her immediate and daily increasing harmony with the facts of the physical and political geography comfort me now. Otherwise I do not believe much will have changed for me here, whether for good or bad. Except that the chaotic initial stage has to be endured once again.

I can be brief, because everything consists merely of variations on familiar phenomena and conditions. The journey on Monday in part torture. Pain in the early morning on the way to the station, walking behind the porter's handcart. 6 heavy and unwieldy pieces of luggage, in addition the tomcat in his cardboard box, who engaged E.'s attention entirely. At Stettin Station [in Berlin] fortunately the ADN car (ordered by teleprinter); but the train arrived very late and then at Anhalt Station a most pig-headed capo, who raised difficulties about allowing me onto the service train and who repeatedly chased me up and downstairs between booking office and platform. At the very last second onto the train, which was almost moving off, with all our things – E. lugged, a conductress helped ... Very serious pains, my heart about to give up, deepest depression. In Halle at 3.30; after some waiting and telephoning Himpich appeared with a car.

Here the anticipated chaos of the most inadequate provisional arrangement – but good will on all sides and, see above, E.'s good mood. The chests from Dresden are here – when will the things from Greifswald arrive? Himpich has had a couple of impossible items of furniture placed in the apartment, which is in itself pleasant and decently renovated. A double bed, onto which the mattresses do not fit – I am sleeping on the floor, nowhere to put things away, no tables etc. A terrific muddle. But Volkssolidarität [People's Solidarity] is going to deliver further provisional pieces and soon – so they swear – new ones which will belong to us. [...] Everywhere papers, half-unpacked chests, a kitchen range without stove pipe, lamps without bulbs etc. etc. Great distance from the town – but wonderful woods and heath ... This whole day I have not read or written a line, constantly on the go and in the evening dead tired to bed at 10 or 10.30. It will go on like this for days yet – especially as I am speaking in Leipzig on the 30th (Kulturbund), on 4/5 Sept. in Schwerin (KB and GSS).

I shall summarise the most important facts:

Letter from Gusti Wieghardt: Maria Lazar[45] already died at Easter. Shook me very badly. Visit by Gusti to be expected in Sept.

Very friendly reception by the KB – already elected in absentia to the regional committee (unfortunately not the executive ... nevertheless!). Secretary Finke. Even more warmly by the GSS. Secretary Heinrich Wagert, chairman Winter, who lives above and is His Magnificence, the Rector, Prof. of East European History, lively fifty-something, Sudeten German, very close to the SED, except – diplomatic! – *not* a member. Wagert immediately helped me with a telegram to Schwerin, with cigarettes, with his car. – Page proofs have arrived a) of the 2nd ed. of the *LTI*, b) of the 3rd ed. of the *Modern Prose* (non omnis moriar??[46] And if so – is it a comfort?). [...] Yesterday evening young Vahlen was here, the civil servant who deals with the actual higher education work under Thape and Halle. [...]

Towards evening

Especially exasperating and wearying errands for a little food. We shall not obtain our regular food coupons here before 1 Sept. at the earliest; the univ. – an estate owner as in Greifswald – will have to help. From pillar to post.

[...]

29th August, Sunday afternoon. Halle

Still chaos without end. [...] New identity cards with finger prints are being demanded here – police, labour office etc.: that will cause us x vexations yet, and the problem of food ration cards for 1 Sept. is still unsolved. Further complicated by the present shortages and by the necessity of obtaining an OdF [Victim of Fascism] identification for E. [...]

1st September, Wednesday forenoon. Halle

[...]

Leipzig on Mon. 30 Aug. (my first, my first in my whole life, talk in Leipzig).

[Klemperer first calls at Teubner, his publisher.] I consider it a great triumph, how much I am now valued at Teubner. The conversation [with 3 editors] turned almost immediately to Teubner's periodical plans. [Klemperer argues for a general intellectual forum for the East – with himself in charge – rather than a specialist academic journal. Such a 'popular' publication would deviate from the academic tradition of the house.] I: I used to feel offended, when I was called a 'journalist'. Now – one must be both scholar *and* journalist. [...] I do not want any contributors from the West – I want to show the West that the East is carrying on and giving a lead in extending the Western things. [...] Later Weise [a senior editor] put in: he would keep on prodding me, so that my 18ième did not remain a torso, he wanted my *Modern Poetry* expanded, my collected essays, my 19th Century...

[...]

I telephoned Werner Krauss who was sick in bed. I telephoned the secretary of the Gewifa [Social Science faculty]. The head people all on holiday, but I have announced myself and now everything will get moving, the first contact has been made.

[. . .]

2nd September, Thursday afternoon. Halle

Yesterday evening in the Schützenhaus the Alexandrow Ensemble of the Soviet Army. (Song and dance.) Great crush, most tremendous applause – I, too, clapped until my hands were sore. [. . .] Also performed was the favourite song of the Russian shoemaker soldiers in the yard of our Jews' House in Zeughaussstr. who more or less saved my life.

[. . .]

13th September, Monday. Halle

Berlin trip 7th and 8th Sept. [. . .].
The journey itself relatively good despite the usual aches. There: dawdling 'express train' 5.50–10.30 a.m., back a good service train 12–3.30 p.m. Help through Mackie's car. Usual hostility to Russians and SED on the part of the [travelling] public [. . .]. I add the Berlin disturbances, which Schober told me about yesterday – the red flag pulled down from the Brandenburg gate![47] And His Magnificence Winter's report on people's indifference to the Victims of Nazism ceremonies. Hopeless.

[Kulturbund Executive Committee meeting. Friedensburg is suspended from the KB for 'anti-Soviet and pro-war agitation' and Klemperer joins in condemning him.] Afterwards I asked Abusch whether I had been too harsh. He, beaming, 'very nice if we don't have to do it all ourselves and someone from the country – (this, then, my modest role!) – relieves us of it.' In the evening Mackie told me he had recently spoken to Ackermann about me. A. had said with 'friendly irony': 'the old firebrand, especially when it's against his professorial colleagues – he's sometimes almost too impetuous for us.' [. . .]

[At the invitation of the rector the Klemperers attend a small reception at the university on the occasion of the Victims of Nazi Persecution ceremonies]: light lunch – my first glance at such events now: which set of cutlery? With or without knife = with or without meat. This was *without* knife. A little music, a little conversation, a little boring from 11–1. [. . .] I feel awkward with the VVN pin, I fear, I know the new anti-Semitism. Today I fetched the magnificent and very heavy packet Berthold Meyerhof had sent for E.'s birthday from the railway post and was inadvertently still wearing the needle. Pin plus packet from abroad: decidement trop![48] A gentleman addressed me: 'Juif?'[49] He was one, too, he is being taken to Palestine by air plane, the state of Israel has its own air fleet[50] . . . I shall always remain between stools.

Otto Klemperer, musician, conducted in Dresden yesterday, Mozart and Mahler; we listened on the wireless, Eva speaks of him in the highest terms. He was also supposed to play in Halle. That came to nothing. From Dresden Lotte Sussmann wired greetings to us on his behalf, we should meet him in Leipzig (impossible) or Berlin ... Psychology of the little man: [I] used to be afraid of Otto, enviously afraid. Now I am the author of the *LTI*, on the Executive Committee [of the Kulturbund], double university professor, a big name. But for all of that, I feel inwardly uncertain and small.

Strange feeling: I have lent Anny Kl. 2,000M out of the royalties for the *LTI*. I as moneylender to Berthold's widow. Life is very strange, it all balances out.

[...]

19th September, Sunday evening

[...]

This afternoon a short walk with E. in the curious heath terrain ante portas nostras,[51] the second in these 4 weeks in Halle. Autumnal fogginess, very melancholy mood of the landscape and of my soul.

23rd September, Thursday

[...]

Today Barbusse volumes arrived from the Berlin university library; yesterday I had a letter from Wendt [Aufbau], he would very much like, as I suggested, to publish a small monograph on Barbusse, so I shall now presumably continue working on this child of sorrows. [...]

Telegram from Dressel: 'Annemarie departed this life 17 Sept. It did and then again did not shake us. For us she had long ago become lifeless and virtually dead. But all this survival! We are ancient. 'Departed this life' – happy, he who can think like that. Dressel is married to the daughter of a theology professor. But I still hear and see Annemarie before me. I no longer remember the occasion. I asked her in some connection: 'Can you really believe *that?*' *That* was God and immortality. She responded with almost tender dismay: *'But Victor – Don't you??*[52]

28th September, Tuesday forenoon. Halle

Chaos as before. [...]

Oppressive correspondence obligations. [...] Vossler, sick, sends word, he still does not have *LTI*. I must send him the book. Likewise it must now be sent to the USA and Latin America. [...] Long letters from Marta and from Willy Jelski. [...]

Every evening, every night noise of aircraft. I always thought: Russian exercises. [...] Then I realised: these are Anglo-American aircraft of the 'airlift'.

[...] Perhaps I should devote the remainder of my life not to the Literary

History, but to the Curriculum [i.e. autobiography]. The success of the *LTI* shows after all, that I have something to say and am listened to.

[...]

5th October, Tuesday evening. Halle

[...] Later a Defa feature film *1–2–3 Corona*.[53] Very nice, but can hardly be called educational and new art. [The occasion was the opening of a model cinema by the Ministry of Public Education.] Adolescents going to the bad in bombed Berlin; stealing, black marketeering amidst ruins. Into the middle of this a sentimental circus business. A horde of youngsters look after a circus girl who has had an accident because of them, set up a circus themselves. The two mistakes: *so* many circus talents in one gang! And: the circus as a factor of democratic renewal worth aspiring to, the circus performance as an artistic and moral model deed! ... For all that actually the first time that I again felt gripped by a film as in the old days. [...]

[Klemperer has a conversation about his appointment with Koch,[54] the dean. Kl. had been called by the government, before consultation with the faculty. The more reactionary members of the faculty, according to Koch, had been against Klemperer and for a former pg, Joachim Storost ...] Schober has nothing good to say about Koch or Storost ... Whom can I trust? No one and least of all myself. Everyone is hostile to me and I must conceal my ignorance and play the part of the scholar.

[...]

8th October, Friday

[...]

This morning the 2nd faculty meeting, 20 people. [...] Present was Rita Hetzer, back from [the Party school at] Klein-Machnow, she will now be lecturer in Marxist philosophy at the Theatre and Music Academy. She is quickly to do her doctorate with us. Inspired by Barbusse's *Zola* I gave as topic: The naturalist school's relationship to politics. Later (later because a difficult and lengthy task) she herself wants to write about the influence of capitalism on linguistic forms. I said, as if it were a matter of course for me: 'Study the Restoration period[55] and start with Balzac!' [...]

10th October, Sunday towards evening

I have just read over what I wrote on 9th Oct. 47[56] [Klemperer's birthday]. As far as my inner life is concerned I could repeat it word for word with respect to yesterday. Only: Greifswald was no help, I have achieved nothing this whole year, and in Halle + Leipzig my energies will be even more fragmented than in Greifswald. The Winters congratulated me very nicely, the registrar sent a basket of flowers with official greetings, Becher (personal signature: Johannes R. B., not 'KB' like the last time!) a telegram. Mixed feelings. I must adopt the view:

it makes no difference what use you make of the remainder of life you have been granted. As long as it is indeed made use of. [. . .]

In the evening there was a meeting of the 'University Works Group' at the Party House. About 40 present. Comrade Schober chaired. [. . .] In all faculties, instead of the previous general philosophy class, there is to be an obligatory course of lectures on Marxist philosophy and economics. It is not supposed to be imposed by decree, rather the faculties are supposed to decide on it 'voluntarily'. [. . .] The matter will go smoothly, because with the new revolutionary dictatorial statute WE have an absolute majority in the Halle senate, and, as Winter emphasised, in the faculties the reactionaries have become tame. Voluntary tameness out of fear of forced retirement. (I know, of course, that this is the same method as in the Hitler period. Only – unfortunately! – applied more tamely and less consistently.) [. . .] So on Saturday – E. had baked a great many cakes and arranged a proper birthday table for me: a waste-paper basket she had painted herself, a bedside rug, a fountain pen, an electric lighter – the Winters came to congratulate me. The conversation touched on the Eastern Jews and on Zionism – Wendt has asked me to change the Hitler–Herzl comparison, I had been criticised for it; I replied, that it was clear from my chapter that Herzl was no Hitlerian, apart from which I detested Jewish nationalism – I could not change anything in my text – and Winter proved to be very philo-Semitic and almost Zionist. The Eastern Jews were such good people, and if the Jewish nationalists were also behaving very badly (just now: the murder of Bernadotte),[57] they nevertheless deserved our compassion and were very brave. [. . .]

13th October, Wednesday evening
So yesterday I lectured for the first time here at Halle University; I had a bit of stage fright beforehand. Will I be able to conceal my ignorance until the end here also? – Fewer students than in Greifswald; there I was an attraction, here I am one among many. The Voltaire Lecture Theatre seats 98 people – there were about 50, Rita H. says, that many had never come to a Romance literature lecture here. After that I gave out Staël papers in the seminar. I think 15 participants, all, except one, senior or very senior students.

[. . .]

15th October, Friday evening. Halle
Yesterday [annual] dies academicus. [Inter alia, Winter officially replaces the 'theological and reactionary Eissfeldt' as rector. Klemperer expresses interest in taking a joint seminar with Winter, a historian . . .] Topics and plans everywhere and nothing will come of it all. [. . .]

21st October, Thursday morning (and later). Halle

So yesterday, 20 Oct., 3–7 p.m. lectured in Leipzig for the first time. What an inner triumph, and how small and pitiable de facto! This Jews' school, this chaos, this badly organised Party institution which calls itself Gewifa and is domiciled on one floor of 3/5 Goethestr.! The 'big name' professors had not yet begun, no one had announced that I would really come on the 20th, the students had not been informed. A good dozen did nevertheless turn up, I consoled myself with the thought that the number would increase and those present appeared to like my Voltaire. But then the seminar – here they said 'study group', which corresponds more to the Party language. Six people, comrades. Not one could speak French, not one had a clue as to what lay behind the title of my class, none of them had ever heard the name Staël before. In any case: the whole arrangement of the Culture lectures, the whole Culture Working Group was new, *I* was the first person to have a teaching appointment for it [. . .] I now explained to them who Staël was, how much could be learned from this book, and how it was the task of the SED to have intellectual weapons in its hands etc. etc. Finally, students, comrades, you must win over the others, *not* for me, but for the cause . . . etc. etc. They said, the seminar would no doubt be a success, I would also find people to give papers using German translations; one female student even wanted to try to read the French text . . . I do not see how I shall make something of this seminar [. . .].

Our luggage has arrived, one bookcase has been set up, first attempt to clear up the chaos – naturally also time-consuming. My proof copy of the *LTI* has turned up, and so before anything else that has to be read through – I have already had a reminder. [. . .]

31st October, Sunday evening. Halle

Work and dissipation of energy overwhelming, everything is at a standstill because of this too much . . . E.'s health very poor – coughing, affected lung? Heart? [. . .]

Very brief addenda

On Saturday 23 and Saturday/Sunday 30/31 Oct. at last read *Massacres de Paris* in E.'s excellent translation, for which I am to provide the afterword on the Commune. Ordered Lavisse yesterday.[58] Leafed through Aragon a little for the Modern Poetry, which is supposed to be ready in 2 weeks! That, apart from rushed and inadequate lecture etc. preparations, is all that I have managed recently. Terrific arrears of correspondence.

[. . .]

On Sunday 24 Oct. Lotte Sussmann here, who was completing a psychiatry course in Leipzig. [. . .] She complained [. . .] bitterly about anti-Semitism. In the psychiatry ward a female patient refused to allow herself to be treated by 'the Jewess' . . . Then she talked about her meeting with Otto Klemperer. His conducting was brilliant, he had been very cordial to her [. . .]. He had left Los Angeles because of the anti-Semitism. He had to engage 10 new people for his orchestra. His choice had been refused, because 8 of the 10 were Jews. In Budapest on the other hand his situation was good, the city was called Judapest. One son is an actor in New York and a daughter is a secretary or correspondence clerk in London or Paris. He had emphatically asked after me and Lotte had immediately had to give him the *LTI*, about which the Wangenheims[59] had told him in Berlin. She had wired me on his behalf. (But so far he has not written to me. *I* cannot run after the famous cousin – 'Are you related to the famous musician?' Still: the difference is no longer as great as before. I am an important figure and author of the *LTI* [...]).

On Wed. 27 Oct. Leipzig. A) at the station *here* meeting with Weise/Teubner [...]. Discussion of the Mod. Poetry. It should be before the unpredictable 'Cultural Advisory Council' by mid-November. Werner Krauss is to provide an opinion on the Mod. Poetry as an 'essential textbook'. 'If the names Klemperer *and* Krauss are underneath it, then they cannot reject it.' [...] B) Journey to L. With E. immediately to Krauss in the Romance Languages and Literatures Department for several hours. After we had discussed our Mod. Poetry business, there appeared the just appointed Hans Mayer ('Your Büchner book is one of the best that I have read recently' – 'I'll return the compliment immediately: Your *LTI* ...' etc.) [...] He is director of the new Culture section of the Gewifa. [...] My lecture again only poorly attended, but a little better than the first time. And it seemed to find favour. After that the seminar. I now ran it as a colloquium and talked almost the whole time and almost alone about *culture and civilisation*. [...] Trude Öhlmann is without any doubt whatsoever at death's door. An awful resemblance to the late Annemarie. The fat swollen face, the terribly swollen hands. She says starvation oedema, says she weighs only 6 stone. Once again this wasting away leaves me terribly cold. And again, as so often in recent years, this hideous sense of triumph: I am 12 years older and will go on living. And always this mixture of indifference and dull fear: when will it be my turn?

On Wed. and Thurs. 28 and 29 Oct. in Berlin. Out early together feeling very, very tired. [...] The professional central point of the trip was *the* unpleasant *LTI* discussion with Wendt, which Abusch also joined. The Zion chapter is held to be impossible; Wendt says even a negative comparison with Hitler is offensive, Abusch declares obstinately, *any* similarity, because Herzl was not a Fascist. I am made out to be a an anti-Semite, a pistol is held to my head. Delete the chapter or alter it fundamentally, otherwise the new edition cannot appear. For a moment I wanted to abandon publication, but that would mean a rupture with the Kulturbund. [...]

[...]

5th November, Friday

Never-ending excessive rush, everything is left lying, health suffers – nevertheless again and again it gives me pleasure. Vita activa, tempestuous old age, one has to be a fatalist and not reflect too much.

On Tue., 2 Nov., after the lecture a couple of minutes with Rita Hetzer. Curious shared home: the illegitimate couple, Robi[60] and Rita and both their mothers

[. . .]. Then to the newly opened 'Government Guest House'. At small tables Paul Wandel, Thape, Halle, Vahlen, Elchlepp, His Magnificence Winter and the one and a half dozen SED academics of the 'uni'. [. . .] Paul Wandel – this was the purpose and the main point of the evening – made a serious speech about the new university line. The crucial sentence: *'The second phase has begun.'* Since for the time being we have been definitively separated from the West, and since our SED forces at the universities have grown a little, we can now reform more vigorously. Our goal is the Socialist Republic and we are preparing the way for it. We can co-operate with the democrats for the moment, we do not need to throw out all the bourgeois academics – but where someone seriously impedes us, he has to go. [. . .] Overall the speech was an evident declaration, now we were going to be in earnest about the Red university. [. . .] It was a very pleasant evening, I came home after 1 a.m. with Winter in the Minister's car feeling very buoyant [. . .].

On Wed., therefore, I was in Leipzig, where I ran into Behrens, the dean of the Gewifa [Social Science Faculty]. [. . .] He, too, lamented Werner Krauss's poor state of health. He wants me to be firmly and permanently associated with the Gewifa. [. . .] It seems I shall sort everything out in a friendly fashion. Except the whole Gewifa makes a really unfortunate impression on me: a Party school attached to the university, without a proper programme, still feeling its way, and with very poorly prepared students, very disadvantageously separated from the old faculties and even more isolated and unscholarly than the education faculty. And Behrens complains that the students preferred to say 'Comrade' and did not maintain the necessary respect towards professors.

[. . .]

14th November, Sunday. Halle

Ratschow has diagnosed E. as having severe coronary dilation, she is evidently seriously ill.

[. . .]

On Sunday, the 7th, the big and exhausting anniversary of the October Revolution. In the morning from 11–2 a big banquet with plentiful alcohol in the municipal Schützenhaus [. . .]. More than 200 guests, senior officers of the SMA, toasts with interpreters. German speakers: Winter, Koenen,[61] Hübener,[62] the prime minister [of Saxony-Anhalt]. Looks like a dried up accounts clerk, speaks well, educated, with sense of humour, noticeably cooler than our [i.e. SED] people. It [Russia and Germany(?)] should be a 'marriage of inclination', deriving from marriage of convenience – love matches result in so many divorces, inclination can turn to love … Everyone else, including the Russians, spoke of friendship, common efforts for peace, for a united Germany … Came back very fatigued (all the food, all the drinking!), with the pressure of the evening before me. – Then in the Volkspark [. . .] over 1000 people. Wagert recited Mayakovsky's 'October Revolution' He spoke very well, and for the first time I got something from Mayakovsky and I could place him in a context: Whitman. Then myself. While speaking I was constantly thinking: is it suitable in front of this crowd, is it suitable in front of this majority of workers? Culture, civilisation, humanism – entirely without the cliches and bellowing of the functionaries. Afterwards Thape shook my hand: 'Only now do I see what a good catch for the university we made with you!' Ambiguous compliment in that place! No one else expressed a word of thanks. Hübener, whom I had after all addressed: 'Prime minister, Ministers' etc., disappeared like all the other bigwigs from the parties etc. I stood by myself. Albrecht, the secretary, said: 'The Party bosses will say, it wasn't political enough.' In the days that followed I heard everywhere in response to my question: Very nice, but for the workers (who had probably not been expected in such large numbers) perhaps a little too high-flown. The whole thing has left something of a bitter taste. I am squandering myself.

[...]

On Wed. 10 Nov. Leipzig. [...] Then Hans Mayer's guest for lunch. Very elegant furnished apartment, very sumptuous meal. M. very evidently the political VIP with important foreign connections. He is the senior chairman of the VVN for its foreign relations, in the next few days he's flying to an international meeting in Brussels. That absorbs him more than his chair in Cultural History at the Gewifa. He is a trained lawyer [...] was able to emigrate to Switzerland – bachelor, [...] simple and unpretentious, not conceited in his manner. We wanted to co-ordinate our lectures [but were interrupted ...]

In recent weeks I had 3 letters from the Vosslers, 2 from him, one from Emma V. Very warm appreciation of my *LTI*, very bitter complaints about Munich conditions. [...]

Letter from Lerch with the typescript of his completely bloodless review of my *LTI*, politically and philologically equally bloodless, nothing but a lexical compilation. He has thus far attempted in vain to place this harmless stuff with *six* Western newspapers and asks me whether I can explain these rejections.[63] Of course I can: because my book smacks of the Soviets, because it talks about the Nazis. The enmity of the two Germanies is now quite blatant.

[...]

16th November, Tuesday forenoon

[...]

On the return journey [talk to trades union representatives at the Leuna chemical plant], from 12 until about 1, dense crowd on the market place: opening of the 'Free Shop' [i.e. no ration cards required'[64]] *LTI*. Most questionable business.

[...]

25th November, Thursday afternoon

My present life must lead to catastrophe; it is becoming ever more rushed and fragmented – and I cannot make up my mind to change it – and as things stand I cannot even really change it. Weise said to me: 'one day it will be said: "earlier he wrote important things, then he slid into politics." ' There is some truth to that.

[...]

3rd December, late afternoon Friday. Halle

[...] I shall have to complete the Modern Poetry during the Christmas holidays. To be able to concentrate on the silly Surrealists (Nadeau[65]) today (and yesterday a little) was the exception, lectures and talks eat me up, Leipzig is a great strain (because of the travelling, the wasted hours in between, also the preparation) because I cannot present anything aesthetic and philosophical to *this* audience at the Gewifa and so have a great need of material. [...]

On Friday, 3 Dec., came the setback. Thape, the education minister has gone to Berlin west and has written to the Party from there, that he is not coming back. Treachery! The abandoned ministry. Otto Halle in Klein Machnow, Thape in Berlin west, Ludwig Einecke a novice, Vahlen young and in ill health. Who will be minister? Frau Winter says: '*You* would be the right man.' I really would be and it could tempt me. But of course it will be some non-academic functionary [...].

[...]

12th December, Sunday forenoon

[...]

On the aft. of Friday, 10 Dec., KB session. [...] In the further course of this meeting [...] I was then elected second regional chairman of the Kulturbund [...]. The election was of course fixed beforehand. – At about 5.30 I drove to Magdeburg in a rented car with a cautious elderly driver. We reached our goal at about 8, the lecture had been announced for 7, a few of the audience had already left, but I nevertheless made a very big impression – Barbusse – on about 50 people [...]. I was virtually feted. [...] Home at 2 p.m., E. got up, we drank tea – then preparation for 'internal instruction' (my 'Workers' Blood, Students' Blood' with an expanded section on students in modern times). To bed at 5, out at 7, at university in the car by about 8. From 8.15–almost 10 spoke with absolute freshness and conviction. The great hall really half full. But who followed, who understood? These political instruction sessions are obligatory, and are belligerently rejected as SED compulsion, those in the back rows are said to be sleeping, reading etc. And not believing anything ... And again: Who understands? Listeners: from the cleaning woman to the registrar – all of the university's employees. [...] But I flatter myself, that I did nevertheless touch one or other person ... To a certain extent I can have some respect for my achievement: Thurs. *LTI*, Fr. Barbusse, Sat. Students 1848–1948 – My old topics to be sure, but I always have to spin them out differently, prepare my thoughts, concentrate ... Is it worth it? I waste and abuse what is left of my strength. The eternal dilemma. Vanitas.

[...]

16th December, Thursday forenoon

Yesterday concluded the first half-semester at Leipzig with a sense of deep disillusion. [...] Chaotic playing around and pseudo-university. 4, 5 people there at the beginning, gradually turning into a dozen. I preached (not for the first time): 'Don't let our enemies have it their way, they are always taunting us about our sham scholarship, take the elements of education seriously!' It is the same every Wednesday: at the beginning there's no one there, they run off before the end: we *had* to go to *that* meeting, we must go to *that* paper, etc., etc. [...] Presumably the situation is at its worst in the new 'Culture' section, but I do not get the impression that there is any greater discipline in the other departments. [...] Between 7 and 9 Werner Krauss was with me in the secretary's office. Some of his conversation is so learned, that I always say only yes, yes and inwardly feel like a nonentity. The rest: bitterness towards Wartburg and Neubert; but he wants neither himself nor me for the Berlin chair but his personal friend Auerbach, who is stuck at a small USA university. He spoke very harshly of S[...], who had been a very active Nazi in Austria and had betrayed a student Résistance group in Strasbourg ... Lerch was a 'twit'. [...]
[...]
On Thurs. morning – I am in a bad way again – to the skin clinic at last. Another sulphur rub, which of course attacked my skin. Prof. Jacoby [...] was in Sachsenhausen concentration camp, is on the executive committee of the VVN, speaks very pessimistically.[66] Constantly increasing anti-Semitism, also in the SED. His daughter is isolated and discriminated against at school. If the Russians were to leave, we would immediately get a new Hitlerism. [...]

17th December, Friday afternoon

Yesterday morning I undertook a doctoral examination for the first time in my life. At 67, after having been a professor for 28 years. Gisela von Remitz, 32, widow of a senior civil servant, [...]: *Vital consciousness, Love and Women in German Neo-Romantic Drama*. Much Freudisme, representation of the prostitute, of the sex drive etc. A great deal of material, nothing in terms of ideas. French as subsidiary subject, and a chapter of the dissertation superficially compiles French influences [...]. I had actually intended to give the woman a hard time: but she certainly knew her stuff. I gave her a II but shall make sure that she is marked *Good* (cum laude) and not *Very good*, as Schneider, her supervisor, would like.
[...]

24th December, Friday, Christmas Eve

The most hypocritical festival in every respect, generally and personally, always uncongenial to me and deeply depressing for me even today. Although actually no particular cause for depression. If we were both not suffering from heart disease and fairly close to the pointless end of a fairly pointless life, and if I were not terribly tormented by scabies and even more terribly by the *Mod*.

French Poetry, we could in fact be content. Above all by comparison with the previous Christmas in Greifswald. [...] For E. I bought a pound of green coffee for 110M – illegally through a miss from the regional bank, and 'good' cigarettes at 80 pfennigs each and a little perfume, and she is to get a picture by the executed Schulze for 600 or 700M.

[...]

28th December, Tuesday night

After scaling the heights of taedium[67] and despair yesterday and today, I resolved to add to the Poetry volume a short appendix, which will deal *only* with the Résistance and only include a couple of decipherable poems by Aragon and Eluard.[68] My starting point Vossler, to whom I shall perhaps dedicate the book.

[...]

31st December, Friday evening

In the morning in a cold wind with E. – a rare walk together – over the Brandberge, freshly dug foxholes and stretches of trench from a Russian exercise, frozen puddles, the strangely wild bare landscape, [...] the woods, the wintery fog, at the edge of the city ... To the police office for the new identity card, the uniform one for East Germany. Povera piccola Germania.[69]

We were supposed to spend this evening with a very small circle of the friends of the GSS in the guest house; there was no car, we are here alone. On the wireless as usual: 9th Symphony and *Fledermaus.* Thoughts: how many dead! And whether one will ever know, what was the point of it all? I am not at all afraid of the 'eternal judge' – only nothingness irritates me.

Résumé 48

In fact produced nothing at all. The Students–Workers address and a couple of little articles. But have asserted myself as a university teacher. In Greifswald, in Halle, in Leipzig. And many lectures.

The newly added worry: E.'s poor state of health.

In the last few days: the *Modern French Poetry.*

The Zion annoyance in relation to the *LTI.*

[...]

1949

3rd January, Monday forenoon

Old people should not have any feast days. I am glad to have survived it once again.

[...]

While out walking yesterday Bennedik called on us with dog and little foster son. Passionately radical. He is now considered the favourite to succeed Thape. His advantage over other candidates: in 1945 he joined the SPD and not the KPD – 'quite by chance'. And now, for the sake of parity, it *must* be someone from the SPD and not the KPD. But Ludwig Einecke is a KPD man. (And Klemperer is, too.) And Max Lange is 'unreliable'. And Winter – there were people who doubted his sincerity. I said I thought him sincere, 'but simply an Austrian, hence pretty limp'. Horrible characteristic of the times: everyone suspects everyone else. [...]

Aside from that spent the whole day brooding over the Poetry and finally, finally concluded the contortions of the short study. I must now devote the remainder of the holidays to completely finishing off the new edition, but essentially I have this work, which I have found so unspeakably difficult and unpleasant, behind me and can more or less enter it under 1948. [...]

12th January, Wednesday forenoon

[...]

Evening

I telephoned Teubner at 8, Weise returned the call at 10, he was here at 1.30 and until late afternoon (with a teabreak) went through my 'Appendix 1948', he left with the ms – now I really have been relieved of this nightmare. [...] The Teubner publishing house is being more thoroughly socialised [...] the whole house is being incorporated into some large state organisation, appears to be becoming a section of a book combine. [...]

On Sunday, 9 Jan., Vahlen visited me ... About the ministerial question. The Party objects to professors. The question whether KP or SP is not important, Bennedik has no prospect – probably Einicke. We talked about the Party's disregard for the intelligentsia. With that I was on to the Rita Hetzer issue again. She is to take over an important official post, in charge of the student secretariat, a kind of 3rd deputy rector. 'Only part-time' – she can carry on the doctorate on the side. But 'on the side' she is already lecturing on Marxism at the drama academy, and 'on the side' she has x political tasks. I told Vahlen on the telephone today: There are laws for the protection of pregnancy – allow Rita to give birth to her book! She is to be my successor. The Party urgently needs scholars etc. etc., my same old song. [...]

16th January, Sunday evening

[...] Compromise [Rita Hetzer]: she will be occupied by this business [student secretariat] for *only* half a year and only half the day, nevertheless see to the department and muddle on with her doctorate. – Most interesting topic of our visit [to Hetzer/Schober]: the reciprocal mistrust inside the Party, the fanaticism of the younger generation: to these people no-one is 'a proper Marxist'. Virtually an atmosphere of inquisition. Some young people had also said it about me – Rita had forcefully defended me, the Party thought highly of me (really?) [...]

28th January, Friday forenoon

No possibility of seriously keeping the diary. Worries of all kinds and chasing around, work and pointless activity, too little sleep and ever more frequently the feeling: I wish it were time to sleep, and always surrounded by the dead, and always with the embittered revulsion against nothingness!

[...] Food supply: the abundance of the Christmas days has been followed by weeks of increasing shortages, very bothersome with respect to tea and coffee. American and English parcels appear blocked, if not, indeed, confiscated. A couple of weeks ago we bought a $\frac{1}{2}$ kilo of coffee for 110M, from that E. gets a cup a day. We have enough tea for another 2 days in the house, and black tea is not to be had anywhere ... The chaos among my and E.'s books and papers becomes ever more of a tribulation: we lack bookshelves and cupboards ... All of it together: a steadily more distressing burden.

[...]

The *Modern Prose* is in the shops at last. But all trade in books with the West is blocked.

At the faculty meeting last Sunday (22 Jan.) I moved that Vossler be given an honorary doctorate [...] and have probably already carried the matter to a victorious conclusion. [...]

Weise says: since 1945 you have produced only 'trifles', from a scholarly point of view *LTI* is 'only raw material and stimulus'.

[...]

2nd February, 4 p.m. Wednesday afternoon. Gewifa office, Leipzig

[...]

KB Executive Committee, Berlin, Tue. 1 Feb. Drove at 7 in the morning with Hopp. Ghastly snowy and frosty weather the day before, now clear frost. Very fast journey, at 10.30 at the sector boundary in Berlin. Very strict check. German policeman: 'There are Jews(!) coming from the West, I make them get out, if they're walking stiffly, they've got a pipe with foreign currency down their trousers, I've already caught 4 out of 13 ...' Why Jews?? Ineradicable. [...] Very good breakfast at Jägerstr. Telephoned Wendt, he sent a car. He was pleased when I accommodated his doubts – he 'had tried to make changes' over Christmas – with the following suggestion: omit 'Zion' now, put it in again in the 3rd or 4th edition. He immediately telephoned the printing works: carry on with *LTI*! It will appear, mutilated, in 2–3 months. [...] I discussed the Dr h. c. for Vossler with Naas. The Central Administration will approve, especially as Vossler is now to be a member of the Berlin Academy. – There was nothing new at the committee meeting itself. [...] The big federal congress is to take place in Eisenach-Wartburg and Weimar – Goethe anniversary![1] – Anny Kl. had me called out around midday – I had asked Peter to come. Difficult talking to her, when waiters are swarming around. Is she really so poor, or is she just becoming senile? I gave her 400M to help with Peter's studies, after I had transferred 300M, my Reutlingen fee for the *Salammbô* introduction, from the French to the English sector for her.

3rd February, Thursday night (actually 4th February, because it is almost 1 a.m.)

[...]

I received a pile of new books from Aufbau, and leafed through them longingly. Time, if only! Feuchtwanger's *Success*,[2] Kantorowicz's *Spanish Diary*.[3]

[...]

At dinner during the Executive Committee meeting I met Arnold Zweig. Fat, dull ice-grey eyes behind thick spectacles, very old, very vain. He showed off with being translated into Chinese.

4th February, Friday evening

[...]

Very depressed by E.'s state of health. She walks with a stoop, is frequently short of breath, in the evenings is almost always racked by pain, evidently seriously ill. The medicine, the second now, does as little good as the injections did. On top of that the terrible chest cough, which reminds me of Annemarie.

[...]

12th February, Saturday afternoon

Anniversary of father's death. If I had the childlike faith, that he was looking 'down at me', then he would have less of a mixed pleasure in my life than I do myself. I wear myself out and flee from my proper work. Every day wearier, inwardly less satisfied – and always taking on more and always in a state of slight intoxication when I re-shuffle my same old couple of topics and am applauded for it. Hardly a day any more without a meeting or a paper or the like, my appointment book ever fuller, each lecture leads to invitations to give three more, and I never refuse. Correspondence and work piles up, I am unable to collect my thoughts. – My heart ever more burdened, ever weaker. And the increasing worry about Eva, who has heart problems every day, without the medicines applied being of the least use.

[...]

I have forgotten the most important thing about the KB day before that [on the 10th, part of a round of congresses and meetings]: Adolf Hennicke [the East German Stakhanov].[4] He came from a big meeting in the same building and spoke a few words to us. Fine figure of a man with a clean-cut head, could just as well be a senior SS officer. Speaks quite well and clearly, sticks to the essentials: that he is not bringing *more* work and extra burdens, but simplification and planning. All of it of course in the tone of a functionary, of the practised speaker who has said the same thing a 1000 times, of someone officially celebrated and supported. He is accompanied by a small retinue, two policemen also remain at the entrance to the hall. Afterwards Kreuzig, the driver: there are always police with him, they are afraid he might be attacked. I remember people cursing him in Bitterfeld a while ago, that I was told there were whistles in the cinema when he appeared on screen. Many there consider him an exploiter and slavedriver of the underfed workers. [...] What is the truth? What did he really accomplish? What are he and the *activists* (LQI) really all about?

[...]

Letter from Vossler; he gripes about Thomas Mann's 'narcissism', what a 'sorry figure', who 'still finds fools enough, here and in America, to admire his exhibitionism'. [...] I replied at length: about the Dr h.c. proposal, about the 'Appendix 1948', about the *LTI* and Zion. He complained again that the *LTI* does not get as far as Bavaria.

LTI: Old intelligentsia, new intelligentsia.

[...]

The Israeli state is hoping for financial support from 'WORLD JEWRY' [Weltjudentum] (so as to be able to avoid the Marshall Plan). Official wireless news on 7 Feb. 49.

[...]

8th March, Tuesday forenoon. Addenda

1) Berlin and Magdeburg, 1 and 2 March. Journey there with E. and Menner. [...] Tedious meeting. Preparation for the Kulturbund Wartburg celebration [...] Many, many speeches at cross-purposes, sterile repetition. E. at Volk und Welt meanwhile. – At 5.30 began our expedition to Judith Kwiet, school doctor in the American sector, Friedenau, 30 Offenbacherstr. Snowstorm, cold, ice, darkness, no car. Underground to Rüdesheimer Platz. Then groped our way. The grave danger of our path between ruins, from which stones etc. were crashing down. The wind so strong, that it almost blew us over.

No street number to be discerned, the house, when finally found, locked up. Shouted. E. and I both shouted. At last, from 4 flights up came help. Guided up with a few matchsticks. The west of the city has electricity only twice a day for 2 hours. Upstairs, candles and a tiny petrol kitchen lamp. But very warm welcome in heated room. Some of the children abroad, Rena, Hans and the two smallest together with Ursel [...] there. Everything, inwardly and outwardly, as in Greifswald. Good food and cordiality. [...] Night in unheated room, there were holes in the windows, but we were under warm blankets. – E. stayed until the aft. and then went back in the car to Halle with Hopp as well as Dr Hoffmeister. I went to Friedrichstr. Station with Hans, the drama student. Journey to Magdeburg from about 9.30 to 1. [...]

Saturday/Sunday 5/6 March: Bärenstein. I took the usual train to Leipzig at 10.30; at Teubner had a discussion with the half-Jewish production manageress, Fräulein [Landsberger], then talked over details of the celebration on the 17th. [...] At Teubner indignation at some people of the SED management, who want to banish Latin and Greek from *all* schools. I shall go into that in my speech. It will be called: 'Transformation of Humanism'. [...] [Difficult wintry journey from Leipzig to Schloss Bärenstein near Dresden: training course for People's High School teachers. K. speaks on 'The People's High School in the Goethe Anniversary Year.'] In charge, Wilhelm Adam, the department head responsible for the People's High Schools in the Saxon ministry [...] Rewarding: Adam, the new man, with whom I shared a room and chatted to a great deal.[5] Very tall and slim, fair, a little Red Indian-looking [...] mid-50s, Rhinelander, his family in the West. Was at Stalingrad, adjutant to Paulus,[6] back from Russia only a few weeks ago. On the executive committee of the National Democratic Party. From him I heard about the party in greater detail for the first time: We are *national* and *without class struggle*, that is the programme and it is successful. [...] Except unfortunately: in the West they name all the Stalingrad officers who lead the party and talk about a camouflaged Communist Party. Nevertheless Adam believes in the success of the thing. He himself gave Plievier material [for his novel *Stalingrad*], says Pl.'s portrayal is almost entirely right. Except that he, Adam, judges Paulus, who is also highly considered by the Russians, more favourably. [...] [Referring to his own talk Kl. says that now the Goethe salad – or mixture – is taking the place of his Russian-culture salad, a topic which can be infinitely adapted to suit place and audience. In passing, he laments how much of Goethe he does not know.]

[...]

20th March, Sunday evening
[...]

[Another round of talks for the Kulturbund: Dresden, Löbau, Görlitz, Mond. 21–Wed. 23 March.] E. will not be accompanying me; it would only be an effort for her, and the deaths of Steininger and of a friend of Lotte would cast a shadow on the friendship part [of the trip]. But I have a bad conscience, for it is in fact a relief, if she does not come with me – I am always somewhat constrained and depressed by concern for her state of health when she accompanies me on a trip ... I wish I were already back.

[...]

10th April, Sunday
Saxony trip 21st–23rd March

The journey out with the worthy Kühne as driver. Very picturesque and full of memories the stretch of the Elbe from Meissen on. Couple of minutes rest in Leipzig before that: Fräulein Zillner, Weise's right hand at Teubner, got the task of obtaining a wreath for Trude Öhlmann, whose death notice had arrived the day before. A deliverance for Trude Ö. and for us. We were dragging a dead woman along with us. [...] In the evening [of the 22nd, after Klemperer had promoted his interests at the Dresden education ministry] up at Renn's Cultural Sciences Institute. Full house. Loud applause. 'The Social Novel'. The serious people, Lotte Sussmann and Blume from the KB, said my really rounded achievement had been the Aragon [the previous evening], the Social Novel was more of a relaxed chat. – In the crush after the lecture Erich Seidemann handed me the *LTI* folder, dedicated to me, from Dölzschen elementary school: essays and drawings by 13-and 14-year-olds after my *LTI* and the related schools broadcast. At that moment I was unable to thank him warmly enough and on Wed. afternoon drove up to Dölzschen. S. told me he was about to take the 'Current Affairs' lesson, extraordinarily important for those about to leave school, very much sabotaged by the passive resistance of the children, supported by the parents, to everything political. There, for the first time in my life, I gave a short political address to the children of an elementary school. Not pure SED in content, but for a necessary politicisation of thinking. [...]

Kogan gave me Hermlin's attack on my *Modern Prose* in the *Tägliche Rundschau* newspaper.[7] He said: Write a reply, because it's an advertisement for your book, and you earn something as well! However, this ever-growing affair is not such a cheerful matter after all. On Sunday the 27th [...] I wrote a letter to Hermlin until 3 in the morning, the 'Dung Hill of Literary History', which I have meanwhile read to several people [...]. Will the article appear? In the meantime Theodor Lücke has written much more gently, but also critically in a lengthy article in *Aufbau* ... I shall not go into detail here, because there still remains a great deal to be said in public and in print. But seen privately, my position is also at stake in this. Between stools, always between stools – that should be my ex libris!

[...]

On Thurs., the 31st, [. . .] to the faculty meeting. There I passionately supported a request from Jena University for backing in their struggle for hard-pressed Latin. Yesterday, at the request of a librarian, I wrote a page with a similar argument for the wall newspaper of the only humanist educational establishment here, the Franckeschule.[8] [. . .]

On Saturday, 2 April, I travelled to Leipzig, quickly settled everything at the Gewifa, then spent a long time at Teubner, where they are anxious because of the Hermlin critique. [. . .]

On Sunday, 3 April, coffee visit by Rita and Schober. Short walk in the woods. Always in a state of exhaustion. In the evening a real tonic for a few minutes, listening [on the wireless] to a boxing match in Leipzig; a true Mark Twain scene, the dissatisfied crowd KO'd the referee.

[. . .]

On Thurs., the 7th, I was in Leipzig again. Preliminary discussion for my lecture course: Thurs. 11–1 French Classicism, 2–4 colloquium on the lecture. Embarrassing farce. Half a dozen people. What will I do with them? If I were not concerned about the appearance of being professor in Leipzig *as well*, and about the 500M a month . . . God knows, with what I shall fill the colloquium.

[. . .]

Then yesterday, Sunday, 10 April, I. M. Lange was here all morning, the Vice-President of the Cultural Advisory Council [i.e. the censorship body] and chief editor of the Volk und Wissen [People and Knowledge] publishing house, the powerful man, who is very important to me:[9] I made his acquaintance by chance on the telephone during one of my recent stays in Berlin [. . .]. After that there arose a correspondence on the Modern Poetry. [. . .] Recently he wrote 'in great sorrow' because of Hermlin's attack. Did I not want to send Hermlin my Modern Poetry for advance perusal!!! – A grey-haired pale-eyed man, born 91. He spoke here on Saturday about modern literary studies . . . He is very amusing, very vain, very sure of himself and his own importance. He is a veteran journalist and man of letters of the extreme left, despite illegal work somehow saved his hide. He wants to 'help' me. Sympathetically, as one helps a bourgeois of good will, whom one can make use of, in whom one disregards one thing or another, from whom one learns one thing or another. He wants to supply the right titles for the individual sections of a new edition of the *Modern Prose* – that is what counts! – In his favour: he is not really dissembling, he makes no bones about what is de rigueur. In literature he knows his stuff, he is familiar with the French. – Awkward really. He is so nice to me, because he can make use of me: because he wants to take his doctorate, and that's not possible in Leipzig, because he has fallen out with Werner Krauss. Besides, it is also a pleasure to patronise a respected professor and to present yourself to him as a powerful provider or denier of favour. And I for my part naturally have x reasons to keep in with the man. So we were very pleasant to one another for several hours over liqueur and cigarettes. He promised 1) to rush through the Teubner pamphlet and to reassure the publisher, 2) to make sure that something from my *LTI* is included in a school reader, 3) to make sure that my *PLN* review finally appears in *Forum*. [. . .]

Up to date at last with the diary ... As if I could ever get around to my Curriculum! But yet one always has to pretend to oneself, that one believes this and that.

[...]

18th April, Easter Monday forenoon

[...]

The affair of my *Modern Prose* has given me quite a shock. Theodor Lücke in *Aufbau* on the whole quite negative. Most unpleasant the letter I got from I. M. Lange yesterday. Humanly and politically unpleasant. Almost fawningly polite, since he would like to take his doctorate with me, after Werner Krauss turned him down – he, the vice-president of the secret court, had a theoretical conflict with Krauss over Marxism – simultaneously firmly against my conception. At the same time hypocritical. The book must, 'taking account of all objectivity, of all devotion to scholarship, nevertheless above all be couched in such a way that it meets all the demands of our new democratic educational reform, which of course mutatis mutandis also applies to the universities ... Revolutionary times must on occasion make do with considerable abridgements in order to accentuate the political line more strongly' ... 'What is important to me as an admirer, and if I may say so, also in a small way a student of your writing, is not only that your reputation as an internationally recognised scholar is safeguarded, but that political progress also has a claim on you: and we must make this claim tangible and comprehensible to all.' – Revolting! Where is freedom. Linden [Nazi historian of literature] says *race loyalty*. Now the word is *class-conscious*. Not quite as poisonous, but it does not have anything to do with scholarship either. (*Race loyalty > class conscious: LQI.*)

[...]

23rd April, Saturday evening

[...]

The honorary doctorate for Vossler has been approved by Berlin. It appears that I could present the diploma to him [in Munich] in person [...]. Mode has just reported that to me. But also that Vossler seems close to death. [...] With complete lack of feeling I said to myself: Then I shall speak at his grave, and then his oldest student has a chance of succeeding him in the Academy.

[...]

Every day my eyes are worse – double vision. Every day I feel more washed out.

[...]

25th April, Monday afternoon

[...]

With bitterness I see that the *Tägliche Rundschau* is not printing my reply to

Hermlin. Kogan told me Colonel somebody, one of the editors there, will be writing to me – thus far nothing has happened.

[...]

[A Russian music evening. Reflecting on the dances on stage, Klemperer wonders:] did we need the October Revolution for that? It's like the imperial divine service and Napoleon in Nôtre Dame. Likewise the acrobatic dancing: these are nice variety members. Musically I liked a pianist, an exciting toccata by Prokofiev, in some way reminiscent of Ravel's *Bolero*, nothing but rhythm, jungle drumming ... Afterwards the big and elegant dinner at Pottel and Broskowski. But E. disappeared, came back feeling unwell – outside fainting-fit and vomiting – inside she collapsed again immediately. We led her outside; lift, car, to bed. It was wretched. The next day she was washed-out, otherwise all right. But always the bad cough, always the physical inhibition. We are both seriously threatened.

[...]

7th May, Saturday

[...]

Sunday, 1 May, was taken up with the May Day celebration. The tram was not running, a university car picked us up. Assembled by faculties on the university square. To one side Paula Hertwig with her well-ordered regiment of white-capped nurses. Bernard Koenen harangued from the steps of the main building. That was at about 9.30. Slow march off. Eva at the back in the disabled van – she was unable to see and hear anything. I with the rank and file. Beside me Mode, behind me Kofler and a number of female students. This row was able to sing, sang very nicely, very revolutionary and very international. 'The Song of the Red Sailors' ('Battleship *Potemkin* has cleared the decks!'[10]), 'Avanti popolo alla riscossa, bandiera rossa!'[11] We marched in a fairly tight circle around the university for perhaps an hour. Crowds lined the route; somewhere a balustrade decorated with flags, drawn up in front of it a police detachment, behind them a good dozen beautiful horses – the present army of the state of Saxony-Anhalt. Finally we marched to the market square, many thousands were already standing there [...]. From somewhere the loudspeaker conveyed scraps of the usual address, to which no one listened. People chatted, craned their necks to see the arrival of new groups. The police army came, their riders to the fore, and was applauded. A cart with some kind of agricultural rig-out as in a carnival procession ... People stood around, chatted, the loudspeakers didn't stop, but no one listened. At about 12: 'The rally is concluded.' The market emptied very quickly. [...]

[Klemperer notes with satisfaction a growing number of students at his Leipzig classes ... Has a meeting with Werner Krauss, the first for some time:] Much knowledge, an astonishing amount of knowledge and much bitter arrogance in Krauss. At the same time hardly concealed ambition. I would like to know what he really thinks of me. [...]

[...]

17th May, Tuesday towards evening

Everything in an utter rush.

On the morning of Wed. 11 May at last elected 1st chairman [of the Kulturbund in Saxony-Anhalt], after Hopp resigned out of consideration for his private profession. Everything settled in friendly fashion [...].

I already appeared as 1st regional chairman in the group photograph in the *Freiheit* the following day [...], my article on Intelligentsia and People's Congress, which had just been published in the *Tägliche Rundschau* in Berlin, was printed with the picture.[12]

[...]

20th May, Friday forenoon

[...]

[There is no let-up in the engagements Klemperer has taken on:] The evening before last, Goethe at Zwickau Kulturbund, back the same night, did lecture for Thurs. (Montaigne, Descartes), to bed after 4, yesterday the two two-hour sessions at the Gewifa, GSS car to Halle, in the evening Barbusse lecture in the new GSS house [...] tomorrow ... etc. etc. It is beyond my powers.

[...]

[On 15 May the Klemperers cast their votes for the People's Congress. VK notes activities in opposition to the election and concludes:] A third voted no [to the unified party lists].[13] Inwardly I am completely without hope, as far as German democracy is concerned.

On Mon. the 16th, our xth wedding anniversary, I was then busy working up and giving my main lecture and children's seminar (Renan.[14] – The Taine text from my Modern Prose) – my feelings about 16 May subdued by the feeling of being close to the end.

[...]

Then today, while I was sitting over these notes this afternoon and nodding off, news by telephone of Vossler's death. Already on the wireless yesterday, said the university – so he must have died the day before yesterday, 18 May. On the surface the obvious: I would have liked so much to go there, partly out of vanitas [...]. On the other hand: I would have had to drop many things here [...]. Now the delay with the interzonal pass has made it all irrelevant ... Below the surface: *my* world is fading away. I was so closely connected to Vossler. Next to Eva he was the strongest influence on me.

A whole number of my plans have been destroyed in the last few days. 1) Teubner has finally rejected my 'Humanism' [periodical proposal]; Lange does not appear to be willing to take over the essay for the *Paedagogik*. Teubner is also hesitating over the edition of the Poetry. [They say] they have to be cautious with publication of earlier books, and so far there had been no reply to Hermlin's attack. Uhse[15] writes, he does not want any polemics against 'our friend Hermlin' in the *Aufbau* periodical, I should respond in the *Tägliche Rundschau*! Nor could anything be said yet about the date of publication of my Surrealism article ...

Sole comfort: Mayer wants to arrange a conversation on the topic for the Leipzig broadcasting station. [...].
[...]

24th May, midday Tuesday

Extreme tiredness, at the moment also of alcoholic origin. Yesterday from lecture and seminar to the new house of the GSS, where I spoke on Barbusse last Thursday. Reception in honour of André Simone, whose *The Fall of the 3rd Republic* I own and leafed through a few months ago.[16] Czech, probably not Jewish, more blonde Czech type, greying, about 50, elegant, German his mother tongue, cosmopolitan journalist, now professor at the Academy of Journalism in Prague. He wrote the *Fall of the Republic* in *English*. [...]

Vossler haunts me. With his slouch hat and his floppy moustache, with the feline suppleness of his fencer's figure and posture, half brigand, half Renaissance cavalier, with his chivalresque theatrical manner at the lectern, one hand akimbo [...]. And then with a short greying moustache, grown older, but still the mature height of elegant virility in 1928, when he became *my* honorary doctor in Dresden. And then, an old gentleman, tiring easily, not hearing very well any more, but still very sympathetic, still unbroken in 1945 in Munich [...]. And then in 1946, during the VVN meeting, very old, softer, almost tender and clinging; the way he accompanied me down to the car wearing his slippers, down the stairs and the few steps around the Maximilianeum (and Frau Vossler whispered to me: 'Just let him – he likes doing it!') It was evidently a real walk for him, a link to a world that was receding. And then in the last letter with the very shaky signature: I cannot go down the stairs any more, I am too weak ... In V. I have seen the finest bloom of manhood and its transience. His figure fills my life. Where is HE now, is he playing with our back tomcat Nickelchen?

26th May, Thursday. Ascension

[...]

After the research assistantship meeting [the previous day] I spoke to Vahlen, regretting that I had not managed to go to Munich. He: I should go nevertheless, take the diploma to Vossler's widow – on behalf of the government and the university! That was agreed immediately, and now I am to undertake this journey after all. I am thrust ever more deeply into politics. The right path??
[...]

29th May, early Sunday. Friedenau, Berlin, at Judith Kwiet's, 30 Offenbacherstr.

Most significant is the pervasive feeling of being abroad, in a hostile, absolutely different world – and that a couple of streets away from my familiar Berlin. The money, you can't pay for the tram, the goods in the shop window. People's calculations – 2M for the cinema, and for you it's eight – and their thinking, their thinking! And on top of that all the time the airlift, all the time, at intervals of a few minutes. Day and night, despite the 'lifting' of the blockade.[17]

[To his ageing female cousins, the Frankes, with their hostility to the Russians . . .] And worse than that: Whatever I say – disbelieving, superior, pitying smiles, pity for the whim of a befogged mind (whereby it is left open, and is a matter of indifference, whether I am so senile or so eccentrically innocent and enraptured as to believe all this, always and ineradicably these pitying smiles, whenever anything pro-Russian is said . . .) Thus with the Frankes, quite openly: we do not believe what you are saying, we know it is different. With Judith one degree better: they're both lying, but on many counts the West is in the right, the Soviet Union in the wrong.

[. . .]

French film somewhere in Schöneberg: *Les Maudits*.[18] In April 1945 Nazis flee to South America on a U-boat. A French doctor, whom they have brought on board by force, narrates. Crude thriller plot full of brutality and glorification of the grand criminel, in our uncivilised Russian zone it would be banned. [. . .] Before that the newsreel: American-English generals, the English foreign minister, Mr Bevin, reception at a Berlin airfield, signature in London of some agreement to protect Europe etc.[19] The other world. And it has its effect. I become uncertain, I feel isolated, in the minor state of East Germany, so many of whose inhabitants are disloyal. And I feel the isolation of Russia. Not until I return to my East patria – 10 minutes from here! – does it really hit me again, how many millions are in the People's Democracy. But from the point of view of the West these millions are the mob, the inferior races etc.

Hans Kwiet, the Reinhardt[20] pupil: all the good artists are leaving us, going to the West (10 steps away). There they get more money and better parts, they don't want the plays they have to do in the East. And they're not risking anything! If they want to return, the East will take them back immediately. Because it's so lacking in artists! In every way, therefore, the Soviet Zone disregarded, in a wretched state, enslaved. One sees, hears and reads nothing else. How should hundreds of thousands of people withstand that? On the train recently I heard: I want to have enough to eat, I don't care about anything else! [. . .]

30th May, early Monday, at Judith's

[. . .] The morning very dreary [at the 3rd German People's Congress]. All in the most familiar way.[21] The three papers identical to one another and each one precisely what one knows from 100,000 lead articles and has said 100× oneself. [. . .]

31st May, Tuesday forenoon. Halle

[. . .]

I did not go back into the oven of the State Opera [where the Congress was being held], sat on a step in the vestibule, heard parts of Grotewohl's speech, the only one with content (against the Bonn statute), walked around, made conversation, shook hands with x people. Profoundly disgusted by this congress, by politics altogether. Forever the same mush of phrases, not a single new thought. And full of lies, which everyone knows to be lies. [...]

And then related to that the farce of the election to the Volksrat [People's Council]. You are given a paper (almost a brochure) with some hundreds of names, divided up according to parties, organisations, 'individual personalities', and drop this torche-cul[22] in the 'urn'. I did not bother. Who put forward this list? The Kulturbund has ten names, among them people who are nothing to do with the KB. The 'personalities': indefinable mixture, all over the place. The Saxony-Anhalt regional leadership is missing, no Hopp, no Klemperer. I roused Hopp, we challenged Gysi and Abusch. No one is responsible. At the last moment a Party committee turned everything upside down with its horse trading. The 'expanded National Front', the NDP, the KB – whispered Abusch – must not have too much SED, and must give prominence to 'technical intelligentsia'. [...]

[After a bit more horse trading] It is almost certain, that *I* shall go to the Volksrat, but I am no longer pleased about it. The whole thing is hopeless. [...] A tragedy. We should give up all hope of an amicable union [of East and West], aim for a dictatorship in the East. *We* – and I should give up politics and work on literary history. But I do the opposite.

Contributing to my most profound depression: the affliction of my skin complaint. Judith had arranged a consultation with Löhe for me [...]. Dermatology Clinic at the Charité. Ice-grey man, who plays the Berlin lout with *such* a degree of exaggeration, that one recognises it as an act and is not offended. An ointment as topical treatment: 'I cannot say what you have, I don't know. You *must* stay in bed in my clinic for a couple of days. I cannot give you any worse treatment than the worst manual worker ...' [...] What now? I am repelled by the idea of lying in bed in such a hospital, nor do I have any confidence in it. On the other hand ... The Charité is a garden suburb amidst ruins. [...]

[Difficulties with Aufbau because Klemperer's conception – in a foreword – of the 'Rococo' as a 'trait éternel' does not] fit with the pure doctrine of Marxism, not with the sociological tendency of the literary history aesthetics desired now...

[...]

4th June, Saturday
[...] Hoffmeister and I dealt with Kulturbund business [at the KB office]. Delegate meeting on Friday. The requested 'comment' on the 'National Front',[23] on the explicit drawing in of Nazis of good will. I consider it a foolish policy. Imitation of the NEP[24] – but the West, too, knows that we are copying and no one believes us. Then the Bolsheviks were strong enough to digest the augmentation for the right, the augmentation from the right will eat *us* up. We issued a declaration

of approval to the press, which became a 'resolution' the next day: the KB had always striven to be 'above party' … […]

At last, yesterday, Friday, the long outstanding delegates' meeting in the splendid music room of the GSS. At first it looked as if we were not going to get a quorum. Gradually 15 persons entitled to vote trickled in, and that was enough. They have therefore democratically – what a farce! – confirmed me as 1st regional chairman [of the Kulturbund] and as representative in the Volksrat. […]

   […]

7th June, Tuesday evening
[…]

Now I am supposed to set out for Munich tomorrow, have already sent telegrams to three offices […] and still do not have a pass. Also, no one, not the Reichsbahn, not the travel agency, knows when the express train from Plauen/Ölsnitz leaves for Munich. […] I'm in the dark about everything, although KB, university and, especially, Edelberg of the SMA have made great efforts on my behalf. I have not yet informed Frau Vossler, who wrote truly touchingly to me and has invited me; I first want to see how the political plan develops. […] I do not feel well physically; I fear this long journey, which is more difficult than a Nile expedition. […]

8th–13th June, Monday–Wednesday. Munich Trip
[…] perhaps […] important for the Curriculum is the moment of loneliness in Gutenfürst on the afternoon of 8 June, as I stood on the 500-metre no-man's-land strip of the autobahn on the far side of the Soviet barrier, without money, feeling completely uncertain and empty with Eva waving to me from the other side. I was as if on an emigrant ship, already abroad and helpless. I have never before felt so ALIEN. (And how powerful the feeling of homecoming when on the 13th I crossed in the other direction and found the KB car and E. walking back and forward in front of it.) Then a stranger, to whom I spoke, took me to Hof in his car. En route it turned out that the man was thoroughly anti-Russian, anti-Communist – very awkward for me. He set me down, very politely, but on the outskirts of Hof nevertheless – it was only 10 minutes to the railway station and he had business here. For him it would have been 5 minutes, for me it was an exhausting half-hour walk with my little suitcase. At the station I had to pay two hundred East Marks for 30WM: usual black-market dealing by the waiters, [but] evidently a quite official and not at all excessive price. […] In the waiting room I sat for a long time over a very scanty supper (afraid I would not manage with my money!). Then an express train to Munich (which no one in Halle, no office either, had known anything at all about!), taking from about midnight to near 6 a.m. Astonishing – just as in peacetime. The lighting, the complete emptiness – one could stretch out on the seats in every compartment, the cleanliness, the suspension of the carriages, the regularly swift and gentle

pounding of the rail joints ... In this respect the West is wealthier. Then early in the morning in Munich the café-restaurant next to the station [...] with its abundance of cakes, real coffee etc. That was of course very seductive, that is *the* seduction of the West. In the Curriculum I would like to call it *'the sweet lie'* ... A long early-morning walk through the town to the River Isar. It seemed more tidied up in some places than the last time but on the whole little changed. A city of ruins with a vigorous life. Many goods in the shop windows.

[...]

[...]. First of all I sought out the Party and felt secure. Above all: from then on I had a car permanently at my disposal. With good Georg Kellner as driver, who, hungry for knowledge, soon displayed an almost infatuated admiration, his highest praise was: 'You are a professor and speak like a proletarian!' [...] *The drivers.* They see themselves as the charioteers of their heroes. [...]

When I arrived at Emma Vossler's there was a room ready for me in the immense Maximilianeum apartment, and an elderly (Molière-like) faithful maid took care of everything. [...]

In my memory it is as if I had lived with Frau V. for days – yet in fact I passed only two nights there, one night with the Neumanns in Pasing and one [...] with Kellner, my driver [...]. The big rooms in the Maximilianeum, Vossler's study, Frau V. had placed his picture on the stove, she laid the diploma down in front of it. Odd mixture of moods: she was certainly most deeply affected by his death, which must nevertheless have been a release for him and for her as well and which was expected, indeed also probably longed for – by him and by her. At the same time, however, she also felt proud as his widow, as guardian of his fame [...] revelled a little in the many honours which he was paid, answered letters of condolence with dignity and not quite without a touch of pleasure in the situation. [...] Her rancour against his political opponents, against the people who now want to take the apartment from her, who award her an ungenerous retirement pension, brought her closer to the East, to me. [...]

[Klemperer gives thumbnail sketches of a couple of the Munich KPD officials.] No less highly regarded by the Party, and a member of the Bavarian regional leadership, is Arno Haucke, one of the heads of their culture section, with whom I drove to Nürnberg. He was in the army, is uneducated, talks about the cowardice and lack of cleanliness of the Jewish soldiers, makes derogatory remarks about the Jew Mode [...] and is a member of the Communist Party. Admittedly the eastern Jews appear to play the most unsavoury role in Munich. One is said to be able to get 'everything' in Mohlstr. [...]

The Party offices in the West (I had the same experience in Mainz) exist in an atmosphere of illegality, conspiracy, in a constant state of alert.

[...]

2nd July, Saturday evening

[Klemperer again expresses his scepticism, indeed fear of the 'dreadful *National Front*' – see above p. 289].

The West connection. The results for me thus far: 1) the [...] Munich trip, with press sequel and my article for the *Tat*: 'Expedition to Bavaria'.[25] And yesterday the anonymously posted newspaper cutting 'Salon Bolshevism' with my picture and written on it in ink: 'You should be ashamed of yourself, if you have any sense of shame left at all.' [...]

2nd–4th July. The Zonal Congress of the Society

[...] Kuczynski[26] announces: from now on [the name will be] 'Gesellschaft für deutsch–sowjetische Freundschaft' – Society for German–Soviet Friendship. Unpleasant the feeling of squandered time – I sit and stand pointlessly around. [...] Even more than before on this second day in Berlin the feeling of absolute futility and waste of time. No one bothered about me. The drawing up of the zonal committee was a farce: sixty-one names, among them male and female workers, a big piece of window dressing, half a dozen people give the orders. I, too, am among the 61. [...]

... Effective speech by a woman doctor from the West. Anyone coming from the West is always greatly acclaimed. – The new customs: We stand up and applaud. *The person applauded claps along!* At the end – LQI<SU – '*Long live peace, long live* ...' The rent of the State Opera cost the society 100,000M. The society is *too rich*, that tempts it into making mistakes, into ostentation and trumping the Kulturbund, even though it absolutely needs the latter. [...]

13th July, 6.30 Wednesday morning

What good is the hope of catching up? The piece of paper with catchwords is getting ever longer, the proper diary quality inevitably evaporates ... My sleep becomes ever less, the mass of work and what is left undone ever greater. [...]

17th July, Sunday

The chaos on my desk, among my books, is indescribable, the scantiness of my sleeping time likewise. What is unsettling me is the National Prize. Erich Wendt says: he has to 'pour cold water' on my hopes. In this first year 'the old fellows had to be got out of the way', next year it would be the new people, and the year after that they would 'already have trouble finding candidates'. [...] That was on the day of the [KB] Executive Committee on the 13th. At the ceremony for the University anniversary, 12 July – the University of Halle was founded on 12 July 1694, it is also E.'s birthday, and so I was able to avoid quite a lot – a proportion of the professors wore gowns again for the first time, and His Magnificence Winter announced the university's nominations for the Academy and the National Prize. I am named in both categories [...] My gown (dark violet) excessively long, heavy, too warm, the squared cap too tight and cutting into my forehead. Very significant in cultural historical etc. terms, that the East zone has recourse to such formal dress again – the Revolution appropriates tradition, the Soviet Union glorifies Tsarism.

[...]

20th July, Wednesday

Forenoon Leipzig. Hans Mayer's inaugural lecture: Goethe and Hegel. 'The Primitive Phenomenon and the Absolute'. Qu'en ai-je su? Qu'en sais-je maintenant?? Tout et rien ...[27] [...]

20th–24th July, Wednesday–Sunday. Mainz Trip

[K. travelled to Mainz to give a lecture at the university there and to meet his colleague and fellow-student of Vossler, Eugen Lerch, for the first time since 1928.]

29th July, Friday afternoon

[...]

To the state of exhaustion were now added feelings of bitterness: *Not* included in the list of writers nominated for the National Prize. Werner Krauss elected to the Academy and – it's unbelievable: Neubert. I can tell myself a 100×: the National Front is to blame and other people are also disappointed: [...] it hurts most bitterly and I thought of resignation, because I can become professor emeritus from 9 Oct. 49.

Under the pressure of this setback I sat at my department's frugal term party in the refectory dejected and resentful and, which was unfair, did not open my mouth. Very simple and very nice performance of *Maître Pathelin*.[28] With it potato salad and rolls with dripping. And a student played the accordion, and there was dancing. [...]

Gusti Weighardt is awaited – telegram from Weferlingen.

2nd August, Tuesday morning

When we came from Weimar yesterday – Thomas Mann – [we were] not among the 'select few' of the evening reception,[29] I found the list of prize winners in the *Tägliche Rundschau*. Not *I*, and *again* Krauss. Fatal blow for me. Its most fatal effect: neither Teubner nor anyone else will ever print my 18ième, nor can there be any question of a new edition of my Literary History. Weise has left Teubner, Marx intimidated by the business of the *Modern Prose*. – The little pig was so very puffed up; now he is not only deflated, but has finally burst. Left over is a wee journalist. To have died a little earlier would have been no bad thing.

2nd August–24th August. Holiday weeks in Dölzschen in our own house

5th August, Friday

[...]

On 2 Aug., Kreuzig drove us here, arriving in the late afternoon. Much work for E. packing; I complained and scolded because of all the baggage. It was stowed away. The tomcat also. Very hot but good drive. [...] In Dölzschen, the plot very overgrown, green wilderness, otherwise in tolerable condition. A few weeks ago Schottländer was in part 'dismissed without notice', in part bolted – subsequently the police were after him. [...]

[On Wednesday, the 3rd] to the Neustadt, Timeusstr., to Gusti Wieghardt. She telegraphed recently from Weferlingen, wanted to come to us, was fetched to Herbert Gute in Berlin, telegraphed her address here ... We met, embraced; I helped her as guarantor at the Victims of Fascism office and at the police, we drove to our house, long get-together, Lotte also turned up. [...] Emotional reunion. She is little changed, does not look her 62 years, her hair has remained almost black – except she hisses a little, her teeth must be poorly made. Karl W. [her son] is working in London at the moment, for the Royal Navy, literally for the enemy, therefore. He still teaches aero-dynamics at Göttingen. [...] She will take charge of broadcasts for young people and children here, the Sachsenverlag is publishing a German edition of *Sally*, also of *Jan auf der Zille* [Jan on the Barge] [...]. We talked about 100 things at once – everywhere the dead on the way. She speaks with warm affection of the English as individuals. Her various posts as cook appear essentially to have been gentleman-cook positions on the basis of friendly relations and recommendations. She lived through the air attacks on London, V1 and V2 and did fire-protection duty.

[...]

Weimar. Freeman Thomas Mann

I feel sure no one will report the most characteristic moment. On account of the 'National Front'. Thomas Mann in the introduction to his altogether passable speech, in fact given $3\times^{30}$ and afterwards distributed in printed form, said: '... insofar as here in Weimar one can speak of "East" at all'. Immediately demonstrative applause, even if probably not by the whole of the packed house. Mann may be innocent, he presumably wanted to say: we here are simply Germany! but the applause said: we here are West Europeans! I looked at Eva, we were both aghast. [...] This meek pleasure: Mann has come to us, too! He was escorted from Gutenfürst [the border crossing] like a ruler. The Kulturbund was the most arse-licking. [...then] Becher spoke, beginning each sentence with 'You, Thomas Mann', finally apostrophising him 'Dear Beloved' – a hymn of conventional phrases. Then came Mann. The audience gave him a long and thunderous standing ovation. Good-looking for his 70 or so years of age. Like a clean-shaven American dollar man. Very prominent cheekbones, reddish-brown skin, deep-set little eyes, powerful nose, blackish hair, thin, medium height. On a table next to the lectern lay 2 folders, one the document bestowing freedom of the city, the other presumably the Golden Visitors' Book. The mayor addressed him, Mann stood self-confidently. After that read out his speech, speaking only the introductory words, including the ominous sentence, off the cuff. [...]

8th August, Monday after dinner

First we shivered at night, now great heat. Changing mood. Should I resign? Will they let me go? – The bitterness of the affront. – I try to manage a little reading, a few notes in these vacation days, to sit alone as much as possible in our green wilderness.

[...]

Constant tiredness, forenoon: fall asleep. Senility.

E. full of plans to renovate and extend; I believe: in her element. Advantages and disadvantages of being here, quite apart from the financial side, constantly go through my mind. Will I be able *bear* the peace? Will I *have* peace?

Visitors all the time. Lotte was here twice so far. She finds the hill difficult. Gusti was up here twice. She is full of activity. The Heinschs came on their motorcycle with a comical delivery box next to the vehicle itself. He told us of Schottländer's last days. One had to admire the stubborn way he stood up for his convictions, it had been wrong to make a martyr of him by sudden dismissal, he could have been checkmated with less fuss. [...]

9th August

[...]

Günther Schmidt here. He makes me anxious. Went from Jena, where he was threatened with arrest, because he refused to inform on West-oriented fellow-students for the Russians, to the 'Free University' [in West Berlin]. I warned him against a stay in Dölzschen – *I* would not betray him. He jeopardises me. And his fate also makes me waver in my attitude. No doubt, the Russians are acting in self-defence and have greater legitimacy on their side. But the individual case is grievous and not the only one. Where is freedom and where complete purity? [...] I am so tired of the university. If the scholars – Frings, Wartburg, Stroux – reject me, call me a 'newspaper writer', why should I not be a newspaper writer in the end? Why not take possession of my special place 'between stools'.

Oppressive heat, semi-thunderstorm.

11th August, Thursday

The day before yesterday towards evening: Gusti. With her driver – that's our style now [...]. Gusti delighted with her post at the Dresden broadcasting station. That is, like on a local rag. So many people here modestly delighted with subaltern positions: they are leading lights on a local scale, on a county scale etc. etc. Why am I dissatisfied? Would fame be any greater if it extended to the 'zonal scale'? And yet the deep dissatisfaction. All the deeper, for knowing that I *really* am only a newspaper writer.

[...]

14th August, Sunday

The hot period is long past. [...] I go out as little as possible, catch up on the diary, read Ehrenburg.[31] Every day is full of visitors. All the neighbours, everyone gossips ... Gusti. She brought the comrades Elsa Froehlich and Erna Rentzsch. All these local leading lights and functionaries. The SED bearers of culture with their deficient education. With their Party slogans and their incorrect German. With their – my coinage [...] – their 'asparagus-tip knowledge'. They know the asparagus tips of Marxism. Being determines consciousness, quantity turns to quality (very popular lately) etc. ... Inwardly Gusti has not changed. Also outwardly very little, despite her 62 years. 'I am very much against you having included a Gobineau[32] text [in the *Modern French Prose*], our students do not need to know that.'

My inner insecurity and depression do not change. In my life two phrases have always alternated, the one in which I looked forward to going to sleep, the other in which I looked forward to waking up. At the moment I feel happiest when I go to sleep. I am very tired, and I am tired of things, and I am sceptical of a great deal regarding the SED and the SU. I tell myself again and again: my time is past. – E. revels in building plans.

17th August, Wednesday

[...]

Invitation to the Weimar ceremonies (awarding of the National Prizes by Stroux etc.[33]) opens the wound once again. – In town yesterday – to the accompaniment of bad memento pains. A summons to police headquarters. I thought: concerning Schottländer. Instead: 'what is your opinion of Lang, the charge hand of the Jews at Bauer?' The whole situation of those days was immediately brought back to me. The question was asked by a very young, very likeably circumspect woman police officer and comrade. 'He has an important director's post, we're keeping a close eye on him.' I: he has a bad character [...], guardedly courteous towards me, harsh towards those socially beneath him ...[34] on the other hand: Caution with accusations against wearers of the star! It was doubtful whether Lang was guilty of any crime, 'Gestapo collaborator' is an unpleasant phrase. The young woman said, my reflections tallied with everything they had heard so far, but 'a close eye had to be kept on him'. Naturally we also talked about Neumark. Everyone had made statements in his favour, but the Russians are supposed to have relied on documents in Berlin which told against him. His fate unknown,[35] likewise that of his family.

[...]

24th August, Wednesday morning

[...] Today the Kulturbund car is supposed to take us to Halle.

Now what was the content and achievement of these last weeks?

The constant desperate and fruitless discussion of the pros and cons of retiring and moving. It is certain that E. inclines towards here. She is once again deep in building plans. Furthermore the house *must* be renovated in spring, if it is not to fall into disrepair. [...]

I read Ehrenburg [...]. Took very few notes. I leafed through *Les grands cimetières sous la lune* by Bernanos, of which I understood very little [...].

25th August 1949, Thursday evening. Halle

When I turned on the wireless in the afternoon, the prize winners were just being announced. Werner Krauss, Member of the Academy, because he has given literary history a fundamental sociological orientation. – It is very bitter – I have been defeated by the hostility of Leipzig: Frings, Wartburg.

[...]

30th August, Tuesday forenoon. Halle

Yesterday Kulturbund committee meeting. [...]

At this meeting I gave Agricola my resignation request.[36] He was 'shocked'. [...]

2nd September, Friday

[On Wednesday, 31 August, Klemperer attends the ceremony to welcome back the participants in the 2nd World Youth and Student Games in Budapest.[37]] After the song ['Youth of all Nations'], which presumably comes from the SU, and which I probably first heard at a Russian concert here, frequently after that, the ceremony appears to be over. But now music: fanfares and kettledrums from the hall doors and to the accompaniment of these strains the parade of flags. Of the music at the entrance to the hall I see the pale drumsticks rhythmically and repeatedly swung into the air and crossed. This movement, these crossed drumsticks in particular, does nothing but revive for me the image of the Nazi years. Hitler Youth and flags and march and anthem: certainly the Nazis stole it from the Bolsheviks. But the reminiscence of the Nazis remains more than unpleasant nevertheless. And the fundamental similarity of the totalitarian remains, les extrêmes se touchent.[38]

[...]

[Klemperer and his wife see the Polish film *The Last Stage*[39], an *'unbearable ... magnificent indictment of Auschwitz'*.] The film is a great work of art, but it will fail in its purpose. The malicious will say: An anti-*Jew Süss*, and just like the Nazi *Jew Süss*[40] mendacious and made to order. The mass in the middle will say: It may have been bad, but as bad as that – we don't believe it, that's impossible. And then: We want to forget it, we the innocent. And the truly well-meaning will simply be unable to bear it, it will weigh too terribly on their souls. All the solemn words which were spoken before and after will be of no use: this film will not be endured. Too much boundless bestiality is laid bare, and it is not universally Fascist, but specifically German,

specifically Nazi. Nothing but Ilse Kochs[41] and Heinrich Himmlers, proud and rational beasts. [...]
[...]

6th September, Tuesday morning
[...]
On LQI: TO LIBERATE. No one conquers any more, everyone 'liberates': the armies of the 'people's democracies' do it, the partisans did it [...] the West wants a *crusade* in order to *liberate* the Balkans, a crusade for Christendom, for Europe, for *Atlantic* culture.
[...]

9th September, Friday forenoon and later
Every most minor and every most important thing poses the question 100× a day: Halle or Dresden? And the answer always stands 50:50.
[...]
[Another Berlin trip: Calls on publishers in relation to translation work for Eva Klemperer.] Then to the Volk and Wissen publishing house. It was very important for me to talk to I. M. Lange, because the evening at home revealed the whole calamity of the *Modern French Poetry* and Teubner's fear. First I was too red for them, now I am too pink and bourgeois. The Hermlin condemnation remained unanswered, then behind my back they asked Th. Lücke for an expert opinion, he finds the book 'dangerous', now they want a discussion between the company, Lücke, I. M. Lange and myself to debourgeoisify the book! – How fortunate that yesterday I confirmed my shared interests with Lange. The three of us drank coffee in his room, on the 14th (KB executive meeting) he will drive here with us and stay the night. At stake is *his* doctorate, and my affair. For the time being I have swallowed my anger and not replied to Teubner. Then the *Büchergilde Gutenberg* [a book club]. [Here the Klemperers and the publisher agree on a translation (by Eva Klemperer, introduced by Victor Klemperer) of master novellas by Maupassant. Eva Kl. has fallen out with the Volk and Welt publishing house over her translation of Aragon ...]
[...]

16th September, 2 p.m. Friday
[...]
On Wednesday the KB executive meeting. The usual journey – with E. and Hoffmeister. Small group. About the National Prizes, about the federal conference, which is now at last supposed to take place and which is always postponed. They want people from the West present, want to make a demonstration. Abusch promised I would get the next free place in the Volksrat [People's Council]. [...] I complained that our drivers were badly fed and got the reply from Becher, that 'levelling' was out of place. [...] [I. M. Lange returns

to Halle with the Klemperers, reads through the Modern French Poetry.] [...] and then yesterday morning discussed everything over an endless breakfast. The business left a deep feeling of embitterment in me. Certainly, IM will speak up for me (he knows why) [...] but he says Lücke is 99.99% right; my book is 'dangerous' – I should revise, accentuate, cut etc. etc. when I get the proofs. [...] Awkward also is IM's desire for a Ph.D. For what? The Party can make him a professor without further ado, but for what should the faculty award him the *regular* degree of doctor (not, for example, a Dr h.c.) if he can present nothing of consequence? He imagines it's as easy as pie. [...] *And so on.*

Evening

[...] Georg was right: Steer clear of politics! I do not wish to go to the West, but I wish I could live somewhere infinitely far away from Germany.

Frau Ubben, very upset, weeping, came here in the car that drove me. Hoffmeister, who was supposed to be back from Berlin today and telegraphed that he would come tomorrow has, because of some gossip, come under suspicion of fleeing to the West with his wife. The gossip and what occasioned it is still completely confused and obscure, but that such a rumour arises immediately and is taken so very seriously is a characteristic feature of the situation.

22nd September, Thursday evening
The shocking Hoffmeister affair dominated the week.

[...]

Mon. and Tue. were then the real typhoon days. On Wed., the 14th, H. had driven to Berlin with E. and myself. He wanted to attend his secretariat meeting on Thurs., attend to some business at the Investitionsbank etc., return on Friday. He sent a telegram, saying that he would be here on Saturday. Immediately after that there were suspicious circumstances, a trades union official warned Frau Ubben, that, on an evidently untruthful pretext, H.'s mother-in-law had made a request to deposit furniture somewhere and sell it ... We waited until Monday, then Frau Ubben and Kreuzig drove to Allrode. H.'s parents lived there [...] H. had for a long time been trying to obtain an interzonal pass for his father, who had a gall-bladder complaint and was supposed to go to Mergentheim for treatment. Perhaps in Berlin H. had suddenly had an opportunity to help his father, or he had suddenly been called to the seriously ill man ... Result: the house completely empty, the neighbours said: 'They sold everything, are over the border!' [...] Their 'clearing out' was long premeditated, therefore. Then to the Party offices, Leni Berg.[42] She laughed in my face, when I talked about trust betrayed. There was no such thing in politics, one could be betrayed by the closest comrades after years of working together. She wanted me to go to zonal headquarters with Frau Ubben herself ... We left at 6 on Tue. morning – I was supposed to speak in Thale at 8 ... In Berlin no one was at all surprised, neither Gysi nor Willmann. H. had simply lost his nerve, he had had enough, he had a brother in Hanover who was on the editorial staff of a newspaper ... and it happens all the time now. [...]

25th September, Sunday forenoon
[...]

On Friday morning another little faculty meeting. [... Discussion of Auerbach as Klemperer's successor.] I should actually be glad, that they are willing to let me go – I also immediately spoke in favour of Auerbach, and Weyhe, the old English scholar said: 'he also has a very good reputation as a real philologist, even Wartburg praises him!' – so actually I should be glad, but I felt as if I were lying in my coffin, and the journalist is going to have a real scholar as his successor.

[...]

2nd October, Sunday forenoon
The essentials of recent days:

[Klemperer notes the 'fiasco' of the 'World Day of Peace' following only a month after the 'German' Day of Peace.] The worn-out formulae of the functionaries no longer have any effect. Old Goebbels merchandise. [...]

... For some days now [...] the existence of the Russian atom bomb is constantly being thrown onto the scales on the side of peace – a monstrous comedy.

[...]

4th October, Tuesday after dinner
Just the thing! The Bonn West state *must* be opposed by an East state. On the other hand: 'East state' means acknowledgement of the West state, of the division. Which is why the SED had refused [...] Now yesterday the solution. The government and popular representation for the whole of Germany will be constituted in the capital of the whole of Germany, Berlin. A fiction – but it means action. [...] At all events linguistically and politically this is a turning point, something new. [...]

Towards evening
Call from Kirsch: News agency representative with him: at the request of the central government in Berlin the Kulturbund must issue an immediate declaration. I: [What about] The Executive Committee, the members, democracy! – [Reply] Time short, tomorrow crucial Volksrat session. – Who has sent the man? – Soviet Military Administration. I hesitate. Democracy? On the other hand: I am certainly in favour. I dictated over the telephone: 'The Kulturbund of Saxony-Anhalt also urgently demands the immediate establishment of a government and a popular representative body for the whole of Germany in the national capital of the whole of Germany, Berlin. Signed, the first regional chairman Victor Klemperer.' Thus did the populace spontaneously surge, that is democracy – thus and no differently was also how it was done in Hitler's day. Except that now it is the real republic that is at stake. – I'm curious to see whether I meet my end in bed or on the gallows. But fundamentally it's all one.

And I am convinced, that ultimately, ideologically and practically, I am on the right side. 'And practically' the conviction is not quite as solid as ideologically. 23 million Germans at most are supposed to be living here, 40 million in the Western zones. Of the 23 million in the East, 10 million at the very outside are truly Russophile and truly Communist.

[...]

6th October, Thursday
[...] Yet I am convinced that very few know what a declaration of war this 'thing' [conversion of Volksrat into Volkskammer – People's Chamber – establishment of an East German state] is. Most people are apathetic. In the West they'll say: Russian orders, Russian comedy. (Are they entirely in the wrong?)

[...]

10th October, Monday evening
[...]
My birthday yesterday. Winter here in the morning, Rita and Robi in the afternoon. Vahlen the day before. People are very effusive, court me – but are letting me go nevertheless and thinking of Auerbach. I feel very much at the end of my tether. My heart, my skin complaint, my 68 years.

[...]

12th October, Wednesday evening
'The German Democratic Republic'[43]. There's been nothing else on the wireless since yesterday. The presidential election, the parades, the speeches. I do not feel comfortable with it. I know how everything is fixed and how spontaneity and unanimity are prepared. I know that under the Nazis it sounded just the same and proceeded in just the same way. I know how little reality there is behind it. 20 million are not even a third of the German people, and of the 20 at least 12 are anti-Soviet. I know that internally the Democratic Republic is a lie, the SED supports and desires a Socialist republic, it does not trust the middle-class parties, and the middle-class parties distrust it. At some point there will be civil war. I was sent a mischief-making sheet from Berlin – 'Resistance of the oppressed' ... 'Copy this' ... Remember who the traitors are ... the SED crimes will be punished, etc. etc. Editorial address, Zehlendorf [in Berlin]. Postmark Berlin. Sender Dr Rita Hetzer Halle. I telephoned Rita. She had received the same leaflet. Sender Prof. Bennedik. Presumably *and so on*. The dispatcher must be very well informed about the situation here and wants to confuse and scare us. US. I am counted one of the Russian lackeys, I have been marked down, I shall probably 'not die in my bed'.

[...]

14th October, Friday midday

[A Kulturbund Executive Committee meeting the previous day. Familiar inconclusive debates, notes Klemperer.] [...] Afterwards with E. to Anny Klemperer's for half an hour. A very instructive half-hour. Anny repeats with bitter conviction what the West says; I also glanced at the *Kurier*. The Democratic Republic is 'illegal', is a Russian and Communist sham and fiction – Bonn on the other hand is democratically elected, expresses the will of the people. And the Americans truly want to help us, and in America there is 'freedom'. And here people 'disappear' into the uranium mines, and here the old people and the bereaved of the army, of officers in particular are starving – here the distress of her own relatives and friends is weighing heavily on A. – Wretched opposition of the two Germanies, wretched and hopeless. – E. used the day to break finally with the Volk und Welt publishing house (Aragon); she would rather not have any payment for the work done than have those people botching her work. She had further discussions with the Kinderbuch and Dietz publishers. The Quiroga is coming out, the Izcaray ditto.[44] She is very proud and fulfilled – but her heart problems are getting worse. During the discussion yesterday I myself had very ominous angina pains. [...]

[...]

20th October, Thursday towards evening

The first step of my withdrawal has been taken. [...] I shall no longer lecture in Leipzig. [Nevertheless the form and occasion of the decision was not a happy one for Klemperer: rather opaque hostilities and intrigues.] If I had not felt the Leipzig affair to be defamatory and had I not been dead tired of the whole wretched Leipzig undertaking, I would have gone on lecturing even for less salary. But rebus sic stantibus,[45] I take the whole matter as a sign of fate. [...]

[...]

28th October, 11.15 Friday evening

[...]

What, however, touches me more than all of this, although I do not want to admit it, although I again and again repress it, is, since Tuesday (or is it already longer ago?) the Neubert affair [...], N. has gone over to the 'Free University of Berlin'. It can be assumed [according to the telephone conversation], that he will be expelled from the Academy, that I will be admitted in his place, and his chair given to me. I consider it to be out of the question, *want* to consider it out of the question and am nevertheless poisoned by the thought. [...]

6th November, midday Sunday

E.'s heart attack yesterday over dinner at the Soviet Friendship Society has shaken me very badly. She was sitting happily beside me. Frau Behnke opposite us says: She's not well. E. has fallen back in her chair, her eyes fixed, her mouth is open, she gasps for air, is pale, unconscious. I feared heart failure. Behnke and Ludwig Einicke to her. We were sitting near the door. After a while the two of them took her out. She recovered in the armchair by the window. Then she got worse again, a choking vomiting. It had been exactly the same at the Revolution anniversary last year, I had taken her with me this time only with some considerable anxiety and inner reluctance. We then drove home, she slept well, is still sleeping now – but my anxiety remains, and E.'s bitterness remains. Always the pressure: 'How much longer?' and 'Who will be the first to go?' And every philosophical and now even religious consolation is lacking. Eva said yesterday: 'I have had an altogether interesting life.' Once I had got her to bed at 2, I completed – flightily and devoid of feeling – my Molière essay, then put together my revolution talk for today and did not go to bed until 4.15.

[Eva Klemperer collapsed at the reception to mark the 32nd anniversary of the October Revolution. Klemperer describes this stiff event – at the officers' club of the Soviet Military Administration in Halle – in some detail.]

10th November, midday Thursday
[...]

In Berlin they don't want me as Neubert's successor, I'm too old, they would soon have to change again. They want to make do with guest professors and are thinking of Auerbach for later on. They are doing that here, too. Yesterday a letter from Lerch: he had proposed Auerbach for Munich 2 years ago, one could not blame a Jew for not wanting to come.

[...]

15th November, Thursday forenoon
Friday (11th) poorly attended final Kulturbund Executive Committee meeting of the session. Under discussion was the drawing-up of the lists for the election. [...]

Abusch informed me: Russian objection, the name Barbusse must not be mentioned in connection with Stalin's birthday. My essay will not be printed [...] Abusch himself had to remove all references to Barbusse in his Stalin monograph, my Barbusse for Aufbau is naturally now also untenable. My kind of freedom! I. M. Lange writes with respect to my *Modern French Poetry*, one could perhaps come to an agreement ... with Lücke ... Now that we are *sovereign*, this thraldom will presumably get even worse. – Only: is one any more free in the West? The best thing would be: to work only for my desk and for posterity.

[...]

The wheel of fortune at Anny Klemperer's. *I* am paying Peter's tuition fees

(215M) and A. asks me in a letter virtually point-blank, whether I can also pay for the necessary books. I am received quite officially by Peter and his girlfriend, who absolutely counts as the illegal daughter-in-law.

[...]

I said to Becher: Your national anthem is splendid:[46] two strands of tradition: 'Deutschland über alles'[47] and Luther chorale. Very simple verses. But the broken rhythm of the concluding line and the emphasis on peace is modern. – 'Yes (he said), it is all very cunningly done.' I was pleased, that he did not affect the poet, but acknowledged the craft. [...]

Towards evening on Saturday I had Rita Hetzer here. Her research assistantship and post-doctoral degree programme. Dependent on me and my staying. I myself am making my staying dependent on a place in the Academy. She set out her work schedule. The habilitation thesis is to be 'George Sand'.[48]

[...]

23rd–27th November, Wednesday to Sunday. Congress. The Berlin days

[The Second Federal Congress of the Kulturbund ... On the Wednesday evening Klemperer takes part in a confidential meeting – 'only a few *reliable* comrades' – to fix who will get on the lists for election to the committee. Half *these* decisions are later overturned.] I then drove to I. M. Lange and we discussed all my business. Marx from Teubner had called on him – all my Teubner things are to go to Riemerschmidt [Rütten & Loening publishing house]. [...]

[...]

10th December, Saturday forenoon. Halle [...]

[...] Accumulated correspondence: Emma Vossler. Otto Klemperer London. He would like to see East Germany for himself and asks whether he will have any 'difficulties'. Evidently – and he even says so – he has no idea of our circumstances. He mentions the *'iron curtain'*.

[...]

16th December, Friday night

E.'s state of health is not good and is worsened by being tied to the house so much by the foggy weather. [...] Her depression affects me, and I already feel bad enough anyway: this terrible inability to produce and the bitterness of having come to the end. [...]

A letter from Berthold Meyerhof, touching and tormenting. He sends us a package and writes us an article [as if] from an encyclopaedia about a stretch of land he had got to know. What else should he write to us. He views the world in which we live with complete incomprehension and hostility, we no longer have any common ideas, interests. We are so utterly isolated, the people of our world are dead or for us intellectually dead. Scherner†, Annemarie†, a few Meyerhofs still alive, but no longer for us. And where is Sebba, where is Frau Schaps? etc, etc. And sometimes the most tormenting thought of all: What am I still to E., and how far does she share my thoughts? I am often so tired now, physically and mentally. I have a horror of the nothingness and nevertheless wish everything were over. I try to persuade myself to believe in the Soviet cause, but in my heart of hearts I don't believe in anything and everything appears to me equally trivial and equally false. The ghastly similarity to Nazi methods in the propaganda for the Soviet Friendship Society, in the hullabaloo around Stalin's birthday cannot be denied.

22nd December, Thursday afternoon to 23rd December, Friday afternoon

Drawing breath in a state of complete exhaustion. In good humour incidentally. I do have some effect after all, and an atom of me will remain after all. Even if I do not get to Berlin and into the Academy, even if I no longer receive the National Prize, which is becoming like the Iron Cross, Second Class. Why this momentary peak? Because I had a speaking success yesterday, and because my *LTI* and my and E.'s Cassou[49] are in the newly opened works library of Agfa Wolfen. [...]

[...]

Mond. aft. unprepared to the Descartes seminar; afterwards the dreaded Romance Languages and Literatures Department Christmas party. [...]

On Tue. to Berlin for the Soviet Friendship Society's Stalin celebration. [... Commenting on the cancellation of a visit by the new President of the GDR, Wilhelm Pieck, to the Soviet Union, Klemperer comments:] *I* found the announcement of the visit somewhat servile. Perhaps Moscow said to itself: Stalin would have to return *this* visit and things haven't got to that point yet. (But when I said that to Steinitz, he said: why shouldn't Pieck travel to Moscow, if Mao Tse (or whatever the new Chinaman is called) does? [But] *He* represents a greater power than Pieck after all. Curious: this treatment of China and Germany as equals moved me; the old estimations of worth are very deep seated, and in this case are also intellectually justified. *We*, the piccolo mondo antico,[50] we after all founded culture, we white people from Palestine and Europe. [...] I sat beside Steinitz and talked a great deal with him. The Berlin chair: Auerbach – if he does not come, Krauss or I. But, and this was the unpleasant new note: 'Our comrades, too, are only lukewarm in their support of you, you must have done something in Greifswald.' So because of that! Franz Wohlgemuth ... Furthermore they are only going to appoint guest professorships for the time being. [...] On Monday it was long past 2 by the time I got to bed. [On Tuesday] I was again very late, and the Wednesday, Stalin's 70th birthday, was a great strain.

[...]

The Thüringer Volksverlag [publisher] at last sent the Rameau with my Diderot sketch.[51] Reading it over cheered me up: whether they fetch me to Berlin or not, I know what I am capable of and what will remain of me.

[...]

26th December, Monday evening

[Klemperer is exhausted by giving talks on German and Soviet peace policies.] After that, serious work on the Maupassant. In an express letter Victor[52] presses us to deliver by 4 Jan. – and after all 20,000M is involved. Thus the struggle to complete this study [i.e. the foreword] fills the Christmas days. – In the evening we had the goose, we put up the two pictures, instead of a tree we had a little wreath, in which E. had placed brightly coloured baubles, as if in an Easter egg nest, and on which she had mounted candles. The evening passed tolerably – what more can one ask of such an obligatory festive evening? [...]

31st December, midnight precisely, Saturday

Our New Year's Eve: All day long (and already yesterday) E.'s terribly tormenting coughing as she ceaselessly took down my dictation: the Maupassant study, become much too long and heavy for its popular purpose, has to be delivered in quadruplicate; I have spent the whole of these holidays struggling to finish it. [...]

1949 saw the Goethe rumpus, which was given a political twist; for 1950 there has been likewise heralded, for the last few days in the newspaper, just now most solemnly on the Leipzig broadcasting station, the Bach rumpus.[53] For a united German culture. [...]

Eva, quite apart from her cough at the moment, is very sickly, the coronary dilation troubles her every day – and I am repeatedly in pain while walking and climbing stairs. How much longer? And who will be first? And then nothing.

And while I should be indifferent to everything, I was nevertheless tormented by the defeats of this past year: the failure to get the National Prize, to get the seat in the Academy, to get the Berlin chair. And yet I know, that in truth none of all this is due to me, that never in my life have I been a philologist. And that I owe the successes which have come to me since 45 solely to the absolute lack of competitors in the East.

My feeling and my situation with respect to retirement and the move to Dresden are quite uncertain. It tempts me and I fear it in equal measure. – The complete decline in my ability to write, the failure of my memory for names. [...]

We are so terribly alone. Most of our circle are dead, the living either unattainably remote – Martha, Walter Jelski, Sebba -or even more remote because of their hostility to the Soviet Union: Berthold Meyerhof, the Frankes.

What have I produced in 1949? Hardly anything new. A couple of lectures, which I then gave dozens of times 'and more' in x places, even more frequently for the Soviet Friendship Society than for the Kulturbund. Hundreds of repetitions and combinations and the same things over again. *That*, probably only *that*, is what I can still manage. And if in Dölzschen I no longer have that, and I can no longer write? [...]

Political high point of my appearances was the 21 Dec. In front of 6000 workers at Wolfen Agfa and in the Halberstadt theatre. – I also became First Regional Chairman of the KB only this year – last year, because it is now 1.40 a.m.

1950

7th January, Saturday evening

I do not quite remember the content of this first January week. [Klemperer notes nevertheless continuing dictation of the Maupassant study, a political committee meeting and writing a newspaper article.]

[...]

Deutschlands Stimme [Germany's Voice] has written to me: eyewitness article for 13 Feb. 1950, Dresden's destruction. I read over my diary, read it to E., rather. Until now in some difficulty. Because I do not want to write about the Jewish memory, I must remain general. But that means worn-out material.

11th January, Wednesday forenoon. Halle

On Sunday, the 8th, wrote the article 'Shrove Tuesday, Dresden 1945'.[1] Successfully.

[...]

12th January, Thursday forenoon

[...]

Yesterday evening at the Kulturbund. Bloch, Leipzig, on modern philosophy. Against Heidegger, Jaspers – 'The Category of Hope'. I understood only with difficulty, but [...] the man impressed me immensely. Furthermore, profound humanist knowledge. Large grey head, probably early 60s. Personally acquainted with Georg and Otto musico (at present in Sydney). The session in front of a 150 man hall lasted until 11.30. I learnt a great deal, more precisely picked it up.

[...]

17th January, Tuesday. Halle

[... Kulturbund meetings, appointments with I. M. Lange, with Walther Victor.] The new Executive Committee hardly any different from the old one – still poorly attended ... Nothing of interest occurred ... [...] I agreed a Maupassant study in *Sinn und Form* with Becher. – At the Frankes in the late afternoon. Hostile foreign land. Worse than the three old women their unlovely niece, Walter's daughter, 25 years old. Derisive rejection of the Russians. I made my opinion very clear. The girl employed by the Americans for five years. Sad, this absolute separation in one and the same city. [...]

Yet another Berlin pleasure: suddenly I'm told: we were too nervous about Barbusse, you can write the monograph. – And who will give me the time for it? – I must get out of this empty rushing around.

[...]

31st January, Tuesday forenoon

Continuing frost, 12 below zero, failing heating. Myself with a heavy cold. Increasing worry about E., she evidently has a serious heart problem.

[...]

3rd February, Friday evening

Frost, ice, snow, failing heating; E. in the little room, I at my desk in my coat. E.'s condition unchanged. She has become very fat, walks with a stoop, does not get out of the house, is often in pain. – We have finally given notice on this apartment, negotiations with removers have commenced. In the summer semester I shall have a room in the Stadt Hamburg hotel. [...]

We eat too well, we don't know what to do with our money, and Frau Stahl is a voracious soul of a slave, happy if she can go shopping and cook for and dine with her rich master and mistress. [...] But in a few weeks things will come to an end here, and it will be impossible to keep house in the same way in Dölzschen.

[...]

8th February, Wednesday forenoon

Worry about Eva.

[...]

A letter from Walther Victor which put us both out of humour: our book had disappointed him. Me he accused of making the Maupassant study too sombre and of neglecting the social historical aspect. Both nonsense. In Eva's text there were errors in the translation and instances of poor style and both had to be 'retouched'. The ms was being set – we would find the 'retouches' in the proofs ... That is very offensive and will lead to a quarrel.

[...]

16th February, Thursday
Semper idem: With all the pursuit of trivia I forgot the day of father's death, 12 Feb. Dear Lord – if one could imagine him watching you! *He* would be amused. *I* feel embarrassed by this rushing about, this emptiness, this vanity, this nothingness around me and before me. – Mon. the 13th was very bad. Unproductive work on the final lecture (Beaumarchais[2]) [...]. Then I drove to the departmental party of my Romanists in the refectory. Actually they are very sweet. The catering: a plate of potato salad, half a roll (literally – no sausage, nothing) a glass of beer. Later they also got some ersatz coffee and rubbery tasteless cakes. [...] Yet nevertheless content and cheerful. About 20 students, the elderly lecturer Rummel, Popinceanu, Macchi, Rita – very pretty and with a deep décolleté Jo Agricola. I don't fit in. [...] I fled. Home at midnight very depressed. [...]

18th February, midnight Saturday
On the evening of Thurs. 16 at the Leipzig KB high school group [...] at least 200 people, Bloch chaired – 'Nation and Language'. Success. In the discussion Bloch was somewhat too polemically wordy and almost ill-humoured, [alleging] I had set the language of the intelligentsia above the more vigorous one of the people. [...] I defended myself briskly and was applauded. [...]

The semester has come to an end.

24th February, Friday forenoon
[...] My time is increasingly claimed by meetings in which the same thing is chewed over and over again, in which I sleep, which I must *nevertheless* attend and at which from time to time I pick up a crumb. *Must* I really? Yes, if I am still out for a political career. Why am I still? Ambition? Fear of real work, of failing at creative work??

[... Klemperer is deeply impressed in more than one respect by an FDJ commemoration of the Scholl resistance group on Wed. evening, 22 February.] [...] The ceremony on Wednesday was downright martial. Honecker[3] had announced in Berlin: we are fighters for peace, we have grasped hammer and spade, we shall pick up rifles *only* to defend peace ... [...] Further: At Whitsun Berlin will belong to the 500,000 [All-German Youth Meeting], all Berlin with all its streets. We will knock the truncheon out of the hands of Stumm's police.[4] And if they drive at us with police vehicles – the Ruhr miners have shown us how to overturn them. And the tanks Schuhmacher has threatened will not prevent the youth of the West from coming to us! [...] 'We will march through all of Berlin in our thousands.' Is that not absolutely a 'March on Berlin'? The tone has changed. Behind the tone there must be *divisions* (which call themselves unarmed People's Police ...) It smacks of civil war. The minute's silence very impressive. The hall in semi-darkness, *one* flag at a time dipping as the names are read out, the flags consistently called the *'blue battle flags'* of the FDJ. Altogether strong emphasis on closeness to the Komsomols, on its own *proletarian* character and on Communism, nothing non-partisan at all. This really in contradiction to the National Front. It pleased *me*. [...] Meanwhile I have been presented with another honour so late and so much from sheer necessity, that now what I long for to some extent leaves me cold. Letter from Friedrich, Rector of Berlin University: invitation to give 'a guest lecture at the Humboldt University'. [...] *After* Krauss, who is lecturing just now, and *only* because Auerbach is not coming and not because there is no one else. And it says: *one* guest lecture? I have asked for details. [...]

4th March, Saturday
[...] My heart feels very heavy. Vahlen called on me yesterday, they are trying to keep me, want to transport me around in a university car, I am also a rectorial candidate (only my Party membership is against it!) – all of that goads me on, tickles my vanity – on the other hand: separation from E., impossibility of writing. I do not achieve anything any more. [...]

7th March, Dresden–Dölzschen Am Kirschberg

8th March, Wednesday evening
So, back in Dölzschen again. Last chapter? Chapter at all? Or the same old rut, only a little more uncomfortable than before?

Very disagreeable days. [...]

Mon. the 2 packers, Tuesday the whole crowd of removal people, 6 or 7 apart from the packers. Then in the aft. with Kreuzig at the wheel and with lots of luggage and the cat, we drove to Dresden. [...] to Gusti. Weisser Hirsch, Collenbuschstr. Welcome, conversations, warmth – everything just as a couple of months ago. We stayed the night there, our tomcat got on with Gusti's black cat. No comfortable bed, no time to wash, Gusti's tenant is head driver at the Dresden Broadcasting Station. He drove us here at 7. The big removal van with the trailer and the helper tractor appeared at 10 with 7 people; unloading took until 2. We've acquired quite an imposing amount of property in these last few years. We had nothing at all any more and are now very amply furnished. Almost too amply. [...]

11th March, Saturday evening. Dresden
[...]

Yesterday, Friday the 10th, Executive Committee meeting in Berlin. There with Kneschke (and wife). Picked up at 5.45 a.m. [However, probably the most interesting thing about this trip for Klemperer was the agreement on his guest professorship in Berlin:] I shall lecture for 4 hours once weekly: Romance Influences on Germany and [Lessing's] 'Hamburg Dramaturgy'. Just as in Halle. On Tue. in Berlin, on Wed. and Thurs. in Halle. But the transport question is unsolved. Meusel [the dean] told me, Krauss has 4 guest hours. I am therefore not ranked lower. [...]

The next few months – until June – will show whether I can achieve the heights of the vita activa and of outward honours in which I would bask for another year or so – striven for and interlocking: the badge of honour of the FDJ, the National prize, the rectorate, the Moscow delegation, the seat in the Academy [...], the seat in the Volkskammer [People's Chamber] – or whether I sink back into nothingness and plunge into my scribbling. This *or* would be far and away more sensible and better for my posthumous fame.

[...]

19th March, Sunday evening. Dresden

Chaos and cold until two days ago; since the day before yesterday springlike, but the chaos almost the same as on the first day. None of my uncertainties resolved. [...] Nothing has been unpacked ... I am most wearisomely labouring over the essay 'Humanism'. We sit opposite one another with our typewriters. E.'s mill clatters away with Spanish. Mine makes a sound every couple of minutes. [...] The villagey-neighbourly life up here is hardly changed. We sit quietly at home, Eva working hard, I making an effort to work hard.

[...]

31st March, Friday forenoon. Dresden

[Extensive reading as ever – Klemperer finds himself developing an antipathy to Goethe – completion of Humanism essay and an article on Lessing. Also the final break in relations with the Teubner publishing house.]

Yesterday Frank Forbrig was here for a very long time. He has resigned from the SED [...], very uncertain whether this the right thing to do. He evidently has qualms. There is boundless rabble-rousing and slander from the Right, they call the new Ministry of Security [Staatssicherheit] the *SS Ministry*. [...]

3rd April, 1 a.m. Monday night. Halle

[...]

Tomorrow into the unknown. An SED courier car is taking me to Berlin at 8. I have been clearing up until now. – Worry about E., who was in considerable pain yesterday evening. – For whom all the building, for whom without her? But the building work gives her pleasure. She lives more naively than I.

[...]

6th April, Thursday, 7 p.m. and (mainly) 7th April, Good Friday. Halle. Romance Languages and Literatures Department. My room

[... Berlin: Quarrel with the new editor of the Kulturbund periodical *Sinn und Form*, Peter Huchel,[5] over the Maupassant article Becher had commissioned; I.

M. Lange promises once again that Riemerschmidt (of Rütten & Loening) will take VK's Literary History and his French Poetry. Meanwhile the Maupassant translation by Eva Kl. with an introduction by Victor Kl. has now been bought for bookshop sale in addition to the book club.] Here *we* contractually have a share in the profit. Never before has a book made us so much money and been a cause of such aggravation. [... Rita Hetzer and her partner gave Victor Kl. a lift back to Halle.] Then there was another halt because of a flat tyre. At this point, under a full moon on the autobahn, Rita told me that she feared – Robi did not yet know – she was expecting a child. 'My post-doctoral!' I told her it could be combined very nicely and she should be happy. Incidentally the couple will be able to marry in a couple of weeks, husband no. 1, 'missing' for so long, has now been declared dead. At the 'Stadt Hamburg' at 3 on the dot.

The Stadt Hamburg is a big hotel opposite the main post office. Rented by the university. Institutes, rooms for a number of students, for guest professors. It was a battle before I was given a room for the whole semester. It is an 'apartment' with bath, but unfortunately without warm water and without an electric plug. I have to pay 80M for it, but live altogether elegantly. The university is especially generous in its provision of food coupons for the Stadt Hamburg. [...] Curious: to be living like this in the centre of a city. I have not done so for endless years now [...]. Above all no peace and concentration. Too much consultation, arrangements, change-over, too much 'chatting'. [...] Efforts are being made on my behalf. The university car will take me to Dresden ever Friday and fetch me from Berlin every Tue. evening. [...]

8th April, 7 a.m. Saturday morning. Stadt Hamburg

[...]

This first outside week ends today. It really is quite uncomfortable and depressing. I have often felt very cold, food is difficult – above all always the weight on my mind: when will you be home? Certainly: I telephoned E. on Thur. evening, but it is not like being together after all. And nor do I believe that I shall get down to serious work. But perhaps everything will work itself out. Perhaps I should long for nothing more ardently, than *not* becoming rector. But I am afraid of disappearing completely. Leaving Halle [University] means giving up the Kulturbund chairmanship etc. [...]

11th April, Tuesday evening. Dresden

[...]

For many years I have been tormented by my ignorance. I am forever thinking: will I manage to conceal it this time, too? I am like a gambler, who leaves his winnings on the table and continues playing the roulette wheel. I devoted all of today to the lecture 'Romance Influences'. It's pure repetition, but also costs me a whole day's preparation. [...]

I. M. Lange sent me his Fontane[6] dissertation.

[...]

In our garden beautiful spring. But very cold April weather.

Very odd this brief being-on-a-visit. My life very absurd. This therefore Easter 1950.

[...]

16th April, Sunday afternoon. Dresden

[...] Here tiredness, I. M. Lange – in order really to enjoy his thesis I would have to know Fontane's novels in detail; good sociological and historical analysis, as literary history it dangles in the air; I constantly have to repeat: Lukács[7] is the concentrated antidote to aesthetic contemplation, but simply no more than an antidote [...]. Mere mechanical repetition of Marx–Engels. And what narrowness, [to say] that a writer is capable of describing *only his own class*! Altogether *class* here is what *breed* is for the Nazis. That belongs in my LQI and one is not allowed to say it. [...] since I've been sitting around in the department all day, there has been increasing intimacy, I use the familiar 'du' [you] with nearly all the seminar students; when an older comrade addressed me as 'Victor' during a class, it did indeed give me an odd feeling, but there were only half a dozen of the most loyal present [...].

26th April, 8 p.m. Wednesday evening. Seminar room, Halle

The days in Dresden very depressed because of E.'s poor health. The terrible cough which affects her heart. And the conflict inside me, the bad conscience. [...] The lecture [at Berlin Univ.] came off this time. About 50 people in a lecture theatre that was far too big. I think they kept up. Seminar on Lessing,[8] a good dozen or so. I spoke almost alone. As yet there is nothing good or bad to be said. But the aura of Berlin University has gone for me. I seem to get along better *here* ... Return journey from Berlin immediately after the classes. [...] Then here from 3–7. Tremendous attendance at my lecture, certainly over 120 people (chairs dragged in, sitting on the steps). I spoke astonishing wisdom about the Provençals. [...]

28th April, 7 a.m. Friday. Stadt Hamburg, Halle

[...]

[More talks in different towns; seminar on the novella and Maupassant. Ever present in Klemperer's mind is the question of the rectorship. However, his colleague Jo Agricola suggests that her husband also has considerable achievements to his name and perhaps Klemperer should rather give the world another couple of books.]

29th April, Saturday evening. Dresden

Yesterday drive to Dresden. Usual construction chaos. Eva better. [...]

Notice of death of Martha Wiechmann (63 years)
My generation – one after the other. [. . .]

4th–5th May, 3 p.m. Thursday. Director's room, Halle

Excessive tiredness, excessive rushing around, pains – how much longer? The rectorial election will be a trial by ordeal. Prospect *fifty-fifty* – Agricola is no longer my opponent, but someone from the bourgeois parties or a natural scientist.

In Halle I finished reading Makarenko,[9] but I find Wilhelm Meister[10] repugnant. Then drudgery on the lecture. [. . .] Then Neumark's secretary Frau Jährig was here, anxious because the Association of Victims of Nazi Persecution intends to check to what extent she was involved in his affairs. She told us: N. is supposed to have been sentenced to 10 years and so far only to have served 3 or 4 of them. Presumably in Russia. His wife and his stepson, Dr Kretzschmar, in Munich, K. working for a ministry. [. . .]

The wireless on the evening of 1 May. First the Rias: Today 500,000 free people demonstrated for freedom on the Platz der Republik – while 'behind the Iron Curtain at the Brandenburg Gate' people were compelled to march, and 'some will have remembered a comrade from last year who is now doing forced labour in the camps or mines' . . .

[Klemperer's lecture and seminar at the Humboldt University are a success, but his satisfaction is clouded:] [. . .] then I learned from Frau Steinhoff, that Krauss is functioning as deputy professor and department head. That weighed very heavily on my spirits again. I should free myself of this damned vanitas. – Frau Steinhoff told me, her husband, previously first minister of Brandenburg, was now Interior Minister of the Republic. SED. Evidently a Jewish lawyer and Victim of Fascism, in some way close to the Schaps family (with its former Reich Supreme Court judge).[11] [. . .]

10th May, midday Wednesday. Director's Room, Halle; ditto 11th May, Thursday

[A new Maupassant problem has arisen, this time not to do with the article for *Sinn und Form*, but in the form of objections by Wendt, the editor at Aufbau Verlag, to Klemperer's introduction to Eva Klemperer's translation of Maupassant novellas.[12]]

The man is seeing pink elephants! I, I! glorify the SS, an anti-Marxist, etc. Sentences torn out of context, arbitrary emphases. [. . .] The letter was waiting for me on Friday night. Gusti W. was with us on Saturday evening. I: 'we are in a madhouse.' G. 'It's quite natural, it was just the same in Russia, it is impossible to avoid such a stage. Restrain yourself as much as possible, keep in the background – soon the people who have not made fools of themselves now or who have not compromised themselves will be needed.' She advised me to withdraw the piece. As already said, my free days were entirely soured, E. found me intolerable . . . Lotte also visited us.

[...]
[Going to Berlin on 9 May, Klemperer notes the rigorous checks on travellers to the city from the Eastern Zone of the GDR. At a Kulturbund meeting Klemperer's Maupassant introduction is heavily criticised for lacking a Marxist evaluation of Maupassant's views.]
[...]

18th May, Thursday afternoon, Ascension Day. Dresden, with the obligatory thunderstorm

[Klemperer gives up his resistance over the Maupassant introduction, and thinking of rectorship and National Prize tells I. M. Lange:] – *'Do what you like with it, I give you carte blanche and will let myself be surprised, I don't want to see the thing any more.'* [...]

[His faculty in Halle recommends Klemperer for the National Prize. But there are other honours for Klemperer. The chairman of the Student Council and of the FDJ (Communist youth organisation) at Halle University presents Klemperer, who is honorary chairman of the student FDJ, with an official invitation to the all-German meeting of the organisation. Klemperer would have a place on the VIP rostrum, though he would not yet have honorary membership, the first batch of such awards would go to senior political figures.] They then brought me the blue shirt [of the FDJ], I had to put it on immediately and wear it in the department, am wearing it even now. [...]

24th May, Wednesday forenoon. Dresden

On Monday I read in the *Tägliche Rundschau*, that the Central Committee of the FDJ in Berlin had presented honorary memberships not to 2 or 3 ministers, but to x people, to Tom, Dick and Harry, but not to the crétin moi.[13] I contracted a 'kidney inflammation' and sent a corresponding telegram to Berlin and an express letter to Rita Hetzer, had my lectures cancelled and am now sitting here quietly without interruption [...] until 1st June (from 18 May). I find the great quietness, after the excessive activity of recent months, very difficult, but I shall get used to it. The failure in the FDJ business, very bitter for me, once again accentuates what I suffered last year with respect to the National Prize. This is now the beginning, perhaps already the verdict in my 'trial by ordeal'. Serves me right. Why am I always chasing after vanitas?

Perhaps more bitter than this defeat is my great divergence from the SED on all intellectual matters. But I cannot just move over to the West – it is even more repugnant to me. In the SED it is only scholarship, only the temporary hysteria, the 150%ers, that I loathe, but over there it is *everything*. But this 'only scholarship' sours the rest of my life and keeps me after all in my old place 'between stools', or, rather, it throws me back there, after I appeared to have succeeded in getting a better place to sit. [...]

I have just had the vexation of the Maupassant. On Saturday I wrote my discussion notes on the 'sick German language': they will no doubt not be printed thanks to the '150% purism'. On Sunday I wrote the article 'West German spoken here', for *Aufbau*, the review of the Hausenstein anthology *The Drunken Boat*. It will no doubt not be printed, because I include Rimbaud among the Decadents, and Stephan Hermlin for one (inter alia honorary member of the FDJ) swears by him and Eluard. I have especially rotten luck with French poetry – whatever I do, always in splendid isolation between stools! [...] I shall be forced back into the situation of the Hitler years: working for my desk drawer. Perhaps someone will publish it one day.

[...]

27th May, Saturday morning. Dresden

[...]

Reading: Sayers and Kahn *The Great Conspiracy Against Russia*.[14] Where does the truth lie?? It all seems like a novel by Sue.[15] I do not see what Trotsky's[16] power was based on. I do not see how Lenin–Stalin could maintain themselves against him, *if* he really had that power. I do not see how Stalin could hesitate so long before beginning the counter-offensive and then still be able to win. I cannot explain the behaviour of the accused in the Moscow Trials.[17] Nor Trotsky's end.[18] And above all: what was the substantial dispute between Lenin/Stalin and Trotsky? What is, what did Trotskyism want?[19] Again and again I miss a clear answer.

[Klemperer regards with a degree of equanimity the spiralling costs of repairs to the Dölzschen house.] We are secure – to the extent that there still is any security. At all events there is a sufficient financial reserve – for whom should we save it? If E. gets enjoyment from building, let her build. There is nothing I would have to do without because of it. [...]

At least a year ago Hans Meyerhof wrote me a letter, which I did not answer because of its strangeness and empty phrases. Yesterday from Dresden City Council the copy of a letter from Hans Meyerhof, commercial representative, Palermo, to the Lord Mayor. He inquires a second time, whether anything is known of the friend of his youth, the Romance literatures scholar, Victor Klemperer. Provides particulars about himself: 70 years of age, 4 years in a concentration camp, not only as racially persecuted but also for his political stance, his family in Germany exterminated ... I shall have to reply.

Evening

A review of the week on Hamburg radio. Against the 'Communist youth meeting'.[20] About the recent conference of the Western powers.[21] One hears exactly the same as from our side. Only where we say the SU, they always say the West [...]. The West protects freedom, is forced to spend more and more on armaments, because Russia wants to attack Europe and crush it. The West wants German unity, the West is rebuilding Germany. *Where does the truth lie?* – The only certain thing is, that war is being openly prepared. [...] I believe, nevertheless, that the real truth lies with Russia.

Today I wrote a couple of lines of 'The Rending of Language', a lot of correspondence. Letter to Hans Meyerhof [. . .]

30th May, Tuesday evening. Dresden
[. . .] Neumark's secretary was here again today, with her daughter Brigitte, the Russian teacher. Frau Jährig is fighting for recognition as a Victim of Fascism; she has to defend herself because of her post then. The obscure Neumark case. He is said to be serving a ten-year sentence. Was he *completely* innocent? [. . .] I had to advise Frau J. on what to write to the Association of Victims of Nazi Persecution. In such a way that she is completely exonerated, that he is not incriminated.

[. . . Klemperer hopes he can come to an arrangement with the publisher Riemerschmidt – of Rütten and Loening – Teubner having let him down.] I'm curious, but not passionately worried. I no longer rightly believe that I shall complete my 18ième . . . [. . .]

1st June, Thursday forenoon. Dresden
[Klemperer completes 'The Rending of Language'.]

[On the – GDR – wireless, outrage at the detention at the inner-German border of Western participants returning from the Youth Meeting in East Berlin. Klemperer is sceptical of the militancy of the language used . . .] What on earth does 'the *struggle* for peace' mean? I ask myself that again and again, and now, an hour ago, it was reported: the Bonn government has ordered the raising of the blockade. I am more disgusted than ever before. The situation of the day, the historical course of events, which as an activist I am right in the middle of and not at all at the deepest spot, is completely opaque. History can never be known. Because I live through it myself, and because I have not lived through it myself. Stand where one will – one never *knows*.

4th June, Sunday afternoon. Dresden
In a few minutes, everything that I had built up for myself over 5 years, has completely collapsed. All influence and power of my position gone – a has-been. 'You are on the wrong track, Comrade Klemperer – you want to move ahead too quickly, the Party is strong enough to stay in the background: the university, the Kulturbund must be led by members of the bourgeois parties.'

On Thurs., 1 June, I was driven to Halle as usual. Rita immediately told me of the Party's position. I dealt with my seminar papers. After that the 'council' in the main hall. [. . .]

[Klemperer's Kulturbund humiliation actually takes place on the Saturday morning.]

Drive back after 3 p.m. Very hot, very exhausted, inevitably an irritable clash with E. [. . .]. We had to drop Gusti at the Weisser Hirsch . . . Landscape beautiful. Here after 8 shattered. – *At the end of my tether.*

[. . .]

I have frequently been leafing through Gerhard Rohlfs' *Romanische Philologie*[22] [. . .] and wrote him an emotional (perhaps *too heart*felt) letter 'with a quiet sense of shame' at being mentioned so frequently and so generously by him, whom I had thought to be my enemy. It really is very important to me. (Acknowledgement in the West, survival of my things, so long ignored. – He did not mention everything, of course, but essential parts nevertheless.) Apart from that the book is a great help to me [. . .].

Letter from Inge and Peter Klemperer. The first letter from him. [. . .] Birth of a son. Caesarian. Already quite lively after 4 days. She writes: *'Blue flag outside the window, the first Klemperer pioneer.'* Oh Grandfather Berthold!! [. . .]

8th June, Thursday afternoon. Halle. Department, my room

[. . .]

Mackie Kahane came to the club. In Berlin with his family until the 20th, but wants to go back [to Prague] permanently. [. . .] In the courtyard of the university I met Peter, young father, very happy. I told him: if your father were to look down from heaven – he would start spinning round... [. . .] Robi's mother feels flattered, that Rita, the intellectual, is now getting 'properly married' to her Robi, formerly a carpenter. The new class structure [. . .] educated and uneducated. [. . .]

During the drive [from Berlin] and here the next day conversations about my future. Great bitterness for me, lengthy hesitation. Final decision: I shall become emeritus, but retain my position here. [. . .]

9th June, Friday forenoon. Department, Halle

[Klemperer has a very encouraging conversation with the editor from Dietrich, Rudolf Marx. Once again Klemperer begins to make plans for future publications. Later that day he is further cheered by the popularity of his classes.]

[. . .]

16th June, 4.30 Friday morning. Stadt Hamburg, Halle

[Klemperer discusses the preparation and arrangements for the elections of 15 Oct. to the GDR Volkskammer and to regional and local assemblies.]

21st June, Wednesday forenoon. Director's room, Halle

The chaos of the house-building, the oppressive sultriness. E. in a satisfactory condition.

[. . . More problems with crudeness and inflexibility in cultural politics, with the '150%ers'.] 'If someone plays the super-patriot', said E., 'then everyone is afraid.' The 'super' can be Junker or Red or Nazi – semper idem. Yesterday evening with I. M. Lange in the HO café. He cannot publish my contribution to the discussion on the 'sick German language'. [. . .] 'there is a very sharp wind blowing' ... 'we have to be very careful.' – Everything points to war, civil war, terror. The cultural course of the SED is odious to me, and at the moment I am constantly its victim – but theoretically and practically there is no other place for me, in all this wretchedness in self-defence it stands for the only true cause.

[...]

[...] On Monday evening it had been announced on the wireless: Prof. Kuczynski resigned[23] [as chairman of the German–Soviet Friendship Society], in order to devote himself entirely to his sociological institute – scholarly work, too many commitments ... I: 'What has happened?' E.: It might be the truth for once. I: Of course even the truth is not impossible, but it is the least probable. – Kneschke: 'Both Kuczynski and Mark, the regional secretary, were émigrés in England. Impossible in the long term!' Then in the evening Lange said Mark had also resigned, the new president is Ebert,[24] the mayor of [East] Berlin.[24] The ever more tense situation evident in this respect also: no one, not even the best comrade, is accepted for the People's Police if he has relatives in the West.

[...]

25th June, Sunday evening. Dresden

[...] 'Have the honour of announcing the wedding on 23 June 1950 of Dr Rita Hetzer née Tomaschek and Robert Schober.' [...] Registry Office (1904) Genthiner Str.:[25] '... I declare you united in marriage, the charge is 3.75, the next party please ...' [In the past] all solemnity was left to the Church. Now the registrar first says a couple of sentences about the structure of the state, which is founded on the family, then conducts matters with dignity and says in conclusion: 'As a sign of your union now exchange the rings in front of me.' The rings were attached to the ribbon of the bride's bouquet.

26th June, Monday forenoon. Dresden

[...] Crippling tiredness. – New and only half-digested: Stalin's essay on linguistics.[26] I already got a telephone call about it in Halle. I still have to think seriously about it. – Now first the lecture.

30th June, Friday morning. Stadt Hamburg, Halle

War? Korea looks bad.[27] Rita in complete despair yesterday: 'what have *I* (my generation) had of life so far?'

[More problems with censorship. South American novellas which Eva Klemperer had translated should never have 'passed'.[28] On the other hand it turns out that Werner Krauss had written a positive and flattering report of the French Poetry book rejected by Teubner after the objections to French Prose.] Meanwhile a Writers' and Cultural Congress of Westerners and anti-Soviet people is meeting in Berlin West.[29] IM leafs through the Poetry again, which was already castrated in 48: 'Romains[30] has to go, of course, the swine is sitting down with Gide over there! I: 'Romains is central, also to the study' [...] Great agitation on both sides. He: 'we have thrown a 72-year-old out of the Party, the same would happen to you, the publishing house would lose its licence, if Romains appeared ...' I: 'then nothing at all any more by me ... stupid slavery ...' etc. We parted barely reconciled ... [...]

1.30 p.m. Department
Terrific heat.

[...] Back home I made ready an express letter for E. with a packet of cigarettes and a few words of love – 'well then, I love you!'[31] for the 29th. For the same 46th wedding anniversary I bought her sumptuous chocolate things in the HO shop. – To bed at 2.

Yesterday, Thursday 29th June, mood in the department dominated by the sudden threat of war – battles in Korea. Rita said: 'What do *I* have from life? I want to have my husband now, I want to establish myself as a scholar – is everything going to be smashed again?' Frau Stahl said, she would rather die than suffer the calamity of war again. *I* thought about our little house – before it has been completely renovated, it could have a bomb through the roof ... Today the world looks a bit calmer. For how long? [...] The seminar in the afternoon was cancelled because of a peace demonstration [...]

5th July, midday etc. Wednesday. Halle, Director's room
Terrible sultriness, serious exhaustion, journey in the hot slow diesel carriage was torture.

Essential points
[...] The SPD man [who had been making critical remarks about the SED on the train] also said: 'I can also procure coffee for you more cheaply than your man in the KB. I get it from *the Jews*, they don't bother about West and East, they do business between the sectors and abroad.' I responded: *Only* the Jews? He: of course not '*only*' ... but the Jews nevertheless. He also thought that the former pg's had been treated too harshly. There had been Socialism there too! [i.e. in the Nazi Party].

[...]

6th July, 5.30 a.m. Thursday. Stadt Hamburg, Halle. Pyjamas
[...]

Here on Wednesday altogether exhausted and wretched. Waiting for me was a *Guest delegate card* for the SED Party Congress[32] – I was a delegate to the first, not to the second. I was very pleased, although it will be the same old thing nevertheless. [...]

[...]

9th July, 1 p.m. Sunday. Dresden

[...]

[To Anny Klemperer's new apartment ...] Anny gave me newspapers on the Writers' Congress [i.e. the Congress for Cultural Freedom in West Berlin], which is costing me the Romains chapter in my French Poetry. – Who is *Koestler*?[33] I have already encountered the name several times. This complete isolation from the people over there! Anny will get an important place in the Curriculum. Entirely senile, stone deaf, with a long ear trumpet and completely agile, proletarianised, [...]. At the same time pulled to the Right by her eldest son. Did I already write, that this Georg Klemperer warned his cousin Lotte against me? Yet married to a Jew.

[...]

13th July, Thursday afternoon. Department

[...]

[Klemperer has been invited to attend a ceremony of the Academy in Berlin,[34] he attends, although he feels very bitter about not having been elected himself. His mood is not improved when an Academy member reads out the names of the new foreign corresponding members and mispronounces the Italian city of Pavia.] ... Pah-via [...] I thought it was a disgrace. I am already exasperated when I hear foreign names mispronounced on the wireless. But here in the elite centre of democratic education! [...] A Halle car really did come at 3 and slowly drove me and Stern[35] home, with an engine repair on the way. Stern related very interestingly [...] that he was, and is, a member of the Austrian CP, and is here on 'Party leave', that he was in Moscow from 36, where he advanced to the post of Professor of Modern German History (lecturing in Russian) at Moscow University, took part in the war at the front with the Red Army as officer and propaganda speaker, then became professor at Vienna University, is now in the closest contact with our Party leadership. I would really like to know whether this huge man, who looks more like a heavy dark-haired grey-eyed Russian than anything else, who drives his own car, knows a bit about the engine, goes hunting wild boar in the Harz – whether he is Jewish. I don't think so – but Leo Stern from Vienna?? He has a good opinion of me. I had the 'Party grip'. That was a Russian expression and meant a no-nonsense way of acting for the Party ... [...] He advised me to concentrate on my Halle professorship, refuse all other teaching and lecturing activities – write.

[...]

20th July, 5.15 Thursday morning. 30 Brückenstr., at Ladendorf's, Berlin-Niederschöneweide [Klemperer's quarters for the Party Congress]

[...]

Awake since 3.45 – latent excitement and overfatigue. The rectorship affair.

[...]

21st July, 5.30 Friday morning. Pyjamas

[At the above meeting news came through of the arrest of anti-nuclear weapons protestors in West Berlin, who had been gathering signatures for the Stockholm Appeal.] Yesterday at the Party Congress: of the 1200 arrested, 500 are still imprisoned in the French Sector, brutally treated ... Storm of protest, resolution, demand to the French commandant.[36] [...]

Party Congress

[...] Characteristic of this whole congress: at every step, *whenever* entering or leaving, dozens of times, always the strictest check, always the most careful comparison of delegate's card, identity card and party membership book. Once yesterday I left my delegate's card inside the hall, Rita had to fetch it, otherwise I would not have been allowed in. The *justified fear of West Berlin*. Likewise on Thursday morning, when Rita had to go to the checkpoint, the same fuss. Here Becher happened to be standing beside us. I did not immediately recognise him, he spoke no word of greeting. Nor did I. As I was explaining to the steward who Rita was, Becher said coldly to me: That's pointless. You might as well explain existentialism to him ... Since the *Sinn und Form* Maupassant business I find Becher *even* more unpleasant than before. I have no friends in the Berlin KB, I shall neither enter the Volkskammer nor get the National prize. [...]

Features of the Congress: food very abundant, barbaric – but one is lost in the mass, has to wait endlessly, can't find a bus, can't order anything in the foyer, in the electric light-bulb factory [where the Congress canteen was], is left to one's own resources. The vast hall of the Congress.[37] Thousands. The huge square in front of it, with the chaos of cars. Former central cattle yard. Now Leninallee-Stalinallee. Perhaps one says 'great Stalin' too often at this congress, perhaps one stands up too often in his honour, claps too long. The contradiction: the presentation is entirely as Communist Party and as a Soviet country – I *very* much approve of and *very* much like that – but there is also an emphasis on *the Bloc* and *the whole of Germany*. [...] And Pieck: here he is Comrade P., Party leader, Communist, workers', emphatically *workers'* leader; and yet also President of GDR, which wants to represent *all* of Germany. The profound contradiction of the Congress, of our situation altogether. And ever stronger the claim to be all of Germany, and ever stronger the imitation of the Soviet party as 'party of a new type'[38] [...]

22nd July, 5 a.m. Saturday morning. Pyjamas, at Ladendorf's

What I noted yesterday emerged even more emphatically in the course of the day, in Grotewohl's speech – and most drastically – in the march-past and in the speech by the Volkspolizei [People's Police]: *the contradiction*. We want to be Bolsheviks and we want to represent all Germany with an all-encompassing National Front ... [...]

Everyone's mood enthusiastic, really sweeping me along. Always at the back of my mind: it's like Nürnberg, but this time you yourself are in the Party and on top – but then again always: but this time by God it's the cause of mankind and of good. [...]

The strictly legal treatment [by Grotewohl] of the Potsdam resolutions on the Oder-Neisse Line[39] and of the 'Bonn puppet state', above all of the behaviour of the occupying powers there. The speech will no doubt appear as a pamphlet. It will be most important material for the LQI: from Party language to state language, of German Bolshevism.

[...] Along with Social Democratism, opportunism and sectarianism,[40] *'self-criticism'* is the most characteristic catchword of this Party Congress. [...]

The two big parades. First the FDJ. Enthusiasm at the Friendship Song. A robust FDJ girl from the line of demonstrators next to me grabs my right hand, the person sitting beside me grabs my left hand, and during the Friendship Song we swayed from side to side linked together. Remarkably my heart bore it. All the clapping and rising to one's feet. Where does the clapping rhythm come from? The clapping with raised hands a little Nazi-like, Hitler Youth. [...]

Above all the Police demonstration. Little Nürnberg, little Red Army. In their greenish khaki shirts with the peaked SA caps, the set faces, the military commands and marching! I cannot get rid of memories of 1933–45. But the enthusiastically cheered words of their speaker: 'We are the first police force, which is not marching against the workers, but for them ...' [...]

Always this mixing up and merging of Party, leading Party, state as such. [...]

23rd July, 8.30 Sunday. Conference hall

[...] Always the two sides of this Party Congress: CP and all of Germany, peace and war. One cannot even say that they say one thing and mean the other; they say *both*, quite openly and in the same breath. Are they naive enough to believe that they will be believed? I think, they really are.

[...]

Changing mood: now it's a waste of time, a vanitas – now an experience, a page of the Curriculum. Yesterday Ulbricht's day. An ugly Socrates with a little beard. An outstanding speaker and *satirist*.

24th July, Monday morning. Niederschöneweide

Today I feel almost chilly. But the most important feature of this Congress after all remains the longing for my pyjamas, the terrible sweating, the shirt hung over the chair to dry. Ulbricht's closing words strengthened the impression of his speech: satirical humour, tremendous optimism, Berlin cheek *without* personal arrogance [...]

Again and again in Ulbricht's speech 'the alliance between workers and "technical intelligentsia"', always only '*technical* intelligentsia'. We poor small fry [...]. In his closing words Ulbricht mentioned Becher and described the task of the Kulturbund as solely (really!) to encourage the young writers and artists to write stories, exemplary ones, about work and the work ethic of today, it should support 'progressive writers'.

[...]

Everyone is against 'pragmatism', everyone for 'self-criticism' and for *competition*. Everyone confesses sins, gladly accepts the other's charges, vows improvement. [...]

Every speaker concludes with homage to Stalin. The formula is unfailingly: *'Our leader and teacher'* (rabbi!)

[...]

26th July, 3 p.m. Kulturbund, Berlin

The suffering is over. It was tremendously exhausting, especially because of the heat and because of the lack of underwear and water, after that because of the rush, on a full stomach, to the buses outside the light-bulb factory; it was often dreary, I dropped off – but it was tremendously interesting and truly historic.

[...]

Peaceful! The demonstration yesterday in the Lustgarten. As our buses rattled up, it was still raining. Later it cleared up. The forest of flags, the crowd of people, the slowness of the passing procession, the thinning out on the road. But then came the police march-past. No goose step, but in very good order, arms swinging, with the salute by the officers in front, with the Nazi-like and traditional arm position of the flag-bearers. *Without* weapons – but thousands [...] And at the rear the 'Marine Police'. This is the new Reichswehr. To 'preserve peace'. Then when one heard Pieck's closing address! Hate-filled Go home, Yankee; it is difficult not to judge this speech a war speech.

29th July. Dresden

[...]

The actual Party Congress ended late on Monday afternoon. There was a pause during the meal at the light-bulb factory. Queuing up: the Saxon textile industry presented each of the almost $2\frac{1}{2}$ thousand delegates with cloth (with lining and the rest) for a suit or a dress. The light-bulb factory presented each of its guests with a 40 watt bulb. Before that we had already received a large valuable packet of books. The breakfast paper bags were each time so abundantly provided with butter, conserves, sweets, even chocolate, that I gave a lot to my nice hosts, brought some of it home. [...]

29th July, Saturday

[...]

Yesterday, Friday the 28th, started out at 7.30, here [Dölzschen] in good time, coffee with the driver and his wife. Afterwards just us. Very great mutual delight [...] at being together again. [...] The centre of attention [...] throughout the last few days the *rectorship*; a) my inner conflict, b) the external still continuing uncertainty.

[Essentially Klemperer's hopes have once again been dashed. It appears that the Party wanted a 'bourgeois' figure to represent the university, even though at this point assuring Klemperer of its support. Perhaps also there were disagreements between different fractions, between the region and Berlin, which led to the extraordinarily drawn-out and inconclusive proceedings which so frustrated him.]

30th July, 10 p.m. Sunday. Dresden
[...]

For weeks I have been carrying Bert Brecht's *Threepenny Novel*[41] back and forth between the cities. Having read about a third, I am now laying it aside. Very witty, biting satire, a great deal of esprit – but unbearable in the long run. Eva is right: these are no people, everything human is absent.

In fact, whatever we do or say, we are both constantly obsessed by the thought of the rectoral election. After all, the shape of our old age depends on the outcome. – When I left Halle on Friday, I was the Party's candidate – am I still? Will it muster 8 of the 15 votes? I shall find out in 18 hours.

[...]

2nd August, Wednesday morning after 7 a.m. Stadt Hamburg, Halle
[Then on Monday afternoon Klemperer learns that another academic, Stubbe,[42] has been elected, he feels like throwing in the towel as far as his academic posts are concerned, but later still that same day it turns out that Stubbe has declined the offer!] I tried to suppress all feelings of hope – and yet all day I played around with the formulation of the telegram to E., if I became rector nevertheless. I asked Prokert to leave a note for me in the Stadt Hamburg, saying how the vote had turned out. Against my judgement I kept on thinking there would be a bouquet of flowers and congratulations on my table. [...] Back [from Berlin] about midnight. No flowers. [...] So still Stubbe after all or Agricola.

[...]

I cannot suppress an awful feeling of bitterness, even though I know that nothing bad has happened to me. Vanitas. I cannot get rid of a double load of remorse with respect to Eva. On Monday I was ghastly to her the whole morning: the agonising wait for the car, the frightful, frightful paint-stinking chaos of the rebuilding, the costs forever rising to insane heights. And secondly: E. feels cut off from the world in Dölzschen – she lacks *a car*. D'où prendre?[43]

At this very moment a letter from Prokert. Stubbe has declined. Election postponed to 15 September. – The noose loosened again. Stubbe – I learned from a telephone call from Vahlen – appears to be keeping himself free to succeed Stroux (Director of the Academy).

[...]

16th August, Wednesday evening. Dresden

[...] All day the noise of rebuilding, in the evening E. does not feel well. – Today finally I had a car come up and drove with her to an appointment with Rostoski at the Friedrichstädter Hospital. [...] Very elderly gentleman, hard of hearing, trembling lips – but as was our experience in the past he appears to practise his trade with care. He seemed to find nothing disquieting with respect to the heart – but now the usual business of the X-ray etc. examination arises: Stomach? Kidneys? There is no cause for joy, one is always afraid.

[...]

18th August, Friday evening. Dresden

Again to the Friedrichstädter Hospital with E. X-rayed, examined once more by a younger senior physician. No cancer, etc., heart not too bad. But blood pressure 140. The doctor said to me: 'Condition at the moment not bad – but with such high blood pressure, sudden death is always possible – I have to tell you that.' It weighs heavily on me. [...]

23rd August, Wednesday afternoon. Dresden

I work as much as I can. Much distraction during the day. In the evening I fall asleep immediately after our meal. Later, when E. has gone to bed – she lies down very early – I pull myself together. On a bad evening I leaf and browse until about midnight; on a good one I work intensively, sometimes very late. Yesterday, today rather, I finished the *Bel Ami* afterword[44] at 3 in the morning, and it has turned out well and is more than mere repetition. [...]

The propaganda trip to the West on behalf of the German–Soviet Society now intrudes into the holidays. The discussion at the Society's offices here took place on the morning of Mon., the 27th. [...] The plan: speakers to the existing, not banned, not permitted Soviet Society groups in the West, preparation for a congress of the Society set for 16–17 Sept. in Düsseldorf, where our new name 'German–Soviet Friendship Society' is also to be proclaimed over there. The plan seems far too bold to me, when I think of the constant Western agitation against us. [...]

On 'leafing and browsing'. Erich Weinert: *The Interlude*.[45] (Volk and Welt send us all their new publications at cost price, although we have completely fallen out with them.) Why did I know nothing at all of the man during the Weimar years? *A crucially important question.* I see from the foreword, that everyone who is in the government now, was in the old Communist Party and served on the Russian front, usually as propagandists. Why do I know nothing whatsoever about all of that? My blindness during the Weimar years crucial to the Curriculum, because the blindness of a whole stratum. – Aufbau's 5th anniversary almanac. (Why without me? Why is the *LTI* not in any shop window? Why have I disappeared from the *Aufbau* periodical? Unpleasantnesses. Invitation to the Aufbau publishing house banquet – I am almost glad that I am forced to decline, because on the 4 Sept. in question I shall be on the front line of peace, in Stuttgart or thereabouts.) [...]

25th August, Friday morning. Dresden

Completely knocked out by days of heat and sultriness. [...] Today in Berlin, Seelenbinder Hall, the *National Congress*.[46] A most elaborately mounted demonstration. I have often asked myself: What is, what does the *National Council*[47] do? Likewise: what do the *Peace Committees* do? Everywhere the same gestures and speeches, one knows them by heart. Must there be this deadly monotony – does it not have a deadening effect? The old question, which I repeatedly ask myself – and what good are 'protests'?

I listen to Rias every day. It says the same about the SU as we say about the USA. Exactly the same. The USA has released war criminals from Landsberg prison, Dietrich and business leaders.[48] *We* denounce. Rias says: And Sedlacek? And names others besides. It reports on a mass trial in Waldheim, of which I have never heard, on hundreds, thousands rather, of very long sentences, it names individual judges and prosecutors, a number of whom are explicitly described as 'notorious'[48a]. [...] The latest is the official strengthening of the 'police' over there, who must be strong enough to be able to balance our 'police'. Etc. etc. And in Korea a proper war, a proper full-blown war. And today a Chinese note about Formosa,[49] nothing less than an ultimatum: 'We will not tolerate ...' I can hardly believe, that we shall avoid war and civil war. I do not believe that the Rias accusations are false – because we have a Communist state or are at least striving for one, LDP and CDU *have* to go along with it, are three-quarters fictitious, we are an organ and part of the SU – and I do not believe, either, that in the long run the Communist system can exist innocuously next to the capitalist one – but for all of that: the *more* just cause – on earth there is none that is entirely just, the Lord above is to blame for that – WE are the *more just cause* ... But freedom for scholarship? [...]

29th August, Tuesday evening. Dresden

Eternal tiredness – wearisome work on 'Goethe 1949' for the Essays.

LTI royalties account for first half-year 1950: 1937 copies sold, 2356.99M. More copies could be sold, the publisher does little for my book, which is mentioned nowhere, but it trickles on nevertheless. And it will last. [...] That provides a degree of consolation as non omnis moriar. [...]

[...]

1st September, 11 p.m. Friday evening. Dresden

[...] I am now supposed to be 'over there' from the 10th–18th, first of all speak several times in the Frankfurt area, then participate in the Düsseldorf Congress. I don't quite believe it yet, I believe that the Congress will be banned and the talks stopped before I get there. [...]

That means the 4 Sept. is now free: the 5th anniversary of the Aufbau publishing house. I had already turned down the invitation – not unwillingly, since I do not feel at ease in the Berlin Kulturbund. Now today I have belatedly accepted – very reluctantly, since apart from costing me time and money the affair could also put me out of humour: somewhere the VIPs are gathered around Pope Becher, and I hang around with the *misera plebs*.[50] I am not valued in Berlin, there I am old, from the provinces and done with. [...] I am going, so as to dutifully 'show my face'. [...]

E.'s health is a very little bit better, continues to worry me greatly. She is much aged, much weakened. I tell myself repeatedly, that neither of us still has a right to health and a long life. There is a certain dull resignation in me and [yet] in everything I do I am pursued by *vanitas vanitatum*. Money, house, outward success, writing – what is the point of it all when one is at death's door? And yet I cannot leave go of the vanity and the desires. I try not to reflect and still to absorb as much as possible.

My diaries and my experiences are once again 'paper soldiers'[51] – I store up and do not ask many questions.

3rd September, Sunday evening. Dresden

[...]

Kulturbund in Halle writes, I am now finally a candidate for the Volkskammer, confirmation from Berlin has come in. I am already telling myself: the Volkskammer is empty decoration.

The puzzle of the absolute contradiction. Given the greatest prominence in the *Tägliche Rundschau* (and *Neues Deutschland* etc.) yesterday 2 Sept.: in accordance with the decision of the Politburo the Central Committee of the SED expels Central Committee member Paul Merker from the Party (the man who attacked my Zion chapter) as well as half a dozen others [yet others are removed from all posts ...][52] because they sided with the *class enemy*, because in exile they irresponsibly allowed themselves to be taken in by the agents of American imperialism, because a) those expelled still directly rendered assistance to the Americans until 1949, b) those removed from their posts did so indirectly, because they betrayed pure Bolshevism. [...] I have just found the newspaper. [...] 'Because of association with the American Secret Service agent Noel H. Field[53] and extensive aid to the class enemy ...' Merker etc. were recruited by the Americans in Marseille – then still Roosevelt! which is why they saw in every American an anti-Fascist – because they had lost their *class consciousness* and lacked a *'firm political-ideological foundation'*. They *'took up Trotskyist positions'* ... 'The enemy concentrated ... on *petit bourgeois elements*, on members who had already deviated from the Party line once before or had belonged to groups hostile to the Party, on former Trotskyists, fractionists, Right opportunists, Left sectarians, especially if they had lived in Western countries for a long time'. – Therefore be alert in each factory and everywhere, report everything to the Party! It is forbearing, where it sees good will.

This then is the *language* of the Bolsheviks without disguise, the closest imitation of the SU, the most intransigent Communism. *How* is that to be reconciled with the broadness of the National Front, with the canvassing of votes for 15 October? It must inevitably put off all of the middle classes and also very many workers, and it gives Rias and co. every possibility for counter-propaganda. Is the SED making such big mistakes – or does it have reasons, which we do not know? Or does the SED do nothing but carry out an order from the SU? And what is determining for the SU, whose policies are so carefully considered? Complete puzzle. – Pay attention to the linguistic aspect!! Extremely important document. First of its kind in the GDR.

Slow work on 'Goethe 1949'. [...]

[...]

7th September, Thursday

[There is still some uncertainty whether Klemperer will actually go on the 'propaganda mission' to West Germany on behalf of the German–Soviet Friendship Society. Evidently there are doubts as to his suitability and whether it is worth him risking imprisonment.]

10th September, 2.30 p.m. Sunday. Dresden

The Society's car is supposed to pick me up at 5. I have an interzonal pass, ticket to Frankfurt, 250 West marks and two Frankfurt addresses. Otherwise a journey into the unknown.

Half an hour ago I completed the 'Goethe 1949'. Agony.

[...]

12th September, 7 a.m. Tuesday morning. At Dr Hahn, Frankfurt/Main

[The 'speaking tour' on behalf of the Society was not a success. After one meeting is prohibited and another stopped by the police, Klemperer does not see any point in continuing. There are frictions with his Communist Party hosts, some of whom feel he should risk speaking despite the ban and also go on to the Congress in Düsseldorf. Klemperer, however, has had enough and is determined to return. No doubt, the harassment of peaceful meetings by the West German authorities and police, the experience of the state of siege in which Communists in West Germany lived and carried on their activities, did a great deal to confirm his negative view of West Germany.]

17th September, Sunday after dinner

In recent days I have not overcome my exhaustion. The two little articles [on his experiences in West Germany] for *Sonntag* and for *Friedenspost* [Peace Post] are costing me a great deal of effort, most of the time I sat around doing nothing.

[...]

Tomorrow Rita Schober is to come to stay for two weeks.

The day after tomorrow Executive Council in Berlin.

Yesterday above Albertplatz [...] a squadron of 17 air planes. They are supposed to be GDR air planes. It does not look much like peace.

[...]

20th September, Wednesday forenoon. Dresden

Yesterday Executive Council in Berlin. [...] A couple of interesting speeches. [...]

In the evening, I was waiting for Bergmann (Secretaries' meeting), Mackie Kahane came into the club; I had heard [...] he is now remaining in Berlin, Doris is to follow him in mid-October with the children. He reproached me, I was frittering away my energies, I should leave off politics, the travelling, write my books, at most work on political theory – my 'Culture' brochure was really bad, he had not read it to the end, he hoped it would not be in my volume of essays ... I would certainly not get the National Prize. [...] I am somewhat shocked by what Kahane said. [...]

Nice books from Aufbau, among them Lukács' *Goethe*. I leafed through it: the exact opposite view of my study.

[...]

29th September, midday Friday. Dresden

[...] Eva's health is seldom really good and since yesterday very bad – she had a temperature. At the same time the workmen still in the house, above all the painter with the stink of his paint. I am unable to finish off [the essay volume]. At the same time Rita Schober is constantly with us. She is not well, she suffers from the imminent child. [...] Our never-ending professional conversation is regularly about the Party censorship, which is becoming ever more tyrannical. One trembles at every single word, in case it could be seen as anti-Marxist. In both of us there is a constant resistance to the senseless narrow-mindedness of this uncontrolled censorship, resistance to our whole inconsistent and often threadbare SED cultural policy.

The *Scholarship and Politics* essay volume has been packed up. I am taking it with me to Halle. [...]

30th September, 10 p.m. Saturday evening. Dresden

At 3 o'clock yesterday afternoon to Halle with Rita, 9.30 Stadt Hamburg. [The rectorial election is cancelled once again. The current rector, Winter, is sick, while one of the potential candidates has fled to the West.] And in Korea the Americans are winning and the Russians don't intervene.[54] *They* have the money, *they* are the stronger.

Two anonymous communications referring to the *LTI*. I was a 'Nazi manqué', in the *LTI* I had attacked what I was now going along with, on a postcard simply: '*LTI*, p. 43 middle'. (Unified list) In a letter: 'valiant sounds like an obituary' – I should look at the war reports about Korea and altogether the LQI was identical to the LTI. There is unfortunately a great deal of truth to that [. . .]. In the morning a troop bugled, drummed and drilled outside my window exactly like the Hitler Youth, but wearing blue shirts. [. . .]

Unpleasant surprise when I delivered my essays at the Mitteldeutscher Verlag. The whole of the old team is gone – no one knew about my contract. The house is now publishing only belles-lettres, is allocated paper only for that. In charge a Comrade Schiedt(?), altogether pleasant and obliging man. I told him I did not want a court case between Party comrades, but a contract was a contract and business was business.

On Wednesday Rita and I were supposed to have a discussion in Leipzig with Marx of Dieterich; she got a telegram, he was 'away indefinitely'. There, too, we fear a one-way trip to the West. Marx owes me a thousand marks for my essay 'On the French narrative in the 19th century'.

A few too many unpleasantnesses for *one* day.

[. . .]

7th October, Saturday afternoon. Dresden

[. . .]

With unctuous words the Mitteldeutsche publishing house refuses to recognise the contract dated 1 Feb., I should recognise the needs of planning. It will pass on the ms to Dietz with a 'recommendation'. I shall threaten it with legal action. [. . .] Grounds: I should have been warned, informed in good time.

[. . .]

Many set-backs recently. Mitteldeutscher publishing house, promotion of French in *Forum* magazine, Frankfurt articles – nothing appears. And today the National Prizes were awarded in Berlin. Not to *me*. Incidentally with much less fanfare than the first time.

10th October, 7.30 Tuesday morning. Dresden

My seventieth year – it sounds loathsomely like dodderer. One has to get used to it as one does to angina. A couple of the usual congratulatory telegrams: Kneschke [. . .], Aufbau – Wendt. Masterbuilder Linke. Brigitte Jährig sent 3 girl pioneers with a basket of flowers and a blue neckerchief. Otherwise alone. [. . .] This whole day *only* the lecture. [. . .]

Depressed about politics. Terrible propaganda on Rias – and not all of it is an absolute lie. [. . .] And why at the beginning the big victory reports from Korea. [. . .] And why is Stalin dropping Korea?[55] As yesterday Spain and Greece. As tomorrow *us*? – Lotte at present at the regional Party school, Seifersdorf nr. Radeberg: she encounters animosity, is not 'proletarian' enough, displays 'idealistic residues'. – Is it any different for me, for Rita? [. . .] Congratulatory card from Anny Kl. in Zürich. 'Paradise!'

[. . .]

11th October, 7.30 a.m. Wednesday morning. Halle, Stadt Hamburg

[Klemperer speaks at an election meeting for regional parliament and Volks-
kammer]. (I had beforehand been secretly informed of the questions the candidates were to expect – Agricola had a written list – incidentally they were not
adhered to.) When it was my turn [to speak], there was immediately such
tumultuous applause, that for quite a while I was unable to begin. I said: my
eyes had been opened in the First World War, but not yet wide enough, I had
still believed in the dogma of the unpolitical scholar. Now I wanted to catch
up. [...]

12th October, 9 a.m. Thursday morning. Halle, Stadt Hamburg

Not a minute free for work, uninterruptedly busy. [...]

I. M. Lange's doctoral examination

A farce as far as I was concerned. I asked literature (Realism and Enlightenment);
he replied, incomprehensibly to me, sociologically Marxistically; I let him talk
and said: very good. [...]

14th October, Saturday evening. Dresden

[Arrives late to give a talk for the Friendship Society in Zerbst – no one there
any more.] But on the return journey! A battery of huge long-barrelled guns
with heavy vehicles pulling them, heavy trucks on the road by some woodland.
An officer gets out of his car, a few waves of the hand: and like wasps the giant
guns buzz nimbly into the wood and in two minutes are swallowed up. It made
a tremendous and cheering impression on me. Somewhere, hidden from us
city-dwellers, the Red Army is in position and protecting us. In the wood
romantic open camp fires could be seen.

[...] I find the Middle French seminar easier now. The beginning was amusing.
I had to impose order. The night has been passed in my room a couple of times,
the couch there is tempting. [...]

16th October, Monday evening. Halle

The 'open' ballot shocked me at first. As soon as I heard about it on the wireless;
then on Saturday evening, E. was already in bed, Erich Seidemann called on
me, and he, too, declared it a danger. Rias anyway declared, the result of this
election was as certain beforehand as in Goebbels' days. Then yesterday morning
in the polling shed! A ballot paper without the possibility of a Yes or a No – it
is dropped into the box without further ado. If one goes into the cubicle, then
one is revealed as a No voter. I was shocked. I walked back with Maria Neudeck,
the returning officer. She, too, shocked and full of apprehension. The people
complain so much! Hardly anyone else will come. Our reactionary Dölzschen!
What shall I do if I have less than 30% voters. I am to count every ballot –

whatever is on it! – as a Yes. The comrades have to be there in the evening and not let the people from the middle-class parties near the table! … But in the evening when I returned to the polling station, the mood was very different: *everyone* had come to vote, over 1,000 out of 1,026 people, only 4 had gone into the cubicle. Not many people were present, the count was carried out very carefully: 4 ballots were crossed out, with three of them there was a slip of paper with a 'No', on one words of abuse: 'Blackmailers! Scoundrels!' Over a 1000 ballots cast intact. Now today the same news from everywhere. 95–99% turnout, 12 million Yes, some 30,000 No. Perhaps it is an honest success after all, because people could have refused to vote en masse. Also Maria Neudeck thought: people's complaints had only been directed at the *open* poll, they had agreed with the election itself. Or am I merely allowing my mind to be befogged after the event by the number of Yes votes? [...] At any rate Rias, and all enemies, will talk of fraud – and it really was not a clean business either. – Afterwards I was congratulated, and I felt heavy at heart. [...]

I made use of these last few days to finish off my *Modern French Poetry*, i.e. to castrate it. I deleted the whole of Jules Romains. This work, too, depressed me greatly. All the things I am now covering as a deputy of this regime! Our neighbour Frau Schmidt was here this afternoon. Her husband 'disappeared' years ago, sentenced without really being guilty. Her son studying as a 'refugee' in West Berlin, because Russian headquarters in Jena demanded he be an informer. [...]

19th October, Thursday morning. Berlin, Niederschönhausen, at Mackie's

[On Wednesday, meetings in Berlin.] Mackie joined me at the club, was my guest. Then he drove me to the news agency. [...] Then home with Mackie, stayed the night as I used to. [...] Very pessimistic with respect to war. 'He says, the SU was *still* too weak: it produces *30* million tons of steel, the USA around *80*! That was crucial. Hence the temporising. Hence the USA was willing to go to war. I: Will *we* be sacrificed like Korea? He: *Perhaps*. [...]
[...]

4th November, Saturday afternoon. Dresden

[...]
If one is away from our government offices and organisations for a month, one encounters completely new faces and situations on one's return, and is oneself entirely forgotten. How often recently have I remarked these *landslides* in publishing houses, authorities, here and there! A dismal feeling. It tells me again and again, that I am on the wrong track. I should give up the vita publica and work for myself. I fear it and this fear is undignified. [...]

8th November, 5 p.m. Wednesday afternoon. Berlin, Kulturbund

Very, very disillusioned. Bit part and the most boring waste of time, emptiest pretence of tan in representation; the Volkskammer. Everything is passed unanimously and without standing up, today I have passed two basic laws on an increased number of regional chambers and of ministers, I know less than nothing about it. And I have risen from my seat and applauded the great leader of the SU.

The dreariest business – and I won't get on to the committees, because the Kulturbund fraction has only very few members and a superabundance of professors, who are National Prize winners, rectors etc. etc. If only for once I could get rid of this damned vanity and spend the remainder of my life more usefully.

[...] Luisenstr. [in East Berlin] about 11. [Kulturbund fraction meeting – Klemperer feels his role as an extra confirmed. He also hears that a new candidate for rector at Halle has been found.] *I* shall also have to attend the SED's fraction meetings. Even more time-wasting and being an extra. – I was assigned a room [as an MP] in the Albrechtshof.[56] Wretchedly shabby for 10M. A hole. I dragged my suitcase there. I walked through *my* oldest Berlin. [...] The room rounded off my depression. [...]

Arnold Zweig muttered strong protest as we accepted the two quite unfamiliar laws, but he, too, raised his hand; he muttered an even stronger protest, when we rose and applauded for veliki Stalin – great Stalin – but he rose and clapped along.

[...]

11th November, 4.15 Saturday morning. Stadt Hamburg, Halle

I fell asleep at 8 in the evening during the meal downstairs in the restaurant; I went to bed at 9 and woke up at 4. To tiredness was added depression. Rita told me: 'Yesterday I was with Krauss in Leipzig, all the languages research assistants had been summoned to him as the supreme head. In the long term I could not be with him as a human being, somehow he is all at once alien to me – but he can do so much, complements you so well! But he was in contact with scholarship for many more years than you, he has close links with contemporary France, personal ones to the French CP, in addition he's well-versed in Marxism – he's just working on a modern bibliography of France ... He speaks of you with warmth and respect and wants to contribute to the Festschrift for your 70th ...' It all hurt me so terribly badly, because it is entirely true. But I can no longer be a subordinate. I *must* go. I have agreed to stay until the end of the summer semester, until autumn 51 ... What then? What will happen to E. without a car? How will I bear the peace and quiet? What point does my outdated 18ième still have?

[...]

20th November, Monday morning. Dresden

[...]

Up early on Saturday, here shortly after 10. Tiredness and visitors always rob me of time here. On this occasion only the Sunday afternoon occupied by Gusti Wieghardt. Eva's condition unchanged. She is fresh for a few hours, then repeatedly short of breath, tired, often with bouts of pain. [...] She walks with a stoop. But the never-ending work on the house, and now even of the gardener, gives her pleasure. [...] All this building is a great luxury. For whom should we save? As long as it makes her happy and makes her happy for a long time. My heart is heavy. [...]

25th November, 7 a.m. Friday morning. Stadt Hamburg, Halle

[...]

Rita is making arrangements for 'my' Festschrift – Krauss has taken a lively interest. But all power is concentrated in Krauss, and I sit on the sidelines as honoured greybeard.

25th November, 9 p.m. Saturday evening. Dresden

In Halle I found the report on the new syllabus, as elaborated by the Romance research assistants under their supreme head W. Krauss in Leipzig a couple of weeks ago. The plan is good – but all without me, Krauss rules. Bitterness. According to it Romance linguistics is to be studied solely by professional researchers at the Berlin Academy. Special institute, now already under Krauss's direction. At the universities only literary history. Main emphasis: 18th and 19th centuries with particular reference to the social. French Classicism from the same perspective. Those taking it as a subsidiary subject need know nothing of the 16th century, nothing of Old French. In fact, therefore, grist to my mill – but it is no longer mine – *go home* vieillard![57]

7th December, minuit Thursday. Stadt Hamburg, Halle

Yesterday's lectures hard – Rabelais. I lack the vigour of youth. [...] I got to bed after 1, up at 5 – the icy walk to the train, the hot, overheated compartment, the inadequate breakfast. At the station [Berlin], the university car, as arranged. [...] Riemerschmidt turned up unexpectedly with an abundance of good tidings. *Three* contracts signed by him: Maupassant, Barbusse and Barbusse translation for his 'Insel Library' [a classics imprint] [...] E. and I will again work together on the Barbusse. Plan to bring out the *Modern French Poetry* by the summer semester, plan to publish 'Scholarship and Politics', *he* was the right person for it, the provincial houses are to be cut back. If only a part of all these good things comes true, that will be welcome enough. My spirits fell as soon as I got outside – I dragged myself painfully to the university. [...] Jusques à quand, Seigneur?[58] And what good will the contracts and the money be to me?

[...]

15th December, 2 p.m. Friday. Fraction room, Volkskammer, Berlin
A great success, a dream of my youth fulfilled: the loud applause of the 'high chamber' for my 'poche ma sentite parole'.[59] It was a considerable test of my nerves, and my heart hurt again (as in recent days all too often and almost all the time.) Yesterday before the beginning of the committee session (which I, as senior, opened at 12) Rolf Agricola came up and with an air of secretiveness led me into the SED room. Apart from him a comrade from the Politburo present: '*You* must take on the report on the Peace Law[60] – we are not leaving it to the LDP or CDU, and it must be a respected man, preferably from the KB.' [...] Afterwards it occurred to me: one has to pull at people's heart-strings with a couple of unrehearsed words. [...] 'Law for the Preservation of Peace, Law Committee before the Second Reading, Reporter Prof. Dr Klemperer', and I had to trot the whole length of the chamber, literally from the corner seat in the last, top row to the speaker's lectern below. My actual 'speech', apart from what I read out, lasted 10 minutes at most. Throughout the whole of the long walk back to my seat, there was loud clapping. Afterwards really from many sides [...]: it had been very good, from several: a *natural* speech, *at last* an extempore speech, of the kind that has so often been demanded. Agricola: he 'sweated blood' [...] I should have given a precise definition of false pacifism, 'nation' had not been right either, it should have been imperialist government ... but it had been a big success nevertheless. – Now we shall see what further effect it has, if at all. For the moment I wallow in vanity. It was after all a great, almost a 'historic moment', and I did well. Behind me the government, in front of me the Volkskammer and above me the broadcasting microphones and the eternal stars ... And still the empty foolish thought: perhaps *this* will after all get me the [...] rectorship.
   [...]

17th December, Sunday about 7 p.m. Dresden
   [...]
   With respect to the chamber speech I am completely deflated. The wireless broadcast 2, 3 sentences from it, the *Tägliche Rundschau* printed ditto – and already it's all forgotten, ousted by other names. Vanitas!
   [...]

23rd December, Saturday evening. Dresden
   [...]
   I discovered a completely hostile review of my Molière study[61] in the Jena University newspaper: I was not the man for a 'new view', the 'Molière legend' had to be destroyed. That means, evidently, that he must be turned into a revolutionary Bolshevik. I am accused of allowing him only to reprove 'naked vice', but not to practise social criticism. There was *no* vice which was not produced by society. (A nonsense!) [...] The author has evidently mixed together a couple of half-digested cliche phrases from Party aesthetics with complete

unfamiliarity with the material and cannot forgive me for underlining the non-revolutionary element in Molière. This critique wounds me all the more, because it will have exactly the same effect as Hermlin's of my *Modern Prose*. [...] Inwardly it puts me off the SED. – Immediately after that I received from West Berlin a pompously lyricising challenge from a former student, pseudonymous of course. He describes a gloomy rainy day last year in Halle on which I talked 'fascinatingly' as always about the French Enlightenment. And then outside [the FDJ had paraded past] with their fanfares (accursed, he's right about that) – and I had sunk down. 'In this fleeting moment there seemed to be nothing in the room except a little twitching crease around your silent mouth and a sudden dimming of the fire in your eyes' ... 'Klemperer, the friend of youth, your new harlequin's costume does not sit well with your grey temples and your stooped back! It sits even less well with your reputation as a scholar and with your clear judgements in the analysis *Lingua Tertii Imperii!* You do indeed know very "concretely", what totalitarianism is, behind its official stage sets. Do you not think so, too, Comrade, Friend of Youth, Professor Kl.?' ... So it goes on, not untalented, for three typewritten pages, with flatteringly long quotations from the *LTI*. [...]

30th December, Saturday night

Very unproductive and unlovely holidays. Neither E. nor I could overcome our influenza [...]

[...] Otherwise profound loneliness. Outside kitschily beautiful snowy winter landscape, but very slippery and difficulty breathing – last night the thermometer fell below 20. I pay for a shopping errand with pains and great exhaustion; if at all possible I stick at home.

The wireless news monotonous and gloomy. I do not believe we shall avoid *war and civil war*. I am sceptical of everything that is reported here about opposition to the Adenauer course and the Americans [in West Germany], about support for Grotewohl's offer of negotiations.[62] Those are the couple of Communists, who manage no more than 5% in any election. [...] Adenauer claims to speak for the whole of Germany and 'to be defending occidental values', which is why he is contributing Germans to the general European army.

Yesterday after a power cut lasting hours [...] Bernard Shaw's *Saint Joan* was broadcast as an abridged wireless play and gripped me again as it did in the old days. After all Elisabeth Bergner as Joan was the greatest theatrical impression of my life.[63]

31st December, midday Sunday. Dresden

On the scale of world history will the GDR be next to the Munich Councils Republic, next to the Paris Commune or next to the Soviet Union? No one alive can say, no one knows, no one truly rules, not even Stalin. [...]

The vita activa et politica was dominant for me this year. I have written little, trivial and politicising things. The volume *Wissenschaft und Politik* – will it ever appear? – merely condenses and warms up what I have been chewing over repeatedly since 1945.

I have lost the chair of the KB in Saxony-Anhalt in return for the unimportant 'honorary chairmanship'. Lectures within the KB and the Society have not become any less but they have become less important. I did not become rector. Instead I have got as far as a deputy in the Volkskammer and had my big day there as spokesman of the Law Committee on the Protection of Peace Law. I was also delegate to the 3rd Party Congress of the SED. But I ask myself, what real importance such political positions possess in the GDR – see above.

[. . .]

In accordance with E.'s wishes we have enlarged and furnished our house very expensively, we have put very many thousands into it, we are richer than ever before, E.'s Maupassant alone covers the whole of the alteration costs, we are both earning more than we can spend – but we are both very old and not very healthy. I can no longer get rid of the death and night thoughts, I am all the time tormented by the question: 'which of the two of us will go first?'

With all this permeation by the thought of vanitas, with all this scepticism of the GDR as of its honours, nevertheless this piercing ambition, this constant feeling of being disregarded, of being third rate ... Very foolish and quite ineradicable.

The crucial facts of the year: the move back to Dresden, the guest professorship in Berlin, the seat (and the single performance) in the Volkskammer, all the money, all the travelling around, the inner conflict between the desire to write and for recognition in public life. The frustration of not being elected rector, not receiving the National Prize, being pushed into the background compared to Werner Krauss.

Eva's now very questionable health and agility. Her work as a translator.

The complete isolation with respect to former companions. Those not dead are divided from us by politics. That is all on the West side, and contact with all West people has broken off: Berthold Meyerhof, the Frankes, the Gerstles, the people in Palestine: Sebba, Walter Jelski. My only surviving sibling, Marta in Montevideo, without any knowledge of our situation, demanding help from me, which I cannot give her.

The inner pressure, the inner vacillation: I want to be a Communist, I want to go with the SED – but what they do in the cultural area is often so fundamentally wrong. Only: what is done in the West is 1000 × more odious still.

Finally: this 'struggle for freedom'. It cannot be conducted peacefully. There will be war again. And civil war. And we are no doubt preparing for it, just as the West is preparing. And I believe: we must prepare for it and must conduct it.

1951

3rd January, 6 p.m. Wednesday
[...]

New Year's Eve passed tolerably enough, a little boring, a little depressed. Lotte Sussmann and her friend Lotte Hoerger with us. [...] We ate and drank elegantly, towards 12 listened to Pieck's empty New Year's message, were in bed at 12.30.

For many years now the times in which I prefer going to bed alternate with ones in which I prefer getting up. For a long time now I have preferred going to bed a 100× over.

[...]

5th January, midnight Friday evening. Stadt Hamburg, Halle
[The rectorial issue has *still* not been decided.]

13th January, Saturday evening. Dresden
[...]

My dispute with Rita. She: there is no question that Marxism ultimately considers insoluble. The question as to the ultimate wherefore and why does not exist. I: it [the question] must not lead people astray, and so because it does lead most astray, towards lethargy, fatalism or mysticism, and inhibits reason then, wherever we are unable to get any further, we wall up the abyss – 'Strictly no entry!' – but we, *we thinkers*, must surely know, that behind the wall there is something unknown, we have to stoically accept that. But you say and you echo Marxism: 'There *is* no final and insoluble question, it is not there.' I answer this denial in Vossler's words: 'I can only congratulate you on that!' But seen practically, Marxism is, of course, right: there *must* not be an ultimate question which confuses people.

14th January, Sunday forenoon. Dresden

[...]

The programme for the summer semester was to be talked through. All of the organisational work for the department is effectively in Rita's hands. It is ever more painfully evident that I live outside Halle. From sheer necessity I announced: From Petrarch to Tasso[1] and French literature 1870–1920 with a seminar on the latter with particular reference to lyric poetry and prosody. [...]

In Berlin the lecture and the rest as usual. But immediately before the lecture I find, on my desk, a letter dated the end of December. Ulrich Riemerschmidt [the editor at Rütten and Loening] sends good wishes for the New Year and at the same time informs me, 'that for personal and practical reasons' he is leaving the management of the company and wishes me further successful co-operation with R & L. That may, yes probably will, have catastrophic consequences for me. I have a *contract* only for the three bagatelles: Maupassant, Barbusse for me and for E. But my *Modern French Poetry*, my 18ième, the collection *Scholarship and Politics*, the reprint of my Literary History! [...] Everything is up in the air, it all looks very black. [...]

19th January, 1.15 Friday night. Stadt Hamburg, Halle

Final flickering up and extinction of hope in the rectorship. Leo Stern solemnly announced himself for 5.30 in the afternoon in my department. I thought: Bearer of the Party decision, put together my 'ministry' with Rita. He solemnly brought me the Party's appreciation, and that for practical reasons it had decided in favour of Agricola. It expresses its particular regard for me, I can expect other honours from it and apart from that they expect me to keep Party discipline. I said to Stern: I agreed to Agricola and would vote for him and congratulate him. But I was weary of chasing with outstretched tongue after a sausage being held in front of me and wanted to leave at the winter semester. [...]

Riemerschmidt had carefully prepared his departure to the West [...]. The Rütten and Loening house, re-established in Frankfurt, is likely to be wound up here. So reports I. M. Lange, who halfway agreed with the shameless Maupassant critique in the *Sonntag*[2] [...]. Depending on which wind is blowing he is becoming ever more of a 150%er.

20th January, 4.30 p.m. Saturday. Dresden

Ever more depressing conditions. I feel I am an intruder. Eva lives her little-woman life here [...] with Frau Richter, the craftsmen, the tomcat, the flowers. I introduce disturbance, ill humour. I arrive exhausted, dejected, my desk is in a muddle ('tidied up'), at every moment there are gardeners, joiners, carpenters swarming around. Then immediately there's an exchange of words, a sharp expression, offence taken, E.'s breathlessness accusing me. [...] I feel so bitter. And she feels like a prisoner up here. [...]

27th January, 6.30 Saturday morning. Stadt Hamburg, Halle

As arranged Gerull[3] turned up at the KB, man around 50, energetic, chubby, dark hair and eyes, deputy manager and Party representative at Rütten and Loening. [...] Suddenly the pleasant Party comrade in a leading position, whom I. M. Lange so strongly recommended to me, is exposed as a 'criminal', psychopath, the most cunning fraud. [...] The certain result for me, however, is an absolute catastrophe. Rütten and Loening will be somehow reorganised [...] joined to Aufbau or Volk und Welt [...]. All my agreements with Riemerschmidt: Literary History reprint, *Modern French Poetry*, 18ième, Italian renaissance reprint – all of it, literally all of it rendered invalid. There remain the signed contracts: Maupassant for me, Barbusse for E. and me are being 'put on ice', for the time being the house is not allowed to publish anything new. [...] I am suddenly without any publication possibilities. [...] My volume *The Century of Voltaire*, my *Modern Poetry* [...] were returned to me, the volume of my essays has *disappeared*. Perhaps it is a good thing if I hold back all publications now. Until the insane course of our censorship and cultural policy has been surmounted. The criticisms of my Maupassant essay, of my Molière, the fate of my *Modern French Poetry*, each and every thing has for some time shown me that I can no longer write with decency, that intellectually I can no longer breathe. I repeatedly have to tell myself: *because of that* I must nevertheless *not* be untrue to the cause of Communism, this is an unpleasant side-effect or interlude of the giant transformation. I also have to explain it to myself in terms of the GDR's situation: in order to paste together the all-German state, the Party *must* come to terms with the middle-class parties; and for that very reason, it must as a Party maintain its own line with utmost radicalism. For sure – but *I* am a victim of this situation. There is in addition, the fact that I am constantly aware, with wretched bitterness, of the dreadful shortcomings in the intellectual sphere; intellectually we are just as barbaric and fanatical as the Nazis. So say nothing, efface oneself, wait. [...]

All of this is provident in another respect also: if there is no prospect of publishing, then it is more practical to transfer my attentions completely to university activities etc., i.e. *not* abdicate. For I am not certain if I can summon up the heroism to write only for my drawer, nor do I know, whether I am still capable of producing at all. [...] On the university I learned from Rita: There are very big and most unpleasant reforms imminent in accord with the 'pure line'. The specialised study of philology is to be even further restricted, the training of secondary-school teachers to be entirely affiliated or subordinated to the Education Faculty. Above all a) theory of education b) Marxism – 35 (thirty-five!) professors are being appointed for the various branches of the obligatory study of Marxism,[4] so that the mass of the students can be consistently instructed: Which means, of course, that 35 Party officials are being made into university teachers. The actual study of philology will be cut back and take place by the way. What then remains of the external reputation and inner value of our GDR universities? Rita said: probably the Party had decided in favour of Agricola as rector because I would have resisted the reform. Agricola asked me to call on him at midday yesterday. Friendly meeting. He: he would have preferred if I had been elected, and he would at last have been able to do scholarly work. (This is probably halfway his true opinion.) I shall sit in the senate again, he will support me with respect to the car question and the Academy. *I* promised loyal collaboration for 'a couple of semesters', until Rita can step into my shoes.

[...]

[Klemperer is not re-elected to the central committee of the Society for German–Soviet Friendship, the committee is largely 'proletarianised'. Klemperer reflects:] Thus I am rid of a part of my external honours.

[...]

31st January, 6 p.m. Wednesday. (Yesterday the big Volkskammer day in Berlin)

[The previous day Klemperer had been one of 13 speakers called on at short notice to support an unconditional offer of negotiations to the West German government – against militarisation, proposal of a joint council with the West German parliament etc.[5]]

2nd February, 10 p.m. Friday. Halle, Stadt Hamburg

[...]

[Reading: Lukács, Russian Realism, Maupassant, preparation for the Zola study. The formal business of the rectoral election is at last carried out:] The whole thing was very, very awkward; I would not like to have been elected like *that*. Still: Agricola will wear the chain, travel to Peace Congresses and Moscow, have everything that I would so much like to have had.

[...]

10th February, 1 p.m. Saturday. Dresden

The Party pressurises people to subscribe to *Neues Deutschland*. It is right – but it is pressure, just as it was applied under the Nazis to subscribe to the *Stürmer* etc. [...] Robi [...] gave me a page of the *N.D.* of 6 Feb.: 'Resolution of the 4th Congress of the Central Committee: the coming tasks in the universities and high schools.' Content and tendency was already familiar. Here I am interested in LQI formulations. 'Strict organisational concentration in one ten-month academic year.' – *stimulating 'progressive scholarship'*, 'Conducting research as a guide to action means, stimulating the development of a new German scholarship serving the interests of peace.' Against 'all apologetics of capitalism and all scholastic bookishness' ... 'Transition to the ideological offensive' ...

'ideological struggle against objectivism, cosmopolitanism and Social Democratism' ... [...]

Who rules? I almost think: only the Central Committee. Schröder[6] is talking
about whether Werner Krauss is now coming to Berlin or staying in Leipzig: 'I'll
speak to Ernst Hoffmann.'[7] He is the department head in the Central Committee,
not the minister. Leo Stern and Rolf: 'the Party will make sure that you get into
the Academy.'

[...]

Just now, 6 p.m., our Agnes from Piskowitz has turned up after years. [...]

13th February, 9 p.m. Tuesday evening. Dresden

Agnes stayed until Monday morning. [...] Then late in the afternoon Gusti
appeared and stayed until late evening ... [...] She said, readers' letters in the
Sonntag had defended my Maupassant against Antkowiak.[8] [...] After Gusti had
gone and E. was in bed I buckled down to the lecture and myself went to bed
at 2.30.

[...]

14th February, 10.30 Wednesday evening. Halle, Stadt Hamburg

[...]

From 4–7 an interminable faculty meeting, at which I proposed and pushed
through Rita's assistant professorship *before* she hands in her habilitation thesis.

[...]

18th February, Sunday afternoon. Dresden

On Friday, the 16 Feb., the meeting of the Executive Committee of the Kulturbund. [...] The Executive Committee is a facade like the Volkskammer. The
praesidium or the 'working committee' proposes something and it is accepted.
Someone, I no longer remember who, told me: 'they get guidance on everything
from the Central Committee.' – It appears that the CC is now the sole ruling
power. Its general secretary: Ulbricht ... Who topples whom, who fears whom
on the Central Committee? [...]

[...]

20th February, Tuesday morning and later. Dresden

[...]

The very interesting pages [in Ernst Fischer] on Th. Mann[9] made me reach for
the appropriate *very good* chapter in Hans Mayer's *Thomas Mann*. Fischer criticises
Mann for not having described 'the social roots and background' of the German
collapse. [...] But a novelist does not have a duty to write the history of society
from the beginning. He has to make a start somewhere. – Gusti related: some
hall in Chemnitz is to get a realist mural. The commission dissatisfied. 'What

do you want?' asks the painter, the Russian officer replies: 'Reality – but a little nicer!' Everything now has to be tailored to optimism and joie de vivre. *Keep smiling!*[10]

21st February, Wednesday forenoon. Dresden

[...] Yesterday in the car with E. to buy a suit, possibly also a rug on Kesselsdorferstr., the big shopping street. [...] Complete disappointment: there are crowds of people in pitiful state and non-state shops and there's the greatest shortage of textile goods everywhere, the little available poor quality and exorbitantly expensive. [...] Again the experience that Dresden is a thousand times more wretched, village-like, denuded than Halle. – So what is the situation of our GDR? Have we risen, or is, and to what extent is, our rise eyewash? Que sais je?

[..]

Despair over Lukács, it is as if I were reading Chinese. At some point I must free myself of this nightmare and simply keep on writing my own stuff, or give up scholarly writing altogether and make an attempt at my Curriculum.

[...]

10th March, 2 p.m. Saturday. Dresden
10 p.m.

In the afternoon Frau Bauer called on us for an hour with her not very attractive friend, Frau Kroch (or Koch?) – very large almost maliciously twitching grey-blue eyes, constantly rolling, mobile mouth. It turned out that this appearance the result of serious hardships and illness. The woman: Jewish, the only one of her family to survive, Riga camp, Ravensbrück, death march, last group of women about to be murdered; the soldiers lost their way somewhere near Stolp, at the last moment the Russians appeared as liberators and bearers of food. The starving women wolfed down so much, that many died of it; Frau K. was ill with typhus for weeks ... She also related that Neumark (the mysterious case – I can blame neither him nor the Russians) died in Bautzen of tuberculosis. I remember his delight when I saw him again in 1945, then he was active on a committee preparing the new constitution. [...]

17th March, Saturday forenoon. Dresden

[...] The altogether *new* and *good* thing about this session of the Volkskammer, was that several speakers censured this or that in the government programme or wanted to improve or extend it. In the afternoon the government benches were very empty and at one point Dieckmann[11] is supposed to have said – unfortunately I was outside – to much applause, he would consider it proper if the ministers demonstrated rather more interest in the chamber. So that for the first time a little parliamentary life entered the proceedings. [...]

24th March, midnight Saturday. Dresden

[...]

Very warm letter from Lerch, the young father – from another world. He is travelling to a literary historians' conference in Florence. He asks in all seriousness, whether I am going, too. How to arrange that?! He writes: 'You're well off. $\frac{3}{4}$ of the Western literature no longer exists for you (insofar as it does not describe the depravity of the bourgeoisie.)' True. But for him no Soviet, no Marxist literature exists. *Two worlds*. He writes: 'Now I implore you: leave off the politics and complete your 18ième! The politicians, whatever their colour, deal only with abstractions after all, and not with people; they are an inferior species. And politics eats its own children [...].' That's what I thought, too – and then the devil Hitler came and got me. And he's not going to get me again. And literature as art pour art is in turn an abstraction. [...]

[...]

30th March, Friday afternoon. Dresden

[... Kulturbund Executive Committee meeting ...] Gysi, only yesterday still omnipotent, has suddenly disappeared.[12] 'Given leave.' I asked why. Secretiveness, no one knows anything, whispering: there was always probably some problem with the Party. Again and again this human waste, this uncertainty. [...]

Yesterday and today E. in a very bad state – very depressing. Myself very worn out. I wrote to Hans Meyerhof; of course, I should have sent him the *LTI* long ago, now made up an excuse. Have still not brought myself to write a letter to Marta. Wretched. [...]

2nd April, 6.30 Monday morning. Dresden

[...] we fetched Gusti W. [...] She knew of Gysi's disappearance. Presumably a Western connection or tendency from the exile years has again been uncovered. (For fear of which Kahane, too, is quaking).

[...]

7th April, 6.15 Saturday morning. Stadt Hamburg, Halle

[...] The stroke of luck: Werner Krauss is so ill, that he can only manage a 2-hour class once a fortnight, so that now my lectures in Berlin are nothing by the way, but absolutely necessary. That I am *the* literary historian and *the* professor in the field in Berlin, that they cannot do without me.

9 p.m. Dresden

[Steinitz, the Berlin dean, now pulls every string at his disposal to have a car (and driver) made available for Klemperer's personal use, so that he can cope with the added teaching load in Berlin, in addition to that in Halle, while still continuing to live in Dresden. The end result:] at the end of next week a new

BMW would be ready for me in Erfurt. In part I am sceptical of such an assurance, in part I fear the gift, on which I shall permanently have to spend half of my income. But the conversation with Steinitz also awoke other hopes. He has just been elected to the Academy and has been awarded the National Prize (he bought a car off it), and I complained to him about being neglected. He: Of course I had to be in the Academy, my 70th birthday was grounds for that – then my money difficulties with regard to the car would also be resolved, because that brings in 1,000M a month. [...] Krauss was in Berlin for the Academy session and a lecture. I had not seen him for a long time. Looked terribly unhealthy. [...] Very friendly – we had *so* much to discuss. Nothing came of it. [...] Into the car at 7.45 very elated and *very* knocked out, fast drive to Halle, to bed before midnight.

8th April, Sunday forenoon. Dresden
[...]

Eva's health very bad. What good to me is the house and the car, if neither are there for her? The garden full of spring. The chestnut outside the bathroom window, the little spherical buds on the cherry trees etc. A French phrase always goes through my mind, from someone of the decadence period: le leurre éternel du printemps.
[...]

14th April, 8.30 Saturday evening. Dresden
My worry about E. I found her a little bit better, but her freshness does not last: two minutes in the garden and she is completely short of breath; now at 8.30 she has again gone to bed exhausted. [...]

As arranged Adam picked me up yesterday. [...] He [...] was recently very pessimistic about the prospects for peace. 'The Americans are coolly calculating businessmen. If they invest so much money in armaments, then they will also wage war.' I asked, how things looked for us. Tanks, aircraft, appropriate training in the SU. And how did things look when it came to generalship? He: he himself was probably capable of commanding an army. Likewise the NDP colonel Vincenz Müller, who had already held very high rank in Hitler's army.[13] Then there were another 2 generals to whom a division, perhaps a corps, could be entrusted.
[...]

At home in the evening I found Gusti Wieghardt, who had kept E. company for 48 hours.
[...]

15th April, 7 a.m. Sunday morning. Dresden
Everything repeats itself and is then nevertheless different. Now I am full of 'the car' as I was in 1936. [...] Today I am expecting Wünsche, the boss of the

Sternring petrol station and haulage company on Tharandterstr. He is to fetch the car from Eisenach for me. The enormous costs – I vacillate between fear and laughter at our financial strength. [...] Once again the old weight on my mind: will I manage to play my part right to the end, will no one notice my ignorance? It has increased since earlier days. Once it was only Provençal, Old French, Portuguese, Romanian and French, Spanish, Italian etc. grammar, Latin and philosophy that I did not know – now on top of all that I do not know any Marxism. [...] Why do I stay in my post? Fear of earning too little, hopes of the harvest of my seventieth birthday, fear of the barrenness, when, in retirement, I sit down to write and am no longer able to do so ... Meditating on it does no good. I have to muddle on. [...]

16th April, Monday morning. Dresden
Yesterday morning, driver applications. A man of 52, Lindner, hired. Later, consultations with Wünsche, who is fetching the car from Eisenach tomorrow [...]. I gave Wünsche two crossed cheques,10,000 from E.'s account, 4,750 from mine. Sensation for me.

[...]

22nd April, Sunday afternoon. Dresden
[...] At the centre of all things here, THE car, dark grey, big and elegant, 4 doors, 25 cwt, 55 HP, Wünsche had brought *Bel-Ami* (I thought of the name yesterday) on Wednesday evening and the next day E. had already been driven to an SED meeting in Dölzschen community house. I am convinced the whole village will now be saying: 'Bossdom just like under the Nazis. House extension, big car – when are we going to hang the Jew Klemperer – Hitler was right.' This and the heavy financial burden means I cannot feel entirely happy about the business.

[...]

27th April, 6.45 Friday morning. Stadt Hamburg, Halle
[...]
But at the centre was naturally the car. [...] The car is a blessing and a vita nova for E. The improvement in her health is *probably* 40% due to the warm spring weather, but certainly 60% it's to the car. She is mobile again, is delivered from her winter imprisonment. She drove with me to Chemnitzer Platz, bought flowers, drove to a nearby picture framers; on Monday afternoon we went to Kino Schauburg [...]. Back without being tired out, and when Gusti W. turned up unexpectedly, E., who otherwise quite knocked out, goes to bed immediately after eating, stayed up, cheerful and excited, until after 11, and was cheerful and fresh the next day, even worked a little in the garden. [...] Lindner acts both as servant-chauffeur and maid of all work. [...] but the real elixir is simply

Bel-Ami, which gives her back a life in the world. [...] I hope our finances will always be sufficient. But at any rate: it makes me happy that E.'s spirits are reviving ... [...]

[...]

30th April, 10 p.m. Monday evening. Dresden

[...]

Frau Kreisler brought along two witnesses to say that she had borne the name Sara. At first I wanted to state only that on 13 February 45 I had to deliver the evacuation order to her. Then it occurred to me: Compliance with a Gestapo order – I could end up sharing Neumark's fate. So we made the statement and had our names verified by the Party office. [...]

[Drive with E. and Gusti Wieghardt to the estate under construction where the latter is getting a house.] Dreadful identical unlovable boxes, one after the other. [...] What interested us about it: here we were very close to 15b Caspar David Friedrichstr., to the place, places, where we experienced the worst. The dead of Caspar David Friedrichstr.! The last journey of our 'jalopy' along Teplitz-erstr. to the scrapyard![14] And now: our Bel-Ami. I only suggest everything that has to be set forth in my Curriculum – if I get around to it, *if.* [...]

[...]

5th May, Saturday afternoon. Dresden

[...] More significant a conversation with Frau Steinhoff: Krauss's serious illness, the Humboldt Uni. without a professor on the spot. And yet a Romance languages centre should be established here, because the French are conducting tremendous propaganda through their Centre de culture [in West Berlin] and are drawing our students: over there they have the most modern periodicals and books, lectures by the best French professors and all for nothing and all in line with anti-Eastern policy and ideology. [...]

[...]

8th May, midnight Tuesday. Dresden stopover

[...]

Note: when I asked Agricola for permission to absent myself from the Liberation Day [8 May] ceremonies, he said something like: 'When the Nazis organised an act of state, everyone came, everyone had to come. We must manage that, too. And *we* (he meant the Party and the Left in the senate) must lead the way.' He was not entirely wrong, and I stayed. But the Nazi-like pattern did get very much on my nerves again. Particularly in the theatre. The constant clapping and standing up, the unvarying formulae: veliki Stalin! [...]

12th May, Saturday before Whitsun. Dresden
[...]

At the station [coming from Halle] Eva and Lindner. That was a real joy. I would so much like to bring E. back to her old self. – On Wed. 9 May, alarm at 3.30 a.m., 5.50 express train to Berlin. [...] Plenum [Volkskammer] at 12. Ulbricht spoke. Content good and brusque, vocally and formally not as elegant as Grotewohl, who is on leave. Climax as in all declarations this week: we shall force through the referendum[15] *against Adenauer's ban* even in the West, we shall defend peace 'to the utmost'. I asked myself and everyone else: what does 'to the utmost' mean, and no one could give me an answer. To the utmost corresponds to the last resort, after all ... [...] I left before the end, took the 6 p.m. train from the Ostbahnhof, found Eva at the station again, this time at 9.15. Then the next morning the usual trip to Berlin in the car.

Berlin
[...] Krauss case. He is so ill, that he does not come at all any more. [...] Then it emerged: Krauss has agreed with Harig,[16] that Romance languages are to be 'given up' in Berlin, that Leipzig will be the 'centre', that Krauss, is taking his actual [Ph.D.?] students [...] with him to Leipzig. That would then leave me in Berlin with a drained remnant and the task of winding things up. [...] And Krauss has all, literally all the trumps in his hand. He came to us stripped and naked from Marburg as martyr and brave renegade: then a member of the Academy, National Prize [...] member of the Central Committee; [...]. Sometimes I have the greatest respect for his things, then again I resent his obscurity, which so impresses all the world. [...]

13th May, midday, Whit Sunday. Dresden
[Klemperer inevitably continues to complain that he is overworked and is spreading himself too thinly – but he can't stop, promises to write an article on 'Americanism and Cosmopolitanism' here, provide a foreword there, give a talk to writers, has to attend the KB Congress etc.]

18th May, midday Friday. Department, Halle
[Leipzig Congress[17]] [...] Conversation with Hans Mayer and Walther Victor – important: through H.M. met Hermlin [...]. *Pleasant* meeting. Blond handsome neutral-looking young man. He said, that back then he had not wanted to attack me as a scholar. My texts were *dangerous* in the hands of dangerous teachers. In that he is right. But then: Let them read Resistance literature *instead*! With that he misunderstands everything. [...]

20th May, Sunday evening. Dresden
[...] At 8.30 [on the 17th] I drove to Berlin [from Halle], where everything was as usual, Frau Steinhoff accompanied me from the university to the institute as

always, the subject of Werner Krauss was again discussed, with questions left open. Frau Steinhoff in favour of Berlin remaining capital with respect to the university as well, she says, we can withstand the competition of the Centre de culture, I also had West Berlin auditors. [The next day Harig speaks to the faculty of Halle University to win them over to the coming reforms, concluding:] the university must quickly and reliably train functionaries and teachers of the democratic state, the Soviet Union was the great model, research need not suffer as a result. [Later Klemperer discusses the Berlin arrangements with Harig, who concedes two centres for Romance languages in the GDR.] I walked very slowly to the Stadt Hamburg with a very exhausted heart and very mixed feelings. On the one hand: In what condition is Berlin University today?! [...] What kind of discarded, torn gown am I being offered as chair – and only because there is no one else, and because Krauss is moribund, and because Krauss egocentrically wants the 'centre' transferred to Leipzig. On the other hand: Berlin is the capital and the flag and must not be given up, and whoever is professor in Berlin is, despite everything, at the very top. And subjectively: that at the age of 70 and with one foot in the grave, Berlin should after all fall to me! Vanitatum vanitissimum vanitas! And yet I am once again in agony, and am quaking for fear that at the last moment this could once again miscarry like the rectoral business. Examiner in Berlin, Director of the Romance Languages Institute (not just department!) ... in my imagination it's something tremendous ... it brings back to me Georg's longing[18] etc. etc. And then again: the Humboldt University is a ruin! On the other hand it is being built up, is, despite everything, *the* university of the Republic. Etc. ad infinitum, I could not get it out of my mind again, I go to sleep with it, I wake up with it.

[...]

24th May, 6.15 Thursday morning. Dresden

On Wednesday aft. with E. to the Saxon Switzerland from 4–7. As far as Kirnitzschtal, there a slow walk in the woods for a few hundred yards. It gave E. a great deal of pleasure – but what melancholy pleasure: in 1945 we walked the many hundreds of miles from Munich to Dresden. The landscape we had not seen for a long time, the 'rocks', the River Elbe, Bad Schandau and Königstein town from above under an overcast sky, fresh greenery, clear view wonderful.

[...]

26th May, 5 a.m. Saturday morning. Halle

[...] In Berlin usual daily round: Frau Steinhoff congratulated me [...], Christel Näther and Winfried Schröder (the seldom-seen actual assistant and favourite of Werner Krauss) acted as if I were certain to get the Berlin professorship, as if Krauss, even for Leipzig, had become an uncertain factor. But I repeatedly emphasised to the others and to myself, that nothing was decided yet. Harig can do nothing without Steinitz, Steinitz, the dean, nothing without the faculty. And Rita says: all of them together can do nothing without the Central Committee, that in our case – also in *her's*, which is closely linked to mine: does she stay in Halle, where she is supposed to become one of the 4 prorectors, or does she go to Berlin, to the ministry, or to Berlin, to me, or to a double post in Berlin, which would create a tremendous position for me – in our case has not spoken yet ... *The Central Committee!* [...]

[...]

30th May, Wednesday morning. Dresden

[...]

The day before yesterday Berlin trip with E. and Rita. How are decisions taken in the GDR? What does the Ministry decide, what the Central Committee, *who* is the one, *who* is the other, what are the ultimate motives? [Klemperer and Rita Schober have discussions at both on this occasion.] It is evidently Rita's opinion and evidently corresponds to the truth, that all final decisions emanate from the Central Committee. Who there holds the university in his hands? People who know nothing of it, nothing of scholarship, who are SED functionaries and catechism people. [...] Overall therefore: the administration of the high schools of the GDR, in whose hands is it? [...]

5th June, Tuesday morning. Dresden

[Other Berlin discussions: It looks *bad* for my entry to the Academy; Steinitz, elected with Rompe in February, for reasons unknown still unconfirmed by the government, Krauss was never available, and if, as I said, Frings is my enemy ... Things do not look good for my National Prize either: Krauss keeps on promising the 'laudatio' and does not provide it. [...] [Later that day – Thursday – Krauss himself turns up in the department and a discussion develops between him and Klemperer – Krauss again proposing the removal of all significant scholarly activities to Leipzig.] I vigorously rejected that, neither Berlin nor I would be satisfied with second place – two centres! Krauss: then he would give up Leipzig, install *his* people at the Academy [...]. We both avoided quarrelling. [...] We parted amicably, the actual point at issue is to be discussed tomorrow. [...]

[Klemperer takes Eva to hospital again for examination – injections, dietary and hygiene prescriptions. Eva regards it all with a degree of mockery.] What remains with all of that is the high blood pressure, the shortness of breath, the disablement, the worry.

[...]

After that: yesterday morning to the vote [Plebiscite against the re-militarisation of West Germany and for the conclusion of a peace treaty between the Allies and Germany]. Why does it last three days? And does it have any real purpose, will it achieve anything?[19] I listened to Rias for a long time and on it the review of the West German newspapers. They say: 'Propaganda – we all want peace, but not (*my* expression) the *pax sovjetica*'. [He also listens to a broadcast on science research and exclaims:] That is world-class scholarship, and *we* are isolated. And: that is scholarship, while over here now there is monotonously, boringly, from morning till midnight, the never-changing political cliche...

[...]

12th June, 9.15 a.m. Dresden
Last week's tour: Thurs. 7th, Berlin, Friday 8th, Halle, Leipzig
[Leipzig meeting with Krauss and others.] So everything was very nice – except: Krauss shot his mouth off, I had to translate his Marxist and philosophical theory into ordinary German for myself and I could only say yes to everything in an essentially simpler form. And Krauss took it as a matter of course to claim for himself, for Leipzig, the leadership of the whole of Romance languages studies in the GDR, just as he has top place in supervising the coming generation of academics. [...] I had mixed feelings: partly depressed, partly like someone who is playing chess several moves ahead. Berlin will be what I make of it in collaboration with Rita at the Ministry. [...]

[Klemperer now has an additional source of anxiety: 'Review' of his Party membership.[20]] Rita telephoned me yesterday from Halle, that I had nothing at all to fear. Nevertheless ... I know nothing about surplus value, nothing about the history of the German working-class movement, nothing about empiriocriticism[21] etc. etc., rien de rien.[22]

[...] On Monday a letter from Peter Klemperer and his wife: their second son was born on 5 June: *Berthold Victor*. The names snap at one another.[23] [...] Inge and Peter both want to take their state examination in the spring, he has caught up with her, since she has fallen behind bearing children. He changes nappies, bathes etc. the offspring, so that *she* has time to study. 'My grandmother does not understand it' – (and the grandfather is spinning in his grave). *Berthold Victor!*

[...]

15th June, 6 a.m. Friday morning. Stadt Hamburg, Halle
[...] Professor in Berlin (unanimously accepted by the faculty) and 'reviewed'.

The review the day before yesterday from 6 p.m. until well after 7. Climbing the stairs to the Senate Hall [at Halle University] severe pains and shortness of breath – *I* notice no excitement, but my heart notices it and complains [...], to such a degree that the young woman (probably a secondary-school teacher), who was the spokeswoman, said a couple of friendly, reassuring words to me. I sat in the hallway until they had examined my questionnaire and my curriculum vitae. I was the only candidate present. Who was the commission? Everyone introduced themselves, I did not catch a single name. A black-haired very quiet man, certainly about 50, chaired, the young lady was the examiner, about 8 other young people, two of them women sat there silently. All of them from the start and in increasing measure with an expression of the greatest sympathy. As I came in I said with a smile, I was anxious – the unfamiliar situation of

being examined after so many years examining! One of the anonymous observers likewise smiling: 'Perhaps *we* are just as anxious.' Then everyone sat down,
the actual examiner began: 'Comrade Klemperer, please tell us something about
your long life.' – 'What would you like to know?' – 'Your relationship to the
working class.' – At that I [. . .] got into my stride and followed up with Georg's
treatment of Lenin and pieces from successful lectures, repeatedly threw in that
I was at home in the field of culture and cultural policy, could 'do' Montesquieu,
regretted the lack of a handbook on the German working-class movement, was
not at all at home in Marxist theory especially financial policy and science,
reaped evident success with that, was not asked anything at all, on the contrary
was consoled, that *one man* simply could not take in everything, and sparkled
for a whole hour. Between myself and the examiner there was a lengthy disagreement conducted in cordial and lively fashion on Goethe's democratism –
[. . .] the chairman muttered sympathetically, Goethe had also been debated at
the Party schools, there was room for differing opinions [. . .] Afterwards there
were friendly handshakes; I: 'so on the whole satisfactory?' *she*, the Party was
delighted that I was its comrade, I was 'in the front line'. So that was a weight
off my chest. I have heard many unpleasant things about these reviews, the
young students, I am told in Berlin, are treated roughly, the functionaries really
are tested (dates etc.) like schoolboys. Frau Dr Steinhoff on the other hand (of
course!) relates beaming, how nice they were to her … Moral: 'He that has,
shall be given.' [. . .]
   [. . .]

20th June, Wednesday afternoon. Dresden

[. . .]
   [The Klemperers drive to Piskowitz to visit their former maid Agnes, who
sheltered them when they were on the run after the bombing of Dresden in
February 1945. Klemperer encourages Agnes's 13-year-old daughter to attend
the Third World Youth and Student Games in August in East Berlin. (Her mother
had been anxious about the girl going to the big city and about the costs
involved. Klemperer leaves 50M.)] Home at 7. Fatigued, depressed, fell asleep at
my desk. If only I were consistently convinced, that I was really supporting the
right cause.
   The car! Like the army boots in the Russo-Japanese war: cardboard soles.
Recently the ball bearings, then a screw breaks, then the wrench breaks, then
the cap of the petrol tank cracked – the steel, again and again the steel, 'we
can't replace the Swedish steel!' This morning the petrol pump fails – the
membrane has to be obtained from the West! In the BMW workshop here there
are 40 cars, as new as ours and as broken down as ours. It is not simply the
constant financial burden, not simply even the feeling of uncertainty. But
something more general: how does that accord with all the boasting about
economic progress, about the 5 Year Plan,[24] with all the fine speeches and
writing? What if the whole of our GDR is like our beautiful BMW, on which

there is no guarantee, and whose every bone has been creaking from the very start.

Something else: With the afternoon post came the *Hamburger Romanistische Jahrbuch* [Hamburg Romance Languages Yearbook] vol. 3. *Six hundred printed pages* and all of it pure scholarly work. And here in the GDR there is no possibility of publishing scholarly philology. And the big lexical study [...] by Lerch. Where can I get the time to work like *that*? I shall never be a philologist the way he is [...] but my 18ième, my Barbusse, I could still very well manage that, if I did not wear myself out in the vita activa. And again the general feeling of depression: is *our* scholarship here more free or just as free or even perhaps less free? [...]

[Klemperer is outraged when he hears that some committed academics are singing Communist songs with their students at the conclusion of lectures. He exasperatedly asks himself if there is not after all too much in common between Communist and Hitlerite youth organisations.]

22nd June, 6.30 Friday morning. Stadt Hamburg, Halle

[...]

[In Berlin] I now drove [...] to the Volkskammer, the Central Council of the VVN was meeting in the SED fraction room, Schumann took me into a side room and informed me [about the International Congress in Vienna]. In the department after the second lecture I met with Rita and Robi who had the invitation from the Central Committee to the Stalin Language Conference tomorrow.[25] So my semester finishes with a *drum roll*.

25th–26th June, 11 p.m. Monday evening. Dresden

[On Saturday morning from Dresden to Berlin.] ... at 5.30 on Saturday morning to the 'Theoretical Party Conference' on language questions on the anniversary of the Stalin publication. It was a very hot day and in the relatively small theatre with a not especially high ceiling in the 'House of the Press' the temperature was completely suffocating. [... Klemperer is worn out and frequently falls asleep.] But the morning was extremely and doubly interesting. 1) [...] Oelssner [the keynote speaker] only touched in passing on the core and actual linguistic part of the thing, instead expatiated more generally: language degeneration, quoting my *LTI*. [...) On the whole it is all a bit like dogma and dogma interpretation, synod and Talmud school. Then again Oelssner was altogether liberal in his emphasis on tradition, the merits of earlier times. 2) the trappings. Wilhelm Pieck (in white shirt) and Ulbricht present all morning. The tempestuous greeting, the ritual standing up and applauding, whenever holy names are mentioned, is too byzantine for me, the ritual is still the same as at the 3rd Party Congress. 3) personally valuable contact with many VIPs. [...] In short: the pleasant feeling of being part of things and being seen. When Oelssner mentioned my book, Rita nudged me: 'You can expect the National Prize now.' But again it will get no further than the expectation.

27th June, 2 p.m. Wednesday. Director's Room, Romance Languages Department, Berlin

View of the Kupfergraben [arm of the River Spree]. In front the flags of the Chinese exhibition, on the other side the facade of a destroyed museum, on which building work is being done, on the surviving pediment the inscription: Artem non odit nisi ignarus.[26] River barges on the dark-dirty channel; building workers come with barrow loads of rubble and unload them into the barges. Yesterday evening a little bit of the usual private life on the boats, as befits a novel of old Berlin. This now my department and my director's office – but there is bitterness underlying the success. From his Charité bed the sick Werner Krauss is trying to snatch all the power for himself (as a dying man tries to snatch the blanket?) At issue is the training of assistants, students, faculty members ... and the real first place in Romance Language Studies. Also, in this department *only* the director's room is better than the least dive in Halle. The other rooms (on the ground floor of the vast, massive building) are smaller than in Halle, and there is hardly anything left of a department library. [...]

[...] I sit here making notes – all alone, master of the department – and without any feeling of being master, on the brink of my first journey across the postwar German border, and without any pleasure in it. I will be without any contact with Eva for a whole week ... It's possible that in this widowed week she will feel better than usual. The strophantin injections have not been any help so far. She is going to fetch Trude Scherner to us in the car. [...]

[On Wednesday, 27th June, Klemperer left Berlin to attend an international congress of the Victims of Nazi Persecution in Vienna, returning on 4th July; the conference largely left him jaded, nor could he summon up any enthusiasm for the city, which he had not seen for several decades. Only a few notes and quotations from this trip.]

[Among his fellow delegates were Rosa Thaelmann, the widow of the pre-1933 German Communist leader Ernst Thaelmann, who was murdered in Buchenwald, and Alfred Kantorowicz, who was to become a friend;] Kantorowicz, the disproportionately large aquiline nose, the twinkling eyes, the somewhat tilted angle of the head. Very friendly contact; literature and Nazi period. He was in England, translated Mao's 'Speech to artists and writers' from English.[27] [...]

30th June, 5.30 a.m. Saturday. Vienna

I have little interest in the streets and buildings. They are the same famous old buildings, houses, names, that I encountered long ago, and which do not surprise me. Herrengasse, Spiegelgasse – on one of these I called on [the writer] Marie von Ebner-Eschenbach.[28] The elegance of the shop windows. In front of each clothing or manufactured-goods shop or perfumery Julius Meyer lectures us, that the [GDR state] HO is cheaper and better. Only for leather goods does he make an exception. He has no interest in bookshops. I come across no book that might be familiar to us. Different authors or such people as are no longer made available in the GDR. [...]

2nd July, 5 a.m. Monday morning. Vienna

[. . .]

The everywhere identical (Soviet) pattern of these conference habits, the clapping and the clapping along, the standing up, the rhythmic clapping, the nullity of the debate speeches, the pure formality of the votes and elections – everything has been laid down beforehand by a small circle, every plenum votes as it is told, 'contribution to the debate' worked out collectively beforehand.

8th July

Everything grows hazy. Again and again the cafés, there are so many of them, again and again the same speeches sweeping past – I have a typescript of what is most important and will prepare my paper from that.

[. . .]

The journey [back] was pleasant, uneasy only because of the customs inspections: I had 2 lbs of coffee in my suitcase and 170 cigarettes. But we got through – the others equally burdened – without problems; greatest strictness at the GDR border. [. . .] All these notes would have been fuller, if I had not found unwelcoming conditions in Dresden, and if I were not so incurably tired.

8th July, midday Sunday. Dresden

[. . .]

At 5.30 p.m. on Wednesday I called from the station, to send the car for me. The car with E. and Trude Scherner in Bad Schandau, Frau Richter sick with influenza.

Very inconvenient circumstance: Frau Richter a patient since Saturday and definitely in need of care for another week. Lindner is now helping out in the house as best he can, but he cannot do everything, and he is not here on Sundays. E. constantly receiving treatment and not improved. Thus I am very much taken up with domestic matters. On top of that extreme tiredness, stifling heat and mental depression. A mountain of work to do.

[. . .]

I must now deal with: 1) the paper on Vienna and the VVN (Schumann wants to give it to the *Sonntag*). 2) the article on LQI for Oelssner (*Einheit* Party journal), 3) the Goncourt study to accompany *Germinie Lacerteux*.[29] In addition during the next few days trips to Berlin, Halle, Burgstädt (KB). – When holidays? When Maupassant? When the Spanish lecture?

[. . .]

8th July, Sunday night

Eva must have suffered a heart attack between 8.30 and 9.30. She was lying stiffly on her back, mouth and eyes open – but quite peacefully and uncontorted, when I brought her tea to her bed at 9.30. When she lay down at 8.30, she said she did not feel particularly well, complained, as often recently, about pressure in her chest. It was no different from 100 times recently, an hour later I usually found her reading or sleeping. – I called Trude Scherner, Frau Richter came, all three of us saw immediately, that it was over. I telephoned in vain for a doctor - Frau Frenzel, a duty doctor, the police, Dr Grube – [...] finally Grube came. He said immediately: dead – probably an hour or longer ... The stifling heat – just at that moment there was a little thunder. He said: gentle death, no suffering, the most desirable. I have purely egoistical feelings: What will become of me? I am quite alone, everything is valueless for me now, childishly I lack only the physical courage to follow her, but I lack such courage entirely.

I do not know what to do with this night. I was upstairs once, at about 12; we have left the table lamp on and opened the windows. It is so hot, the decomposition will begin quickly. I lack the physical courage to sit up there. Wake – all of that seems so literary to me. I try to raise memories, I try somehow to 'behave' – it would only be literature, in accordance with a model, 'the done thing'. I am merely completely numb and wish this night were over. – What will happen then? This house! Weller made an effort to complete my expensive birthday present for E. in time: the gravel paths. The amount we have put into this garden! And how much it was E.'s delight. Truly her last bit of happiness – thank God that I did not spare any expense on it. The garden and our blind tomcat, who today cannot sleep in the hollow of her knees as usual. I have just fed him, he sat on my page here for quite a while. – What now? On Tuesday and Wednesday examinations are set in Halle and Berlin. Call off? It's probably the proper thing. – But what will I do with myself here? Again and again: what will I do at all? What still has value to me? – I am very egoistical; I think only about myself, I think it is a harder blow for me than for her.

Everything about me is literature. That I begin a new page here: si morte di Madonna Eva.[30] Everything about me is blunted and false. Only the emptiness, the fear of the emptiness of the rest of my life and the fear of the emptiness of death is genuine. I shall be absolutely alone. Who has true feelings for me – for whom do I have true feelings? [...] I am absolutely alone. And all property and all honour, that which I have and that which I am striving for – it is all worthless.

In the late afternoon Gustl had cut our hair. Yesterday E. bought herself a pair of slippers and a pair of sandals. A couple of days ago, while I was in Vienna, she drove with Weller to Schellerau, where there's some kind of botanic garden for Alpine plants. Lindner took a whole number of photographs: E. in conversation with the gardeners, bent down studying the flowers, walking carefully and elegantly along the stone paths [...] – everything so fresh and animated. No sign of the stoop, which sometimes worried me during the last year.

The little tomcat would so like to get into the bedroom.

E.'s greatest sorrow was probably the loss of her compositions. No one knows how creative she was. She lamented, that everything she created was destroyed: her compositions, her pictures [...]. The Maupassant volume is all that remains – and is unjustly again and again ascribed to me. I have always found it depressing, that all the outward honours went to me. She was a 1000× more talented than I: musician, painter, philologist, and she was 1000× braver, more moral, more altruistic, free, independent, more adept than I, and she was, in complete contrast to me, never envious and never ambitious. The only thing that soothes my conscience: I never denied it and told her so a 1000×.

No one will see this death as tragic. 'A beautiful death' ... 'reached a good age' ... 'much happiness' ... But I, I am so dreadfully alone.

It is past 4 and bright daylight. I have written to Marta – I had finished the corresponding letter to the Compensation Office, when I brought E. her tea, 20 minutes later than usual because of this letter.

9th July, after 12 on Monday night

The first day without her. Constant activity. [...] I brought Gusti Wieghardt over here in the car. Long heartfelt visit over lunch and coffee. From her came the suggestion of an official funeral. Phoned Hilse. [...] Long late evening visit by Grube. Imbecilic philosophising. Of course the notion of 'a loving God' is a blasphemy, but this denial of an innate question as to beginning and end is childish. All human reason asks about beginning and end. Grube's: *'being'* exists *'always'*, is senseless. The best thing: a robust Catholicism. E. said, she 'wanted to let herself be surprised'.

12th July, 5.30 Thursday morning

E. would have been 69 today, her garden was supposed to be finished today. Yesterday at 1.15 on 11 July her funeral took place in Tolkewitz.

The day before yesterday, the 10th, I was in Berlin, and that was a good thing. As long as I am involved in public business, I don't think of anything. [...] At 5 Mackie came to my department; he was very upset. Doris and the children in Weisswasser, somewhere near Bautzen [...]. He sent her a telegram.

Yesterday the ceremony. It turned into a big event. And childishly I felt caressed, even though I know how little it all means. Letters of condolence, telegrams, flowers; in the early morning from Halle: the university. Kitzing driving the big Mercedes: Rita, Reitzenstein for the faculty, Hadwig Kirchner[31] for the department, Frau Stahl. From the Halle KB Frau ... the name's gone, my right hand when I was in charge there and the young student representative – that name is gone, too, also a new man to me for the Dresden KB. I found the Halle University group already here when I returned from the bank. Horrible things [...] there. Whether I had authority 'beyond decease'? The answer proved to be yes – otherwise there would have been legal problems. I merely had to swear on oath that there were no relatives of the woman in existence entitled to inherit. Frau Richter swimming in tears and rapture all day. Both equally genuine and equally intensive. Very beautiful wreaths and flowers; Weller could not do enough – when we came back from the cemetery, there were new flowers in all the rooms. [...] The ceremony was really dignified and really flattered my vanity. Over 100 people present, a profusion of flowers, wreaths, ribbons, Brigitte Jährig with the VVN flag, with its black crepe, standing by the grave, pretty organ and cello playing: two Bach preludes, a very calm speech simply read out by Gusti W. without pathos, a likewise altogether dignified and rhetorically decent shorter speech by Hilse, Gusti humanely private and literary, Hilse political for VVN and SED. Really offensive only the proprieties as directed by the same man, who had already fetched the coffin here and now gave instructions: 'The next mourners to take their leave, please' whereupon one then had to stand by the coffin for a minute ... 'the next mourners to pay their last respects', whereupon one then stood in a small group, while the coffin sank, and the flag signalled the descent, as if it were a car getting a place in a car park etc. etc. always in a jolly voice, and then I slipped the man the 20M which he had certainly counted on, given the number of wreaths, and the departing car got a last warmly sympathetic farewell, and then 'the next gentleman, please', I don't know if another notable and another estimate of 20M. But the drollest thing was, that I nevertheless felt myself in some degree pleasantly moved by the whole spectacle. Just as in Italy they used to say of a newspaper: è pagato and believed it anyway ... Besides: there was quite evidently genuine warmth in the two speeches and likewise evidently on the part of a proportion of those attending. (The procession of hands to shake – I did it quite decently.) Late in the afternoon our guests drove off animated; Doris stayed, I sat until ten in the evening with her and Trude, alone after that dosing and leafing through books until about 1.

14th July, Saturday afternoon. Dresden

[...] Yesterday in Leipzig. The whole of Romance Studies, the curriculum. Baldinger present, von Jan, Brummer, Rita, myself, Krauss [...], Thalheim. Krauss looked more like a corpse than E. in her coffin. He went out after a short time, and then we were told he had to go home to bed. Moribundus. [...] I enjoyed being able to dominate a little. I formulated a resolution against the swelling up of the Education faculties – signed by everyone ... [...] I then came home in the evening very worn out and hopelessly depressed. The desk covered in letters of condolence and other bits of paper – I in front of it all dosing and paralysed.

15th July, towards evening. Sultriness and thunder

The Saturday also passed in a state of paralysis. Every time, when I wanted to start some kind of work, some visitor or other. [...]

A week has passed since E.'s death. I now bear no kind of responsibility any more, have no binding tie. I am therefore more free than before, I have nothing to fear any more – I fear only nothingness. Both the nothingness of my life, which has to be numbed and the nothingness of death.

Am I still vain, do I still have pleasure in success? Yes, almost against my will and at the next moment ridiculing that Yes. As when Rita said to me – Leo Stern had told her under seal of silence – my name had been mentioned for the Berlin rectorship, as when I think of my new professorship.

[...]

19th July, Thursday forenoon. Dresden

Everything just goes so dully and steadily on. Still ambitious for this and that, at the same time always a sense of wronging E., a sense of betrayal and disloyalty, as it were, and always in every bit of ambition an agonising feeling of futility. Again and again: I am still alive out of cowardice, not for the sake of some 'mission'.

The worst was the Tuesday morning. Frau Richter had tormented me, the urn's place in Tolkewitz was unworthy – a closer cemetery, what do I know? I gave her a free hand. Together with Weller she has – she enthused – found such a beautiful spot. Dölzschen cemetery, truly a wonderful place for an outing, behind the Pfeifers' farm up in the village, a view into the far distance and down to Dresden, surroundings – view for whom? Frau Rasch, Frau Richter, Frau Stahl, the three attendants, Weller, Lindner and myself. A black metal can (a bit like a pound of peas or fish or perhaps a small mess tin, so says Trude Scherner) is presented to me. 'Satisfy yourself that it's the right one.' The official who has brought the can from Tolkewitz, laboriously deciphers the stamped letters: Eva Klemperer † 8/7/51, *Königsberg. 12/7/82. He has pulled the little tin out from under a black cloth, covers it again: 'Please follow me.', strides with dignity to the burial place. And then the final straw: He presented the can to me again: 'Place your hand on it for the last farewell!' I really did, although I would have liked to hit the fellow in the face. The others also placed their hand on it. Then a very small hole had been prepared in the big grave. The man puts the tin into it, remains standing with his head bowed, commands: 'A minute's silent remembrance!' After a couple of seconds, in which I felt nothing at all, I stood up straight with a jolt. The loathsome event [...] was at an end. I said to Weller, I found the business revolting, during the 'silent remembrance' the man had been thinking about his tip, Weller should decide how large it was to be. Five marks, said Weller, for the official from Tolkewitz and five for the cemetery superintendent here, and now he, Weller, would 'arrange' the grave. A rockery, rhododendron, a very simple stone for both of us – because I get an adjoining hole for my tin. – The can haunts me. – Eva's 'I want to let myself be surprised.' This cannot be all, these few ashes. But the dear Lord, in whatever form, cannot be either: The question as to beginning and meaning is unscholarly and obstructive and dangerous. Well and good. But to deny the question is unmarxist, for it is posed by reason and therefore to the highest degree altogether real. It is not innate to reason, but only culturally developed?? But it is already, after all, *potentially* contained in the dimmest jungle ape and in the remotest protoplasm. Everything that exists today and will exist tomorrow is given in the first seed, even the human reason, that examines this finest seed. One has to let oneself be surprised and will most probably not be surprised at all and end up being deceived and looking stupid.

[...] Meanwhile next door poor Frau Schmidt is dying so agonisingly of cancer of the liver, without being given any morphine, that I consider Eva lucky.

I sleep so well and peacefully next to her empty bed, on which she lay dead, on which ... I think it is the same piece of furniture which since 1906 she has frequently painted, decorated, somehow touched up. What a story. Take your pick: in the style of Crébillon fils[32] or Anatole France[33] or Bossuet.[34] Not a single thought in me which is not literary, not a single true feeling – always only emptiness, the fear of emptiness, professional thoughts and vanities and difficulties again and pangs of conscience about it all. E. was so much braver, courageous, important than I. What was she really, what was I to her, what did she know and think of me? In these last months (since our return to Dresden) there was already so much distance between us and we had drifted so far apart. But always whenever that overwhelmed me, whenever it gripped me, when I saw her moving around *stooped*, then I could embrace her, feel her, talk to her. And now the tin can. And the tomcat sleeps peacefully on her empty bed, just as he slept beside her, and I – no different from the tomcat.

[...]

Our old dining cubicle next to the kitchen has now been fitted out, my study relieved. E. painted two mighty cockerels on the cupboard downstairs, martial beasts with Bersaglieri tails. Everywhere E. and everywhere emptiness. In the garden never-ending abundance of fruit. We give it away on all sides.

24th July, Tuesday evening. Dölzschen

I am so terribly alone and empty. I cannot work. [...] I am glad of every distraction. [...] On Sunday I had Horst Heintze as guest from midday to late afternoon. He is in barracks in Königstein on a training course – interpreters for the [Youth and Student] festival. A good lad – but what can he be to me? On Monday evening Katja Scheinfuss[35] ate with me – alone with me up here – the household downstairs. Shop talk and gossip. What can she be to me? This morning Frau Steinhoff appeared quite unexpectedly: she had accompanied her husband on an official trip, she stayed until 2. I showed her the house, the garden, I drove up to the cemetery with her – the grave with the wilted wreaths, soaked ribbons looks ghastly. Conversations touching on religion. [...]

27th July, towards 11 p.m. Friday evening. Dresden

In Berlin yesterday. [...] I allowed myself to be included in a [KB] commission as representative of Romance Studies and Literary Studies. I pursue all matters of business and ambition as if they really still meant something to me, and in the course of this pursuit I also still believe in their meaning, I am roused by the honour and the money, feel this interest with a pang of conscience – disloyalty out of cowardice! – but afterwards there is the ghastly feeling of nullity, the emptiness to be numbed or forgotten in sleep.

[Rita Schober is now in a powerful position as a senior official in the Education Ministry in addition to her academic post.]

29th July, Sunday afternoon. Dresden

It is very funny, but my life is to great extent determined by the two factors *tomcat* and *petrol*. It is probably the cat which ties me most closely to this museum house. He is E.'s legacy, he is alone a great deal, in his blindness he can exist only here, he still has many years to live – who will look after him? I do not have absolute confidence in Frau Richter in this regard ... But I probably have to be in Berlin *two* days a week and one in Halle. (Do I *have* to? After all I could retire from everything. Did I *have* to leave E. alone so much before? My disloyal ambition ...) [...] I have asked Doris, if she was serious, when she said she could give up two rooms and a garage in her house to me.

[Discussions on preparations for a Festschrift for Klemperer to mark his 70th birthday]

[...]

A letter from 'honey', i.e. Elena Meyerhof in Palermo. Hans died quite unexpectedly of a heart attack on 1st June, and she had thought that she would be first, because she has serious heart problems, is in addition deaf and has eye problems. He was a pantheist – she includes corresponding verses by him – freemason, rabbi and happy in poverty. His lodge has buried him very nicely 'in the cemetery by the sea, where there are only foreigners' and taken a collection for her – she is entirely propertyless and helpless. By selling some household effects she hopes to get by until her expected and probably near end. I read it all quite coldly. [...]

Surrounded by death on all sides, everything goes on, and yet I am afraid, am more afraid of it than of emptiness. Pitiful.

[...]

3rd August, 11 p.m. Friday evening. Dresden

Since Wednesday brooding over my article 'Stalin's theory of language and the German linguistic situation' – or something like it.[36] [...]

[Disagreement with Krauss becoming more explicit.] At the meeting [on syllabuses] Rita tacked between us, and I spoke my mind very clearly to Krauss. I do not forgive him for offering Rita an assistant professorship at Leipzig, I accused him of an appetite for dictatorship and of forming cliques ... [...]

[...]

11th August, towards midnight Saturday evening. Dresden

[...] Extremely slow progress of the Stalin language study.

[Krauss has revived the idea of establishing Leipzig as the sole important centre of Romance language studies in the GDR. Klemperer has difficulty overcoming his own lethargic indifference despite the urging of Rita Stober and Frau Steinhoff.]

I ate lunch with Rita and Lindner, and the afternoon was then devoted to the World Youth Games. The streets are full of colour, crowds of young people with curious neckerchiefs and sporting emblems marching, drumming, bugling. Really very bright, a great crush, masses of young people at Alexanderplatz. [...] But I know now how things happen in Berlin. The comparison with the Olympic Games is not right. Here sport is only *one* factor among many. The democratic sector [of Berlin] is truly a great festival ground, decorations everywhere: flags, coats of arms, pictures on wooden scaffolding, flowers, the decorations and the new buildings between ruins and half-finished new buildings. 'Cultural' and 'National' programmes are advertised every day in x places, also performed in the open air. But the most important thing is everywhere the international mingling of young people. [...] Then the exotic figures. Korea and China are being fed in the KB on Jägerstr: a dainty brown Korean girl with fine features ... It is said not everything is a success [...]

[...]

17th August, 7 a.m. Friday morning. Dresden

About to drive to Halle. (Tax Office, Univ. administration.)

[...]

8 p.m.

The dreariness and the terrible feeling, that it will never end. I was back from Halle shortly after 6 p.m. Coming back is always the worst. [...]

[...]

24th August, minuit Friday. Dresden

[...] Wretched Romance languages. What are Krauss and I fighting over? I thought 20 or 30 new registrations. But in the whole of the GDR only *six* have registered for French. Because the subject was so long considered as being without employment prospects.

[...] At lunchtime a couple of minutes with the stonemason, Schleider [...]. E.'s gravestone, the inscription. [...] For a while I was uncertain whether the text should remain. Schleider said, the text – and that was also something to bear in mind – would form quite a good bar between E.'s name and mine; it would fill up the space on the stone very nicely! It was almost funny. I decided from now on to place these words at the front of *all* my books yet to appear. How many will it be? 'You have always gone before me, oh heart, by day and night!'[37] [...]

[...]

29th August, towards evening, Wednesday. Dresden

[...]

Unhealthy, dreary, monotonous life. Smoking, working, sleeping, no movement, dullness, bitterness, when I go out into the beautifully blooming and tended garden. Trude Scherner, good-natured, quiet, can give me nothing. I rarely see her, she is mostly with the 'domestics' in the garden or in the kitchen, she goes to bed at 8.30 – I at 1.30.

Yesterday evening at the grave, on which work has been completed. Very beautiful and elegant, my text looks good. What use is it to E.? Most wonderful view into the distance.

[. . .]

The Heinschs are supposed to come this evening. It's probably about the Dr h.c. [to be awarded by Dresden Technical University] – my seventieth birthday. Idiotic ambition: I want to live to see it and reap outward honours. The honorary doctorate, the Festschrift, the National Prize, the rectorship – it all entices me, and at the same time I feel the futility and am ashamed. Sometimes I lie to myself I am also achieving something lasting and of worth to Eva with my own honours. [. . .]

[. . .]

8th September, Saturday evening. Dresden

Most profound oppressive, almost impossible to numb, loneliness. Nothing has any meaning without Eva. I cannot believe in her continued existence, just as little in her non-existence. I often ask myself, whether I was really good enough to her. In the last few years I sacrificed her to my ambition. Had we drifted apart? What, really, was I to her, what did I know of her?

[. . .]

12th September, 7 a.m. Wednesday morning. Dresden

[. . .]

On Tuesday, the 11th, glorious, but very exhausting 6 hour start [to semester] in Halle. Delegation from Leipzig: Werner Krauss completely out of action, in a sanatorium in the Soviet Union for a semester – *I* am *also* to lecture in Leipzig; after hesitating I agreed to 4 hours on Mondays. – Home at 9 p.m. very exhausted and flushed. Today to Berlin.

I am teaching therefore: 18ième lecture and seminar in Leipzig 4 hours, in Halle and Berlin 5 hours, 17ième in Berlin 2 hours, Problems of the 20th Century, Halle 1 hour. In the Halle lectures I have a good 50–60, in the seminar $\frac{1}{2}$ a dozen students. [. . .]

13th September, about 9 a.m. Thursday morning. At Kahanes, 34 Tschaikowskistr., Niederschönhausen, Berlin

Reorganisation: The whole of Romance Languages at Leipzig is being transferred to Berlin, this where the main emphasis and the centre is. Should Krauss come back from the SU cured, then he will be professor in Berlin *alongside* me, we will then be on an equal footing. Should ... it is not too likely. [. . .] At the department there was a letter from Krauss (written before he knew about his evacuation to the SU.) He begs for the maintenance of our friendship and co-operation, he himself will only be able to lecture very little, will 'draw in his horns'. That is now outdated. But I shall write very warmly to K. today. To which there is much hypocrisy and egotism. [...] I am the one-eyed king of the GDR, I am the better horse. [...]

22nd September, Saturday forenoon. Dresden

The preparation of the lectures is eating me up, the days between the trips – insofar as they leave time and vigour to work at all – are completely taken up with it [...]. Consultations with Rita. Great power in Berlin. 20 Leipzig research assistants and students to me, Leipzig department shut down completely. Like-wise Jena and Greifswald, only Rostock remains. Berlin entirely the 'focal point'. Krauss as moribundus [...] to the SU. [...] On Mon. afternoon I am to speak at the Physics Institute on 'Germany and France': I am being put on display a little in Dresden. And with all of that, in between all of that always (purely visually) the tin can, E. dead in bed, in the coffin ... It disappears, is for hours no more than a dull pressure, not at all present, and yet always there.

[...]

25th September, 6 a.m. Tuesday morning. Dresden

In the late evening at Gusti W.'s for a while. There, as also related by Brigitte J., as at Sunday lunchtime – more visits! – by Grube, as – more loss of time – by Weller, the same thing: extreme dissatisfaction of the workers; they are in many cases in a worse position because of the collective contract, there's a shortage of butter, of electricity, the pace of work is too great. [...]

29th September, Saturday forenoon. Dresden

[...]

In Berlin my 18ième very good, my 17ième passable. Consultation with Rita, now the government. They are preparing a doctoral ceremony for me in Dresden, and Berlin and Halle will send delegations. [...] In Berlin I received a telephone call from Inge Kl., that Peter had been arrested and was in Moabit Prison[38] ... I should have gone to the Jewish Community, to the Office for Compensation Claims on behalf of the Jelskis. Iranische Strasse is in the French sector, a long way from elevated or underground railway. I didn't dare go. [...]

6th October, 7 a.m. Saturday morning. Romance Languages Institute, Berlin

[...]

I am with Gusti a great deal. The car, the intellectual isolation, the shared memories and habits of thought and education of the same disappearing gen-eration. Gusti is even more sceptical of present conditions than I am. The intellectual nadir, the intellectual straitjacket. She, too, talks at length about the great dissatisfaction of the workers. The intelligentsia are getting everything stuffed into their mouths, the workers are being kept short, squeezed, the collective contracts frequently place them in a worse position than before. Gusti believes in and wants a Soviet dictatorship here.

[...]

Then in the afternoon (Friday, 5 Oct.) Inge and Peter Kl. came to the [Berlin] KB, we had coffee together. Peter looking more manly (energetic and broad-shouldered, very sharply cut features, no longer so soft and pretty as he still was until recently), wearing the FDJ pin. He was in custody in Moabit Prison for two days, because his name is on a Peace Committee invitation, he has to report to the police and is awaiting summons to appear in court. [...] I chatted to the pair of them here in the department for a long time, [...]

13th October, Saturday midday. Dresden

[...]

Pieck is to award the National Prizes on Sunday afternoon. Nothing has gone to me. Among the few humanities scholars of this series are *two* of the Halle bourgeois party members – *I* am only in the SED. [...]

Tue., 9 Oct., my seventieth. Set out for Halle already at 6 (with Katja). [...] A couple of professors, Heusler as dean, Stern, Hausherr, Reitzenstein present – formal congratulation and addresses. Lengthier speech full of long Greek quotations by Reitzenstein. The Graces[39] had stood by my cradle, I was able to enthral like an artist. Those of ill-will had warned against me – a hint that in Halle they had been braced for a Red agitator – but I had won everyone over through my humanism ... In my reply (a little moved, which subsided later) I made a profession of belief in my Party, in the new humanism. – I found my department re-furnished, two pictures of me on the wall, a great quantity of flowers and baskets of flowers ... First of all I gave my usual lectures 3 hours 18ième, 1 hour Issues of Literature (German language situation). The seminar in the afternoon was cancelled – instead a big coffee table – in addition the Anglicists, also (above all) the Leipzigers. Addresses, the prettiest by Hadwig Kirchner. Then I spoke. In Halle I was at home, in Berlin at the front. [...] Presents, above all the beautiful photograph album.[40] [...] At 7 Kulturbund, reception at Gustav Nach-tigallstr. Here the big speeches, the masses of presents. Frau Sasse, Karl Kneschke, Frau Sternbeck,[41] Minister of Education for the Prime Minister, the mayor of Halle – the latter also a colleague from the Volkskammer, praising the fact that I spoke without notes there, everyone listened to me! – etc. Ernst Hoffmann from the Central Committee on behalf of Ulbricht. A huge basket of flowers, the congratulations of the Central Committee, as printed in *Neues Deutschland*. There, too, the article by Hans Mayer, which talks of my good fortune at still having E. as the companion of my days. Mayer is evidently not to blame, he was in the West for some time. [10 Oct. Volkskammer, Berlin ...] Grotewohl spoke in the morning; in the afternoon before the debate a long commemoration of my 70 years by Dieckmann, deputies rose from their seats, clapped. [...] That and the telegram from President Pieck, mentioned in the newspapers are my principal honours. But the newspapers are full of the pictures of the National Prize winners – and everyone is asking himself why I am on the sidelines. –

From the chamber to the faculty meeting, where I was congratulated somewhat matter-of-factly. Steinitz moved that Krauss be offered a chair in Berlin immediately. I spoke warmly in favour, to avoid Krauss thinking that he was in any way being pushed aside; emphasised that we were friends and both had a place in Berlin. [. . .] In the evening at the Kahanes'. Great warmth, presents. [. . .] On Thurs. evening I had the actual private party at the Kahanes'. Very touching. If only the children there were not so naughty and if everything were not quite so chaotically bohemian. On Friday, after the lecture, spent time with Peter and Inge at the KB. I like Inge, who had already visited me at the department on Thursday, more and more. Refined, calm, confident, educated. Present: *L'Enfer*[42], a second-hand copy, in which Barbusse has written a dedication for someone. – In Dresden after 8 p.m. [. . .] Flowers in profusion as in Halle. Huge number of letters of congratulation.

[. . .]

17th October, midday Wednesday. Dresden

My dream: I am driving a car. There's a clatter – and the whole body falls off; I continue driving on the bare chassis, crash into a wall and the whole frame dissolves into nothing. Yet I am unhurt, untouched by any kind of fear, not even by the moment of shock – it's just the way it is. As at E.'s death. As at the now constantly appearing pictures of her corpse and her tin can.

[. . .]

On Monday, 15 Oct., the Kahanes arrived here at 10. [To take Klemperer to the award of the honorary doctorate by Dresden Technical University.] Later, during his toast, Seydewitz said, that I had sat there like a prisoner awaiting sentence. It was probably true, I did not know where to look and ducked my head. Dähne said, in my praise, that I was able to deliver learning and opinion 'with a smile'.[43] [. . .] In purest Party jargon, Lohagen [. . .] praised me as an upright man of the 'old intelligentsia' who had joined with the working class. [. . .] Katja also among the guests at the TU and the Hotel Astoria ... [. . .] The Kahanes drove us, had a coffee here, then drove with me up to E.'s grave. It is kept very nicely by Weller, fine and elegant – but what good does it do *her*? And what good does it do *me*, if I stand up there. [. . .]

[Commenting on his desire to be elected to the Berlin Academy, Klemperer concludes:] Vanitas! But yet not quite. The place in the Academy would allow me to keep up the car even after retirement. And it would also mean recognition outside the GDR. – But in the middle of all this the tin can before my eyes and the feeling of loneliness.

[. . .]

29th October, 9 p.m. Monday evening. Dresden

[. . .]

Thurs. evening at the Kahanes'. It had been Doris's birthday the day before – 26. I brought her one of the rings, which Kätchen left E. [. . .] I only discovered after the event, what valuable presents Mackie gave me: a folio volume of Lafontaine fables illustrated by Doré, a Henriade[44] from the 18th century ... [At an executive committee meeting of the VVN Klemperer is co-opted onto the committee.]

At the VVN meeting a speaker from the West decidedly *anti-Semitic*. Very unpleasant. – On the train I heard once again: 'The Jews are trafficking in coffee.' It really is supposed to be 'the Jews'.

4th November, Sunday evening. Dresden

I completed reading the proofs of the *Histoire véritable* without interruption – yesterday and today. [. . .] paragraphs of it were written by Eva. [. . .] Eva's handwriting – I am particularly depressed today; I withheld so much from her. She should have had the house earlier, the new car earlier. In the last year she sat up here imprisoned and too often alone. Then the Greifswald exile. I frequently tormented her with my tight-fisted hesitation, etc. etc., I am so heavy at heart, I am so alone – and yet still ambition, still fear of the end, still life ... Just don't think... [... Addressing Ulbricht in the corridor of the Volkskammer, to thank him personally for the 70th birthday honours, Klemperer finds him friendly but evidently without any idea who he is.]

[. . .]

7th November, 7 p.m. Wednesday evening. Dresden

[. . .]

With my overtiredness I lost my rag twice yesterday. As I began the lecture on humanism, the FDJ began to bugle and drum. They had taken up position outside the window, I constantly saw the movement of the two raised crossed hands with the drumsticks – the damned Hitler Youth gesture. I sent someone out, to tell them to stop. Another song was drummed. I sent someone out once again – they marched off. I said bitterly, things could not be done like *this*, we were 'working with our heads', I was a friend of the FDJ – but like *this* it harmed itself and us. There was some stamping of feet – by a few, most sat there embarrassed and silent. The second emotional outburst in the seminar [at one student attacking another and using only cliches and dogmatic phrases from Party schooling].

These two lapses – they could have consequences – belong at length in my Curriculum; it is very possible, that because of them and some similar occurrences I shall soon have plenty of opportunity to continue with it. [. . .]

10th November, Saturday afternoon. Dresden

[... Klemperer has a brief altercation with Rita Schober, who feels constantly overworked as well as overburdened by the move to Berlin. Klemperer:] I felt I had to keep running after her – she accused *me* of having pushed her into the government job, and she was doing more for my institute and my person than for anything or anybody else. In short each accused the other of a certain lack of gratitude. [...] I wish I were free. Surely I could gradually begin to concentrate on writing. If not the 18ième then the Curriculum [...]

[...]

[In a seminar Klemperer curtly tells a 'dull-witted or obstinate or at any rate absolutely ignorant' student:] 'You can study thanks to taxes paid by the workers, you are under an obligation to really study or to give up your place to someone more hardworking.' [...]

13th November, 6 a.m. Tuesday. Dresden (before drive to Halle)

[...]

Saturday. Invitation in the evening to Frau Bauer. A tasteful, well-to-do villa on Bernhardstr. Completely undamaged inside and out, entirely surrounded by ruins. The fat little woman in trousers particularly little and fat. On altogether elegant services an altogether elegantly served just sufficient meal. [...] Topic of conversation: the general losses, particularly the Jewish ones of the Nazi years. A Dresden Jewish chronicle. Frau Bauer lost her only son. Concealed mixed race, as a young soldier went missing somehow and somewhere in the Mark Brandenburg in the last days of the war. Frau Koch(?), her friend, lost *all* her relatives in Riga. Paul Kreidl was hanged there. I asked after Lissy Meyerhof. 'From the last Berlin transports only the clothing sent on for the SS came; the people were already killed en route.'

[...]

15th November, 5 p.m. Thursday. Director's Room, Romance Languages Institute, Berlin

Sensation: Winfried Schröder reports with a radiant face, Krauss has just returned to Berlin by air plane. Full of plans and energy. For the moment has gone on to Leipzig. What now? [...]

[Berlin University SED group meeting.] I saw Comrade Hager[45] for the first time, the Central Committee's man in charge of higher education and who lectures on political economy in the faculty. Very mild-looking middle-aged man. Under discussion was the list of lecturers to be elected as full-time members of faculty [...]. At the faculty meeting, which lasted until 9 p.m., Rita Schober was elected along with [...] several others ... Afterwards to the Kahanes'. [...]

[...]

26th November, Monday morning. Dresden

[Klemperer expresses his fears of the threat that Krauss's return represents – he might even have to share the director's office! But he wants Krauss's support to secure his election to the Academy.] How much treachery on all sides. To say nothing of my liking for Hadwig Kirchner. And yet E. is and E. was my only love, my only support, and again and again I feel so empty and wretched. I wish it were time to go to sleep and then again I don't wish it. [. . .]

28th November, Wednesday morning. Dresden

[. . .] Brigitte Jährig said: 'if you were 40 years younger, I would have married you.' They are very nice, this Brigitte and Hadwig – whom I gave a 1 in the state exam yesterday – but substitute or temptation? Really not.

   [. . .]

29th November, after 4 p.m. Director's room, Berlin

Around midday in Dresden yesterday expedition to the State Library, where many people still know me. I am given an instruction by voters, to ensure that the library gets a new bus connection. [. . .] Meanwhile Krauss looms and is supposed to appear tomorrow. According to the Leipzigers, he seems to want to have his old suprematism back. While this is depressing, Rita has just telephoned triumphantly: first meeting with Wartburg and Frings [of the Academy . . .] – things look 'positive' (LQI) for our matter, I should not worry about Krauss.

   [. . .]

2nd December, 7 p.m. Dresden

[. . . Meeting in Berlin to prepare a language conference.] Regret at Krauss's absence – and he turned up after all, he had arrived at the Anhalt Station. Looking somewhat recovered, immediately playing the leading role, reporting on Moscow [. . .] – the man with the great political, philosophical, Marxist, philosophy of language knowledge, truly overwhelming me with all his abilities, halfway silencing me. How will it go on, how long will I go along with it? [Later:] we drank coffee [during a meeting of the SED university members] and decamped after a quarter of an hour. At the buffet outside Krauss invited us to a second cup of coffee; then we drove to our Institute and discussed Romance languages business: Rita, Krauss, myself. All very harmonious, very friendly. Everything is to go ahead jointly with completely equal rights: Krauss has the Spanish, I the Italian – French we share, the research assistants' colloquium we take together. I have two fears, and the second moderates the first: Krauss will greatly surpass me in the colloquium; after a few weeks he will be sick again – as he is already explaining now, he must not overload himself for the time being, and he will have to repeat the cure. – But what does my health look like? My heart lets me down more and more – while walking, while climbing the stairs – my exhaustion becomes ever greater. E. Hoffmann of the Central Committee said to me, I would have to take a holiday soon; everyone knew that my heart was not all right. But I do not want to stop until the Academy is won.

   [. . .]

   [. . .]

22nd December, 5.30 p.m. Dresden

This last week before the holiday that began for me today has exceeded every-thing that preceded it, in terms of chasing around, the variety of things to be done and exhaustion, and I must now get down what still sticks in my mind.

[...] I always drive to my Institute as early as possible, where I then never get down to work. [...] Always my lack of confidence in the face of the 'Leipzigers', ever more difficult my relationship to Krauss, who remains as invisible and dominant as Tartuffe in the first two acts. On the morning of Sat. 15 Dec. there was the Romance Languages session chaired by Rita, for the sake of which I had to remain in Berlin. [...] The day before I had seen what a position Rita has now acquired for herself. She now really is fully in charge of all of philology in higher education, including Slavonic languages and German. [...] The session chaired by Rita concerned a) the courses of study and the examination regu-lations for *non*-teachers and b) in the presence of the relevant Ministry depart-ment heads, the setting up of an academic periodical. [...] I suggested a common but voluminous periodical for Romance and English Studies and that met with general approval. Editorial board Klemperer, Krauss, Lehnert [...] The one missing person was Krauss, although in Berlin and announced. He is gradually getting on everyone's nerves. [...] It appears now, that he wants to play the role of the researcher and push me into the role of the schoolmaster of the GDR. But I cannot afford a quarrel with him, he must propose my admission to the Academy. [...]

[Halle:] Tuesday, lectures [...] After that to the department Christmas party. [...] I took Hadwig Kirchner, who had come over to the party, home to her parents in the car. [...]

On Thurs., the 19th, out again at 6. To Berlin with Katja. I only had to give my Montesquieu lecture [...]. But a great deal of government business. [...] Because of the Stalin celebration our Institute party in the refectory could not begin until 9.30. [...] Finally towards 12.30, at Frau Steinhoff's urging, we broke up. Very dangerous drive [back to Dresden], since Lindner, partly overtired, partly in considerable pain, drove very erratically and as if distracted. Here towards 4, in bed at 5. [...]

I am ready for action for the planned holiday workload: Balzac study and Henri IV + Ranke.[46]

26th December, 2 p.m. Wednesday, second Day of Christmas. Dresden

Soon this holiday will be behind me; even when E. was alive it was not pleasant, now it is odious. [...]

1st January, 1.30 a.m. Tuesday – New Year therefore

After dinner I was at Gusti's, good old Lindner brought me back at 12.

The Grundigs, Erna Fleischer and her son from Berlin, a couple of neighbours, the time was passed quite pleasantly and emptily. It would have been nothing for E, too hot, she would have fainted. It weighs heavily on me how frail she was in these last years. And yet I always hoped she would pick herself up again. And probably, certainly, I lived at too great a distance from her.

She died on 8 July. And I have become professor in Berlin and honorary doctor here and am striving after the Academy and am ambitious and feel the futility of the whole thing and perceive my life as a betrayal and have the most foolish fear of death and am on the whole blunted. I am busy with 100 things, and amidst them E. always comes into my mind, as corpse on the bed, in the coffin, as tin can. Sometimes I am up at the grave, and that always seems especially foolish to me. – I have hardly written anything this year; the essay for *Einheit* is merely an expanded revision of my earlier language study. [...]

1952

3rd January, midnight Thursday. Dresden

It is always considered to be especially horrible, if some ghost appears, or if someone dead makes themselves known. I sometimes think, when I enter the bedroom at night, it would after all be very cheering, if E. would somehow make herself known. That would be a marvellous demonstration, that something could be expected. No matter what – just not the absolutely imbecilic nothingness ... E. always said: 'I want to let myself be surprised.'

[...]

My life will become easier, once the loneliness of the holidays is over. I must live in a rush and in external contact with the world – my great books will probably remain unwritten.

6th January, Sunday evening. Dresden

[...]

I am happy that the holidays, which are none at all, are coming to an end. Wednesday Volkskammer. – Lea Grundig related, how her parents cursed her, when she went out with the goy Hans Grundig. [...] Hans Grundig's splendid concentration-camp painting has not been admitted by the Berlin art exhibition.[1] It is not optimistic enough, it is 'formalist'. In painting the mischief is running riot to an even worse extent than in literature.

8th January, 10.30 p.m. Tuesday evening. Dresden

[...]

A couple of days ago I received another anonymous letter, I was betraying my convictions, because the present regime matched the Hitler one and I should write an LQI. The abbreviation LQI really was in this letter, and linguistically the man is right, also I have long been making notes on it anyway – but practically he is simply altogether not right – even if with respect to literature I feel myself confined and tyrannised.

[. . .]

12th January, midday Saturday. Dresden

[. . .]

[Once again Klemperer is overcome by the boring pointlessness of the Volkskammer sessions.] There are no debates, only the same things drearily read out. There is no tension – everything is settled beforehand. And the proposals and appeals to Bonn: one knows the answer in advance. [. . .]

Sitting next to me – present for literally the first time since he was elected on 15 Oct. 1950 [. . .] – was Johannes R. Becher. He said to me: 'A letter has been sent to you in Halle, saying that we have admitted you to the PEN Club.' I was overcome by a quite stupid warm feeling of pleasurable ambition. Although the business did seem a little mysterious, because the members of the Pen Club are belles-lettrists. (Only just now have I discovered in the new Duden dictionary: Poets, Essayists, Novelists, and *LTI* consists of essays after all.) When Becher then rushed off, I caught up with him on the stairs and asked, how I had come by this honour. 'We have just elected another 20 . . .' and was gone. Afterwards I learned that the actual [German] Pen Club had 'split', and a GDR group had made itself independent, for which, therefore, recruits were required[2] . . . I was deflated; I come to this club as I came to the Humboldt University and shall come to the Academy. *That* is what my honours look like – and I chase after them and thereby betray Eva, whom I should not have outlived.

[. . .]

The holidays are at an end, the lectures have to be prepared. There is a bittersweet comfort in that: I have to find my feet in a part of the 18ième still unfamiliar to me. The difficulty begins with the Contrat Social.[3]

[. . .]

19th January, 1 a.m. Saturday night (actually Sunday). Dresden

[. . .]

Inner anxiety: '*Krauss*'. I have a serious and all too justified inferiority complex. [. . .] I always have the feeling K.'s research assistants look down on me. How will the shared colloquium turn out? We decided to systematically discuss the passages on French literature in the 'Classics', i.e. in Marx, Engels, Lenin, Stalin, Mehring.[4] At least it will not be empty talk – but how shall I come off? – On the other hand: Krauss is a sick incapacitated man [. . .].

[. . .]

27th January, Sunday forenoon. Dresden

Betrayal? Sentimentality? Frau Richter's illness has set everything in motion. [...] It brings up the whole question of my continued existence here. From the other side: everything is pushing me towards Berlin. My life is a constant betrayal of E. Is it less of a betrayal, if I'm sitting here? [...] Besides and below the emotional: what is to be done with this house? [...]

Since Eva's death I have not had a really good day. Only benumbed days. Always a bad conscience. Which I already had in Greifswald, in stronger measure since then. But if I have this nonsensical ambition and this cowardice – if I go on living: am I then any less disloyal than in Berlin?

[...]

Hadwig Kirchner said: she could not contemplate joining an 'atheist' party. That is when I learned she was a Catholic. [...]

30th January, 11 p.m. Wednesday evening. Dresden

[...]

On Sunday afternoon at Konrad's – cf the Nazi time. The man is in his 73rd year, more vigorous than I am. His wife has got over a mild stroke, but makes a good impression. The two old people, she 69, live quietly and happily on their pension, together they have 500M. He helps her with the cooking and the washing-up, is minyan man[5] of the Jewish Community, which now has 150 people *and* a small synagogue once again, and is enjoying the evening of his years. [...]

[...]

10th February, Sunday afternoon

[...]

Here the miserable situation again: what is to become of the house, my cat and me? [...] My thoughts go back and forth: give up this house? Keep it? One thing as distressing as the other. [...]

In recent days I have called off a few things. [...] That still leaves me more than enough, my appointments diary is full to the brim. Victor Hugo in Freital, in Dresden, in Weimar and twice in Berlin[6]. On literary criticism in the Writers' Association here. Yesterday the Saxon Interior Ministry, whether I could contribute to a training course on language. I agreed. And a number of KB papers.

[...]

19th February. Director's Room, Halle, inter lecturas

[Victor Klemperer has an unpleasant altercation with Max Kahane at the latter's birthday dinner. Max accuses him of Western anti-Marxist views, of believing Stalin to be a bloodthirsty spider pulling all the strings. In fact, according to Klemperer, he had merely expressed the view that because Stalin had to think in the long term, he might in the short term have to abandon some positions, e.g. the GDR.]

I returned to Dresden inwardly and outwardly weary and there I met with work and chaos. [...] I needed the Saturday for preparation and to give my talk to the Writers' Association. 'Questions of literary criticism'. *My* cosa vecchia:[7] personality–form–society, which is chalked up against me as 'idealist'. [...] On Sunday I worked up the Victor Hugo. Première yesterday evening [...]: Freital trades school, 60 people – applause. Gusti: much too idealist [...]. She's probably right in that – I shall touch it up. [...]

20th February, Wednesday forenoon. Dresden

[...]

I am in every respect dead tired. I am most of all tempted, although I have serious reservations, by Gusti's offer to take the upper floor of her house and to write there in retirement. One of the reservations: Gusti, too, has serious heart problems, what happened to E. can happen to her any day. [...] We always both laugh, so that no real argument arises. [...]

All my lectures and seminars, in Berlin as in Halle, are a desperate struggle for the freedom of the intellect.

On Sunday evening Dr Grube, who closed E.'s eyes, visited me, as he sometimes does. He knows my troubles and spoke some words which touched me considerably: 'What you are carrying on here, is PRESERVATION OF A MONUMENT.'

[...]

25th February, Monday afternoon

[...]

Frau Richter in St Joseph's. I visited her there today. The sight of the city is a shock. The whole of Pirnaische Platz and the surroundings an empty, already partly green space. Nothing, absolutely nothing of the old cityscape remains after this clearing up. I did not know my way. Lindner said: 'the Mohren Pharmacy was here.' It was less strange, when there were still ruins standing. Grunaerstr.: a row of very new houses. Floral decorations on the grass left over from 13th Feb. [anniversary][8] Imagine what's underneath! [...]

Yesterday morning to Altenburg with Lindner, on Marxism and Language in front of 300 people in the theatre there. [...] Back towards 3 p.m. Then until after 1 in the morning completely finished the 18ième, so that it will finally be delivered to Thomas in the morning. It is a good book – it is solidly bourgeois and liberal, and I now had to delete a number of attacks on Rousseau and on the 'frenzy' of the Terror, in particular the concluding sentence: 'Voltaire could be simplified, and Rousseau hardly needed to be simplified.'

[...]

2nd March, Sunday afternoon
[...]

[The previous Friday a long-awaited conversation with Ernst Hoffmann of the Central Committee on Klemperer's acceptance into the Academy and on the Romance Languages Institute. After lecturing he goes to meet Rita.] We discussed the Academy business, there was in addition discussion of the re-organisation of my life – a house in Berlin. I was deeply unsettled by Rita's suggestion: take in Hadwig as a kind of housekeeper. You can make the poor thing so happy, and she will look after you! I said, that was a little like procuring, Hadwig was too young for that, I liked her, sometimes I already felt as if I were betraying E. – what would happen if I had H. with me in the house? – besides I could not marry her, would also not like to make a fool of myself. Rita said, whoever goes on living has of necessity the feelings of someone who is still living; she was evidently surprised at my resistance. Since then my imagination has been unpleasantly agitated. So *that's* what a great love and fidelity looks like. Eva has been dead for less than 8 months. It has not been very nicely done. [...] Work and don't think of anything!

Evening and night from Thurs. to Frid. at the Kahanes'. There was a great shortage of foodstuffs, no meat, no sausage – for about 10 days there has been nothing in the shops in East Berlin. No one, including the news agency, knows the reason. The holding back of the goods is somehow connected with some financial operation – but which certainly does not mean any devaluation of the East Mark. [...]

Today I found my article 'Linguistic Patriotism' in the Friday edition of the *Tägliche Rundschau*. In the afternoon Erich Seidemann appeared and reported, that Rias had attacked me yesterday because of this article. 'Prostration before Stalin' and perverse reversal of my *LTI*. What I had censured there, I now praised, *LTI* and Stalin's language were alike.

[...]

8th March, Saturday evening. Dresden
The Hadwig affair – now really an affair – is an immoral play, which has got mixed up with reality, which weighs on me and does not let go of me. On Thursday lunchtime in the staff club Margarete Steinhoff again chattered foolishly away in the presence of Hadwig and Christa N., Hadwig should get a room in my Berlin house and look after me in my 'Biblical age' I made a joke of the idea [...]. Hadwig was silent. Later in my room I spoke very seriously and very flirtatiously to her. I told her, I did not know what to say. I was aware of my ridiculousness, my faithlessness, the impossibility of the thing; I could be her grandfather – but I was not, and could not help my feelings ... again and again I tried to make fun of everything ... [...] But for all that we looked at one another very seriously, and Hadwig said, she for her part could not make a declaration of love either, and it was good, that I as an older person thought about the world, she sometimes took the view, that she 'didn't care a pin, what other people said'. In short, it would have been up to me to act. I said: You need

a handsome young man. Once I also said, I asked myself, whether sins in thought were not in fact worse than real sins. That was no more than sophistry, she thought. As I said, we parted in a very serious mood. [...] Now, after H. and I have spoken seriously – now the situation is quite awkward. In the Institute and while speaking and glancing during lectures I must constantly make an effort to be at ease.

9th March, Sunday afternoon

[...]

The Hugo series. Done so far: 1) Freital 2) Halle 3) Weimar 4) Soviet Berlin 5) Berlin Univ., still to come: 6) Leipzig (after all!) 7) Sangerhausen 8) Peace Committee Pankow.

[...]

The Hadwig affair is constantly on my mind, I flirt and play with her and she weighs uncomfortably on my conscience. If E. were alive, it would not have come to this. I once said to her, Hadwig Kirchner (whom she did not know) would be the only one who could lead me into temptation.

[...]

14th March, after 11 p.m. Friday evening. Dresden

As long as I tell myself: Her absolute ignorance of my long life – Eva as burden of conscience on my heart – the ridiculousness [...] – the fear of her family – [...] What do I know of H.'s past? – [...] then there is no time for it to be so bad. But what a joy to see this face, pale narrow spirited at once sensitive and intellectual, childlike and very mature, to feel the truly warm friendship, I almost believe: the true sympathy, the responsiveness. And the truthfulness and calm knowledge in everything. [...] At any rate: she is very close to my heart, moves and attracts me more and more, and in fact we have already come very far in mutual confessions and confidences – always on the dividing line of or wavering between jesting and very great seriousness. It should be up to me to embrace her, and she is very close to making a start. But I am the seducer after all, and my uprightness and whole behaviour is flirtatious and a pretence. [...]

[...]

23rd March, Sunday forenoon. Dresden

Monday – or Wednesday? – it has become very serious, very bitter-sweet. Hadwig kissed me first and told me, she really *loved* me. It all sounds so comical – and the comedy of the thing is almost the first of my anxieties. [...] I have pointed out to H. in every possible way how physically used up I am. In addition the pangs of conscience with regard to Eva. Then the outward difficulties. Rita, whom I have taken into my confidence [...] said: people will find you comical; but when they see you together, they'll understand and not laugh any more ... [...] And in all of that always the grave up in Dölzschen before my eyes. And the empty bed … When tonight the storm created the most frightful din all around, I was truly gripped by a superstitious shudder. But Eva would forgive me … But *I*, how can I forgive myself?

[…]

[In Berlin, after a faculty meeting.] I then brought the very fatigued Rita home to her housing estate, where I, too, would now like to have a little house and begin a vita nova with Hadwig. (Everything about this plan is up in the air, is almost utopian). […]

[…]

On Friday aft. following the Hugo lecture […] the decisive *Central Committee session about the Academy.* Hoffmann, Steinitz, Rita, someone representing Naas and then descending from the clouds, prima donna, deity, high priest, Stefan George[9] – Krauss. He wrote a very nice opinion on me – but he has made sure, that the Institute was decided on now in accordance with his plans and with him as director. I am to be elected after that. [Nevertheless Klemperer is assured that he is co-director with equal rights.]

Sole content of today, Sunday: this report. My exhaustion is too great. And all too great the confusion of my emotions. This betrayal of Eva, this impossible new relationship.

[…]

29th March, Saturday afternoon. Dresden

Hadwig. On Tue. night there was a letter from her here. Between playful lines much love. On Thurs. evening I was alone with her in the Director's Room for an hour. Invitus invitam dimisit.[10] Rita is in the know, and after speaking to H. – 'she really loves you' – she is in agreement and thinks the matter is realisable; only we should await the upshot of the Academy business, which would otherwise founder on the ridiculousness of this marriage and on Krauss's intrigues … After the very beautiful evening, I have spent all morning writing a long letter to H., which sets forth everything, that I recently outlined here. My bad conscience, my depression with regard to Eva […] and yet my great tenderness and love. I am completely imbued with it, everything else falls away.

[…]

On Thurs. morning to Berlin by train […]. At […] 9.30 I reached Friedrichstr., and I was in great difficulty on the short walk to the Institute. I arrived exhausted and depressed – and thus I go a-courting! – surreptitious togetherness, Christa always has to be included, I always hide behind banter. Do Christa and the others really not notice? […]

31st March, 11 p.m. Monday evening

Hadwig. A childlike loving letter from her. What mischief have I caused? I cannot find any peace, make up my mind, am constantly wavering. The love matter made simultaneously more complicated and easier by the house business. I must begin a completely vita nova in Berlin. I am as if paralysed and fatalistic.

Do I know Hadwig? Does she know me? Is real common ground between us at all conceivable? How is it possible for H. to look over the half-century, the wall of this half-century, that I have lived through before her, lived through with E.? In H.'s presence will I not feel like a ghost d'outre tombe and thus be even more lonely? Always these tormenting thoughts [...].

5th April, 10 p.m. Saturday. Dresden

Hadwig. Thursday to Friday 10 p.m.–6 a.m. in my Director's office. I cannot relate and analyse it. It is so beautiful and sad, so ridiculous and so comical – so serious and actually so tragic. And there is a young creature, who is a mystery to me, incomprehensibly touching and at every second very remote and very close. Happiness, despair, guilt, fatalism, self observation and yet much, truly much love.

[...] On Thurs. to Berlin by train, Lindner came on Friday morning with the car. The train punctual this time. At Ost Station at 8.30 – then *Hadwig* appeared, she had been sent by the department to pick me up. We invented a delayed train and sat a long time in the waiting room over a cup of coffee. It was *just* like that I sat in the Stettin Station [in Berlin] in 1904 with E., who had come from Königsberg. We are so terribly open with one another. I related it to H., and she told me that she had been in Jena to make a clear break with her boyfriend, who remains her friend. [...] She says, she has not yet been loved, she said the purely sexual was not so important for a woman. What does *says* mean? We then had this mysterious night, after all, and the next day she was as affectionate as before. The Thursday first of all passed half-normally. My two lectures, in between the faculty club with Margarete Steinhoff, Christa and Hadwig, then Baldinger's[11] language colloquium with H., then another colloquium for an hour, in which the syllabus for the 19th century was laid down – and then everyone left and Frau Voigt brought me my bedding and coffee arid sandwiches, and I did not know for certain, whether H. had really hidden in Room 4, and at 10 she really did appear ... I was at my desk at 4.30 and let H. sleep until 5.30. And then the first charwoman already came before 6, and H. was still with me, and it was a very long and awkward hour, until H. managed to get back to Room 4 and remain shut in there until the normal opening time. A discovery would have made us both absolutely impossible.

Today feeling completely knocked out I sent a letter to H, dealt with a small amount of correspondence, shelved the huge new packet of books from Aufbau publishing house – completely knocked out and my emotions in a state of complete chaos.

[...]

12th April, 6 p.m. Saturday. Dresden

A diary letter to Hadwig took up Good Friday. [...] Accompanying everything tiredness, confusion of emotions, helplessness. Very laborious preparation of lectures. [...] Wednesday morning to Berlin by train, at Friedrichstr. Station I met Hadwig – and then from first to last H., day and night, when will it become obvious, what will become of it? But beyond the confusion of emotions and the physical wretchedness it is bliss. And I believe in H. and her love. On Wednesday I had no reason to be in Berlin – only Hadwig. I did not leave my Director's office at all – pretext: deal with all business before Easter, too many appointments on Thurs. The night. At 5 H. hid in the next room, last week she had slipped in too late, there were already charwomen in the building. This time she came out too early. Excuse: fault of her alarm clock. We breakfasted together. [. . .] Overtired and overwrought, I found it impossible to really complete the Lafontaine lecture. I made an excuse and concluded a quarter of an hour before time. Afterwards out to Rita with H. [. . .] She is entirely on our side, counsellor, admonisher, matchmaker, convinced that we belong together. Fear and joy mixed up, the tangle of Hadwig, Academy, home, Krauss. [. . .]

Yesterday I also read Hadwig's 'Weilerproblem' [The Problem of the Hamlet – i.e. Hadwig Kirchner's undergraduate dissertation on place names]. Such rigorous philology, such clear thinking – and real belief in God, real Catholicism. But I love her, everything about her is true. – I would like to have her in the SED. From deep inside: 'If I only knew, if they really don't have any concentration camps . . .' I: I definitely believed *not* – and if, then self-defence. And where is the boundary between prison and concentration camp?

[. . .] Confusion, confusion and tiredness in me. E. chose the better half. But so much love in H.

14th April, 10 p.m. Easter Monday
Diary letter to H. Excepting it and the many times I fell asleep devoted the whole day to Lafontaine. Despite which I shall only be able to make notes tomorrow. I find everything difficult – tiredness and confusion of the emotions.
[. . .]
Just now, towards 11, a telephone call from Hadwig in Berlin. Just like that
. . . [. . .]

17th April, 3 a.m. Thursday morning. Director's office, Berlin – I shall lie down for another hour afterwards
[Vita nova! exclaims Klemperer once more. But meanwhile difficulties are accumulating at home in Dölzschen. He is forced to dismiss Frau Richter.] God knows, what it looks like at home now. At any rate, it *must, must,* come to an end, my now absurd Dresden life. Gusti, too, said, I was living in a 'coffin', agrees with my slogan *vita nova* and docs not know how true it is. I was close to a confession, but remained silent after all.

And then the bliss of yesterday here – poor betrayed Eva.

Hadwig at the Ost Station, more delightful than ever. I gave her E.'s inherited watch and gold chain. [. . .]

H. accompanied me to the Academy at about 9.30, the Jätgerstr. building. A proper congress, perhaps 200 philologists[12] [. . .] I was about to join them at lunch in the KB when the surprise came. Messenger from the State Secretariat: requested by Poland. [i.e. to be part of a GDR delegation ... Klemperer is also to give a number of lectures. Meanwhile Hadwig Kirchner's parents are in Berlin to visit their daughter:] unsolved question: Secret or put my cards on the table? They are supposed to be in the department today. [...]

18th April, 7.30 Friday morning. Director's Office, Berlin

[Klemperer notes his ignorance with respect to some of the themes and terms discussed at the conference. And yet:] among the new works on language: Klemperer's *Language of the III Reich – me*, me in a programmatic German Philology and Linguistics lecture of the Academy!! *He walks on air.* But what is a phoneme,[13] which the Russians have discovered, the Germans never paid attention to?? [...] [then] H.'s parents. He: very fat grey-haired and bald, 61, somewhat depressed, she (57) imposing, close-cut grey hair under a net, very lively, evidently the intellectual power in this marriage, *he* in somewhat poor health, *she* very active. Both pleasant, kind-hearted, both evidently very impressed by my position, whose power they completely overestimate. He LDP, Protestant, she non-party, very close to our ideas. What holds them back is more the cultural uncertainty and the growing pains of the Party rather than the fundamental character of Marxism. I always preach: join and have an effect from the inside!

19th April, Saturday afternoon. Dresden

On Thurs., the 17th, after a very mediocre lecture delivered as if in a daze, I was invited to H.'s together with her parents. To talk to her mother about Heinrich Mann's *Henri IV*, she is reading it for the second time. A tenement building, quite reasonable from the outside but pretty terrible inside, opposite the 'Babylon' cinema.[14] A small furnished room, couch instead of a bed, simple, decent – very simple. I managed to find a way to start while we were still drinking coffee. I had been welcomed with a little too much respect, especially by the father; he had doubted whether I would come and we did arrive very late, because it was so nice to be alone with H. [...] I spoke very earnestly, without pathos, plainly, paternally – but they must have noticed the great affection. I also talked about Eva, also about the comedy and tragi-comedy of the situation, also about the religious and political aspects of the thing, also about money – people will say, she's marrying my car, will laugh about me, etc. etc. etc. Listened to me and were really moved and straightforward. Hadwig said nothing at all [...]. The parents in fact immediately sympathetic. Objections: her mother: H. was motherly, she would miss children – but she would be kept busy as an aunt. (Her younger brother's wife is already expecting a baby.) He: whether she would be able to replace Eva intellectually. Both repeatedly emphasising: H.'s own decision. Finally her father, and this was already half-comical, said: 'so I give my blessing.' [...]

Today I am unable to write, I shall now, 7 p.m., fetch Gusti here.

20th April, 6 p.m. Sunday afternoon. Dresden

H.'s parents left towards 8 on Thursday. [...] We ate supper [in a restaurant], it was so nice, being together. I drove back with H., took her to the house door, then took the underground to Friedrichstr., walked slowly up and down in my director's room ... I have come full circle: in 1904 my first great love in Berlin, then on Potsdamerstr. and the adjoining western part of the city; now in 1952 in 'democratic' Berlin, amidst the destruction and reconstruction, at 70 years of age with a new, disloyal love for a young girl, who is a stranger, really, and yet so close to me. I shall never again be able to put this confusion of emotions behind me. H. wrote to me, she loves E. in me – *I* am now giving her what remains of E.'s jewellery, it should live on with her, and not be scattered.

[...] Towards 3 p.m. we, i.e. Hadwig and I, drove to Halle. [...] I told her to eat supper with Lindner in the Stadt Hamburg, after that she picked up her parents from the station in the car. [...]

In between I attended a [university] senate meeting, from 6.30–10.30. An unusually interesting session. Preparations for the celebration of the 450th anniversary of the foundation of Halle-Wittenberg University. [...] It is intended to be a large-scale international cultural celebration: *the progressive German university*, it is also intended to demonstrate the tolerance of the GDR and emphasise the 'Martin Luther University Wittenberg-Halle'. The religious and bourgeois circles are to be won over, the CDU is trumps; that, at least, is how I see the situation. [...]

[...] What will Gusti say about my devout Hadwig?

What do *I* say to Hadwig? Worlds between her and me, two generations between her and me. Are we really strangers to one another, am I [...] deluding myself? [...] But beneath the feeling of happiness my conscience: betrayal! I have not managed to go to E.'s grave again. Which would only be sentimentality anyway.

[Then preparations for the trip to Poland.]

22nd April–7th May. Poland trip

[Only a very small proportion of the entries will be translated here. Klemperer visited Warsaw, Breslau, the Baltic coast, Krakow and Auschwitz.]

1st May, 4.30 p.m. Warsaw, Bristol

The rightly feared monotony and strain of the 1st of May is essentially over and done with – tomorrow life will be more interesting again, also the beginning of the final part [of the trip. The day before, Klemperer had flown for the first time, from Breslau to Warsaw.]

2nd May. Hotel Bristol, Warsaw – inter somnia

[...]

4 p.m.
No post. In very low spirits because of H.'s silence.

5th May, 6 a.m. Monday morning. Krakow
The Saturday afternoon was dismally taken up by Auschwitz. [. . .] I was given a guide who spoke very good German. [. . .] My own state during these endless hours: bored, without feeling, depressed at the inability to feel, repelled [. . .]. Drive through nondescript landscape. Auschwitz is less than 40 miles west of Krakow, about 20 miles east of Kattowitz. [. . .] Of the town of Auschwitz only a church tower is visible in the distance. Bleak heath land. A group of symmetrical barracks-like buildings for the SS or for administration purposes, a group of solidly built barracks, wire fence with metal posts surrounding them, with watch-and machine-gun towers, as they are familiar to me from Buchenwald. Altogether again and again Buchenwald, except spatially and in every other respect multiplied by a 100. 4 million dead! Probably 5 million. Area of 25 sq. miles. But once one is away from the main camp mostly all that one sees is fenced-in heath. The guide leaves the main camp to last. A thickset blond man in his forties speaking good German (with a Polish accent); he was interned here from beginning to end – but somehow in a work team in a semi-privileged position, but was very badly treated a couple of times. He speaks as fluently as a guide in a castle, but with genuine feeling in his voice, is a true FIR[15] [. . .] comrade, knows Diermayr,[16] Leo Stern, gives me greetings for VVN people. Long walk through the 'sub-camps'. Little to see. A couple of wooden barracks buildings, a railway track, a blown-up bunker, a water course through the somewhat swampy terrain, a little wood, the watch-towers, a couple of water-filled pits – nothing special at all. But the explanations! 'This is the death train.' 'This the ramp, where the *selection* took place.' 'This is the women's camp.' One sees nothing more than the usual prison and barracks mattress frames. But: 'just *one* such mattress had to be shared by up to eleven women, lying feet to head, feet to head. When they arrived, they weighed about 110–132 lbs, later none weighed more than 55 lbs . . . The long way in a shirt to the latrine.' A particularly large barracks building, round seat next to round seat. Here they exchanged letters, news, here the '*shit of a forewoman*' fried herself potatoes . . . Beside that a water purification plant – everything was utilised for chemical production, oil and soap produced. The brutalisation of the women, forced to strip, clothed in the pus-covered, bloody uniforms of captured Russians, is particularly emphasised by the guide. 'Here in this blown-up concrete room is where the gassing took place. It took 15–20 minutes until everything was quiet. Then we had to pull out the corpses. Here, where these water-filled pits are, the pyres burned day and night. The ovens couldn't cope any more. A layer of wood, a layer of bodies and petrol over them: The terrible air! . . . We built this channel . . .' All of it known, all of it evoked by the place and the report . . . The main camp, which is shown last, is different. Here much has survived, on the one hand for a natural reason: more substantial buildings, well built, because this is the prison displayed to the international 'humanitarian' commissions (with an orchestra,

decent food etc.) Then: because it has been renovated and extended as a museum. Layout as in Buchenwald. The cells, the holes in which prisoners had to sleep standing after their day's work – many deaths; the (decorated and renovated) 'death wall' for shootings, the mass gallows like a frame for beating carpets – 'but Hoess'[17] (the camp commandant, later captured and handed over to the Poles) 'we hanged at the camp entrance, he could not be allowed to die in the same place as our comrades. He admitted *three* million ...' From the sub-camps on the heath, I am still carrying a cross and a board with a Hebrew inscription. 'We have allowed it – but on the whole we don't like it, *human beings* were murdered here, without distinction of nation, of faith ... only human beings.' Museum rooms. A huge glass case with women's hair. Mattress and cushion stuffing was made out of it. Another glass case with a mountain of empty tins: they contained the zyklon. In front of them a broad strip of whitish crystal grains: the zyklon itself. Posters with diagrams, statistics on the walls. In huge letters on one wall: *4,000,000.* The guide adds: it is supposed to have been almost 5 million. Soap, sealant made from ashes, the gold teeth melted down to gold ingots are mentioned. Room for sterilisations, room for experiments – leprosy injections! Etc., etc. 'We show groups round every day ... 500 people are coming tomorrow ... We have to inform ... educate youth, keep the memory alive. We are in the service of humanity.' It is all spoken in a really genuine tone. The details (figures, precise statements: 'here stood' ... '135 Russians were shot here' ... etc. etc.) has been learned, the grief and the horror and the sympathy are genuine. The Polish state has, in other words, turned Auschwitz into an obligatory educational institution ... *The* hell of the 20th century, the technical and scientific hell, the German hell ...

I was repelled and exhausted, I was numb as ever. In the hotel at about 7, knocked out. Early to bed.

[...]

6th May, 10.30 Wednesday. Hotel Bristol, Warsaw

[...] We reached the plane at the last minute. Flight [from Krakow] now already familiar, 70 minutes from 7–8.10. [...]

4 p.m.

When we got back at 1 p.m. there was a letter from Hadwig here, very warm lines from 24 and 26 April, so sent airmail at latest on the 27th! I travel back in a calmer mood [...]; I shall have the Hadwig letters, which are undoubtedly on their way, sent back to Dresden.

[...]

That essentially concludes the Polish trip; unfortunately the train does not leave until 10.45 and unfortunately only arrives in Berlin at 10.

Certainly it went well. I was the first exchange humanities scholar to come here [...].

And now into the unknown. The house, the Academy, the Soviet Union holiday – Hadwig!

Everything is uncertain. I shall let myself be carried along. Nothing is *long term* for me any more.

[. . .]

11th May, 8 p.m. Sunday evening. Dresden
On Wed., 7 May, from the station to the Institute, long joyful conversation. [. . .] Invitation to Rita's. Telegram to Lindner: be at Rita's midday Thursday. Welcome by Rita as warm as it was natural. We are considered a married couple [. . .].

14th May, 2 p.m. Wednesday. Dresden
From Thurs. to Friday we continued our beautiful togetherness out at Rita's. At the Institute early, 14 intermediate examinations, coffee together in my room, then started for Halle. [. . .] At 7.30 an hour late for the senate. The meeting lasted until 11.30, began very brusquely, closed temperately. Revolt by the natural sciences faculty – Gallwitz, the dean – against the 10 month academic year, against arrests, against the Republic. An impudent resolution, an impudent attack on Leo Stern. Franz Wohlgemuth sent by the State Secretariat. Tremendously cutting with his quiet voice and cold haughty brutality – would be outstanding as Alba.[18] We value you as a scientist, Herr Gallwitz, otherwise you would not be where you are – but in political matters you are a complete ignoramus. Finally Gallwitz was forced to withdraw his faculty's impudent resolution, declare it non-existent and make his faculty bring forward a new pro-government resolution. The threat that otherwise the State Secretariat would take drastic measures was quite unmistakeable. [. . .] The Halle Gallwitzers had joined ranks with the Rostockers. There was also talk of abducted and arrested students – in part it is supposed to be tittle-tattle, in part elimination of elements hostile to the state. [. . .]

[On 10 May Klemperer speaks in Dresden on the anniversary of the Nazi Burning of Books:] Buchenwald, Auschwitz – how little do a couple of burned books weigh against them! And yet: here the beginning, the principle. [Klemperer also speaks out against the continuing refusal of the Dresden mayor to provide a bus service out to the State Library in its new, more remote location.]

We drove up to the cemetery, and Lindner placed the tulips in a jar in front of the gravestone. The grave is very beautiful and well-tended, very aesthetic – for whom? More a numbing of the emotions than confusion.

In kitchen apron H. proved to be an able cook and conquered Lindner's heart with meat rolls. 'You should stay here all the time, Fräulein Hadwig. Herr Professor will certainly pay you a good salary.'

After the meal drove to Gusti: there as guest, Helene Weigel,[19] whom I have never seen onstage. In ordinary clothes she looked just as on the *Mother Courage* pictures. Friendly and natural. She was en route to Chemnitz with her ensemble. [. . .] H. gave a good account of herself. [. . .] I arranged another visit with Gusti on Sunday morning. So then we sat with her on the garden bench

[...]. She knew everything immediately; she and 'Helly' had already noticed it yesterday.

18th May, Sunday forenoon. Dresden

[...]

The house business is uncertain. The Academy even more so. – Decision: the marriage will take place immediately. Whatever comes of it – perhaps it can be kept secret.

[...]

22nd May, 6 a.m. Ascension Day. Dresden

We shall take the 7.28 train to Berlin: invited by telegram to the Writers' Congress.[20] [...] At 9.45 on Friday we shall be wed at a registry office ceremony.

[...]

23rd May, 7.40 a.m. Friday. Director's Room, Berlin

[... At Writers' Congress:] Shook many hands: Purpose of our presence. Kantorowicz. Immediately raised H.'s doctorate. 'Influence of the French Résistance on German Literature.' Rita set the topic, joint supervisor. Why not I? – Because we are getting married tomorrow! [...]

25th May, towards 9 a.m. Sunday morning. Dresden

[...]

So on Friday morning, the 23rd, Lindner appeared. We picked up, one after the other, Hadwig, Rita and Robi (from the Central Committee building), were at the Berlin Mitte Registry Office on Elisabethstr. in good time. Comical-dignified-embarrassing ceremony, the registrar, a crumpled amusing personality, in part displaying a dignity learned by rote, in part a particularly obsequious cordiality, proud of the special case, concluded by giving a solemn speech with many quotations and with the 5 Year Plan at the end. Rita had absolutely wanted to force little bunches of myrtle on us for dress and jacket lapels – we had to have them, it is good luck – we had stuffed the bunches into our pockets. It did after all affect me very deeply that H. is now completely legally tied to me. – To the Institute, Christa Näther was speechless with surprise, Frau Limberg [the secretary] already knew, otherwise deserted. To the caucus meeting at 11, back at the Institute at about 1. [...]

Yesterday – first day of the new marriage – all kinds of accumulated correspondence attended to with H.'s help, began clearing up the chaos. After supper to Gusti's. Grundigs there. H. very tired. I brought breakfast up to her bed at 10 and let her go on sleeping. It is now midday.

Did I say anything about the foundering of the Academy business? Actually it hasn't foundered, merely been postponed. Nothing is going to happen for the time being because of the political situation; if it comes to a break with the West, then no more 'concession figures' will be needed and a more radical line can be pursued [. . .]. With all of that Krauss's game of intrigue continues. I don't have much hope any more. [. . .]

29th May, forenoon Thursday. Dresden
Our days here pass, insofar as we are alone, honeymoon-like, and sometimes the various weights on my soul are numbed and sometimes not. [. . .]

3rd June, Tuesday morning. Dresden
LQI: Doubt as to whether diversionaries[21] and splitters are identical. [. . .]

[On Sunday the Klemperers are guests at the wedding of one of his students.] H. sat mockingly beside me [during a very political, pro-Communist, address by the officiating Protestant pastor]. But then, when the concluding Lord's Prayer came, she prayed in a loud voice and with deep conviction. That shook me greatly. [. . .] At H.'s parents' I was affected by the great tangible tenderness between father and daughter. I am, whether I like it or not, always jealous. Of H.'s past, of H.'s future. I know, how profoundly unjustified and egoistical that is, I must and do wish her a later marriage and children with all my heart. I offended her, when I talked about 'the sinister power' of the Church and of confession, which stood between us. She offered to refrain from confession – I firmly rejected that. [. . .]

[. . .]

9th June, towards 7 p.m. Monday. Dresden
[On Friday Klemperer dealt with academic business in Berlin.] During the discussions E. was shopping – that she was also buying something in West Berlin made me a little anxious – but we ate together at Friedrichstr. Station, drank coffee in the Press House. [. . .] Out to the Kahanes'. Only Doris there. She took the news of our marriage well and without much surprise. [. . .]

Early yesterday afternoon – H. was sleeping – the Grubes, father and son, here. No one is surprised at my new marriage. Poor Eva. No one suspects how much love and how much bad conscience there is behind the new partnership.

[. . .]

16th June, 6 p.m. Monday
[Klemperer attends the regional conference of the Kulturbund on 13th–14th May. At the close he is unexpectedly elected honorary chairman.] Afterwards it turned out that I now really have the same KB position in Saxony as in Saxony-Anhalt. That certainly represents an increase in power and honours and just as certainly a further fragmentation. Always the same dilemma. [. . .]

20th June, 8 p.m. Friday. Dresden

[Volkskammer: lively discussion about the tedium of the sessions. The writer] Kuba[22] as enfant terrible: it was so boring, that one was ashamed to be a deputy. [...] The desire for real opposition, votes etc. is always disposed of by the pig-headed with the objection: 'We are not a bourgeois parliament!' [...]

[...]

2nd July, Wednesday morning (and later). Dresden

[On Friday, the 27th, Klemperer travels to Berlin with Hadwig. Discussion of theses, not least those of Rita Schober and of Hadwig.] Then Ruben told me I had been proposed for the National Prize by the Humanities Faculty, and Steinitz [said], that the Academy elections had been set for November, I was on the list and was absolutely certain to be elected. [... Problem of a student expelled from the FDJ as a Western 'agent'. In such cases:] The State Secretariat orders relegation *without* disciplinary proceedings [...] or for such students, who have not committed any crimes, but have clearly shown themselves to be opponents of the GDR and supporters of the West etc., a temporary interruption of studies. They are directed towards other professions, are kept under surveillance, the question of a later return to university is left open, if they prove themselves. [...] Privately I have repeatedly, passionately and fruitlessly discussed the matter with H. She says: this is the path to denunciation, to new concentration camps, to new violence, it was a mistaken policy. She says: action *only* where proven crimes not because of talk ... *Good*. But yet wrong. The Nazis were allowed to talk freely for so long until they were able to commit their crimes. [...]

7th July, 5 a.m. Monday morning. Dresden

Tomorrow E. will have been dead for one year. On Friday one of her posthumous books arrived, the Izcaray, published by Dietz.[23] I do not know the content, have even now read only the first few pages and admired the pure German. We were *so* far apart during the last part of her life that I did not know her work any more! And now ... Disloyalty to her, disloyalty to Hadwig. But there is such great love between H. and myself. Yet I am depriving H. of her right to youth. I shall never again have a really clear conscience. Always the ghastly feeling: did E. die in time for me to enjoy youth once more? There is no time to pursue such reflections. I must go on living despite it all.

[...] Whenever I see H. with her naked legs and feet happily watering the garden, E.'s garden, now at its most splendid! and now with everything that E. created (stone by stone, flower by flower, cherry by cherry!): always this doubly disloyal feeling: have I acted rightly?

(I am unable to get through the daily pile of newspapers, leaf through them – the never-ending repetition! – quite cursorily ... But yesterday a very fine speech by Ilya Ehrenburg about America.[24] Mocking, superior and yet also deeply felt – altogether humane and wise. On the whole, however, we have been living off the *one* idea of a new humanism. Nothing has been added to it, and we are marking time. And with us in the GDR or SED theory and practice are very rarely in harmony. And the general mood is poor.

9th July, Wednesday morning. Dresden

[In Halle on Tuesday, Klemperer learns, at a faculty meeting, that he is not going to be proposed for the National Prize by the university. His faith in Leo Stern is shaken. According to the latter, Klemperer is not as highly esteemed in certain quarters as by the university, and it would be an embarrassment if the university were to put his name forward for the third time and be turned down again. In the meeting discussing the issue Klemperer is criticised for not having produced sufficient new work. Finally it is agreed that a list of three names, including Klemperer's, should be put before the university senate, but with outside 'opinions' to follow.]

11th July, Friday morning. Dresden

[...]

Conversations (already beforehand with H. and – on the telephone – with Gusti) about the 'Second Party Conference'.[25] The tremendous crassness of the contradiction and of the sudden *LQI* alteration. Talk of peace, unity, 'free elections as before' – and *beginning of the construction of Socialism, national armed forces* and – above all: the War of 1813[26] was 'a war of national liberation'. Previously it had been 'the "so-called" Wars of Liberation'. It is impossible for me to sufficiently emphasise this 'so-called'. [...] Is it Hadwig's moral and human reservations, is it my old liberalism and scepticism, is it the ever more oppressive unpleasantnesses of the SED, which make me ever more doubtful? The West is rotten, and I belong to the East: there is no doubt of that for me (nor for H.). But inwardly I am very tired and sore.

[...]

13th July, Sunday evening. Dresden

Leo Stern was my patron and has now let me down. He always used to say to me: 'You have a particular friend in Fred Oelssner.' Now in his programmatic speech at the Party Conference Ulbricht has spoken very harshly of Oelssner.[27] Could Stern's desertion be related to this fall from favour? I do not trust a soul. Everyone is trying to stand upright on a slippery floor, and every day someone loses his footing and when he slips, others, *still* standing have to change their position.

[...]

20th July, Sunday evening. Dresden

[...]

Teweleit[28] was here on Friday morning. The publishing house is called 'Deutscher Verlag der Wissenschaften' [German Publishing House for the Sciences]. T., about 30, was Rita's colleague at the ministry – responsible for English. [...] X plans – which of them will be fulfilled? Immediately the *Siècle de Voltaire*,[29] immediately a reprinting of my 19th Century in 2 vols., periodical for Romance Languages with Krauss, Baldinger, Rita, periodical for literary theory and criticism with Hans Mayer. The sore point Krauss, my National Prize. [...]

[...]

28th July, Monday. Dresden

General feature of the last week: The parents-in-law, very likeable and very time-consuming, since I repeatedly get caught up in earnest and unproductive conversations (on war and peace, on the errors and virtues of the republic etc. etc.). Once a walk together into the village and to E.'s grave. [...] sheer agony of the faltering work on the article for the Festschrift.[30] Yesterday at last completely finished and ready to post.

[...] On Tuesday the invitation to the celebration of the Polish national day in the Polish Embassy in Pankow. I have never seen such a number of cars in one place, never such a sumptuous trough of a cold buffet with so many delicacies, such a crowd, such gorging and boozing. Only chairs were missing. [...] One promenaded, chatted with one person or another. We: with Harig, with Leonhard,[31] with Wilhelm Koenen, very tipsy ... with several whose name and position I did not pick up, but they were all VIPs. In the crush we saw Ulbricht, Grotewohl, Anna Seghers etc. It was all very amusing, since the two of us could always observe together. And gorge and drink and feel oneself to be important ... [...] We left towards midnight once we had at last enjoyed the longed-for coffee. The car was called by telephone. Lindner, somewhat indignant himself, reported the 'mutiny' of the drivers: they had each got only a bockwurst and a glass of beer ... [...]

[At a meeting of DFD[32] and Kulturbund deputies of the Volkskammer, there are attacks on Becher for his non-appearance.] I thought: If you speak it'll cost you your National Prize. But I pulled myself together and spoke vigorously against Becher, called the post of Volkskammer deputy 'the highest honour'.

Here in Dresden [an] interesting visit, Erich Seidemann and wife. He is facing a Party court, because at a neighbourhood meeting he had spoken out vehemently against the Party and against the Russians. He is caught up in the reactionary Dölzschen milieu, says: 90% of all workers were against our government, there was more to eat in the West, every day people deserted from East to West, never the reverse, the way the Russians had behaved here at the beginning would be remembered for centuries [...] etc. etc. I advised him to retract – but it appears to be too late for that. [...]

My *Histoire véritable* [novella by Montesquieu] has at last appeared – but my name is only in small print somewhere as translator.[33] [...]

Today a long letter from Lisel Sebba in Haifa – after years! She writes: Dear V., dear E.! – Not a line from Jule, he appears to be paralysed.

3rd August, midday Sunday. Dresden
[...] I have received an assurance from Teweleit's scholarly publishing house, that printing of the 18ième will begin in a few days, and that the proofs will be submitted to the National Prize Committee.
[...]

5th August, Tuesday morning. Dresden
Yesterday Halle. To bring back the Kirchner parents. Complete holiday hush in the department. [...]

In Halle mainly the house of Kirchner. Brother Gottfried[34] visited with his young wife. [...] Gottfried: very handsome, powerful, very intelligent, energetic bold face. Lectures very enthusiastically on phonetics and phonology and the phoneme – absolutely new to me. *I* have to pretend that of course I have looked at Saussure's[35] book – I did not have a clue about Saussure, he has only very recently mysteriously cropped up a couple of times. [...]
[...]

15th August, 4.30 a.m. Dresden
The constant professional torment of the last week: the fruitless work on Diderot. I read Katja's selection, I brooded over the D'Alembert,[36] began my study; i.e. I endeavour to adapt and trim the chapter of my 18ième. But I don't make any progress and write nothing at all new. But the torment increases with every day – because again and again I see, how *impossible*, how *bourgeois* my 18ième looks. I fear it will not be printed at all. And *if* it is printed -what will the effect be? Worse than that of my *Modern Prose*. And my National Prize? And my admission to the Academy?? Every day these thoughts. [...]

Yesterday in the most sultry heat I granted both of us – H. is learning Russian like a schoolchild – a day off: I began reading Stefan Heym's *The Crusaders*[37] aloud. Very strong interest. (Borrowed weeks ago from Gusti, with whom relations are strained at the moment. She said: *the* book of our time.)

17th August, about 8 a.m. Sunday morning. Dresden
[...]

In Berlin on Saturday (16th Aug.) [...] At Rita's in the afternoon where we plotted to make history. In the Leipzig University periodical Krauss has boasted about the work his people have produced and claimed the re-orientation of the study of Romance Literatures for himself. Now *we* are going to publish our work and theories in the Halle periodical. [...] Krauss's latest plan: not to lecture at all in Leipzig, only to teach his research assistants, be high priest, floating high above the everyday university business. [...] I no longer believe in [...] Ernst Hoffmann's power. Who has the power?? Nepotism and intrigue and greased floor, on which one can stumble at every step, *anywhere!* Not just in our little Romance corner, not just everywhere in our whole area of culture – everyeveryeverywhere in the Party. [. . .]

[Difficulties of a planned visit to Hadwig's parents who live in the Harz Mountains but within the 3 mile prohibited zone along the East–West frontier.[38]] As things stand, from the 18th–20th we shall be in Halle and the Harz, on the 25th we want to go to Heringsdorf [on the coast], and I may already have to be in Berlin on the 23rd, because I have asked for an audience with the newly appointed Education Minister Else Zaisser.[39] At the parliamentary group meeting recently Zaisser led the attack on Becher in which I warmly supported her. [. . .]

[. . .]

21st August, 7 p.m. Thursday. Dresden

[. . .] At 2 p.m. we started for Wernigerode. Very poor roads, there at 5. I have frequently passed through W., have probably also spoken there. The general picture of the mediaeval wooden town was familiar to me, above it, like a toy, the castle, probably rebuilt in the 19th century. [. . .] H.'s parents were waiting for us, for them our visit was a big event. The touching affection which the members of this family show to one another, Hadwig's intellectual superiority and great love. Her mother had found a wonderful bay-windowed room – unfortunately stinking of floor polish – in the Hotel Meyer; view of the castle. We stayed there very happily. It was really our first non-'official' trip, the short time from Mon. evening to 2 p.m. on Wed. seemed very long to us. [. . .]

23rd August, 8 a.m. Saturday. Dresden

[. . .]

Today we have been married for 3 months. I love H. more and more, and my guilt towards her and towards E. is present in my mind in complex fashion every day.

[. . .]

24th August, 5 p.m. Sunday afternoon

[. . .]

Today completed the article 'State of Romance Languages Studies' for the *National Zeitung* – my third piece of journalism recently[40] [. . .].

There remains: Packing and a little bit of clearing up. Tomorrow, therefore, to the Baltic via Berlin. For the first time without Eva. I love them both very much, and my heart is never quite at ease. I owe it to myself and to Hadwig to make of this improbable remainder of my life what my heart and head allow.

26th August, Tuesday afternoon. Heringsdorf

[Victor Klemperer and Hadwig stay only 10 days instead of the planned fortnight.]

Here in 1904 with E. and now with H., Swinemünde now in Poland ... no time for atmospheric descriptions and reflections.

[... Accommodation] primitive but nice, Lindner drove back to Anklam last night. What bliss without driver, without supervision, without car – free!

27th August, 6.30 a.m. Wednesday morning. Heringsdorf

Central is the bathing question. [...] There are no bathing establishments, no cabins any more. Beach still very busy. The undressing problem. More easily solved for H. than for me. Crowds of young people – conspicuous age. With a belly (weighed over 12 stone yesterday! twelve!). After lengthy consideration H. bathed – the first time in the sea for her. Today we, *me included*, will look for a quiet spot in the quiet late afternoon on the way to Bansin. [...]

28th August, 7 a.m. Thursday. Heringsdorf

[...] I thought I recognised the Seehof where I was happy with E. in 1905(?) [...] The swim did me no good – shortness of breath, fear: I shall not repeat it. H. swam happily. Old man, young woman. My depression weighed heavily on her. She always worries about me, tries to 'console' me, to help me. Sometimes I doubt whether her good humour is genuine. Every kind of self denial, self castigation, lying out of consideration and good nature can constantly be assumed on her part. I torment myself and her and myself again, because I know I do not strike the right note ... Nevertheless much love and happiness and probably also much genuine pleasure for H ... Idiotic waste of time this diary tone.

[...]

Formal appointment accompanied by congratulations as 'Chairman of the Academic Advisory Committee for the Subject Area Romance Languages and Literatures'. Members: Krauss, Baldinger, Böhme, Brummer, Storost, von Jan, Rita Schober, Manfred Naumann – i.e. all, literally all the professors in the GDR. 'I had you appointed,' Rita, who has meanwhile lost her ministerial post,[41] recently told me. [...]

30th August, 6.30 Saturday morning. Heringsdorf

[...] Yesterday almost classically beautiful the strong swell of the steely sea with its crests, the clearly visible coast with the Swinemünde lighthouse – in POLAND – why does this 'Poland' here give me such a feeling of pain, why did the Soviet Union make Poland smaller and compensate it here? [...] We talked about it and did not come to any conclusion. Nevertheless with all its failings and inconsistencies the SU is our salvation and the better future of the world. [...]

In the afternoon and the evening I read aloud, in the mornings I write and read for myself. Thus one struggles through the 'holiday'.

[...]

4th September, 5 p.m. Thursday afternoon. Heringsdorf

Today – for loo purposes – I bought a newspaper – the first in two weeks. Everything in it is the same as before, treading water and varying the repetitions. The Soviet Note, for which the Volkskammer is meeting tomorrow, is likewise a repetition.[42] The Soviet Union's desire for peace and readiness to negotiate, proposals which will once again, of course, be rejected.

[...]

13th September, Saturday forenoon. Dresden

[...]

Interesting and not disagreeable: it is impossible to conduct the seminar on the Modernists with the 32 new first-year students, since a large number of them begin as absolutely illiterate in French. We have replaced the seminar with language exercises conducted by the foreign language assistants. [...]

22nd September, Monday morning about 9 a.m. Dresden

The excess of work and fragmentation. I spent all of yesterday on a Zola article for the *Berliner Zeitung*, this morning already 2 Leipzig examination scripts and Katja's Sainte-Beuve introduction dealt with. The Leipzigers fluently get down the usual political cliches about imperialism and Socialist Realism in halfway polished French; they don't have a clue about actual literary history and aesthetics. [...]

The trip to Kamenz on Saturday was nice. Essentially visiting Agnes in Piskowitz. We fetched her from work – on a nationally owned estate, at 75 pfennigs an hour, we saw her field, the destroyed little house, in which she sheltered us in 1945. Her son Juri has turned into a hugely strong good-natured and intelligent-looking lad of 21 – FDJ, *not* Party. I particularly liked his attitude to Marka, the upper-school pupil. 'She's studying – I'm only a dirty worker!' said with affection. Still the cramped hut. No money to build [a house], although there have been promises and assurances. It's a matter of 4,500M. They already have the building materials. [...] I have promised them the money, either as an interest-free loan [...] or as a present. That is in accordance with Eva's wish and also with Hadwig's. [...] Agnes welcomed Hadwig with friendly matter-of-factness: 'But you couldn't remain alone, Herr Professor.'

[...]

27th September, Saturday evening about 8 p.m. Dresden

The terrible excessive burden [of work] and the chasing around. The diary is suffering greatly.

[...]

Nice, almost habit now, the bohemian supper in our [i.e. Hadwig's] room followed by cinema and then to the state restaurant at Alexanderplatz for a spritzer or a dessert wine, since the ice cream was already sold out.

[...]

28th September, 7.30 Sunday morning. Dresden

[...]

Everything merges into everything else in the chaotic rush of recent days. When was the changeover of rectors [at Berlin University]? I think, only the day before yesterday on Friday, the 26th. Deutsches Theater. Gowns, trying them on. Grey velvet the economists, blue the philosophers, red (in various shades) the law and medical people, etc. We sat on the stage; at a table in front of the professors, three blood-red beadles. Investiture ceremony. Is it appropriate for us? Friedrich,[43] old man, now President of the Academy, read a long report, very good. A true historical overview, comprehensive, dignified, always measured and simultaneously emphatically bringing out the will to democracy. The new man, the jurist Neye,[44] cut a most embarrassing figure by comparison. By tone and content a 'middling' sort of Party functionary. [...]

I saw Peter and Inge Klemperer again after a long gap. They are both in the middle of their state exam. We are going to visit them in Friedrichshagen[45] at the same time as Peter's mother (who has meanwhile been in Switzerland).

[...]

Today is the 28 Sept. The award of the National Prizes takes place on 7 Oct. in the 'President's official residence'. Were I to be included, I would already have an invitation ... Unpleasant and bitter.

[...]

5th October, Sunday evening. Dresden

Back from Berlin yesterday evening, to Berlin again at 6 tomorrow morning, to receive the National Prize, of which I learned with certainty on Thurs. afternoon, 2 Oct. In between, the most chaotic, exhausting, exciting Berlin week with all the charms and drawbacks of bohemian life, cramped conditions etc.

[...]

12th October, Sunday morning. Dresden (until 5 in the aft.)

The National Prize affair passed off, all in all, somewhat depressingly, even disgustingly, at any rate tastelessly and boringly and I base this *not only* on my 'third class'.[46] – From the stage of the Staatsoper, the curtain closed, one was called out as if for a military roll call and assigned to seats. Certainly a good 100 people – very many collectives – [... most] industrial – 'Sulphuric Acid ...' 'Rolling mill ...' – 'Coach Builder ...' etc. I sat in the very front row, but in front of me there was a very long table with piled-up books – the large and somewhat crudely prepared diplomas. Then, from the podium in front of the benches,

Pieck read out a short dull speech, then stepped in front of a little table in the middle of the stage and read in rapid succession the names of the prize winners and their contributions (these latter extremely brief), stumbled over the chemical names and all the time – Weinert excepted – spoke like an automaton and held out his hand. Yet there was perspiration on his face. [...] as mentioned the majority of the prizes, whether first, second or third class, went to collectives, and each time it was announced in detail: A receives 15,000M, B 9,000 the rest shared equally ... [...] the audience clapped enthusiastically for Erich Weinert and his 100,00M prize – after that mechanically and dutifully. The overwhelming share of the prizes went to industry, after that to medicine, veterinary medicine, chemistry and the like. Very few to art and literature, [...] only two humanities scholars – the other a historian of recent German history, a politician therefore. I was the only prize-winning philologist – povera e nuda vai ...![47] The diploma very schematic and lacking content: 'For services to German Studies and Romance Languages and Literature'. The monotonous ceremony lasted from about 11 until almost 2, in great heat. Afterwards we drove to Rita Schober's and at 5 we were sitting in the opera house again, this time the two of us together in the stalls. The 'State Occasion'. Suffocating heat and terrific boredom until almost 9 o'clock.

[...]

The VVN gave me a big basket of flowers, in Halle there were also flowers, letters, telegrams. But in the press I came off poorly. Only the *Berliner Zeitung* printed my picture. Today I had a delegation here from the Dresden West KB group. The pupils' group of Dresden West Upper School is to bear my name.

[...]

On Frid. afternoon a conference in my [Berlin] director's room: Teweleit, Görner,[48] Rita, Baldinger, myself on the Romance Languages periodical to be founded, editorial board Klemperer, Baldinger, a Westerner – editor Rita. Everything depends on the still-to-be-found Westerner. [...] Success doubtful. Baldinger attended a Romance scholars' congress in London. The most unbelievable hair-raising ideas about Russian barbarism and slave-holding in the 'Eastern Zone' are widespread.

[...]

At the centre of things here yesterday the great still-unsolved question of the '*evening dress*' for the Halle celebrations next week. H. tried on [dresses] in the state HO store, but has not yet found anything suitable. To me it all still looks so like fancy dress, looks tarted up, conspicuous, old-fashioned. [...] But all these costume questions are very topical nevertheless. It was widely noted that at the last diplomatic reception Pieck wore tails, in Halle new gowns and birettas are being made, at the installation of the Berlin rector there was a big fancy-dress celebration – representation, ties to historical traditions, the Russians do it likewise – 'extensive display' of our dignity! ! [...]

[...]

23rd October, midday Thursday. Dresden
Never-ending autumn rain, never-ending electricity cuts. Yesterday from 5 p.m. until almost 9, today since 7 a.m. Hadwig says: because of re-armament, and is probably right. [. . .]
 [. . .]

25th October, midday Saturday. Dresden
[Klemperer gives a detailed account of the ceremonies, processions, speeches and banquets to mark the 450th anniversary of the University of Halle-Wittenberg, 18 and 19 October. Hadwig changes dresses 3 times on the Saturday – Klemperer says he feels like a grandfather introducing his granddaughter into society.] Incidentally only very few ladies were wearing evening dresses and H.'s was undoubtedly the most elegant, dignified and most beautiful. [. . .]

[Away from the festivities and back in Berlin VK is doing his best to encourage the teaching of French and of linguistics.]

After a very long time a letter from Otto Klemperer in London. In a very friendly tone a family report on his two grown-up sons, one a doctor, one a chemist, both in research institutes, the youngest son in a boarding school, his German wife a schoolteacher. Visit by his brothers, who have wives and children, from the USA. – A very faraway world, completely closed to me, despite the closest blood relationship. How little blood counts! O. writes – and so also still new and impressive to him: 'They all came in a tourist air plane,[49] which flies from New York to London in *one* night.' – We are cut off here.
 [. . .]

26th October, Sunday forenoon. Dresden
The tomcat has disappeared since yesterday evening. I fed him at 7.30 [. . .]. There was certainly no door or window open. We did not notice the disappearance until late [. . .]. Between 1 and 2 we searched outside with lights, we rummaged through the house, every corner, every cupboard. The animal was clumsy and fat, probably also already a little lame. We expected and expect a heart attack. We searched and are searching everywhere for his corpse. In vain – a complete mystery. – The tomcat is E.'s legacy. Did he lack affection after her death? Hardly, I think . . . As usual my feelings are cold. My usual selfishness: easier life without him. Yet I did my very best to look after him. Poor Eva.
 [. . .]

1st November, Saturday forenoon. Dresden (until about 8 p.m.)
Having a search made, placing an advertisement have been no help – the tomcat must have perished somewhere. It weighs doubly on me. On the one hand because of the animal itself via Eva, on the other because of my lack of feeling. For days I don't think of the animal, for days don't think of E. [. . .]

In addition Hadwig: She now has her diploma as academic research assistant and has her commitments. She will not always have business at the Institute on the same days as I.

[...]

[Klemperer discusses with several other academics the right terms in which to refer to Stalin in a lecture-cum-pamphlet he has written.] Conclusion: It seems to me like the resolution of the French National Assembly, that God exists. Moscow must decide and resolve what language, what literature is. In these things there is a harsher dictatorship than in the West. But I regard this intellectual dictatorship as temporary – temporarily necessary – and one that will relax, and I believe, within this dictatorship we are more progressive and humane than the friends of the Yankees. [...]

In the morning someone said our tomcat had been sighted up in the village. In the afternoon Lindner, Frau Duckhorn and Weller conducted a search lasting several hours until well after darkness had fallen. In vain. [...] The whole neighbourhood has been alerted.

[...]

8th November, 8.30 a.m. Saturday. Dresden

[...] (The army is already replacing the People's Police at the checkpoints [i.e. at the entries to Berlin] and wears such Russian-looking uniforms, that one doesn't know whether one is looking at Russian or German soldiers.[50])

9th November, midday etc. Dresden

[... Klemperer is confronted with difficulties in the recruitment of qualified students. The prorector Havemann[51] – at the Humboldt University – is particularly eager in his application of new guidelines: Why should students with a bourgeois background be allowed to study, if they're just going to go off to the West, for example. Also students with addresses in West Berlin are being dropped.] Similar [...] to the matter reported [to me], the measure against shopkeepers, whose shops are over here and whose homes are in West Berlin: A sudden police action has brutally shut down their businesses.[52] How much grist to the Rias [broadcasting station] mill! Mutual fear and everywhere the situation is worsening.

[...]

16th November, midday Sunday. Dresden

On Thurs. 13th Nov. in Berlin (alarm set for 4 – lecture). First news: Romania trip – 2 to 16 December. [... Academic Advisory Board meeting, Klemperer chairman, for forthcoming lecture programmes, he succeeds in removing the cliched Marxist titles which Krauss has employed for courses, such as 'Voltaire, the genius of the big bourgeoisie'.] The whole thing was a bit of a triumph for me. The tension between Krauss–Klemperer now engages the whole of Romance Studies in the GDR. [...]

Wilhelm Pieck's declaration: Friendship with France! is of the greatest significance for my efforts on behalf of French.[53] For years I have been saying and writing: Our allies of tomorrow! Still unaware of this declaration I had myself officially charged with urging Wandel to introduce the teaching of French in the People's High Schools. Reason: we need already trained secretaries and shorthand typists in our Romance Languages and Literatures institutes.

23rd November, Sunday forenoon. Dresden
[...] In the afternoon we had been for two minutes at E.'s grave, which Weller had put in order very nicely – because today is the day of the dead, and today I have been married to H. for six months to the day. Never again will I have completely clear feelings. Don't reflect – go on obstinately living and working, and make H. as happy as possible. There is not a single feeling inside me that is not mixed.
[...]

26th November, midday Wednesday. Berlin, Institute
[...]
Shocking gangster letter from the 'Association of Free Lawyers for the Exposure of Injustices Carried out by the Governing System of the Soviet Zone'. I must try to make a copy before handing it over to the Party or police. My National Prize was bribery. I should clearly distance myself from the terror regime, by supporting the persecuted with my money. I should keep receipts of such support in a safe place, because then on the 'day of the re-unification of Germany' I would be able to prove, that ... etc.[54]
[...]

29th November, midday Saturday. Dresden
On Thurs., 27 Nov., after normal lectures – the close of the semester for me: a) Montesquieu, b) overview up to the Résistance, to Eluard, who has just died. Fine conclusion. Elan in both lectures [...]. [Reception marking the Month of Soviet Friendship.] We sat – with the usual good 'cold buffet' at a table with Kantorowicz, Hadwig's 50% doctoral supervisor. Animated by wine he spoke very bitterly of Becher's baseness and unscrupulousness as a human being. B. had prevented Kantorowicz's already agreed election to the Academy [of Arts] from taking place and instead had his creature and bootlicker, Abusch, admitted in his stead, he had also undermined Arnold Zweig's presidency and would shortly no doubt be the latter's successor,[55] he was omnipotent and could not be brought down, because Ulbricht, absolutely ignorant in literary matters, supported him. [...]
[...] and now I drove to Paul Wandel. It turned out a success: French in the schools and People's High Schools! He called in his department head; a commission is to be set up: State Secretariat, Ministry of Popular Education,

myself: and after the holidays in advance of my France speech to the Humboldt University and the Peace Committee important measures for the improvement of the position of French will be decided and officially announced at my speech. [. . .]

Romania

1st December, 2 p.m. Monday. Berlin, Institute
[. . .]
Hadwig at Kantorowicz's lecture. He has circumscribed her doctoral thesis: French influences on H. Mann's late novels.
[. . .]

4th December, midday Thursday. Budapest, German legation
Tuesday evening to the station with H. and Lindner. [. . .] H. very melancholy with fixed smile – it haunts me. [. . .]
I am sitting in a private room on the 2nd floor – some nondescript elegant street, an elegant normal house, downstairs waiting room as in Warsaw as everywhere with flags, Pieck, Lenin, Marcks and much red [. . .]

Towards 7 p.m.
[. . .] Our train is due to leave at 21.55.
The broad Danube impresses me. But it is not blue here either.
[. . .]

7th December, 6.30 p.m. Sunday. Bucharest, Hotel
[. . . The trip is not as pleasant as the previous one to Poland. The Romanians seem uncertain what to do with their academic visitor, there are few opportunities to lecture and Klemperer finds political conditions much more oppressive than in East Germany.]
[. . .]
[. . . Klemperer attends the final day session of a peace congress.] The Stalin cult. Ours already seems oriental to us. But here! Literally at least five times more so. Every five minutes (at the latest) standing up, rhythmically clapping a whole slogan: Slava lui Stalin! [Praise to Stalin] and then a drumming of feet. Also much more oriental than Warsaw. [. . .]
[. . .]

10th December, 5 p.m. Wednesday. Bucharest
[. . .]
Fear and narrow-mindedness appear to be general here. [. . .] The professors

are only allowed to lecture reading from monitored manuscripts and are not at all allowed to speak extempore.

11th December, after 8 a.m. Thursday morning. Bucharest
[...]
I now, thank God, have half of this not very pleasant trip behind me. The second half will probably not drag on so agonisingly, since I'll start travelling and that in the direction of Berlin and Hadwig.
[...]

19th December, 10 a.m. Friday. Director's Room, Berlin
[...]
Lindner was waiting for me at the station at about 7 p.m. Everything all right at home. [...] Night in Dresden, most indifferent welcome by the tomcat, then had a bath yesterday morning, to Halle – ice and winter landscape, with H. at 10. [...] – most heartfelt joy. Then at midday we carried on to Berlin – [...] Bought mince and ate supper in our little stove corner. Afterwards – unfortunately – the department's Christmas party in the Institute's rooms. [... There are skits taking off the professors.] Holger[56] unfortunately presented me as such a bent old man, that I felt really miserable. [...]

24th December, Wednesday morning. Dresden
Thus far the usual nice and oppressive waste of time. Of the Diderot,[57] which I am fed up to the back teeth with, few lines written. Christmas shopping in dreadful crowds. [...] Since yesterday evening until beginning of January H.'s parents here [...]. I abstain from analysing my Christmas feelings and all the other feelings related to it. The best thing: not think of anything at all, take delight in H. and get through the time.

Received the very interesting *Romance Languages and Literatures Yearbook*, vol. 4 from Hamburg. Lerch's touching and in many respects quite uncomprehending article on my 70th birthday.[58]

2nd January
The last week of 1952 passed very uneventfully – pleasant and simultaneously busy and empty.

In fact always at home, once a little walking crawl up Grenzstr. to the 'goat place' below the cemetery. 'GDR standards' [...]. If I did not believe all of this to be transitional and growing pains, if I did not know that in the West everything is equally dulling – here aiming at a great goal, over there at a base one ... Admittedly for *me* it is easy not to despair; for E.'s mother as a schoolteacher it is dreadfully difficult. I admire her and her attitude very greatly. Suffering because of her knees and legs, she spends most of the time sitting in a club chair, completely surrounded by books and always reading – as long as I don't come anywhere near her, because then I am overwhelmed with stories and questions. In everything she says there is her passionate and genuine feeling, her enthusiastic mind, her great education. In everything her conscience and her goodness. She is very good – merely a little time-consuming ... H.'s father is different. Terrible embitterment, which he hides or tries to hide behind forced humour, he evidently really has problems with his heart and his nerves, but there is perhaps also a little self-indulgence involved. He sleeps an enormous amount, also during the day, he goes for long and lonely walks, he gets on the nerves of wife and daughter, who love him dearly and whom he loves dearly. – H. as mediating daughter demonstrates such sincerity and affection, such a sure, slightly humorous, never condescending or impatient intellectual superiority, at the same time showing respect with such naturalness and daughterliness, that I cannot admire and love her enough for it.

In short: the Kirchner family filled the last week. At Christmas we had Gusti here, on New Year's Eve we were alone. A very pretty little tree – there were moments when the whole thing weighed on me ... The feeling of guilt towards E. inside me, I am trying to balance, so to speak, by the greatest possible repayment of what H. has given me.

[...]

The main things 1952
23rd May 1952: Marriage to Hadwig. – Before that Poland. (The pleasant trip). – Afterwards in December, Romania (The expedition).

In October: the National Prize. – Printing of my 18ième: *The Century of Voltaire*. (Proofs ongoing.)

Own work only trifles.

1953

2nd January, Friday forenoon. Dresden (since this morning everything picturesquely covered in snow)

Rita had sent me a eulogy intended for publication, in which there was rather too much talk about the son of the rabbi, Jewish suffering etc. I wrote to her most unequivocally: I found philo-Semitism just as unpleasant as anti-Semitism. I am a German and Communist, nothing else. Besides the consequence of philo-Semitism was certainly only a reinforcement of anti-Semitism. [...]

I also add a characteristic scene of desperation, which I experienced with Weller, the gardener. The man came to me on Christmas Eve completely distraught: he was crushed, he had just been informed by telephone that he must vacate his leased nursery garden on 1 January. We immediately told him, it must be a deception, either because of personal envy, or to make him an enemy of the GDR.

[...]

8th January, 10 p.m. Thursday. Dresden

[...]

The period of calm is now coming to an end. Tomorrow Berlin again: KB Executive Committee and 'reception' in honour of Becher's Stalin Peace Prize. [...]

Continuing proof reading of the 18ième. [...]

12th January, 8.30 a.m. Monday. Dresden

Even less time, even greater fragmentation, inability to work than ever. [...]

[...]

[After a Volkskammer session.] The fiery protests, the conscience of the world!!

It makes me want to throw up. Does anyone believe that the Rosenbergs,[1] who were of course also discussed, and who are to be executed on 14 January, does anyone believe that they will be saved. The USA won't be moved by paper protests – anzi![2] But it's propaganda *here*. The Rosenbergs are secondary and will be forgotten tomorrow, replaced by other names. [...]

Then on Friday evening the reception for Becher, bearer of the Stalin Prize. We both shook his hand, were then seated very much out of the way in a distant room, ate our fill at the cold buffet and left early. [...]

19th January, 7 p.m. Berlin, Institute

Politically upsetting news of recent weeks: [...] Soviet action against the doctors' conspiracy in connection with the *Joint Distribution Committee*.[3] (My Zion chapter need no longer be missing from the next *LTI* edition. My request to Rita: No philo-Semitism, is justified!) – The heads of the GDR Jewish communities, in particular Loewenkopf and Julius Meyer[4] are supposed – Joint Distribution Committee! – to be in the West.

[...]

I am not a good human being. Today Baldinger assured me, Lerch really was dead; my feeling at that, solely the wicked triumph: 'Hurrah, I'm alive!'

[...]

Yesterday afternoon curious coffee party here: the Konrads, Lisl Steininger, Frau Bauer, Frau Stefan-Hamann. There was much talk, remembering of Jewish matters. The flight of Loewenkopf and Jule Meyer was also mentioned; I did not believe it.

[...]

22nd January, Thursday. Berlin, Institute

Between 12 and 2 (language exercises 2–4) Comrade Joseph: her father with the Jewish Community in Leipzig. Jule Meyer came from Berlin, urged flight, all community heads from Berlin, Jena, Leipzig fled to West Berlin – Zion – Joint, in some newspapers there had already been printed 'The Jew' so and so – that's how it had started in 1933, too.

24th January, Saturday forenoon. Dresden

I said to Joseph: *You* are a comrade after all, you must know that anti-Semitism is impossible here – our theory ... our liberation by the Russians ... we are opposed to Zionism allied to the USA, to capitalism ... Yes, she appreciated all that, 'but one is shocked nevertheless, one doesn't know what's true, all Jews are said to have been expelled from the Soviet army!' I tried to speak words of comfort. – Meanwhile expulsion of those gone to the West (Meyer, Loewenkopf) expressed in the harshest terms – 'casting out' of the 'guilty agents and traitors'.[5]

These people have collaborated with the Joint (which sent packets to observant Jews) and had contacts with the state of Israel. Odious. At the same time triumph of my Zion chapter in the *LTI*.

[...]

We drove back from Berlin at about 6. – I have achieved nothing [...] with respect to strengthening the teaching of French. The red tape in the GDR is just as crippling and recalcitrant as red tape anywhere. Especially exasperating the question of French teaching at the People's High Schools. [...]

30th January, 1 p.m. Friday. Berlin, Institute

[...]

I did not get down to much work [on Wednesday], because I learned of Krauss's attack. He has written a malicious letter about me. So malicious, that it met with opposition in the Academy, even on the part of Frings. As far as I have been able to find out, he has accused me, inter alia, of failing to establish a school. But until Halle I have never had an opportunity to do so. I was stuck in Dresden – the proper universities were closed to me. My bitterness of those years: Frankfurt, Vienna, Hamburg. The poorer candidate was always preferred. Hamburg: 'We already have the Jew Cassirer.'[6]

[...]

14th February, midday Saturday. Dresden

[...]

On 5th Feb. the class elections of the Academy are to take place, on the 12th the definitive election. It was a childish wish of mine to be elected on the 12th, the anniversary of father's death (12.2.1912! It is a mistake that I am still alive!). Steinitz told me on the telephone, it had been postponed again, to 19 Feb. This has been going on since spring 1952.

[...]

21st February, about 9 a.m. Saturday. Berlin, Institute

[...]

On Wednesday, in the Babylon, sitting in our fine box with Lindner, we saw the *Rembrandt* film,[7] which H. already knew. Beautiful and frequently affecting. Biographical. [...] Great performances by the actors – big names almost all unknown to me – the twelve Nazi years. But in the auction scene a group of buyers like a caricature in the *Stürmer*. The film was made under Hitler. How could the film have been passed now – especially now! cf Joint! – I am going to raise it at the VVN.

[...]

22nd February, Sunday midday etc. Dresden
[...]

[Klemperer attends a meeting of the Central Council of the VVN – Association of the Victims of Nazi Persecution. A decision is made to wind up the organisation. On the one hand, suggests Klemperer, because of a general process of centralisation in the GDR, on the other, because of the flight of the 'Zionist Jews' – and the VVN was seen by many as representing Jews. There remained an Anti-Fascist Committee maintaining links with abroad.[8] I spoke of my profound antipathy to Zion, related the fate of my Zion chapter – said further, I was probably the only wearer of the star on the committee [...] I had just witnessed the alarm among the Jews (case of Elisabeth Joseph), it was necessary to be careful. A scene like the *Stürmer* image in the Rembrandt film was impossible. Incidentally I regarded it as a piece of good fortune, that our group, which fell apart into smaller groups, was now becoming an essential part of the people as a whole. Beyling immediately said there had been a number of democratic criticisms of the *Rembrandt*, film and it would be withdrawn in the next few days. It was [...] a gratification of my vanity, to have been placed on this committee. The session was over at 1.30, and I then had lunch together with the others. [...] With Kantorowicz, who is very important to me for H.'s sake, but whom I also really like for his own sake. [...]

We brought the record player with us, which we had already bought a week ago and decided on since the National Prize, Lindner set it up. 20 records have already been bought, more are to follow. In the evening we had a concert, and it will continue today. Thus the gramophone days are being repeated at a technically higher level.[9] Then Eva taught me to dance the tango.

[...]

28th February, Saturday afternoon. Dresden
[Klemperer's goal of election to the Academy is achieved at last.]

Baldinger brought me the first news during the faculty meeting on Wed. aft.: 'very secret and illegal congratulations' – official announcement would follow later. Then on Thurs. morning Dr Irmscher, a new man to me, secretary of the Social Sciences Group or Section of the Academy.[10] [... Finally Naas at the KB Executive Committee meeting:] 'We are expecting great things of you. You must build up the new Marxist history of literature.' [...] Afterwards I took Doris, whom I had not seen for months, along to Hadwig's room on Linienstr. [...] She told us, Hansen was no longer head of ADN [news agency], but on the Central Committee. Mackie has not been promoted in his place [...]. Because of his time in France Mackie is evidently not considered absolutely reliable.

All afternoon while I was writing these lines, H. had the record player on; we already have some 50 records of every kind.

[...]

2nd March, 7 p.m. Monday. Dresden

[...] Today only lecture preparation – although for the first time in many years I read the 2nd vol. of my 18ième and was very taken with it.[11] When I revise the Rousseau, the sections to be removed or changed will be put in my Curriculum (R. as defender of Hitler!)

[In the visual arts Klemperer takes pleasure in attacks by the GDR leadership on 'cosmopolitanism and formalism'.]

[...]

6th March, Friday forenoon. Berlin, Institute – my room too cold – in No. 6 Böhme and Rita's – but alone

Stalin died yesterday, 5 March, in the evening; expected, since the announcement of the stroke the day before yesterday. – At the beginning of the Renaissance lecture, on Holger's advice, a few words: Tremendously great side by side with Alexander, Caesar, Napoleon – unlike them *only* in the service of humanity and in particular *our* liberator. There is no need to fear for the Soviet Union as state, it is a co-operative achievement and remains as cohesive as before. (What I did not say, but certainly discussed with Holger etc.: danger that the USA might think it has to take advantage of the *supposed* moment of weakness. If that is so, then woe betide them! but also woe is us!)

At 3.30 in the afternoon Ruben as dean[12] gave a pretty little speech two floors above me in the stairwell of the German Studies Institute. The man of irresistible Marxist scientificity in politics and strategy, the most successful politician, who was never wrong and could never be wrong. Which is why even after his death the Marxist party *must* go on being victorious.

[...] Short meeting: we must pull together even more closely than before and bury all personal differences. Rita in tears; Rita and Holger, Rita and I shook hands. [...]

11th March, midday Wednesday. Berlin, Institute

Stalin's death has turned everything upside down. On Friday there was supposed to be a Karl Marx commemoration and academic festival. [Cancelled along with various lectures and talks Klemperer was supposed to give.] And – main question – what will now become of the Academy election? It was supposed to take place on 19 March in conjunction with the Karl Marx commemoration and unveiling of a bust. *All* Karl Marx celebrations have been postponed until May.

[...]

An obscure and unpleasant business: coffee. Constantly rising in price, now 64M for 400 gm. Franke, the KB porter tells me and H. has heard almost the exactly the same at her hairdresser's: 'Soon, when West Berlin is cordoned off, there will be nothing at all in the store ...' Which 'store'? – 'Well, the one *the Jews* keep here, the police know all about it.' – Why Jews? – 'It's *only* Jews, *mine* is a Czechoslovak. They have the connections, they live in the West and have their stores over here.' Surely there is something rotten here tolerated by higher authorities. The *Jews* get the blame, the *Party* gets the blame. Gusti W., whom we brought a pound of coffee last week, says: better without coffee, better to stay out of it. [...]

13th March, 4 p.m. Friday. Berlin, Institute
The journal for Romance Languages and Literatures has been licensed. We shall now publish it, even if Friedrich in Freiburg refuses to join in, *even* if Baldinger refuses. Editorial board Klemperer and Böhme, editor Rita. [...]

18th March, 2 p.m. Wednesday. Berlin, Institute
Spring. – Excessive rush – high spirits – extreme tiredness.
    Saturday–Sunday in Dresden. Probable completion of theory study – at last! [...]
    Tomorrow, 19 March, the *receptio academica*[13] after all, at last the official notification: elected, and confirmed by Grotewohl, installation at 3 p.m. [...]

22nd March, Sunday forenoon. Primaverissima[14] Dresden
[...]
    Then on Thurs., 19 March, the great day of the admission to the Academy. After the cancellation of the Marx celebration it proceeded very prosaically. [...] H. says, I am depressed after every longed-for success.
    [...]

5th April, midday Easter Sunday. Dresden
Hadwig has gone to mass with her parents, here since Thurs ... My customary conflicting thoughts. But H. is dearer to me with each day that passes – and E. ever more remote. My life is too sinfully long. [...]
    The plenary session [of the Academy] was for me – and for half, at least half of those present absolutely incomprehensible. First a chemist with never ending formulae, then a 'sun physicist' on the 'sun's magnetic field'(?). [...] ... they might just as well have been speaking Chinese. Afterwards questions by several chemists and physicists. [...]

11th April, Saturday evening. Dresden
[...]
    Home after 9 p.m. Topic of conversation, very shocking for days now: a few months ago the Soviet doctors' trial with the anti-Zionist slant. [...] Followed by dissolution of the VVN, panic among Jews here ... Now, immediately after Stalin's death: [...] everywhere the *Pravda* article, there is justice in the Soviet

Union.[15] A minister dismissed and imprisoned along with a perfidious official, release, rehabilitation of the emphatically entirely innocent who had been 'forced to confess by strictly forbidden interrogation methods'!![16] Should one rather be shocked or should one admire this frankness? H. said, she regarded it as a break with the terrorist past and a promise of a better future. All three Kirchners, in particular father Kirchner, believe with much bitterness, that previously there had *not* been real justice in the SU. Darkest aspect: the usual confession of guilt. How extorted??

[...]

25th April, Saturday afternoon. Dresden

The excess and variety of commitments is gradually wearing me out; I do not get around to reading or to writing, I envy Hadwig, who is truly studying, doing Russian, social science and modern literature, at the same time managing the pile of newspapers and completing the translations for my 18ième. I myself ... nothing is really completed any more.

[...]

[An Executive Committee meeting of the KB on 24 April: Klemperer speaks out against the proposed abolition of the 12-year school career. (At issue here was the qualification of pupils for university and the teaching time for Classical languages.) There are also very sharp comments by others present on the uncritical acceptance of Soviet science, and even barely concealed criticism of the continuing secret arrests.]

On Wed. in our 'Babylon' again. A moving and outstandingly acted Italian film: *Bicycle Thieves*.[17] [Klemperer briefly summarises the plot of the famous film before concluding:] Very significant (*and different from here!*): all crude black-and-white depiction of the bourgeoisie or the property-owners is avoided. The system is to blame, not an individual. [...] The police also quite human. All the more oppressive the hopelessness of the end. Name: The programme bill mentions only the director Vittorio de Sica.

[...]

26th April, Sunday after 3 p.m. Dresden

[Gusti Wieghardt has meanwhile become an editor at the Children's Books publishing house.]

To be used as characteristic. Vossler spoke contemptuously with reference to psychometrics of 'locksmiths of the soul'. Stalin or Lenin affectionately called teachers and authors 'engineers of the soul'.[18]

[...]

29th April, 1.30 p.m. Wednesday. Berlin, Institute

[Inter alia, Klemperer discusses possible changes to his French Literary History of the 19th century. At a literature conference he meets again after several years

Klaus Gysi and his wife, who had been demoted to lesser publishing jobs. Klemperer notes: 'Both lost their prominent positions, because they – although not incriminated – were émigrés in the West.']

7th May, Thursday forenoon. Berlin, Institute

[...]

Once [in Dresden] we met Weller, the gardener. He was outraged, and we hear similar things from all sides, at the brutality of the new distribution of ration cards. Owners of tiny grocery shops are having their cards taken away because they are self-employed business people. (Likewise the lawyers, because they do not have a productive profession!)[19] In the state shops no fat, no sugar to be had. Widespread, most profound discontent. But in the newspapers everything is going splendidly for us, and the 'Karl Marx Order' has been founded to mark the 1st of May and Chemnitz has been renamed 'Karl Marx Stadt' [Town].

On Tuesday afternoon a young fanatical-looking teacher from the Kreuz Grammar School called on me. A new teacher and a scholar of Greek! Passionately in favour of upper-school Latin and Greek.[20] Against which public opinion has been stirred up for weeks now. [...] The Volkskammer, the university! [i.e. have not been consulted] No instruction by any minister! [...]

Drove here yesterday at 6 in cold rainy weather. In the morning Dietz of Greifenverlag publishing house came to see me. He, too, depressed at the terrible amount of ill-feeling and the government's mistakes. [...]

[At a faculty meeting Klemperer is successful in having a proposal agreed that the dean ask the government about its intentions on school education.]

17th May, Sunday afternoon. Dresden

[On 10–11 May Klemperer attends a joint East–West PEN Club 'German Centre'[21] meeting in Berlin, the first day of which took place in West Berlin. He notes his feelings:] ordered Lindner for 3 p.m. at Friedrichstr. Station and drove off. *With immediate stabbing pains in my chest.* A journey into enemy territory, into the combat zone. It was quite uncertain whether the meeting would end without any arrests. This entirely justified feeling of fear was actually the most significant element of the day. As soon as the Brandenburg Gate has been passed, one is on hostile territory. It's been years since I was there. [...] The hotel on Kurfürstendamm [...] very elegant, meeting in a handsome room, undisturbed. 15 members, half West, half East, in addition a couple of female secretaries and clerks. A couple of people with real names, the majority unknown. For the first time I saw Brecht, a wry crafty face, looking neither like a genius nor kindhearted, but with a very calm, quite unaffected natural way of speaking without raising his voice. *He* was elected chairman instead of Becher. [...]

The meeting itself was entirely about the desired reconciliation with the Federal Republic part of Germany. [...]

A certain Lestiboudois,[22] a very well-disposed West German publicist was proposed as a new member; he had only once published a spring poem in the *Schwarze Korps* [Black Corps – weekly newspaper of the SS], after that there had been fierce hostility between him and the SS. Ehm Welk[23] said, he believed he had encountered L.'s name several times in the *Schwarze Korps*. I: 'Impossible to accept the man.' Frau Kern[24] [who had proposed L.]: 'Whether Black Corps or White Corps', we have to forget that. I: with some vehemence: 'You don't know what plague you're talking about!' Kern: 'But we've heard, after all ...' I: 'You don't know anything, if you were outside.' [Kern had been in exile in London.] Brecht: in principle he agreed with me. An admissions committee was formed. [...]

18th May, Monday morning. Dresden

[...]

[At a meeting of the Romance Languages and Literatures Advisory Board Klemperer again organises lobbying against the proposed school reform, including a memorandum to the Education Ministry, and a request for an audience with Grotewohl, GDR Prime Minister and joint chairman of the SED.]

New edition of my *Literary History of the 19th and 20th centuries*. Rita, who is supposed to provide an opinion, takes the following very sensible view. Revision of the artistically complete work would be destruction, would take years and put me at the mercy of 100 critics. Apart from 'insupportable' details, I should change nothing. Instead a) a lengthy foreword by me, b) a specialised Marxist one by herself. [...] next Friday I intend to speak to Hager (Central Committee) about the matter.

[...]

What shakes me politically is 1) that the acceptance of the Europe Treaty by the upper house of the West German parliament[25] is almost completely ignored – after there had been fiery protests for so long. 2) the removal from office (or arrest?) of Franz Dahlem.[26] (On the autobahns there's a sign *'Danger! Slippery surface!'* It should be put up in all the ministries, in the Central Committee and in all government offices.)

Horrible was the visit in Berlin by young Frau Bucur. Her husband, a now stateless Romanian,[27] [...] was dismissed by us as Romanian assistant, when Draeger, the academic came. But now his wife wept that he had disappeared 6 weeks ago, evidently arrested, and she could not find out where he was. These disappearances are ghastly – why can they not straightforwardly say: in custody?

19th May, Tuesday morning. Dresden

[...]

The agreed article on the school business for the *Berliner Zeitung* has become irrelevant, also the audience with Grotewohl: Yesterday the decree of the Council of Ministers was already in the newspaper: abolition of the 12-year school (of course put opaquely). Without consulting the university, the Volkskammer, after a brief dictated 'enlightenment' of public opinion. That is called: Democracy and raising the cultural level.

[. . .]

22nd May, 6 p.m. Friday. Berlin, Institute

[. . . Class meeting of the Academy on 21 May:] The class authorised me to interview and warn Grotewohl, also in its name . . . At this meeting I realised, that I am the only literary historian amongst linguists. How *one* word betrays a position. One of the bourgeois linguists: Zucker, God knows, which field, they are all Arabists, Egyptologists, archaeologists etc.[28] said to me during the plenum: if Latin is cut, then we shall be entirely '*de-Europeanised*'. Lord, protect me from my friends!

[. . .]

28th May, 5 p.m. Thursday. Berlin, Institute

[On 27 May Klemperer listens to a speech by Ulbricht to the Kulturbund on the role of the intelligentsia.] It sounded good, but coincided only in part with the real truth. Freedom of scholarly discussion! Elevation of learning. Everything here, of course, is oriented to industry, engineers etc. *must* be trained en masse, some 20 new polytechnics are to be established – the universities are supposed to float above all that, and themselves be expanded. [. . .]

Just before the lunch break [. . .] *I* spoke. Poche ma assai sentiti parole.[29] For foreign languages, for Latin; above all: the schools question is decisive for all future Five Year Plans, it must not be settled by any 'decree', it must be discussed by the Volkskammer. Much applause from this assembly, at least 75–90% of whom were engineers, many chest pains.

[. . .]

9th June, Tuesday forenoon. Dresden

[. . .]

We brought Gusti over to us, she is making notes from my Curriculum for her text about me in the *Neues Leben* booklet series: the winners of the National Prize. [. . .] Gusti, too, told us, what I had heard from others, that [later] at the intelligentsia meeting Zaisser had attacked me, and that there had been a stamping of feet.

[. . .]

15th June, 8 a.m. Monday. Dresden

On Wed., 10 June, the Communiqué of the Central Committee had appeared which retracted and cut back all measures of recent weeks as 'mistakes'[30]: food distribution, persecution of large farmers, recall of the refugees etc. etc. How greatly the populace as a whole was agitated by it: The unpolitical Lindner immediately told me: 'excitement everywhere in the city!', brought the *Berliner Zeitung* up to my director's room. 'They' are afraid ... The Russians, the 'High Commissar', were behind it. He then told H. – he was probably afraid to tell me as an SED member – it was rumoured, *Grotewohl had shot himself!* [...]

For days the newspapers at all the kiosks in Berlin are said to have been sold out. [...] In the Academy: Relaxation, all the money is no longer to go on armaments, prospects for my Literature Institute.

[...]

18th June, Thursday forenoon. Berlin, Institute

We drove here early yesterday quite unsuspecting. From about Grünau [outside Berlin] on: probably a works outing. Then another, further groups. Then workers in the gateways of their factories. H: it looks like a strike. I: 'impossible here'. At a crossroads two policemen, one bent over a shiny gun barrel. Lindner, a minute later: 'Did you see? He was loading his submachine gun.' We drove the usual route to the Institute past Marx Engels Platz – I did not notice any large crowds, the scene was hardly any different from usual. Then at the Institute the news. [...] We sat here quietly all day listening to the wireless reports, then later [heard] the clanking of the tanks and the sound of the warning shots. And in the evening at the Erdmanns[31] listened to the triumphant Rias. A week ago at a moment of great optimism – Korea, Italy,[32] our communiqué[33] – Böhme had said at a Party discussion: now a disruption and provocation was due ... Rita Schober spoke with dignity of the need to stay calm ... According to her there had been a building workers' demonstration on Tue. evening and work targets had been withdrawn.[34] Altogether peaceful. Only after that had Western hooligans poured in through the Brandenburg Gate, and now there had been scuffles. And today – probably 10,000 were demonstrating on Marx Engels Platz – so stay calm! Meanwhile she got a call from Robi: things were more serious after all – come home! Lindner reported: Soviet tanks had crushed two workers – the anger of the crowd. Then at midday: 'State of Emergency!' At about 4 we walked home. At lunchtime H. had eaten with Holger and Möller in the professors' refectory, afterwards bought sausage and bread here for several people, since the shops were shut. Inge Klemperer came to us. She wanted to fetch Peter from his clinic in Ziegelstr., missed him. There was no public transport or traffic, news of wrecked cars frightened people – she had to go to Friedrichshagen and is expecting a child in July. She declined to stay here or come with us. A young FDJ member, whom she knew and was going the same way, turned up; they both wanted to get out of the city – out there something could be organised ... [...] The rest of the empty and confused day – at any rate ... (interrupted, don't know what at any rate I wanted.)

19th June, Friday forenoon. Dresden

[On Wednesday morning nevertheless a discussion of Klemperer's proposed

Literature Institute. But Krauss is again a hindrance, it will not be agreed without him as co-director.]

Then sat at home doing a little proof reading. Listened to the triumphant Rias.

Yesterday morning Lindner fetched me in the car as normal. At the University *and* the Academy [...] everything has been cancelled. A long, all-too long visit by Hans Fischer who is giving up his job as department head with a feeling of bitterness and Hendrick Becker, the grey-haired, 50-year-old somewhat eccentric son of Phillip August, whom I have already met a couple of times. From him I heard for the first time, what all the world knows, the nickname '*goatee*' for Ulbricht. (I would never have called his rectangular piece of facial hair a 'goatee' ...) [...] Becker: Ulbricht had walked down the Stalin Allee discussing. The workers had calmly and soberly said: 'The goatee must go!' Only after some hours had rioting hooligans put in an appearance [...] Fischer related the attack on the Ministry and how Selbmann had been badly beaten up[35] ... At home in the evening the leading article of today's *Neues Deutschland* was broadcast.[36] It very much impressed me as a political and literary achievement, and I also give it credence – only things are inevitably somewhat glossed over. It admits the government's mistakes; but the 17th June had been started and controlled from the West as 'Day X', as finis reipublicae ... In Berlin matters had taken a more violent course than we had been aware of and believed: storm on the ministry, looting, fires, shooting[37] ... Agitation against the Russians. Pool of blood of someone run over by a tank, cross put up beside it ... Overturned, burnt-out cars ... At 3 p.m. we were still sitting in our restaurant on Unter den Linden – quite normally, but Russian vehicles and tanks were parked protectively at the Brandenburg Gate ... From 4–7.30 p.m. as normal to Dresden. Just outside the city a large quantity of Russian artillery on the road. – In Dresden telephoned Gusti, we learned that there had been disturbances here also and throughout the GDR, and that a state of siege had been declared. At that I cancelled the lecture in Görlitz set for yesterday.

Towards 11 p.m. in the evening
In the afternoon two hours with Gusti W. Present Hermann Duncker,[38] Schrammel, Party Secretary, the [...] sculptor[39] who lives with Eva Schulze-Knabe. We heard further news: very violent disturbances in Görlitz.[40] A first lieutenant in uniform with the Iron Cross, 1st Class, had been mayor for a couple of hours, the town in the hands of the Fascists, People's Police forced to the edge of town. Then Russian tanks and an end to the uproar. Serious disturbances in Magdeburg, Halle (political and other prisoners freed) etc.[41] In short: the pre-planned 'Day X', strike a pretext, cover, starting point. Failure of many, many workers, government offices etc. Duncker, who had me inform him in detail, fiercely against weakness, incompetence and zig-zag course of the government. [...] Who is to blame, who is accountable to whom?? I: in parliamentary countries the cabinet resigns after such mistakes or failures. What should happen in our case? Gusti and Duncker: that was not certain ... D: the Politburo had to answer to the Central Committee, the whole Central Committee to the Party

as a whole, represented by delegates or a congress. [...] I: and the Volkskammer? Duncker: yes, they would have to get a hearing too. (So at first he had completely forgotten about it.) Then he remembered his old profession as a teacher: [...] the Party did not speak simply enough, the masses were not yet trained. Those are generalities which are no good to anyone.

H. photographed us all enthusiastically.

20th June, Saturday forenoon. Dresden

Current catchword: The 17 June 1953 was intended as *Day X*, on which the GDR was to be *rolled up* from Berlin. The *Fascist adventure* has been frustrated. (LQI.) Nauseous the way the Party plays the victor. But only the Russian tanks were any help.

I add from yesterday the wide sentry and tank cordon around the court and *prison* at Münchener Platz. I, too, was once imprisoned there![42]

Sickening the declarations of especially firm confidence in our government. Today the finest picture of Grotewohl in *Neues Deutschland*. Not a word about Ulbricht. In the *Sonntag* [newspaper] *Aufbau* is presenting a supplement to mark Ulbricht's 60th birthday.[43] I have not yet signed my Institute's congratulatory address and have held it back.

Wireless report: the Rosenbergs were executed at midnight.

[...]

22nd June, Monday afternoon. Dresden

[...]

I do not see how I can finish the Rabelais introduction for the Greifenverlag publishing house before going to Ahrenshoop. Too much dissipation of my energies.

[...]

The political news very gloomy. On the wireless it was said today: calm in the cities, but disaffection and outside agitation in the countryside, air planes were setting down agents, including armed ones, a gang on the autobahn from Leipzig to ...? Gusti said, the books of the 2nd Party Congress, that is the programme of Socialist construction were being pulped, all similarly oriented texts were banned, in particular withdrawn from school curricula – we are now for the big farmers, for the young [Church] congregation, we are in repentant retreat. On the wireless the courting of the workers, the confession of sins continues, at the same time the declaration of ruthless severity towards all enemies, of whom many have already been arrested and many others have still to be caught. [...] For myself I can only repeat what I said in Munich after Vossler's death: *To me the Soviet tanks are like doves of peace*. I shall feel safe in my skin and position for just as long as Soviet dominion lasts here. If it ends, then that's it. Gusti says: Under no circumstances will the Russians leave here.

[...]

24th June, midday Wednesday. Berlin, Institute

Yesterday in Halle, H.'s parents, especially her mother, in very depressed mood. Her report complemented today by Hans Schneider. I shall sum up. The demonstration in Halle: 'Free elections!' The pictures of Marx and Engels were not touched – but only these pictures. One column carried a picture of Thaelmann. Fejö Schneider [an elderly professor of German] joined one of the columns! E.'s mother lamented: there was no opposition to the Party. [...] Hans Fischer: terroristic measures were being taken, with mass arrests! In Halle people were shot by the police, *not* by the Russians. 'Without Semyonov [the Soviet High Commissioner and ambassador to the GDR] we would already have civil war.' Throughout West Berlin, in West Germany and in the Western countries flags were being flown at half mast for the victims in the GDR. [...] I ask myself quite egoistically: what will become of me, of Hadwig, if...

[...]

1st July, Wednesday forenoon. Berlin, Institute

[... Class meeting of the Academy. Klemperer presents his Literature Institute plan ...] I got support from Frings. [...] An institute for literary history was necessary, my plan sensible, the institute itself agreed on for many a long day - I should give him, Frings, my plan and he himself would work on Krauss during the coming holidays.

[...] On the afternoon [of Tuesday] at the Kirchners. Depressed mood there; I had the impression they believed the Western news reports more than our own. *I* believe neither one nor the other. – In the car on the way here there were a few impetuous words between H. and myself, which we both regretted afterwards. The question: what is the role of the Volkskammer? How will it behave, if there is a vote? How will *I* behave in this case? H. 'You will want to sit in the next chamber, too!' She would prefer me not to attend the next session. For moments we were in a huff. She: I want 'humanity', I am on the side of the workers. I: Your mood inclines to the West ... Afterwards we made up again. I, too, believe: the government should go. (There are said to be executions still taking place. The worst thing: in everything one is dependent on rumours, the government is silent, no one believes the press.)

[...]

2nd July. Berlin, Institute

[...]

All kinds of details to report. First of all a thought. What jubilation there was that day at the Party Congress, when the PEOPLE'S Police marched into the hall. No longer *against* the workers – your brothers and sons, *your* protectors!! And now? They are more hated than the Russians, who maintain discipline and don't shoot to kill ... [...] As soon as someone puts on a uniform, he is separated from the people, from the workers, is in a class of his own. Here, too. In Zola's

Débâcle,[44] I think, it says: 'As soon as they put on red trousers, they are against us' (or something like it) [...].

[The Klemperers spent the fortnight from 6–21 July at Ahrenshoop on the Baltic coast.]

6th July. Ahrenshoop. Berlin addenda

[...]

At the KB Executive Committee meeting on Friday there were very sharp words, Becher made a great show of opposition. Likewise Brugsch, Franck, Deiters, Arnold Zweig. The uncertainty of the legal situation! Deputies arrested, no defence lawyers, partiality of the judges ... [...] The most important thing: What was the role of the Volkskammer? Dieckmann, in his double capacity, as President of the chamber and representative of W. Pieck, should have summoned the chamber on 17 June. Chambre introuvable![45] – The *school reform* should be discussed by the chamber. [...] All the complaints of the intelligentsia had been compiled in one declaration. Franck, Kleinschmidt, Abusch and myself were entrusted as a committee with adding supplementary material on chamber and school. [...]

On Saturday 4th July we drove out of Berlin punctually at 4 a.m. [...] In Ahrenshoop towards midday and Lindner sent home.

13th July, Monday. Ahrenshoop

[Once again Victor Klemperer does not feel entranced by the seaside. He counts the days. He says he has always found such vacations questionable:] I would like to be able to travel with H., as I travelled with E.: the Atlantic!

On 8 July I did not for a single second think of the anniversary of E.'s death; on the 11th it oppressed me, and yesterday, on her birthday I thought about her a great deal. Why analyse here, what torments me? I would like at least to get as much happiness as possible for H.

[...]

One day I spent some time in the newspaper room of the KB House. The Beria case troubles me.[46] Is he a 'traitor' and 'imperialist agent', when yesterday he was still Interior and Security Minister and the second most powerful man in the state?

19th July, midday Sunday. Dresden

[...]

Inge Klemperer announces the birth of the 3rd son in very humorous fashion. He is called Peter *David* – David is what he is to be known as. [...]

22nd July, 4 p.m. Wednesday. Berlin, Institute
[...]

Prime Minister Grotewohl let me know, the audience with him was no longer necessary, since 12-year schooling and Latin were now going to stay. Details should be discussed with Frau Zaisser. I once again called the head of G.'s office, and asked to be allowed to speak to him in any case. I would encounter resistance from Frau Zaisser [...]. Also I was in some small degree the delegate of those with an interest in the issue, and they would be reassured, if I were to have access to Grotewohl. [...]

23rd July, 8 p.m. Thursday. Dresden
[...]

The reception at the Polish embassy – exact copy of last year's, was something of a disappointment. [...] H. made a conquest in Arnold Zweig, who let her have his seat from time to time, while she was useful to him (he is $\frac{3}{4}$ blind) in fetching food. He talked uninterruptedly and always interestingly. He had finished his novel 'only today' and now wanted to write a critical survey – perhaps for his desk drawer – of the 5 years he has now spent in the GDR. He speaks very critically, very outspokenly (not in the Party, *no longer* president of the Academy),[47] very proud and at the same time very unaffected. H. has loved him for a long time. [...] He studies the Western press, regularly visits West Berlin, is surprised that we do not go to the theatre and cinema over there. He interrupted the conversation with H. and myself only once, when the correspondent of the *Daily Worker*[48] addressed him – he is published in English newspapers ... [...]

Zweig left towards 10. We left immediately afterwards.

1st August, 4 p.m. Saturday. Dresden
On Tue. aft. I drove to Gusti. With some solemnity: she was my oldest friend and comrade – what was to be done?? Fechner[49] dismissed as an enemy of the Republic, the hated Hilde Benjamin minister of justice,[50] Ulbricht triumphant, Herrnstadt and Zaisser removed from the Politburo as appeasers,[51] the workers embittered and provoked – what was to be done? Gusti: One could do nothing, the alternative was useless martyrdom, joy in the West. But the Party would split. Everything was opaque, here and in the Soviet Union (Beria!). Personally she warned me against vanity. Stay quietly in the background!
[...]

[Volkskammer 29th July:] On the first day of business Ulbricht, general secretary of the newly designated Politburo, sat in his place as stiff as an idol, was absent on the second day, but now appears in the press with a big picture and big speech to the plenum of the Central Committee, is again the big man, comme si de rien n'était. For how long??
[...]

On Thurs. the speaker of the – much despised! – FDGB [Trades Union Federation] – put on the most noble performance. With the greatest pathos he described how on Day X the workers had victoriously defended *their* republic against Fascists, agents and the misled. [...] During the interval I talked to Adam, who was present in civilian clothes. I said that I was speaking amicably with a heavy heart. He, like Gusti, I must howl with the rest. He is well aware of the embitterment of the workers, expects the Party to split, and says, such a split means the end of the GDR. What will happen, and what is going on in the SU, he does not know either.

[...]

8th August, 6 p.m. Saturday. Dresden

[Romance Studies at Halle is being run down.] I remain there as guest professor and institute director and give 4 hours of lectures as before (18ième, parallel to Berlin, I can be partly relieved of lectures and seminars by the assistant Erwin Silzer, art historians and historians can also take it as a minor subject). [...]

[A session of the Antifa Committee – which was all that remained of the VVN.] I learned all about the 'new course'[52] and the crushed 'Fascist adventure of Day X', which I have now already heard 1000 times. The whole world is loyal to the core to the SED and Ulbricht a wise and mighty man. [...]

On Friday an amusing, somewhat eerie trip to the cinema in Wölffnitz. [As Klemperer is watching the film *The Woman of My Dreams*,[53] a German musical comedy produced during the war, he realises it is a remake of a silent film he saw in the 20s with E.] ... Kitsch with happy end [...]. And yet I was just as happy as the rest of the cheering house to be delivered for 2 hours from politics, Socialist Realism and the eternal repetitions of propaganda. [...] Altogether silly and reprehensible – but brilliant and witty acting and music and – as already said – a 2 hour deliverance. [...]

15th August, 6 p.m. Saturday. Dresden

[...]

[On 14 August, Klemperer, Hadwig and Lindner went for an outing in the woods and waterways of the Spreewald south-east of Berlin.] From Lübbenau the Spreewald proper. In 1906 or 1907 Whitsun excursion here with Eva and the Sterns and probably Lissy Meyerhof. The four women dead, Lissy and Caroli Stern gassed. [...] We were in the punt for hours, we fed the countless ducks [...]. Another memory: 1897 or 98 a cycling trip to Lübben with Berthold. At the time we were only interested in the cycling itself, this brand new sport. B. was even more tired out than I was, and we saw nothing at all of the landscape. B. probably gave up cycling immediately afterwards – I cycled a great deal for years. [...] At 5 we landed at our Lübbenau starting point, we were in Dresden just after 8.

[...]

31st August, after 9 p.m. Monday. Dresden
[...]

Today visit by Frau Bauer, who has returned unchanged from her illegal flight.[54] She has her factory again, her house, too. [...]

Tomorrow begins the great pilgrimage of this week. Halle – Leipzig (Barbusse lecture, Trade Fair) – Berlin (Thurs. Academy) – Dresden – Frid. Halle again (Senate), Saturday/Sunday: Lecture Görlitz.
[...]

6th September, 5 p.m. Sunday. Dresden [...]
On Thurs. morning H. passed her intermediate examination in social science with a I, also learned that she is getting a I in Russian. I was as relieved as a grandfather, admired, also envied her; H. is an all-round talent, and she is enormously receptive and well-informed. It is my fate, that my women surpass me. [...]

13th September, 7 p.m. Sunday. Dresden
On the evening of Mon. 7 Sept. officially delegated by the Volkskammer [...] to speak to a residents' meeting at Alaunplatz on the Soviet Note [Renunciation of further reparations claims, further normalisation of relations between Soviet Union and GDR[55]]. And that on the day of the tremendous Adenauer victory: 12 million for him, 7 million for the SPD, 600,000 for the KP, and a minimum of votes for Wirth-Elfes![56] [...]
[...]

26th September, 7 a.m. Saturday morning. Dresden
[...] On Thurs. [...] from 10.30 until almost 4 KB Executive Council. At issue is a new basic statute, essentially what was in the '14 points' [in favour of greater freedom of expression for artists and intellectuals[57]], which were attacked by the Party [...]. Wendt as official speaker backed down on several matters – someone complained he was sounding a retreat not a fanfare. Franck, the psychiatrist, Schwarz, ever the charlatan rhetorician, Kleinschmidt, Deiters, Bloch spoke very vigorously. Opposition 'on the basis of the Republic'. [...]

Treadmill and extreme tiredness.
[...]

4th October, 7.30 a.m. Sunday. Dresden
On Friday and Saturday – when I am too tired for anything else after the days away from home – it has become usual for us to drive to Gusti or have her fetched over here. [...] Yesterday Gusti was particularly ailing. Which of the two of us will speak at the grave of the other? She is more philosophical than I – also less bound to life. She has evidently really taken Hadwig to her heart.

Yesterday she said: 'In the car you don't notice it as much as I do on the tram etc. There has never been such absolute and general ill-feeling towards the government. *Everyone* criticises everything, it is to blame for everything. *It cannot be made good with money.*' That is our impression and our opinion entirely. The secret tyranny, the secret corruption, the oldest course under the cloak of the new. Quo vadis?[58] But again and again Gusti's conviction [...] 'under no circumstances resign from the Party! Work for cleanness, even if the dirt wins.'

5th October, about 8 p.m. Monday evening

[Klemperer is to give a 'festival lecture' at Halle University.] The problem is almost a quite formal one. To give new shape to what is worn out. In addition also: No exuberance and yet still be positive! There is a lie involved too: the 17 June did not founder on the overwhelming majority of supporters of the Republic and the calm Soviet protection, but *solely* thanks to the Soviet tanks. [...]

9th October, Friday. Dresden

Birthday – unimaginable: 72, young wife, buried wife, death, meaning of the whole thing ... don't reflect. In addition extreme tiredness, and here there is a mass of correspondence and work. [...]

[On the 6th Klemperer gives his festival lecture at Halle – anniversary of the foundation of the GDR. He complains at the lack of professors in attendance.]
  [...]

17th October, midday Saturday. Dresden

[Klemperer is told that there have been criticisms of his Halle lecture. He notes the complainants' hostility to the intelligentsia.] This, too, reinforces me in my decision to step down, which I have talked about everywhere in recent days.
  [...On the 14th the KB fraction of the Volkskammer holds a discussion.] There were some quite interesting things here, although the topic 'More influence for deputies on government and media' hardly made progress. Zweig distracted from the subject for a long time, by speaking out for the release of the Germanist B[...] who had been given a two-year sentence and used the opportunity to inveigh against para 175[59] with heavy Freud artillery. [...] At the meeting Wendt as chairman said, we were not quite as powerless as we were represented, *my*, Professor Klemperer's, agitation had largely contributed to keeping 12-year schooling. [...] (Meanwhile my *Aufbau* article [On teaching at university and upper school] had already appeared, which according to Frau Kirchner has caused a sensation in Halle.) [...]
  Reading yesterday: began Rita's habilitation thesis – Zola's Theory.[60]

25th October, Sunday afternoon and later. Dresden

[...] The most beastly thing again and again the Krauss affair, or, rather, the corruption which underlies it. We had been invited to the Central Committee for Wed. afternoon: Rita Schober, Holger Christiansen and myself; from the other side Krauss with Naumann and Bahner; there was supposed to be a final discussion 'at the highest level', i.e. in the presence of Wandel and Hager. Instead there was only young Eckert, who simply declared, the journal was postponed, the Academy Institute buried – so that every possibility of dis-agreement between Krauss and myself was removed; the question of blame would not be investigated, and the Party would 'distance' itself from both comrades. Krauss made an impertinent speech, in which he demonstrated the impossibility of the Institute and of the journal, treated Böhme and Rita with contempt, was elevated philosopher and high priest. I declared with passionate emphasis that he was saboteur and underminer, demanded with the greatest emphasis, that he undergo medical examination. He: slander, *crime*, inves-tigation of my mental health. I had very bad heart trouble, still felt ill the next day. An investigation before the Party's Control Commission – Hermann Matern – can probably no longer be avoided. [...]

[On Tue., 20th October, Klemperer had to submit to a 'discussion' of his lecture to Halle University. This was friendly enough, but he was well aware of its warning character with respect to adhering to 'catechism formulae' inside the university as well outside.]

30th October, Friday towards 8 p.m. Dresden

One immediately after the other, two wonderfully good French films which once again really made me feel the greatness of the French and the monotonous poverty of the state of literature here. Wed. in the 'Babylon': *Sans laisser d'ad-resse*[61], here this afternoon – too tired to work: *La Putain respectueuse* by Sartre.[62] [...]

This time Halle was completely normal – albeit with a reduced number of students, because everyone was 'in action for the sugar beet harvest'.

[...]

31st October, Saturday forenoon. Dresden

[...]

Very curious, that Sartre comes over to our side now. How he joins with us, we with him. In *Sans laisser d'adresse*, a satirical scene takes place in the 'Club of the Existentialists'. The hideous chanteuse in black men's clothes steps out of an upright coffin and back into it.

[...]

5th November, Thursday midday and afternoon. Berlin, Institute

[...]

In Dresden I rummaged through the slim publications of the Seghers publishing house: the most modern Communist poetry in France. That is to be turned into a wireless speech on new French poetry due on 25 November. Thus I am not really lazy – but I feel my way and my energies are fragmented and I hope for the time – and fear it! – offered by retirement. Which, in order to force myself to do something, I am everywhere announcing for 1st September 1954.

[...]

11th November, 7 p.m. Wednesday. Berlin, Institute

Followed Hadwig's advice: Tomorrow in the Academy I am speaking on Delille and not on literary theory. The way the [latter] study was written in March, I would not have been able to deliver it.[63] Also there too many places where I could put my foot in it; but for the lecture I had first of all to condense the big Delille work. Absurdly I have stage fright. Although the majority of those present will certainly know nothing about it.

[...]

28th November, 8 a.m. Saturday. Berlin, Institute

[...]

The meeting of the Academy: It had been repeatedly emphasised, one should speak for 30 minutes. I took advantage of that, said I was presenting a sketch of my detailed study and spoke without notes in my usual way for 30 minutes: What impression?? Applause is not allowed [...]

29th November, 1 p.m. Sunday. Dresden

[Wed., session of the Academy, strengthening the role of the SED. Klemperer hears that after he left, Hager had issued a reprimand] because disputes between comrades were being carried out in front of a bourgeois public. He named 3 pairs: Klemperer–Krauss, Meusel–Stern and Kuczynski–?

[...]

13th December, Sunday forenoon. Dresden

The confusion, the stream of visitors, the meetings: all this chaos was more exhausting than ever. [...] After the last visit of Frau Görner – [of the Verlag der Wissenschaften publishing house] – it is now certain, that I will be allowed 63 printed sheets for the 19ième [...]. Delivery date: vol. I: 1 Sept. 54, vol. II: February 55, 18ième vol. II: 1956; if possible between these the *Modern French Poetry*. [...] Dr Künzel, SED, of the Akademieverlag, wants to publish a volume of collected essays (before and after 1945), I have promised compilation by February 54. The essay volume for Greifenverlag (Balzac, Maupassant, Barbusse) is still pending – how shall I manage it all – to say nothing of the Curriculum! – if I do not get a free hand? [. . .]

[. . .]

19th December, Saturday afternoon. Dresden

The longed-for first day of the holidays.

[Meanwhile, however, Klemperer (under pressure from the Ministry, the Central Committee, Rita Schober) has been persuaded not to retire, though the Berlin directorship goes to Rita Schober. He retains one day's lecturing and classes each in Berlin and Halle – which should leave him four to five days a week in Dresden to devote to his own work.]

[. . .]

In the evening [16th December] after a very long interval at the Kahanes' again. [. . .] Really like in the old days, great warmth.

[. . .]

24th December, Thursday forenoon. Dresden

[. . .]

Holidays began a week ago. The Kirchner parents here since Sunday – with their agreeable and disagreeable sides. And today the usual painful Christmas mood. The festival has to be borne with composure.

[. . .]

Résumé 1953

This past year 1953: I have entered the Academy and thus far have had little joy of it. I am conceited because of the title and yet I know, that this Academy is no longer respected, and that I got into it because of my Party membership and am out of place in the Language Class.

I have published nothing except the Rabelais study and the Humanism booklet. I have been completely taken up with all my chasing around. The intention to retire did not come off completely, it has been botched: I shall be rid of the authority and keep the work and the rush.

With Hadwig I am very happy anew each day, and every day in connection with her the same gloomy thoughts, the same feeling of double infidelity.

There's a pretty line: 'with you, Lord, is clarity and bright is your house!'[64] If one could believe in it. But I cannot get rid of even the smallest fraction of my scepticism. It is absolute – sometimes even in politics. Ultimately Anatole France is my man after all.

Yesterday evening Gusti and Ludwig Renn here. A formal supper, Renn talked a great deal, the Kirchner parents were good listeners, and so we comfortably passed the time until 1.

Now another one or two days – then back to the old routine, and all reflection is submerged thank God in work and activity.

Finally as memento there came a telegram, saying Böhme has suffered a heart attack and is likely to die.

Work: Stendhal and Rolland diary.[65]

1st January 1954, Friday forenoon. Dresden

1954

9th January, Saturday evening. Dresden
[...]

H.'s parents departed last Sunday, very quiet here since then. Böhme died the same Sunday; it affected me very *egoistically*; he was five years younger than I, and I, too, have a bad heart.

[...]

9th February, Tuesday. Dresden, in bed, music room
On Friday, 15 January, I was already feeling very wretched during the day, very severe pains. In the evening drove to Weisser Hirsch nevertheless. There a Dr Ernst was called by telephone; he gave me a couple of strophantin-valerian drops, said, there was nothing worrying about my heart, I should come to him on Mond. for an ECG examination. Then for about an hour I spoke with some effort on Rolland to about 80 listeners. Again, this time very much supported, the dreadful steps from the house to the road.[1] [...] Bad night, in the morning awful vomiting; during the day, and on Sunday as well, I crouched over my desk, incapable of reading even a single line. At last on Sunday evening Grube came, percussed me. To bed, tomorrow he would call in a specialist. I have now been lying here without moving since Mond. 18 Jan. and am to go on lying here until 20 Feb. After that another ECG and decision about what follows. Probably complete, or as good as complete retirement. It *was* pneumonia, which was swiftly tackled with penicillin; there is a cardiac insufficiency. In short: I'm finished. Taking great care I can perhaps last another couple of years. Poor Hadwig; as nurse she is even more devoted than usual [...] – was born without original sin. [...]

During these weeks I read, *without* notes: Feuchtwanger's outstanding *Foxes in the Vineyard*, Erckmann-Chatrian's charming *Madame Thérèse* (in German), I began Feuchtwanger's *Privilege of Fools* (on Rousseau)[2] and a Rolland-related study[3] [...] (To be reviewed for the DLZ)[4] ... [...]

I write a paragraph at a time. In between the *Privilege of Fools*, dozing, conversation with Frau Duckhorn [the housekeeper], who is good-natured and keen to be educated.

The doctors

[...] Grube comes as friend and family doctor almost every day, stays for hours. [...]

After the examination the long conversations. Basically always the same topic and the same views: The Party's mistakes. Grube and I comrades. G. was already a Socialist student in 1918 in Munich. He is now senior medical administrator of the district. He complains: we attempt too much, do things for the sake of appearances [...] Schmeiser, early 40s, plump, calm, German from Bohemia, head physician of the Neustadt Hospital,[5] very socially oriented, strong moral sense, he left the SED shortly before the beginning of the new course. At the time he offered to resign from his post – he remained in it, he's needed. He is quite evidently pro-GDR, emphatically rejects West Germany, which he knows well and where he has relatives, but complains about the constant mistakes and injustices of the Party: discrimination against willing children from middle-class homes, slavish and stupid echoing and idolisation of the Russians (Pavlov cult).

[...]

I completely repress all thoughts as to the length and content of an absolutely uncertain future, and see what can be got out of a day in bed. A minimum.

17th February, Wednesday afternoon. Dresden, in bed

I have now been on my back for a month and am to lie here for another month, and my active life is probably over.

[...]

I sometimes dictate shorter correspondence to H. But she is [already] far too distracted from her proper work. In Kantorowicz's research assistants' seminar she is to give a paper on [Heinrich Mann's] *Henri IV*. Nursing and the endless doctors' visits take up all her time.

[...]

2nd March, 2.30 p.m.

[...]

The doctors say: On 10 March allowed up for the first time, in May perhaps the garden, from Sept. two-hour lecture once a week in Berlin. I.e. retirement. Possibly in August after France. [...] Poor H.

Yesterday Schmeiser complained with particular bitterness: One of his senior physicians was 'taken away' in the middle of the night. A nurse just now returned after several years' imprisonment. With bone tuberculosis. What she related, and she is absolutely reliable, is not so very different from what one heard about the Nazi camps. In Bautzen, Sachsenhausen, Waldheim over-crowding, poorest food and hygiene, confessions, signatures extorted by beatings etc. etc. People condemned to death by the Russians in the 40s for spying, sentences commuted to 25 years. The half-guilty and the innocent. Just now a completely arbitrary partial amnesty ... And the GDR proceeds hardly any differently from how the Russians proceeded and proceed. If only a quarter of all of that is true, how do they expect to face the next 17 June? And where does my conscience stand in relation to the Party??

[...]

Also on the topic of education a conversation with Frau Duckhorn today. It angers her, that a young person is not allowed to go on to upper school because her father is a dental technician, 'bourgeois', therefore, so that a young girl – tears! – is forced to become a metalwork apprentice.

[...]

8th March, Monday forenoon. In bed

On the 10th I am to get up 'for 5 minutes'. In Schmeiser's certificate for Berlin it says: he advises me to retire from university and to give up the Volkskammer seat.

Finished Feuchtwanger's *Goya*.[6] Final chapter [...] weaker. But the thing as a whole is once again magnificent. F. is not merely 'humanist' in the GDR sense but also entirely *humane*. He knows all about politics and the social, but also about the *absolutely human*. And he knows everything that goes to make up a *single* human being. He is a sceptic like Anatole France and like him believes in progress. I was probably under something of a delusion as far as my adherence to the Party was concerned. In the end I am liberal. And also the Barbusse quotation, every scholar is a Marxist, even if he himself does not yet know it, is only partly right; in the very last analysis people like us are liberal.

[...]

16th March, Tuesday forenoon. Desk

Since the 10th a couple of minutes morning and afternoon at my desk. But nothing comes of it. The sitting down does not tire me out, but the few steps there and back.

[...]

I am preoccupied with the thought of a foreword to the 3rd part of my Curriculum. My changed inner situation. The leap into Communism. The recent re-emergence of liberal ideas. The inner insecurity. [...] But I have depressions every day, which tell me that I shall never get down to any production again. Just lie here, read novels, let myself be nursed by H. and love her very much with a very bad conscience.

[...]

10th April, 7 p.m. Saturday. Desk in my dressing gown
Everything unchanged. Morning and afternoon out of bed for an hour. Great tiredness, unsteady on my feet, incapable of work. Nothing but correspondence. [...]

Today the Verlag der Wissenschaften announces the distribution of my *Century of Voltaire* [...].

[...]

24th April, 9 p.m. Saturday. Desk
Rita here yesterday until the evening train, today likewise Holger Christiansen; then when I wanted to note a couple of diary lines, Grube came. [...] Business matters with Rita: Proposal to the University Secretariat: 3× a month Berlin, 1× a month Halle. In Berlin [...] I shall read two *full* hours each week, with an interval between them. In addition a research assistants' seminar every two weeks and chair of the Advisory Committee. In Halle 2 hours every four weeks, overall charge of the Institute, Senate. – A full professorship for Rita has been proposed.

25th April, Sunday forenoon. Desk
[...] Holger's Berlin mouth. To see me and call out: 'Like in Molière!' was something. And, truly, in the dressing gown I look like the malade imaginaire or the guardian in *Ecole des femmes*.

[...]

29th April, 2 p.m. Saturday. Desk
[...]

My reading is all over the place. Good or bad? I should be taking notes, I should be sticking at it. Then again: there is so much to catch up, so much to repeat. [...] But: *what* am I reading *for*? *Only* for my own pleasure, *only* to enjoy my retirement? In that case it does not give me any pleasure. But to concentrate on writing, means rummaging in the past, finally giving up the present. [...] And there is so very much to read. [...]

When I was confined to bed, it was the depth of winter. Now spring is in bloom outside. And I am not allowed out of my room, I'm sitting around in nightshirt and dressing gown, the doctor still does not let me go up any stairs. [...] Then I take heart again nevertheless. H. always constant in her great love and consolatoriness.

1st May, 7 p.m. Saturday. Desk
In trousers and pullover for the first time since 17th January, admittedly over the nightshirt. But it is an improvement on the baggy dressing gown nevertheless. But the bed still remains down here, and sitting at the desk takes up

only a few hours in the morning and a few towards evening and in the evening, and stairs and garden are forbidden. [...]

2nd May, 8.30 a.m. Sunday morning. Desk

[... There is an unpleasant altercation between Hadwig Klemperer and Gusti Wieghardt. Gusti accuses H. of being too negative about the 'Republic'; H. responds that G. is too negative about the German people. Only a matter of minutes and the two make up, but the incident leaves Victor Klemperer very depressed.]

13th May, 5.30 p.m. Thursday

[...]

Yesterday *The Century of Voltaire* arrived. Mixed feelings. Of course proud of it. But more 'between stools than ever'. Over here it will be said: too bourgeois! And in the West: research since 1930 has not been taken into account. In addition disgraceful misprints. [...]

16th May, Sunday afternoon

H. came back from Jena yesterday evening. I went in the car to the station, my first outing since 15 January. But still the terrible weakness and inability to work. – I now venture into Gusti's garden with H.

[...]

Today is 16 May – 48 years ago the registry office with E. What is fidelity? Am I flirting with my bigamous feelings? In truth I am attached with everything that is alive in me to Hadwig. And I face death uncomprehendingly and more unwillingly than ever.

[...]

25th May, 9.30 Tuesday

Hadwig to Halle; on the 31st she will go to Berlin for the Russian examination – and that should be the last time she goes alone. I am making good progress now; I am still unsteady when I walk and get a little tired, but on the whole I am halfway cured. [...]

On the evening of Thurs., the 20th, Peter and Inge Klemperer came here to round off their holiday trip to the Harz and stayed until yesterday evening. [...] Both very pleasant people, strong bond between them and Hadwig. Their confidence in the Party is badly shaken, especially Inge's. A friend of theirs, Heilmann, senior official in the FDJ, is in prison for 5 years 'for Fascist intrigues'; his wife, now released after 2 years, relates vile things about Gestapo methods. Peter closer to the viewpoint: revolutionary transition stage, self-defence etc., Inge: humanity! What is actually happening, neither knows [...], Peter thinks, personal power struggles and vengefulness could be involved [...]. At any rate the fact is: here, too, shattered faith. Admittedly both are constantly exposed to Western influence. My sister-in-law Anny! And his brother Georg in Switzerland! [...]

5th June, Saturday forenoon

On Sunday 30 May, *Mother Courage*[7] in the Large House, right at the front of the stalls, 3rd row from the stage [...]. Bad acoustics (beside Gusti, who had got the tickets) – but able to follow the outstanding acting very closely. [...] The evening made a big impression on me. The next day I read *Courage* (for the first time!), together we looked through the Theatre Book of the Brecht company.[8] [...]

Thanks to this performance my old dilemma became especially agonising. I know nothing of Brecht, of his theory of epic drama, I know next to nothing of the whole of modern literature from West and E, I could spend the whole day reading, I pick up 5 things at a time – and I have to put it all aside, if I want to bring *my* things to a conclusion. [...] In the three months of illness I have *only* read, without making notes, without producing. How little I have read, how little of what I have read has definitely remained mine!
[...]

14th June, Monday

Inability to produce and the feeling of being half-buried while three-quarters dead. In private life as in the vita publica.
[...]

Reading: a Rowohlt volume of Sartre plays. I have a lot of time for him after all. A deliverance after the childish simple-mindedness of our Soviet to the nth degree way of writing. [...]

Sterile snail's pace work on the Stendhal essay.[9] – Resignation with respect to my 19ième. I cannot rewrite it. [...]

20th June, after 7 p.m. Sunday. (Very oppressive heat)

On Tue. the 15th in Halle for the first time: examined a little, with H.'s parents a little – all as before the collapse. On Frid. the 18th in Berlin. In the Institute vanitas Ritae, party the next day for the end of the students' year with flowers, general invitation, meal in the professors' refectory – self-assured assumption of power.[10] [... KB Executive Committee:] More interesting the subsequent speech by Bloch, brilliant, not quite as hegeled in style as usual, about the 'category of the practical' to which belong not only technology, natural sciences and political economy, but also what used to be included under intellectual history. [...]

Thrilling reading, demonstrating the absurdity of our blinkered aesthetics: Hemingway *The Old Man and the Sea* [...]. What was the name of the novel and what happened in detail in it, which gripped me so powerfully during the Nazi years? The collapse of the Italian front, Italian Fascism, the fate of a woman, who dies in childbirth ... Alive in me now is only the general impression of human tragedy and outstanding form and exciting plot. Now a very simple story with extraordinary technical realism. [...] Here despite all tragedy: *Optimism*. Why is such great writing not allowed to appear here,[11] why is it not 'Socialist Realism'? The blurb epithet 'Homeric' is entirely justified.

4th July, Sunday afternoon. Dresden

[The GDR State Secretariat has approved a 3-month French vacation (1 Aug.– 31 Oct.) for the Klemperers. Doris Kahane is expecting her third child on 10 July. Dietz, of the Greifen publishing house, asks if he can brush out the party badge in a photograph of Klemperer to be used in the West for publicity purposes. Klemperer agrees.]

11th July, Sunday. Dresden

[...]

The work on the 19ième is agonising. The Napoleon chapter is beyond saving, yet indispensable. The whole effort is so sterile.

8 July – the anniversary of E.'s death. The gardener had to remind me of it ... It was raining so hard, that we were unable to go up. Did not go until yesterday, the 10th [...]. Nowhere do I have fewer thoughts of E. than up there. It is always a matter of the done thing and knowing it, one counts to 100, makes cynical remarks, looks at other graves, praises the view – everything up there is false. But the grave is kept very nicely and there is plenty of room for *my* tin can. – Always, not only up there – the loathsome thoughts: what is fidelity, what remains, were E. and I really still so deeply attached during the last years, how do I stand now between E. and H.?

[...]

19th July, Monday forenoon. Dresden

[...]

From time to time H. gives me something by Heinrich Mann which has a connection with France. I am always irritated by his obscure snobbish style, which curiously enough H. has no difficulties with and which she likes. She loves her author and I anxiously keep my distance from her dissertation. [...]

H. thinks I am working hard. But nothing comes of it any more.

[...]

6th August, Friday forenoon. Dresden

We were in Berlin from Frid. 30 July–Mon. 2 August.

[... Problems with planned French stay: There must be a French invitation and after 'attestation' it takes 2–3 months until the French authorities issue permission to enter France.] Ergo, the journey has been postponed indefinitely and I have to start my lectures in September. Very dejected for a couple of days, now already – thanks to H. – recovered my equilibrium. [...]

On Sunday aft. [...] at Rita's for coffee. [...] Horst Heintze with his [...] Edith also there. I read out my 19ième foreword [...]. It met with such great approval, that Rita now wants to dispense with her foreword and justify this to publisher and censor. [...]

[Klemperer and Hadwig then visit Doris Kahane in hospital, where she has given birth to a daughter a week before.] Mother and child in the best of health, and the father (present, turning very grey) happy. I always feel so sorry for H., when I see her joy in children.

[...]

10th August, Tuesday evening. Dresden
[...]

LQI: Philology, intellectual history, Idealism, cosmopolitanism: words that are disapproved of.

16th August, Monday afternoon. Dresden
[From the Academy comes word that it cannot do anything with respect to the France invitation, because of Klemperer's 'positive attitude to the GDR'.]

[...]

5th September, Sunday evening. Dresden
On Thurs. 2nd Sept. Executive Committee in Berlin. Candidatures for the Volkskammer. It could not be more undemocratic. The Presidium has discussed things with the National Front; *we* propose. This time we have only 15 instead of 20 representatives (instead more in the district councils). [...] It is presumably not much different in the other organisations. And then the electors elect the 'united list' [...]

6th September, Monday morning. Dresden
[...]

Yesterday I at last had the first part of the 19ième ready for the printers. Since Friday I had been agonising over the Mérimée[12] section. The book will turn out like an old pair of trousers with new patches sewn onto it. [...]

17th September, Friday morning. Dresden
Three days Berlin Tue. 14th–Thurs. 16th

Very exhausting, before the first lecture in 9 months I almost had a little stage fright, nor was it so easy for me physically to get through the *full* hour. Admittedly this time there was a lot of to-ing and fro-ing – but to make up for that there are two full hours the next time. The third years, I was warmly welcomed, and even more so afterwards; I stated my principles, I talked about *Liaisons dangereuses*[13] ... But I felt dethroned nevertheless. The Institute has been re-arranged a little, my director's room is now a seminar room – I share Room 6 with Rita, it used to belong to her and Böhme [...]

At 2 a.m. yesterday [16 Sept.] there was then also a meeting of the Party members of the Academy on the new elections for Vice-president and for Secretaries. Frings advances to Vice in place of Stroux[14] [deceased], the former's successor in our class will be Steinitz, whose deputy Grapow was Vice-President under Hitler![15] [...]

[...]

2nd October, Saturday forenoon (and later). Dresden

[...]
On Thurs. the 30th and Frid. 1 Oct: in Berlin, Class meeting of the Academy. Krauss present in glowing health. From the minutes that were read out, I discovered to what extent he has outplayed me. [Krauss had succeeded in establishing a 'Working Group on the History of the French and German Enlightenment' in the Historical-Philosophical Class of the Academy.] It hit me hard. Since it is work on behalf of the Party and since it will be attached to the Historical-Philosophical Class, there is nothing I can do about it.[16] [...].

[...]

11th October, Monday forenoon. Dresden

My birthday passed quite pleasantly without any reflection. Now it is slowly coming at me out of the torpidity – but within a couple of days I have got used to my new year. Nevertheless: the thought of death is really always with me ...
[...]
The journey to France. What an effort it cost me yesterday to write three short letters to thank the chers collègues, who are doing their best on behalf of my trip! On Thurs. I am to go with Cornu[17] to the Maison de France [in West Berlin].
[...]
[...]

16th October, Saturday forenoon. Dresden

Oppressive the unending quantity of cars [in West Berlin]. The mass of people, the full shop windows, the cinemas – but everything in shacks, stage-set buildings, and behind and above there are ruins – but lit up in the evening. All that is probably only true of the Kurfürstendamm and the beginning of the side streets. In the Maison de France the sacred rooms of the consulate at the top. They're friendlier on the first floor. [...] The rest of the palaver – the application now goes to the Foreign Ministry in Paris – is supposed to take only a few weeks. H. is optimistic – and flexible; I have little hope and in fact more fear than longing. Cornu went off in his car towards 5. We went back to Zoo Station on foot. I felt as if I were in an enemy country. H., who has of course been living in Berlin as a research assistant, makes her way through West Berlin as a matter of course and maintains, that 'all Berliners' do so. It is also possible, that as a 'functionary' I feel particularly inhibited.

[. . .]

20th October, Wednesday forenoon. Dresden

Grube here yesterday evening. Utterly incensed at the election.[18] The mistake of open voting. The evident, yet unnecessary falsification of the results. Ballots had been declared valid which were not so, the 5% of *No* votes had been turned into 0.7%. What for? 5% opposed would not have been a bad result and a credible one. But now no one believed in any statement. Tyranny of a tiny minority in the Party – fear and absolute impotence of the great mass. He, Grube, had expressed the same opinion to a new Party secretary, had met with the most obstinate hostility. He seemed virtually to fear for himself. [. . .] He sees no way out. – In *Neues Deutschland* a very well-documented article by Girnus: 'Is Hitler dead?', about the terrible Nazism and anti-Semitism redivivus in West Germany. *We* are the lesser evil – but if the mistakes of the SED continue to increase – what then??

24th October, Sunday evening. Dresden

[. . .]

In Berlin we saw *Rome, 11 a.m.*[19] in the Babylon. One of the very best and most shattering of recent films. Thank God: 'only' *critical* and not hope-celebrating socialist realism! A flight of stairs collapses, because 200 women are crowded onto it queuing for *one* advertised shorthand typist position. Individual fates, one death – who is to blame? Unspoken answer: The social situation. – Splendid acting. Great art.

[. . .]

3rd November, Wednesday forenoon. Dresden

On Monday aft. the Dietzes [. . .] were here for coffee. [. . .] Dietz [Greifenverlag] is urging me to give him the first volume of my Curriculum. Hadwig, enthusiastic about the novel 'Josephus',[20] wrote a long letter to Feuchtwanger – a touch too warm to my mistrustful mind. But she is 45 years younger than I and has much more trust in people.

To Gusti the same evening. There, too, at great length: the Curriculum; set everything else aside, give up your offices, ambition and money earning – concentrate on what is most important, the Curriculum!

[. . .]

11th–12th November, Thursday and Friday morning. Berlin, Institute, inter proelia[21]

[...]

In Dresden, Konrad, my old friend from the Hitler years, had telephoned, there were piles of books stored in the Jewish Community – did I want to look through them and pick out anything I could use. We drove there together on Tuesday morning. Bautzenerstr. A big apartment in an old building, very high winding stone stairs, 2nd floor. The middle room converted for prayers – but now there is a new synagogue or synagogue chapel somewhere. Large office rooms. Konrad present (my age) and a certain Levinsohn, diligent little man, 62, looking older, furrier, now pensioner and synagogue employee. Ante Hitler Dresden alone had *5000* Jews, now by itself it has 45 and as district community (inclusive of Görlitz, Freiberg etc.): 90. Non-capitalist Jewry. (Levinsohn was a *journeyman* furrier, a tradesman. He said, the trades here were doing quite well now in terms of tax and otherwise. Pieck's picture on the wall ... We talked about the flight of Jews (the panic – Beria – the Jewish doctors in the SU). Levinsohn (the ordinary tradesman): 'Well, we are just the *seismographs*.' – In a storeroom huge, somewhat damp stacks of books, everything mixed up, most of it Hebraica, but frequently German, French, even a couple of English books in between. [...]

[...]

30th November, midday Tuesday. Dresden

[...]

Yesterday (with Lindner and Frau Duckhorn) to the French film *Maitre après dieu*.[22] Both acting and content remarkable and moving. The captain – maître après dieu – discovers the Bible and his conscience and scuttles his ship, to prevent the 150 Jewish refugees being returned to the Nazis. Humour repeatedly breaking through the tragedy. [...] Names to note: Pierre Brasseur: captain; Jean Mercure: rabbi.

[...]

4th December, Saturday forenoon

Yesterday in Berlin: France visa refusé.

Negotiation with Akademieverlag publishing house. Essay collection *Vor 33 – nach 45* [Before 33 – after 45] *will* appear. [...]

Romance Languages and Literatures Advisory Board. Basically a farce. [Decisions made by the ministry without any consultation.]

5th December, Sunday forenoon

[...]

Gusti related via Lea Grundig, who had been to the FIR [...] meeting in Vienna, that the numerous French in attendance there had cut the GDR in an unpleasant way and regarded *only* the Adenauer state as Germany. Gusti links that with my refusé and considers it a compliment to me. But I do not believe that I am in any way personally known over there. E. R. Curtius has been made Dr h.c. of the Sorbonne and my services remain unknown.

22nd December, Wednesday forenoon. Dresden

Mother-in-law is staying in bed for a day, apothecarised, H. has a two-storey life. In the evening the family plays skat upstairs; I myself encourage it – but sit down here feeling very lonely, cannot hide it from H., when she appears again at 11 – almost tears, and I reproach myself. That or something like it sometimes ... H. said: 'my mother is suffocating as a teacher and her pupils are suffocating, too.' Therefore one must understand her mother's complaints and her pessimism. Certainly ... but ... H. always stands between her parents and me. And always: she cannot do right by anyone ... And always feeling of guilt on my part and a feeling of loneliness. And yet I love her more with each day and know that she returns it.

The agony over Bergson,[23] over the 2nd vol. of my 19ième has begun. [...]

25th December, Saturday forenoon. Dresden

The dreaded Christmas Eve passed peacefully with presents and alcohol in moderation [...]. Beforehand a few rocks [to negotiate ...]. Mother-in-law precipitated a conversation about religion; she said, the crucial point is, that one must *want* to believe. I call that (although I did not say so) self-mutilation. I also found very awkward the parents-in-laws' determined questioning as to what festivals were celebrated in my parental home. Perhaps I shall again address the problem of the *Jew* in my Curriculum. Later, as already said, things proceeded peacefully. (And boringly and depressingly.)

26th December, Sunday forenoon

[...]

We buy so many books, I leaf through so many things – and do not find time for anything. Lying on the Christmas table for H.'s parents are Thomas Mann's *Joseph*, Feuchtwanger's 'Josephus' – How I would like to!! [...]

31st December, Friday afternoon, New Year's Eve 1954. Dresden

[...] The godly holidays [...].

It was not a good year for me. I fell ill on 15 January, I was on my back for almost 4 months, since then I have been basically an invalid. I have returned to my posts in appearance only. Rita Schober rules in Berlin, I am powerless in the Academy, am without influence in the KB, despite my position on the Education Commission. Politically I am marginalised. The West repels me – but what the SED is doing is hardly any less repellent to me.

Probably it would have been better for me if I had kicked the bucket on the 15th. [...]

I have no longer worked productively all this year. The revision of the 19ième is a dreary occupation and will not bring me any success. More than ever 'between stools' and in every, really every respect. Afraid of death and afraid of life. Never at ease in my mind even for an hour. And always tired.

H. has driven up to the Weisse Hirsch with her parents. They are going to walk around a little, then sit down at Wachendorf's, which is now a state-owned café. I know that, caught between her parents and me, H. feels just as heavy at heart as I do. Of course I was asked to come along. Symbolic, that the car only has room for 3.

So: *Vallès.*[24]

1955

4th January, Tuesday forenoon. Dresden
[...]
I feel very depressed that I am no longer at all able to get around to reading the modern Germans. H. is at home with both Manns [...], also I have still not read anything of H.'s dissertation in the making.

Sterile and cut off from life.

6th January, Thursday forenoon
[...] To bed at 2 in the morning (now usual for us – *I* then sleep until 9, H. until 12 – in the evening alcohol, music, since the departure of the parents-in-law a soothing browse) in bed, therefore, H. informed me about atoms and the periodic table, which hangs in every classroom. Why should not this most minute thing that moves, that is movement and matter in one, why should it not be called *God*? But to know of *this* God, and to know the history of the religions (*plural*) and to have studied and be completely enlightened and tolerant and for all that and despite all that to be loyal to orthodox Roman Catholic dogma: that is absolutely, with the best will in the world incomprehensible to me. But H. has the sharpest and most practical mind and her knowledge is superior to mine. I do not understand that, *that*. But I love her infinite goodness, her sense of justice, which is impossible to deceive, her impassioned Socialism (which the SED is betraying, almost she believes, at least of the leadership, *consciously* betraying), I love her love of me, I love her youth – I even love her – *only hers* – Catholicism.

[...]

10th January, Monday forenoon. Dresden
[...]

A grammar-school teacher, Dannewolf, writes to me from Tübingen in West Germany, a copy of my 18th Century had fallen into his hands by chance – in the name of many colleagues he requested a re-publication of my 19th Century. He had heard me speak in 1930 at the Modern Philology Congress in Berlin, I must be rather old by now etc. He writes very warmly – I shall write a nice reply and send him a couple of offprints. It warms my heart all the more, since not a bloody soul here takes any notice of my 18th century, as I grow ever more isolated.

The *youth initiation*.[1] H. says: a provocation of the churches, emphatic atheism [...]. The newspapers: Tolerance of every declaration of belief! Intolerant attack by the Church on our declaration of belief! I find the matter unpleasant and tasteless; it seems mediaeval to me. And coming from the Marxist side: unworthy. It must not get itself up like a religion, not imitate ecclesiastical customs. Science and the beyond have nothing in common. Indeed, science says: I do not know. Religion says: I know and takes fairy tales seriously.

[...]

17th January, Monday evening. Dresden
[...]

Today, in English, from the Nobel Committee of the Swedish Academy – a printed circular, but addressed to me personally, the invitation to propose a candidate for the 1955 Literature Prize. That is very flattering, although it must presumably go to all members of the PEN Club, and although I know that my membership of the PEN is of no significance. I will nominate Feuchtwanger. In a letter of thanks to Dietz, he included a couple of friendly words on my Rabelais essay[2] ... [...]

[...]

12th–13th February, 6 p.m. Saturday and forenoon Sunday (Anniversary of father's death, 12th February 1912). Dresden
[...]

Berlin: a) Lecture. My actual course, Thurs. 12–2 again to a good 100 people. Mérimèe and Sainte-Beuve. My old song: take account of the West *as well*. Frid. 3–5: to the 4th years, about 20 people, in the Institute the first of 3 agreed lectures on the 20th century. [...] b) Friday from 10.30 a.m. to past 2 the Education Committee on Latin teaching. [...] All agreed: *More Latin*, the present situation a nonsense. [...] The Ministry of Popular Education gave an assurance: there was no question of *abolition* of Latin teaching.

[...]

25th February, midday Friday. Dresden

Yesterday in Berlin alone, back at 10 p.m. In the Institute I worked on the 19th Century, then Academy in the afternoon. Very disillusioning, no longer even annoying. We lower everything to the Iron Cross, Second Class, first the National Prize, now the Academy. 60 have become 120, yesterday another 30 were added. One puts crosses beside names without having the least clue. What do I know about mathematics and engineering, what do the medical men know of philology etc. etc.? [...]

[...]

15th March, Monday evening. Dresden

[...] The really depressing thing is my diminished capacity for work. [...] Sometimes – often – I feel so much at the end of my tether. My tiredness, my disappearing memory for names.

[...]

Constant deep political disappointment. Our cultural and other policies are *so* stupid and mendacious, they simply represent no more than the 'lesser evil'. And where is certainty? [...]

We put down our names for a holiday in Varna, Bulgaria, organised by the Academy. I would like to still give H. something ... Not a word about France.

21st March, Monday morning. Dresden

[...]

Thurs. and Frid. in Berlin. Rita ill. My lectures successful; to the 4th years essentially on Proust with and against Curtius. Really arduous preparation. In the same place I shall give a third and last lecture on Neoromantic poetry. [...] My essential point here and in the public lecture to which 100–125 people are still coming: get to know the bourgeois, the Catholic, the *other* France! And again and again barely veiled criticism of the conduct of our teaching and cultural affairs.

[...] On Friday second session on Latin. It turned out that basically my demand is being acceded to: Latin is to be taught for 4 years, not 2. Admittedly at the expense of French. I said: Latin is more important. [...]

Meanwhile the copy of the 3rd volume of the 19ième arrived. Now has to be proofread yet again. [The Klemperers admire the comic talents of Gérard Philippe[3] and his company in *Ruy Blas*.[4]]

28th March, Monday evening. Dresden

[...] At the university from 12–2 my lecture to students of Romance languages and Germanists, from 3–5 p.m. a third and final lecture to the 4th years: From Baudelaire to the most recent poetry. I said plainly: this to some extent was my testament: do not forget bourgeois France, which is yesterday and *half of today!*

[...]

30th March, 9 a.m. Thursday. Berlin, Institute

[Annual meeting of the Academy. Klemperer meets the distinguished French philologist Marcel Cohen,[5] who is a corresponding member of the Academy.] My dominating feeling: I hope I have not cut too triste a figure either linguistically or substantially.

[...]

From the store to the Kahanes. We had been promising to come for a long time, were honoured with a festive dinner, soup, wines (plural!), cognac, coffee; soon Peter and Inge also turned up. It was nice. – Kahane has just left the news agency, is about to start as an editor at the *Tägliche Rundschau*. [...] Kahane believes war inevitable. But there could be peace for a while yet, because both sides were still arming. But the USA definitely wanted war. The SU had now conceded everything that the USA itself had been demanding a few years ago; now the latter was not yielding anything – it wanted and had to have war. [...]

[...]

18th April, Monday evening. Dresden

The last volume of the 19e agonisingly completed – leaving only the Barbusse chapter which has to be rewritten [...]. Aesthetically the Deux Frances thesis is difficult to sustain.[6] I have to conclude that in France form and tradition are ultimately more firmly established than here, that a new fusion of the two strands of literature will no doubt take place. A [...] consolation [...] that my *Modern Poetry* is at last supposed to come out again. If I really get a contract, I shall start work on it immediately [i.e. revising it] and emphasise how strongly the Communist literature is linked to all this decadence.

19th April, 7 a.m. Tuesday (before going to Halle). Dresden

[...]

On Friday morning Executive Committee meeting: Commemoration ceremony: 10 years since liberation by the Soviet army. Kneschke's speech – little about the Soviets, really only a review of what the Kulturbund has achieved in 10 years. I slept through a historian's [...] speech. [Further speeches praising Soviet help for artists in the early days.] (if only, with all of that, one did not think of the rapes! Which no one mentioned of course ... which does not mean I want to be an enemy of the Russians. But the old objective liberal mind, understanding everything, breaks through – 'the lesser evil'.) [...]

23rd April, Saturday forenoon. Dresden

[...]

On Friday morning I prepared my 'Humanism lecture', [...]. In earlier lectures I had enthusiastically celebrated Socialist Humanism. Humanism for *all*, smashing the form (the bond with Latin, with tradition etc.) Now: the pendulum has swung too far. Form necessary, tradition necessary. *Critique*: Intelligentsia in the Workers' and Peasants' State, insofar as not 'technical' intelligentsia, mistrustfully tolerated. At ceremonies the humanities merely used as decoration. Tradition cultivated one-sidedly, 'undialectically'. [...] Conclusion: Humanism conceptually overstretched to [mean an idea of] humanity. An aesthetics which sees only the class and not *the* person, the private and the common humanity is false. [The lecture is given in Potsdam, but Klemperer cannot stay for the discussion.] ... curious as to how the thing continued. On 3 May I have to speak to the Press Club in Halle, on the 16th in Zwickau to the teachers of the district, about language; I shall say exactly the same thing on both occasions, yesterday it had the title: 'The old and the new humanism'. [...]

Vehement agreement with my 'Responsibility for the language' article together with complaints about the present situation from an upper-school teacher called Reichert in Hildburghausen. 'We upper-school teachers are very grateful to you ... Unfortunately we only have one Klemperer. And he sometimes seems to me like a voice crying in the wilderness ...' That fills me with delight, and I shall reply very graciously.

[...]

30th April, Saturday forenoon. Dresden

[...]

In Berlin on Thurs. long discussion with Kortum[7] at the Ministry. Result: I shall become emeritus on 1st September. I shall lecture – for Germanists as well – once weekly in Halle (Rousseau). I hope to see H. appointed in Halle after she has taken her doctorate ... Convenient and inconvenient aspects of the new situation: it will not take much work off my shoulders – not take much external honour and external fields of activity from me. Nevertheless, as an emeritus I have the right at any time to stop lecturing and at any time to resume lecturing in Berlin and in Halle.

[...]

[...] Halle is not to get any new Romance Languages and Literatures students, but the old ones, who still have 2 or 3 years to go, are being left there, it is being allowed to 'run down'. I acquiesced in that, because in 2–3 years the situation can change x times over. I want to claim the credit for having saved the threatened traditional chair in Halle. I want to cut a dash in Halle in splendid isolation. Vanitas vanitatum. [...]

[...]

7th May, Saturday forenoon. Dresden

[...] On 3 May I lectured the last time this semester at Halle, and in the evening I then spoke to 50, 60 people in the Press Club on 'Language and Humanism'. Just as recently in Potsdam. I got considerable applause and thanks. [...] The next day a letter from Wenzel about Potsdam. In the discussion after my departure: Half of those present indignant: I had *not made a 'positive critique'*, talked about the 4th Reich (LQI), underestimated the achievements of the GDR, etc. (Opposition also with respect to Latin.) Obviously my audience in Potsdam had been teachers and people from the teacher-training college, in Halle people with a university background. [...]

Letter from the SED organisation, Halle University: Could I use my influence on Silzer who had expressed himself inappropriately during language teaching: a) the SED, with its agitation against the SPD was *also* to blame for the E–W. split, b) why in our impotence do we have to raise an army?! ... I wrote, I would talk to him personally. What should I tell him?? That he's right and that he should not put his foot in it. Very disagreeable.

[...]

17th May, 7 p.m. Tuesday. Dresden
[...]

Weimar – Schiller Celebrations – Thomas Mann
[...] At the ceremony on the morning of the 14th we sat directly behind Thomas Mann, second row of the stalls. I noticed the uninterrupted slight trembling of the bony head and the large ears. His daughter beside him,[8] looking very like him, but also like the mother, whose face has become remarkably like that of her husband. He probably spoke for a good hour, curious mixture of schoolteacher, clergyman, grandad, practised actor with plenty of gesticulation, with humorous-ironic notes. All very warm, very simple – passing lightly over philosophy and aesthetics. But emphasising [Schiller's] language, his trenchancy, his theatrical effect. Disregarding politics, emphasising humanity. – Becher introduced him: altogether with dignity. Mann has been honoured with a degree of submissiveness, welcomed like a king at the GDR border ... [...]

Then on Saturday evening and Sunday evening: *The Maid of Orléans* (Weimar theatre), *Maria Stuart* (Stuttgart theatre).[9] The applause on Sunday incomparably greater: much of it a political ovation for the West. Presumably also because *Maria Stuart* goes down more easily than the knight's tale. [...] I have noticed in these last weeks how little I still know of Schiller and in fact ever knew. I would so much like to immerse myself – but I must, I must bring my meagre producing to a conclusion, I am not satisfied by mere reception.

[...]

19th May, Thursday afternoon, Ascension Day. Dresden
[...] Yesterday alone in Berlin. The Foreign Policy Committee [of the Volkskammer], which I imagined to be something special, disillusioned me. Between a dozen and a dozen and a half mostly younger people, who hardly opened their mouths. [A report on the setting up of the Warsaw Pact military alliance[10] as an answer to NATO and West German re-armament within the NATO structure.] ... and in less than an hour the session was concluded. A sham like all our parliamentarism. [...]

Holger sent me the April issue of *Trygée*.[11] In it Wagner[12] attacks the Ministère de l'Intérieur, because it refused me a visa. However, I am regarded only as an object, the praise for me is intended only to confirm my harmlessness. My 19ième, on the new edition of which I wanted to work in the Bibliothèque Nationale, becomes *un ouvrage de référence*, a reference work. Bitter! Hardly sweetened by my *production scientifique des plus honorables*[13] ... I was 'perhaps the only professor for the history of literature in East Germany', my only blemish was this: M. V. Klemperer se trouve aujourd'hui à l'est de cette ligne idéale qui sépare, nul ne l'ignore, deux mondes, celui de la liberté et celui du despotisme, celui de l'humanisme et celui de la barbarie![14] ... That's how Croce protected me in Naples in 1915: an innocent fool.

25th May, after 8 a.m. Berlin, Institute
[...]
On Monday *wedding anniversary*, three years! My most undeserved happiness, dearer to me each day, and every day in every respect burdening my conscience.
[...]
Started work on the last 19ième chapter: Vallès and Barbusse. I looked up my diary: this sterile torment since the beginning of May last year. [...]

30th May, Whit Monday evening
On Sunday I was notified of my emeritus status, sweetened with a big eulogy from the State Secretariat. Drily added by Neye – the sergeant-major rector – my retirement as director of the Institute of Romance Languages and Literatures, which need not necessarily have occurred simultaneously, and which is an act of rancour on the part of His Magnificence. – I was annoyed for a day, really no longer than that.
[...]

5th June, Sunday. Dresden
Still incapable of work. And tomorrow Berlin and Wednesday Jena. [...]
How greatly the moderns interest me in every respect! If I were like H.'s father, receptive and without ambition and vanity, then I could now revel in all of that, retired like him and *without any* financial worries (a wealthy man!). But I *must* get my stuff finished.
[...]

The set aside Munich notes
1 and 2 June, journey there 31 May, journey back 3 June

The tremendous amount of driving around, the mass of cars, in between them the tiny 'scooters', in the morning also the tremendous stream of cyclists, simple ones and mopeds, coming from the suburbs. All that was racing down

Leopoldstr., while we waited for the tram. World city and former village [...].
People were in every respect very friendly to us. – Including Rohlfs, white-
haired, imposing, precise when he spoke, altogether as a colleague should be.
He did not bear myself or Vossler any animosity. Especially cordial was Wilhelm,
the Catholic [professor at Tübingen]. Grey, with very dark eyes, very southern
type. But his wife! In all innocence. In our part of Germany preaching was not
allowed, after all, or attendance at church! It was virtually impossible to persuade
her otherwise – 'we are so mistrustful!' Her husband signalled desperately to
her, to break off the conversation. [...]

[Receptions. Instead of going to one at the Italian Institute, the Klemperers]
went to a cinema on Arnulphstr., sat over an espresso afterwards, and then
slowly walked the long way back.

At the cinema the newsreel; Adenauer at the formal 'declaration of sov-
ereignty'. – A pretty documentary film, very American scenes (revolver, erotica)
in the previews. Then Zuckmayer: The Devil's General.[15] Strong impression.
Why forbidden by us? It is impossible to be more anti-Fascist. [...]

[A bus trip, with H., into the Upper Bavarian countryside, the still snow-
covered peaks of the Alps clearly in view.]

7th June, Tuesday forenoon. Dresden
[...]

I negotiated in 'my' Institute with Kowen and Pommerenke about my *Modern
French Poetry*. I am now getting a contract, it will appear next year, edition of
3000 copies [...]; I am adding a Résistance chapter.
[...]

16th June, Thursday forenoon. Dresden
[...] ... correspondence to be got through [...] and travel preparations. [...]

We read *The Devil's General*, talked about it for a long time. The play is even
better than the film. [...]

Tonight or, rather, tomorrow morning at 4 the journey to Bulgaria begins.
[...] Mixed feelings. Hope, that H. gets full pleasure (not too greatly impaired
by me) out of it. I myself a little blunted and sceptical.

6 p.m.
We bought two caps for 5M and spotted in passing *the* small refrigerator we
have been hunting, for years it seems. We bought it immediately, since it was a
much-admired single item. Difficulty of paying: 665M – I did not have that
much on me [...]. Paid a deposit, went to the bank, closed – back home, fetched
savings bank book and cheque book – cheque up to 500M was allowed, we gave
the rest in cash. *That's* how difficult some things are here. Poor East.

17th June–11th July. Bulgarian Trip

23rd June, forenoon

[Just as on previous holidays with Hadwig on the Baltic coast, Klemperer is plagued by worries, bad conscience and fits of depression.]

[The travel group drawn from various professions.] ... our group consists of some forty people, Party officials, writers, theatre people etc. We know very few of them, have contact with very few of them. [...]

24th June, Friday forenoon

Hotel Balkan Tourist: Mixture of elegance and primitiveness. On our arrival late at night (1 a.m.) it appeared virtually barbaric. No water. Now we know: Abundant during the day, off from 6 p.m.–6 a.m. One fills the wash-hand basin for the night, one tries to avoid using the loo if possible. In the open hall the most sumptuous supper, all around it, however, uproarious clamour. There are not only Germans here. Also Czech and Hungarian groups. Bulgarians also. Probably Russians and Poles, too. The eastern temperament, the eastern joy in singing. Added to that, of course, but not unpleasantly, hardly dominant in fact, alcohol. People singing in chorus. People singing something at every table, now and then communicating from group to group. It was deafening. Chasing between the tables, despite the late hour, children and infants, playing, shouting, bawling. For exhausted and unwashed people shaken to the core by the terribly bumpy bus it was an inferno. I thought: 20 (twenty!) days: Now it's better. [...]

27th June, Monday forenoon. Varna

[...]

Yesterday evening a discussion among the comrades took place here [...]: a professor's young daughter was stopped (arrested? It remained unclear) by soldiers, because she was photographing gypsies. Explanation: they had suspected press photography of Bulgarian 'backwardness'. Gypsies: the backward Bulgaria. One is suppose to illustrate the Bulgaria being built!

[...]

[Late nights, not least with the Dresden doctor, Alfred Schmeiser, who is with another party.]

[...]

17th July, Sunday evening. Dresden

Slowly back to work: Concluding piece Barbusse. I hope to be finished in the course of this week.

[...]

27th July, Wednesday evening. Dresden

Today at last took the Barbusse chapter to Ullmann, so the real work on the 19ième is now completed after a good $1\frac{1}{4}$ years. Now proofreading of the manuscript volume.

[...]

Everyone full of the progress of peace at Geneva[16] and of Adenauer's obstinacy. Yesterday in Berlin drive home delayed by the masses congregating for the demonstration: Bulganin[17] and Krushchev[18] back from Geneva, guests of the GDR.

[...]

I dreamt of my mother, I saw her on the window seat of the connecting room, saw her almost blind on the sofa, asked her how far she recognised me. I really did that at the time. But when was 'the time'? Vagueness of my memory. And did I go to her funeral in Berlin? I truly do not know any more. I only know that I received the telegram of her death in 1919 in the Munich pension. It was during the chaotic days of the revolution[19] ... I sometimes do not know what of myself and of my past is still alive.

2nd August, Tuesday forenoon. Dresden

[...]

Now first proofs of *Vor 1933, nach 1945*: 'Is there a Spanish Renaissance?' I fear these old essays.

[...]

10th August, Wednesday forenoon. Dresden

We have mostly had the heating on, the weather is so bad.

[...]

Very detached and disgusted with respect to politics – above all bored by it. Both sides lie, hush up, slander, I can no longer feel any enthusiasm for 'us', I merely find the Federal Republic '*even* worse', I feel ever more strongly the confinement, the isolation, the futility of the situation here, especially my own. I am particularly irritated every day by the emptiness of our news reporting, above all on the wireless. I usually switch off the 'Commentary' of the day – after 10 words I know the rest.

Tito! What abuse was heaped on him. Now he is vir bonus.[20] [...]

16th August, 3 p.m. Tuesday. Dresden

[Volkskammer] At the group meeting Zweig spoke passionately against the 'bandits' in the Bonn government, against the Hitler luminaries they've brought back. But the mood is for reconciliation. Although again and again it is emphasised: we shall not give up anything of our achievements. Now the next sensation: Adenauer is going to Moscow.[21] Que sais je? What has been fixed up?

Next to politics the big event is Thomas Mann's death.[22] H. said (and it's obvious) he let himself be celebrated to death like the old Voltaire.

[...]

21st August, 7 p.m. Sunday. Dresden

[...]

Since their Berlin trip H.'s parents long for the West more than ever. Her father would get a good pension in West Berlin whenever he wanted – he taught there for a long time; they are afraid only of the separation from their children who are bound to the East. [...] I know, at least of H.'s mother, that she is dissatisfied with Western policies but both parents regard the GDR as a prison and as the worst of states ... [...]

23rd August, Tuesday evening vers minuit[23]

[...]

Just today I am sitting over the essay 'World literature and European literature'. It was written in 1928 and dismisses the Russians as chaos. What am I supposed to do now with this essay. But more profoundly I grieve at my blindness. *That's* how I went through life, and now I've come to the end. Then I was alone – Jew, irresolutely liberal and in a society which did not respect me; today I am in a society which disregards me. [...]

[...]

3rd September, 6 pm. Saturday afternoon. Dresden

[...]

LQI. The Israeli state, the Israelis. On the warpath against Egypt and Arabia, with tanks and jet fighters. Cock fighting. The Israelis have American masters and American blades in their claws – the Egyptians are 'looked after' by the Russians ... I cannot say what an aversion I have to politics and how repugnant to me both sides are.

[...]

6th September, Tuesday evening. Dresden

Today the beautiful chestnut in front of the bedroom window was knocked down. Necessity: the dampness of the house, the imminent draining and insulation ... When the house was built, the masterbuilder planted two chestnuts. The masterbuilder – his name?? yes: Praetorius[24] ... died long ago, E. is dead, the very splendid tree has been chopped up. I spook around.

[...]

Tomorrow and the day after Berlin. We have tickets for the inaugural month of the Opera.[25]

11th September, Sunday forenoon. Dresden

[The Klemperers see a production of Wagner's *Mastersingers* at the newly
restored State Opera, which they enjoy. Subsequently lively discussion between
the two of them on Wagner. Klemperer is favourably impressed by the
number of working people at the performance, tickets distributed through
organisations.] H.'s beautiful evening dress fairly lonely, barely half a dozen
in corridor and foyer; altogether giving the impression of an exception, a
costume.

[...]

After that [Thurs.] I gave my lecture – the room again packed and the
greeting almost an ovation. But the whole proceedings are no more than a little
pleasurable vanity, which costs me far too much time and strength. [...] ... à
quoi bon? 50% vanity, 50% petrol coupons, coal etc.

[...]

16th September, 7 p.m. Friday. Dresden

[More wrangling over Klemperer's position – and that of Romance Languages
and Literatures – in Halle. In the end:] resolution of the Party group: complete
detachment of my person from Berlin: full teaching post as emeritus in Halle,
retain senate seat. – That was carried unanimously – still open: payment, petrol,
coal; Stern agreed to every preference – rejection of Heintze as deputy, dispute
over that settled; I can come and go as I please. I then arranged with Silzer: 2
hours 19th century, 2 seminar hours 'Lessing and France' [...]. God knows if I
have made the right decision. Hadwig seems in agreement.

[...]

23rd September, Friday forenoon. Berlin, Institute

[...]

I had the most packed house of my life. The room had to be changed. Over
200 people, the undernourished Germanists, in addition 10 French students as
guest group, to whom I addressed a few words, and who thanked me with a few
nice words in German ... [...]

[...] Rita wants me to lecture here every four weeks. I accept, but *without* a
fixed date, but whenever I have business in Berlin.

We drove (that, too, with a heavy heart and after long consideration) to the
senate meeting in Halle, today at 6. Left towards 1.

[...]

[At the meeting Stern, the rector, relays the Party line: For unification, but no
giving way ... but in the long term building Socialism and the future.]

[...]

29th September, 5 p.m. Thursday. Berlin, Institute

[...]

[Volkskammer, Berlin, 26 Sept. The group meeting discusses constitutional change necessary to allow conscription – essential condition of the establishment of GDR armed forces. But no discussion provided for in the chamber itself!] Protest (where I had not expected it) from the 150%er Havemann, from Meusel [...], from Zweig [... both against the lack of discussion and the principle of conscription itself]. *I* said, and paid for it with palpitations, shortage of breath and pain, if the chamber passed [the measures] in silence, I would consider that a disaster, 'I underline a disaster.' 'There's always talk about raising the standing of the deputies. If they now once again keep their mouths shut – what are we here for?' [...] Then on the wireless and in the newspaper I learned of the 'unanimous passage'.[26] [...]

12th October, Wednesday afternoon. Dresden

The somewhat feared birthday passed quietly, all the usual congratulations and telegrams came – only those of the Party organisations were missing. [...]

Yesterday in Halle where I calmly presented my 19ième and calmly took my Lessing seminar [...], I felt better for a little while; but today, as I'm trying in vain to answer the pile of congratulations, I again feel quite incapable of work. I have outlived myself, I should have called it a day before I was kicked in the backside [...] for how long will I still be able to teach in Halle, for how much longer will my books be allowed to appear? [...]

13th October, Thursday. Dresden

Article in German Teachers Newspaper, 24 Sept.: 'Digging potatoes made interesting'. 'Secondary-school pupils and students are being sent to the belated potato harvest. The teachers evaluate the action with particular reference to the educational aspect (patriotic education, education for work, respect for work, importance of the alliance between working class and peasants, all round education).' That's written by 'Colleague Faulwasser from Altenburg'. The article adds: 'Such work will very quickly drive out the intellectual presumption from some heads ...' [...]

20th October, 7 p.m. Thursday. Dresden

[Klemperer speaks in Leipzig on Balzac etc. as *writers*, not as material for social questions. He also mentions his interest in the work of Hans Mayer, notes the parallels, regrets Mayer's closeness to Krauss and his sometime agreement with Hermlin's annihilation of Klemperer's *Modern French Prose*.]

21st October, Friday forenoon

[The Klemperers buy tickets in advance for the French film of *The Red and the Black* by Claude Autant-Lara.[27] Long queues for it everywhere.]

Additions from 13th–20th

(In recent days I have been even more rushed off my feet than before my retirement.) [...]

So on the 14th I attended the Executive Committee meeting in Berlin [...]. Long speech by Comrade Hager about the political situation. General, but clear summary, the familiar things. New to me. Hager's indignation at the West's sentimental and propaganda effort for the returnees, the generals. [As a result of the visit to Moscow of the West German chancellor, Konrad Adenauer, the Soviet Union had agreed to release the remaining German prisoners of war it still held.] [...] Kleinschmidt's retort to that: his wife senior nurse at the border point in the Frankfurt on the Oder camp. Much wretchedness, by no means only generals, poor devils as well, women and children as well. The nursing staff, the public deeply moved, rejection of the cold behaviour, the isolation measures on our side. [...] the opposite point of view of Hager's official one.

[...]

27th October, Thursday forenoon. Dresden

I am 'written off' everywhere, no longer exist. I no longer exist in the Kulturbund and Aufbau, no longer exist in the Academy. My 18ième ignored. Not present in the 'Fundamental Positions of the French Enlightenment' edited by Krauss. Only Naumann in his Holbach monograph mentions me, with a contemptuous [...] remark.[28] [...] My 'Montesquieu' does not exist for the 'Fundamental Positions' either. For the French, by the way, equally non-existent ... Eva once said bitterly: nothing of her would remain. [...] *I* am forgotten in my own lifetime. Sometimes it appears to me like retribution. What faith have I kept with Eva? In the last few days I went for a walk to Rosstal with H. and her father. Across terrain quite unfamiliar to me – I hardly get into the open air any more, and I see nothing – I do not find my way about in Halle, never have done, and I don't here either. [...]

13th November, Sunday forenoon etc. Dresden

Of 16 days I have only catchwords. I notice no relief through my retirement. Perhaps the tiredness of old age slows me down. Everything piles up.

[...]

On Friday and Saturday 28 and 29 October in Berlin. [...] In the Advisory Council on Saturday [...] there was discussion of who to send to an international Romance Languages and Literatures Congress in April 1956 in Florence. [...] now the State Secretariat wants to send a larger delegation to Florence, including up-and-coming academics. Naturally everyone wants to go to Italy [...]

[...]

In Halle 2 weeks *beet harvest*, the whole university shut down. How is one supposed to complete one's course?

[...]

Mackie Kahane is reporting for the *Berliner Zeitung* [newspaper], his wife Doris is now interpreting in Hanoi.

[...]

15th November, Tuesday. Dresden

In the Weimar years it was the 'captains of industry'. Now it's the 'nuclear physicists'. Among the members of the re-constituted [Executive] Committee [...] is Herr or Baron von Ardenne [nuclear physicist].[29] I first heard the name from Schmeiser [...]. Herr von Ardenne arrives from the SU. Unimaginably wealthy. Builds a villa using the most expensive materials, luxuriously furnished, has an elite superlatively exclusive club set up. The Russians picked up Herr von Ardenne in 1945 and now send him back as our and their cosseted friend. If Hitler had held out another three months, then Ardenne would have provided him with the almost completed magic weapon (V3?) – if Hitler had then finally been destroyed anyway, Herr von Ardenne would now be 'war criminal no. 1'. What do we know?? My Curriculum is intended to record precisely this *not knowing*.

[...]

24th November, Thursday forenoon and later. Dresden

Sunday 18 Nov. was filled with visitors. [... among them] Dr Günther Schmidt, our neighbour's son, who returned to the GDR one and a half years ago, is now a dermatologist in Chemnitz [...] No doubt Günther Schmidt represents 90% of all Germans both West and East. They are fed up to the back teeth with politics, they would like to have a state of peace based on a tolerable compromise, with butter and without travel restrictions (and with books and newspapers from everywhere in the world). This last in brackets, because only a couple of members of the intelligentsia care about that.

[...]

27th November, Sunday forenoon. Dresden

[...]

Letter from Marcel Cohen, whom I sent the *LTI* months ago. Wants to review it, wants to publish the foreword (Heroism) in *L'Europe*. That would push open the door to Europe for me, that would at last get me the France trip and, honoured, from there make possible the trip to England ... to Palestine to the Israelis ... etc. etc. [...]

11th December, Sunday about 2 p.m. Dresden

[...] Ever greater workload and inability to work and dissipation of my energies. The proof reading! Yesterday I received the ms of *Modern Poetry* [...] That and the 19ième and the Essays: how can I think of serious study on the 18ième before Easter? [...] I feel so impoverished, uneducated and obsolete ... Yet constantly the longing, aroused by H.'s work, to brush up my former knowledge of German literature, extending it to modernism. [...] And likewise acquaintanceship with French modernism. The sphere of what is interesting, longed for, grows ever larger, the capacity for receptive, still less productive activity ever less. [...]

24th December, midday Saturday. Dresden

[...]

H.'s parents here since Thursday. So far everything has gone well – and this time I do not dread Christmas Eve quite as much as usual.

[...]

Again and again depressed by the diminution in my ability to work – tiredness – sleeping long – reading slowly – resignation etc. The terrible search for names that have escaped me. I see the people in front of me, since yesterday Annemarie's compagnon in Pirna,[30] whom I last met, when I spoke in the upper school there. What is his name?

[...]

25th December, Sunday afternoon

The hour of the lit Christmas candles, the records of devout music and the standing and sitting around with tree and presents was very depressing after all, but I coped quite well, and I felt somewhat more at ease at supper. [...] Going to church and the usual religious conversation associated with it has also been got through. Tout passe. Today still a walk, correspondence and *the* bird; tomorrow beginning of the ms proofreading of *Modern French Poetry*.

[...]

Résumé 1955

Emeritus, quarrel with Rita, pushed aside.

Halle my place of retirement.

No productive work accomplished any more. Only the never-ending revision of the old things for new editions.

Daily feeling of having outlived myself.

Vita exterior: the summer trip to Bulgaria.

Depression because of my age as compared to Hadwig's.

The one thing I can do every day: work on, obstinately, *not think!*

Profound political disappointment. Of my enthusiasm there remains only: *we* are the lesser evil. And: Marxism is a) better than our SED government, b) a religion like other religions – and I cannot believe.

[...]

1956

5th January, midnight Thursday
[...]

Today after strenuous, dull-witted work I completed checking the *Modern French Poetry* ms. In part I no longer understand the content, it has become so foreign to me. [...]

13th January, Friday morning (9.30!). Dresden
[...]

We indulge in going to bed late. During the day we sit at our work – in the evening with lighter reading. Then we become lively. Yesterday stopped after 2 a.m. [...]

16th January, Monday forenoon. Dresden
[...] For the Curriculum also: H.'s Catholicism. Yesterday this moved me: Communion. She *cannot*, because she lives with me without a church wedding. But she goes to mass, pays church tax, will, if she wishes, be 'administered to' in extremis. (She calls that 'club rules'.) Her mixture of freedom and restriction again and again remains incomprehensible to me [...]. Eva must forgive me: I have never loved any human being as much as H. (Senility, the psychologist will say.)

[A boring KB meeting in Dresden. Klemperer concludes: I] also know and say, that I am laughed at as vieillard vénérable[1] – is it worth it? Vanitas vanitatum – I cannot stop myself and on Wed. will go to the Volkskammer in Berlin [...].

Konrad is humiliatingly smarter. His wife died in November. He informed me weeks later, I invited him over, he was here on Saturday afternoon. 76, hissing through badly fitting dentures, good posture, modest, calmly confident in himself, a wise man. He has his small pension, is in the SED, is active a little (without giving talks: 'my memory is no use any more, I've also given up reading Lenin, Stalin, I don't keep it in my head'). He is an observing Jew. 'Our service is usually just chatting. For a proper service we need 10 men, of course; which we rarely manage – just one needs to be ill, then it's not possible.' (*Club rules!*) He has a foster-daughter, whom he took in as a child, in 1945. [...] How does he fill his day? 'I cook, I take care of the house – my foster-daughter is on duty for 8 hours, after all. [...] He vegetates, evidently not without happiness, en philosophe.[2] Before Hitler he was a respected wealthy businessman. Now the small pension. Sometimes he sells a piece of a saved porcelain collection.

23rd January, Monday forenoon. Dresden

[On the Sunday Lessing lecture in Kamenz.] We left after lunch on Saturday. First to Piskowitz. Agnes in her new house, her own. Much still to be done. But spacious, neat. Her son, Juri, 24, unbelievably like her, largely built the house himself. Engine driver at the nearby coalmine. His mother looks after the holding (a cow, two goats, a pig etc.) also helps out 'with the farmer'. Everything work and exchange, barter economy, no money – yet the young engine driver in Society for Sport and Technology[3] ... And the daughter, previously a pioneer at school, enthusiastically for GDR and Party, cleared off ages ago, because unemployed, to Frankfurt am Main, where she's living at her half brother's and is training as a nurse in a private hospital. Picture of our time.

[...]

On Wed., 18 Jan., I was in Berlin alone. The historic session in which we unanimously approved the creation of a National People's Army. All this playing at parliament: choses farces, farces, farces ... tristes, tristes, tristes.[4] And yet the GDR is the lesser evil. And it irritates me, when I encounter the shoulder-shrugging contempt for the GDR and cannot contradict it. [...] The exhibition of uniforms, whose 'German tradition' is strongly emphasised, made an unpleasant impression on me. [...]

3rd February, Friday morning 6.30 a.m.

[Volkskammer:] Grotewohl on the *National People's Army*. [...] Further: we have been promoting the dove of peace for 10 years, so naturally it's not easy to convince the people of the necessity of the army. But it is necessary, we are the western vanguard of the 900 million strong peace group. It is our duty. (Unfortunately sounds suspiciously like *the Germans to the front*,[5] which is of course also true of the Adenauer army.) [...]

3rd February, 9 p.m. Friday

[...]

Quite unexpectedly the visa for Paris arrived by the early post. To some degree disturbing effect.

9th February, Thursday 8.30 a.m. Berlin, old Institute seat

[...] And an urgent commission by telephone from Volk und Welt publishing house: Afterword to Diderot's *La Religieuse*.[6] I declined at first – old hat etc. for me. They offered 1,500M for 6–10 pages and 2% of further editions. I accepted.

[...]

11th February, Saturday forenoon. Dresden

[...]

On Wednesday evening at the Kahanes', together with Peter and Inge Klemperer. A visit by Willy Jelski is imminent[7] – it will not be possible to see him, we cannot organise a special trip to Berlin. Also he is likely to fearfully avoid our zone and our sector. Partly fear of our side, partly fear of American reprisals. Perhaps Willy is different – but the other relatives fear the 'Communists' like the plague. *My* family!

[...] And now I learned by the way that Marta 'died one or two years ago'.[8] It left and leaves me criminally cold, she was dead for me long ago, I think only of my Curriculum. But this coldness shocks me – I do not have a clear conscience with regard to Marta. But then with regard to whom do I have a clear conscience? – At midnight we were driven back in a Western DKW, which Peter drove. It was given to him by his mother, who is now a wealthy woman again. That, too, for the Curriculum. If only time is left to me for *that*! Instead I dissipate my energies on lectures and articles, and the 18ième is also waiting, and my memory for names fails me more and more.

[...]

19th February, Sunday forenoon

[Reading Laurence Sterne and the French Marxist Henri Lefebvre,[9] Klemperer asserts:] ... But *my* Diderot [in his 18ième] can stand on its own nevertheless, despite the absence of Sterne and Marx. Why do I no longer have what it takes to create like that? – Bourgeois déraciné, désorienté, vieillard stupide.[10]

[Meeting of intellectuals under the banner of the National Front. Klemperer again speaks up, inter alia, for Latin. Dieckmann replies, stressing the necessities of technology ... '*in the past* Latin, Greek and Hebrew were taught in the grammar schools, that could not be done today'.] The next day Gusti told me, she had heard *I* had called for the teaching of Greek and *Hebrew* in the schools. [...]

H. said, she would never publish my Curriculum of her own accord. 'Otherwise everyone will swear, I had falsified it to make it more right wing!'

[...]

22nd February, Wednesday forenoon. Dresden

It was Schmeiser who drew our attention to Mikoyan's speech (20th Party Congress, the first since Stalin's death).[11] Until then I had not read the many speeches at all, assuming semper idem, it had also escaped Hadwig, who is much more zealous. It is of world historical importance. Dead Caesar, become dust and grass[12] – the dead lion given a kick in the backside. How we had to rise to our feet in the chamber every time Stalin's name was mentioned! It was literally a parade ground drill: Lie down – Stand up! – How little, or nothing at all, we know of what is going on around us. [...] What will happen now? Constant discussion, here and yesterday at the Kirchners. [...] For myself I find it unpleasant that Stalin has so completely become a dead dog. He must have been good at *something*. But what? This sudden toppling of the god, this sudden silence about him is fairly loathsome. [...] In short: the Stalin–Mikoyan subject absorbs us in every respect. [...]

[...]

7th March, Wednesday forenoon. Dresden

[A former student from Halle calls on Klemperer to discuss a Ph.D. topic. He remarks that all Stalin's books have disappeared from the displays at the Leipzig trade fair.] We asked ourselves what will happen to the Marx-Engels-Lenin-Stalin plaquettes. Ulbricht writes: 'Stalin is *not* one of the classic authors of Marxism.'[13] The anniversary of Stalin's death has just passed. Not a word about it in our newspapers. Friwi[?] related: broadcast on a Western station: on the anniversary of Stalin's death a sign had been placed on Stalin's mausoleum in Moscow: '*Closed for cleaning*'.

[...]

17th March, Saturday forenoon. Dresden

Still snow and most irksome winter.

[...]

25th March, Sunday forenoon

[...]

Kahane (on Thurs. in the Press Club) said: he did not like Ulbricht at all – but Stalin had 'exterminated' the cadres hostile to him, for example the Polish ones, despite every warning he had been unprepared for Hitler's attack, etc. etc., altogether, therefore, a serious blight, bloodsucker and despot, in short traitor, since the mid-1930s. (I am, of course, summing up in exaggerated terms). I am not quite convinced ... H. on the other hand completely on Kahane's side. – At any rate politics as a whole disgusts me more than ever.

[On Mond. and Tuesd., 19th and 20th March Klemperer was in Halle, first of all for lectures, then to be ceremoniously made an honorary senator of the university.[14]] I was charged with expressing the thanks of those honoured. [...] Outside Halle no one took any notice of the whole business, my honorary certificate is in the linen cupboard, next to the Dr h.c. folder. For me the honorary senatorship is something unpleasant: attestation of senility, harbinger of the way I shall be fobbed off on my 75th, third-class distinction.

Thurs. Frid. in Berlin. Got up at 3 a.m., 5 a.m. start – earliest spring – at Wilhelmstr. punctually at 8.30. Complete chaos with prospect to the Florentine business. Nothing properly prepared. [...]

3rd–8th April. (International Romance Languages and Literatures Congress in Florence). Hotel Cavour, Via del Proconsolato [...]

[On the flight to Florence, the second leg from Prague by Swissair, Klemperer is amazed by the packaging of the meal provided – and by the fact that it is included in the price of the ticket.]

[The weather is bitterly cold, the conference itself boring, but offers plenty of opportunity to make contact with other scholars. And, of course, Klemperer is showing Hadwig the city. But there are worries, too, and, as always, memories.]

7th April, 9 a.m. Saturday

[...] The worry about currency! We hesitate over every espresso, that costs 40L.

Yesterday something beautiful, truly beautiful and new to me: the Ponte Vecchio. (What did Eva and I see of Florence in 1915? I remember only the quiet veranda with the ancient tortoise. The diaries will have been destroyed. 'What remains of it all? Ashes, ashes, ashes.' Apart from that, we never felt at home in Florence. I remember incomparably more of Naples and Rome.)

[...]

7th April, Saturday after 9 p.m. Room

[Outing to Fiesole, later also to San Gimignano.]

What remains? The cold, the life-threatening traffic, the espresso and the general Italianità familiar from 100,000 pictures.

[...]

[After the close of the Florence congress, the Klemperers take a Cook's Tour to Naples, Pompeii and Rome. Victor Klemperer notes:] In all of this I am constantly filled by the wish, that the journey will be of lasting importance to H. I have given up thinking about myself. I appreciate the pretty moments and doze through the rest. I have no kind of expectation of life any more.

16th April, 9 a.m. Monday. Marseille, Hôtel de Berne on the station square

Pouring rain, I let H., who has a bad cold and is very exhausted, sleep. We are en route to Paris. [...] Along with the rain great tiredness, also a certain uniformity of impressions – *the* Italianità, *the* Provence, *the* coast backdrop, *the* tunnels in their incalculable sequence, in between a bit of coast, the film landscapes, watering places, hotels, artificially cultivated palms (badly affected by the frost), *the* motor roads, *the* many and large cars and buses, the famous names: Rapallo, Monte Carlo, Bordighera, Cannes, Mentone or Menton, Nice (a big city). All of it a little threadbare, filmed all too often, all of it variations and identical bits of film. The question: am I excessively blunted or does H. feel the same?

Since being released from the care of Cook, the strain is, of course, greater. *I* am clumsy, and my body fails me, H. lugs the suitcases, tires herself, which repeatedly depresses me. A porter is rarely to hand etc. etc. But again and again pleasant moments, impressions, breaks – mostly over a happily snatched, reviving espresso. [...] We hope to be able to lead a calmer and more meaningful life in Paris than while travelling.

[...]

[The Klemperers were in Paris from 17 April to 17 July 1956. Here it will only be possible include very brief extracts from the diaries covering these months.]

19th April, Thursday afternoon. Paris, Cité Universitaire, Maison internationale. Room 2 with its own loo and bath!
[The Klemperers are officially guests of the University of Paris.]

[Klemperer is plagued by the usual depressions and doubts, takes time to get used to the city, which he has not seen for decades. Nevertheless the couple go to the theatre, begin to make contacts, e.g. with Gilbert Badia, a Communist and schoolteacher of German, later to become a distinguished historian of the German Left.]

24th April, 12 p.m. Wednesday. CUP (Cité Universitaire Paris)
[...]

Yesterday and today in the Bibliothèque Nationale. Yesterday in complete despair, because I was quite unable to find my way around the catalogue room. Profound depression. Whereas H. made sense of it immediately. Today was a little better. Not much – I am fighting tiredness and the feeling that I am no longer able to work. [...] What am I looking for in Paris? My 18ième? The right wing of modernism? Paris life? Why am I walking blindly through the streets? What interests me in Paris, what do I take in? To what *end* do I still try to pick up new things? Again and again the feeling of not really existing any more. Poor Hadwig.

[...]

I'm reading a little Koestler.[15]

Anny Klemperer has replied to my letter by card first of all [...]. She writes: we would no doubt experience the beauty of the *free world*. Once the expression would have filled me with indignation. *Now* (Stalin etc.) I can no longer completely reject it. Nor can I ignore Koestler.

27th April, 10 a.m. Friday. CUP
[...]
    [...] *Réunion des enseignants:*[16] *Algerian War problem.*[17] Very large hall. [...] Those present nearly all intellectuals, mostly young, very many women, not a single *coloured* person – it's really only the CUP with its Maison de Tunisie etc. that is coloured. [...]

29th April, Sunday forenoon. CUP
Fairly extensive reading of the *Figaro littéraire*. I learned of E. R. Curtius' death through an obituary by Jean Schlumberger.[18] He died in Rome just after his 70th birthday following a long illness. Picture of a fat man. The 'great German philologist', who already in 1914 had recognised the pionniers de la France nouvelle.[19] He had such sure judgement, because his knowledge was so comprehensive, also of England, of Spain, of the Middle Ages. I must, with bitterness and self-accusation, concede that: he was infinitely more educated than I. My whole life long I have been no more than a journalist with very limited knowledge, I have always asked myself how I managed to get a chair. [...]
    Our life here has assumed something of a pattern. Many hours (stériles et somnolentes)[20] in the Nationale (whose bureaucracy and poor arrangement exasperate me), the hours there and back on the métro, supper and final coffee in a bar, main meal in the refectory – and always the cold, the cold. Today, Sunday, very bad. H. reads in bed wearing her fur jacket, I write with numb fingers. And always the feeling that I am finished.
    What interests me: What is contemporary literature? What is the literary coverage of the press? The *non*-Communist press. I learn more from that than from books. Of course random samples. *Figaro*: Right wing. *Le Monde* (often quoted in the GDR) evidently bourgeois-liberal. [...]

8th May, Tuesday forenoon
[...]
    A degree of boredom proves to me that I have really absorbed enough of the 'Vie parisienne':[21] the traffic pouring past, the noise, the risk in crossing the road, the métro labyrinth, the sitting beside and on the street, the black coffee, the racial mixture of the Cité universitaire, the abundance of churches, the abundance of monuments and divinities, the splendour of the mass of the Louvre on the right bank, the government buildings on the left bank of the Seine. I am too old, too blasé, too blind for all of that. I am always afraid of weighing on H.'s spirits, of hampering her mobility and receptiveness.
    [...]
[Klemperer attends a meeting of Sorbonne German students addressed by three speakers, including a Communist deputy. The main topic was] getting to

know and maintaining friendship with the GDR. Hostility towards the Adenauer state. It really did me good, to hear so many positive things about the
GDR. Everything looks better from a distance, of course. Also, from a distance
one does not feel the restrictions over there, but only one's own shortcomings.
[...]

On Saturday evening (5 May) there was a surprise phone call from Mackie
Kahane (H. didn't understand his name. 'They're all called that here' – she
meant Abraham[22] and the juiverie communiste).[23] He then came out to us at
about 10 and we sat for a long time in the Babel over a coffee. He has been here
for a week, attached to a trade delegation as a journalist [...] complained about
the low intellectual level of the delegation and his own lack of freedom – he
had hardly been permitted to visit us, they appeared to suspect him. [...] He is
staying another week and wants to come to see us again.

[The central political issue throughout the Klemperers' stay: the Algerian
war.]

12th May, midday Saturday. CUP
Constant tiredness and depression.

Recently on the wall of a palais on the rue Mazarine in chalk: *Go home
juif!*[24]

[It turns out that the earlier refusal of a visa to Victor Klemperer had been
something of a minor cause célèbre, at least in academic circles; there had been
a letter of protest to the government signed by many professors etc.]
[...]

13th May, Sunday forenoon
[The previous day calls on Marcel Cohen.] Moved by the Café aux deux Magots.
I ate breakfast there regularly with Eva. 1914 or 192 ...? But did I really hear
Bergson lecture at the Collège de France, or did I only read and hear of it so
often? In my mind I see only Bédier 1913, Faguet 1903.[25] Touchingly patient,
Cohen would not rest until he had put us on a bus. [...]

16th May, Wednesday
[...]

On Sunday aft. we strolled through the Luxembourg Gardens with Mackie.
Excess of children and statues. [...]

Then to the Opéra Comique [...]

[Klemperer is received by the rector of the Sorbonne, who had also intervened
on his behalf.]

H. was meanwhile photographing monuments. I waited for her in the very
busy inner courtyard. – Addendum to the call on the rector: the functionary in

the antechamber wears a frock coat down to his ankles (like a conductor) and white cravat. How is so much old-fashioned dignity consistent with the constant kissing and embracing of all couples in the métro and on the street which almost amounts to public copulation and is seemingly not only allowed, but virtually de rigueur?

[...]

17th May, Thursday forenoon

At home during the day yesterday – rest and diary. After an early meal in the refectory we went early, having been warned, to the SARTRE lecture. It was supposed to begin at 9.15 in the evening, at 8.30 we found an already con- siderable queue, in which a lot of German was being spoken. The course was supposed to take place in the Salle Descartes. After quite a long time there was called out: Salle Richelieu, situated at right angles to the other hall. At that moment all order dissolved, there was an ever greater crush, soon accompanied by shouting and screaming, a wild pressing forward by fits and starts and storming against the closed double door, an absolute lack of discipline – inci- dentally it all seemed to be normal and was carried on with more humour than anger and brutality. [...] Amphitheatre, balcony running round, about 700–800 listeners. After 9.30 Sartre appeared at last and spoke for 2 mortal hours, to me monotonously. Sentence after sentence the same: loud beginning and then muttering, so that for me a sheerly physical not-understanding – to a lesser extent for H., but still 50% – was the result. Dominant impression: absolute unpretentiousness, in appearance as well – blond, plump man like some German grammar-school teacher, no gesturing, no airs, no mane of hair and no panache. Absolutely unvarnished, absolutely simple French, no images, no esprit. Logical structure and links: Don-que[26] ... Et ... par exemple[27] as the beginning of each sentence. But the content? Probably (following H.'s explanations): Man grows by use of the *tool*, by conquering matter, with the growth of man, the growth of the idea – history: development of the idea in matter, mutual influence and encouragement – Marxism in the right, if human action, if the human idea is central – *idealist* Marxism. Of which I understood the tiniest scraps and H. a great deal, in terms of content it does not seem particularly new. He seemed to be defending the *idealist* Marx against materialist interpreters and reducers ... What does that have to do with Existentialism as nihilism and angst and pessimism?? Repeatedly as catchwords: *action*, groupe. Was Sartre different before, has he developed – or was the way he was presented to us, before politically he became a (half)-ally of the SU, only a *distortion*??? – So with respect to linguistic understanding the evening was yet another failure; but it provided me with a surprising impression of the man Sartre: citizen, modest man, almost dry schoolteacher. One suspects neither the writer nor l'homme d'esprit[28] in him. – We then cooled down over ice cream and coffee at the Porte d'Orléans, once again did not get to bed until 2.

On the whole the stay here for me: a *void*, a dullness.

[...]

5th June, Tuesday forenoon

The Kirchners always write: 'Enjoy!' They do not suspect, how tired we both are, how much sense of duty and effort, to a degree, are involved. The real enjoyment will – must! – come afterwards. It is not the series of difficult-to-bear good days, but the knowledge of being able to take away so little of everything. [. . .]

12th June, Tuesday forenoon

[. . .] The 'empty' hour on Sunday gave us, apart from the study of shop windows, in particular of shoe shops, the church of St. Germain l'Auxerrois, the very Gothic and very isolated tower between church and cloister buildings. In the strikingly narrow and thereby long church a mass was just under way. Astonishing, how well and devoutly attended by people of *all* ages and all social strata: *Catholic* France, *living, believed Catholicism* – against that no Communism will make headway, which ultimately is itself also *faith* and only faith substitute. These convictions impress themselves on me every single day. And every day my scepticism grows stronger in every, absolutely every respect. I shall die more stupid, than I was at my birth. [. . .]

15th June, Friday forenoon

Nothing new in Paris – which is actually not a good sign. We are over-tired and cannot get out of our rut. In the mornings we're very late, because in the evening despite all our resolutions and for no good reason we're always up until half past one and sometimes almost half past two. No reason? It's so nice here when H. is sitting in bed at the desk and I am sitting at the desk and we're quietly reading our newspaper, eating cherries or sweets and philosophising, discussing etc. this and that. And all troubles, doubts, inadequacies, frictions out of love, hesitations are at an end for one day.

We spent one day entirely at home: Correspondence. [. . .] The other days a little *Nationale* [. . .] constant feeling of unease at what is probably a waste of time. Once dinner in our room. A joy and an affliction, both at once: we drink a whole bottle of wine that is better than the ordinaire, tastes wonderful and does not particularly agree with me, we take trouble shopping, the long baguette, the sardines, the cheese – the cheesemonger in Rue Richelieu is H.'s passion, delicate salads; costs double the refectory feed. I reproach myself for materialistically eating and boozing away our currency, I tell myself: *that*, too, is part of French studies. [. . .]

In *Monde* there is already the 7th instalment of Krushchev's secret report on Stalin.[29] H. reads it carefully – I glance at it with repugnance. It is quite dreadful and disillusions me completely. H. will cut out the most important literary or political newspaper articles – I shall anyway not get around to making notes as I had originally planned. [. . .]

18th June, Monday forenoon
[One of the highlights of the Paris visit is a dinner – from apéritif to dessert – to which the Klemperers are invited by the philosopher and historian Auguste Cornu. The latter, who taught at the Humboldt University in E. Berlin, talked, inter alia, about the way he was disregarded there.]

19th June, 9 p.m. Tuesday evening
[. . .]

[An East German art historian, Joachim Uhlitzsch,[30] telephones Klemperer, and they meet in a café.] I asked how the Stalin affair was being treated in the GDR, drew his attention to the publication in *Le Monde*, to *France observateur* etc. etc. He: the GDR press remained silent. He thinks both that and the whole suppression of foreign news to be just as mistaken as we do. He, too, is of the opinion that such isolation is foolish, harmful and *unnecessary*. [. . .] But he, too, realises that this truth cannot be kept secret, despite all isolation and all jamming stations. And of course he will buy the brochure to be published by *Le Monde* and of course read Koestler. – What is to become of the SED, what of the GDR, if the Ulbricht regime continues?
[. . .]

23rd June, Saturday forenoon
[. . .]

The constant press topics of this French quarter year: *Alger, le Cessez-le-feu; la déstalinisation, Adenauer – le dernier Mohicain de la guerre froide.*[31] [. . .]

27th June, Wednesday
[. . . Farewell receptions and dinners, the Klemperers are served ' "Kuskus", a Tunisian national dish' . . .]

[The Klemperers also observe the Chamber of Deputies in session:] For sure: a 'talking shop', for sure a new government every 2 months, for sure the power and corruption of finance, for sure quotation marks around 'free elections' – but for all that a bit more democracy than in our state, where the parliament is completely superfluous and plays the same sham role as in the Hitler state. I caught only one speaker's name: M. Pleven. A fat dark gentleman, in the middle of the very front row, he spoke repeatedly and with passion. Beneath us sat the right wing, the Gaziers said: Poujadistes.[32]
[. . .]

28th June, Thursday forenoon
[. . .]

At about 5 p.m. from the library to the airline office in the Rue de la paix.

[. . .] It is of course again H. who takes care of everything. So we are flying from here to Berlin via Brussels on Saturday, 14 July. [. . .]

4th July, Wednesday forenoon
[. . .]

[. . . Conversation with Pierre Abraham of the periodical *L'Europe* (close to the Communist Party)] General topic: Déstalinisation, émeute de Poznan.[33] I: je voudrais être consolé. J'ai cru a Staline, je suis si affligé. Et j'ai peur pour la DDR.[34] Why do they not make Ulbricht resign? I very much came out of my shell, perhaps too much. A. quoted Goethe: systolic and diastolic epochs.[35] He compared Stalin and Robespierre, agreed that the *Pravda* report was sweetened by comparison with the one in *Le Monde*, on the whole took exactly the same position as I do in my discussions with H., who rejects the Robespierre comparison and speaks of Stalin with profound animosity. [. . .]

5th July, Thursday forenoon
[. . .]

[. . .] we bought return tickets for Paris–Toulouse–Paris yesterday [. . .] [for a holiday in the South of France].

13th July, 9 a.m. Friday morning. Paris, Hôtel du Palais Bourbon, rue de Bourgogne
[. . .]

After sending off our packages we were now completely free, in a better mood, and in possession of some 70,000 fr. [. . .] which I cannot take back to the GDR, without handing them over for a $\frac{1}{4}$ of their West Mark value.

[. . .]

The résumé will now after all be left for Berlin or Dresden.

It is my hope that H. has drawn much profit for her life from this trip. I myself perhaps somewhat more than it appears to me now. Depends whether I have time to turn it to account.

18th July, Wednesday afternoon. Dresden
In Berlin [. . .] exploration of the city, as we explored Paris. Crucial impression – even in West Berlin: the emptiness of the roads, the absence of the stream of cars.

[. . .] Then (15 July) Peter and Inge appeared with their Western car and a fresh shirt for me: Drive to West Berlin to Anny Kl., whom I have not seen for years. Double experience: the woman and the city – West Berlin is more foreign and distant to me than Paris. Anny now over 70, very much aged, somewhat fixed gaze, stiff forced upright posture, absolutely deaf – one shouts into an ear trumpet with a long tube, she tries to read one's lips, one writes on scraps of paper – almost tragically enclosed and cut off from the world by this deafness. At the same time displaying the greatest, tormentingly tyrannical warmth, a self-consciously wealthy, simultaneously generous and calculating woman. She lives in an elegant pension on Meineckestr., close to Kurfürstendamm. For a while she was doing badly, now former property owners have been very well compensated in the Federal Republic, whereas the little people have not been compensated. [...] We invited Anny to visit us in Dresden, and she will no doubt come at some point. I was simultaneously moved and depressed by her, even a little shocked.

There was talk of family members, whom I knew as young people, and who are now well past 50 and in part already grandparents. – A few months ago Willy Jelski and his wife were in West Berlin, passed on greetings and left pictures of the children for us. – Felix's youngest son, Wolfgang, a doctor, on the American side during the war, is now a brain surgeon, F.'s daughter has married a second time and been divorced a second time (USA), Felix's eldest, Kurt, formerly training for the law, has opened a factory making cameras in South America (Buenos Aires?), he is childless and they have adopted a German child. One of Georg's sons studied agriculture and is now a farmer ... etc. etc.

And I with my 75 years am now the senior of the family and should have been buried long ago.

All day Tuesday I was still incapable of work, and even today everything is still lying around and has not been cleared up and this diary entry is all that I have managed at 6 p.m.

[...]

On Monday I found 25 copies of my 19ième, vol. I, here, and am really quite taken by the foreword, which I wrote *before* the 20th Party Congress or (but this very definitely!) before the Stalin business became known. [...] Gusti got the first copy of the 19ième. [...] Gusti has only now started corresponding with her son Karl again – after many years. He is a reader at Hamburg University, and sends greetings 'to old Klemperer', delighted, 'that he is flourishing again', which could not have been assumed in 1940 (on Karl's fearful visit to Caspar David Friedrich Strasse).

28th July, 7 p.m. Saturday. Dresden

Back to the same old thing [...] tiredness, dissipation of energies – when will I get around to new and complete work?

[...]

3–4 days careful, continuous reading of H.'s *Henri IV* dissertation.[36] An exemplary effort. Major historical survey, most meticulous use of materials, succinct statements, calm and independent aesthetic judgement – if this thesis came to me from a complete stranger, I would certainly give it a I. I have learned a great deal from it, and H. Mann's oeuvre, which I could never quite plough my way through, has come alive for me. – Except unfortunately I could not stop myself suggesting reconsideration of individual turns of phrase etc. And H.'s nerves are completely gone as far as this thesis and the following examination are concerned. At the same time she is still working on a couple of footnotes and addenda [. . .].

But already the proofs are eating me up again. The first sheets of vol. II of the 19ième are here, today a chapter from the second volume of the 18ième arrived [. . .]

[. . .]

9th August, Thursday evening

Postcard from [. . .] Falkenstein: 'Frau Gertrud Scherner succumbed to a stroke on 2 August.' It shook me, also weighs on my conscience. Why did I no longer go to see Trude Sch. in the last few years, as I occasionally intended after all, why did I no longer write to her? It was not just the difficulty of visiting Falkenstein in the restricted area of the Wismut zone, nor simply the lack of time for private correspondence. Rather Trude Sch.'s mental decline [. . .] after the death of her husband repelled me. [. . .] In addition to the bad conscience there is naturally the dreadful feeling of outliving my generation, of being forgotten by death – for how long?

[. . .]

19th August, Sunday forenoon. Dresden

Yesterday, 18 Aug., 'act of state' for Brecht – died unexpectedly on 14 Aug., heart attack, 58. I received an invitation by telegram: vanitas, 'showing one's face', combination with other business and went. Theater am Schiffbauerdamm, onstage only a lectern, behind on a white screen the Picasso dove, underneath in big letters Brecht's signature. Good seat in a box in the dress circle, but badly dazzled by the electric lights, voices of the speakers much too quiet (to the point of incomprehensibility). One did not miss much. All emphasised the Communist, the writer took second place. Ulbricht and Becher aiming $\frac{9}{10}$ at the ban on the KPD [in West Germany],[37] more propaganda than funeral orations. Then Wandel, then in very strongly accented German, expressing simple things complicatedly, Lukács [. . .]. In between, standing by the wings, in which the piano was concealed, Ernst Busch singing: 'Reih dich ein in die Arbeiter-Einheits-Front' [Take your place in the workers' united front].[38] That was the best thing. It all lasted an hour from 11–12 [. . .]. Shook hands with Abusch, Bloch – what snobbish nonsense, his lines under the Brecht picture in the *Sonntag*! – Hans Mayer.

What is the point of the 'blazing anger', the demonstrations against the KPD ban? – Where is the party freedom or any other kind of freedom here? We are merely the 'lesser evil'. [. . .]

20th August, Monday forenoon

[. . . Klemperer discusses with Rita Schober his teaching duties at the Humboldt University.] Conclusion: I lecture every last Wednesday in the month, altogether

6–7 double periods of Rousseau, summing up of the big, yet to be born Halle Rousseau course [. . .]

I justified what I had in truth simply forgotten: in the Zola footnotes in the 19ième I mention only her printed foreword not her ms post-doctoral thesis. I also said, that our views diverged, that was simply a fact. – 'Ah Victor, the divergence isn't so important any more.' She had added to her knowledge, she had put *one* stage of development of Marxism behind her – the recent events – shock: some people must have known. [. . .] Embitterment and worry: why does Ulbricht not go as Ràkosi[39] has done? – [. . .] Finally we agreed that the GDR was nevertheless 'the lesser evil' compared to the Federal Republic.

[. . .]

9th September, Sunday forenoon. Dresden

[. . .] Otherwise: reading and hesitation about the three overlapping topics: Rousseau, Feuchtwanger, Marie Antoinette, i.e. for my lectures, for the Greifen almanac article, for a study: Rousseau in the 20th century. I have not got as far as writing any of it. Also mixed up with this is my lecture: 'France after 30 Years'. It is to be delivered for the first time tomorrow in Erfurt. [. . .] On top of all that I also got my teeth into the odious, in terms of style and content – yet not uninteresting – Lukács (*The Historical Novel*).[40] [. . .]

[. . .]

1st October, Monday forenoon

On 26 Sept. [. . .] Rousseau lecture in Berlin. Very well attended, great deal of applause – but that was for the entertainment provided by friendly oppositional chat, in opposition to the Party, the running of the university, Rita etc. A little bit the role of a popular old cabaret artist.

Important on this Wednesday was meeting Walter Jelski[41] and his wife again. I recognised him immediately: face, voice (very Jewish), character. Not dis-likeable, not really likeable. Talented, unsound, opaque circumstances, a touch of the genteel schnorrer.[42] Had an adequate position as an insurance man in Jerusalem, has some debts there at the moment – but a savings account for the future. Left because of unbearable barbarism. Has very little money at present – but was in Switzerland for some weeks (relatives of his wife), is staying with friends in West Berlin, is slowly making his way to the USA, invited by Willy to join his travel agency. Will decide when he gets there . . . All uttered very easily, very cordially, very flamboyantly. Carefree, self-confident, not overbearing. Favourite word – still, and he is 52 or 53! – 'fantastic'. [. . .] The State Opera on Unter den Linden 'fantastic' – but the GDR otherwise deplorable and *HE* cannot live in such a totalitarian state. The best place is England – we read English books, German – we can no longer bear German voices. [. . .] The Jelskis continue their journey on 6 Oct.

This whole West–East split increasingly gets on my nerves, and in the long run the fact that it also to some extent runs through my own house cannot be ignored.

[. . .]

7th October, Sunday forenoon

[. . .]

My 75th is coming very horribly closer. It has been impossible to talk the Kahanes out of coming with their 2 children, the Humboldt Univ. is sending Rita, Heintze and Lilo. A 'reception' (hosted by the Federal Executive of the KB in Berlin and the District Executive Dresden KB) in the evening at the club house.

14th October, midday Sunday

My 75th is gradually ebbing away. Ocean of flowers, above all chrysanthemums, luxuriant and transient, honours, delegations, telegrams etc., from Pieck, from Grotewohl, from Dieckmann (especially long and cordial), from Justice Minister Hilde Benjamin, an address brought in person from Berlin by Central Committee member Heinz Herder [. . .], a delegation from Humboldt Univ.: Rita, her assistants Pohle and Lilo Limberg, wireless interview, newspaper articles – the best, surprisingly, in the *Sonntag* – but no Silver Order of Merit, *no* 'scholar of outstanding merit', *no* reprinting of my *LTI*. I shall go to the grave with my body lying askew. The 'reception' arranged by the Federal Executive of the KB in the club house on the Weisser Hirsch. Since the neighbouring Luisenhof with its kitchen has meanwhile burned down [. . .] the cold food was much more pitiful than recently for Laux, nothing but sausage sandwiches. And a couple of the customary toasts and a substantial speech by Rita; theme, with some variation: 'Inter sedia, between stools'. She should print it as my obituary. [. . .] The Kahanes were our guests for the day and until the next morning. With their two boys, who have developed nicely and become well-behaved. [. . .] Frau Duckhorn, who watched over them in the evening, admired their intelligent chess-playing. – What should I say of my feelings? My vanity was not entirely satisfied and the thought that I was attending a dress rehearsal for my own funeral never left me for a moment. It is time to find my way back to the numbing business of everyday life, 'my 76th' is really no different from my 75th. Senility one way and another.

[. . .]

Addendum to my 75th. The KB – Federal Exec. – sent a fine very modern wireless (Sachsenwerk-Olympia), our Super-Nova, taken from Nazi-Berger, bears the date 1928. If only I knew something of technology and had more time to listen to the wireless. Becher sent a telegram, Kneschke sent a much more friendly and intelligent letter than I would have imagined that worthy earth-bound proletarian and opponent of the intelligentsia to be capable of. From West Germany only Julius Wilhelm sent congratulations in a very warm-hearted letter, from France *only* Cohen.

[...]

What of the *big things* (18ième and Curriculum) will be completed? I lack the courage to draw back from everything else. I take flight into all the rest.

17th October, Wednesday forenoon

Yesterday Halle. Between lecture and seminar a small ceremony in the department. [...] Basket of flowers, speeches – the longest by a woman student, a pigskin-bound volume, probably first edition 1721 by Pufendorf: *De officio hominis et civis* [Of the duty of man and citizen].[43] When will I read it? [...] The most important thing: the folder with a part of the Festschrift study,[44] above all with Kunze's bibliography. Touching with its 350 entries, it both upset and humbled me. It begins with *Aus fremden Zungen* [From Foreign Tongues],[45] 1906, 5 pfennigs a line. I began as a journalist, have been one all my life and have remained between stools. Fame in the little cage of the GDR and only today and tomorrow – actually no longer today. On the whole it was after all a dress rehearsal for my burial. [...]

Then to the parents-in-law as usual.

The 'honours' for my 75th have truly not made me vain, in fact the contrary. And the bibliography is the last straw. I am a journalist – for life.

Vanitas: Kunze has nevertheless forgotten the very first article, in the *Börsencourier*, on Figaro, probably 1905. And an essay on Wilhelm Jensen, which I dictated to Eva until late at night – and then we took it from Wilmersdorf to the Anhalt Station.

Constantly on my mind, and new names keep occurring to me: everyone who did *not* congratulate me.

25th October, Thursday forenoon. Dresden

[...]

Profounder depression: for all mutual tenderness, consideration, assumption of blame – again and again truly grievous disharmonies. We returned from Berlin yesterday, H. had handed in her thesis, deliverance! We were going to celebrate. We bought a pretty unpolished opal in the little antique shop on Chemnitzer Platz. Then over to H.'s photographic shop where recently there had already been bother because of the delivery of the wrong little frame box. The response to my complaint about the manufacturer had been evasive, H. warned in advance that I should not upset myself. I became furious nevertheless, threatened as a deputy to make the case public as fraud. H: You are behaving like an informer, the people are afraid of being *taken away*, the Volkskammer is unpopular, they know you will be found to be in the right – if it was against a state shop and not a retailer, you would lose ... etc. All undoubtedly correct, all from the perspective of the opponent of the GDR, behind it all the equation of Nazism and Communism – all justified, *ultimately* justified, and yet so hurtful. And at the same time H. hates the West German money economy as much as I do. – Then we make up, then comes the wireless news, veiled language about

the uprising in Budapest[46] – 'Lindner already told me about it this morning' ...
'*You* are told by Lindner, by your parents ...' 'I wish I hadn't said anything ...'
That is H.'s involuntary exclamation of despair, which strikes me quite physically, I feel myself literally cut off from life, shut into a sick room, in my
anguish – truly angoisse, not fear – I fight for breath, and am in pain. H. acts
out of love, wants to protect me – I know that, and it is painful to me ... The
planned bottle of champagne was not drunk. Naturally there is immediate
reconciliation in mutual contrition, but the weight on my soul remains. I feel
more sorry for H. than I do for myself. She has given her heart to dying people.
Her father is worse again, she is constantly worried about *my* heart, I often talk
to her about my imminent demise. She will remain alone – childless. [...] I love
her greatly, and she is better, less corruptible, less vain, more steadfast than I.
[...] In short deeply black low spirits. To blame at present: the Hungarian
Uprising and its immediate consequences for me.
[...]

30th October, 9 p.m. Tuesday evening. Dresden

[...]

Constantly listening to Western broadcasts. To the confused and bloody news
of the Hungarian Revolution – against whom, for what? Truly a 'fight for
freedom' against the Russians?? Since yesterday evening the Israeli attack on
Egypt[47] – likewise completely opaque. Great agitation of my parents-in-law,
their absolute anti-Sovietism.

[...] Volkskammer scheduled for Friday – we shall therefore be there for *three*
days. The Kirchners would have liked me to stay at home. Yesterday Schmeiser
found my heart worse than usual, advised rest – but realised himself that *now*,
of all times, I did not want to miss this session of the chamber.

[...]

7th November, Wednesday afternoon

[On 30 Oct.] I received – a ray of hope – the [...] letter from Feuchtwanger,
whom Dietz [of Greifen] had sent my *Widow Capet* piece,[48] without my knowing.

Truly: the only ray of hope amidst tiredness, fragmentation of work and –
even more! – the feeling of hopeless disgust. Hungary[49] and Egypt – we always
listen to the squeaky Western stations – who stinks, who lies more, who is more
cruel? Are the *three* Kirchners right, if the West appears less inhuman to them,
is (or was?) the Hungarian 'counter-revolution' really a Fascist business? All this
murdering is unspeakably sickening.

Details, chronicle of the last week:

We were in Berlin from Wednesday, 31 Oct. until Friday, 2 Nov. Concern of
the Kirchner parents, we could be driving into a revolution (concern or concern
and hope?) [...]

Thurs. afternoon, KB parliamentary group meeting. I was outraged at the
plebian tone, in which Kuba delivered his 'statement' on Hungary.[50] [...] Arnold

Zweig and Franck complained about the language of the press [...]. Then on Friday the plenary meeting. Large force of police, in the foyer a whole lot of all-too-harmless civilians, whom with a bit of good will one could take to be drivers etc.; evidently secret police. The platform fuller than usual. Grotewohl: what he always says, for 2 hours, only even more imploringly than usual, virtually beseeching. No disunity, trust, no split, our friends in the East, the wicked Horthy people[51] etc. Rapturous applause, in which I joined, a little bit moved, a little bit sceptical, a little bit bored. And again and again – Ulbricht was sitting beside him – *we* are not replacing anyone in the government! [...]

9th November, Friday evening. Dresden
[...]
Yesterday telegram and telephone call from Berlin: I am now after all receiving the Fatherland Order of Merit in Silver. It depresses me, that H. (rightly!) to some extent despises this distinction and puts up with my vanity with unintentional mockery.
[...]

15th November, Friday forenoon. Dresden
[...] Hungary still depressing. The West talks of Hungary, the East of Suez – but for *us* Hungary remains the actual catastrophe. Always and everywhere the question: what is going to happen here? to Ulbricht? I personally: inwardly irresolute, hard-pressed by my nearest and dearest, sometimes even virtually alarmed. Gusti, for whom of course I am too bourgeois said, half-derisively, of the reactionary character of the *10,000* students here: 'They'll hang you, too.' Je n'en doute pas. Yet at least 60% (60% is the law) of the 10,000 TH students are from working-class homes. Tormenting for me personally are the attacks of our press on Cardinal Mindszenty.[52] His picture in the *Sächsische Zeitung* – very emaciated surrounded by soldiers – the 'Christian' (in quotation marks) with counter-revolutionary soldiers. H. regards the man as a martyr. [...] In France demonstrations against the PCF, a party building in Paris set alight [...]

Tues. aft. from Halle to Berlin. Yesterday in the 'official residence' there, conferment of the order. The big bare room in the palace [...]. High white walls divided by yellow longitudinal stripes (marble?), white putti in the corners of the high ceiling, in the room half a dozen leather armchairs in front of a desk. A few persons to be decorated, a couple of officials [...]. It was all conducted rapidly and without much ceremony. [...] After some waiting [President] Pieck arrived. Fairly thin, walking somewhat stiffly. [...] I said my two sentences: For the 3rd time I had the good fortune to be standing in front of the President – the first time, on 5th Feb. 1946, you chaired the Central Cultural Congress of the Communist Party of Germany. How much has been achieved since then! Our thanks: further confident work ... Then a servant brought half a dozen glasses of champagne on a tray – we drank standing, Pieck smiled at everyone around him and left. At the door Pieck's daughter shook my hand: 'It was so nice that you recalled 1946.' The whole show lasted less than fifteen, the act itself less than five minutes. [...]

[...]

2nd December, Sunday afternoon. Dresden

[On 29 November, after more than a year, Klemperer attends the meeting of his class at the Academy. The topic of discussion: foreign language teaching. Priority, French or English?] Feeling of triumph, I was glad I was no longer isolated with respect to the Academy, but it was a very ambivalent feeling of triumph. They consider me no more than a journalist. I strongly supported what had already been decided in the praesidium: to be represented [on this issue] by Franck, a natural scientist. [...] After the meeting I asked for a private talk with Franck. 'Why am I not in the Saxon Academy? – it offends me deeply, and Krauss will never propose me.' [...]

This afternoon – commemoration of the dead a week ago! – we drove up to Eva's grave. Because it's the done thing. I do not know what to do with myself up there. We walked back. Piercing wind, I felt very bad, H. shocked, I without philosophy as always.

[...]

12th December, 11.30 a.m. Wednesday evening. Dresden

Yesterday in Halle the usual. Very exhausting, as my day began at 4.30: torture of the Rousseau lecture. [...] Niemeyer publishers [Halle] are at last taking over the *LTI* – at last, if it passes the censor. Will it? Hitler's 'unified list' [of candidates] and election propaganda. They could feel it described them. On the other hand the Zion chapter becomes acceptable. It is anti-Israeli, after all, I triumph, so to speak.

For the past 2 weeks Wolfgang Harich, editor at Aufbau,[53] has been under arrest, and also, as I have just heard from Doris Kahane, Walter Janka, his boss. [...] Mother Kirchner has already brought the rumour: Kantorowicz also.[54] The rumour, and the fact that it is believed or thought possible! We told ourselves, then Hadermann will have to examine H.'s thesis. But at home a telegram was waiting, Kantorowicz wants to speak to H. tomorrow morning. Now there!

[...]

20th December, 6.30 p.m. Thursday. Dresden

[...]

H. meanwhile had a conversation with Kantorowicz. He was, therefore, *not* arrested? But he was, said H., very depressed, uncommunicative and gloomy. He was very reluctant to say it – there are people in the Party, who are his enemies. [...] H. suspects, no doubt rightly, that K. was 'picked up' for an interrogation and – provisionally? – released. That could happen to me, too. At

any rate I am further away from the firing line and a little bit of a *protected species*. An old gentleman like me no longer needs to be taken seriously.
[...]

22nd December, 5 p.m. Saturday

[...]

Short friendly letter from Otto Klemperer in London. He is now a 'double grandfather'. One grandson by his eldest, who is serving as captain in the medical corps at present, the other by his second eldest, who is a chemist at Melbourne University; his youngest is just preparing for his school-leaving certificate and is going to study history. What a family story! From Rabbi Klemperer, my father, by way of his son, who treated Lenin, to his son, professor of physics in London, to the child just born in Melbourne. Material for how many novels! How limited the Comédie humaine, the Rougon Macquart[55] measured against it!

26th December, Wednesday forenoon

Kitschy snow-covered picture-postcard Christmas – frost and snow began on the 24th precisely. H. is getting her first skiing practice [the Klemperers were planning a skiing holiday in Czechoslovakia ...]. Usual sentimentalities on all sides, usual depression on my side. [...] Peace over gramophone records and goose and wine ... the same, the same, the same (bête, farce, triste), and always the loathsome feeling of the closeness of death. – Nevertheless: so far we have got through the time quite well.

Even a little work. [...]

The parents-in-law gave me *The Diary of Anne Frank*. So far, as Mother Kirchner predicted, disappointing. But I am only at the beginning and am leafing more than reading. Some of it is already familiar, from others' accounts, many press reports of the worldwide success of the stage version, which is being performed in the Youth Theatre here. So far a poor kid – but still a vain and silly, somewhat snobbish girl in her teens and nothing more. But I am at the first days of the warehouse imprisonment.

[...]

30th December, 8 a.m. Sunday. Dresden

[...]

In *Neues Deutschland* an intertitle in bold letters in a programmatic *Pravda* article: '*There is no Stalinism.*' Mother Kirchner recently, as a visit to Gusti (who has 'flu) was being considered: 'I'm always afraid my husband might see the *Stalin picture* in her room.' (On this 1) I myself have never seen it: 2) Gusti's political obstinacy also gets on my nerves, hardly any less than the Kirchners' opposite tendency.) [...] Notice in *Berliner Zeitung*: Kantorowicz invited to give lectures in France. In the New Year's Eve edition of *Neues Deutschland* a short extract from Kantorowicz's *Spanish Diary* [. . .]. Immediately we both conclude: 'So he is not out of favour after all!'

31st December, Monday evening, New Year's Eve
Résumé

Superficially a successful year. The Italian–French journey April–mid-July: the honours on my 75th, the Festschrift, the Order. Re-published my 19ième, vol. I and *Vor 33–Nach 45*.

In fact: not a day on which I was not aware of my decline. Failing memory, tiredness, inability to work, the constant thought of death, of nothingness, of the absence of individual consciousness. France without any achievement, repeatedly, especially in the Bibl. Nationale the terrible feeling of emptiness. New work, nothing but the preface to Diderot's *The Nun*, and the *Widow Capet* article. Otherwise constant proofreading and sterile preparation of lectures, which I find ever more difficult. Without hope of really being able to complete the 18ième and the Curriculum.

[. . .]

I would like to be able to maintain the appearance of courage and not be a burden on Hadwig for too long. My greatest wish: to kick the bucket without a long sickness.

1957

2nd January, Wednesday forenoon. Dresden
The year began with a *terrible cold*, which suddenly and cruelly descended on me. H. went alone to practise skiing for an hour, after last Sunday receiving initial instruction with Schmeiser and his two little daughters in Oberbärenburg.
[...]

9th January, 8 a.m. Wednesday morning. Dresden
At 9 I'm going to talk in the Dresden Teachers' Centre on German–French literary relations in the 19th century. Preparation cost me almost half a day.
[...]

Afternoon
With the teachers – 150–200 – again a suspiciously large amount of applause, they are happy at everyone who speaks more freely, and when I say of myself, 'I am to some extent a protected species,' then the jubilation is of course particularly great. [...]

13th January, Sunday forenoon
[...]
   A great deal of tiredness. – Also much grievance in political matters. Father Kirchner's fanatical hatred of the Soviets, altogether the mood of the Kirchner parents does to a certain extent rub off on H. In her impassioned feeling she does see more blood-letting, more force on the Eastern side than on the Western. Perhaps, probably even, it is egotism, more than anything else, that binds me to the GDR. *Here* I am someone, *here* I am wealthy, here I am a great scholar. What, of all that, would I be in the West? My belief in the pure intentions, the

pure humanitas of the Soviets is long gone. But over there they are not any better, only more polished. And we here are the lesser evil nevertheless. Besides I am more insensitive and egotistical than H. . . . No time, to think over that.
[. . .]

19th January, Saturday forenoon. Dresden

[Volkskammer. . .] 1) Lengthy Grotewohl report on the new treaties with Moscow,[1] which is giving us a loan, to whom we remain utterly loyal with respect to Hungary, explicit thanks to the Soviet troops as saviours of Communism – hostility to Adenauer, rejoicing over China (meeting with Chou En-Lai). 2) Final acceptance of the Laws for the Extension of Democracy. The core of it is not quite clear to me. a) Central authority – autonomy for lower bodies – that always remains contradictory to me. b) if then 'the people' themselves really are the rulers, if the Volkskammer really is the supreme authority – what is the Party, what the central Committee, what the Politburo, what Staliniculus Ulbricht?? And why the game with *parties*, when only *one* rules? I do not understand it, I am an old liberal, and my temporarily suppressed liberalism is showing ever more strongly through the layer of red make-up. [. . .]
[. . .]

29th January, Tuesday forenoon

Politics ever more loathsome and agonising, at home and outside. On Thursday, the 24th, closed session of deputies. For hours nothing but the torture of the absolute waste of time (and of shivering in the badly heated large chamber). The democracy extension law was discussed at great length, I did not understand the details. [. . .] Internal politics: there must be no split between working class and intelligentsia. The intelligentsia arrives at its Socialism all too deeply rooted in the idealist side, overlooking the economic etc. necessities. [. . .]

At home often disagreements, upsets, bitterness because of politics. Again and again I feel sorry for H. But it is easier for her, because she has her faith – and her parents. Marxism is a faith like Catholicism – *I* am without faith.
[. . .]

1st February, Friday morning

[. . .]

Stimm,[2] the Tübingen man, has declined the chair and accepted an assistant professorship in *Saarbrücken*. Saarbrücken rated more highly than the Humboldt University! How many sad conclusions can be drawn from this trifling fact! With respect to the general GDR situation, with respect to me personally. Always in the place where one does not properly count. From Jews' star to Jews' star. Ever since I have been a big name in the GDR, its Academy, its Humboldt University, the GDR, the Academy and Humboldt University wear the Jews' star.
[. . .]

20th February, 7 p.m. Wednesday. Dresden

[...]

Very limited 'pushing forward' of Voltaire and Feuchtwanger.

[... Schmeiser, Klemperer's senior doctor friend, long critical of conditions in the GDR, after complaining about the technical and scientific backwardness of both East Germany and the Soviet Union, relates the following:] Schmeiser has appointed a doctor, who was pardoned and released from Bautzen Prison after $4\frac{1}{2}$ years. Was sentenced to 8 years because as police doctor he had out of pity passed on secret messages from prisoners. Many doctors had been sentenced for the same reason. [...] Treatment at the beginning very bad, later a little better. But even now still methods to wear the prisoner down: sleeplessness through searchlights, the sound of running water ... As one has heard of it from the SU, as one has heard of it from the USA ... On the (eternally jammed) Western station they call themselves the 'free world'. It makes me angry again and again. Is one really a little more free there? Immoral in a different way to make up for it. Terrible times – I believe in fact 100× worse than before 1914. Or is that no more than the vieillard's 'good old days'?? – *Deep depression.*

27th February, 7 p.m. Wednesday. Dresden

Berlin Thurs. and Frid. 21–22 February was especially interesting (and exhausting) this time. In the forenoon lecture from 10–12, hence up shortly after 4, departure shortly after 6. On the *Contrat Social.*[3] I repeatedly emphasise: I am the counterweight to the 'Leipzig School', I am a literary historian. [...] After the Class meeting [of the Academy] a short private conversation with Frings. Substance: I: disappointed by my [Party?], disappointed by West Germany – I am a Communist. He: 'We all are, but what is happening here is a "shameless betrayal of Communism".' Frings is a Catholic, related to Cardinal Frings,[4] dissatisfied with West German conditions, even more so with conditions here. [...]

Evening: Volksbühne, Sartre's play *Nekrassov.*[5] Actually two worn-out themes intertwined. [...] But with Sartre every word is clever – *so* clever, that at speed I miss a great deal; and every word is satire, and the satire thrusts at Right and Left. [...]

[... Friday morning, Kulturbund Executive Committee meeting; condemnation of intelligentsia deviations etc.] More interesting than this official stuff was Bloch's defence.[6] He first of all mentioned an Ulbricht letter, according to which he is confirmed in his post – but he has resigned (or been forced to resign??) from his lectures as a 'revisionist' and because he had taken a stand against the university basic course. I do not know what is true, I have not followed the whole affair; but in the Academy plenum I told him without further ado, I stood by him; he replied: he had not doubted that for a moment. (We are de facto quite alien to one another, I do not care for him as a snob and as an intimate friend of Werner Krauss.) At the Executive Committee, therefore, he spoke in a quiet voice and with considerable dignity: no one could have any doubts of his Marxist past. And in the present he had evidently been denounced by blockheads or by the malicious. He was not against the basic course as such, but very much against the complete lack of education of many university teachers, whose ignorance and narrow-mindedness caused mischief. And 'revisionism'? He could not repeat mechanically, he had to go on developing ... Sparse applause. [...] I (having applauded ostentatiously [...]) [...] said the mistaken hostility to education [of e.g. the Minister of Popular Education] appeared to be linked to some degree with what Bloch had expressed. [...]

1st March, Friday evening
Once with Gusti W. [...] She was especially doddery and moribund. [...] H. sees as a sign of the approaching end, the fact that several months ago Gusti re-established contact with her renegade son, Karl. He is now assistant professor in Hamburg, he is coming to Dresden for 10 days, giving a lecture at the TH – which for an academic from the West is almost an act of courage. [...] Gusti very contradictory. Always the especial love of England and always obstinately Marxist-Russian; always surrounded by the most stupid female Party comrades, always full of contempt for the Party's hostility to education.

[...] This is the 'Day of the National Armed Forces';[7] the newspapers have been full of the appropriate pictures and articles for a while. H.'s profound aversion to the regime depresses me greatly. I can no longer contradict her with complete conviction, have been unable to so for a long time – but I am attached to our cause and hate the Nazism of Bonn even more than our stupid and unimaginative dictatorship. I have sunk deep into scepticism and apathy, fear nothingness, and yet already feel myself to be in that nothingness. Fundamentally I am indifferent to what happens to Germany, to a world in which my time has run out. All I still care about, is compensating H. for everything which I can no longer offer her. [...]

A little while ago Lindner bought a film camera and showed us the first results this evening. I was shocked at my appearance. Walking between department and university in Halle beside Silzer or Heintze. Bent, tentative, an old man of 80. Everything foretells my end. I no longer have a right to life. And I am unable to rest content. I should read nice things for pure pleasure and give up wanting to produce. I cannot do it and torture myself.

17th March, 7 a.m. Sunday morning. Dresden
At 9.30 we have to start out on our journey to Tatranska Lomnica [for the skiing holiday] which I am not much looking forward to.

The past good two weeks passed historyless, as it were, for me. Apart from the usual routine I wanted at least to finish the Feuchtwanger, and I don't want to mention the Voltaire at all any more. [...] tiredness, irresolution, sleeping too long, ever new lecture-course difficulties.

[...]

[...] H. is dearer to me every day, and every day I see the impetuousness of her nature in questions of conscience and conscientiousness. That gives rise to hysterical outbreaks, followed by remorse. Problem point no. 1: politics, Stalin, Hungary, the political trials, all murders, all breaches of the law etc.; point 2: the preparation for the oral examination ... I told her that Kantorowicz judged the thesis magna cum laude, had particularly emphasised the scholarly worth of the concordances. [...]

[...]

20th March, Monday forenoon. Hotel – desk [Lomnica]

[The Klemperers spent three weeks in Czechoslovakia, staying overnight in Prague both on the journey out and on the return trip.]

[Klemperer had frequently been in Prague as a young man, and both his parents had been born and grown up there, before the demolition of the old Jewish ghetto. The Klemperers look at the oldest synagogue and arrange for a guided tour of the old Jewish cemetery on their return journey. Klemperer feels a sentimental-literary attachment.]

[...] I did not tell the guide, at least not for the time being, that I am very closely connected to Prague; he will in any case have got that from my name in the visitors' book. [...]

I have begun Feuchtwanger's *Josephus*. It gripped me from the first page. But 3 volumes, 1500 pages, and I read so slowly.

[The routine of the first part of the holiday is that Hadwig goes up to the practice ski slopes until the afternoon, while Victor reads etc. in the hotel.]

30th March, 11 a.m. Saturday. Desk

[...]

I made notes on the second vol. I can't put the book down, I get so much from it. – Josephus – Voltaire ... I would still so much like to write a few things. And again and again depression. Too old. I find the smallest slope, flight of steps difficult. Memento. And my failing memory for names [...].

10th April, Wednesday. Dresden

[...]

On Friday evening (5 April) the car took us [...] to Poprad. In the sleeping car we had a bigger compartment than on the journey out, it also had well-made beds, but apart from that it was shockingly dusty and dirty [...]. After almost exactly 12 hours we arrived in Prague at 8 a.m. on Saturday. This time the Cedok[8] man waiting for us was an elderly painter, who then left us to ourselves until the early afternoon of Sunday, 7 April. We got a good room in the Palace Hotel in the city centre [...]. After a thorough wash and a coffee snack we spent the morning shopping. [...]

The next morning, Sunday, 7 April, to the Old Synagogue. We found it, but not the entrance. A young man, fabulous oriental eyes under the round kippa, observed us for a while. Then to me: Are you a Jew? No, but we were looking

for the entrance. He showed, asked in jargon, naively importunate, whether H. my daughter? No, my wife. 'Such a young woman, such a beautiful young woman!' He shook her hand. What beautiful warm hands! I did not know, whether to be outraged, or whether I should accept his behaviour as oriental courtesy. H. laughed, very amused. Meanwhile the tourist guide came out of the synagogue, recognised us immediately – [...] took charge of us, left the bocher[9] standing, who looked at us in surprise. The cemetery immediately adjoining the synagogue: a confused forest of gravestones in a small space. The dead are supposed to lie 7 deep one above the other. The guide told us a great deal. Animal pictures: the *Hirsch* [deer] family, Bär [bear] etc. – The bride under the chupa[10] – but *without* a face ... Pebbles on the edge of the Rabbi Loew's[11] monument. (To H.: place a stone on it, then you'll do well in your doctoral examination.) The man was widely travelled, well read, in comparison to the bocher the purest European. We had written our names in his book 3 weeks earlier, under hers H. had written: De profundis clamavi;[12] that gladdened his heart. – There was a shower of rain after H. had taken her last two photographs. [...] Lindner was waiting for us at 6.30 a.m. [on the 8th].
   [...]
   Then the catastrophe. Telegram and telephone call from Berlin: H.'s doctoral examination brought forward to Mond., 15 April, my 'secret' with Rita [Klemperer had known of the change of date, but had been sworn to confidentiality] has depressed me all this time. Now the effect is incomparably worse than I had expected. Truly hysterical breakdown. [...] She feels betrayed, betrayed in her dignity as an independent decision-making person, treated like an 'Ibsen woman', like Nora in the *Doll's House*. [...] I have never seen H. so desperate and so angry. I feel helpless. Her mother is better able to deal with her; already yesterday she engaged H. in revision conversations. [...] Now in the evening (10 p.m.) H. seems a little calmer. Will it last? Really, I am glad that her parents are coming tomorrow.
   [...]

15th April, 5 p.m. Monday. Berlin, Romance Languages Institute

For an hour now H. has been examined upstairs in the German Studies Institute by Rita and Kantorowicz. She was deathly pale and completely shattered when she was taken upstairs by Rita, Lilo and others, the last few days were an unending torment. [...]
   I gave my Rousseau lecture (*Nouvelle Héloise*)[13] from 12–2, then went to the State Secretariat. [...]
   Here since 3, waiting since 4.
   [...]

19th April, 11 p.m. Good Friday. Dresden

At 6 p.m. on Monday H. came down to the Romance Languages director's room delivered. Dr phil magna cum laude. 'Since she is your wife, it was impossible to give her summa cum,' said Rita. With that the worst was over. – We bought our supper and a little bottle of wine at the state shop on Alexanderplatz, sat quietly in our room and soon went to bed utterly exhausted. The next day [. . .] we left for Halle after 7 a.m. [. . .]. [This was for the celebrations marking the 80th anniversary of the chair of Romance Languages and Literatures at Halle University.]

20th April, Saturday forenoon

At 2 p.m. on Wed. the closing speech. In the 'Urquell' another meeting with Rheinfelder and Wilhelms [West German academics]. In private conversation Rheinfelder told me in the East dialectical materialism ruled, in West Germany common materialism plain and simple. He was evidently pleased to hear, that H. was a believing, 'practising' Catholic. Later mother and daughter Kirchner asked me whether I was right to have attributed the predicate 'practising'. The answer was not quite unambiguous. The annual communion, the sacrament of marriage . . . [. . .]

30th April, 7 a.m. Tuesday morning. Before the drive to Halle

After 5 years of marriage: ' "Practising" made me think of it – we should get married.' Yesterday evening, at first I didn't understand. With much squirming, she did not want to torment me . . . but then she could go to communion. And nothing would be asked of me, no profession of faith, no prostration – the business with children did not apply anyway – and only in the sacristy and no one would know about it, and the priest would promise to keep silence under the seal of confession . . . Add to this: a) the witnesses, chance, the parish register, Rias [Western radio]? The danger of being a laughing stock to the world, if not of even greater harm. The old man gets religion, is tied to his wife's apron strings etc. b) the inner depression: so great a difference between H. and myself. I am unable to understand this way of thinking and feeling. And why more strongly now? c) With what right could I refuse? If it is a matter of conscience for H.? What is it for me? Inwardly nothing at all. [. . .] How can one be *so* alien to one another and yet *so* love one another?

1st May, Wednesday morning

I hung out the heavy red flag – with very mixed feelings. H. had to come to my aid.

[Klemperer is irritated by a discussion with the publisher who wants to bring out a new edition of *LTI* – only 2000 copies to be printed, and a demand for changes to phrases and passages which might be misunderstood in the contemporary context.] I said: I would not change a word, either the historic text appears, or it does not appear. I can wait. But it is ignominious for the GDR. I could at any time publish with Rowohlt or in Austria or Switzerland. I promised *not* to do that, because I do not want to harm the GDR, no matter how little I agree with its cultural policy. Redslob [the editor]: of course the West would publish the book – over there they would think nothing of publishing it in the same historical series as Hitler's memoirs! I declared that I was withdrawing my book.

[...]

15th May, Wednesday forenoon

Towards 8 p.m. on Saturday (11 May) in the church (sacristy or consulting room) as arranged. It was, of course, still very light, but around there Bernhardstr. consists of many ruined houses and is deserted. The mere feeling that one does not want to be seen is unpleasant. Father Huber, a cheerful Swabian, about 40 at most, does not yet know anyone in Dresden – H. said: not pompous in the pulpit either, hearty rather; approached the business with man of the world amusement – Jesuitical? naive? both? at any rate in an obliging way. I emphasised: 'inward and outward position'. Faith: a blessing, which I lack, [but] responsible for my wife's tranquillity of conscience. (Why after 5 years???) – Made ridiculous and harmed if it becomes public ... He: it will certainly remain secret, and no one would inquire as to *my* faith. Only [there was] all kinds of paperwork. To my surprise H. had my Protestant baptismal certificate with her (the second!).[14] I said, I had left the church many years ago. That did not need to be noted, [but] I had been baptised; otherwise there would be greater difficulties, a higher authority would have to be approached: whereas like *this* the bishop was sufficient. Bishop Spülbeck in Bautzen [...]. In Bautzen no one would pay attention to the name, such cases simply had to be dealt with properly and officially. I: to my regret I doubted that our postal confidentiality was absolute. [...] Father Huber: then the documents could be sent by courier ... Afterwards we conversed for quite a while. I talked about the Order of St Vincent[15] nurses and about the reading room of the arch-episcopal seminary[16] in Paderborn and about French Catholic poetry and was very pro-Church and tolerant ... But I do not feel quite at ease with this business in any respect ... Amusing was the Father's argument delivered with liveliness and evident conviction. Of course nothing can be proved rationally, of course one must have the *blessing* of faith, of course it was 'simply a mystery'. But if there were no justice, no compensation in the world to come – I had said 'Your ethics is also mine, except that I cannot apply love thine enemy to bloodhounds' – '*if* that were not so, then the whole of existence would be meaningless!' But that is precisely the issue: *whether* it has a meaning! – H. was very contented, and we walked home in the protective darkness. He would let H. know as soon as the documents were back, the whole thing would last 'two minutes', there were witnesses in the house, and no one would get wind of anything, the father assured me once again. He could also come to us, but that would cause more of a stir.

Halle yesterday (Fénelon[17] lecture) normal.

Other business: Voltaire, a couple of pages of *The Good Woman of Sezuan*.[18]

My signature on the protest against the Brecht–Horst Wessel comparison of [West German] foreign minister Brentano.[19] [...]

[...]

23rd May (and probably 24th May). Berlin, Romance Languages Institute

[...]

24th May, Friday

[...] On Tues. 21 May, in Halle, there were two great gratifications. 1) Hadwig's lecturing appointment. In Hadermann's World Literature department – (German Studies overcrowded) – French influences on the 19th century German novel. [...] 2) *LTI* (cf 1st May) my emphatic no had an effect after all. 'Censorship' had evidently only been a pretence, and only the general fear of the Party on the part of the publishers had been involved. Redslob brought me the signed contract. 'Unaltered reproduction of the first edition'; half a dozen lines as foreword: any change would efface the value of the historical statement. The book is to go to the printer immediately. Only 2000 copies, probably at 11–12M. I am agreeable – as I still have hopes of Reclam for later on.

[...] In the evening we were at the Kahanes'. Max badly affected by concentrated inoculations; in a couple of weeks he is going to New Delhi as correspondent, the family is to join him three months later. For a 'few years'. – What will have become of us in a few years? Kahane's confidence in the present course also appears to be extremely limited.

[...]

29th May, Wednesday forenoon. Dresden

[I used] the Sunday and Monday to prepare my last Halle lecture, i.e. I studied my Figaro chapter, which had long ago slipped my mind. It is so good, that I shall perhaps publish it by itself in the university periodical. This volume 2 of the 18ième *must*, it *must* be completed.

[...]

30th May, after 6 p.m. Thursday. Ascension Day. Dresden

[...] Now [...] this momentous 29th [of May ...].

Then after 7 p.m. down to our Father Huber on foot. There was great bustle in the courtyard, adolescents for a singing lesson. The father came out and asked us to wait for a while. We walked up and down the empty yet for me still too busy street, the children dispersed, the father appeared again in plain clothes – awkward mood [in me], almost as in the restaurant in Falkenstein in 1945 – who knows me?[20] The father very nice and unaffected, he understood the awkwardness of my situation. He offered me the church with candles; I asked for the sacristy and complete lack of ceremony. He had a nun come and a gentleman in plain clothes – Hadwig told me: his colleague, soutanes and white copes were hanging on the walls, he put on both in front of us, placed the stola on top, read a very short prayer from a sheet without any solemnity, asked: do you of your own free will? ... I said yes, H. the same. 'Then place your hands together.' He wrapped a tip of the stola around them. I declare you joined ... now a very short prayer ... the father congratulated, the two witnesses congratulated and disappeared. The whole thing had lasted two minutes at the very outside and was simpler and less formal than the registry office wedding 5 years ago. It had given the father evident pleasure to take part in a little conspiracy and to make the matter a little easier for me. He reassured me, I was not the first case of this kind. As already 2 weeks ago I had rather more an impression of good-tempered naturalness than of Jesuitical cunning. I gave him 50M 'for the poor'. He said, that was too much – his church evidently looks after very simple people, H. is a very rare bird there. We invited the father to visit us next week. He gladly accepted, he would be dressed entirely in mufti, even come without his 'tradesman's licence' (he meant the clerical collar) and on his moped. H. was outwardly very calm, but I felt the agitation from her cold hands. The conclusion of the absolutely unceremonial ceremony was a brief sign of the cross over H., who crossed herself and then, as we went out through the dark space of the church, knelt before the altar. – Today she was up early and went to mass. Now she was allowed to receive communion. On an empty stomach – we breakfasted after her return. We normally do not breakfast before 12 or 1 anyway. During the whole ceremony I stood around with my arms hanging down, I am also inwardly quite detached. All that matters to me, is that H. has her peace of mind. That she takes the matter – the 'club rules' as she and her mother call it – so seriously now, is evidently a reaction against the pig-headedness of the course here, and was occasioned by Rheinfelder's question about practising. And I myself? Am I merely tolerant? Or am I, too, not acting somewhat Jesuitically – not with respect to faith, but with my see-sawing between the parties? [...]

8th June, Saturday afternoon
[...]

On Thurs. evening (6 June) Father Huber visited us – like a conspirator [...] his clerical collar [...] hidden under a scarf. [...] We got on well. Why, he says, should God not have the right to work miracles. The resurrection is 'proven' after all, Lourdes, too, has acknowledged miracles to show etc. etc. H. listened quietly amused. She and the father simply have the blessing of faith; with him, a good-natured nitwit without much education (seminary without university), it's understandable, with her – a miracle. Father Huber is satisfied with me, a) because the Jews – he takes that literally and racially and completely seriously – simply are the chosen people, and b) because with my ethical views I am 'close to heaven's gate'. [...] It then remained comically undecided, whether his 'close to heaven's gate' referred to my great age or to my great morality.

[...]

[From 9 June the Klemperers attend a Romance Languages and Literatures Conference in Mainz, West Germany. They stay on in the West until the 22nd.]

13th June, 10 a.m. Thursday. Mainz, Hotel Mainzer Hof
[...]
My mood: as always when travelling. The constant undertone: Why still? Forgotten by death, 'written off' etc. But as long as I am still vigorous, I take everything offered and make an effort – with about 75% success – not to cast too much shadow on H.'s pleasure. [...]
We left Dresden at 9 p.m. on Whit Sunday, in Frankfurt at 9 a.m. on Monday. The train very slow and empty. [... In Frankfurt:] always the *one* perception: poverty of the GDR, impotent struggle against steel, coal etc. etc. property. [...] Recovered a little on the train to Mainz (about 45 minutes).
[...]

18th June, 10 a.m. Tuesday. Tübingen, Hotel zum Ochsen
Politics
The mayor in Mainz. Reception in the town hall. Cordial, the guests from 'Middle Germany'[21] receive a friendly mention. [...]
[The 17 June holiday:] Because this 17 June yesterday is a *'National Holiday'* here in memory of the failed liberation uprising in the GDR. All shops, schools etc. shut. [...]

23rd June, 'Election day'. Dresden
[...]
Our passport was valid until 22 June – because after all the famous democratic election was taking place on the 23rd.[22] [...]

1st July, Monday forenoon. Dresden
Since return on the 22nd fragmented and overwhelmed by too many demands.
[...]
Main work, yesterday the introduction to Voltaire memoirs at last sent off.
[...]
On Tue. 25 June in Halle. The contingent of new students. Ten allowed (not many more for Berlin and Leipzig either), three of them impossible – without knowledge of French, of Latin. – Hartmut Haress 'taken away'.[23] Doctoral candidate, comrade, Russian lecturer. A group has been 'taken away' – leaflets – house searches. His wife (two children!) also studied under me, came to tell me. Did I note my reply in Tübingen to Schneider's [East German historian] question: Where would you like to live? *'On the moon!'*

Now in addition to that the *Sonntag* affair 'fiction and reality' [In an article entitled 'Fictions and Realities' in the newspaper *Sonntag* of 26 May, 1957, the chief editor, Bernt von Kügelgen, had attacked the organisers of the conference marking the 80th anniversary of the Romance Languages and Literatures Department at Halle University. He accused them of propagating a 'non-committal fictional re-unification' by using 'phrases like love, understanding and common language'. On 3 June Klemperer sent a letter to the newspaper protesting against the article, and emphasising that simply by appearing publicly in the GDR the West German participants had demonstrated the courage of their convictions: Klemperer's letter was not published.] [...]

[...]

8th July, Monday forenoon

Only as I am writing [...] do I remember: 8 July, 1951, the day Eva died. And I sit here in the wealth and the happiness of my new marriage. It would be proper for me to go up to the cemetery and place flowers. But that would be a troublesome and mendacious gesture. I shall be lying beside Eva soon enough. And I cannot conceal from myself, the fact that I am disgracefully happy with H. and love her more and more ... No time for lyrical flirtations. [...]

[...]

21st July, Sunday morning

I shrink back from the 18ième: *not* because of fragmentation, too many commitments, also *not* out of fear of no longer being able to produce, but because the book is wrongly structured, because the division 'here Voltaire – there Rousseau' does not work. [...]

26th July, Friday forenoon

In the Central Committee in recent days speeches in the Culture Section entirely in accord with the rabble-rousing tendency. Against Hans Mayer, against Kantorowicz, against Becher himself. The dirtiest prole mouth: Kuba. More moderate but following the same line, Hager etc. What do I still have in common with these people? What purpose does the Kulturbund still serve? [...] Kuba demands radically political professors in place of Mayer and Kantorowicz.

[...]

10th August, Saturday forenoon

We drove to Berlin on 7 August, back in the late afternoon of the 8th. Unique event: Krushchev gave a long speech in the Volkskammer, in Russian, interpreter beside him translated a paragraph at a time.[24] There is nothing to be said about the content of this session; it repeats in every respect what has long been chewed over. First Grotewohl elaborated for the umpteenth time his federation programme and Ulbricht in his unpleasant castrato voice underlined what had been said by G. and Kr.[25] In between Kr. repeatedly emphasised the familiar Soviet standpoint, that they wanted peace and friendship with the whole of Germany, but that Adenauer wanted to be at enmity with the SU, falsely attributed aggressive intentions to it etc. etc. The man does not make a bad impression on me – but, the But! The most senior Party member of the Soviet Union is speaking in our chamber! *We* have received instructions beforehand to give an enthusiastic reception, on the stairs we welcome the delegation with tumultuous applause, rise from our seats as in the Stalin times, we repeatedly break out in spontaneous enthusiasm, when we are assured of Soviet aid – and *we* are sovereign, but in the West they are in thrall to America. And things are going so very well for us, nothing but progress and unity. And what nonsense, [to suggest] that Krushchev wanted to intervene in the election campaign![26] – I am so disgusted, I see the mendacity on both sides and everywhere. Everywhere it is power that is at stake, between states, between parties, within parties. Everyone constantly talks about morality, and everyone lies. At the moment things are evidently more brutal, Asiatic here than in the Adenauer state. But over there is the most blatant return to Nazism – here to Bolshevism. De profundissimis.[27]

11th August, Sunday forenoon

[...]

Recent work: Ploughed through my 18ième vol. II ms [...]. I now know how to continue. [...] But there were moments of exasperation beforehand, which made H. unhappy. But it will take a lot of work yet, a lot of time. But it no longer satisfies me. I do not have the right approach, I no longer care to borrow everything second-hand, and it is impossible for the literary historian of a century to do more than read samples. [...]

17th August, Saturday forenoon

[...]

Here the non-appearance of Bulganin, whose visit had been announced, has been passed over in silence. Over there they say: B. has been toppled, he was too conciliatory to the Molotov group.[28] However that may be: there are constant power struggles within a small group behind closed doors. We are unable to get rid of Fascism: here in a somewhat more Asian, in the West in a somewhat more European form. In Bonn one is allowed to be in opposition and gets two or three years in prison; here one absolutely has to keep one's mouth shut and gets 10 years hard labour. To make up for that the old SS, the old anti-Semitism rules over there with shameless frankness.

[...]

On Thurs. evening – *25 August, Sunday forenoon* – Lindner came, he had not quite made it out, but he thought he had heard the name Kantorowicz on Rias. Then at 12 we heard Kantorowicz's declaration ourselves, he had sought asylum from the brutal government of the GDR ... H.'s parents have a West Berlin paper with his full declaration. Our press calls him a traitor. I feel sorry for him, I would even have understood, if he had got out and not said anything. But to seek 'freedom and security' in the Bonn state, to publicly support the Bonn regime! I find that odious, whereas my Kirchner people see it as martyrdom, sacrifice of property and livelihood. I am unable to pursue all of this, which affects me greatly, in detail. [...]

Today, 25 August, 1957, after an interruption of 15 or 16 years (at some time in Caspar David Friedrichstr. they took away my typewriter, I don't have the time to dig up the diary), today, therefore, I am going to continue with the ms of the 18ième interrupted at that time.[29] I am beginning with Laclos. [...]

Our black tomcat ill for 2 weeks. [...] Parents-in-law and H. to church [...]. During mass Lindner to the Reyck Animal Hospital with the beast. Somewhat belatedly discovered kidney problem. Can perhaps be saved. [...]

31st August, 9 a.m. Saturday

In the last few days: To the Ardenne Club with the parents-in-law. Film: *The Threepenny Opera*.[30] Seen for the second time, only now appreciated its greatness, resolution to see *it* again, to see *every* more important film *twice*.

[...]

West German reading, Dürrenmatt young Swiss author, crime novel with irrationalism: *The Judge and His Hangman*.[31] Keep an eye on the man!

About to set off on the Black Sea trip.

[The Klemperers were away on their Black Sea trip from Saturday 31 Aug. until 25 September. Apart from the cruise from Odessa to Batum and back, they also spent time in Kiev, Odessa and Moscow.]

2nd September, about 4 p.m. Monday. Kiev, Hotel Intourist

[...]

Saturday afternoon and evening at Doris Kahane's with Peter and Inge, accompanied to the station by *everyone*. Night journey and half of 1st September to Brest-Litovsk. Compartment for four, no opportunity to wash, only a little jet of water in a tiny basin, enough for one's hands. Like *that* and unshaven to Kiev. Embarrassment when undressing only on the first night.

[The following extracts from the diary for this period will be very brief.]

4th September, 8 a.m. Wednesday. Kiev

[...]

I add from Berlin: Peter has – peaceably – resigned from the Party. My question, how he had contrived this 'peaceably', remained unanswered. Perhaps he did not want to talk in front of Doris. Inge was 'still in'. She herself only uttered a few angry sounds. Something like: 'these dirty dogs!'

[...]

20th September, 7.30 a.m. Friday. At sea, Sochi–Odessa

The Wednesday lying in the roads of Sochi was very restful. Constant conversation: *when* are we going ashore, how continuing? – Some were seasick, a few were bored, everyone was anxious about the big trip into the mountains. General dissatisfaction at receiving so little information. That has preoccupied us throughout the journey: Russian mistrust, Russian passivity, *internal iron curtain??* The formula has 'just occurred' to me, really just; but we have been brooding over the subject for a long time. I have often considered H. infected by the West – but she is evidently right: the Russians put up a smokescreen around themselves. Never any precise information, never a binding confirmation, least of all a written one! Is it the expanse of time, of space, Eastern passivity? Is it the political mistrust *knocked into* everyone?? The very simplest pieces of information are avoided or overturned at the last moment – e.g. time is wasted, because a meal is set for earlier and then served later after all; the daily programme is announced too late and incompletely, they always say, we don't know yet; whether one asks the interpreter or the courier or the Intourist official – no one knows (or is forbidden to know, or does not have the confidence to know) . . . The regular steamers we encounter every day – the *Admiral Nachimov* is pointed out to us – but what is its tonnage, or that of our *Pyotr Veliki*[32] or of the others, the *Lensoviet*, the *Rossiya* etc. (Little Karin Heinsch told us, there are not the most minimal statistics available on the civil aircraft of the SU. They are all displayed 'publicly', but in truth a 100 times less is told than by the Americans.) Everywhere the *internal iron curtain*. [...] During supper it was officially announced at last: The ship will put into port tomorrow – Thurs., the 19th, at 5 a.m., breakfast already at 7.30 immediately followed by a day excursion in *open* buses to Lake Riza.

[...]

26th September, 9.30 a.m. Berlin, Romance Languages Institute

[...] At Schönefeld Airfield Lindner awaited us with the sad tidings that Mauz had been missing since Sunday (my lack of feeling!) Then we were here at the Institute for a while, at Doris Kahane's for an hour – in the evening dead tired in Linienstr.

What should I add now?

[...]

Details:

[...]

The Jew

A young woman from tourist class, probably in the FDJ, chatting innocently to

H. in the swimming pool: 'You're waving to *the Jew* up there.' She no doubt meant nothing malicious by it – but . . .

The worst thing about this trip: Everyone suspects everyone else, fears 'report', denunciation.

The 'bourgeois' avoid and fear Schwandt, the metalworker and zealous Berlin functionary – 'they break off their conversations, when he comes anywhere near them' [. . .] All are against Wernecke, the pliable and clumsy [. . .] courier, the head porter at the government guest house. Who is making 'reports' on whom?? – the mood of the Third Reich.

Moscow: America and 1001 Nights, modern and most modern times and the Middle Ages, passivity, indolence and fever. Europe was lacking, a calm present was lacking, normal situation and atmosphere was lacking.

27th September, Friday afternoon. Dresden
Yesterday in Berlin my cobbled-together introductory lecture to modern French poetry.
[. . .]
Mountains of newspapers pile up embarrassingly unread. Work on the lectures, on the 18ième, on Voltaire weighs on me – on H. her first lecture.
[. . .]

3rd October, towards 7 p.m. Thursday. Dresden
[. . .]
On Tue., 1 Oct., H.'s première passed off well.

I began my lectures. Yesterday and today, reading the whole time [. . .]. Two days for half an hour's lecturing! And the 18ième? And Voltaire–Frederick [the Great]?? Fragmentation – and I no longer manage anything. And tomorrow to the Executive Committee in Berlin.
[. . .]

6th October, 10 a.m. Sunday. Dresden
The Executive Council in Berlin – government guest house, Green Salon! – an absolute nullity. [. . .] What does *old* intelligentsia, *young* intelligentsia mean? – Wendt said to me: we want to make the group of deputies younger. *You and Zweig* . . . I: all right by me, but I wished to remain on the Executive Council. He: naturally . . . Curiously, H. who would so much like to see me give up all politics, was put out: they simply wanted to get rid of all the moderates.

[Klemperer is resolved to give up the chair of the Advisory Council on Romance Languages and Literatures.]

The Festschrift
Niemeyer [the publisher] is shaking with fear. Not only is nothing being done about the Festschrift; he is also not bringing out the printed and already

advertised *LTI*, because – says Silzer – after the contents page [usually at the back in German books] the Festschrift is advertised with Kantorowicz's contribution. I asked Meusel [historian, Academy member etc.] for advice. Reply: Omit Kantorowicz's contribution to the Festschrift, publish the *LTI* even with the taboo name.

[...]

Most embarrassing piled up correspondence arrears. Cohen urged me to do something for J.-R. Bloch;[33] Besthorn[34] invites me ('and your dear Hadwig') to give a lecture in Greifswald, Noyer-Weidner [West German academic] wants to review my Literary History. Etc. etc. Did I mention the friendly and considerate article in the *Berliner Zeitung*:[35] a good Literary History, since we have no other, important, even if Bergson means nothing to us today? Cohen, too, admonishes: Write the continuation up to today! – Too late for me. And yet I would so much like to. But today's literature is rushing past me. The French, the German, the English. I see what H. is buying. – I would so much like to read this and that and all just for my own pleasure. I feel myself so foolishly obliged to bring my little things to a conclusion.

And the ever-present final feeling: it is all so meaningless and unimportant. Yesterday the first Soviet little space ship was launched.[36] What is politics, GDR, what Romance literary history compared to that?

[...]

Muschel-Mauz, the tomcat, has been brought back to us as a corpse and been buried in the garden in my absence. Frau Duckhorn inconsolable.

10th October, Thursday forenoon. Dresden

The dreaded birthday passed off quite well and about 99% more quietly than the last one. Few telegrams (government, Volkskammer – only a few leading figures). Personally I was pleased by the congratulations of the Aufbau publishing house, or rather of Gysi, its director.[37] Reminder of my former closeness to the Kulturbund and its publishing house. Gysi had to stay in the background for many years. Now he is on top again and I am slowly fading into the background.

[...]

23rd October, Wednesday afternoon. Dresden

'Our conscience is shaped by society; if we do not know that and take it to be a kind of Geiger counter of good and evil independent of all social facts, then we are terribly deceived ... (Thus) the Party is the final judge of our conscience and we have to act in accordance with this judge ...' *Neues Deutschland*, 15 Oct. 1957, article by Heinrich Schwartzer, lecturer in the philosophy faculty, Leipzig. Polemic against Bloch and the 'third way'.[38] – Very characteristic of the general tendency of the Party in all its intellectual decisions. The sentence can just as well be maintained from the point of view of the Inquisition, the Jesuits, the orthodox Catholic Church.

[...]

As a political plus I would like to note here the recognition [of the GDR] by Tito[39] – but here, too: how deplorable is our situation. Apart from that, I find politics ever more loathsome – they both (East and West) lie and stink far too much; I read the newspapers only fleetingly, as far as possible I avoid political discussions with H.

[...]

My diary entries are getting ever shorter. I lack the time and the belief that I will ever be able to turn them to account? What happens to my day? It runs through my hands like water.

6th November, Wednesday forenoon. Dresden

Triumph of Sputnik II,[40] military jubilation over it, dismissal of Marshal Zhukov,[41] because he reduced the influence of the Party commissars in the army, constantly growing tyranny of the SED and now a piece of *Western* news, the Soviet Union has withdrawn from the [UN] disarmament commission.[42] On top of that H.'s double burden on Tuesdays: her lecture and the mood in her parents' home. Thus yesterday evening there was a brief but very convulsive outburst: 'The Russians are *extortionists*, there will be war, no matter how much talk there is of the fortieth anniversary of peace.'[43] Combination of revulsion at violence, dictatorship, war of extermination, combination of momentarily overstrung nerves and instinctive hostility to the Soviet Union. But very logical combination and very well founded: Softer line of the 20th Party Congress, Hungarian reaction, new reaction and return to Stalinism ... Of course one can also put it the other way around: Western-fomented Hungarian counter-revolution, war policy of the USA, self-defence and defence of peace on the Soviet and GDR side. I vacillate a great deal, but *my* hate turns instinctively against Bonn with its Nazi and Jew-murderer ministers. Then again all of H.'s outbursts demonstrate the absolute goodness of her heart, whereas I regard things half apathetically and *wholly* egotistically. I sought to pacify her and soon succeeded, too, but I feel greatly for H., worry greatly about her and love her ever more.

[...]

On Friday I gave my Berlin October lecture on poetry, and in the evening we saw *Galileo*[44] in the Berliner Ensemble. Brecht is a great writer, but his alienation folderols, here the foolish chorus boys before every scene, can spoil one's pleasure and his epic theatre is no technical novelty, cf the historical scenes of Vitet, Mérimée, Gobineau. Splendid acting [...]

On the morning of Sunday, 3 November, Dresden Kulturbund delegates conference, preparation for the Federal Congress in Leipzig on 5 Dec. I sat on the platform, was presented with flowers and a book on China. Laux gave a long speech obediently following the Party line: all parties are welcome, but the

Kulturbund has a Socialist orientation, entirely in every respect obstinately Socialist, utterly blindly obedient to the Party. I expressed thanks for being honoured and then turned to Laux, whom I – unusually – addressed familiarly, and repeatedly called Comrade Laux. He had demanded 'fanatical' dedication, he should read the chapter 'Fanatical' in my just published *LTI*; he had spoken of reprehensible *decadence* just as our State Secretary, Abusch, had recently done at the Culture Conference of the SED. That was only possible at a political meeting; but to the intelligentsia of the KB I had to speak as to my students, to whom I repeatedly explained the connection between Comrades Barbusse, Eluard etc. and Decadence; one also had to be careful when it came to the ivory tower. We are the Kulturbund, we have an obligation to think. [. . .] it is a matter of *self-defence* against the West, as intellectuals we must observe and act with a clear mind . . . Sparse polite applause and then as next speaker a Party secretary. 'We are not, as Prof. Klemperer says, on the defensive, we are on the offensive, we consort with no decadence,' etc. He, too, got sparse applause, that was my consolation. I left before the lunchtime break, while the talking was still going on. It can be assumed that this 'contribution to debate' in the Elbe Hotel will cost me my place on the Executive Committee at the Federal election in Leipzig. Which would actually be a blessing for me.

I have declined all the many invitations to the 40th anniversary [of the October Revolution] (Academy, Berlin Univ., Halle Univ., KB Berlin, KB and SED here etc.) The endless celebratory din makes me even more refractory than I would be anyway, thank God that tomorrow is the 7 Nov. at last.

[Yet meanwhile Klemperer has taken on more work writing introductions, despite his dissatisfaction with the inevitable superficiality of such tasks.]

[. . .]

20th November, Wednesday evening
In the last 2 weeks I have at last – a whole 5 pages! – managed to finish the Laclos; the reading for it began even before the SU trip in August! [. . .]

Apart from that: 12–14 Nov.: Greifswald–Berlin. Tue. 12 Nov. – beet deployment in Halle. [Greifswald lecture on Feuchtwanger.]

[. . .]

23rd November, Saturday forenoon
[A namesake of Klemperer's, a Dr Joseph Klemperer, calls. The latter, after leaving Germany, had spent some years in Israel before departing in disgust at atrocities against the Arab population.] Once again: Joseph Klemperer seemed credible to me, because he is literally quite apolitical. A Jew and repelled by the state and attitude of Zion, gone to West Germany, because he draws his pension there and can pursue his 'hobbies'.

H. opposed with some indignation my expression, that the Jews against the Arabs were 'worse than the Nazis' [. . .]. (Besides [continued H.] today's refugee

camps in Egypt, like those in West Germany, were 'conserved injustice', deliberately conserved as political propaganda.) I: certainly there are Dantesque
stages of hell, and Auschwitz is the very last pit of hell. But that the Jews are in
the penultimate circle of hell – precisely as Jews they shouldn't be there.

29th November, Friday
The 3rd edition of my *LTI* has appeared at last. On the last page my Festschrift
advertised for 1958. The name Kantorowicz is mentioned among the contributors. To make up for it they've forgotten the table of contents. I complained
immediately. Apart from that: very good paper and good binding. H. thinks, on
the one hand I'll get into trouble, on the other have success in the West. *I*
believe, I shall be ignored. On the same day (yesterday) letter from Marcel
Cohen: Chap I of the *LTI* (translated by his daughter) is about to appear in
L'Europe. [...]

Letter to Feuchtwanger. Sent him both *LTI* and *Vor 33 nach 45*. Asked him
whether he could have a chapter of the *LTI* published in English (mentioned
L'Europe).

4 p.m.
Just now, by way of a telephone call from the Antifascist Committee in Berlin,
the possibility [...] (at once tempting and very inconvenient) has turned up, of
attending an Antifa Congress in Paris from 16–17 Dec. It is almost impossible
to obtain a French visa at such short notice. [...]

12th December, Thursday after 8 a.m. Berlin, Institute
The improbable story appears to becoming reality.

X weeks ago a Paris invitation from the Antifa [...]. About 3 weeks later:
Antifa meeting in Berlin. Spielmann to me. Nothing decided on Paris yet. I
thought no more of the matter. Then – less than a week ago – telephone call
from Berlin: I should go, with wife – only: *I* should obtain the visa [...]. I shall
not regard the thing as certain until we have passports, visa, currency, air-plane
tickets in our hands. [...]

[Volkskammer, 11th Dec.] But really important and upsetting for me in the
afternoon was Dr Hilde Benjamin's long speech on new criminal law measures –
a terrible shame, that I am no longer on the legal committee! – theoretical
justification of Socialist justice. Humane! more humane in private – boundlessly
cruel, obstinately and stupidly cruel, where the defence of the Socialist GDR
is concerned. Penalties for 'enticement', for 'flight from the Republic'! Then
everything is a crime, then one can turn everything into high treason, prison
for up to 15 years, even life, at the extreme even the death penalty can be
dictated.[45] (It weighs heavily on me that in the chamber I myself once spoke in
favour of the death penalty.) After Frau Benjamin's speech I left. [...]

13th December, 7 p.m. Friday. Berlin, Institute

In the morning here I first of all castrated the Frederick ms as desired.[46]

Then Executive Committee in the tall building on Strausberg Platz. Speech by Klaus Gysi – general situation, 'knocking into shape' (says H.), toeing the line. Pre-arranged heavy attack on Bloch, as carefully discussed yesterday at the SED preliminary meeting. So yesterday this preparatory meeting in the government guest house with, as main speakers, Erich Wendt, Kurt Hager, the extremely agitated and sickly Karl Kneschke. According to them Bloch is a traitor and confidence man and enemy of the state and responsible for a 'Bloch Circle' and a *Telegraf* article by his 'favourite student' Zwerenz.[47] – Today Bloch's impassioned defence [. . .]

[The Klemperers were in Paris from 14–20 December, apart from attending the congress sessions and gala performances for the participants, the couple took the opportunity to go to the theatre and cinema, and to shop.]

22nd December

[. . .] *Comédie*. Gala for veterans. A military band in the entrance hall, lining the stairs cuirassiers in golden helmet and plume and presenting drawn swords. And the Marseillaise on the arrival of the president of the senate . . . Many orders worn, big ones on a red collar. Molière's *Critique de l'école des femmes*[48] and *Amphytrion* were performed. I understood almost nothing of the text, but I was familiar with the content after all.

The real literary pleasure of these days (*Films: La Garçonne* and *A King in New York, Molière in the Théâtre Français + Liberté*): Chaplin and *Liberté*.[49]

Friday 8 p.m.

Return flight with Eberlein. [. . .] At Schönefeld Lindner decently on hand. Slow drive back with ice and a broken exhaust pipe. Here at 6 p.m.

Paris was a nice *recapitulation* for us.

So now the actual two session days of the Rencontre Européenne sur le problème allemand[50] or the Colloque sur l'invitation d'un Comité de résistants français, présidé par le sénateur J. Debu-Bridel, les 16 et 17 décembre à Paris.[51]
[. . .]

Since aggression on all sides and by all sides was avoided, the result [. . .] was a generalised wishful thinking. [. . .]

Pastor Niemöller,[52] welcomed with ovations, guest for a couple of hours on Tuesday. I would have judged him in his 50s at most, slim, finely chiselled face, very natural simple manner of speaking. He proposed (says H.) disarmament in both West and East Germany. This clause was dropped from the final appeal.
[. . .]

22nd December, 6 p.m. Sunday. Dresden
[...]

I merely glanced at the piled-up newspapers. Semper idem. But those bought in Paris: *France Observateur* and *Le monde* I shall try as far as possible to read.

[...]

Provisional travel offer by the Academy. I immediately thought of buying two tickets for a China trip in Aug./Sept. 58. [...]

30th December, 7 p.m. Tuesday. Dresden
I get through the holiday with Christmas tree, parents-in-law etc. with my usual and often fixed moods – on the whole tolerably this time.

Résumé 1957
This is the first year without a publication. I have laboriously managed to prepare my worn-out lectures, gave a couple of worn-out talks, fled from myself into sham activities (meetings), have laboured over the Voltaire–Frederick theme, over Feuchtwanger – did not really produce anything.

Apart from that the year of travels: In March the Tatra Mountains, in spring Mainz–Tübingen–Lake Constance, in Aug.–Sept. the Black Sea, the Caucasus, and at the very end Paris. Despite it all essentially numb. But Hadwig should get some benefit out of it, and I get through the time. Death always present in my mind. [...] Catholic marriage to H. – Completely disillusioned with respect to politics.

1958

2nd January, Thursday forenoon

I coped well with Christmas, on New Year's Eve I misbehaved over the drinks question – champagne? not champagne – over family memories and family bonds: Gottfried called from Leipzig, bliss, especially of mother, who is constantly trembling in case Gottfried gets arrested. (All it needs is one of his Slavonic Languages colleagues in the SED to name him as witness to some expression or other ... Not even an unjustified fear! Nazi conditions.)

On 1 January I pulled myself together. During the day dealt with an enormous quantity of correspondence; in the evening the deferred New Year's Eve bottle of champagne.

[...]

24th January, towards 9 a.m. Friday. Berlin, Institute Director's Room

[Work on the Frederick pamphlet to be presented to the Academy. In *Neues Deutschland* an article by Girnus, Germanists should put the Middle Ages in the museum and work on modern writers. At the Academy session:] I greeted Bloch. House of the Atrides.[1] The Dr Horn who instigated the affair against me hanged himself 2 weeks ago.[2] Reason unknown. Immediately afterwards he told another Academy member in exactly the same words [...].

25th January, about 8 p.m. Saturday. Dresden

[...]

[Klemperer has mixed feelings on reading Kafka for the first time.[3]]

There was much discussion – H.'s parents stayed until 9th Jan. – of literature, of Feuchtwanger's *Jephta and his Daughters*,[4] which I have not yet read.

Feuchtwanger wrote to me – I had said to him, when I sent the 3 copies of *LTI* he requested, if the 18ième were not weighing so heavily on me, I would most of all like to write a monograph on him (which is true, it's not flattery) – so he replied with comic immediacy, 'of course my 18ième was more important', but it would nevertheless be 'marvellous', if I were to write a book about him, so much that was foolish, mediocre, superficial was written about him; nor was anything much to be expected of a portrayal published by Rowohlt and addressed to a wider audience. I on the other hand! [...]

26th January (Addenda)

I feel quite alien in the Academy. [...] I am an outsider there, and I always think that I am disdained by everyone. For one group I am an SED journalist foisted on them, for the other a senile bourgeois. I always have heart problems after I've been there. Perhaps the Frederick thing is only foolishness on my part. Then again: I place it under the Academy's protection. *Hic et semper et ubique: inter sedia.*[5]

Magnificent on Thurs., the 23rd, *Fear and Loathing in the Third Reich.*[6] Schiffbauerdamm, 1st row of the stalls. I have never read all the scenes, know much only from H., who can recite them by heart. [At one point] I said quite loudly: 'Like today.' I am haunted by a sentence of Hilde Benjamin which I noted for the LQI from the *Berliner Zeitung* on 12th January: 'Dr H. Benjamin emphasised, that the law (Criminal Law Supplement) was a wise, generous and partisan instrument of the administration of justice of the GDR.' Partisan justice!

14th February, 6 p.m. Dresden

[...]

Political situation: Girnus, the State Secretary for the universities, with his hostility to education, is only a minor figure. The whole; and this whole is concentrated more and more on the one Ulbricht, is ever less distinguishable from Nazi attitudes and methods. Say working class instead of race and both movements are identical. Tyranny and narrow-mindedness increase with every day. Agitation against [religious] belief, youth initiation, struggle against 'ideological co-existence', against 'fractionism', against 'petty bourgeois arrogance' – all of it is LQI. Latest concrete facts: Oelssner, Schirdewan, Wollweber (the State Security man, alias police minister) have been kicked out of the Politburo,[7] Kuczinsky (a second Bloch case in the offing) has been attacked as anti-Marxist in a long article in *Neues Deutschland*, because in a book on the origins of the First World War he mistakenly asserts – mistakenly! But I saw it with my own eyes! – that the workers went to war voluntarily, they had failed as Socialists. There is a picture with the article: Workers' protest meeting against war. If one looks more closely, then under the picture there is the date 1911!

[... Federal meeting of the Kulturbund in a factory hall – Ulbricht on the platform, Becher speaks for 3 hours, for dogmatic Socialism, Ulbricht etc.] The most sickening speech of the congress was delivered by Frau S[...] with her usual pathos. To the accompaniment of repeated invocations of his holy name she crawled so far up Ulbricht's a-hole, that she should have left her visiting card outside, had one not, even invisible, been able to recognise her by her sweet morality. Good was Gysi's plain matter-of-factness: we are forced to take 'harsh measures', if we want to maintain ourselves as a Socialist state. Dreadful a Christian, who emphasised his 'primitive Christianity'. Questionable, but not entirely bad, Havemann who stood up, to some extent idealistically, for unlimited free research [. . .]. The votes were fixed, everything was carried 'unanimously' and quickly. [. . .] I myself am again elected – anonymously submerged in the enlarged mass – to the Executive Committee.

[. . .]

In the evenings we each time ate in our room, before that on Friday to Giraudoux's *Amphitryon 38*,[8] on Saturday to the *Diary of Anne Frank* in the Studio Theatre [. . .]. The Anne Frank – I did not warm to the book – made a deep and really shattering impression on me as a play. [. . .]

15th February, Saturday forenoon

Yesterday spent half the day on 'Frederick and the administration of justice' for Langhoff's theatre programme [for Peter Hacks' play The Miller of Sanssouci[9]], the other half on my diary. [. . .]

On Sunday aft. 2 Feb. to the Grubes. Their apartment, very elegant, empty because of its great spaciousness, on the 5th floor of one of the new buildings on the Altmarkt above the big state shops. [. . .] the view from the windows magnificent and shocking. That *was* Dresden. Now a not very large empty space, planned city with green spaces and cleared streets. In the middle of the clean emptiness, of the spread-out three-dimensional map stands an isolated yellowish not yet demolished block. That was the Ufa cinema on Waisenhausstr. I would not be able to pick out the individual city streets of former days. Modern Pompeii. Yesterday evening bells were rung on the 13th anniversary of the destruction. – I am like a ghost.

[. . .]

27th February, Thursday evening. Dresden

Private and political aspects of the last ten days partly interwoven.

Main content the Voltaire–Frederick study.[10] Completely corrected – poor typesetters! – Yesterday sent off to Neuendorff, to be passed on by him to the Akademie publishing house, since following decision of the plenum it is to appear in the series of the proceedings – like the Delille, only shorter [. . .].

On Thurs. 20 Feb. I gave the lecture in the plenum, speaking summarily and without notes – reading the whole thing would probably have taken two hours, 30 minutes are prescribed, I will have spoken for 45. In the Academy there is no applause, but I had the impression that I was heard with pleasure and attentiveness. Afterwards Meusel spoke. Not at all aggressive and basically only paraphrasing what I had said: that Mehring had regarded it as a duty to oppose the Frederick cult. [...] I responded [...] that in the enthusiasm of speaking I had expressed myself too tersely on Marxism and personality – Marxism only repudiated every form of *hero worship*. Meusel immediately agreed. (Oh Stalin! Oh Walter Ulbricht!) [...] On the stairs I met the ostracised Bloch. He paid me many compliments. At last an *electric* session with real discussion, not just the usual metalworking and boredom! I had spoken as freely as was possible 'under these circumstances' [...] The same thing will happen to you as to Kuczynski. [...] I was very proud, felt like a conspirator and heroic martyr, ascribed the lecture a certain significance in the history of the Academy ... Later the air went out of me somewhat. I am and will remain a small fry.

[Changes are demanded in Klemperer's Voltaire–Frederick book introduction. Klemperer refuses and requests the return of his ms, adding, the editor was sure to find many contributors who would write the 'desired foreword'!]

This private Fridericus trouble is of course closely linked with the radicalisation of our politics. LQI symptoms. In every context, where previously a resolution or congratulations, or the like, was signed 'the Central Committee' or the 'Politburo' it is now 'the Central Committee (or the Politburo) *with Walter Ulbricht at its head*.' [...] I was humanly shocked by the extraordinarily agitated stammering, the constant repetitions with which Grotewohl begged for unity in the Party, with which he emphasised his closeness to Ulbricht. The other speakers, too, were greatly agitated. It is a power struggle between individuals. A couple of times a special tension is evident between the lines: *We* were in the concentration camps, *we* are the martyrs and heroes! and the others: *we* got our training and our overall view outside (in the Soviet Union), *we* are on the side of progress.

13th March, Thursday evening. Dresden

[...]

Latest heretic: Kuczinsky, who humbly recanted. He had dared to say that in 1914 the workers went along with things just like everyone else. [...] At the group meeting yesterday [in the Volkskammer] – there were only $\frac{1}{2}$ a dozen of us – Franck greeted him: 'Congratulations on your confession of sin.' Both laughed.

[...]

26th March, Wednesday forenoon

[...]

In Halle, in the last few days, there was a 'council' on the socialisation-Marxisation of the university. The discussion is supposed to have been very bad-tempered. Reitzenstein had offered to resign his professorship, the pharmacist Mothes[11] (considered important) had been even more vehement in his opposition, His Magnificence, Leo Stern, had tried to be conciliatory ... [...]

[...]

2nd May

The Academy – H. has made a copy of Meusel's opinion [...] – is afraid to print my Frederick, I shall withdraw it; Fascism right and left.

[...]

9th May, 7 p.m. Friday

[...]

On Saturday, 3 May, in Berlin alone for the Advisory Committee and back immediately. The new curricula entirely tailored to the training of teachers, to the ten-year school, to Marxism, factory, de-intellectualisation. I said and had it minuted: Romance Languages and Literatures as a university subject was thereby extinguished, we were practically giving instruction at a teacher-training college, it would be more honest if we taught at a college and did not call ourselves professors. No one contradicted, Rita said, she had said it all at the crucial ministerial and Party meeting, but we had to acquiesce. It was a kind of mourning session. I also said: as in the SU. On the visiting cards of their scholars there is only 'Academician'. Only within the Academy are they scholars. Universities are mere secondary schools, are not mentioned. [...]

14th May, Wednesday forenoon

My Fridericus has just come back from the Akademie publishing house, written on it the note: accepted by the Academy, withdrawn by the author ... *Ex ossibus ultor.*[12]

[...]

7 p.m.

[...] Since last night – Rias report on military coup in Algiers[13] – eager to know French developments. In our press, our broadcasts *not a word*.

2nd June, Monday

Intense interest in France, we listen to London and Rias, and our latecomers.

H. shares my hostility to de Gaulle,[14] she is equally hostile to all armies and every dictatorship. Rias is emphatically anti-Gaullist – London not. [...]

The other political event of these last 2 weeks: the abolition of food ration cards,[15] which we were the only people still to have, which we have had continuously since 1938. Wireless and press make their usual mistake: they boast about the success, talk about our superiority over the West, whereas our belated arrival, our poverty are quite evident, whereas no one is completely satisfied. I was at the solemn Volkskammer session on 28 May in Berlin, drove there at 5 without H., took part in the group meeting at 8, in the plenum until 11, in which Rauh announced and explicated many price details – bockwurst down from 1.20 to 80 pfennigs provoked joyful laughter. [...]

Last Sunday we listened for the 3rd time to Kantorowicz's lecture series broadcast from London. He defends himself and goes onto the offensive. The fundamental principle: keeping silent so as not to help the enemy was wrong. Yesterday with especially intemperate animosity against Ulbricht and his 'ale-house slang'. My heart is very divided. [. . .]

Cultural treats: On the 14th to the Ardenne club: *Kuhle Wampe* – afterwards the director Slatan Dudow spoke, discussed.[16] The unemployed on their bicycles – always just the wheels, the mute searching – made the most impression on me. [. . .]

By contrast a more direct and shattering pleasure: *Die Mörder sind unter uns*. [The Murderers are among us]. One should see every good film 2×, at least twice. I already remembered this one as very important. This time an even greater impression. [. . .]

[. . .]

15th June, Sunday forenoon

The French business drags on. Coup d'état in slow motion [. . .].

From Sunday, the 8th, until Wednesday the Kahanes were here, who are flying back to Delhi in July. (With all 3 children!) He is unappreciative of my intellectualist complaints, nor does he really believe in the general discontent here; as a *Neues Deutschland* correspondent more or less loyal to the Party he sees the foreign policy successes(?) of the GDR, considers my intellectualist education worries to be petty, unimportant etc. [. . .]

Gottfried Kirchner has been attacked in the Leipzig University newspaper because, out of sheer necessity, he used the text of the Gospels to teach Church Slavonic and has recourse to the German New Testament as a necessary aid. They write that he is giving 'grammatical Bible instruction' [. . .] In Halle I was welcomed by the news that Brummer, Rostock, had 'left the Republic'. What Romance languages professors are left to us? [. . .]

[. . .]

23rd June, Monday

The de Gaulle business drags on enigmatically, there is now a worsening of the general situation [here] because of the Nagy affair in Budapest. In 56, having been promised he would not be prosecuted, he came out of the Yugoslav Embassy, was then nevertheless arrested, and has now – now! – more or less unexpectedly without much ado been executed with 3 other people. Every such political killing is more or less judicial murder, this one especially objectionable because of the broken promise and the lengthy passage of time.[17] Why now? And yet certainly on Soviet urging. What a gift to Bonn, Rias, de Gaulle! The new catch phrase: return to Stalinism – first used by the Yugoslavs, now by the West. On our side: *against revisionism*. [. . .]

29th June, Sunday evening

Anniversary of Eva's death: 8 July, her birthday: 12 July, our registry office marriage: 16 May[18] – I always think of these dates (it's only that I go rarely and reluctantly to her grave). But 29 June, which was after all engraved on both our wedding rings, was the real beginning! It weighs heavily on me today, and I believe I have not taken any notice of it in recent years. Our beginning 54 years ago – and what remains of fidelity, of passion? I feel so disloyal, towards Eva and towards Hadwig, both. And I feel like a ghost, without a proper right to my still being alive, and I still have so much desire to live and such horror of non-being. And so much love for H. I always feel at ease, when I am with H., and when I am reading and writing – and always wretched, when I think about myself. There is nothing in me I can hold on to, I am non-existent, when I reflect on myself, I do not know my name.

[...]

Der Sonntag: a special issue for Ulbricht (65). Likewise of course the news-papers. Becher, Brugsch etc. idolise him. HE is the 'central figure', the leader, the little Stalin. In a leading article all in the same breath: We have no 'heroes', the working class brings forth progress ('working class' – in literally every line of Becher) and: leader personalities, who lead the class ... [...]

5th July, Saturday forenoon

[...]

Suddenly the Party Congress,[19] which has been filling the newspapers and the broadcasts for months [...] – I no longer read and hear the never-ending repetitions – suddenly it descends on me. Only yesterday (belatedly) invitation from the Central Committee in Berlin. In the afternoon a functionary in a car here from our local Party headquarters: I have to be there on the 14th, when the comrades of the Academy in person greet the Party Congress. And I must also be there before that, of course. In short 9th–14th July inclusive in Berlin! Honour, duty – and personal security require it. [...]

The Festschrift is supposed to have been printed; I wish it were already out, otherwise they might cut the Brummer[20] as well. The Festschrift should no longer to be called: *In the Service of Language* (which is in any case misleading, because it is not linguistic), but *Ten Little Niggers*.

[...]

Two 'pledges to myself':

1) I am now going to tackle the 18ième and take on nothing – [...] nothing else at all, until I have delivered the volume. [...]

2) Then, if I have [also] managed the Curriculum, and am still alive after that, I want to really *study* the whole of Feuchtwanger and write a mono-graph on him. *If.* Feuchtwanger, to whom I wrote that, and who would like me to write a book on him, replied, *he* still wants to write another thirteen novels.

[...]

10th–16th July, Fifth Party Congress

10th July, 4 p.m. Wednesday. Institute

Yesterday morning at 10 – good weather, very warm, to Berlin.
[...]

We resolved to get as much personal pleasure out of these dreary days as possible. In the late afternoon to the cinema with Lindner. *Amphitryon*.[21] Seen once before very incompletely from a very poor seat. This time completely enjoyed it in all its witty Offenbachism. [...]

More important the surroundings and what H. told me. Delta Cinema, Wollinerstr., a couple of yards from the sector boundary, one sees the policeman, who stops everyone and allows only the Berliner, *not* the GDR citizen from outside Berlin to pass. [...]

12th July, 1 p.m. Institute

[...]

The Party Congress

Over 4000 people in the huge hall, 3000 delegates downstairs, guests etc. on the balconies. The sessions are from 9–11.30, from 12–2, from 4–8. On the first day I lasted until 2 hardly sleeping at all. The only speaker, morning and afternoon, was Ulbricht. Absolute pig-headedness: Against revisionism. Only technology – he knows no other kind of scholarship. The whole educational system directed towards it. [...] Literal laying down of 10 commandments of the new morality, he said '10 points' and read them out like a catechism. Not mankind, *only class*. Only Socialist philosophy of work. On Thurs., the 11th, only from 9–11.30. Krushchev's speech [...]. K. spoke in Russian and the speech was simultaneously read [through headphones] in German by the translator. [...] Major effort. a) foreign policy in general: alliance against revisionism and the West, b) against Tito, bitter at a revisionist-Western wing of the Communists splitting off, c) for German Federation, vehemently against Bonn. From 1 Jan. 1959 the GDR gets a remission of 600 million DMs of the cost of the occupation. Jubilation and standing up and three cheers as in Stalin's day. He is a good speaker, often very emotional, impetuousness immediately mitigated by a bon mot, a witticism [...]

Today – only from 9–11.30. Dreariness of the 'discussion'. The naively enthusiastic peasant woman, in the Party and collective for 3 years, with her earthy bits of popular wisdom, such as butter, milk and eggs don't grow in the state shop, that we women have to join in too, that it's no good if only our menfolk are in the Party etc. etc. ... [...] Then a long speech by an officer: our National People's Army, entirely Socialist, entirely the sons of workers and peasants, the most modern weapons, side by side with the glorious invincible Soviet power ... Endless speech by an industrial worker. About God knows what method, which saves the lathe operator 3 minutes, which amounts to a total financial saving of 1.9 million marks ... [...] I am determined to miss tomorrow entirely. Then on Monday the famous delegation of the scholars. I am counting the days, they are putting a great strain on me.

[...]

13th July, 6.45 p.m. Sunday. Linienstr.

[...] Today entirely private. Very great heat, in the night towards morning a thunderstorm, since then oppressively sultry. H. to church in the morning, then breakfast here together.

[...]

Now we are waiting for Lindner. He is driving us to the Theater am Schiffbauerdamm, Berliner Ensemble: *The Mother.*[22] Two free tickets, performance for the Party Congress.

15th July, 7 p.m. Tuesday. Dresden

Mon. evening: *The Mother.* Weigel's great artistry. *The* epic theatre. The content of each scene announced on a white cloth. The naturalistic little house on stage. Behind it town or factory as painted backdrop, the stage area around the house (the empty street). Here entirely idealistically, cabaret and opera-like: the songs, speech-songs of individuals and of groups. The monologues deliberately primitive: I am now going to do this and that. Extremely deliberate destruction of illusion: *this* is how the flag-bearer falls whom I am now portraying. H. is right: *only* through the magnificent acting is the effect, the restoration of illusion, re-established from scene to scene. The extension to 1917 – with cinema images of the storming of the Winter Palace – is unnecessary and excessive ... I should read the novel.

[...]

On Mond. 14 July breakfast on Invalidenstr., then the Party Congress. At first I fell asleep. Harig, the former universities state secretary, was sitting beside me and woke me up: the delegation of scholars. What an impression the 3rd Party Congress made on me, how honoured and elated I felt. This time – how much on the sidelines and what conflict within myself and how very much aware of the pretence! I feel so ludicrously helpless and superfluous.

16th July

[... The scholars' delegation:] In one room of the 'coffee house' breakfast had been laid for about 75–100 people, scholars and 'up-and-coming' academics – I knew very few. A whole number of rectorial chains (the mass of our polytechnics), mass of decorations. And this was the very day I forgot my gongs; usually H. pinned them on for me in the evening and took them off again as soon as I was back. A couple of handshakes – out of place. [...] (meanwhile yesterday, 14 July, landing of American troops in Lebanon; Iraq!)[23] At 12 we then trooped to the front of the hall where there were two rows of seats for us. For the first time I recognised the faces on the platform. Tremendous clapping, standing up, 'tumultuous applause' – I know it all; that's the way miners, athletes etc. are greeted. Spontaneous repetitions. Thiessen spoke, Hager replied, we marched out again to the same din as when we had marched in. At 1 p.m. the Party Congress (which only closes today, the 16th) was over for me. [...]

I got nothing at all from the Party Congress, it only bored and exhausted me. But we made the best of the days in Berlin.

[...]

22nd July, Tuesday afternoon. Dresden

[...] but the feeling of no longer being able to manage my 18ième has been reinforced once more. The book is souring my last years, gets between me and my true interests. I know that I am no longer accomplishing any real work with the 18ième, only journalisme superficiel,²⁴ only superfluous belated stuff. All the modern reading, that tempts me and that remains unread! On the other hand: I want to bring it to a conclusion nevertheless. [...]

Gottfried [Kirchner] told me in confidence, he had been interrogated by 'State Security' in January; he is a friend of Ralf Schröder,²⁵ who is in prison. 'We are not interested in you' but they want statements. Gestapo rediviva.²⁶ Gottfried has now been attacked because of his 'grammatical Bible instruction'. On the other hand he is supposed to speak on his adverb dissertation at the Moscow Slavonic Studies congress in September. He was really depressed when he talked to me; his parents, his sister are not supposed to find out about the interrogation. (But H. knew about it long ago.)

[...]

2nd August, Saturday afternoon

[...]

Early on Thurs. morning in the car to Buchenwald, where H. had never been before. (*3 Aug.*) [...] There is not much to see any more, most of it has been erased, most of it overgrown with lush grass and beautiful wild field flowers; only outlines marked out and rough boulders bearing the names of the former blocks. Preserved are the ovens for the corpses and a few main buildings. Characteristic: flower arrangements have been placed in the ovens. Everything is too beautiful and too cared for. The big monument is to be unveiled next month,²⁷ they're still working on it. H. thinks all sense of the horror is now alleviated and distracted by enjoyment of art. I think of the Auschwitz camp, where the dreadfulness is preserved and prepared and heightened – the cases with cut-off women's hair, the black earth where the funeral pyres were etc. etc. – Memorial hall for the victims, which was crowded with people, made no impression on me. Pictures of execution victims, texts etc. H. is tireless in carefully studying such things – *I* prefer to read them up in books ... A film was

just being made on the Appellplatz: Groups in camp clothing, SS uniforms, a far-too-new and clean-looking swastika flag on the tower at the entrance ... At 1, in fine weather, we drove through the beautiful landscape to Rudolstadt, ate a bockwurst in the little town, and then drove up to the Greifenverlag publishing office in the castle. Both Dietzes looking much aged and quite careworn. He very nervous, distrustful and frightened. Repeatedly: 'are you sure no one can overhear? – There was a door open again ... my wife is so thoughtless ...' Embittered: throttling of the private business, harassment, spying ... They had tried in a dirty way to blackmail a girl who had been working for him for 13 years into spying on him. 'They', that is 'the Security'. A new decree requires all proposed publications to be submitted with two opinions – my essay volume also has to be presented in this way ... Feuchtwanger's *Devil in France* can no longer be sold – because of Kantorowicz's afterword ... [...] We sat there over coffee, cakes, whipped cream, and the atmosphere was as if we were threatened by the Gestapo again. [...] When we took our leave at 6.30, D.'s last words were (he was so grateful for our visit), 'it does me so much good, to be able to pour out my heart for once!'
   [...]

7th August, 8 p.m. Thursday
[...]
   Apart from that a little Sainte-Beuve and for almost two days listlessly and without any new idea prepared the lecture for Saarbrücken [the Klemperers would be in West Germany 8–16 August, primarily to attend a Franco-German peace conference], above all, brooded over it, tapping in the dark.
   [...]

17th August, Saturday. Dresden
[...]
   Two pleasant surprises :1) In the West German literary monthly *Welt und Wort*,[28] which no doubt thanks to Weinert I have been receiving for a few months, each time from a different address as a 'gift parcel', and which already once printed a short appreciative review of my *Modern Poetry*, there is now in the June 58 issue an article which is a perfect paean of praise of my 'magnificent' Literary History, reviewing all 3 volumes of the new edition.[29] 2) [On our return] I found the Festschrift here with the famous Kesting photograph.

21st August, Thursday afternoon. Dresden
Wolfgang Klemperer, Wolfgang W. Klemperer, MD, Seattle 1, Washington, if you please! entirely, emphatically American. *He* was in the army and in action, and his cousins, Georg's sons were not and he does not like them. Felix, his father, was always in Uncle Georg's shadow and yet – we know this from

Schmeiser – was more important as a scholar. But Georg was more versatile, sociable. (And, this I add for my own part, [Felix] was burdened by his wife, the daughter of Goldschmidt, the money Jew, whereas Georg's wife was the Aryan bourgeois from a highly respected family in Wiesbaden. And he probably as little allowed his sister-in-law to take part in his representative gatherings as his own parents, as his father, the rabbi, who in the curriculum vitae at the end of Georg's dissertation was called a 'country cleric'. But despite all that the Imperial university did not give him a chair, and the Nazis threw him out, and his brother-in-law and medical competitor, Prof. Umber, became a Nazi and disassociated himself from Georg.[30] All that went through my head ...) And so Wolfgang, born 1913, whom I remember only as a boy of about 12 or 14, emigrated with his mother in 1936. Now a man of 45, certainly looking like his father, except more thickset and broad-shouldered. Emphatic determination to obliterate his Jewish origin. His children baptised, as he repeatedly mentions. Anti-Semitism was widespread in the United States – but the second generation, if it grows up entirely Christian and entirely American, does have opportunities to escape the curse. 'I would *never* have married a Jewess, my wife[31] is entirely *Aryan* and entirely *American*.' (34, dark-haired, slim, friendly, without any knowledge of German.) Wolfgang truly warm-hearted. But quite naive: Uncle Victor, do you really believe *that*? By 'that', he means the Soviet Union and the GDR and Communism and the 'Iron Curtain' y todo – and he does not have a clue about any of it – and America despite anti-Semitism [...] is nevertheless the truly humane land. Once I said, the policies of the USA amounted after all to those of big business. Lively disagreement: it always helps out disinterestedly, and all atrocities in Korea had come from the Soviet–Chinese side ... But as already said, aside from this absolute Americanism, a most warm-hearted man. On the Kurfürstendamm he photographed us from every angle. He had a little box of slides with him, had made an arrangement beforehand with a big photographic shop on Ku-Damm and there he projected a large number of beautiful colour views of his home onto the wall. Long, one-storey wooden house in Seattle in the north of California, nearby, visible through trees, a lake, around the house a flower garden, in the middle of it – a source of particular pride, not yet old, a special colour effect: the *swimming pool*. Pictures taken in summer and with some snow, the city, a long bridge – and naturally again and again the children, the whole family, Betty Klemperer,[32] exactly the same age as me (born 8 Oct. 81), now a severe lean face, the grandmother. Once, a face completely unfamiliar to me: W.'s older brother, Kurt, formerly a trainee lawyer, now a well-to-do photographic dealer in Montevideo, I think ... W. emphasised repeatedly, that he himself was not especially well-to-do [...]. But the 4-year education of a son at college costs 14,000 dollars and 3 daughters as well – all 4 are still children, the marriage was in 47. But there are also pictures of a morning ride and this European trip is costing 2500 dollars ... If I were a writer and could put the history of the Klemperer family down on paper! In the car yesterday I talked to H. about the confessional question and the ambition in our family: Georg, Felix, our parents, the Jelskis ... I said repeatedly: It is impossible for you to understand emotionally...

I have been somewhat shaken by a death: *Walter Jelski*. Last year in Berlin I found him so unpleasant! [. . .] He was afraid to visit the GDR, he went to the USA, quite evidently to rely on his brother Willy, whom everyone, including Wolfgang, describes as good-natured and helpful [. . .] Walter, in Berlin as healthy and unreliably big-mouthed as ever he had been, at least 20 years younger than I, was diagnosed with a tumour and died after a couple of months in hospital. Wolfgang knew nothing of the fate of his likeable widow.

We had driven to Berlin on Tue., the 19th, for this meeting – and nothing else. [. . .]

Inge Klemperer is working on a dissertation: History of the medical faculty at Berlin University. She is full of the battles of the 1840s for and against the right of Jewish doctors to lecture. She will possibly move over entirely to the history of medicine. She is convinced, that under *this* government she will never get a teaching position, as she has turned her back on the Party. I said to her, she should really dedicate a *historical* work to *me*, the only *Professor* Klemperer of Berlin University.

[. . .]

25th August, 7 p.m. Monday

Everything is a burden to me, nothing is finished any more, the day runs through my hands – I am incapable of work. On top of that the distress of the weakness of my brain. Just now I could not remember the word 'Buchenwald' – I only recalled Auschwitz. On 14 Sept. we shall have to go to the big Buchenwald ceremony. a) complimentary ticket, b) invitation to speak 'introductory words' at a 'scholars' forum'.

[. . .]

31st August, Sunday forenoon

Three Kirchners at church. – Father Huber here on Thursday for supper. Also in the company of the parents-in-law he was as pleasant company as usual, likeably open-minded and without any aggression or affected piety. Earlier, however, I misbehaved for an embarrassing moment. Kirchner senior asked: 'What shall we do about grace?' I, somewhat agitated, I was absolutely tolerant, the Father was free to act as he saw fit, but 'in my house *I* am in charge' . . . Kulturkampf, persecution of Christians, informing, my position, my 'between stools' – it's ghastly. Afterwards I apologised, Father Huber did not even make the sign of the cross, and everything was soon well again – only I was left with a disagreeable feeling.

[. . .]

Private reading in tiny morsels very late in the evening: Fontane's 'Schach von Wuthenow'.[33]

[. . .]

Now doggedly on to the revision of the Marivaux typescript.

10th September, Wednesday forenoon
[...]
Flight of the university teachers is 'almost' the main topic [Reitzenstein, professor of classics at Halle and Hämel, rector of Jena University, had just fled to the West]. In first place, in general and quite personally for us, is of course China. Really war between USA and 'Red China',[34] and thus cancellation of our journey? Probably clamour, histrionics and horse-trading and nothing more. We have at any rate paid for our trip. [...]

14th September, Sunday before 6 a.m.
[...] On the evening of the 12th phone call on Gusti's 71st birthday. She gave me news of a death: Hans Grundig. Lengthy illness, he died just before his National Prize. [...]
[...] *My* first thought everyone around me is dying and is younger than I: Grundig 57 [...].

19th September, midday Friday and later. Dresden
Red China – People's China. Things look ever more warlike – but it's probably all bluff, negotiations are under way in Warsaw – but there is plenty of shooting ... etc. Aside from the political situation – I increasingly dread my own bravery: Will my health hold out, does the trip have any point for me? Does it for H., who is handicapped by me and looks after me? What can H. gain from it? I myself can no longer gain anything, I am incapable of taking anything in ... But on the other hand: It is after all quite an adventure for H. – and later on will she be able to undertake something like this on her own behalf? ... Don't think, let yourself be carried along...

The Chinese nightmare prevails. Tomorrow to the doctor for inoculation once again. I reacted a little, H. hardly at all.

Additions
On Sunday 14th Sept. Weimar-Buchenwald. [...] The road up to the Ettersberg congested, organisation inadequate, overwhelmed by the mass of cars and buses, by the huge crowd of people. [...] Grotewohl's speech – H.'s correct criticism – too general and too remote from the dead, just as the pompous monument is remote from Buchenwald concentration camp, only the outlines of which are still preserved [...]. In fact Grotewohl really spoke only about West Germany and nuclear plans. He spoke about the Hitlerism over there and of course ignored the Hitlerism over here. After that the usual cliches from the 18 delegations corresponding to the 18 pillars and braziers of the perimeter wall. The whole spectacle, impressive because of the crowds of people, lasted about 2 hours. I shook a few hands, did not really know whose – but was in this way present. [...] We ate all too well in the International – we could have stayed and eaten there for 3 days. What vast amounts this ceremony, this monument must have cost. And the hospitals, the kindergartens, the old-age pensions??

[...] In the afternoon we drove up to the Ettersberg again and now looked at the whole layout in relative peace, walked right round it. [...] The Cremer monument at the front not very impressive.[35] Too theatrical. Gusti W. said: Like a group of actors when the curtain rises again at the end. Nor do I feel very happy about the 'stelae', which are copied from the stations of the cross: from the building of the camp to the Liberation.[36] I am irritated a) by a certain primitivism, a deliberate stiffness and clumsiness; b) the material. The shell limestone makes everything look weathered and worn already. What will happen, when there is real weathering? Beautiful the view into the distance, the rolling plain, the distant hills. Very beautiful the peaceful sunset.

[...]

[Class meeting of the Academy on the 18th. Complaints about the government's school and university policies, the loss of humanist intellectuality and education, absence of historical knowledge, classic literature.] I [...] talked of the inadequate German of the Romance languages students – (Frings: 'since when have they been writing their main essay in German?!!' – 'They don't know enough French.') [...]

[...]

25th September, Thursday forenoon. Dresden

This afternoon we are driving to Berlin, will spend the night in the Kahanes' empty home, have to be at the underground station tomorrow morning at 6 (six!). With that the China trip begins. Great suspense, very mixed feelings on the part of H. as of myself.

Yesterday the Volkskammer: preparations for the election on 16 Nov.,[37] today Academy meeting – with China as pretext I have cried off both. Ambivalent feelings. It's good for me to withdraw; it is hard to lie down in one's grave a bit at a time. It is good that I am giving up my political role; it will be difficult for me, I would so much like to have been a member of a genuine all-German parliament, in a decent Socialist party.

Yesterday I managed to read and make notes on Sainte-Beuve – without hope of being able to complete my 18ième. At 2nd and 3rd hand I don't want to any more, at 1st I would still need years.

[...] I am taking on the journey: Feuchtwanger's *False Nero* and Mann's *Lotte in Weimar*.[38]

Yesterday evening we drank a bottle of Soviet champagne – to the preceding *23rd* and to the journey.

[...]

Once again, all alone and without complaint, H. has taken care of everything technical, practical etc., all the packing as well, naturally. I let myself be carried along.

Tomorrow evening in Moscow.

[The Klemperers were away on their China trip from 26 September until 25 October 1958. The tour took them to Peking, Wuhan, Canton, Hangzhou,

Shanghai, Nanjing and back to Peking. The entries for this period have largely been cut.]

26th September, 10 p.m. (Moscow time) Friday. Moscow, Leninskaya

[...] The alarm clock at 4, Lindner at 5.30, the travel agency at Strausberger Platz at 6. [...] Our flight: a twin-engine Aeroflot. From 8–10.30 to Vilna. Normally and quietly above the clouds at 8000 feet. [...] After that from about 12–2.30 the fatiguing second leg to Moscow. [...]

28th September, 8 a.m. Sunday morning. Moscow

Very murky autumn weather, grey, wet and warm.

[...]

In France today de Gaulle gets his Hitler dictatorship.[39] Tonight we fly to Peking. [...] The prospect of the Tupolev flight is in every respect alarming. At a height of more than 30,000 feet and a speed of 500 miles an hour – how will my heart respond? And how will it cope with the exertions of the coming weeks? And what pleasure will H. get out of it all, if she is constantly worrying about me, and if keeping up with the group [...] is a strain on me? I *must* keep up, there must be no more 'if only'.

[...]

5th October, 7.30 a.m. Sunday. Wuhan

[...]

This trip required preparation, and it would require extensive study afterwards. I had and have time for neither. But perhaps at some point H. can make use of what for me remains a fleeting impression. [...]

7th October, 7 a.m. Tuesday, 'Day of the Republic'. Wuhan

5 years ago I was given the National Prize by Pieck. Then I was still a believer. Today ... I was supposed to speak here. H. stopped me, I suggested Brekenfeld[40] as the Ministry man. Afterwards we tossed for it, the speech went to him. I'm very glad – there are already a few people here, who know my opinion of the Ulbricht dictatorship.

[...]

9th October, towards 10 p.m.

The terrible sweating, the long journey here from 10.30 in the evening in Wuhan to 10.30 in the morning in Canton. A degree of pagoda fatigue, the cold caught from H., rushed to some extent, because we are supposed to make up lost time, off again tomorrow evening. In short a little depressed, especially as H. out of sorts. Apart from that my 77th birthday in a curious situation.

[...]

24th October, after 7 a.m. Friday morning. Peking

[Klemperer, after conversation with Paul Wandel,[41] former Kulturbund colleague etc., now GDR ambassador to the People's Republic of China, and reflecting on what he has seen:] In the course of the afternoon it became clear to me, that Communism is equally suited to pulling primitive peoples out of the primaeval mud and pushing civilised peoples back into the primaeval mud. In the second case it sets to work more mendaciously and is not only stultifying, but debasing as well, in that in every way it trains people to be hypocrites. Thanks to my China trip and fully acknowledging the prodigious achievements here I have finally become an anti-Communist. *This* cannot have been Marx's ideal condition.

To Wandel's remarks I add the speech, which the lecturer Graefe gave in Nanjing. Graefe, probably in his late 30s, director of a pre-teacher-training institute in Altenburg, *not* university educated, for a couple of years now teacher of German at – roughly technical and agronomical – Nanjing University [...] Graefe's task naturally was to show everything in a favourable European-Marxist light. [...] I asked Graefe what he taught and expected 'language'. No, literature as well. Bredel, Seghers etc., 'I have dealt with the more well-known names; during this semester the unknown ones: Turek, Grünberg[42] ...' This is German literature for the Chinese! The 'rest' unimportant.

25th October, 4 a.m. Saturday morning. Peking

It is now definite that we fly to Moscow at 7 with the Tu, whether there will still be a connection to Berlin today is uncertain. Since the day before yesterday there has been a great deal of talk [in the group] about the crash of the Tu on 16th Oct.(?), very matter-of-fact, very witty, very cynical, and today – H.'s observation – everyone will of course be especially cheerful and witty but the feeling of closeness to death is of course preying on everyone's mind. On top of that the unpleasant fact of being virtually unable to inform relatives about the delay. A telephone call has only been made to the travel agency in Berlin.

26th October, 6 p.m. Sunday. Dresden

[...] H. woke me: beneath us a huge city of lights – Berlin. Gentle landing, it was 10 a.m. Berlin time. Lindner in attendance. [...]

27th October, Monday afternoon. Dresden

At home since Saturday night; still utterly exhausted, incapable of work. H. feels exactly the same. [...]

General news:

Becher has died.[43] In the Party obituary: 'the greatest writer of our time'. Even if one were to restrict [the claim] to poetry it would still be wrong.

De Gaulle elected with about 80% of all votes.

[. . .]

The election propaganda; the rejuvenation of the KB group. I have been discharged and replaced by Laux, who under Hitler worshipped the Führer.

I have lived too long and feel very superfluous.

[. . .]

Only my Curriculum and Feuchtwanger still tempt me. Instead I shall again labour to finish the wretched 18ième.

Again and again I was moved by the inkpot which H. lugged all those thousands of miles for me.

Not to forget: the slippers everywhere, the cotton masks over mouth and nose, the wiping up, the tea, the ungummed stamps, the little blast furnaces, the children with naked backsides . . .

29th October, 7 p.m. Wednesday. Dresden

The evening before last the Schmeisers here for dinner. On Mond. morning he had examined me very thoroughly at his clinic, I also had an ECG. As a result in the evening he decreed 2 weeks of absolute rest: a double dose of digitoxin, a heart diet without salt and liquids, lying on my back most of the day – i.e. almost the same regimen as during my serious illness. I submit very unwillingly, but am really very tired and sleep a great deal and with resignation. H. keeps me away from the kitchen stairs and watches over and waits on me in the familiar way.

[. . .]

10th November, 9 p.m. Monday

Tomorrow in Halle for the first time, perhaps still without a seminar. Preparation (Chateaubriand, de Staël) naturally cost me Sunday and Monday again, without adding anything new.

The second 'rest week' not quite as bad – no longer *just* lying, just sleeping, just relaxation, the diet a little less strict – nevertheless still very restricted and always a slight feeling of dizziness as soon as I walk. Curious about tomorrow.

Much Feuchtwanger: after the Nero, the Oppermanns.[44] But took no notes. From F. himself a friendly letter after a long gap [. . .].

12th November, 9 p.m. Wednesday

Halle yesterday depressed me greatly. The lecture (despite my constant unsteadiness while walking) went altogether well and I handed the seminar over to Silzer, only because I had promised Schmeiser and Hadwig that I would do so. [However the real cause of Klemperer's depression is a conversation with the editor Redslob of the Niemeyer publishing house, which has taken over Klemperer's major scholarly publications: thousands of copies remain unsold, the earlier contracts are no longer valid – and as for the future, the editor feels under pressure from the censors and compelled to produce practical, technical texts. Interest remained in the second volume of Klemperer's 18ième, but no date was set for publication.] I was so shaken, shortage of breath, pains in my left arm. I took nitrangin, I said in the introduction to the (well-attended) seminar, which I handed over to Erwin,[45] that I had to keep the seminar course very simple, since the new curricula made it impossible, given the diminished number of hours available, to cover what I regarded as absolutely necessary for taking Romance languages and literatures as a major subject, for a proper university education. There need have been only one 100% comrade among the listeners, then I am *even* more written off than I was before.

On the journey back I considered very seriously whether I should not rather leave off the 18ième and write on Feuchtwanger. Most secret thought: physically and intellectually I am no longer capable of producing – if I *read* Feuchtwanger, then at least I have a (melancholy) pleasure and do not get on H.'s nerves so much with my bitter complaints. I still feel more sorry for *her*, than I feel sorry for myself. She said yesterday (and not for the first time), she was not so attached to life, 'the people I love, are dying – why go on living?' [...]

19th November, 6 p.m. Wednesday. Day of Repentance
[...]
I thought the election on Sunday an impudence. We were at the [polling station] at about 10 [...]. I was shocked that one was not even allowed to place a cross, but dropped the paper 'just like that' into the box, it was 100× more shameless and stupid than the poll in 1954. There is supposed to have been a cubicle with a curtain somewhere. What would one have done in there? [...]

20th November, 10 a.m. Thursday
Last Monday I spoke [in Jena] in the University Kulturbund club about André and Marie-Joseph Chénier.[46] I promised the lecture long ago – I have been turning down all other outside lectures, the invitations have almost ceased anyway. [...]

29th November, 10 a.m. Saturday
[...] Yesterday my state burial by the KB. Prof. Max Burghardt, President, in a letter of thanks to me, dated 26 November: 'In the Volkskammer's 3rd term the German Kulturbund will greatly miss your advice and help in its group. I am sure, however, that you will support us on the Executive Council in word and deed. With best wishes for further co-operation I remain your M.B.'
[...]
Always weighing on me: I have lived too long. The same fear in the physical

respect. The increasing inability to remember names. Yesterday evening for the first time also old man's mistrust. [...] But the fear: I am no longer being taken seriously, merely pityingly cared for as an old man. [...]

I remember from the remote past: 29 Nov. was my parents' wedding day. I assume 29 Nov. 1863, because Georg was born in 65 and before him a child that died young, who is buried in the cemetery in Landsberg. My parents so far back, all my siblings dead – I am like a ghost among the people of today.

[...]

23rd December, Tuesday forenoon

Yesterday morning Keysch telephoned from NDL [*Neue deutsche Literatur* – New German Literature]: Feuchtwanger died Sunday 21 Dec. It affects me deeply in every respect. But I must set aside all feelings etc. and write a study for *NDL* by 6 January, which I had offered for *May*.

26th December, Friday forenoon

[...]

F.'s death affects me very humanly and very egoistically. I truly (and enviously) love him, il est ma voix[47] [...] Egoistically: I had hoped for a closer association with him, for a closer association *through* him with the USA, for my *LTI* to become well known through him.

[...]

Second factor with double effect on this Christmas: immediately beforehand, on 23 Dec., verdict in the Halle-Leipzig student trial – Harress, the two Schröders – two to ten years in prison.[48] [...] So far we know only hints from a telephone conversation with Gottfried (safe and sound), and summary remarks on Rias; our newspapers remain silent. Double effect on our Christmas holiday. On the one hand casting a shadow. On the other hand: Gottfried appears to be saved, so to speak. And likewise on the other hand: *I* am able to say less than ever to counter the Kirchners' embittered hostility towards the East, because I, too, am more and more disgusted by our regime. Without, admittedly, that making the West any more attractive to me.

[...]

31st December, Wednesday night, New Year's Eve, 1.30 a.m.

New Year's Eve passed more innocuously and pleasantly than had generally been feared, childish crackers improved our mood, and Soviet champagne.

During the day as throughout recent days I agonised over the Feuchtwanger study, very depressed at my no longer being able to write. It will hardly be finished by the 6th of Jan., but the content is good.

The résumé of this year is very paltry. Studies: Fridericus and Marivaux,[49] compilation of the essay volume 'Aus 50 Jahren' [From 50 Years].

Politically out of favour and discharged and without sympathy for, not for the West and not for the East. Germany is an earthworm cut in two; both parts squirm, both contaminated by the same Fascism, each in its own way.

Always the awareness of my 77 years, of post equitem sedet atra mors,[50] of being unable to cope with the thought of death, exacerbated by my thoughts of Hadwig, who has attached herself heart and soul to nothing but old people, who should have children and will only be an aunt. The journey to China September–October.

A couple of pages of my 18ième.

1959

11th January, Sunday night (after 12.30)

Today I sent off 'Feuchtwanger's Central Novel'[1] to NDL by express post – Keysch telephoned urgently from Berlin the day before yesterday – and then spent until evening putting the quotation page references into the uncorrected copy. Keysch telephoned with news of the death on 22 Dec., I promised a study by 6th Jan. Since then [...] I have been working on the *Success* study like a man possessed – uncommonly slowly, and then when I read over [the essay] I was not very pleased with it. Perhaps because I was too tired. [...]

18th January, Sunday forenoon

[...] Gottfried was involved, as a witness, in the disgraceful trial of the Halle-Leipzig student group, which was supposed to have conspired against the dictator Ulbricht. Among them my doctoral candidate Hartmut Harress, whose dissertation on Vogüé was with us, to protect it from confiscation. The people were in prison awaiting trial for almost one and a half years. Gottfried, interrogated by 'State Security' once, always in danger of being arrested himself. [...] The group has now received sentences of up to 10 years in prison – that was announced by Rias, not by our broadcasting stations and press. My parents-in-law constant fear, which even now has not been allayed. [...] Tensions and conflicts as in the Nazi years. [...] Harress got away lightly. About one and a half years, most of which he has already served awaiting trial. In fact the whole group can have committed no serious crime. Nothing but discussions against Ulbricht among themselves. They had no power to do anything else, contacts with Bonn were out of the question.

For a couple of days I have been reading the complete *Novels and Tales* of

Voltaire in the Dieterichsen edition. My introduction [to the short novels[2]] is
to be *variation* at least, not mere *repetition*. [. . .]
  [. . .]

19th February, Thursday
Yesterday evening at last stuck down the envelope with the Voltaire ms. All
these weeks only HIM – and yet so little added to my Literary History.
  [. . .] I feel myself ever more out in the cold. On 29 Jan. There was a *Figaro*
première at the Berlin Opera House. The dramaturge had requested an article
from me: I *and* Feuchtwanger were to write on it in the programme. [. . .] I was
promptly paid the agreed 300M – then silence and 2 weeks ago the most
tortuous, courteous and mendacious letter arrived from the evidently decent
dramaturge [. . .].
  In addition to the small private worries the big general ones: A group of
student conspirators has been arrested at the TH. With great emphasis on the
serious conspiratorial intention – plotting with Western agents, possession of
weapons.[3] The Technical High School! Centrepiece of our 'culture', full of the
sons of workers and peasants!
  [. . .]

21st February, Saturday afternoon
Feuchtwanger has come back on me again and took up several hours today: The
NDL study has appeared, Dietz telephoned, he wants to reprint it (with my
picture) in a special booklet for the commemoration. From my ms I added the
passages which are missing from the *NDL* because of lack of space. (Dietz on
the telephone: But, please, no problems with the censors! They raise so many
difficulties for us. I shall see if I can 'perhaps get your essays through after all'.
[. . .].)
  [. . .]

12th March, Wednesday towards 6 a.m.
The day before yesterday Halle, today Berlin. H. has to attend to passport matters
[Klemperer had been invited to an international Romance Languages Congress
in Lisbon[4]], I give my Corneille lecture. Impossible to deal with the topic in *one*
double class a month.
  Extremely bitter at the rejection of my essais.[5] The 'opinion' passed on to me
by the editor Wenig [who had replaced Karl Dietz, who had died] is an insult.
Who wrote it? Did the publishing house, which kept me in suspense for months,
present the ms to the Literature Office [i.e. the censorship body] at all – as it
maintained? We doubt it. At the same time a further cut in my Feuchtwanger
essay was demanded. (The sentence: Rousseau would hardly have agreed with
Robespierre.) I withdrew my imprimatur, wrote a final refusal, forbade further

advance notice. Finis. I am probably doing the poor swine an injustice – they are not to blame. But why put me off and lie to me?

[...]

25th March, Wednesday afternoon

[...]

In Halle yesterday Harress, who has now been released from prison, called on me. 38, two children. He said, he had come to his sentence like a lamb to the slaughter. He is a completely unpolitical man. He now wants to work as a translator. There is a demand for editors etc. When [interviewers] see the prison entry in his pass, he is turned down. Cf Jean Valjean on his return from the bagno.[6]

[...]

Trip: International Romance Languages Congress, Lisbon

27th March, Good Friday evening. Dresden

H. has finished the packing, is trying out her camera. [...]

Travel mood? My attitude to the whole enterprise is one almost of apathy. It is a linguists' congress, and I do not know a word of Portuguese. H. has had all the running around to do, likewise the packing. [...]

28th April. Dresden

Hic incipit tragoedia.[7] Sequuntur H.'s notes,[8] dictations, efforts. Today H. in Halle alone for the first time. Expected back at 6.

29th April, Wednesday evening

Every day for over a week now I have been sitting at my desk for a long time. But I am so unsteady on my way to it that H. has to support me and my hand trembles so badly that I can hardly manage a signature. Schmeiser maintains, this is only a matter of weakness and circulation, after Whitsun I shall be at my lectern again.

It distresses me, that H. has hardly any time left for her own work.

[...]

Reading: 100 pages of *Napoléon* by Tarlé, in French – *Der Fall Deruga* [The Deruga Case[9]] by Ricarda Huch; in contrast to H. I did not warm to the latter. Neither with respect to realism nor with respect to psychology.

Now *Jew Süss* [Feuchtwanger[10]]. Invitation from the Academy of Arts tempts me.[11]

Betrayal by the Greifenverlag repels me.

I have lost all belief that I might have an effect. All belief in right or left. I live and die as a lonely literary journalist.

30th April, Thursday
Jew Süss. I find it hard.

Still extremely unsteady on my feet. It's all right when I'm sitting. My hand trembles, these few notes are already progress. I cannot imagine, that I will be ready for duty again in 4 or 5 weeks. Politically completely indifferent, newspaper and wireless bore me. I reproach myself for making use of H. for private dictation.

Already 2–3× at my desk now, but slow-witted and listless. The way here and back, the way to the bathroom, a great effort. Impossible to clean myself properly. What H. is doing is caring for an infant. In the mornings she shaves me with the new soapless electric razor.

3rd May, Sunday
I sit at my desk for a couple of hours every day. But I can only unsteadily get as far as this leaning on H., the feeling of dizziness is always there now. I can also only write laboriously. Also nothing occurs to me. I no longer believe, that I shall bring even one of my three topics to a conclusion. On the other hand: to read 'just for the sake of it', as my father-in-law does con amore, does not satisfy me. If I really wanted to complete the Feuchtwanger, then I would need at least two years. Same amount of time and concentration for the 18ième. To say nothing of the Curriculum. And always the feeling: None of the 3 plans will be completed.

At the moment, therefore, *Jew Süss* – reading mind you, not any notes. Great writing, but inwardly profoundly irresolute. Ultimately altogether mystical, ultimately religious after all [...].

8th May, Friday afternoon
I am still creeping to my desk for two or three hours and back to bed in my nightshirt and H.'s dressing gown, leaning on H., tottering; I still find it very difficult to write with a pen – in any case nothing occurs to me. The doctor talks about improvement; I myself feel, physically and mentally, that I have outlived my time. H. is convinced, if I'm 'grumbling', that's a sign of improvement. But even if I should get over my weakness and my fear of the night – there is always the sense of futility. I constantly feel sorry for H., she says I am impatient, is offended if I am not in 'cheerful' mood, etc.

Many visitors, far too many for H. Nursing, house like a hotel, in addition constant calls by the doctor and always the pressure of her lecture preparation. Running up and downstairs, she has become thin and looks terribly pale and gets too little sleep.

[...]

9th May, Saturday afternoon

Again at my desk in nightshirt and H.'s dressing gown. But today in sunny-warm weather went for a one-and-a-half hour drive with H. wearing a suit. On the heath, Radeberg – Fischhaus, sat at the edge of the wood for half an hour. But the terrible unsteadiness, the trembling of my hands, the weakness almost unchanged.

[...]

Have I noted that Gusti W. was also here at some point? In between she was in hospital in Berlin-Buch, was much examined, treated, even had a small operation, is just as moribund as I and yet is quite calm; sees the stupefaction, the cultural mendacity etc. of the Ulbricht dictatorship just as well as I do – and still swims with the comradely current and is carried along by it. Whereas I am a dead man. On this point H. is completely right: 'You speak out, you play the martyr – and then you are annoyed when you're struck off.'

Reading *The Ugly Duchess* [Feuchtwanger]:[12] But I must – I *must* – at least note down a couple of catchwords on *Jew Süss*. After that back to the 18ième, *even if* the lecture for the Academy of Arts is finally agreed.

My depression with respect to H. grows ever deeper in *every* respect. She is having a very hard time.

11th May, Monday forenoon

The awful feeling of dizziness while standing and walking very slowly. It is supposed to be nothing more than weakness and circulatory trouble after being on my back for so long. Therefore: On my feet. On the other hand: my heart needs rest. Therefore: lie down. I creep about a little. H. still has to support, wait on me etc. etc. for every little thing. All this is called convalescence.

Peter and Inge Klemperer were here from early Thursday, Ascension Day, afternoon, until yesterday evening at 7.30. Various retrospective family conversations. Georg the 'son of a country cleric'.[13] Inge's doctoral thesis. Jewish themes not looked on with favour in the GDR.

12th May, 1.30 a.m. Tuesday

[...]

Inge Kl. related: Mette, Volkskammer colleague, psychiatrist, study on Hölderlin, already in the Ministry of Hygiene for some time, recently also Professor for the History of Medicine – without a clue, time or institute funding for it, is her boss. A big Festschrift is to appear for the 150th anniversary of the Humboldt University in 1960,[14] Mette responsible for history of medicine – Inge's dissertation is to appear there, in brief and as free of Jews as possible. Her actual larger topic: Jews in the Berlin medical faculty, is to be cut back. Characteristic of the GDR ... And characteristic of me: I would very much like to see the Jewish theme and have it dedicated to *me*. We talked about it and about Georg's position.

LQI: *Sächsische Zeitung* 23.4.59. 'Colleague Schubert, day nursery teacher at the 12th Primary School: with some groups in our nursery we have got to the point that the children are already working independently and *learning leadership* ... From lunchtime, under the supervision of a nursery teacher, the children themselves take over. Thus we try to *teach leadership* to our worker and peasant children; because one day they will be in charge of the state.' Purest Nazism, in *even* worse German! [...]

I finished the *Ugly Duchess*. Very disappointing. [...] I do not really believe I shall complete even one of my three plans.

[...]

17th May, 8 p.m. Whit Sunday

On Thursday night like a bolt from the blue, so to speak, I had a minor relapse. When my pulse reached 120, H. telephoned Schmeiser; the good man came out in the middle of the night. Since then I have been getting sleeping pills, lie in bed a lot, stagger about all day like a drunkard and have lost all faith of ever returning to a normal life. H. is having a hard time with me; I would so much like to conceal from her that inwardly I feel finished and yet do not manage it. Always the fear of the night, of the next attack, of dying. Awful. Poor H.

[...] I manage ever more rarely to read our newspapers. We learn literally nothing about Geneva [4 power conference on Berlin, German unification, European security and disarmament].[15]

20th May, 7 p.m. Wednesday

A lot of digitalis, a lot of sleeping pills, anxiety as soon as I am lying in bed upstairs about 2 a.m., a 'thriller', fall asleep about 3, wake up between 11 and 12, then lie downstairs, fall asleep again after breakfast, then here at my desk after 4 the most urgent correspondence, then Schmeiser comes, finds my heart satisfactory, talks encouragingly etc. All this is called living. I would have much preferred not to die off bit by bit like this with the constant fear of dying.

[...] Last items of serious reading were *Jew Süss* and the *Ugly Duchess* – the sheet with no more than the beginnings of notes is lying on my desk. Meanwhile word came from the Academy of Arts, it has been decided that an official Feuchtwanger ceremony will take place in 'a Magdeburg factory', while *I* should give a Feuchtwanger lecture at the end of June [...] in the rooms of the Academy. At that I cancelled, as my health had not yet sufficiently improved and my opinion of Feuchtwanger was well known. No doubt in the Magdeburg factory Abusch or one of his people will give prominence to F.'s inclination towards the Soviet Union and dismiss everything else as bourgeois original sin, talk a great deal about the Adenauer state and as little as possible about the Jews, and *Neues Deutschland* will print a big and enthusiastic review of it all – while my lecture, given behind closed doors to 40–50 brave people would have been ignored.

[...]

Today I took a few uncertain steps around the garden, tomorrow by car to the hospital for an ECG. I no longer believe in the lecture in Halle on the 26th.

[...]

21st May, 9 p.m. Thursday

Last night with too small a dose of sleeping pills for H. and me no sleep until almost 4 a.m. In the morning to Schmeiser's clinic for the ECG. At 7 he brought the result here: distinct improvement but not good – ban on lectures for the whole semester. I expected nothing else and am nevertheless very, very shaken. Especially as I believe the 'distinct improvement' is a friendly lie. The truth is: mai piu.[16] I had sometimes almost come to terms with the thought of death. But this dying bit by bit, the fear of every night, the staggering about (particularly bad again today) as a result of 'circulatory trouble' – poor H.!

I stick to my *thrillers*. Tonight we both read until it grew light and the birds cheeped. [...]

23rd May, Saturday evening towards 10 p.m.

Married seven years. I am very heavy at heart. The staggering does not stop, I have completely lost any hope in recovery.

24th May, Sunday evening

Very depressed – condition unchanged.

Yesterday afternoon at Gusti's for an hour. [...] Gusti probably just as moribund as I, but on the one hand more philosophical on the other less sensitive than I am to the dreadful stultification of the Party, thirdly as much buoyed up by success, as I am abandoned by it. Constantly new editions of her books.

Triumph and bitterness: Two letters from the Academy of Arts: the principal ceremony to mark Feuchtwanger's 75th will now take place in Berlin after all, I am to give the lecture, Helene Weigel the reciter. – On Schmeiser's urgent instructions I had to decline. He has written a doctor's certificate for Halle: Another 6–8 weeks of complete rest; it was 'extremely likely' that I would be able to resume lecturing next semester. To me he maintains that my most recent ECG (21 May) shows significant progress, the unsteadiness will stop etc. but I no longer believe it.

[...]

For a couple of days now (since H: and I had an almost completely sleepless night) I get a big dose of kalhypnon at 11, afterwards read down here until about 12.30, but then fall asleep immediately. The next day begins in the afternoon, and I no longer have a whole day.

[...]

27th May, 6 p.m.
[...]

Nothing changes in my condition; I am unable to make H.'s unpleasant task any easier. Yesterday she brought her new dress from Halle and delightedly showed it to me. I was unable to suppress my egoistical bitterness. As if for a school leavers' ball in summer, really very charming. And *I* forgotten by death and waiting for it without composure.

1st June, Monday evening towards 10 p.m.
With an interval of three days we saw the same film, first in Niedersedlitz, the second time today in Trachau: *Wir Wunderkinder* [We Miracle Children – a West German film]. Quite outstanding, especially the songs (influenced by Brecht ...)[17] [...]

My state of health continues to be hopeless; I no longer believe Schmeiser's encouragement – the dizziness remains unchanged, my eyes are very bad [...].

Deeply depressed. – I completed a footnote to the de Sade section [of the 18ième], will now tackle the Charrière, but without any hope.

My actual reading, Werfel. Now *The Forty Days of Musa Dagh*.[18] The Armenians, he says, the Jews, he means – but he has genuinely studied the Armenians. As writer and artist he undoubtedly surpasses Feuchtwanger.

[...]

On Saturday afternoon at Gusti's again for an hour. [...] Probably we both think the same thing about each other: After such a long friendship what is the point of discussion with a moribund old dodderer? I mostly leave the conversation to Hadwig, who negotiates all obstacles with her benevolently superior Jesuitism and her irony. [...]

6th June, 7 p.m. Saturday
Always the same feeling of dizziness. Last night with a smaller dose of kalhypnon fell asleep at 6 a.m. Poor Hadwig. – Schmeiser repeatedly explains, my heart is considerably better – and when it is *even* better, he will deal with the dizziness.

The day, therefore, begun after 1 p.m., from 3–4 with Gusti in her garden. There as here most beautiful leurre éternel [du printemps], a profusion of roses. She just as ill as I, but happy in activity, success, Party. [...] I talked about Werfel's *Musa Dagh*. Gusti coldly disapproved of it. H. afterwards: 'If the Armenians were Communists then Gusti would be interested in it.'

I repeatedly try to get back to my 18ième, leaf futilely through old disordered difficult-to-decipher mss, then resignedly go on struggling through the *Musa Dagh*. It has almost 800 closely printed pages, I shall probably get to the middle this evening.

[...]

7th June, Sunday 10 p.m.

A tiny bit better for a while, now tottering about again.

Most beautiful weather. With H. in the car to Tharandt, Hartha, Grillenburg, sat there in the wood for half an hour. Parked cars everywhere – people taking the country air.

I am looking through my 18ième. It is subjective literary journalism – but very good literary journalism. I should finish the book off. I *should* – but I cannot put down *Musa Dagh*. [...]

11th June, 10 p.m. Thursday

Semper idem. Dizziness, kalhypnon, digitalis – the doctor is 'satisfied'.

Semper idem. [...] Sleep until midday and *Musa Dagh*. And that's called convalescence.

Headline in the *Sächsische Zeitung* yesterday 'Bonn terror justice, eleven years jail'. If one reads the report, then these eleven years are spread over a large group of defendants facing political charges, of whom not one got more than 9 months at most.

Decent little Father Huber. At Whitsun after the sermon he said in the presence of parents-in-law: 'We pray for a sick man.' He recently told H., he had prayers said for me. The most comical thing about the story: for a long time we were unable to invite the man here, because otherwise I might even get the reputation of 'asking for Catholic consolation in the face of death'. Now that I am out of bed half the day, am also going on excursions, he can come again sometimes. (Naturally as a disguised motor-cyclist.)

[...]

25th October. Hospital Writing Room

The day before yesterday, 23 October 1959, it was exactly seven years and seven months since we were married and exactly seven months since I had the serious cardiac asthma attack in Brussels, from which I only partly recovered, before then being admitted here on 26 June after another relapse on 24 June. This is the first diary entry after a number of correspondence notes, and could be the beginning of a new volume of the Curriculum.

Peter and Inge, our guests while attending a psychiatrists' congress in Dresden, visited us here every day. We went for drives in the surrounding countryside with Inge. My every step is unsteady, Lindner pulls me into the car. Both consoled me about the most distressing symptom, which causes me to doubt my mental recovery, *déjà vu*. I trust the psychiatrist even less than any other doctor and yet allow them to comfort me.

I have now got to the point, that I can wake up in the night without a start, and without calling H. to help, can think over a few things.

As I do so one event repeatedly comes to mind and the belated vindication of an attack which at the time I felt to be unjust. I must read up the details in my diary. At the time of my election to the Academy there is supposed to have been an article in a Frankfurt newspaper about the older professors at the Humboldt University. The older university teachers who remained loyal to it were either idiots or had been bought – in the case of Klemperer, both were true. At the time incomprehensible to me. In the plenum of the Volkskammer, as spokesman of the Law Committee, I had demanded with complete conviction the re-introduction of the death penalty for the most serious political offences – e.g. blowing up bridges, I condemned everyone who went over to the West. Why do I not publicly recant now? when I am convinced that Russian policies are being pursued here, and that the Russians are pursuing imperialist power politics just as much as the West Germans, only in somewhat more bloodily Asiatic fashion than the cultivated West. Why am I content with remaining silent, and am even afraid of disapproved silence? For H.'s sake. It is hardly likely that I will be harmed. But if the promised pension were taken away from her?

I am much too cowardly for suicide. But if I were not (*if!*) then I would not be waiting night after night for the next attack.

[...]

26th October, 7 p.m. Writing Room

The infinite length of this one day and one night since yesterday. Excursion in a handcart[19] – H.'s physical exertion. At the same time constant attempts at consolation. Excursion in the car, Lindner tugs me in. I experience everything twice over. They want to talk me out of it. I am supposed to stay here until December. What does H. gain, if she alone is saddled with me at home? What for me from lingering on, if I can no longer produce and no longer believe in the worth of producing? Make an end, Lord, make an end . . .

H. has noted the names of my hospital visitors in these last months. [...]

Once Klecker, the eye specialist, reassured me about the state of my eyes – but they get ever worse, the reassurance does not hold up.

28th October, about 8 p.m. Writing room with almost correct chair and table height and not too glaring lights

H.'s advice: Concrete details, not general complaints about my condition! Patiently practise my hand!

Yesterday a big day. Drive to the Malther dam. Long conversations with Pastor Bach. Purest hospital film scene. Serious depression in between. [...]

Today drive in the car as far as Altenberg.

Today good fortune in my Fontane reading: *Before the Storm*. After having struggled through his *L'Adultera* and getting nowhere with *Jenny Treibel*.

[...]

29th October, after 8 p.m. Writing Room

It took me more [than] one and a half hours to write a short birthday letter to Anny Kl. My head failed me much more than my hand. [...]

But even the short pieces of dictation to H. [...] cost a great deal of effort, since I found it difficult to make up my mind about the wording. Apart from that a short drive into town in connection with the will and very lengthy walking exercises in the hospital grounds.

Halting and yet very enjoyable reading of *Before the Storm*.

At night fear and frequently interrupted sleep as before.

[Victor Klemperer died on 11 February 1960.]

ABBREVIATIONS

ASSO Assoziation revolutionärer bildender Künstler Deutschlands (Association of Revolutionary Artists of Germany)

CDU Christlich-Demokratische Union (Christian Democratic Union)

FDGB Freier Deutscher Gewerkschaftsbund (Free German Trade Union)

FDJ Freie Deutsche Jugend (Free German Youth)

GDR German Democratic Republic (i.e. East Germany)

HUB Humboldt Universität Berlin (i.e. the old Berlin University, situated in the Soviet sector of the divided city)

KPD Kommunistische Partei Deutschlands (Communist Party of Germany)

KB Kulturbund

LDP Liberal Demokratische Partei (Liberal Democratic Party – in West Germany and West Berlin, later changed its name to Free Democratic Party)

LDPD Liberal Demokratische Partei Deutschlands (Liberal Democratic Party of Germany – part of the National Front in East Germany)

LTI/*LTI* Lingua Tertii Imperii (the Latin name – Language of the Third Reich – Victor Klemperer gave his diary notes and subsequent book on the uses of language in Nazi Germany)

NDL *Neue Deutsche Literatur* (literary periodical published in East Germany)

NDPD National Demokratische Partei Deutschlands (National Democratic Party of Germany – part of the National Front in East Germany)

PHS People's High School (for the German VHS – Volkshochschule)

SED Sozialistische Einheitspartei Deutschlands (Socialist Unity Party of Germany)

SMAD Sowjetische Militäradministration in Deutschland (Soviet Military Administration in Germany)

SPD Sozialdemokratische Partei Deutschlands (Social Democratic Party of Germany)

TBE *To the Bitter End: The Diaries of Victor Klemperer 1942–45*

TH Technische Hochschule (Technical High School – usually Dresden)

USPD Unabhängige Sozialdemokratische Partei Deutschlands (Independent Social Democratic Party of Germany)

VVN Vereinigung der Verfolgten des Naziregimes (Association of the Victims of the Nazi Regime)

NOTES

Preface

1 Erich Kästner, *Notabene 45. Ein Tagebuch* (Frankfurt/Main, 1965), p. 140.
2 Of course, this is not really a concluding paragraph at all, because the diaries flow on unstoppably. Nevertheless, the account of the long journey – on foot much of the time – from Bavaria to Dresden (26 May–10 June 1945) does constitute a distinct unit within the diaries, written up after the return to Dölzschen. In literary terms it is a form of Romantic 'Wanderung'.
3 Rammon Reimann,' "Ex oriente lux": Warum Victor Klemperer den Osten dem Westen vorzog. Eine Sicht auf Briefe von und an Victor Klemperer ab Mai 1945', in *Germanica*, vol. xxvii (2000), p. 209.
4 Kulturbund zur Demokratischen Erneuerung Deutschlands – Cultural Union for the Democratic Renewal of Germany. At first an ostensibly non-party grouping of intellectuals established under the auspices of SPD and KPD in the summer of 1945. It effectively became one of the channels of official cultural activity, first in the Soviet Zone, then in the German Democratic Republic which took its place.
5 *Victor Klemperer: Leben sammeln, nicht fragen wozu und warum. Tagebücher 1919–1932* (Berlin 1996).
6 A decree of the Soviet Military Administration had made it necessary to join a political party in order to be eligible for compensation as a victim of fascism, but there was no compelling reason why that party should be the KPD. In the Soviet Zone and East Berlin the Social Democratic Party and the KPD were united as the Sozialistische Einheits Partei (SED) – Socialist Unity Party – on 23 April 1946.
7 A passage from the diary entry of 16 August 1936, much quoted since the diaries were published, gives some idea of the depth of anger he already felt then, and which helped propel him leftwards: 'If one day … the fate of the vanquished [i.e. after the defeat of Nazism] lay in my hands, then I would let all the ordinary folk go and even some of the leaders, who might after all have had honourable intentions and not known what they were doing. But I would have all the intellectuals strung up, and the professors three feet higher than the rest; they would be left hanging from the lampposts for as long as was compatible with hygiene.' *I Shall Bear Witness: The Diaries of Victor Klemperer 1933–41* (London, 1998), p. 225.
8 Max Kahane, the husband of Klemperer's great-niece Doris Machol, reported to Klemperer the amused comment of a then senior Communist, Anton Ackermann (13 September 1948): 'he had recently spoken to Ackermann about me. A. had said with "friendly irony": "the old firebrand, especially when it's against his professional colleagues – he's sometimes almost too impetuous for us." ' Considerably less indulgent had been the remarks of the Communist Interior Minister of Saxony, Kurt Fischer, a couple of years earlier. At a regional committee meeting of the SED (2 October 1946)

he described Klemperer as an 'enemy of intellectuals' and a 'political child', and ensured that he was unlikely to be elected to the Saxon parliament. (From documents held by the Saxon State Archives, quoted in Michael Richter/Mike Schmeitzner: 'Einer von beiden muß so bald wie möglich entfernt werden.' Der Tod des sächsischen Ministerpräsidenten Rudolf Friedrichs vor dem Hintergrund des Konfliktes mit Innenminister Kurt Fischer (Leipzig, 1999), p. 91.) Klemperer's own diary entries (1 and 3 October 1946) do not reveal whether he was aware of such hostility. Nor does he describe with any clarity why, at about the same time, he felt forced to step down from his adult-education post, though his resignation does seem to have been related to lack of support on the part of the SED. At any rate the incident demonstrates that Klemperer's rise in the Soviet Zone and the German Democratic Republic was far from smooth and in part dependent on power struggles of which he seems to have been only dimly aware.

9 Another factor was his fear of a revival of Nazism. In common with many observers he completely overestimated such a possibility, though it was hardly surprising in a Jew who had survived the Nazi genocide, when so many around him had not. In truth, however, Nazism as a political force was already dead before Hitler. 'People felt they had been betrayed by their leader' – Sebastian Haffner, *Anmerkungen zu Hitler* (Frankfurt/Main, 1981), p. 154.

10 When the strikes and riots usually known as the 'Uprising of 17th June' take place in East Berlin and East Germany, Klemperer is critical of government and Party, but simultaneously believes the official line that a 'Fascist' plot with the aim of bringing down the Communist regime had been responsible for the violent incidents in Berlin and other cities.

11 Ironically this also seems to have been a criticism of one of Klemperer's most brilliant colleagues and rivals: Ernst Robert Curtius was accused of being 'more a belle-lettrist than a scholar'. (See Walter Boehlich, 'Ein Haus in dem wir atmen können. Das Neueste zum Dauerstreit um den Romanisten Ernst Robert Curtius', in *Die Zeit*, 6 December 1996). Leo Spitzer, a protégé of Karl Vossler (also teacher of Victor Klemperer and perhaps the most important intellectual influence on him), commented, in a postwar review, on Curtius's 'journalistic vein'. Spitzer had earlier also criticised Victor Klemperer's 'Feuilletonismus'. (Reported 29 July 1934 in *Ich will Zeugnis ablegen bis zum letzten* (Berlin, 1995), p. 126 of the fuller German edition of the Klemperer Diaries.) I owe these last references to Hans Ulrich Gumbrecht's *Vom Leben und Sterben der großen Romanisten* (Munich, 2002). It contains biographical essays on Karl Vossler, Ernst Robert Curtius, Leo Spitzer, Erich Auerbach and Werner Krauss, and is a brilliant study in intellectual history and of a tradition of German scholarship. It is, not least, essential to an understanding of the context of Victor Klemperer as scholar and university teacher.

12 Rolf Schneider, *Von Paris nach Frankreich. Reisenotizen* (Rostock 1975), pp. 66–72. The full account from which I have quoted extracts here throws up some further questions and contradictions with respect to Klemperer (and perhaps in part they derive from Schneider rather than Klemperer) but they are of minor importance. I am very grateful to Gunhild Muschenheim of the Goethe Institut Library, London, for drawing my attention to this book.

13 Hans-Joachim Petsche, 'Victor Klemperer – ein Mißverständnis?' in Karl-Heinz Siehr (ed.), *Victor Klemperers Werk. Texte und Materialien für Lehrer* (Berlin, 2001), p. 248.

14 For reasons of space it is not possible to include here a discussion of what will remain his most important completed work, his study of Nazi language, *LTI*, first published in 1947.

15 In my introduction to *I Shall Bear Witness. The Klemperer Diaries 1933–41* I stated that *all* of Victor's brothers married non-Jews. It is a claim also made by other commentators. In

fact, the wife of Felix, Victor's second-oldest brother, was Jewish, Betty née Gold-schmidt. See Victor Klemperer's interesting but brief remarks in the entry for 21 August 1958.

16 See e.g. diary entries for 19, 22 and 24 January 1953.

17 See footnote 13 above.

1945

17 June

1 Ernst Neumark, lawyer. The German authorities had appointed him the local Dresden spokesman of the 'Reichsvereinigung der Juden in Deutschland' (National Association of Jews in Germany), i.e. to act as liaison between the dwindling Jewish community and the orders and demands of Nazi Party and state.

2 Bavarian village north-east of Augsburg. It was the final stopping point in the Klemperers' flight after the bombing of Dresden on 13–14 February 1945 (and after Victor Klemperer had removed his Jews' star). The Klemperers were in Unterbernbach from mid-April to mid-May 1945 before returning to Dresden.

3 Willy Katz (1878–1947), doctor. During the war he was the only Jewish 'healer' permitted to practise in Dresden.

4 Plauen Station; i.e. the railway station in the Dresden district of Plauen, of which Dölzschen village was administratively a part.

19 June

5 Klemperer had given his diaries, as well as some other possessions, to the couple's friend, the doctor and surgeon Annemarie Köhler (1892–1948) for safekeeping. Köhler, together with Friedrich Dressel, had been in charge of a private clinic in Pirna since 1937. Pirna is a small historic town on the Elbe a few miles south-east of Dresden.

6 Will Grohmann (1887–1968), art historian and writer. Occupied a number of admin-istrative positions in Dresden 1945–8.From 1948 he taught in West Berlin. He was a prominent promoter and a populariser of modern art in postwar West Germany.

7 Local grocer; after the Klemperers were forced to leave their home in Dölzschen in 1940 and move into a 'Jews' House', the Nazi authorities imposed Berger on them as a tenant.

8 The Begerburg was a castle-like neo-Gothic residence, originally built for a quarry-owner. After 1933 it was the seat of the local Nazi officials.

9 'In Königsberg, in Bromberg'; today Kaliningrad in Russia and Bydgoszcz in Poland.

21 June

10 One of the Jews' Houses in Dresden, in which the Nazis forced the remaining Jews of the city to live, was in Sporergasse.

11 The Jews' House in which the Klemperers were living when the major Dresden air raids took place was in Zeughausstrasse.

12 Adolf Bauer, owner of a cardboard box company. Victor Klemperer was forced to labour there, and at another business, Thiemig & Möbius, from 1 November 1943 until finally released from forced labour on 23 June 1944, owing to ill health. (Before working at Bauer, he had also worked at Schlüter's, a company producing herbal teas.) Within the limits set by Nazi supervision and deportations, the owners of these companies had done what they could for the Jews allocated to them.

13 Albert Konrad, formerly in business at the Dresden slaughterhouse; representative of the Jewish workers at Schlüter.

14 Anna Mey was an employee of the Technical High School during the 1920s and thirties and friendly with the Klemperers.

15 Werner Lang, economist; acquaintance of Adolf Bauer. Representative of the Jewish workers at Thiemig & Möbius. From May 1945 President of the Dresden Chamber of Commerce.

16 Rudolf Friedrichs (1892–1947), lawyer. SPD member from 1922, senior civil servant in the Saxon Ministry of the Interior 1926–33. Lord Mayor of Dresden May/June 1945, from then until his death chief officer of the state of Saxony.

17 A reference to the period of the Councils Republic in Munich after the First World War, which Klemperer experienced at first hand and of which he had a rather jaundiced view (even though his earlier best friend, Hans Meyerhof, was involved on the side of the revolutionaries).

23 June

18 Maria Kube, a Sorb (the Sorbs are a small Slav minority living around Bautzen and Kamenz near Dresden), was the Klemperers' housekeeper 1929–31. She remained in touch with the couple during the Nazi years.

19 Agnes Scholze, also a Sorb, was the Klemperers' housekeeper 1925–9. The Klemperers found shelter with her on their flight from Dresden (18 February–4 March 1945).

20 From May 1940 to September 1942 the Klemperers lived in the Jews' House at 15b Caspar David Friedrichstr. Julia Pick, one of the other occupants, was often visited by her friend, the former bank employee Karl Steininger. Faced by deportation to Theresienstadt, Julia Pick committed suicide on 20 August 1942.

21 (Italian): on the other hand.

22 Social Democratic para-military organisation set up in 1924 to defend the Weimer Republic.

23 Fritz Salo Glaser (1876–1956), lawyer. Before 1933 frequently defended Communists in the courts. He and Klemperer became acquainted during the war. Glaser was Jewish, but since his wife was Aryan *and* both children had been brought up as Protestant, he had the status of a 'privileged' Jew. This meant, for example, that he did not have to do forced labour.

24 (Spanish): and everything.

25 I.e. complete the diary account of the journey back to Dresden from Bavaria, much of it on foot, between 25 May and 10 June 1945. This constitutes the final part of *To the Bitter End: The Diaries of Victor Klemperer 1942–45* (*TBE*).

26 (Latin): abbreviated from *Vanitas vanitatum, et omnia vanitas* ('Vanity of vanities, saith the Preacher, vanity of vanities' (Ecclesiastes ch. 1, verse 2 and ch. 12, verse 8)).

25 June

27 Frau Rasch, the friendly and philo-Semitic caretaker's wife at the Jews' House, 2 Lothringer Weg, where the Klemperers lived from 3 September 1942 to 13 December 1943.

28 LTI, an abbreviation of Lingua Tertii Imperii, was what Klemperer had called his notes on the language of the Third Reich, and *LTI* was to be the title under which he published his essays on the subject. As early as June 1945, however, Klemperer was making critical notes in his diary on the language of Communism, which he called LQI – Lingua Quarti Imperii or Language of the Fourth Reich – and he continued to do so despite making a commitment to Communism.

29 Willy Schlüter was the owner of the Schlüter herbal teas business, the first company for which Victor Klemperer had to do forced labour (though previously he had been allocated to snow-clearing duties).

29 June

30 Eva and Victor Klemperer had first met on 29 June 1904; when they were married two years later, this was the date engraved on their wedding rings.

31 Vogel, a grocer who had sometimes helped out the Klemperers with food in the early part of the war.

1 July

32 From 1934 until the ban on Jews using public libraries (2 December 1938) Klemperer worked on his *History of French Literature in the 18th Century*. The ms was deposited with Annemarie Köhler shortly before the Klemperers were expelled from their house. Klemperer continued revising and expanding this monumental work for much of the remainder of his life. Vol. I, *Das Jahrhundert Voltaires* (The Century of Voltaire), was published in 1954; the second vol., *Das Jahrhundert Rousseaus*, was published posthumously in 1966.

3 July

33 Emil Menke-Glückert (1878–1948), academic and civil servant. Dismissed in 1933 for his democratic political views.

34 In Ebert's time: Friedrich Ebert, a Social Democrat, was German president 1919–25; probably Klemperer just means the period of the Weimar Republic.

35 Elisabeth Winde had got to know Eva Klemperer through Frau Kreisler (see below) in 1943. Her husband, Arthur Winde (1886–1965), wood sculptor, Professor at the Dresden High School of Design 1918–34, when he was dismissed for political reasons. Taught at the Academy of Applied Arts in Dresden 1945–9. Subsequently in Münster, West Germany.

36 Charlotte Kreisler-Weidlich, singer and singing teacher. She was one of the Glasers' circle of friends.

4 July

37 The German Image of France: a study Klemperer began at the end of 1932 and completed in June 1933. It did not appear until 1961, after his death, under the title 'Das neue deutsche Frankreichbild (1914–1933). Ein historischer Überblick', in the journal *Beiträge zur Romanischen Philologie* (pp. 17–61 and 71–114).

11 July

38 *Nathan the Wise*: classic play (1779) of the German Enlightenment by Gotthold Ephraim Lessing. Set during the Crusades, it pleads for tolerance in matters of religion.

39 Johannes Kühn (1887–1973), historian. Professor at Dresden TH 1928–46, from 1947–9 at Leipzig, from 1949 at Heidelberg. A friend of the Klemperers until the mid-1930s, when Klemperer broke with him because of his (perhaps) opportunistic accommodation to Nazism.

40 Christian Janentzky (1886–1968), Germanist. Professor at Dresden TH 1922–52. Klemperer regarded him as exemplary of the fellow-academics who had failed to support and help him during the Nazi persecution of the Jews.

41 Gertrud von Rüdiger, Germanist in Janentzky's department; revealed herself an enthusiastic Nazi supporter after the seizure of power.

42 Extreme right-wing illegal and semi-legal units of ex-servicemen and students, who helped suppress left-wing revolutionaries and defend Germany's borders after the First World War. Many of those involved later joined the Nazi Party.

17 July

43 (Latin): 'Even if the world perish, the garden shall be made.'

44 Until 17th July, Klemperer's notes are on typed sheets. From the 18th onwards he used the empty pages of a bound notebook, which already contained earlier entries.

19 July

45 Felix Holldack (1880–1954) had taught law at Dresden TH; forced to give up teaching in 1933 because Jewish. Gustav Kafka (1883–1953), philosopher, forced to retire in 1935; taught at Würzburg (West Germany) from 1947. Hans Gehrig (1882–1968), economist and statistician; professor at Dresden TH 1915–34 and again from 1945; forced to retire for political reasons in 1934; at Halle from 1947–52.

20 July

46 Really Muschel, the Klemperers' cat, which had to be put down when Nazi regulations prohibited Jews from owning pets (see *TBE*, 15 May 1942).

21 July

47 I.e. Curriculum Vitae, Klemperer's title for his autobiography of the years 1881–1918, which he had begun in February 1939, when it was no longer possible for him to go on working on his history of French literature in the 18th century. He stopped writing the Curriculum in March 1942, when Gestapo house searches made it too dangerous to continue. In his postwar diaries Klemperer frequently considers bringing his autobiography up to date. It remained an unfulfilled ambition. A German edition of the extant autobiography was first published in 1989, in what was then still East Germany.

48 (Latin): here and everywhere.

49 I.e. the Potsdam Conference from 17 July until 2 August 1945.

50 Former secretary, i.e. a senior administrator, of Dresden TH.

23 July

51 Heinrich Wengler (1889–1946), editor at the Insel Verlag, Leipzig, then Italian lecturer at Leipzig University, from 1928 grammar-school teacher in Dresden; he and his sister Ellen were part of the Klemperers' circle. Wengler was forced out of teaching and imprisoned for a while in the Third Reich.

52 Wilhelm Nestler (1896–1997); his 'Army Bookshop' in Bautzenerstr. had been a secret KPD (German Communist Party) meeting place during the war.

26 July

53 (French): literally, little horses, reference to a game of chance in which little horses revolve on a spinning turntable.

30 July

54 Otto Dibelius (1880–1967), senior Protestant church official from 1925; relieved of his post in 1933; leading figure of the Confessing Church, which resisted Nazi incorporation. Bishop of Berlin and Brandenburg 1945–66 and President of the Council of the Protestant Church in Germany 1949–61.

1 August

55 Trude Öhlmann, a friend of the Klemperers since their time in Leipzig 1917–18. Employed at the Deutsche Bücherei (German Library) in Leipzig since 1921.

2 August

56 The People's High Schools (Volkshochschulen) are a further education institution whose original aim was to make learning and skills available to working people.

(They have meanwhile become the normal channel for adult evening classes in Germany and are administered by local government authorities.)

57 Wife of a colleague of Klemperer at Dresden TH, the physicist Harry Dember (1882–1943). The couple emigrated to Istanbul in 1933, then to the USA in 1941. Until 1937 his wife frequently returned to Germany to visit her mother.

58 Werner Kussi, from 1949 on the committee of the Dresden Jewish community, later emigrated to the USA.

3 August

59 The Potsdam Communiqué, i.e. the statement agreed by the three great powers, USA, Soviet Union and Great Britain, later joined by France, on the future treatment of Germany. Generally known as the Potsdam Agreement.

8 August

60 I.e. the first atom bomb dropped on Hiroshima, 8 August 1945.

12 August

61 Hellmuth von Moltke (1800–91), Prussian field-marshal; Chief of the General Staff 1857–88. Architect of the Prussian military victories over Denmark (1864), Austria and the minor German states (1866) and France (1870/71).

62 Erich Seidemann (b. 1908); in 1929 secretary to Herbert Wehner in Dresden. (Wehner, at that time a senior Communist, was later, from the 1950s, to become one of the most important figures in the Social Democratic Party in West Germany); 1931–3 editor of a Communist newspaper. During the Nazi years he was held in Waldheim Prison and Buchenwald, Dachau and Mauthausen concentration camps. Later trained as a teacher and was also an academic.

63 Elsa Kreidl was a fellow occupant of the Jews' House at 15b Caspar David Friedrichstr. She was married to the former owner of the property, Ernst Kreidl, who was murdered in Buchenwald in 1942.

64 Fräulein Ludwig was the non-Jewish housekeeper of another occupant of 15b Caspar David Friedrichstr., the former bank director Sally Friedheim. Friedheim was murdered in Dresden Police Headquarters on 12 June 1942.

65 Ida Kreidl, Jewish widow of the brother of Ernst Kreidl, with her son Paul also at Caspar David Friedrichstr. Paul Kreidl, whose wife managed to get to England in 1939, was deported to the Riga ghetto at the end of January 1942, Ida Kreidl to Theresienstadt at the end of August 1942. Kätchen Sara Voss – Käthe Voss – also in the same Jews' House, widow of an insurance company director, was deported to Auschwitz on 3 March 1943 with the last big transport of Dresden Jews. (See both *LTI* and *ETB*.) Kurt Hirschel, leader of the Jewish Community in Dresden; his wife Elsa and their two sons, as well as Adolf Kahlenberg, employee of the Jewish Community, and Kahlenberg's mother, were deported to Theresienstadt on 21 June 1943 and later from there to Auschwitz.

66 Rosa Ziegler, fellow occupant of the Jews' House at 2 Lothringer Weg, Jewish Community nurse, was deported at the same time as Käthe Voss; Lissy Meyerhof, sister of Hans Meyerhof, the best friend of Klemperer's young days; Carola Stern, cousin of the Meyerhof siblings, deported from Berlin in February 1943.

67 After the dropping of a second atom bomb on Nagasaki on 9 August 1945 negotiations for a Japanese surrender began the next day. Unconditional surrender followed on 14 August.

16 August

68 Marshal Philippe Pétain (1856–1951), the head of state of the Vichy French col-

laborationist government, was sentenced to death for high treason on 15 August 1945, the sentence commuted to life imprisonment because of his great age. He was exiled to the Île d'Yeu.

19 August

69 Dr Fritz Magnus-Alsleben, orthopaedist and surgeon. Klemperer met him for the first time in February 1942, when both were part of a group of Jewish forced labourers deployed to clear snow from roads.

70 Elsa Kreidl continued living at 15b Caspar David Friedrichstr., the former Jews' House.

71 Sally Friedheim, see note 64 above.

22 August

72 On 23 July 1945 the SMAD (Soviet Military Administration) had ordered the closure of all banks in the Soviet-occupied zone and the blocking of all savings accounts. The municipal savings banks and some other banks were allowed to resume their activities on 12 September 1945.

24 August

73 The 'Kulturbund zur demokratischen Erneuerung Deutschlands' (KB – Cultural Union for the Democratic Renewal of Germany) was founded on 4 July 1945 in Berlin, on the initiative of SPD and KPD as well as of anti-Fascist intellectuals and artists. From 8 August 1945 the president was the Communist poet Johannes R. Becher, vice-presidents were the novelist Bernhard Kellermann and the painter Karl Hofer, later joined by the classicist Karl Stroux.

74 (Yiddish): here meaning, rather, nonsense, but also small fry.

75 Gerhart Hauptmann (1862–1946) was the leading German playwright of the turn of the century, best known for naturalist dramas like *The Weavers*, *Before Daybreak* and *The Beaver Coat*.

27 August

76 Siegfried Lewinsky, an actor, was a 'privileged Jew'. During 1943–4 he frequently supplied Klemperer with books and newspapers. Was due to be deported on 13 February 1945, but avoided this fate thanks to the bombing of Dresden.

77 House of the former court jeweller Jacoby at 2 Lothringer Weg, Dresden-Blasewitz. His elderly widow Jenny Jacoby was deported in September 1942 and the villa was turned into a Jews' House in which the Klemperers, sharing with other parties, lived from 30 September 1942 to 13 December 1943.

28 August

78 Hans Scherner, pharmacist in Falkenstein, and his wife Trude had been friends of the Klemperers since their time in Leipzig 1917–18. The Scherners helped and sheltered the Klemperers, notably during their flight after the bombing of Dresden.

79 Otto Klemperer (1885–1973) was among the most famous 20th-century conductors. A cousin of Victor Klemperer – their fathers were brothers. Early in his career an advocate of modernist composers; director of Cologne Opera 1917–24, director of opera houses in Berlin 1927–33. Emigrated in 1933, first to Switzerland, then the USA; conductor of the Los Angeles Philharmonic Orchestra 1935–9, he returned to Europe in 1946, taking charge of the Budapest Opera 1947–50. Conductor of the Philharmonic Orchestra, later renamed the New Philharmonia Orchestra, in London 1950–64. To judge by the present diaries, Victor Klemperer was so intimidated by his cousin's reputation that he avoided meeting him. (They last met during the First

World War – that there continued to be some contact between the two seems to have been Otto's doing.)

80 Franz Werfel (1890–1945) was a German (and Jewish) novelist, dramatist and poet from Prague. Starting as an Expressionist, he went on to achieve enormous international success with novels like the *Song of Bernadette* and *The 40 Days of Musa Dagh*. Emigrated to France (from Austria) in 1938, in 1940 to the USA, died on 20 August 1945 in Beverly Hills, California.

30 August

81 Johannes Becher (1891–1958); author. Began as an Expressionist poet before the First World War. Joined the Communist Party in 1919, emigrated to the Soviet Union 1933; after his return co-founder of the Kulturbund (see note 73 above). The dominant voice (or channel) of official cultural policy in the Soviet Zone and then in East Germany. He was GDR Minister of Culture 1954–6.

82 The Dresden branch of the KB (Kulturbund) was set up on 23 September 1945. The writer Wolfram von Hanstein was replaced as chairman in November 1945. In the 1950s von Hanstein was President of the 'Gesellschaft der Menschenrechte' (Society for Human Rights) in Bonn.

7 September

83 Theodor Plievier (1892–1955), novelist and journalist. Participated in the sailors' mutiny of November 1918 at Wilhelmshaven, one of the events precipitating the collapse of the German Empire at the end of the First World War. In exile 1933–45, latterly in the Soviet Union. Returned to the Soviet Zone of Germany, but in 1947 went to the West and distanced himself from Communism. Novels like *Stalingrad* (the first volume was published in 1945) were worldwide bestsellers in the postwar years. *The Emperor Went, the Generals Remained* was first published in 1932.

84 Henri Barbusse (1873–1935), French novelist, journalist and left-wing activist. His novel *Le Feu* – Under Fire – (1916) was the most influential anti-war novel of French literature and rapidly translated into many other languages. His experience of the trenches made him a pacifist, but he later turned to Communism.

10 September

85 Helmut Aris (1908–87) was one of the 100 or so remaining Dresden Jews, who were ordered to be ready for deportation on the morning of 13 February 1945. He, too, was saved as a result of the bombing of the city that night. From 1953 chairman of Dresden's Jewish Community. In 1952 co-founder, 1958–62 Vice-President and from 1962 President of the Association of Jewish Communities in the GDR.

16 September

86 Georg Klemperer (1865–1946), Victor's eldest brother and a distinguished medical man; had been one of the doctors called on to treat Lenin during his final years of illness. Forced to retire in May 1933, he and his wife went to the USA in 1937.

87 Eva Schulze-Knabe (1907–1976), painter and graphic artist. In the anti-Nazi resistance from 1933, sentenced to life imprisonment in 1942. Her husband Fritz Schulze (1903–42), also an artist, co-founder of the Dresden group of the Association of Revolutionary Artists (ASSO), likewise active in the resistance, was sentenced to death for high treason and executed in 1942. Planettastr. had been named after one of the Nazis who assassinated the Austrian Chancellor Engelbert Dollfuss in 1934.

88 Between 3rd and 12th September 1945, the 5 Länder (or states) of the Soviet Occupation Zone issued decrees on land reform, as a result of which approx. 7,000 properties larger than 100 hectares (i.e. a little under $2\frac{1}{2}$ acres) were expropriated

without compensation; this land was divided up between farm workers, refugees expelled from eastern Germany and peasant smallholders. (They were later to lose their rights to the land thanks to the collectivisation programme.)

18 September

89 Mikhail Kutusov (1745–1813), Russian field marshal, defeated Napoleon's invasion of Russia. The celebrations marked the 200th anniversary of his birth.

90 Ralph von Klemperer was the offspring of a well-known banking and industrialist family in Dresden.

91 Frau Paul was a non-Jewish friend of Käthe Voss (see note 65 above).

92 'Die Moorsoldaten' was a resistance song composed in 1933 in Börgermoor concentration camp located in the bleak peat bogs of north-west Germany near the Dutch border.

24 September

93 'Edel sei der Mensch ...', beginning of Goethe's ode 'Das Göttliche' – The Divine.

94 (French): poor cake!

95 The twin sons of the Windes had been conscripted into the German navy during the war.

96 Hilde Jonson was Klemperer's niece, daughter of Martin Sussmann (deceased 8 April 1944) and Klemperer's youngest sister Valeska (Wally) 1877–1936.

28 September

97 *Die Frau meiner Träume* (*The Woman of My Dreams*), German film made 1943/44, directed by Georg Jacoby.

30 September

98 I.e. Wilhelm I (1797–1888), Prussian king from 1861, German emperor from 1871.

5 October

99 *Moderne französische Prosa 1870–1920* – study with texts and interpretations. Published by Teubner in 1923, followed by a new revised and expanded edition in 1926.

100 Papesch had been Klemperer's assistant from 1921 and from 1928 was a lecturer at Dresden TH. She was dismissed in 1936.

101 Klemperer's book publications between 1925 and 1933: *Die französische Literatur von Napoleon bis zur Gegenwart* (French Literature from Napoleon to the Present), 4 vols., Leipzig/Berlin 1925–31; *Die moderne französische Lyrik von 1870 bis zur Gegenwart* (Modern French Poetry from 1870 to the Present – a study with texts and interpretations), Leipzig/Berlin 1929; *Die moderne französische Literatur und die deutsche Schule. Drei Vorträge* (Modern French Literature and the German School. 3 lectures), Leipzig/Berlin 1925.

102 On 2 October 1945 the first conference of the foreign ministers of the 5 great powers (USA, USSR, Great Britain, France and China) ended without agreement on a closing statement. There was, nevertheless, agreement on a number of issues including German reparations; unresolved were questions relating to the preparation of peace treaties with Germany's satellites.

103 Frau Streller had been the secretary of Helmut Richter, an estate agent. In April 1942, the authorities appointed him trustee of the Klemperers' house in Dölzschen. An opponent of the Nazis, Richter did everything he could to ensure Klemperer remained owner of the house; he also supported the Klemperers with food and offered to help

hide Victor Klemperer. He was arrested in autumn 1943 and in spring 1944 taken to Buchenwald concentration camp. He died shortly after the war as a result of his treatment in the camp.

12 October
104 (Latin): always the same thing/nothing changes.
105 *Montesquieu* (2 vols), Heidelberg 1914–15; Klemperer's habilitation thesis. The study *Pierre Corneille*, Munich, published at the beginning of 1933, was Klemperer's last book publication until after the Second World War.

17 October
106 Enno Heidebroek (1876–1955), 1912 professor at Darmstadt TH, 1931–51 at Dresden TH (Chair of General Mechanics), rector 1945–7.
107 An interesting misjudgement, Heidebroek (see above) was in his late 60s. Perhaps he was relatively well-fed compared to Victor Klemperer and his acquaintances.

22 October
108 Wilfried Bade (1906–missing 1945) was a senior official in Goebbels' Ministry for Popular Enlightenment and Propaganda; he wrote a history of the Third Reich and in 1943 published a book of poems about the war (*Death and Life*) to which Klemperer refers.
109 (French): I'm going there.
110 Leon Loewenkopf (1892–1966), SPD member since 1908, deported to the Warsaw Ghetto 1940; in Auschwitz, Majdanek and Sachsenhausen concentration camps 1942–5; joined KPD 1945; 1948–52 chairman of Dresden's Jewish Community; 1948–52 president of the Issuing Bank of Saxony. Imprisoned August–November 1952 as a result of false accusations, he fled to West Berlin in January 1953 at the beginning of the anti-Jewish measures which were cut short by Stalin's death in March 1953.

26 October
111 According to the notes of the German edition, Klemperer's diary entry of 4 March 1944 includes the lines: 'Goebbels' leader in *Das Reich* of 20th Feb. "The Life and Death Decision". The same old song: we are protecting Europe against Jewish Bolshevism, England and the USA are mad, should wake up. The tone nevertheless more subdued and hesitant than before. Indignant at Soviet concealment of the ultimate goal: Instead of Comintern [the international organisation of Communist parties abolished in 1943] the word is now Soviet Empire. "The International" is got rid off and replaced by a Russian state anthem. Where did I read, and how was it substantiated there, that all victorious revolutions take a turn towards the nationalistic?'
112 A reference to Russia's defeat in the Russo–Japanese War of 1904–5.

29 October
113 Karl Vossler (1872–1949) was the principal scholarly influence on Victor Klemperer. In 1911, after a number of less prestigious academic posts, Vossler was appointed professor in Munich, where Klemperer was his student. He was relieved of his post 1937–45 for political reasons; briefly Rector of Munich University from 1945. Represented a very aestheticising approach to language studies, drawing on philosophy and cultural history. His main research interests were Italian and Spanish literature. He was also a noted translator, for example of Dante's *Divine Comedy*. Leo Ritter (1890–1979), surgeon and gynaecologist. Friendly with the Klemperers since their days in Munich after the First World War. Senior consultant at the Neues

Krankenhaus, Regensburg. The Klemperers stayed with him in Regensburg on their long walk back to Dresden in 1945.

6 November
114 Marta Jelski (1873–1954), Victor Klemperer's second youngest sister, emigrated to Argentina with her husband Julius (1867–1953) and her daughter Lilly (b. 1910).

8 November
115 Radio Beromünster, a Swiss radio station, 'reddar' i.e. radar; *Freiheitskampf*, a Nazi newspaper.
116 (French): nightmare of having to reply to Hilde in French.
117 Gestapo commissar (inspector) Arno Weser, 'the Spitter', committed suicide. After his duties in Dresden, SS Hauptsturmführer Johannes Clemens, 'the Boxer', was deputy to the German chief of police in Rome, Herbert Kappler, later sentenced for the massacre in the Ardeatine Caves in Rome in 1944. In 1951, Clemens, by then a Soviet agent, joined the Gehlen Organisation, the basis of the West German intelligence service. Given a ten-year prison sentence for high treason in 1963. Numerous references to Weser, Clemens and Köhler in *TBE*.

11 November
118 Between 1920 and 1928 the Hirches had been neighbours of the Klemperers at 131 Holbeinstr. in Dresden-Striesen. In 1931, Klemperer used his contacts with the officers' family of Gertrud von Rüdiger and at the TH to smooth Hans Hirche's path into the officer corps of the Reichswehr and himself acted as referee. At the beginning of 1947, Hans Hirche wrote to Klemperer from a prison camp requesting a testimonial. Klemperer's lengthy letter of refusal (printed as an appendix to *'Und so ist alles schwankend', Tagebücher Juni bis Dezember 1945*, Berlin, 1995) is at once angry and sorrowful.

13 November
119 Friedrich Wolf (1888–1953), doctor then author, primarily dramatist. Joined the KPD in 1928, emigrated in 1933, first to France then the USSR. In 1943 he was one of the founding members of the National Committee for a Free Germany. *Professor Mamlock*, first performed in the Soviet Union in 1934, was an international success; there was a Soviet film version in 1938 and an East German one in 1960.
120 In 1945 the SMAD had permitted 4 parties, KPD (Communist Party of Germany), SPD (Social Democratic Party of Germany), CDU (Christian Democratic Union) and LDPD (Liberal Democratic Party of Germany). The KPD and SPD were soon amalgamated under Communist control to form the SED (Socialist Unity Party), which became the permanent governing party of the GDR. The SED and the two other parties, later joined by the NDPD (National Democratic Party of Germany) and a Peasants' Party, constituted the National Front, which was supposed to bring together all sections of society in support of the regime as a kind of compulsory popular front. These subordinate parties were effectively part of the state apparatus.

18 November
121 The Klemperers had got to know Martha Wiechmann, a teacher in Meissen, near Dresden, on a cruise to South America in summer 1925. Friendly contact broke off in the mid-30s.

20 November
122 A Hebrew term for God.

26 November

123 Previously the home of a student association and song club. (Erato was the muse of love poetry.)

27 November

124 The *Süddeutsche Zeitung* is a liberal newspaper, published in Munich and founded in 1945.

30 November

125 Arthur Simon (1893–1962), chemist. From 1932 professor of inorganic chemistry at Dresden TH, from 1946 for a time in charge of the High School and Scholarship section of the Saxon Ministry of Popular Education.

126 (French): as if nothing had happened.

7 December

127 (French): see below.

128 Werner Lang, president of the Chamber of Commerce since May 1945, was in fact appointed a permanent secretary in the Saxon State Administration.

9 December

129 The two institutions were merged in 1950.

130 Hans Reingruber (1888–1964) was from 1934 professor of rail and transport communication at Dresden TH; GDR transport minister 1949–53. Here there is another example of Klemperer's odd judgement of age: as 'a young man', Reingruber was not much younger than Klemperer himself. Did he feel himself to be so old, was it an expression of his hypochondria, in addition to past and present privations, the lack of food and poor health?

131 I.e. the Nürnberg Trial of 22 major war criminals, which took place before an international military court from 20 November 1945 until 1 October 1946.

132 Ernst Gamillscheg (1887–1971), Ernst Winkler (1891–1942) and Fritz Neubert (1886–1970) were prominent academics in the field of Romance Languages and Literatures.

14 December

133 Johann Heinrich Pestalozzi (1746–1827), Swiss educationalist and writer. Advocated an education which promoted 'natural' ways of thinking and living and schools for poor children which encouraged pupils to think for themselves, instead of learning by rote.

23 December

134 Herbert Gute (1905–75), art teacher, writer. Joined the KPD in 1929, member of ASSO. Frequently imprisoned after 1933. From the end of 1945–1948 senior civil servant in charge of the Art and Literature section of the Saxon State Administration (later government); employed in the Central Administration for Popular Education, Berlin 1948–50; deputy director of the art school in Berlin-Weissensee 1950, professor at the Humboldt University, Berlin 1952, Lord Mayor of Dresden 1958–61.

135 Kurt Liebmann (1897–1981); writer and cultural politician. In 1945 a founder member of the Dresden Kulturbund.

26 December

136 The offending article was published in the *Sächische Volkszeitung*, 24 December 1945.

27 December

137 During the Weimar Republic the Stahlhelm (Steel Helmet) was a nationalist and conservative paramilitary organisation of veterans. After Hitler came to power it was forcibly incorporated into the SA of the Nazi Party.

29 December

138 Willi Leitner (pseudonym of Georg Hansen, 1903–76). Joined KPD 1919, editor of the *Ruhr-Echo* (a Communist newspaper), worked for the Military Counter-Intelligence Service of the Red Army in London; imprisoned 1927–35; was subsequently in Moscow. Editor with the *Deutsche Volkszeitung* 1945, chief editor of the *Sächsische Zeitung* in Dresden 1946. Late 1946 founder of the ADN (Allgemeine Deutsche Nachrichtendienst – General German News Agency) which he headed until 1952, held senior positions at *Neues Deutschland*, the official newspaper of the state party in East Germany 1956–69.

31 December

139 *Der Stürmer*, rabidly anti-Semitic Nazi weekly published in Nürnberg by the Gauleiter of Franconia, Julius Streicher. Particularly infamous were its vicious cartoons of Jews.

1946

4 January

1 Wilhelm Pieck (1876–1960) joined the SPD 1895 and in 1917 was a founding member of the Marxist anti-war group the Spartacus league, as he was of the KPD in 1918, from when he was part of its leadership. Member of the Reichstag 1928–33. Emigration to France 1933, then to USSR; chairman of the KPD 1935, leadership of the newly formed National Committee for a Free Germany 1943. Chairman of the KPD in the Soviet Zone 1945; major force in promoting the amalgamation of SPD and KPD in the Soviet Zone of occupation as the new SED (April 1946), of which he was joint chairman with Otto Grotewohl (formerly of the SPD). From October 1949 President of the newly constituted German Democratic Republic. The meeting mentioned by Klemperer marked Pieck's 70th birthday.

2 Gustav Dahrendorf (1901–54), SPD official, Reichstag deputy 1932–3; sentenced to 7 years' imprisonment in 1944; member of the SPD's management committee for the Soviet Zone; returned to his home town of Hamburg March 1946; Vice-President of the Economic Council of the Bizone (i.e. the US and British occupied zones) 1948.

20 January

3 Berthold Klemperer (1871–1931), Victor Klemperer's third-eldest brother, a successful lawyer, frequently gave Victor material support right up to the time the latter obtained his chair in Dresden.

4 (Latin): after the event.

5 Adolf Spamer (1883–1953), Germanist and ethnologist. Professor at Dresden TH 1926–36 and again 1947; at Berlin University 1936–45.

6 Alfred Rosenberg (1893–1946), leading Nazi ideologist, author of *The Myth of the 20th Century*; shared responsibility for cultural affairs under Hitler and in charge of intellectual and theoretical training in the Nazi Party. Appointed minister for the occupied territories of the Soviet Union 1941. Executed at Nürnberg as a major war criminal.

7 Friedrich Tobler (1879–1957), botanist. Professor in Münster 1911; at Dresden TH and Director of Dresden Botanical Garden 1924–46; in Switzerland from 1950.

8 Georg Wildführ (1904–84), hygienist and microbiologist. Director of the Hygiene Institute and Hygiene Museum, Dresden, 1945–7. Professor in Dresden 1946; chair in Leipzig 1947–70.

9 Eugen Lerch (1888–1952), Romanist. Professor in Munich 1920, and in Münster 1930–35 and 1946; from 1946 professor in Mainz. He and Klemperer co-operated on various editing projects during the Weimar years before becoming estranged in the course of an academic dispute; like Klemperer he was a student of Karl Vossler.

10 Term applied to the big estate owners of eastern Germany.

11 Heinz Willmann (1906–91) joined the KPD in 1925, worked on the *AIZ* (*Arbeiter Illustrierte Zeitung – Workers Illustrated Newspaper*) from 1928; after being held in a concentration camp, emigrated to Czechoslovakia in 1934 and then to France and the USSR. Co-founder of the KB and of the Aufbau publishing house 1945; General Secretary of the KB 1945–50 and later of the GDR Peace Council.

12 Wolfgang Balzer (1884–1968) was from 1923 Director of the Dresden Kunstgewerbemuseum (Arts and Crafts Museum). Forced into retirement in 1933, he was re-appointed in 1945; Director of the State Art Collections in Dresden from September 1946, retired once again in February 1951 in the course of the SED's campaign against 'Formalism' in art.

13 Joseph Keilberth (1908–68), conductor. Music Director in Karlsruhe 1935, Director of the Philharmonic Orchestra in Prague 1940–44, in charge of the Dresden Staatskapelle 1945, and became chief conductor of the Bamberg Symphony Orchestra in 1950; from 1959 at the Munich State Opera.

14 Alfred Baeumler (1887–1968), philosopher. Professor of Philosophy and Educational Theory at Dresden TH 1928; Professor of Political Education in Berlin 1933; Director of the Nazi Party's Scholarship Department under Alfred Rosenberg. For Baeumler's threatening words see the entry for 21 February 1933 in *I Shall Bear Witness: The Diaries of Victor Klemperer 1933–41*.

15 Walter Weidauer (1899–1986) joined the USPD (Independent Social Democratic Party – it broke away from SPD during First World War because in favour of immediate peace without conditions) 1919, KPD 1922, Reichstag deputy 1932. After imprisonment in a concentration camp emigrated to Czechoslovakia then Denmark; arrested 1940 and sentenced to 15 years' prison in 1942. Town councillor and Deputy Mayor of Dresden 1945, Lord Mayor of Dresden October 1946–1958.

16 Hermann Matern (1893–1971) joined SPD 1911, KPD 1919; member of the Prussian Parliament 1932–3; after imprisonment fled Germany in 1934; exile in the Soviet Union. Secretary of the Saxon regional leadership of the KPD 1945–6, later member of the SED Politburo; Vice-President of the Volkskammer (People's Chamber) from 1950.

Otto Buchwitz (1879–1964), joined SPD in 1898, member of the Prussian Parliament 1921 and of the Reichstag 1924. Emigrated to Denmark 1933, imprisoned by the Gestapo 1940–45. Chairman of the Saxon regional association of the SPD 1945; strong supporter of union of SPD and KPD in April 1946, having been disillusioned by SPD failure to stand up to the Nazis before 1933. Member of the management committee, then of the Central Committee of the SED; member of the Party's Central Control Commission 1948–50; member of the Saxon Parliament 1946–52; member of the GDR Volkskammer from 1949.

27 January

17 In German, as, for example, in French, there are familiar and formal versions, *du* and *Sie*, of the personal pronoun of address, where in modern English there is only 'you'. In left-wing parties, in trade unions etc. it was normal for members (comrades) to use the 'fraternal' *du* to one another. But, of course, under other circumstances the

use of the familiar *du* by one adult to another (e.g. a Gestapo officer to a Jew) would be a sign of contempt and lack of respect.

18 Ilse Frischmann had passed on information to Soviet prisoners of war, was arrested for this offence in 1944 and deported to Auschwitz; her mother Elsa Frischmann was sentenced to $2\frac{1}{2}$ years' imprisonment, her father Georg Frischmann was taken to a labour camp in nearby Radeberg, where he died.

19 Klemperer means the Christian Social Union (CSU) founded in November 1945.

29 January

20 I.e. the caretaker of the Jews' House at 2 Lothringer Weg; see note 27, 25 June 1945, above.

3 February

21 From the end of October 1938 Jews had been forbidden to visit theatres and cinemas.

22 Klemperer associated the old Catholic Zentrum Party (banned in 1933) with opposition to the Nazis. The post-Nazi CDU (Christian Democratic Union) was in part a continuation of the Zentrum, but without its exclusive confessional orientation. Klemperer saw the CDU in the Soviet Zone as a refuge for right-wing elements; cloaca maxima, refugium nazisticum (Latin) – main sewer, Nazi refuge.

4–6 February

23 Karl Laux (1896–1976), musicologist. Lecturer since 1922 (1936–48 at the Dresden Conservatory) and music critic. Sub-department head responsible for music and theatre in the Saxon State Administration and Government 1945–48. Founding member of the KB in Saxony; music critic of the *Tägliche Rundschau* newspaper 1948–51; from 1951 chief editor of the periodical *Musik und Gesellschaft* (Music and Society) as well as professor and Director of the Academy of Music and Theatre in Dresden, which became the High School of Music, of which he was rector 1957–63.

24 Hans Grundig (1901–58), painter and graphic artist. Joined KPD 1926, founder member of ASSO in 1930. Prohibited from working in 1934. In Sachsenhausen concentration camp 1940–44; professor at the Dresden Fine Art Academy 1946 and Director 1946–8. Lea Grundig-Langner (1906–77), graphic artist. Married Hans Grundig 1928, joined KPD 1926, member of ASSO 1930. In custody 1936 and 1938–39. Emigrated to Palestine 1940, returned to Germany 1949. Professor at Dresden High School of Art (the renamed Academy) 1950. President of the Artists' Association of the GDR 1964–70.

25 Paul Hindemith (1895–1963), leading 20th-century composer. Prominent modernist who came to the fore in the 1920s, influenced by Stravinsky rather than Schoenberg. Resigned his professorship at the Berlin Music High School in 1937 and went to the United States.

26 Gusti (Auguste) Wieghardt-Lazar (1887–1970), author, above all of books for children and young people. Moved from Vienna to Dresden in 1920. After the death of her husband, Karl Wieghardt, mathematics professor at Dresden TH, in 1924, was in close contact with the KPD. Good friend of the Klemperers from 1926; emigrated to England in 1939. During the 1930s Victor Klemperer had frequently been exasperated by the dogmatism of her left-wing views.

27 Anny (or Änny) Klemperer (1885–1963), non-Jewish wife of Victor Klemperer's brother Berthold. Widowed 1931.

28 Anton Ackermann (1905–73) joined the KPD 1926. In Soviet exile a member of the National Committee for a Free Germany. Prominent in the merger of SPD and KPD as the SED. Member of the latter's management committee, then of its Central Committee. Developed thesis of a distinctive German path to Socialism. Senior

official in the GDR Foreign Ministry 1949–53; lost all his Party and state posts after the Uprising of 17 June 1953 in East Germany. Rehabilitated in 1956.

29 Paul Wandel (1905–95) joined KPD 1926, Soviet exile 1933–45. Chief editor of the *Deutsche Volkszeitung*, the first newspaper to be published in the Soviet Zone, 1945. President of the Central Administration for Popular Education established 11 September 1945. Minister of Popular Education 1949–52, Secretary responsible for Culture and Education on the Central Committee of the SED. GDR ambassador to China 1958–61.

30 Robert Rompe (1905–93), physicist. Joined KPD 1932. Director of the Scholarship and High Schools section of the Central Administration for Popular Education. Professor at Berlin University 1946. After 1950 director of various institutes of the German Academy of Sciences. Member of the Party management committee 1946–50; member of the Central Committee from 1958.

31 In its day the Adlon was one of the great hotels of the world, famous, not least, as the setting of Vicki Baum's novel *Grand Hotel*, which in 1930 was turned into a successful Hollywood film starring Greta Garbo, among others. Following the re-unification of Berlin, the Adlon Hotel has been rebuilt.

12 February

32 Victor Klemperer's father, the rabbi Wilhelm Klemperer, born 1839.

22 February

33 Richard Gladewitz (1898–1961) joined KPD in 1920, emigrated to Czechoslovakia 1933. Took part in the Spanish Civil War and the French Resistance; member of the National Committee for a Free Germany in the West. In 1945 First Secretary of the KPD in Plauen District (Plauen the town, not the Dresden district); appointed to head the Information Department of the Saxon Administration at the end of 1945. Later worked at the (East) Berlin Radio Station. In an opaque case, he was arrested in 1950 and imprisoned for 'kidnapping' and then acquitted in August 1951. Gladewitz was possibly caught up in the campaign against émigrés who had been in the West, rather than the Soviet Union.

23 February

34 (Italian): we shall see.

28 February

35 (French): it's late. The anecdote is taken from a story by Alfred de Vigny published in 1833/35.

36 *Maître Corbeau*: a reference to La Fontaine's fable 'Le corbeau et le renard' – The Crow and the Fox. Thanks to his vanity the crow in the fable is in the end left with nothing.

2 March

37 Gustav Leissner (1890–?), lawyer. Mayor of Meerane (town in eastern Thuringia) 1921–6, councillor in Breslau (now Wroclaw); Lord Mayor of Dresden February–October 1946.

38 Egon Rentzsch (1915–92); prison and concentration camp 1933–9; Director of the KPD's Saxon regional Party school 1945; councillor responsible for education in Dresden 1946; in charge of the Arts and Culture section of the Central Committee of the SED 1950–53; subsequently Secretary of the management committee of the FDGB (the official – and only – trade union organisation of the GDR).

39 (French): 18th century – Klemperer's usual abbreviation for his history of French literature in the 18th century.

40 (Spanish): and everything, everything.

12 March
41 Hermann Weidhaas (1903–78), architect and art historian. Town councillor in Plauen 1945–46; lecturer (1946) then Professor and Director (1948) of the Institute of Art History in Greifswald; Professor at the High School of Architecture and the Arts, Weimar, 1949–68.

22 March
42 Alexander Kociolek – see text entry.

25 March
43 Reference to Churchill's speech of 5 March 1946 in Fulton, Missouri, attacking Soviet foreign policy, in which he spoke of an 'iron curtain' dividing Europe.

26 March
44 The headquarters of the Soviet Military Administration were in the Karlshorst district of Berlin.

2 April
45 (French): the eternal lure of spring.

6 April
46 Karl Kneschke (1898–1959), founder member of the Czech Communist Party 1921, Party official to 1938 when he emigrated to England. Regional Secretary of the Saxon KB February 1946–1951; Federal Secretary then First Secretary of the KB in the GDR 1950–57.

10 April
47 A short book published by Johannes Kühn at the beginning of the Second World War.

17 April
48 The Technical High School Berlin-Charlottenburg was re-opened in 1946 as the Technical University Berlin.

20 April
49 Ernst Jünger (1895–1998), writer. Famous above all for his memoirs of the Western Front in the First World War, *In Storms of Steel*. Wrote for extreme right-wing publications during the Weimar years, but was also close to advocates of a 'National Bolshevism'. Cultivated an attitude of aristocratic disdain towards the Nazis after 1933.
50 Gottfried Benn (1886–1956), poet, essayist, etc. One of the 4 or 5 most influential German poets of the 20th century. Initially welcomed the Nazi regime. Distanced himself from it in mid-1934. Prohibited from publishing in 1938.

25 April
51 Lisl Stühler, her Jewish husband (who died at the end of 1944) and their son Bernhard had been immediate neighbours of the Klemperers in the Jews' House at 1 Zeughausstr. Victor Klemperer had secretly tutored the adolescent Bernhard. (As a half-Jew he was not allowed to attend school.)
52 Neighbours in Dölzschen.

28 April
53 Otto Grotewohl (1894–1964), politician. Joined SPD 1912; Interior and Education Minister 1921–22, Justice Minister 1923–24 in the small state of Braunschweig (Brunswick). Member of the Reichstag 1925–33. Chairman of the management committee of the SPD for the Soviet Zone 1945. A driving force on the SPD side for the amalgamation of SPD and KPD. Joint chairman with Wilhelm Pieck of the united party 1946–54. Prime Minister of the GDR from 1949. The Congress at which the unification was officially agreed took place on 21–22 April 1946 in Berlin. (The unification only applied in the Soviet Zone.)

4 May
54 The work of the PHS had been split into two parts, lectures and lecture courses of general interest on the one hand, courses preparing for school-leaving certificate (Abitur) and university entrance on the other, i.e. the Evening Grammar School. This arrangement was to be the cause of friction with the Soviet occupation authorities and was in part responsible for Victor Klemperer's resignation as director of the Dresden PHS. The actual sequence of events, the conflicting pressures, are, however, not made clear by the diary entries.

7 May
55 I.e. in the International Brigades in the Spanish Civil War.
56 Kurt Schumacher was the spokesman and first leader of the SPD in the three Western zones. He was utterly opposed to a unification of SPD and KPD.
57 Ernst Wiechert 1887–1950), writer. After 1933 made clear his opposition to the Nazi regime's policies. His book *Forest of the Dead* is based on his two-month imprisonment in Buchenwald in 1938.

16 May
58 16 May 1946 was the Klemperers' 40th wedding anniversary.

19 May
59 A plebiscite on a draft law to 'transfer enterprises owned by war and Nazi criminals to the property of the people' had been called for 30 June 1946.

28 May
60 Max Sebba (1880–1959), doctor and surgeon in Danzig, emigrated to England at the end of 1938; his brother Julius (later Yehuda) Sebba (1882–1959), a lawyer, taught international maritime law at the Commercial High School in Königsberg; Julius, a close friend of Klemperer since his days as a journalist in Berlin before the First World War, emigrated to Palestine with his family in 1933. Frau Jenny Schaps (1867–1950), widow of a senior judge, close friend of the Klemperers since 1921 when her younger daughter Elise (Lisl, 1894–1960) married Julius Sebba. Hans Gerstle, owner of a malt coffee factory, was the husband of Toni Schaps, the older daughter of Jenny Schaps; in 1938 the family emigrated to England with Frau Schaps.

29 May
61 Werner Straub (1902–83), psychologist. Professor at Dresden TH 1937–67. Rector of the TH 1947–9.

6 June
62 In this case Otto Klemperer (1899–1987), eldest son of Georg, Victor's brother. Physicist, emigrated to England 1933.

9 June
63 (Italian): on the other hand.

16 June
64 After Louis Bonaparte's coup d'état in 1851, Victor Hugo went into exile, first in Belgium, then on the Channel Islands, all the time remaining bitterly opposed to Napoleon III's (as Louis Bonaparte declared himself) empire. He returned to France immediately after Louis Napoleon's defeat and capture by the Prussians at the Battle of Sedan 1870.

23 June
65 Hans-Georg Gadamer (1900–2002), philosopher. Professor at Marburg 1937, at Leipzig 1939 (rector 1946–7), Frankfurt/Main 1947; at Heidelberg from 1949. His philosophical hermeneutics made him perhaps the most influential German philosopher to come to the fore after the Second World War. Theodor Litt (1880–1962), philosopher and educationalist. Professor in Bonn 1919, in Leipzig 1920–37 and 1945–7, in Bonn again after 1947.
66 Arthur Franz (1881–1963), teacher of Romance languages and literatures. Professor in Giessen 1920, in Würzburg 1927, in Königsberg 1929–45; taught at Jena 1949–54.
67 Berthold Meyerhof, youngest brother of Hans Meyerhof. He and his wife emigrated to the USA in 1933.
68 Walter Blumenfeld (1882–1967), psychologist. Professor of Education at Dresden TH 1924–34. Emigrated to Peru 1935; Professor of Experimental and Educational Psychology at Lima University. He and his wife Grete had been close friends of the Klemperers. Wilhelm (Willy) Jelski (1913–94), son of Victor Klemperer's sister Marta.

30 June
69 (Spanish): nothing.
70 (Latin): death.
71 The draft law on the expropriation of Nazis and war criminals (see note 59 above) was supported by 77.6% of voters with 16.5% opposed.
72 Günther Jacoby (1881–1969), philosopher. Professor in Istanbul 1914, in Greifswald from 1919; compulsorily retired 1937, re-appointed 1945. Dean 1946–8; emeritus 1955 after writing a critical memorandum on philosophy at GDR universities. Probably a somewhat more distinguished figure than Klemperer realised.
73 Schwerin was (and is once again) the administrative capital of the *Land* of Mecklenburg-Vorpommern.
74 (Italian): no one knows what tomorrow may bring – from a Florentine Carnival hymn ascribed to Lorenzo de Medici.
75 Theodor Brugsch (1878–1963), internist. Professor in Halle and Berlin. After 1945 was for a time head of the Universities Section of the Central Administration for Popular Education. Played an important part in the re-opening of the Berlin Humboldt University (HUB).
76 Felix Klemperer (1866–1932), Victor Klemperer's second-eldest brother, internist. As distinguished a medical man as the eldest brother, Georg. Professor in Berlin from 1921.
77 Heinrich Deiters (1887–1966), educationalist. Active as a school reformer in the 1920s. Compulsory retirement in 1933, professor at the HUB 1947; chairman of the Berlin KB 1947–57.
78 Charles-Augustin Sainte-Beuve (1804–69), writer and critic. Established, inter alia, the biographical method of literary criticism.
79 The day on which Eva and Victor Klemperer had met.

12 July

80 (French): Irun is no longer Irun – a quote from Victor Hugo, who had known the Basque town in his youth. I.e. the excitement of seeing and doing things for the first time or when young can never be recaptured.

81 (French): I don't give a damn (or something stronger).

82 Ricarda Huch (1864–1947) was a distinguished writer who had withdrawn from public life after the Nazi seizure of power. Wolfgang Langhoff (1901–66), actor, director, theatre manager; joined KPD 1928, imprisoned in a concentration camp 1933, escaped to Switzerland 1934, worked at the Zürich Schauspielhaus until 1945; general manager of the Düsseldorf theatres 1945, general manager of the Deutsches Theater, Berlin, 1946–63. Bernhard Bennedik (1892–1973), musicologist, Director of the Berlin Music High School 1945–8, later of the High School of Theatre and Music in Halle. Member of the Executive Committee of the KB 1945–7. Werner Krauss (1900–76), Romance languages and literatures scholar; professor at Marburg 1942; arrested that same year for involvement in the Red Orchestra resistance group, sentenced to death in January 1943, but saved by the intervention of distinguished colleagues including his teacher Karl Vossler; in part thanks to psychiatric reports his sentence was reduced to 5 years in prison; professor in Leipzig 1947, later director of research bodies of the German Academy of Sciences; one of the most distinguished scholars of his time in his field, in particular with work on the Spanish Golden Age and on the French Enlightenment. He and Victor Klemperer were to become academic rivals. Horst Lange (1904–71), writer. Max Pechstein (1881–1955), painter and graphic artist; member of the Expressionist group 'Die Brücke'; banned from exhibiting in 1933, professor at the Berlin Art High School 1945. Ferdinand Friedensburg (1886–1972), Regierungspräsident (district president, roughly equivalent to a French prefect) of Kassel 1927–33, removed from his post 1933; a co-founder of the CDU in Berlin and the Soviet Zone 1945; deputy Lord Mayor of Berlin 1946–51; member of the Bundestag (West German parliament) 1952–65; professor at Berlin Technical University from 1953, President of the Institut für Wirtschaftsforschung (Institute of Economic Research) 1945–68. Klaus Gysi (1912–99) chief editor of the periodical *Aufbau* 1945–8, secretary of the KB 1949–51 (more details of his subsequent career in the diaries themselves and below). Karl Kleinschmidt (1902–78), Protestant minister; joined SPD 1928, prominent member of the Association of Religious Socialists; arrested after 1933 and released from pastoral duties for a while. Cathedral preacher in Schwerin from 1935. Founding member of the Mecklenburg KB 1945, Vice-president of the KB 1947–9.

83 Arthur Werner (1877–1967), engineer. The Soviet Commandant of Berlin N. F. Bersarin appointed him Lord Mayor of the city on 17 May 1945. He held office until December 1946.

84 Leo Spitzer (1887–1960); Austrian scholar of Romance languages and literatures. Professor in Marburg 1925, Cologne 1933, Istanbul 1933 (after emigration), Baltimore 1936. Defining himself against Karl Vossler's idealist language theory Spitzer aimed to place stylistics on a new foundation; he also contributed to the development of textual linguistics.

13 July

85 (Latin): in the first instance.

86 I.e. where Klemperer's father had been second preacher. The Reform Congregation founded in Berlin in 1840 made considerable concessions to Christian (Protestant) liturgical practice and ritual.

87 The 'Club of Cultural Producers' was officially opened on 26 August 1946.

88 Franz von Papen (1879–1969) was a right-wing nationalist Catholic politician with close links to industrialist circles. He was briefly German chancellor in 1932, when

he was responsible for illegally removing the Social Democratic government of the largest German state, Prussia. He was one of a group of right-wing politicians who believed Hitler could be made use of and controlled if appointed chancellor. As is well known, the opposite happened. After 1934 von Papen was marginalised in diplomatic posts.

89 I.e. the Reich Chancellery, Hitler's office and residence as head of state.

20 July

90 *Die französische Literatur von Napoleon bis zur Gegenwart*, 4 vols., Leipzig/Berlin 1925–31.

91 See note 101, 5 October 1945.

11 August

92 Richard Woldt (1878–1952), sociologist and political economist; before 1933 a senior civil servant in the Prussian Ministry of Culture; honorary professor at Dresden TH 1928, professor 1945, Director of the Institute for the Social Science of Work.

12 August

93 (Latin): black day.

14 August

94 Karl Kautsky (1854–1938), socialist theorist and politician; the leading thinker of pre-First World War Socialism (i.e. of the generation before Lenin). In 1883 founder and until 1917 chief editor of the SPD theoretical journal *Die Neue Zeit* (The New Age).

95 Carl Heinrich Becker (1876–1933), orientalist. State Secretary in the Prussian Ministry of Culture 1919, Minister of Science, Art and Popular Education in Prussia 1921 and 1925–30; Professor of Islamic Studies in Berlin 1930.

16 August

96 Maria Strindberg (1895–1948), writer; sister of Auguste Wieghardt-Lazar (see note 26 above), wife of a son of the Swedish playwright and novelist August Strindberg.

97 Karl Wieghardt (1913–96), physicist; stepson of Auguste Wieghardt-Lazar; at the Institute of Current Research, Göttingen 1938; at the Admiralty Research Laboratory, London, 1949; professor at the University of Hamburg 1955–82. (See also *I Shall Bear Witness: The Diaries of Victor Klemperer 1933–41*, entry for 15 May 1941.)

98 Eva Büttner, wife of the composer and director of the Dresden Conservatory Paul Büttner (1870–1943). Through the death of her non-Jewish husband she lost the protection of marriage to an 'Aryan'. She faked suicide and survived in hiding.

21 August

99 The Third Punic War, 149–146 BC, set the seal on Rome's domination of the western Mediterranean and ended with the conquest and complete destruction of Carthage.

28 August

100 I.e. work of artists from all 4 zones was displayed.

101 (Latin): poor Germany.

2 September

102 This association had also put up candidates in the local elections.

103 In the local elections of 1 September 1946 in Saxony the SED obtained 48% of the votes and was, therefore, the strongest party, but narrowly failed to achieve an absolute majority.

6 September

104 Doris Machol (1920–76) was Victor Klemperer's grand-niece (married Max Kahane April 1951); graphic artist, painter and journalist; emigrated to Spain 1936, later to France; began her studies at the Académie Montmartre, Paris, in 1939; studied at the Art School Berlin-Weissensee 1951–5. Heinz Machol (1893–1943), Klemperer's nephew, son of his second-eldest sister Hedwig Machol (1870–93). Heinz Machol's first wife, Mathilde Grabowski, was not, in fact, Austrian, but merely acquainted with the leading Austrian Socialist Friedrich Adler (1879–1960).

15 September

105 (French): midnight.
106 Arthur Rudolph (1885–1959); painter and lithographer. After studies in Leipzig, Dresden and Munich settled in Dresden. The Klemperers first met him in August 1922.

27 September

107 The whole expression is: to the dead the laurels, to the living the duty.
108 Brecht's play was written in 1937, after the beginning of the Spanish Civil War.
109 Walter Jelski (1904–58), nephew of Victor Klemperer, eldest son of his sister Marta; briefly lived with the Klemperers in Dresden 1922–3; emigrated to Palestine 1933.
110 Helene Ahrens and the Klemperers had become acquainted in 1941; in the last years of the war she helped them out with food (see e.g. *TBE*, 29 March 1943).

1 October

111 Wilhelm Koenen (1886–1963) joined SPD 1903, USPD 1917, active in promoting the latter's fusion with the then much smaller KPD; member of the Reichstag 1920–32, member of the Prussian second chamber 1926–32; emigrated 1933; member of the Executive Committee of the SED 1946, then of the party's Central Committee; in charge of the administration of the Volkskammer 1949–58.

9 October

112 (Italian): (his) newspaper is paid for or bribed.

16 October

113 Günther Ramin (1898–1956), organist and choir master; organist of the Thomas-kirche in Leipzig from 1918 and of the Gewandhaus concerts from 1920; director of the Thomanerchor (choir of the Thomaskirche) 1940; important interpreter of Bach.
114 Max Kahane (b.1910), journalist; grew up in Berlin; KPD 1932; emigration to Prague 1933; fought in the Spanish Civil War, subsequently underground in France; co-founder of the ADN news agency 1946, later a press correspondent above all for the Party newspaper *Neues Deutschland*, foreign correspondent for some years, in New Delhi and Rio de Janeiro; then a chief political commentator in the GDR media.

24 October

115 On 22 October 1946, on the orders of the Soviet occupation authorities, around 10,000 German scientists, engineers and skilled workers were taken to the Soviet Union with their families. They were supposed to rebuild dismantled plant from the Soviet Zone of Germany and to train Soviet specialists.

27 October

116 Sergei Tulpanov (1901–84), Soviet officer, head of the information section of the SMAD.

117 In the election to the Berlin City Council (from all 4 sectors) of 20 October 1946, the SED had not had the same success as in Saxony. (The majority of SPD members in the city had not gone along with amalgamation with the KPD.) The SPD emerged as largest party, with 48.7% of the votes, CDU 22.2%, SED 19.8% and LDP 9.39%. In the eastern sector the SPD got 43.6%, the SED 29.9%.

31 October

118 'Aus dem Wörterbuch des Unmenschen' (From the Dictionary of the Beast) was a regular column in the Heidelberg periodical *Die Wandlung* (ed. November 1945–April 1948 by Dolf Sternberger with the collaboration of Karl Jaspers, Alfred Weber and Werner Krauss). The texts on terms such as 'Einsatz' (commitment) and 'fanatisch' (fanatical) were initialled. They were written by Dolf Sternberger (1907–89), a journalist, historian and political scientist; Gerhard Storz (1898–1983), a journalist and writer; and W. E. Süskind (1901–70), novelist, essayist, translator. It was 1952 before a book version with many additional articles appeared as *Aus dem Wörterbuch des Unmenschen* (see above).

6 November

119 I.e. one evil deed brings others in its train (Schiller).

14 November

120 Heinrich Barkhausen (1881–1956), physicist; professor at Dresden TH from 1911; Director of the Institute of Communications Engineering. His wife had been an auditor of Klemperer in the 1920s, which led to social contacts.

121 Klemperer means the German People's Council, which later became the Volkskammer (People's Chamber) of the German Democratic Republic.

23 November

122 Jean Anouilh (1910–87), French dramatist; once one of the most frequently performed modern dramatists, he is now largely forgotten. His *Eurydice* dates from 1942.

123 Manon – heroine of *Manon Lescaut* (1731), novel by Abbé Prévost (1697–1763).

25 November

124 For Frida Dittrich see e.g. *TBE* entry for 5 December 1943. Klemperer proved to be a very poor student in the cardboard-box factory.

8 December

125 Herbert Volwahsen (1906–?), sculptor. From 1945 until its dissolution in March 1946 he was President of the 'Saxon Chamber of Artists'. Director of the sculpture department of the Design School in Bielefeld (West Germany) 1956.

126 Town and area about 100 miles east of Madrid fiercely contested (December 1937–February 1938) during the Spanish Civil War.

127 Presumably interned by the French authorities on the outbreak of the Second World War.

128 Left-wing newspaper owner.

129 Traugott Böhme (1884–1954), teacher of Romance languages and literatures; professor at Ohio State University, Columbus, 1927–8; teaching post at the Wirtschaftshochschule (a business school) Berlin 1931–45; department head in the Central Administration for Popular Education 1945; professor at the Humboldt University 1945. He and Klemperer were later to get on rather better than on this occasion.

11 December
130 Concert with works by Paul Büttner – see note 98 above.

17 December
131 Erwin Hartsch (1890–1948), Saxon Minister of Popular Education from 1946.

20 December
132 Nazi propaganda usage; the title of an anti-Soviet exhibition mounted in Berlin in 1942, which was damaged by arson by the largely Jewish resistance group known as the Herbert Baum Group.

25 December
133 Independent 'Opfer des Faschismus' (Victims of Fascism) offices had sprung up all over the occupied zones after the end of the war.

31 December
134 Wife of Erich Meyerhof, a younger brother of Hans Meyerhof. Erich Meyerhof emigrated to England in 1933 (interned in Australia during the war), while his non-Jewish wife remained in Berlin with their sons.

1947

10 January
1 Siegfried Pionkowski had been an employee of the Dresden Jewish Community 1940–2.

11 January
2 The last of a series of Sorb maids employed by the Klemperers.

13 January
3 Georg Klemperer, Victor's eldest brother, died on 24 December 1946.

19 January
4 (Latin): If only I had remained silent. (Adapted from Boethius in his *De consolatione philosophiae*.)
5 Helmut Hatzfeld (1892–1979), Romance languages and literatures scholar; professor in Frankfurt/Main 1929, in Heidelberg 1932; dismissed 1935; emigrated to the USA 1938; professor at the Catholic University of America, Washington DC from 1942. He was a quarter Jewish, in Nazi terminology therefore 'second grade mixed race'.
6 Wilhelm Friedmann (1884–1942), Romance languages and literatures scholar; lecturer then assistant professor in Leipzig; emigrated in 1933.

22 January
7 (Latin): in the hour of his death.
8 Schiller's poem begins (roughly): 'Even what is beautiful must die! That subdues men and gods.'
9 Lange, a carpenter from Dölzschen, had told Eva Klemperer in April 1942 about murders of Jews he had witnessed in Kiev. See *TBE*, 19 April 1942.

26 January
10 Max Opitz (1890–1982); joined KPD 1919, member of the Central Committee from

1929; member of the Saxon Parliament 1925–30, of the Prussian Parliament 1931–3, of the Reichstag 1933; prison and concentration camp 1933–45; police chief of Dresden 1945–9; Lord Mayor of Dresden 1949–51; in charge of the office of the President of the GDR 1951–60.

11 The 4th session of the Council of Foreign Ministers of the four leading victorious powers of the Second World War took place in Moscow from 10 March to 24 April 1947. No agreement was reached on a peace treaty with Germany.

2 February

12 Operetta (1929) by Franz Léhar (1870–1948).

13 Klemperer's cousins Else, Adele and Olga (as well as Walter) Franke were the children of Eduard Franke, a brother of Victor Klemperer's mother and his non-Jewish wife Malvine.

8 February

14 *Luis de León* (1941), a study of León (1527–91), Spanish theologist and writer, advocate of a synthesis of Christianity and humanism; 'Die Welt im Traum' (The World in a Dream, 1941), philosophical poem by the Spanish-Mexican poet Sor Juana Inés de la Cruz (1651–95) which Vossler had translated; the study of Romance language and literature was published in 1946.

11 February

15 Max Sebba had been appointed a schools doctor.

27 February

16 VVN – established in the Soviet Zone on 22/23 February 1947, for all 4 zones in March 1947. Political organisation which emerged from and replaced the largely autonomous committees of Opfer des Faschismus (Victims of Fascism), which sprang up in 1945.

28 February

17 Alexander Abusch (1902–82), journalist and cultural politician; Member of the KPD since its foundation, chief editor of *Die Rote Fahne* (The Red Flag – the Party's main newspaper); exile in France and Mexico 1933–46; chief secretary of the KB 1946–53; Minister of Culture 1958–61; Deputy Prime Minister of the GDR 1961–71.

18 Harald Henschel (b. 1924–?); his father Bruno Henschel was from 1928 head of the Volksbühnenverlages (a theatre publisher). In 1946 Bruno Henschel and Fritz Erpenbeck set up the theatre publishers Henschel und Sohn in Berlin.

19 Gustav Leuteritz (b. 1923, died in Vorkuta, Siberia, declared dead in 1956), writer and journalist; worked as a journalist in Hamburg 1924–33; editor at the *Tägliche Rundschau* 1945; arrested by the NKVD (Soviet Secret Police) in 1948.

20 Max Lange (1899–1963), educationalist; editor of the periodical *Pädagogik* (Education); Professor of Sociology at Halle 1947; went to West Germany 1951.

21 I.e. on the position of the KB with respect to the negotiations on the German question at the Moscow meeting of the Foreign Ministers of the 4 powers.

22 Franz Dahlem (1892–1981), journalist, politician; joined KPD in 1920; member of the Reichstag 1928–33 emigrated to France; was one of the three chief political officers of the International Brigades; interned in France in 1939; handed over to the Gestapo by the Vichy French authorities in 1941; in Mauthausen concentration camp until 1945. Leading functionary of the SED from its foundation but was forced to resign from its Central Committee and Politburo in 1953 in connection with the

trial of Rudolf Slánský in Czechoslovakia, accused of having contacts with Noel H. Field; rehabilitated in 1956.

23 Julius Meyer (1909–79), joined KPD in 1930; in Auschwitz and Ravensbrück concentration camps 1943–56; chairman of the Jewish Community in East Berlin 1946–53; spokesman of the Jewish Communities of the Soviet Zone (then of the GDR) from June 1947; committee member of the VVN. On 15 January 1953 he and other chairmen of the Jewish Communities fled to West Berlin because of the intensification of the SED's anti-Zionist campaign.

24 *Pastor Hall* by Ernst Toller (1893–1939), dramatist and writer; involved in the Bavarian Councils Republic and sentenced to 5 years imprisonment; emigrated to Switzerland in 1933, then France, England and the USA, where he committed suicide on 22 May 1939. The play *Pastor Hall* was written in 1939; Klemperer saw the production premièred on 24 January 1947.

25 (French): not too much.

25a (French): old name.

26 Between 1897 and 1900 Klemperer was an apprentice at Loewenstein and Hecht, in Berlin, a company specialising in the export of souvenirs and trinkets to English seaside resorts.

27 When Klemperer's parents moved to Berlin in 1890, the family lived at 20 Albrechtstr. From the courtyard windows of the apartment the young Victor Klemperer could see into the workshop of a military tailor.

28 It is still standing (December 2002) – trans.

2 March

29 Fritz Grosse (1904–57); prison and concentration camp 1934–45; regional chairman of the VVN in Saxony 1947–9; head of the GDR mission to Czechoslovakia 1949–53.

30 Principal Jewish cemetery in Berlin.

23 March

31 A tension dating back to the 1920s, involving the award of degrees, etc.

28 March

32 For Neues Leben publishing house in Berlin.

33 Armand Salacrou (1899–1989), French dramatist.

34 Presumably Antoine de Saint-Exupéry's *Night Flight*. The writing of Saint-Exupéry (1900–44) was largely inspired by his career as a pilot; he is most famous for his children's book *The Little Prince*.

30 March

35 Eduard Hanslick (1825–1904), influential Viennese music critic.

36 The Valhalla (properly Walhalla) is a hall of fame, in the shape of a neo-classical temple, with busts of famous Germans. It was built in 1830–2 on a hill overlooking the Danube near Regensburg.

2 April

37 Dresden had long been famous for its opera. Before the destruction of 13 February 1945 it had been housed in the so-called Semper Opera House designed by Gottfried Semper. After restoration it was finally re-opened on 13 February 1985.

12 April

38 Ludwig Renn (pseudonym of Arnold Vieth von Golssenau, 1889–1979), writer, gave up his career as an army officer after the First World War. His reportage novel *Krieg*

(War), which appeared in 1928, was a worldwide success. A KPD member, he was sentenced to $2\frac{1}{2}$ years in prison in 1933; fled to Switzerland in 1936. Chief of Staff of the 11th International Brigade in the Spanish Civil War; exile in Mexico 1939–47. Professor of Anthropology at Dresden TH and Director of the Institute of Cultural Sciences From May 1947.

17 April
39 I.e. Stephan Müller, who did forced labour with Klemperer at the Schlüter herbal teas company, later fellow occupant of the Jews' House at 1 Zeughausstr. Before his Jewish origin became known he had been a member of the SA (hence SA-Müller as Klemperer called him in *TBE*, not Gestapomüller as he misremembers here). Stephan Müller was arrested by the Gestapo on 15 November 1944.

21 April
40 Hippolyte Taine (1828–93), French philosopher, historian and literary critic; Applied the rational-scientific approach of Positivism to the study of history, literature and art.

29 April
41 There is no evidence either that Dresden was bombed to stop the Soviets getting hold of it, nor of any Soviet objections to the bombing.
42 (French): eternal characteristics.

2 May
43 I.e. on the anniversary of the Nazi public burning of books of left-wing and Jewish authors on 10 May 1933.
44 Jakob Flamensbeck, before 1945 head of the local Nazi farmers' organisation and deputy mayor of Unterbernbach in Upper Bavaria, where the Klemperers stayed after their flight from Dresden. They were fed on Flamensbeck's farm.
45 Erich Auerbach (1892–1957), Romance languages and literatures scholar; professor in Marburg 1930–5, dismissed because he was Jewish; professor in Istanbul 1936–47, then at Pennsylvania State College and finally at Yale University, New Haven (Conn.). *Mimesis* (1946), his magnum opus, investigates the development of Realism in European literature.
45a (Latin): the old reviving fears.

15 May
46 Werner Krauss's novel *PLN* (the abbreviation for Postleitnummer – a purely numerical postal code devised in Germany during the Second World War) is an allegorical satire of Nazi Germany, which Krauss wrote during his imprisonment. First published 1946 in Frankfurt/Main.
47 Erich Wendt (1902–65), publisher and cultural politician; worked for Communist publishing houses from 1921; in the Soviet Union 1931–47, again involved in publishing. Director of the Aufbau publishing house 1947–51; first secretary of the KB; from 1957 deputy minister of culture or state secretary.
48 Rudolf Schottländer (1900–88), philologist and philosopher; worked as translator and journalist until 1933; protected from deportation by a 'mixed marriage'; forced labour in a munitions factory. Professor at Dresden TH 1947, dismissed on political grounds 1949; settled in West Berlin, where he was dismissed from a teaching post in 1959 for supporting the peace movement. Professor at the Humboldt University, East Berlin, 1960–65.

15–19 May

49 Name of the locomotive in Zola's novel *La bête humaine* (1890).

50 I.e. a book by the Russian writer Maxim Gorky (1868–1936).

51 Catholic old people's home where the Klemperers had stayed in May 1945 on their way to Dresden.

52 Philip Auerbach, himself a persecuted Jew, was the director of the Bavarian Compensation Office, in which capacity he tried to help Nazi victims as unbureaucratically as possible. In 1951 he was arrested and accused of misappropriation. Cleared of the original charges, he was nevertheless sentenced to $2\frac{1}{2}$ years imprisonment for bribery and embezzlement. He committed suicide in prison.

53 Sir Georg (György) Solti (1912–97), conductor of Hungarian origin; student of Bartok and Kodály; at the Budapest State Opera 1934–9; General Music Director in Munich 1947; in Frankfurt/Main from 1952, later in London and Chicago.

54 Heinrich Grüber (1891–1975), Protestant theologian; in 1937 set up an Office for the Assistance of Racially Persecuted Protestants; concentration camp 1940–43; provost of the Marienkirche in Berlin 1945; representative of the German Protestant Church to the Government of the GDR 1949–58.

55 Theodor Herzl (1860–1904), Austrian writer; most influential advocate of Zionism i.e. of the foundation of a Jewish state; called the First Zionist World Congress in Basel, 1897. Martin Buber (1878–1965); Jewish religious and social philosopher of Austrian origin, active in the Zionist Movement from 1898; professor in Frankfurt/Main 1923–33; at the Hebrew University, Jerusalem, 1938–51.

20–23 May

56 Alfred Meusel (1896–1960), historian; professor at Aachen TH. Emigration to England via Denmark 1934; professor at HUB, 1946–53; Director of the Museum of German History in Berlin from 1953.

57 Anna Seghers (1900–83), writer; exiled in France and Mexico from 1933; returned to Germany 1947; Vice-President of the KB; founding member of the Academy of the Arts; President of the German Writers' Association 1952–78. Many best-selling novels, usually dealing with the fight against Nazism e.g. *The Seventh Cross* and *Transit*.

58 Michael Tchesno-Hell (1902–80), film-script writer, journalist, editor; joined KPD 1922; worked as a journalist during emigration (France, Netherlands, Switzerland); set up the publishing house Volk und Welt (Nation and World) in 1947, which he managed for several years.

59 Wilhelm Girnus (1906–85), cultural politician; joined KPD 1929; illegal activities, concentration camp after 1933; director of the Berlin radio station 1946–9; editor at *Neues Deutschland*, the principal SED organ, 1949–53; Permanent Secretary with responsibility for high schools and technical schools 1957–62.

60 Klemperer had read a section of Sartre's essay 'Réflexions sur la question juive' (1946).

61 Romain Rolland (1866–1944), French novelist, dramatist, biographer and essayist. His work is informed by an eclectic mix of Tolstoyanism, Socialism and oriental mysticism. His major work of prose is the 6 volume novel *Jean-Christophe*. He was awarded the Nobel Prize for Literature in 1915.

2 June

62 I.e. invitation to be guest professor at the Humboldt University, Berlin.

5 June

63 According to the notes to the German edition it appears that Willy Schmidt's sentence was not the result of a legally valid procedure; his was evidently one of many cases in which the Soviet authorities imposed arbitrary sentences.

10 June

64 *The Seventh Cross*, dealing with a break-out from a concentration camp, was Anna Seghers' most successful novel. Published in Mexico in 1942, it was very soon translated into other languages and made into a Hollywood film, directed by Edward Dmytryk, before the end of the Second World War.

12 June

65 The Klemperers' housekeeper.

18 June

66 The circumstances of Friedrich's death were never fully clarified and it has been suggested, that as a troublesome stumbling block in the way of a complete Communist control, he was a victim of the Soviet secret police. Erich Zeigner (1886–1949) joined SPD 1919, Prime Minister of an SPD/KPD coalition government in Saxony in 1923; forcibly removed on the orders of the central government he was sentenced to 3 years imprisonment in 1924. Buchenwald concentration camp 1944; Lord Mayor of Leipzig 1945–49.

23 June

67 Thomas Mann's *Thoughts in Wartime* was first published in 1914.

25 June

68 F(ranz) K(arl) Weiskopf (1900–55), German writer and journalist from Prague; emigrated to the USA 1939; in the diplomatic service of the Czechoslovak Republic after 1945; settled in GDR 1953. The lexicon was published in Berlin in 1948.

29 June

69 UNRRA – The United Nations Relief and Rehabilitation Administration established in 1943 and taken over by the United Nations in 1945. Its purpose was to help refugees and displaced persons in territories occupied by the Allies; it was wound up in 1947 and replaced by the UNHCR, the United Nations High Commission for Refugees.

9 July

70 In summer 1947 the trial took place in Dresden of some of those responsible for the euthanasia murders carried out in Sonnenstein sanatorium and mental hospital in Pirna.

17 July

71 Nikolai Ostrovsky (1904–36), Russian-Soviet author. *How the Steel was Tempered* was first published 1934/35.

18 July

72 'Pajok' is Russian for ration; name given to supplementary food supplies to intellectuals and functionaries by the Soviet occupation authorities.

20 July

73 Presumably a reference to the Foreign Ministers' Conference that is had met in Moscow March–April 1947 and was due to meet in London in December 1947.

74 Dolores Ibárruri Gómez (1895–1989), known as 'La Pasionaria' (the Passionate); Spanish politician. Founder member of the Spanish Communist Party 1920; member

and president of the Spanish parliament 1936; in Soviet exile from 1939; from 1942 General Secretary then chair of the Spanish Communist Party.

25 July

75 Jacques Roumain (1907–44), Haitian writer, one of the most important exponents of 'négritude'. Founded the Haitian Communist Party in 1934. The novel *Gouverneurs de la rosée* (1944) made his reputation. Eva Klemperer's translation appeared in 1947 under the title *Herrüber den Tau* (Lord of the Dew).

76 As a 17-year-old, Klemperer turned a number of maxims from the Talmud into rhymed form, which his father then used in his sermons. In the summer of 1905 Klemperer composed more than 400 such pieces, many of which were published in newspapers. Later a selection appeared as a small book. See Curriculum Vitae, vol. I, p. 183 and p. 413 (Berlin 1996).

31 July

77 I.e. *The Protocols of the Elders of Zion*, a forgery, which supposedly represented the record of a secret meeting of Jews in Basel in 1897 to plan Jewish world domination. It was published by the Tsarist secret police in Russia to legitimise pogroms against Jews. A number of trials between 1924 and 1936 proved its fictitious nature.

78 (French): What do I know?

4 August

79 Karl Kröner (1882–1972), painter and graphic artist, from 1920 living as a freelance artist in Radebeul near Dresden.

12 August

80 Becher's *Abschied. Einer deutschen Tragödie erster Teil* (Leave-taking. The first part of a German Tragedy) was first published in Moscow in 1940.

81 A polemical essay on Sartre's Existentialism, published in *Neue Welt*, vol. 2, no. 12 (1947).

82 (French): Where does this pitiless hatred of the Bolsheviks come from?

14 August

83 Residence of Hermann Goering in countryside north of Berlin; blown up on Soviet orders in 1945.

16 August

84 (French): forced smile.

85 Rudolf Brummer (1907–89), Romance languages and literatures scholar; professor in Rostock 1946, and in Mainz, West Germany, 1959–72.

86 Wolfgang Steinitz (1905–67), linguist and ethnologist; professor in Leningrad 1934–7; guest lectures in Stockholm 1938–45; from 1946 Professor of Finno-Ugrian at the HUB; Vice-President of the German Academy of Sciences 1954–63; Director of the Institute of German Ethnology.

20 August

87 In a letter of 13 August 1947, the dean, Günther Jacoby, assured Klemperer that the University of Greifswald was creating very favourable conditions, not least through the purchase of a house and garden, for the accommodation of the Klemperers and of the Romance Languages and Literatures Department.

30 August

88 *St Joan of the Stockyards*, written 1929–30, premièred 1959.

89 *Nietzsche und der französische Geist* (1939), by Julius Wilhelm (1896–1983), Romance languages and literatures scholar; professor in Munich 1937 and in Tübingen 1942–66.

90 (Latin): fame is sweet, youth is sweeter.

2 September

91 The prison in Bautzen was the largest and most notorious in the Soviet Zone (and subsequent GDR).

12 September

92 Gadamer had gone to Frankfurt/Main (later Heidelberg), Litt to Bonn during 1947.

22 September

93 Franz Wohlgemuth (b. 1915–?) was later, 1957–8, Professor of Scientific Socialism in Halle.

24 September

94 Andrei Vyshinsky (1883–1954), the notorious chief state prosecutor of the Moscow show trials in the late 1930s; Soviet Foreign Minister 1949–53; Permanent Representative of the Soviet Union at the United Nations 1953–4. In a speech to the Second General Assembly of the United Nations on 18 September 1947, he accused the USA of misusing the United Nations to promote its own ends and named a number of leading US politicians as warmongers, thus inaugurating an intensification of the Cold War.

1 October

95 I.e. humanism both in its definition of a period, of the revival of scholarship during the Renaissance, and in its more contemporary usage of a concern for humanity and human rights.

31 October

96 Colonel Dymshits was Chief Cultural Officer of the SMAD.

10 November

97 I.e. the pogrom against Jewish institutions and businesses begun on the night of 9/10 November 1939, during which 267 synagogues were destroyed, almost 100 Jews murdered, 7,500 businesses wrecked and 26,000 Jewish men taken to concentration camps. Whoever was responsible for the somewhat trivialising phrase 'Crystal Night' (the allusion is to the smashed glass of the windows of Jewish shops), it was in use almost immediately.

29 November

98 I.e. to a local SED official.

99 Jacob Kaiser (1888–1961), trade unionist and politician; member of the National Committee of the Christian Trades Unions 1924–33; active in the anti-Nazi resistance; co-founder of the unified trades unions (i.e. with the intention of superseding trades unions defined by confession and party political allegiance) and of the CDU in Berlin; chairman of the latter in Berlin and the Soviet Zone 1945. In opposition to Konrad Adenauer's policy of integration with the West Kaiser proposed Germany as a bridge between East and West. In December 1947 he was relieved of his post by

the SMAD and went to West Germany. Member of the Bundestag (West German parliament) 1949–57; Minister for All-German Affairs, deputy chairman of the CDU.

100 On 1 January 1947 the US and British occupation zones were amalgamated in the 'United Economic Territory', the so-called 'Bizone'; the seat of the 'Economic Council' of the Bizone was in Frankfurt/Main. Whereas the USA and Britain presented the Bizone as a step towards the establishment of the economic unity of Germany, the SED accused the (West) German politicians on the Economic Council of being traitors to their country, comparing them to the Vichy French regime which collaborated with the Nazis.

101 Daughter of the dentist Erich Isakowitz, with whom the Klemperers were friendly, and who emigrated to England in 1936.

102 (Italian): little new world (i.e. how small the world has become).

14 December

103 (Latin): to the stars.

104 Rudolf Seeliger (1886–1965), physicist; professor in Greifswald 1918–55, rector 1946–8.

105 Franz Dornseif (1888–1960), classicist; professor in Berlin 1925, Greifswald 1926, Erlangen 1946, Leipzig 1948.

17 December

106 Hans Mayer (1907–2001), literary scholar; emigrated to France 1933, later to Switzerland; political editor of Radio Frankfurt/Main. Professor in Leipzig 1948, settled in West Germany after years of attacks by the SED. *Georg Büchner und seine Zeit* (Georg Büchner and his Time), Mayer's first major work of literary scholarship, was published in 1946 in Wiesbaden and then in 1947 in the Soviet Zone. Georg Büchner (1813–37), author of plays and prose and a revolutionary, little known in his own lifetime, is now recognised as a writer of enormous influence on later literary developments.

107 The London Four-Power Conference ended on 15 December 1947 without agreement on the question of the future eastern border of Germany, on a future government of Germany and on reparations.

108 Following the failure of the London Conference, the regional People's Congresses, such as that in Mecklenburg, were intended to institutionalise the People's Congress Movement 'for unity and a just peace', among other things through the setting up of 'Permanent Committees' at local, county, regional (*Land*) and Zonal level. (Effectively the People's Congress was the forerunner of the People's Chamber – Volkskammer – the representative chamber of the German Democratic Republic.)

19 December

109 Margarethe ('Grete') Riesenfeld (1867–1942), Victor Klemperer's eldest sister. The excursion to the coast with her took place in August 1937.

110 (Italian): i.e. imply a mood of no surrender.

25 December

111 I.e. at the very end of the war, as the village of Unterbernbach was about to fall to the Americans. See *TBE*, 25 August 1945.

27 December

112 In effect the censorship body of the Soviet Zone, though Klemperer does not quite grasp this yet.

1948

1 January
1 (French): cat excreta.
2 Max Burwitz (1896–1974), teacher; joined SPD 1925; dismissed 1933. Lord mayor of Greifswald 1945–9, then of Rostock.
3 Herbert Schmidt-Walter (1904–80), art scholar; professor in Greifswald and Director of the Institute of Art Education 1948; at the Dresden High School of the Arts from 1955.
4 Sartre's first novel, published 1938.

21 January
5 Arnold Zweig (1887–1968), novelist, essayist, dramatist; emigrated 1933 (south of France, later Palestine), returned to Berlin 1948; President of the German Academy of the Arts 1950–53; member of the KB Executive Committee until 1958. Major novelist and essayist, whose anti-war and anti-Nazi novels in particular have never gone out of print, also an acute observer of developments in Palestine/Israel.
6 Editions de Minuit was originally an underground publishing house during the occupation of France. Perhaps its most famous literary publication was the novel *Le silence de la mer* (1942) by Vercors (1902–91).

23 January
7 (French): *blind* and *with* – the two French words begin with the same syllable but have different Latin roots.
8 Ernst Robert Curtius (1886–1956), Romance languages and literatures scholar, one of the most distinguished of the 20th century; professor at Marburg 1920, Heidelberg 1924, Bonn 1929; popularised important contemporary authors in Germany, including Marcel Proust, Paul Valéry and T. S. Eliot. During the Nazi years he concentrated on apparently uncontroversial medieval topics. Victor Klemperer always regarded Curtius' success and achievements with envy.
9 P. A. Becker (1862–1947), Romance languages and literatures scholar; professor in Budapest 1893, in Vienna 1905, in Leipzig 1917–30. After retirement he was made honorary professor in Freiburg.

31 January
10 André Maurois (1885–1967), French novelist, essayist, historian; particularly well known for his 'fictionalised biographies'.

9 February
11 In the first elected German parliament convened in Frankfurt during the Revolutions of 1848, it was the democrats and radicals who proposed the 'Greater German solution' with the inclusion of the Austrian provinces (which had of course also elected representatives to the Frankfurt parliament) which were part of the German Confederation. Ninety years later, however, Adolf Hitler had adopted the term 'Greater Germany' to describe the German state after the absorption of the Austrian Republic.
12 Friedrich (Fritz) Behrens (1909–80), economist; town councillor in Zwickau 1945; professor in Leipzig 1947, founding dean of the Social Science Faculty (Gewifa); founder of the Working Group of Marxist Scholars (including Werner Krauss and the historian Walter Markov); from 1955 director of the GDR's Central Statistical Office. An important influence on GDR economic policy in the 1960s; disciplined for 'revisionism' in 1957, he was forced to retire prematurely in 1967.
13 Jean Cassou (1897–1986), French critic, novelist and poet; took part in the Spanish

Civil War and in the Resistance. His novel *Les Massacres de Paris* (1935 – Eva Klemperer's German translation appeared in 1948) deals with the Paris Commune of 1871.

16 February
14 I.e. the Society for the Study of the Culture of the Soviet Union.

22 February
15 Willi Bredel (1901–64), leading 'proletarian writer'; concentration camp 1933; after release, flight to USSR 1934; took part in the Spanish Civil War 1937–9; founding member of the National Committee for a Free Germany. Edited periodicals after 1945; President of the German Academy of the Arts 1962.

12 March
16 Max and Doris Kahane lived within an area of Berlin-Niederschönhausen which had a Russian military guard. Here senior functionaries and their families lived in confiscated detached houses.

19 March
17 The Second German People's Congress 'For unity and a just peace' elected the German Volksrat (People's Council) with 400 members, 100 from the Western zones, and announced a petition for a referendum in May 1948 on the establishment of German unity.
18 Walter Ulbricht (1893–1973), joined KPD 1919; member of the Reichstag 1928–33; exile in France, Czechoslovakia and USSR. Deputy chairman of the Central Committee of the SED 1946–50, General Secretary, then First Secretary of the Central Committee 1950–71.
19 The planned economy in the Soviet Zone was initiated with a 6-month plan for July–December 1948. It was a preliminary to the more detailed Two Year Plan for 1949–50.
20 Burial place in Friedrichshain Park, Berlin, of 184 revolutionaries killed on the barricades in March 1848.

29 March
21 *De l'Allemagne* by Madame de Staël (1766–1817); her book on Germany (and German Romanticism) was a powerful influence on the development of French Romanticism.

9 April
22 Klemperer gave his first lectures in 1919 as a private lecturer at Munich University and his last lectures before 1948 in 1935 as professor at Dresden TH.

18 April
23 (French): from beyond the grave, an allusion to the memoirs of the French writer and diplomat, Chateaubriand: *Les mémoires d'outre-tombe* (1848–50).

21 May
24 Rita Hetzer (later Schober, b. 1918), Romance languages and literatures scholar; academic from 1946; professor at the HUB 1954–78. Published work on Zola and edited his works; wrote, inter alia, on French Classicism and on Structuralism.
25 Joachim Storost (1905–81), Romance languages and literatures scholar; professor in Halle 1941, Innsbruck 1944, in Halle again 1948, Greifswald 1949; at the Philosophical-Theological High School in Bamberg 1953, in Würzburg 1958–71.

23 May

26 Robert Schober (1911–94).

27 Paul Harms (1866–1945), prominent journalist. The Klemperers became acquainted with him during their time in Leipzig; then leader writer of the *Leipziger Neueste Nachrichten*. Became a full-blooded Nazi after 1933. See entry in *TBE*, 21 March 1945. Kopke, a journalist in Harms' circle, also worked for the *Leipziger Neueste Nachrichten*.

24 May

28 Ernst Bloch (1885–1977), philosopher; emigrated 1933 (Zürich, Vienna, Paris, USA from 1938); professor in Leipzig 1948, forced into retirement 1957; went to Tübingen as guest professor 1961. On the basis of dialectical materialism, drawing on Aristotle, Hegel and Jewish-Christian eschatology developed a 'Philosophy of hope'. Also one of the most acute contemporary writers on the rise of Nazism (see e.g. *Heritage of these Times*).

30 May

29 Presumably a reference to the Frankfurt Parliament of 1848–49 and the proposed 'Greater German' approach with the inclusion of the Austrian territories of the German Confederation. Unfair inasmuch as the black–red–gold flag (now also the flag of a united Federal Germany) was a symbol of democracy as against the flags of the various German states, as well as against the black–white–red of Imperial Germany after 1871, which colours were adapted by the Nazis in 1933, when they got rid of the hated democratic flag.

30 (French) – translates roughly as: 'I shall say it unceasingly, / I shall say it without fear: / You are the nephew of my dreams, / You are the nephew of my heart. // As for me I am a weak poet, / That has always been my misfortune; / So, stammering, I repeat: / You are the nephew of my heart!'

31 Ernst Busch (1900–80), actor and singer, interpreter in particular of socially critical and revolutionary songs; a key member of Brecht's ensemble after the Second World War though he had already worked in Brecht's theatre and film productions before 1933. He is one of the great popular singers of the 20th century.

20 June

32 Alfred de Vigny (1797–1863), French poet, novelist and dramatist.

33 With effect from 21 June 1948 the Reichsmark ceased to be legal tender in the 3 Western occupation zones and was replaced by the D-mark. From 20 June each inhabitant was permitted to exchange 40RM and in August a further 20R at a rate of 1:1, otherwise cash was devalued at a rate of 100:5, bank and savings accounts at a rate of 10:1.

34 Gustave Flaubert's *Salammbô* (Reutlingen 1948) was published with an essay by Victor Klemperer on Flaubert and French Romanticism.

23 June

35 (Italian): on the contrary.

26 June

36 On 23 June a currency reform was also carried out in the Soviet Zone: 70RM per head were exchanged at 1:1, sums beyond that amount had to be paid into accounts and were devalued as follows: balances up to 100RM at 1:1, up to 1,000RM at 5:1 and up to 5,000RM at a rate of 10:1.

37 *Irgenwa in Berlin* (Somewhere in Berlin, 1946) directed by Gerhard Lamprecht; a

prominent and early example of the 'Trümmerfilme' (films in the ruins) made 1946–8.

11 July

38 The Free University in the Dahlem district of Berlin, opened on 4 December 1948.

39 In response to the introduction of the D-mark in the Western sectors of Berlin, the SMAD had suspended all goods traffic to West Berlin. The Western Allies met this blockade with the 'air lift'. West Berlin was supplied by air until May 1949 along the three air corridors recognised by treaty.

12 July

40 (Latin): life and death.

8 August

41 The National Demokratische Partei Deutschlands (NDPD – National Democratic Party of Germany) was established on 25 May 1948, the Demokratische Bauernpartei Deutschlands (DBD – Democratic Peasants' Party of Germany) on 29 April 1948.

42 Edouard Peisson (1896–1963) wrote popular seafaring novels.

43 I.e. a dissertation on the French critic and writer Eugène-Melchior Vicomte de Vogüé (1848–1910).

10 August

44 Jacques Delille (1738–1813), French poet. Klemperer's study of 1934 on Delille and his didactic poem 'Les jardins' (The Gardens) of 1782 could not be published during the Nazi years.

27 August

45 Maria Strindberg, née Lazar, sister of Auguste Wieghardt-Lazar.

46 (Latin): I shall not quite die; from Ovid's Odes III (30, 6).

13 September

47 On 6 September 1948 SED supporters forced their way into a session of the city council; the majority of the councillors left and moved to the British sector. Three days later 300,000 Berliners demonstrated in front of the ruin of the Reichstag against the suppression of political freedom in the Soviet Sector. There were clashes between demonstrators and police and Soviet military at the Brandenburg Gate and a 15-year-old demonstrator was shot and later died.

48 (French): definitely too much.

49 (French): Jew.

50 The independent state of Israel was proclaimed in Tel-Aviv on 14 May 1948, shortly before the departure of the last British troops.

19 September

51 (Latin): before our gates, i.e. at our front door.

23 September

52 See *I Shall Bear Witness: The Diaries of Victor Klemperer 1933–41*, entry of 24 January 1933.

5 October

53 *1–2–3 Corona* (1948), directed by Hans Müller.

54 Herbert Koch (1880–1962), Classical archaeologist; professor in Jena 1918, Leipzig 1929, Halle 1931; emeritus 1953, taught until 1959.

8 October

55 I.e. after the Restoration of the French Bourbon monarchy in 1814–15 following Napoleon's defeat and exile.

10 October

56 In the 'Zion' chapter of *LTI*.

57 Folke Bernadotte, UN mediator in the conflict between Israel and the Arab states, was assassinated in Jerusalem by Jewish extremists on 17 September 1948.

31 October

58 Ernest Lavisse (1842–1922), French historian, in particular of 19th- and 20th-century France.

59 Gustav von Wangenheim (1895–1975), dramatist, film-writer, actor and director; before 1933 one of the advocates of proletarian-revolutionary theatre. Inge von Wangenheim (1912–93), writer and essayist; initially actress, wife of Gustav. In 1933 the couple emigrated to the USSR by way of France.

5 November

60 I.e. Robert Schober.

14 November

61 Bernard Koenen (1889–1964) joined SPD 1907, KPD 1920; member of the Prussian second chamber 1924–9; emigrated to USSR 1933. Chairman of the SED regional leadership, Saxony-Anhalt, 1946–52; First Secretary of the SED Halle District 1952–3 and 1958–63.

62 Erhard Hübener (1881–1958), company lawyer; member of the liberal Deutsche Demokratische Partei before 1933; co-founder of the LDPD (Liberal Democratic Party of Germany) in Halle 1945; President of the provincial administration of Saxony-Anhalt and Prime Minister 1946–9; Professor of Administrative Law at Halle 1946.

63 The review was finally published in the periodical *Südwestdeutschland* (29 November 1948).

16 November

64 On 15 November 1948 the first retail outlets of the State Trading Organisation (Handelsorganisation) HO were opened in which goods were sold without ration cards or vouchers but at high prices.

3 December

65 Maurice Nadeau, *Histoire du surréalisme* (Paris 1945).

16 December

66 The dermatologist Georg Jacoby went to West Germany in 1949.

28 December

67 (Latin): revulsion.

68 Louis Aragon (1897–1982), French novelist, poet and journalist. Starting his career as a Surrealist, Aragon joined the Communist Party in 1927, adopting literary forms and themes more in keeping with that commitment; active in left-wing cultural politics. Paul Eluard (1895–1952), French poet, essayist, critic.

31 December
69 (Italian): poor little Germany.

1949

2 February
1 I.e. 200th anniversary of Goethe's birth in 1749.
2 Lion Feuchtwanger (1886–1958) was one of the most successful authors of the first half of the 20th century and much translated. *Erfolg* (Success) deals with the domination of the extreme right in Bavaria after 1919 and the consequences. Published in 1929 it is one of the first novels to address the rise of Nazism.
3 Alfred Kantorowicz (1899–1979), literary historian and journalist; emigrated to France 1933, exiled in the USA 1941–6. Editor of the periodical *Ost und West* 1947–9; professor at the HUB and Director of its Institute of German Studies. August 1957 fled to West Berlin. He and Klemperer had become friends after the latter began teaching at the HUB. Kantorowicz's *Spanisches Tagebuch* (Spanish Diary) is an account of his experiences in the Spanish Civil War.

12 February
4 Adolf Hennicke (1905–75), miner; the exemplary figure of the Activists' Movement in the GDR: on 13 October 1948 he overfulfilled his daily production target by 387%, thereby setting a new record. His achievement and its promotion was modelled on the career of the Soviet champion worker Alexei Stakhanov, who in August 1935 supposedly produced 14 times the previous best output of a worker on a single shift.

8 March
5 Wilhelm Adam (1893–1973), early member of the Nazi Party; in 1941 First Adjutant to the commander of the German 6th Army, taken prisoner at Stalingrad; member of the National Committee for a Free Germany. Department head with the government of Saxony 1948–9; member of the executive committee of the National Democratic Party 1949–58; Saxon Minister of Finance 1950–52. Colonel with the militarised units of the Volkspolizei (People's Police), then of the Nationale Volksarmee (National People's Army) of the GDR; Commander of the Officers' High School. Retired 1958 with the rank of Major-General.
6 Friedrich Paulus (1890–1957); from the beginning of 1942 commander-in-chief of the German 6th Army on the Eastern Front. After savage fighting in and around the city of Stalingrad his forces were cut off; against Hitler's orders he eventually surrendered his remaining troops on 31 January 1943.

10 April
7 Stephan Hermlin (1915–97), poet, prose writer, essayist; emigrated to Britain, France, Switzerland 1936; radio editor Frankfurt/Main 1945; in Berlin from 1947. In his review in the *Tägliche Rundschau* (25 March 1949) 'A Disservice to German Youth', Hermlin criticised the unchanged selection of French prose since 1926 and the inclusion of texts by less important authors 'meanwhile thrown onto the dunghill of literary history' whereas democratic and Resistance authors had not been included.
8 The Franckesche Stiftungen, endowments founded by the Protestant theologian and educationalist August Herman Francke (1663–1727) were educational establishments (including a grammar school) and libraries, which since 1946 had been attached to Halle University.

9 Actually Hans Friedrich Lange (1891–1972), journalist, critic, editor. Joined KPD 1929 chief editor of Volk and Wissen publishing house 1958.

7 May

10 During the 1905 Russian Revolution, the crew of the battle-cruiser *Potemkin* of the Black Sea Fleet mutinied. (The basis of Eisenstein's famous film.)
11 Famous Italian revolutionary song. The first lines go: 'Forward people to revolt, the red flag will triumph.'

17 May

12 The article enlisted support for the elections to the Third People's Congress, which were held on 15–16 May 1949. Victor Klemperer was one of 77 candidates from Saxony-Anhalt.

20 May

13 At the election to the Third German People's Congress there were, for the first time in the Soviet Zone, no individual candidates or parties standing. Instead there was a 'unified list' of all parties and organisations. Voters had a choice between 'yes' and 'no' to this list. In the event 61.1% of the valid votes were 'yes', 38.9% 'no'.
14 Ernest Renan (1823–90), French scholar and writer; one of the leading French writers and intellectuals of the 19th century, particularly important for his religious studies. He tried to reconcile a belief in human progress, not least in science, with religion, despite his own loss of faith.
15 Bodo Uhse (1904–63), novelist and essayist; emigrated to France 1933, fought in the Spanish Civil War; exiled in Mexico from 1940 chief editor of the *Aufbau* periodical 1948–58.

24 May

16 André Simone (actually Otto Katz, 1895–1952), journalist and writer, born in Prague. From 1922 in Berlin; emigration to France 1933, Spain 1936, USA 1939, Mexico 1941–6. In the Slánský Trial in Prague he was sentenced to death at the end of 1952 and executed. The majority of those sentenced were Jewish and/or had been émigrés in Western countries. He was posthumously absolved of the charges in 1963 and re-admitted to the Communist Party in 1968.

29 May

17 On 5 May 1949 the chief delegates to the UN Security Council of the 4 great powers agreed on lifting the blockade of West Berlin. This took effect on 12 May. The air lift was continued for some time after that in order to replenish basic reserves in the Western sectors of the divided city.
18 *Les Maudits* – The Damned – (1947), directed by René Clément.
19 On 5 May 1949 the foreign ministers of 10 West European states signed the statutes of the newly established Council of Europe.
20 Max Reinhardt (1873–1943), actor, director, theatre manager; with his takeover of the Deutsches Theater in Berlin in 1905 began the development of modern director's theatre; one of the most influential theatre directors of the 20th century. In the USA from 1937.

30 May

21 Klemperer attended the session of the Third German People's Congress on 29 and 30 May 1949. After the Parliamentary Council of the Western Zones had proclaimed the Basic Law (i.e. constitution) of the Federal Republic of Germany, the People's Congress

accepted the Constitution of the German Democratic Republic and elected 330 members to make up the People's Council.

31 May
22 (French): arse-wipe.

4 June
23 The parties permitted in the GDR, which necessarily endorsed the GDR and its constitution, constituted the National Front, i.e. the various parties were essentially organs and transmission belts of government dominated by the Communist Party in the guise of the Socialist Unity Party and only residually parties as they are understood in parliamentary democracies on the Western model.
24 Abbreviation of New Economic Policy, which in 1921 in the Soviet Union replaced the 'War Communism' of the Civil War years and which once again permitted private enterprise as well as making concessions to private companies.

2 July
25 Published in *Die Tat* of 13 August 1949 (journal of the VVN).

2–4 July
26 Jürgen Kuczynski (1904–97), economic historian; economics editor of the KPD organ *Rote Fahne* 1930–33; emigrated to England 1936. Professor at the HUB, 1946–56; Director of the Economic History Section of the Historical Institute of the German Academy of Sciences 1956–68. Kuczynski was one of the few social scientists or historians of the GDR to establish an international reputation.

20–24 July
27 (French): What did I know about it? What do I know now? Everything and nothing . . .

29 July
28 *Maître Pierre Pathelin*, famous medieval French farce composed 1464, first published 1485 or 1486.

2 August
29 On 1 August 1949 Thomas Mann accepted the Goethe Prize in Weimar and was made an honorary citizen of the town.

5 August
30 Thomas Mann had already given the speech in Frankfurt/Main on accepting that city's Goethe prize.

14 August
31 Ilya Ehrenburg (1891–1967), Russian and Soviet novelist and essayist; went into exile in Paris before the First World War; returned to Russia in 1917; went into exile again 1921–4. He was then mostly a foreign journalist for Soviet newspapers until 1941, when he became a war correspondent with the Soviet forces. His early work is both politically and formally very radical, but perhaps his best-known novel is *The Thaw* (1954), which captured the sense of relaxation in Soviet society after Stalin's death.
32 Joseph Arthur, Comte de Gobineau (1816–82), French writer and diplomat; notorious as one of the popularisers of modern racist ideas; he believed in the inequality of races and the intellectual superiority of an 'Aryan' race.

17 August

33 In fact the ceremonies commemorating the 200th anniversary of Goethe's birth took place around 28 August 1949.

34 In contrast to Victor Klemperer's judgement, others (according to the notes to the German edition of the diaries) have emphasised Werner Lang's solidarity with and concern for his fellow persecuted Jews; e.g. Henny Brenner, née Wolf, in whose parents' house Werner Lang hid after the bombing of Dresden.

35 The Soviet investigating authorities accused Ernst Neumark of collaboration with the Gestapo. No documents relating to his trial are known. Neumark probably died in Bautzen Prison around 1950. In the entry of 4 May 1950, Klemperer records Neumark's former secretary as saying she believed him to have been sentenced to ten years and to be imprisoned in Russia.

30 August

36 I.e. application for emeritus status.

2 September

37 The Games were the first in which the FDJ, the East German Youth organisation, participated.

38 (French): the extremes meet (i.e. right and left) – saying derived from the seating arrangements of the French Assembly.

39 *The Last Stage*, Polish film by Wanda Jakowska (1907–98), who was herself a survivor of Auschwitz concentration camp.

40 *Jew Süss* was an anti-Semitic film directed by Veit Harlan (1899–1964).

41 Ilse Koch (1906–67), concentration camp warder; married Karl Otto Koch, camp commandant of Sachsenhausen and Buchenwald concentration camps in 1936; sentenced to life imprisonment by a US military court; pardoned at the end of 1948, but immediately put on trial by a German court and in 1951 sentenced to life imprisonment for incitement to murder. In 1967 she committed suicide in prison.

22 September

42 Helene Berg (b. 1906); trained as a dressmaker; joined KPD 1927, emigrated to Soviet Union, becoming a Soviet citizen. After 1946, inter alia, responsible for SED propaganda in Saxony-Anhalt; Director of the Institute of Social Sciences of the Central Committee of the SED 1951–8.

12 October

43 On 7 October 1949 the German Volksrat (People's Council) declared itself the 'Provisional Volkskammer' (People's Chamber), enacted the constitution and formed a 'Provisional Government'; with that, the German Democratic Republic had been founded. On 11 October in a joint session, the Volkskammer and the regional chambers unanimously elected Wilhelm Pieck State President.

14 October

44 Horacio Quiroga (1878–1937), Uruguayan author; wrote, inter alia, stories about his life in the Argentinian jungle. Jesús Izcaray Cebriano (1903–80), Spanish novelist, journalist and critic; emigrated to Mexico 1939; after 1945 lived in France until Franco's death. Eva Klemperer translated the documentary report 'Castro Garcia Roza' (1947) for the Dietz publishing house.

20 October

45 (Latin): the way things stand.

15 November

46 'Auferstanden aus Ruinen' (Risen from the Ruins), by Johannes R. Becher, music by Hanns Eisler, was declared the state anthem of the GDR by the Provisional Volkskammer on 5 November 1949.

47 'Deutschland über alles' (as it is popularly known) became the German national anthem in 1922; originally a poem entitled 'Das Lied der Deutschen' (The Song of the Germans, 1841) by Heinrich Hoffmann von Fallersleben (1798–1874). The melody was adapted from Haydn. It was made the anthem of West Germany after its foundation in 1949 and of the reunited Germany in 1990, although after the Second World War only the third verse was ever sung, so as to avoid any possible offence to non-Germans and to take account of changed historical circumstances. (The liberal Hoffmann von Fallersleben proclaimed a 'Greater Germany' in his lyric.)

48 George Sand (1804–76), French woman writer and journalist.

22–23 December

49 Eva Klemperer's translation of Jean Cassou's novel (*Massaker von Paris*), with an afterword by Victor Klemperer, had been published in 1948.

50 (Italian): little old world.

51 Denis Diderot, *Rameaus Neffe* (Weimar 1949). Victor Klemperer had written an introduction to Diderot's novel.

26 December

52 Walther Victor (1895–1971), journalist and writer/editor of SPD newspapers. Exile in Switzerland and USA from 1935. Senior civil servant in the Saxon government 1947; in charge of the re-establishment of the Büchergilde Gutenberg in East Germany. (The Büchergilde Gutenberg, originally a book club associated with the Social Democratic Party, was also revived separately in West Germany.)

31 December

53 To mark the 200th anniversary of Bach's death, the GDR declared 1950 Bach Year. (It so happened that both Bach and Goethe, who had been celebrated the previous year, had spent the major part of their adult lives on the territory of what had become the German Democratic Republic – in the case of Bach almost entirely so.)

1950

11 January

1 Published as 'Der Höllentanz' (The Hellish Dance) in *Deutschlands Stimme* (Germany's Voice), 10 February 1950.

16 February

2 Pierre Augustin Caron de Beaumarchais (1732–99), French dramatist; had a colourful career as a businessman and spy besides writing the two anti-feudal comedies which made his name – *The Barber of Seville* (1775), the basis of an opera by Rossini, and *The Marriage of Figaro* (1784), the basis of an opera by Mozart.

24 February

3 Erich Honecker (1912–94) joined KPD 1929; sentenced to 10 years imprisonment 1935. Co-founder 1946 and chairman until 1955 of the youth organisation FDJ; candidate 1950, member 1958 of the Politburo of the SED; later First Secretary and

General Secretary of the Central Committee and chairman of the GDR Staatsrat (Council of State). Honecker effectively replaced Ulbricht as the most powerful man in the state in 1971.

4 Johannes Stumm (1897–1978) was West Berlin's chief of police 1948–62.

6–7 April

5 Peter Huchel (1903–81), poet – in fact, a major one; chief editor of *Sinn und Form* 1949–62; after he was forced to retire he was not allowed to publish in the GDR. Went to West Germany in 1971.

11 April

6 Theodor Fontane (1819–98), novelist, essayist, journalist, travel writer, poet; the most important German novelist of the late 19th century. In English his best known novel is *Effi Briest*. Did not begin to publish novels until he was in his 60s after a chequered career, not least as a Prussian agent in London.

16 April

7 György Lukács (1885–1971), Hungarian Marxist literary historian and philosopher writing mainly in German. His aesthetics was largely based on intensive study of the 19th century European novel. Minister of Culture in the reforming Imre Nagy government, which took office at the beginning of the 1956 Hungarian Uprising, he was arrested at the end of 1956, and removed from his teaching posts, after which his works could only appear in the West.

26 April

8 Gotthold Ephraim Lessing (1729–81), critic, playwright, aesthetician, philosopher etc. Leading figure of the German Enlightenment, but also paving the way for the elevation of feeling in Romanticism. One of the founders of modern criticism, he contributed greatly to breaking French aesthetic domination of German literature. His plays mark the beginning of the modern German theatre.

4–5 May

9 Victor Klemperer had been reading Anton Makarenko's (1888–1939) didactic poem 'The Path to Life', which related the history of the 'Gorky Colony', a reform school for young people set up after 1917 near Poltava in the Ukraine.

10 *Wilhelm Meister*, Goethe's great Bildungsroman, published in two parts in 1795/96 and 1829.

11 Karl Steinhoff (1892–1981), lawyer, civil servant from 1922; Joined SPD 1923; dismissed from his post 1933. President of the Provincial Administration of Brandenburg 1945, then Prime Minister 1946; GDR Interior Minister 1949, dismissed 1952. Professor of Administrative Law at the HUB 1949–53.

10–11 May

12 Walther Victor had shown Klemperer a copy of a letter from Erich Wendt to the Büchergilde Gutenberg, which raised serious objections to Klemperer's introduction to the Maupassant novellas. Wendt described it as 'wrong and harmful' and demanded considerable changes.

24 May

13 (French): fool me.

27 May

14 Michael Sayers and Albert Eugen Kahn: *The Great Conspiracy Against Russia*. The German translation appeared in 1949.

15 Eugène Sue (1804–57), best-selling author of big city mystery and adventure novels which were usually first published in serial form.

16 Leon Trotsky (1879–1940), one of the leading Bolshevik revolutionaries; principal figure in establishing the Red Army in the Civil War; Stalin's chief opponent in the internal Party struggle for power after Lenin's death; advocate of revolutionary internationalism ('permanent revolution') in contrast to Stalin's consolidation of 'Socialism in one country'. The book Klemperer is reading is evidently a Stalinist apologia, bracketing Stalin with Lenin.

17 In the Moscow Trials (the infamous show trials) of 1936–8, former leading figures of the Bolshevik Party, of the 1917 Revolution, of the Civil War period, the associates of Lenin such as Zinoviev, Kamenev, Bukharin, Radek, were put on trial. They invariably confessed to a variety of unbelievable 'crimes' against the Soviet Union, and most were executed. Stalin was henceforth without rivals as the inheritor of Lenin's mantle as revolutionary leader.

18 Trotsky, in exile in Mexico, was assassinated on Stalin's orders.

19 In addition to the idea of permanent revolution, Trotsky's followers argued that the workers' councils (soviets) of the early period of the Russian Revolution provided a model for a future social organisation based on the workplace.

20 See above, entry of 24 February 1950.

21 The foreign ministers of the three Western powers had met in London (12–15 May) to discuss the German question. As a consequence a committee was set up to review the Occupation Statute for West Germany.

4 June

22 Gerhard Rohlfs (1892–1986), Romance languages and literatures scholar; professor in Tübingen 1926, in Munich 1938–58.

21 June

23 One of many forced resignations at this point of those in high positions, who had had 'Western connections' during their exile; they were often accused of being pro-Zionist.

24 Friedrich Ebert (1894–1979), joined SPD 1913, son of the Socialist leader of the same name, who was Germany's first president (1919–25); member of the Reichstag 1928–33. From 1949 member of the Politburo of the SED; lord mayor of East Berlin 1948–67.

25 June

25 The year 1904 because, although Victor and Eva Klemperer had been married in the same registry office in 1906, the date of their first meeting, 29 June 1904, was engraved on their wedding rings.

26 June

26 Stalin's interview-cum-essay 'Marxism and Linguistics' first appeared in *Pravda*, Moscow, on 25 June 1950. The German translation was published in *Neues Deutschland* two days later.

30 June

27 On 25 June 1950 troops of the Democratic People's Republic of Korea (North Korea) crossed the 38th parallel to attack South Korea. Seoul had already fallen on the 28th

and Communist forces swept down the Korean peninsula. Press and media of all the Eastern Bloc states described the North Korean offensive as a counter-attack in response to South Korean actions. The UN Security Council, however, declared North Korea an aggressor, and called on all UN members to support the South Korean government – effectively, US forces, with the help of a number of other countries, came to the assistance of South Korea.

28 A selection of the stories of the Argentinian writer Horacio Quiroga, which Eva Klemperer had translated from the Spanish, but which was never published.

29 I.e. 'The Congress for Cultural Freedom' organised by Melvin J. Lasky, 26–29 June 1950, conceived as a response to the Eastern-dominated World Peace Congress.

30 Jules Romains (1885–1972), French novelist, essayist, dramatist. His lasting achievement is the cycle of novels *Les Hommes de bonne volonté*.

31 A private joke of the Klemperers dating back to their earliest years together.

6 July

32 The Third Party Congress of the SED had been called for 20–24 July in Berlin.

9 July

33 Arthur Koestler (1905–83), English author of Hungarian origin (although the novels that first made his name were written in German); member of the Communist Party 1931–7, then broke with Stalinism, expressing his opposition in a number of novels and reports, most famously *Darkness at Noon*.

13 July

34 The 250th anniversary of the Prussian Academy of the Sciences (proposed by the philosopher and mathematician Leibniz); renamed the German Academy of the sciences in 1946.

35 Leo Stern (1901–82), Austrian historian; member of the Austrian Social Democratic Party 1921–33 and then of the Austrian Communist Party 1933–50. Emigrated to Czechoslovakia, then USSR; participated in the Spanish Civil War; officer in the Red Army 1942–5. Professor in Halle 1950–66 (rector 1953–9).

21 July

36 In March 1950 the World Peace Congress proclaimed the Stockholm Appeal to ban nuclear weapons; 500 million signatures were collected by the end of 1950. The action was banned in West Berlin.

37 The Werner Seelenbinder Hall was specially built for the Congress.

38 The Third Party Congress approved a new Party statute laying down the principles of 'democratic centralism' for a 'party of a new type'; in addition the previous Party Committee was replaced by an 80-strong Central Committee.

22 July

39 On 6 July Grotewohl and the Polish Prime Minister, Józef Cyrankiewicz, signed the Görlitz Agreement in which the Oder-Neisse Line established by the Potsdam Agreement of the Big Powers was fixed as the final German–Polish border. The West German government refused to recognise the agreement and the finality of the frontier. (Formal acceptance only came with the treaties regularising German re-unification.)

40 'Social Democratism' and 'opportunism' designated so-called 'right deviations'; 'sectarianism' was the term for 'left deviations' from the Party line.

30 July

41 *The Threepenny Novel*, which evolved from the musical play *The Threepenny Opera*, was written in 1934 and published in 1939.

2 August

42 Hans Stubbe (1902–89), biologist and geneticist; director of the Gatersleben Institute of Cultivated Plant Research 1945–67; professor in Halle 1946; founder of the German Academy of Agricultural Sciences 1951 and its president until 1967. Resisted ideological deformation of genetics during the Stalin period.

43 (French): Where to get it from?

23 August

44 Novel (1885) by Guy de Maupassant; the edition had an afterword by Victor Klemperer.

45 A collection (*Zwischenspiel – Deutsche Revue von 1918 bis 1933*) containing Erich Weinert's satirical poems from the Weimar Republic.

25 August

46 At the 'National Congress of the National Front' (25–26 August 1950) President Wilhelm Pieck announced a 'Twelve Point Programme of National Resistance' to the political and military integration of the Federal Republic in the West European and Atlantic Community.

47 Leading committee of the 'National Front for a Democratic Germany', which emerged from the extended executive council of the German People's Congress.

48 On 16 August 1950, on instruction of the US High Commissioner in Germany, eight of those sentenced to 6 or 7 years imprisonment at the Nürnberg trials were released early from Landsberg Prison 'for good behaviour'. They included the former Reich Press Chief Otto Dietrich, the former Reich Peasants' leader Walther Darré, the industrialist Friedrich Flick, the director of the IG Farben chemicals combine, Fritz ter Meer, the Krupp director Heinrich Lehmann and Karl Rasche of the board of the Dresdner Bank.

48a From the end of April until June 1950 the summary trials took place of more than 3,300 prisoners, who after the winding up of the Soviet internment camps were turned over to GDR jurisdiction. In the majority of cases there was no hearing of evidence or witnesses or a defence. The charges, on the basis of statements taken by the Soviet authorities, were usually of 'crimes against humanity'; 32 death sentences were imposed and more than half of the accused received prison sentences of between 15 and 25 years.

49 At the end of the Chinese Civil War the defeated pro-Western Nationalist forces of General Chiang Kai-shek took refuge on the island of Formosa (now known as Taiwan), which from 1895–1945 had been a Japanese colony. Formosa was claimed by the Chinese Communist mainland government in Beijing, and there have been repeated periods of tension between China and the Nationalist Chinese – later Taiwanese – governments supported by the USA. These have frequently been sparked by incidents in the sea channel between the mainland and the island or involving small islands close to the mainland also retained by the Nationalist Chinese.

1 September

50 (Latin): the poor unimportant folk.

51 An image derived from Victor Klemperer's childhood memories, referring to the amassing of material without managing to do anything with it. Cf Introduction to 'Curriculum Vitae', vol. I, pp. 5–10.

3 September

52 Those expelled from the SED by the Politburo on the basis of a resolution of the Central Committee of 24 August 1950 were Paul Merker (1894–1963), joined KPD 1920, member of the Central Committee of the KPD 1927–45, emigrated (France, Mexico); member of the Executive Committee of the SED 1946–50. Arrested in 1952, he was sentenced to 8 years imprisonment; released in 1956 and rehabilitated. Lex (really Adolf) Ende (1899–1951); joined KPD 1919; emigrated to France, later Mexico. Joint chief editor of *Neues Deutschland* 1946–9. Leo Bauer (1912–72), chief editor of the Deutschlandsender radio station. Bruno Goldhammer (1905–71), a senior figure in the 'Office of Information'. Maria Weiterer and Willi Kreikemeyer (1894–?), General Director of the East German Railways, whose death has never been clarified. Those relieved of their duties included Wolfgang Langhoff (see note 82, 1946 above); Hans Teubner (1902–92), another Party veteran, rehabilitated in 1956; Bruno Fuhrmann (1907–79), Director of the West Commission of the Central Committee of the SED; and Walter Beling (1899–1988), member of the Central Secretariat of the SED; from 1959 headed the Permanent GDR delegation in Geneva.

53 Noel H. Field (1904–70) was an American anti-Fascist who from the late 1930s, as representative of the Unitarian Service Council, helped numerous émigrés in western Europe. In the show trials of Rudolf Slánský in Prague, László Rajk in Budapest and Traicho Kostoff in Sofia, Field, who had been held in Hungary since 1948, was ascribed the role of the wire-puller of a spy ring.

30 September

54 After amphibious landings by American forces Seoul was retaken on 26 September, and on 30 September UN forces reached the 38th parallel, the demarcation line between South and North Korea.

10 October

55 In the course of October 1950 UN forces occupied almost the whole of North Korea, reaching the Chinese frontier on 24 October 1950.

8 November

56 I.e. on the same street on which the young Klemperer had lived after his father was appointed to a post as preacher in Berlin.

25 November

57 (French): old man.

7 December

58 (French): how much longer, Lord?

15 December

59 (Italian): few, but honest lively words.

60 The law, passed by the Volkskammer on 15 December 1950, threatened prosecution for anyone who 'agitates against those taking part in the struggle for peace because of their activities'. A very elastic clause effectively permitting, for example, criminalisation of criticism of the policies of the GDR leadership.

23 December

61 Victor Klemperer had written a foreword to an edition of Molière's Comedies in the Dieterich imprint. The review in question was written by Alfred Antkowiak.

62 On 30 November 1950 the GDR Prime Minister, Otto Grotewohl, wrote a letter to the

West German Chancellor, Konrad Adenauer, proposing the formation of an All-German Council with equal representation from East and West, to prepare elections to a National Assembly.

63 On 3 October 1925 in the Deutsches Theater, Berlin, Victor Klemperer saw the 150th performance of the German première of G. B. Shaw's *St Joan*. Elisabeth Bergner (1897–1986), one of the stars of the Weimar stage, came to Berlin from Vienna in 1922; emigrated to England 1933.

1951

14 January
1 Francesco Petrarca (known as Petrarch, 1304–74), Italian humanist and poet; established a new relationship to the authors of Classical Antiquity; with Dante and Bocaccio instituted the literary Renaissance in Italy (and beyond). Torquato Tasso (1544–95), Italian poet.

19 January
2 A further critique by Alfred Antkowiak (1925–76), editor; head of the world literature section of the Aufbau publishing house from 1951, later worked as a literary translator. Antkowiak accused Klemperer of shortcomings in the 'recognition of social relations' and a failure to distinguish 'between the *Naturalist* Zola and the *Realist* Maupassant'.

27 January
3 Walter Gerull-Kardas (1898–1978), literary translator. In charge of the Literature Section of the Central Administration for Popular Education 1945; deputy manager of the Rütten & Loening publishing house January 1950 and its head from January to October 1951, when it became part of the Volk & Welt publishing house.

4 The so-called Social Science Basic Course for students in all fields in their 1st–3rd years, beginning in the autumn semester 1951, consisted of lectures in the history of the working-class movement, political economy and dialectical and historical materialism.

31 January
5 On 30 January 1951, following a government declaration by Otto Grotewohl, the Volkskammer adopted an appeal to the West German Parliament, the Bundestag. It proposed the setting up of an 'All-German Constituent Council' to agree steps towards the establishment of a government for the whole of Germany.

10 February
6 Winfried Schröder (b. 1925), Romance languages and literatures scholar; Ph.D. student of Werner Krauss 1950, simultaneously assistant to Victor Klemperer; arrested mid 1957, sentenced to 3 years imprisonment at the end of 1958 for 'treason'.

7 Ernst Hoffmann (b. 1912); arrested October 1933, sentenced to $2\frac{1}{2}$ years imprisonment; emigrated to Czechoslovakia 1937 and to England 1939. With the Propaganda Section of the Central Committee of the SED 1950–52; Professor of the History of the German Working Class Movement at the Institute of Social Sciences at the Central Committee 1952–62; at the Humboldt University Berlin 1963–77.

13 February
8 Two of three readers' letters published in the *Sonntag* of 11 February 1951 defended Klemperer against Antkowiak's criticisms and emphasised his intelligibility and avoidance of clichés.

20 February

9 Klemperer had been reading essays by Ernst Fischer (1899–1972), Austrian writer and politician; joined Austrian Communist Party 1934; exiled in Prague and Moscow 1934–45, when he returned to Austria; expelled from the Communist Party in 1969 for protesting against the Warsaw Pact forces occupation of Czechoslovakia. Wrote plays, novels and essays in addition to theoretical works.

10 The background here is the anti-Formalism campaign initiated 1950/51 in the Soviet Union – that is, the attack on artistic tendencies which did not conform to the Party's demands for an art 'close to the people'. In March 1951 the Central Committee of the SED adopted the appropriate corresponding resolutions.

17 March

11 Johannes Dieckmann (1893–1969) joined the Deutsche Volkspartei (DVP), a moderate conservative party, in 1918; member of the Saxon Parliament 1929–33; founder member of the LDPD in Dresden 1945; member of the Saxon Parliament and fraction leader 1946–52; Saxon Minister of Justice 1948–50; a deputy chairman of the LDPD from February 1949; President of the Volkskammer 1949.

30 March

12 Klaus Gysi (1912–99); a member of the KPD since 1931, was removed as Federal Secretary of the KB, evidently on the basis of suspicions relating to his anti-Fascist activities in Berlin 1940–45, having re-entered Germany illegally after internment in France. Subsequently (1952–7) he was head of the German Literary History section of the Volk und Wissen (People and Knowledge) publishing house; following the purge at the Aufbau publishing house, after the Hungarian Uprising, he was its head 1957–66; Minister of Culture 1966–73, GDR Ambassador to Italy 1973–8; State Secretary for Religious Affairs 1979–88.

14 April

13 Vincenz Müller (1894–1961), professional soldier; appointed lieutenant-general 1943, deputy commander of the German 4th Army 1944; prisoner of war in the Soviet Union; condemned to death in absentia by a Nazi court. Chief Inspector of the Volkspolizei (People's Police) 1948; deputy chairman of the NDPD 1949–52; Deputy to the Minister of National Defence 1956.

30 April

14 A reference to the frequently unreliable Opel that the Klemperers bought in March 1936 (and for which Klemperer took his driving test) and which had to be given up in December 1938 when Jews were no longer allowed to hold a driving licence.

12 May

15 A referendum against German re-armament had been set for 3–5 June in the GDR.

16 Gerhard Harig (1906–66), at this time a First State Secretary responsible for universities, historian of science and functionary; physicist; dismissed 1933; illegal activities; Buchenwald concentration camp 1938–45. Professor at the Social Sciences Faculty at Leipzig 1947–8; first Professor of Dialectical and Historical Materialism in the GDR 1948; Director of the Karl Sudhoff Institute of the History of the Natural Sciences and Medicine in Leipzig from 1957.

18 May

17 The first German Cultural Congress, with participants from both German states, took

place in Leipzig on 16–18 May 1951. It was immediately followed on 19 May by the Third Federal Congress of the Kulturbund.

20 May

18 Although Georg Klemperer was by the 1890s recognised as one of the leading internists in Germany, and was from 1905 an associate professor at Berlin University, he was never given a chair as full professor. This was certainly at least partly due to his Jewish origin.

5 June

19 The 'Referendum Against the Re-militarisation of West Germany and for the Conclusion of a Peace Treaty with Germany' took place on 3–5 June 1951. There was a 96% yes vote.

7–8 June

20 In mid-1951 a general review of all members was carried out in the SED.
21 A reference to Lenin's *Materialism and Empirio-Criticism.*
22 (French): nothing at all.
23 A reference to the sometimes strained relationship between Victor Klemperer and his brother Berthold.

20 June

24 After the Two Year Plan 1949–50, the economy of the GDR operated within the framework and goals of the First Five Year Plan.

22 June

25 Theoretical Conference of the Propaganda Section of the Central Committee of the SED, 'The Importance of the Works of Comrade Stalin on Marxism and of the Questions of Linguistics for the Development of Scholarship' (23–24 June 1951).

25–26 June

26 (Latin): only the ignorant man hates art.

27 June

27 Eva Klemperer had translated the text from the French. It was published as a pamphlet in 1950.

30 June

28 Marie von Ebner-Eschenbach (1830–1916), well-known late-19th-century author; her realist and socially critical stories and novels often dealt with the oppression and injustices of village and rural life. Klemperer had written about her when he was a journalist before the First World War.

8 July

29 *Germinie Lacerteux,* novel by the brothers Goncourt (Edmond 1822–96 and Jules 1830–70).
30 (Italian): on the death of Madonna Eva – an allusion to Petrarch's sonnet 'In morte di Madonna Laura'.

12 July

31 First explicit reference to Hadwig Kirchner (b. 1926), soon to be Victor Klemperer's second wife; studied German and Romance Languages and Literatures; after taking

her doctorate at the Humboldt University Berlin, she held a teaching post at Halle University 1957–59 and 1961–84.

19 July

32 Claude-Prosper Jolyot de Crébillon, known as Crébillon fils (1707–77), novelist; principal influence in the establishment of the genre of 'contes licencieux' (risqué erotic tales).

33 Anatole France (1844–1924), French novelist and critic; Nobel Prize for Literature 1921; representative of the anti-clerical, Enlightenment tradition. His reputation was made, above all, with novels critical of politics, progress and religion, which appeared from the 1890s onwards.

34 Jacques-Bénigne Bossuet (1627–1704), French religious writer and the most famous church preacher of his day.

24 July

35 Katharina Scheinfuss, (1814–86), dramaturge at the municipal theatre, Görlitz, 1946–8; taught at the High School of Theatre and Music in Halle 1948–51, lecturer at Dresden TH; dramaturge for radio plays from 1957; worked at the State Art Collections, Dresden, after free-lancing as a translator etc.

3 August

36 Article commissioned by Fred Oelssner for the theoretical journal *Einheit*.

24 August

37 Line from the ballad 'Das Herz von Douglas' (The Heart of Douglas) by Moritz, Count von Strachwitz (1822–47).

29 September

38 Moabit was the main prison in West Berlin.

13 October

39 The Three Graces: Ancient Greek goddesses, companions of Aphrodite, Dionysos and Apollo.

40 The album contains photographs of Klemperer and colleagues and students taken in the Romance Languages and Literatures Department at Halle.

41 Annemarie Sternbeck, Deputy Minister of Education of Saxony-Anhalt.

42 *L'Enfer*, novel by Henri Barbusse (1908, revised 1917).

17 October

43 In 1950–51 Hugo Dähne was Dean of the Faculty of Education and Cultural Sciences of Dresden TH, which on 15 October 1951 bestowed the title of Dr h.c. paed. on Klemperer.

29 October

44 Epic poem by Voltaire, *La ligue ou Henri le Grand*, about Henri IV of France, a heroic figure to Voltaire, representing religious tolerance.

15 November

45 Kurt Hager (1912–98) joined KPD 1930; concentration camp 1933 followed by exile in France and England. Professor of Philosophy at HUB 1949; Director of the Science, Scholarship and High Schools Section of the Central Committee of the SED from 1951; Secretary of the Central Committee (responsible for Science and Scholarship,

Popular Education and Culture) 1955; member of the Politburo of the SED 1963–89; head of the 'Ideological Commission'. Notorious in the final period of the GDR for his response to Gorbachev's policy of 'Glasnost', declaring that just because one's neighbour changed the wallpaper, that was no reason to do likewise.

22 December
46 Leopold von Ranke (1795–1886), Prussian historian, one of the dominant academics of his time; professor in Berlin 1825–71.

1952

6 January
1 The German Art Show 'Artists Create for Peace', December 1951 to January 1952, organised by the Association of Fine Artists in the KB.

12 January
2 The split was created by the departure of the majority of the West German PEN members. Henceforth there was a Federal German PEN Centre and a German PEN Centre East and West (as well as a German exile PEN in London).
3 I.e. Jean-Jacques Rousseau's *The Social Contract or Principles of Constitutional Law* (first published 1763).

19 January
4 Franz Mehring (1846–1919), writer and politician; leading literary and cultural theorist of the SPD before 1914; on the left wing of the SPD from 1891; leading member of the anti-war Spartacus League from 1916.

30 January
5 minyan (Hebrew): the quorum of ten male Jews aged 13 or over required by orthodox Jewish law before a religious service can take place.

10 February
6 The occasion was the 150th anniversary of Hugo's birth on 26 February 1952.

19 February
7 (Italian): old thing.

25 February
8 It had become customary, on the anniversary of the destruction of Dresden, to place wreaths and flowers at the now-cleared places where relatives had died.

23 March
9 Stefan George (1868–1933), poet; very popular in the first half of the 20th century; cultivated an aura, particularly in the later years of his life, of a seer surrounded by a circle of disciples.

29 March
10 (Latin): against his and her will he dismissed her. Racine claimed the three words were the basis of his play *Bérénice*.

5 April

11 Kurt Baldinger (b. 1919), Swiss Romance Languages and Literatures scholar; professor at the HUB 1948; in charge of the Institute of Romance Linguistics of the German Academy of Sciences 1949–62; professor at Heidelberg (West Germany) from 1957.

17 April

12 The Conference of Linguists and Germanists from 14–18 April was held to mark the founding of the Institute of German Language and Literature of the German Academy of Sciences, which under the direction of Theodor Frings was intended to continue and expand the work of the German Commission established in 1903.

18 April

13 Smallest differentiable linguistic unit, an innovation of the Russian exile scholars of the Prague School of Linguistics, e.g. Nikolai Trubetzkoi and Roman Jakobson.

19 April

14 On what is today Rosa Luxemburg Strasse.

5 May

15 I.e. a member of the Fédération Internationale des Résistants (FIR).

16 Leading member of the VVN whom Klemperer had got to know in Munich.

17 Rudolf Höss (1900–47), officer at Dachau concentration camp 1934, at Sachsenhausen 1938; Commandant of Auschwitz concentration camp 1940–3; organised the mass killing of prisoners, primarily Jews, by Zyklon B gas. Condemned to death in Warsaw and executed 16 April 1947.

14 May

18 Allusion to the figure of the Duke of Alba in Goethe's play *Egmont* and Schiller's play *Don Carlos*.

19 Helene Weigel (1900–71), actress and theatre manager; married Bertolt Brecht in 1929; went into exile with him in 1933 and returned in 1949; from then general manager of Brecht's company and theatre, the Berliner Ensemble.

22 May

20 At the 3rd German Writers' Congress (22–25 May 1952) the German Writers' Association (DSV), previously a part of the Kulturbund, constituted itself as a separate organisation. Anna Seghers was elected president, Kuba (Kurt Barthel) first secretary.

3 June

21 On 24 May 1952 the GDR's highest court sentenced the East Berliner Johann Burianek to death; Emil Möbis and Fritz Henschel were given life sentences. They were accused, as members of the West Berlin 'Combat Group Against Inhumanity' of having, inter alia, prepared 'diversionary' attacks on factories and communications. It was in this context that the term 'diversionary' was widely adopted in the propaganda language of press and radio.

20 June

22 Kuba – Kurt Barthel (1914–67), poet, dramatist, screenplay author; emigrated to Prague 1933, to England in 1939; from 1950 a candidate, from 1954 a member of the Central Committee of the SED.

7 July

23 Jesús Izcaray, *Castro García Roza. Geschichte eines Spanischen Helden*, German by Eva Klemperer.

24 Ilya Ehrenburg, 'Das Sowjetvolk will Frieden mit jedem Amerika' (The Soviet People Want Peace with Every America). Speech at the extraordinary meeting of the Council for World Peace in Berlin. Printed in *Neues Deutschland*, 6 July 1952.

11 July

25 The Second Party Conference of the SED, which took place in Berlin 9–12 July, agreed the 'planned construction of Socialism'.

26 Following the rout of Napoleon's invasion of Russia, Prussia and Austria rejoined the coalition against France, leading to Napoleon's further defeat at the Battle of Leipzig followed by the occupation of France and Napoleon's surrender. In German history books the uprising against French domination is usually referred to as the 'Wars of Liberation'.

13 July

27 In his speech at the Second Party Conference on 12 July, Walter Ulbricht held Oelssner and the Propaganda Section of the Central Committee, of which he was in charge, responsible for shortcomings in the ideological work of the Party.

20 July

28 Horst Lothar Teweleit (1923–95), Romance Languages and Literatures and Arabic scholar, translator and editor; editor at the Deutsche Verlag der Wissenschaften (German Scholarly Publishing House) 1952–4, later with Rütten & Loening, Volk und Welt and Aufbau publishing houses.

29 *The Century of Voltaire*, the first part of Klemperer's History of French Literature in the 18th Century, was published by the Deutsche Verlag der Wissenschaften in 1954.

28 July

30 'Das romanische Katheder und Seminar' (The Romance Languages and Literature chair and department) in *Festschrift zur 450. Jahresfeier der Martin-Luther-Universität Halle-Wittenberg* (Halle/Saale 1957) – Festschrift marking the university's anniversary.

31 Rudolf Leonhard (1889–1953), author and journalist; lived in Paris from 1927; co-founder and leading organiser of the Communist-dominated Schutzverband deutscher Schriftsteller im Exil (Aid Association of German Writers in Exile). Settled in the GDR 1950.

32 DFD – Demokratischer Frauenbund Deutschlands (Democratic German Women's League), i.e. the official women's organisation.

33 Montesquieu's novella, translated and with a foreword by Victor Klemperer and woodcuts by the Berlin artist Werner Klemke, was published by Aufbau.

5 August

34 Gottfried Kirchner (b. 1928), Slavonic languages scholar, linguist and translator.

35 Ferdinand de Saussure (1857–1913), Swiss linguist; his *Cours de linguistique générale* inaugurated a new phase in linguistics, notably with the distinction between *langue*, a language system (shared by a speech community) and *parole*, its actual use in speech and writing.

15 August

36 Jean le Rond d'Alembert (1717–83), French philosopher and mathematician; co-editor of the *Encyclopédie*; wrote on literature, history and philosophy.

37 Stefan Heym (pseudonym of Helmut Flieg 1913–2001), novelist and essayist; emigrated to Czechoslovakia 1933, then to the USA; served in the US army from 1943; settled in the GDR 1952. From 1956 he frequently came into conflict with the cultural policy of the GDR, but after 1989 became a fierce critic of German reunification and briefly sat in the German parliament for the post-Communist PDS. *Crusaders*, originally written in English and published in the United States in 1948, was published in German in 1950. The novel's characters are part of the American D-Day invasion force.

17 August
38 The 'Decree on Measures at the Line of Demarcation' of 26 May 1952 established a 3-mile prohibited zone along the inner German frontier; thousands of inhabitants of places within this strip were forcibly resettled.
39 Else Zaisser (1898–1987); originally a teacher, she was in the USSR from 1931 with her husband Wilhelm Zaisser; lecturer in Halle 1947, Professor of Methods of Russian Teaching at Dresden TH 1949; State Secretary 1951, Minister of Popular Education 1952–3.

24 August
40 'Die Romanistik an unseren Hochschulen' (Romance Languages and Literatures at Our Universities) in *National Zeitung* of 11 November 1952. The German editor of Klemperer's diaries writes: 'a notably blunt description for the period, of the neglect of Romance Languages and Literature at East German universities after 1945'.

28 August
41 Rita Schober had been appointed to a chair at the HUB from the autumn semester 1952; she consequently resigned from her post in the State Secretariat for the Universities.

4 September
42 On 23 August 1952 the USSR renewed its offer of holding a 4-power conference to clarify the future status of Germany and the implementation of all-German elections.

28 September
43 Walter Friedrich (1883–1968), physicist; from 1922 professor in Berlin; rector of the HUB 1949–51, President of the German Academy of the Sciences 1951–6, President of the German Peace Council 1950–68.
44 Walter Neye (1901–89), legal scholar; professor at the HUB 1949–66, rector 1952–6.
45 A Berlin suburb.

12 October
46 The National Prize of the GDR was divided into 3 classes: Class I carried with it a sum of 100,000 marks, Class II 50,000 marks and Class III 25,000 marks.
47 (Italian): the line in full is 'Povera e nuda vai o Filosofia,' roughly: Poor and naked go you, oh philosophy; from Petrarch's 'Canzoniere' (7, 10).
48 An editor at the Deutsche Verlag der Wissenschaften.

25 October
49 In spring 1952 the major airlines introduced, at first as an experiment, a tourist class on transatlantic flights.

8 November
50 The new olive-green (instead of the previous dark-blue) uniforms of the militarised units of the Volkspolizei, as well as new ranks, were introduced on 7 November 1952.

9 November

51 Robert Havemann (1910–82), chemist; sentenced to death December 1943 for anti-Fascist resistance activities. Director of the Berlin research institutes of the Kaiser Wilhelm Society 1945–50; professor at the HUB 1946; member of the Executive Committee of the Kulturbund 1945–58. He was dismissed from his Kaiser Wilhelm Society post because of his protests against American nuclear policy. In the 1960s he became the most important critic (within East Germany) of the GDR system.

52 A decree of 4 September 1952 'to secure assets' permitted the expropriation of companies whose owners were not resident in the GDR and the revocation of the trading licences of company owners etc. who were resident in West Berlin or the deletion of their entries from the register of trades.

16 November

53 On 13 November 1952 Wilhelm Pieck issued a brief declaration on the 'common struggle of the patriots of France and Germany against the revival of German militarism in West Germany', which creates 'a new situation in Franco-German relations'.

26 November

54 The letter urged Klemperer to use his prize money (or part of it) to help the dependents of political prisoners or of those who had died in prison or been wrongfully executed, or by confidentially donating money to an Aid Committee for Political Prisoners in West Berlin.

29 November

55 The author Arnold Zweig was President of the German Academy of Arts 1950–53; his successor 1953–6 was Johannes R. Becher. Zweig became Vice-President in 1953 and Honorary President in 1968.

19 December

56 Holger Christiansen was first an assistant then a teacher and colleague at the Berlin Romance Languages and Literatures Institute. The German editor of the Klemperer diaries provides no information on this frequently mentioned figure.

24 December

57 The introduction to a volume of stories and scenes by Diderot translated by Katja Scheinfuss.

58 In the *Romanistisches Jahrbuch*, vol. 4 (1951), pp. 25–9.

1953

12 January

1 Ethel (1916–53) and Julius Rosenberg (1918–53); the American couple were arrested in summer 1950 accused of betraying atomic secrets to the Soviet Union. They were sentenced to death on 5 April 1951 and executed on 19 June 1953. A death sentence for espionage in peacetime was unprecedented in the USA and there was a worldwide protest movement against it being carried out.

2 (Italian): on the contrary.

19 January

3 On 13 January the Soviet News Agency TASS announced the arrest of 9 leading

doctors, the personal physicians of the Soviet leaders. They were accused of deliberately giving false diagnoses and treatment and of planning the death of high-ranking Soviet army officers. Seven of the nine were Jewish and the uncovering of the 'plot' was clearly part of an orchestrated anti-Jewish campaign presumably related to shifts in Soviet policies towards the Middle East. (Israel had received a great deal of military assistance from the Soviet Bloc but oriented itself to the United States.) The doctors at any rate were also accused of having carried out their crimes as 'paid agents of foreign secret services' above all of the Jewish aid organisation the American Joint Distribution Committee, often referred to simply as the Joint (and not just by Klemperer).

4 Out of fear of the anti-Zionist campaign (which effectively took the shape of an anti-Jewish campaign in the Soviet Union and its satellites and was linked to the elimination of alternative possibilities within Socialism, often associated with figures who had been in exile in Western countries and not the Soviet Union), a number of Jewish leaders in the GDR fled to the West. Julius Meyer, the chairman of the Association of Jewish Communities in the GDR, fled to West Berlin on 15 January 1953, along with Leon Löwenkopf and other heads of Jewish communities. Hundreds of members of GDR Jewish communities left for the West in subsequent weeks.

24 January
5 On 21 January 1953 Julius Meyer, Leon Löwenkopf, Günter Singer and Helmut Looser were expelled from the VVN as 'Zionist traitors and agents'.

30 January
6 Ernst Cassirer (1874–1945), philosopher; professor in Hamburg 1919, in Oxford 1933–5, then in Göteborg, Sweden; from 1941 in the USA at Yale and Columbia Universities. Neo-Kantian, explored the relationship of 'symbolic forms' to the structure of experience and understanding.

21 February
7 *Rembrandt* (1942), directed by Hans Steinhoff.

2 February
8 At its meeting of 21–22 February the Committee of the VVN, on instruction of the SED leadership, resolved to discontinue the activities of the organisation in the GDR, since the 'heritage of the anti-Fascist resistance fighters had become a matter for the whole nation'. It was replaced by a 'Committee of Anti-Fascist Resistance Fighters'.

9 In his diary entry of 5 November 1926 (printed in *Leben sammeln, nicht fragen wozu und warum* [Diaries 1925–32], Berlin 1996), Klemperer records the purchase of a gramophone and the excitement of buying records and having friends round for dancing (to which Klemperer responded with ambivalence – the dance moves were all too sexual, even 'nigger-like' for him).

28 February
10 Johannes Irmscher (b. 1920), classicist; professor at the HUB 1953; Director of the Institute of Roman-Greek Studies at the German Academy of Sciences 1955; ret. 1985.

2 March
11 Klemperer had begun work on the second volume of his *History of French Literature in the 18th Century* in May 1936, but had been forced to break it off at the end of December 1938, when Jews were prohibited from using public libraries.

6 March

12 Walter Ruben (1899–1982), Indologist; emigrated to Turkey 1935, professor in Ankara until 1948; in Santiago de Chile 1948–9, at the HUB 1950–65.

18 March

13 (Latin): admission to the Academy.

22 March

14 From Italian *primavera* – spring; a jocular intensification, therefore: most spring-like spring.

11 April

15 Printed e.g. in the *Sächsische Zeitung* of 8 April 1953: 'Socialist legality is inviolable.' Beria, the Soviet Minister of State Security, who had been relieved of his posts and then executed, was accused of 'political blindness and negligence'; the arrested head of the Investigation Section of 'deceiving the government and political adventurism'.

16 On 4 April 1953 the Soviet Ministry of the Interior announced the rehabilitation of the group of nine doctors arrested in January 1953.

25 April

17 *Bicycle Thieves* (1948), directed Vittorio de Sica (1902–74), Italian actor and director.

26 April

18 Stalin in conversation with Gorky, 26 October 1932.

7 May

19 On 9 April 1953 the Council of Ministers decreed that from 1 May a number of categories of person (entrepreneurs and contractors, wholesalers, artisans and traders employing several workers, the self-employed, retailers, publicans, restaurateurs, house owners, owners of agricultural enterprises) would no longer be issued with ration cards. Thus, approximately a tenth of the population of the GDR was dependent on buying food at the high state-shop prices.

20 Horst Zimmermann later transferred from the Kreuzschule to a 10-year upper school which did not offer Greek.

17 May

21 I.e. the PEN East and West Centre, which had been set up at the end of October 1951 and of which Klemperer was member; see note 2, 1952.

22 Herbert Lestiboudois (b. 1907–?), novelist and essayist.

23 Ehm Welk (1884–1966), author, dramatist, screen writer.

24 Elga Kern (1888–1955), essayist; from 1949 member of the London Exile PEN, later of the German PEN Centre East and West.

18 May

25 I.e. the ratification (19 March 1952) of the Generalvertrag (General Treaty), which defined West Germany's relationship with the Western Allies, and of West Germany's adhesion to the European Defence Community.

26 In mid-May 1953 Franz Dahlem was expelled from the Central Committee of the SED and stripped of all Party functions, accused of 'political blindness in the face of the activities of imperialist agents and because of an un-Party attitude towards his errors'. In 1955 he was appointed Deputy Permanent Secretary in the State Secretariat for the

Universities, politically rehabilitated 1956, and re-admitted to the Central Committee at the beginning of 1957.

27 Theodor Bucur (b. 1915–?), Romanian assistant at Berlin University/HUB 1944–45 and 1948–52.

22 May

28 Friedrich Zucker (1881–1973), Classical philologist, papyrologist; professor at Jena 1918–43 and 1945–61 (rector 1945–8).

28 May

29 (Italian): few but very plain, lively words.

15 June

30 The 'Communiqué of the Politburo of the Central Committee of the SED' of 9 June 1953 admitted a series of mistakes by the government and the SED and recommended the government of the GDR to revoke numerous measures, above all ones that had come into force in the first 6 months of 1953. These had affected the middle classes and peasants/farmers and had led to a mass exodus from the GDR. Promises included the release of those sentenced as a result of these measures, the return of expropriated property on return to the GDR, the readmission to their courses of students and senior pupils who were members of Protestant Church school and student groups, as well as cancellation of all limitations in the distribution of ration cards. Unaffected were the rises in work and production targets – and this was to lead to the strikes and disturbances which began on 15 June.

18 June

31 Georg and Helene Erdmann, the landlord and landlady of Hadwig Klemperer at 226 Linienstr.

32 On 8 June 1953 agreement was reached in Panmunjon on the return of prisoners of war, thus resolving one of the most difficult questions holding up the conclusion of an armistice between the two sides in the Korean Civil War. In the Italian parliamentary elections of 7 June 1953 the governing Christian Democrats lost their absolute majority; the Socialists and Communists made gains, the latter becoming the second strongest party. After the fall of the René Mayer cabinet in France on 21 May 1953 several attempts to form a new government collapsed; not until the end of June was a new prime minister, Joseph Laniel, voted in.

33 See note 30 above.

34 On 28 May 1953 the GDR Council of Ministers decreed a general 10% rise in production targets by 30 June. This led on 16 June to a strike of building workers on the Stalin Allee and a protest march to the seat of government on Leipzigerstr. That same afternoon loudspeaker vans announced that the increase in work targets was not obligatory; the protestors were not convinced by or unaware of this announcement. They called a general strike for the following day. On 17 June 1953 there were then strikes, demonstrations and meetings in more than 270 towns and villages of the GDR. There were repeated demands for the resignation of the government and for free elections. Soviet tanks were deployed from midday and at 1 p.m. a state of emergency was declared in Berlin.

35 On 16 June 1953 almost 10,000 demonstrators gathered in front of the House of Ministries on Leipziger Strasse (there had already been some work stoppages on the 15th); they called in vain for Walter Ulbricht or Otto Grotewohl to come out and

speak to them. Instead more junior Party figures appeared, but were shouted down; the railings at the entrances of the building prevented the demonstrators from breaking into the building.

36 The article 'The Collapse of the Fascist Adventure' (unsigned) in *Neues Deutschland*, 19 June 1953, set forth the argument of a 'Day X' plotted outside the GDR, but nevertheless admitted mistakes with regard to the general rise in production targets. It concluded with the declaration that now 'a new stage in the history of the GDR [was beginning], in which our state will be more just and considerate towards working people'.

37 There were, for example, clashes with demonstrators at the Brandenburg Gate and on Potsdamer Platz, where the police station in the Columbia House, among other things, was set alight.

38 Hermann Duncker (1874–1960); joined SPD 1893, editor of the *Leipziger Volkszeitung*, one of the leading Social Democratic newspapers; from 1907 an itinerant teacher on behalf of the SPD. A founder member of the anti-war Spartakus League and in 1918 of the KPD. Imprisoned 1933–6, then emigrated to Paris, to USA 1941. Professor in Rostock 1947; from 1949 Director of the FDGB (trades union) High School in Bernau, near Berlin. Duncker had been given the nickname 'Teacher of the Party' before 1933, indeed before 1914.

39 Eugen Hoffmann (1892–1955).

40 The demonstrators in Görlitz were particularly militant, hence the effort to discredit their attempt to organise an administration in the town.

41 In the course of disturbances in Halle on 17 June 1953 the prison was occupied and inmates released, including a former SS warder at Ravensbrück concentration camp, Erna Dorn, who was serving a 15-year sentence. She was involved in later protests in the city. The SED used this as evidence of the 'Fascist character' of the events of 17 June. Erna Dorn was sentenced to death on 2 June 1953.

20 June

42 A pardonable exaggeration. After a house search on 11 November 1938, during the 'Crystal Night' pogrom, Klemperer was brought to the Public Prosecutor's office in the court building at Münchner Platz and released again the same day (see *I Shall Bear Witness*, 27 November 1938). In 1941 he served 8 days in prison for breaching the blackout regulations, but in the police cells at Schiessgasse.

43 Due to the events of 17 June the supplement was never published.

2 July

44 *La Débâcle*, novel (1892) – about the French defeat in the 1870–71 war with Prussia.

6 July

45 (French): the undiscoverable (or invisible) chamber, an ironic description by the French Royalists of the powerless (as they saw it) French parliament of 1815–16.

13 July

46 Lavrenti Pavlovich Beria (1899–1953); People's Commissar of the Interior and Head of State Security 1938–46, Deputy Prime Minister 1946–53. Responsible for the running of the Stalinist terror system. After Stalin's death First Deputy Prime Minister and Minister of the Interior and State Security. At the instigation of Nikita Khrushchev, Beria was arrested at a session of the Central Committee on 9 July 1953, subsequently sentenced to death and executed on 23 December 1953.

23 July

47 On 24 April 1953 Johannes R. Becher was elected President of the Academy of Arts, replacing Arnold Zweig.

48 Then daily newspaper of the Communist Party of Great Britain.

1 August

49 Max Fechner (1892–1973); joined SPD 1919; member of the Prussian Parliament 1924–33; imprisoned 1933–4 and 1944–5. In 1945 one of the three chairmen of the SPD in the Soviet Zone; Minister of Justice from October 1949. After 17 June he gave a newspaper interview in which he endorsed a 'limited right' to strike in the GDR; he was thereupon dismissed, expelled from the SED, arrested, tried and sentenced; released from prison in 1956.

50 Hilde Benjamin (1902–89), lawyer; banned from practising 1933; deputy chief judge of the senior court of the GDR 1949–53, presiding over a number of show trials; Minister of Justice 1953–67. Hilde Benjamin succeeded the dismissed Max Fechner on 15 July 1953; she was the wife of Georg Benjamin, a Communist member of the Reichstag who died in a concentration camp in 1942. Georg Benjamin was the brother of the great critic and historian Walter Benjamin.

51 Rudolf Herrnstadt (1903–66), journalist; KPD 1929; from 1930 in Prague, Warsaw, Moscow etc. Chief editor of the *Berliner Zeitung* newspaper 1945–9, from 1950 of *Neues Deutschland*. In July 1953, after the fall of Beria, he and the Minister of State Security, Wilhelm Zaisser, as opponents of Ulbricht, were expelled from Politburo of the SED because of 'activities hostile to the Party' and stripped of all offices; in January 1954 both were expelled from the SED. Wilhelm Zaisser (1893–1958); KPD 1919; during the right wing Kapp Putsch of 1920 he was one of the commanders of the Red Army of the Ruhr; worked for the Comintern in Moscow from 1927; participated in the Spanish Civil War 1936–8 ('General Gomez'). Minister of the Interior in Saxony 1948–50, Minister of State Security from 1950.

8 August

52 The 'New Course' proclaimed after the events of 17 June confirmed the revocation of measures directed against the middle classes and active Christians, which had already been announced on 11 June, as well as cancelling the rise in work targets.

53 *Die Frau meiner Träume* (1943/44) directed by Georg Jacoby. (In fact, it was the first film Victor and Eva Klemperer saw after the war; see entry for 28 September 1945.)

31 August

54 'returned ... from her illegal flight' – see notes 30 and 52 above.

13 September

55 On 22 August 1953, as a result of negotiations between the Soviet Prime Minister Georgi Malenkov and Otto Grotewohl in Moscow, the USSR declared its renunciation of any further GDR reparations payments from 1954; in addition 33 Soviet-run companies were to be transferred to GDR control and the two countries diplomatic missions would become embassies.

56 In the second elections to the West German parliament the CDU/CSU got 45.2% of the votes cast, and the SPD 28.8%; the KPD failed to enter parliament as did the All-German Party of Joseph Wirth (a Catholic politician in government during the 1920s) and Wilhelm Elfes (another Catholic politician), which stood for a reunited but neutralised Germany, a position possibly reconcilable with Soviet offers on the future of Germany.

26 September
57 The '14 Points', which were published in the *Sonntag* newspaper of 12 July 1953, advocated 'freedom of opinion' in artistic and scholarly discussion, the responsibility of writers and publishers, artists and theatre makers in questions of artistic creativity, freedom of scholarly research and teaching, security under the law, and the right to participate in all-German meetings. This contribution to the 'New Course' on the part of the Kulturbund and similar proposals by the Academy of Arts were soon quashed by the consolidated Party leadership. Such proposals, it was argued, would lead to the liquidation of the leading role of the Party in these areas and encourage tendencies to eliminate the achievements 'of the struggle for a national realist art' (*Neues Deutschland*, 19 July 1953). Public discussion of the proposals of the KB and the Academy of Arts was closed down, though, as Klemperer's entries show, it continued behind closed doors.

4 October
58 (Latin): Whither goest thou? (Simon Peter's question to Jesus after the Last Supper. John 13: 36.)

17 October
59 Para. 175 was the part of the German Criminal Code which criminalised homosexual acts. After the Nazi version of the paragraph had been abolished in East Germany in 1946, the regulation of 1871 remained in force until 1957 and then in modified form until the final reform of the penal law in 1968. According to the 1871 formulation, 'coitus-like acts' between men were a punishable offence carrying a sentence of 2–5 years.
60 Rita Schober, 'Emile Zola's Theorie des naturalistischen Romans und das problem des Realismus' (Emile Zola's Theory of Naturalism and the Problem of Realism) (Berlin 1954).

30 October
61 *Sans laisser d'adresse* (1950), directed by Jean-Paul Le Chanois.
62 *La Putain respectueuse* – The Respectful Prostitute – (1952), directed by Marcel Pagliero from the play by Jean-Paul Sartre (1946).

11 November
63 Published in *Sitzungsberichte der Deutschen Akademie der Wissenschaften zu Berlin, Klasse für Sprachen, Literatur und Kunst*, vol. II, no. 3 as 'Delille's "Gärten". Ein Mosaikbild des 18. Jahrhunderts' (Delille's 'Gardens'. A mosaic of the 18th century).

Résumé 1953
64 From the epitaph composed for himself by the Low German writer Fritz Reuter, which goes roughly as follows: 'Beginning and end, Lord are thine. / The stretch between, life, was mine. / And if I was lost and could not find the way, / with you, Lord, is clarity, and bright is thy house.'
65 Klemperer was reading Romain Rolland's First World War diary, *Journal des années de guerre* (1952).

1954

9 February

1 On 15 January 1954 Klemperer spoke at the Kulturbund Club in the 'Villa San Remo' on the Weisser Hirsch.

2 Lion Feuchtwanger, *Füchse im Weinberg* (Foxes in the Vineyard), novel (1947/48); *Madame Thérèse ou les volontaires de 92*, novel (1865) by Emile Erckmann (1822–99) and Alexandre Chatrian (1826–90); *Narrenweisheit oder Tod und Verklärung des Jean-Jacques Rousseau*, novel (1952).

3 A study of Rolland's First World War diary which was published in the *Wissenschaftliche Zeitschrift der Humboldt Universität Berlin, Gesellschafts-und Sprachwissenschaftliche Reihe*, vol. IV (1954/55), part 1.

4 *DLZ – Deutsche Literaturzeitung* – a review of scholarly publications, published by the German Academy of Sciences 1880–1993.

5 Alfred Schmeiser (1914–70), internist; Director of Dresden-Neustadt Hospital.

8 March

6 *Goya oder der arge Weg des Erkenntnis* (1951), novel by Lion Feuchtwanger.

5 June

7 Bertolt Brecht's play *Mother Courage and her Children. A Chronicle of the Thirty Years' War* (1939).

8 Probably *Theaterarbeit. 6 Aufführungen des Berliner Ensembles* (Theatre Work. 6 Productions by the Berliner Ensemble), ed. by Berliner Ensemble and Helene Weigel (Dresden 1952).

14 June

9 Published as 'Stendhal in doppelter Beleuchtung' in *Wissenschaftliche Annalen zur Verbreitung neuer Forschungsergebnisse*, part II (1954), pp. 642–51.

20 June

10 In mid-1954 Rita Schober succeeded Victor Klemperer as Director of the Romance Languages and Literature Institute of the HUB.

11 Hemingway's *The Old Man and the Sea* was published in 1952 and translated into German the same year. Hemingway's novels and stories were published in the GDR from 1956 beginning with *The Old Man and the Sea*.

6 September

12 Prosper Mérimée (1803–70), French writer occupying a position between Romanticism and Realism, his stories invariably tragic and melodramatic, the settings frequently exotic. Best known today perhaps for writing the original story of 'Carmen' on which the composer Georges Bizet based his opera.

17 September

13 Epistolary novel (1782) by Choderlos de Laclos.

14 Johannes Stroux (1886–1954), Classicist; professor in Basel 1914, Kiel 1922, Jena 1923, Munich 1924; from 1935 Director of the Institute of Classical Studies at Berlin University; regular member of the Prussian Academy of Sciences 1937; Vice-President of the Union Académique Internationale. First rector of the re-named Humboldt University Berlin 1946–7 and first president of the German Academy of Sciences 1946–51.

15 Hermann Grapow (1885–1967), Egyptologist; professor in Berlin 1938–45 (dean

1940–5); member of the Prussian Academy of Sciences 1938 and its Vice-President 1943–5.

2 October

16 In mid-1954 Krauss had proposed a 'Working Group on the History of the German and French Enlightenment' in the Historical-Philosophical Class of the German Academy of Sciences. This began work in 1955 under his direction; from 1958 he was the Working Group's full-time director.

11 October

17 Auguste Cornu (1888–1981), French philosopher and historian; joined French Communist Party 1923; participated in the Resistance. Professor in Leipzig 1949, at the HUB 1951–9. Wrote inter alia on the early history of Marxism.

20 October

18 In the elections to the Volkskammer the United List of the National Front supposedly obtained a 99.46% endorsement on a turnout of 98.4%.

24 October

19 *Roma ora undici* – Rome, Eleven o'clock – (1952), directed by Giuseppe de Santis.

3 November

20 I.e. Feuchtwanger's 'Josephus' trilogy: *The Jewish War* (1932), *The Sons* (1935) and *The Day Will Come* (English 1942, German 1945).

12 November

21 (Latin): between battles.

30 November

22 *Maître après dieu* – Skipper Next to God – (1951), directed by Louis Daquin; the phrase 'maître après dieu' (master after God, or no master but God) refers to a ship's captain's absolute authority on board.

22 December

23 Henri Bergson (1859–1941), French philosopher. Parallel to Symbolism in literature, Bergson developed the theory of 'élan vital' – life force – in opposition to the material world, and emphasised the role of intuition. He was awarded the Nobel Prize for Literature in 1927.

31 December

24 Jules Vallès (1832–85), French journalist and novelist; member of the Central Committee of the Paris Commune, 1871; founder of the newspaper *Le cri du peuple*; in exile in England until 1880.

1955

10 January

1 Jugendweihe: A form of secular confirmation ceremony introduced in the GDR to mark the entry of schoolchildren into adult life. It included a pledge to Socialism. It was opposed by the Protestant Church (against which, of course, it was also directed). In diluted form it remains popular and widespread in former East Germany.

17 January

2 I.e. the introduction to a new translation of Rabelais's *Gargantua and Pantagruel* published by Greifenverlag (1954).

21 March

3 Gérard Philipe (1922–59), one of the most popular French stage and screen actors. Klemperer had previously seen him in the film *Fanfan la tulipe* (1951), directed by Christian-Jaque. He was visiting East Berlin with the Théâtre Nationale Populaire of Paris.

4 *Ruy Blas* (1838), play by Victor Hugo.

30 March

5 Marcel Cohen (1884–1974) was a specialist in Hamitic and Semitic languages, but also wrote a well-known history of French.

18 April

6 The Deux Frances thesis: the Two Frances thesis – in the new edition of his history of French literature in the 19th and 20th centuries Klemperer had proceeded from a division in French literature after 1918 into a bourgeois and a Socialist strand.

30 April

7 Hans Kortum (1923–97); until 1952 an assistant to Werner Krauss; employed at the State Secretariat for Universities and Technical Colleges 1954–7; later professor at the German Academy of Sciences.

17 May

8 I.e. Erika Mann (1905–69), also a writer.

9 *The Maid of Orléans* (1801) and *Mary Stuart* (1800), tragedies by Schiller.

19 May

10 On 14 May 1955 in Warsaw representatives of the USSR, Albania, Bulgaria, Czecho-slovakia, the GDR, Romania and Hungary signed a 'Treaty of Friendship, Co-operation and Mutual Assistance', which became known as the Warsaw Pact, i.e. formally a response to the existence of NATO.

11 *Trygée*, French literary journal.

12 Robert Léon Wagner (1905–82), French linguist; professor at the Paris Sorbonne.

13 (French): very reputable scholarly publications.

14 (French): Monsieur Victor Klemperer today finds himself east of that artificial line which, as everyone knows, separates two worlds, that of freedom and that of despotism, that of humanism and that of barbarism.

5 June

15 *The Devil's General* (1955), directed by Helmut Käutner based on the play (first per-formed 1946) by Carl Zuckmayer (1896–1977), dramatist, prose writer, poet and essayist; emigrated to USA 1939.

27 July

16 On 18–23 July 1955 in Geneva the heads of government and the foreign ministers of the Four Powers met for a summit conference for the first time since the Potsdam Conference of 1945. Although there were no tangible results with respect to major problems (Germany, European security, disarmament) there was a sense of progress

towards a reduction of tension between the two power blocs through a policy of détente.

17 Nikolai Bulganin (1895–1975), Soviet politician; Prime Minister of the Soviet Union 1955–8, during this period he and Khrushchev (then First Secretary of the Central Committee of the Communist Party) launched a policy of 'peaceful co-existence'.

18 Nikita S. Khrushchev (1894–1971), Soviet politician; member of the Politburo of the Communist Party from 1939; emerged as the most powerful figure of the collective leadership after Stalin's death. First Secretary of the Communist Party September 1953, also Prime Minister from 1958. Relieved of all offices in 1964.

19 Victor Klemperer saw his mother for the last time on a short visit to Berlin on 29 January 1919; he travelled to Berlin from Munich for her funeral on 22 June 1919.

10 August
20 (Latin): a good man.

16 August
21 From 9–13 September 1955, West German Chancellor Konrad Adenauer was in Moscow with a large delegation. The result of the negotiations was the establishment of diplomatic relations between West Germany and the USSR in December 1955 and the latter's promise to release the remaining German prisoners of war and civilian internees.

22 Thomas Mann died on 12 August 1955 in Zürich.

23 August
23 (French): around midnight.

6 September
24 Karl Prätorius died in January 1937.

25 After several years of reconstruction the German State Opera on Unter der Linden was re-opened on 4 September 1955 with a performance of Richard Wagner's *The Mastersingers of Nuremberg*.

29 September
26 Officially the law passed ('Law to Amend the Constitution. Military protection of the Homeland') made service with the armed services an 'obligation', but did not yet make it compulsory.

21 October
27 *Rouge et Noir* (1954), French film directed by Claude Autant-Lara based on Stendhal's novel *Le Rouge et le noir*.

27 October
28 *Grundpositionen der französischen Aufklärung*, vol. I of the series *Neue Beiträge zur Literaturwissenschaft*, ed. by Werner Krauss and Hans Mayer (Berlin 1955); Manfred Naumann's study of the Enlightenment figure Baron d'Holbach was a contribution to this volume.

15 November
29 Manfred, Baron von Ardenne (1907–97), physicist; in charge of an electronics research laboratory in Berlin 1928–45, after that of a research institute in Suchumi (USSR); from 1955 director of the 'Manfred von Ardenne Research Institute' in Dresden; professor at Dresden TH. Responsible for numerous inventions and developments,

first in electronics, later in applied nuclear physics and finally in medical technology. Von Ardenne was not involved in the development of the V rockets and missiles.

4 December
30 I.e. the surgeon Friedrich Dressel (see note 5, 1945, above).

1956

16 January
1 (French): venerable old man.
2 (French): philosophically.

23 January
3 The Gesellschaft für Sport und Technik (GST), established in 1957. It was responsible for military sports and pre-military training of young people.
4 (French): things farcical, farcical, farcical ... sad, sad, sad. An allusion to a famous sentence in a letter from Guy de Maupassant to Gustave Flaubert of December 1879: 'Je vois de choses, farces, farces, farces, et d'autres qui sont tristes, tristes, tristes; en somme tout le monde est bête, bête, bête, ici comme d'ailleurs.' (I see things which are nothing but farce, farce, farce, and others which are sad, sad, sad; in short everyone is stupid, stupid, stupid, here and everywhere else.)
5 Order given by Lord Seymour, commander-in-chief of the international force sent to raise the siege of the European and US embassies in Peking during the Boxer Rising. The order went to Captain von Usedom, commander of a battalion of German marines after one relief attempt had failed.

9 February
6 Novel (1796, written 1760–1) by Denis Diderot.

11 February
7 Willy Jelski (1913–94), nephew of Victor Klemperer, son of his sister Marta.
8 Marta Jelski, Klemperer's second-youngest sister, had died in 1954.

19 February
9 Laurence Sterne's *Sentimental Journey* and Henri Lefebvre's *Diderot* (Paris 1949).
10 (French): uprooted, disoriented bourgeois, foolish, dull-witted old man.

22 February
11 Anastas Mikoyan (1895–1978), Soviet politician; member of the Central Committee 1923; People's Commissar or minister with various responsibilities from 1926; member of the Politburo. Consistent supporter of Khrushchev after Stalin's death, a First Deputy Prime Minister 1955–64. His speech at the 20th Party Congress of the CPSU in Moscow (14–25 February 1956) began the attack on the Stalinist 'personality cult'.
12 Misremembered quotation from Shakespeare's *Hamlet*, Act V, Scene i.

7 March
13 An article signed by Walter Ulbricht, published in *Neues Deutschland*, 4 March 1956, stated, 'After Lenin's death Stalin undoubtedly made significant contributions to the building of Socialism [...]. Later, however, when Stalin placed himself above the Party and cultivated the personality cult, considerable harm was done to the CPSU and to the Soviet state. Stalin cannot be included among the classic authors of Marxism.'

25 March
14 The occasion was the 10th anniversary of the re-opening of the university after the war.

24 April
15 Klemperer was reading Koestler's novel *The Yogi and the Commissar* (1945) in a French translation from the English.

27 April
16 (French): Assembly of the teaching staff.
17 The revolt against French colonial rule was inaugurated by the Front de Libération Nationale (FLN) on 1 November 1954; the war lasted until March 1962.

29 April
18 Jean Schlumberger (1877–1968), French novelist, critic, dramatist, poet; co-founder of the literary periodical *Nouvelle revue française*. Ernst Curtius died on 19 April 1956.
19 (French): the pioneers of the new France. Victor Klemperer had reviewed Curtius' book *The literary pioneers of modern France* in the year of its publication, 1919.
20 (French): unproductive and drowsy.

8 May
21 (French): Parisian life.
22 Pierre Abraham (1892–1974), French critic and journalist; chief editor of the journal *L'europe* 1949–74.
23 (French): Jewish Communists.

12 May
24 (French): Jew.

13 May
25 Joseph Bédier (1864–1937), French literary historian; likewise Emile Faguet, professor at the Sorbonne when Klemperer was studying there.

17 May
26 Don-que i.e. donc (French: therefore). Klemperer is conveying Sartre's classical pronunciation.
27 (French): And ... for example.
28 (French): thinker, man of ideas.

15 June
29 On 25 February 1956, the last day of the 20th Party Congress of the CPSU, Nikita Khrushchev informed the delegates in closed session about the crimes and mass repression as well as the serious political and military mistakes committed or permitted by Stalin since 1924. The speech, not published in the countries of the Eastern Bloc, was read out at meetings of party branches in the Soviet Union, and led to considerable convulsions in Communist parties worldwide.

19 June
30 Joachim Uhlitzsch (1919–89), art scholar; lecturer at the High School for Graphics and the Art of the Book, Leipzig, 1952–61; Director of the Gallery of Modern Masters (Albertinum) in Dresden.

23 June
31 (French): Algeria, the cease-fire, de-Stalinisation, Adenauer – the last Mohican of the Cold War.

27 June
32 Poujadistes: Formally the Union de Défense des Commerçants et des Artisans, a right-wing populist party founded by Pierre Poujade which briefly rose and fell in 1950s France, appealing to the lower-middle class of shopkeepers, etc.

4 July
33 (French): Poznan Riots; on 27 June 1956 there was a demonstration for higher wages by 15,000 workers from the Poznan locomotive factory. The next day troops and tanks confronted tens of thousands of demonstrators demanding free elections and the withdrawal of Soviet troops from Poland; more than 50 people were killed.
34 (French): I would gladly be reassured. I believed in Stalin, I am so upset. And I fear for the GDR.
35 Phases of contraction and slackening, e.g. of the heart muscle, here applied to historical processes.

28 July
36 Hadwig Klemperer's dissertation was on the relation of Heinrich Mann's novel *Henri Quatre* to its sources and models.

19 August
37 On 17 August 1956, the West German Federal Constitutional Court, in response to a petition by the Federal Government, declared the KPD, the Communist Party of Germany (which had retained the old name because there had been no fusion of SPD and KPD in the Western zones of occupation) to be unconstitutional and ordered its dissolution; the Party's property – real estate, printing presses and 17 newspapers – was confiscated and 33 officials were arrested.
38 Refrain of the 'Solidarity Song' by Bertolt Brecht and Hanns Eisler.

20 August
39 Mátyás Rákosi (1892–1971), General Secretary of the Hungarian Communist Party (later Party of Hungarian Workers) 1945; the most powerful figure in Party and state 1949–53; replaced 1956 and fled to the USSR.

9 September
40 Lukács' study *The Historical Novel* was first published in Berlin in 1955.

1 October
41 Walter Jelski (1904–58), nephew of Victor Klemperer, eldest son of his sister Marta; lived with Eva and Victor Klemperer in Dresden 1922–23.
42 (Yiddish): scrounger, even beggar.

7 October
43 Samuel, Baron von Pufendorf (1632–94), legal scholar and historian; developed the Natural Law theory of Grotius; *De officio hominis et civis* is one of his two major works.
44 The Festschrift for Victor Klemperer's 75th birthday (9 October 1956), *Im Dienst der Sprache* (In the Service of Language), ed. by Horst Heintze and Erwin Silzer, published in Halle 1958. The first item is a catalogue of publications by Klemperer, listing 410 items.

45 *Aus fremden Zungen* (From Foreign Tongues) was a periodical.

25 October

46 On 23 October 1956 there was a mass demonstration for reforms; members of the state security service AVO, in particular, opened fire. On the following day Soviet troops intervened at the request of the First Secretary of the Central Committee, Ernö Gerö, but after the appointment of János Kádár as First Secretary and of Imre Nagy as Prime Minister negotiations led to the withdrawal of Soviet forces on 29th Oct.

30 October

47 On 29 October 1956, after a period of mounting tension and border clashes, Israeli units crossed the Egyptian border and advanced towards the Suez Canal. This was quickly followed by Anglo-French intervention to secure the canal, but US pressure subsequently forced the withdrawal of the English and French forces.

7 November

48 On Lion Feuchtwanger's drama *Widow Capet* (1956); printed in the 1957 Almanac of the Greifenverlag publishing house.

49 On 4 November 1956 János Kádár set up an alternative government in the eastern Hungarian town of Szolnok. He accused Imre Nagy of having increasingly surrendered power to 'counter-revolutionary elements'. This was the basis of his request for help to the Soviet army, which simultaneously advanced on Budapest; there was fierce fighting, which lasted until 16 November.

50 Kuba's text in *Neues Deutschland* of 28 October 1956 (under the heading 'Well-known Writers Give Their Views') included the sentence, 'If out of sheer self-criticism we drop our trousers, show our backside to the enemy, we should not be surprised if he hits it.'

51 Miklós Horthy (1868–1957), right-wing authoritarian ruler of Hungary after suppressing the Communists in 1920; joined the Rome–Berlin Axis in 1937 and brought Hungary into the German attack on the Soviet Union; overthrown by Hitler in 1944 as he was attempting to make a separate peace with the Allies. The renewed intervention of Soviet troops in Hungary on 4 November 1956 was based in part on the assertion that Arrow Cross (Hungarian Fascist Party before 1945) and Horthy supporters had to be prevented from seizing power.

15 November

52 Cardinal Jószef Mindszenty (1892–1975), Primate of Hungary 1945; condemned to life-imprisonment for high treason 8 February 1949; freed from prison by soldiers of the Hungarian army on 30 October 1956; sought refuge in the US embassy shortly after the Red Army advanced into Budapest. Mindszenty spent 15 years in the embassy compound before he was permitted to depart for Vienna.

12 December

53 Wolfgang Harich (1923–95), philosopher; professor at the HUB 1949–56, simultaneously editor at Aufbau Verlag; developed a conception of 'a special German path to Socialism' as well as of a 'peaceful (democratic Socialist) re-unification'; arrested 29 November 1956, sentenced to 10 years imprisonment in March 1957; amnestied 1964. Walter Janka (1914–95), publisher; joined KPD 1932, concentration camp 1933–5, participation in the Spanish Civil War (battalion commander); from 1941 exile in Mexico; director of the publishing house El Libro Libre; 1950 deputy, 1952 effective director of the Aufbau publishing house. Sentenced to a term of imprisonment at the same trial as Wolfgang Harich.

54 Kantorowicz had not, in fact, been arrested or interrogated.

22 December
55 The 'Comédie humaine', Balzac's great cycle of novels, the 'Rougon-Macquart', that of Zola.

1957

19 January
1 From 3–8 January 1957 a GDR government delegation headed by Otto Grotewohl negotiated with the Soviet leadership; the results included a Soviet credit to the GDR of 310 million roubles and a 30% increase in arms deliveries to the GDR in 1957.

1 February
2 Helmut Stimm (1917–87), Romance languages and literature scholar; professor in Saarbrücken 1957, Munich 1965.

27 February
3 I.e. Rousseau's *Social Contract*.
4 Josef Frings (1887–1972), Archbishop of Cologne 1942–69, Cardinal 1946.
5 Sartre's play was first published 1955, translated 1956.
6 In 1956–57 there was an ideological campaign against Bloch's 'philosophy of hope'. Bloch was forced to resign his chair in 1957.

1 March
7 The 1st of March was observed in the GDR as 'Day of the National People's Army'.

10 April
8 Czech state tourist agency.
9 (Yiddish): fellow.
10 (Hebrew): marriage canopy.
11 The High Rabbi Löw (actually Jehuda ben Betzalel, before 1525–1609), rabbi from 1573 mainly in Prague, focus of numerous legends e.g. that of the Golem.
12 (Latin): Out of the depths have I cried unto thee – the opening words of Psalm 130.

15 April
13 Rousseau's epistolary novel *Julie, ou la Nouvelle Héloise*, first published 1761.

15 May
14 Klemperer had converted to Protestantism in 1903, but had himself baptised once again in 1912.
15 After falling ill on active service on the Western Front, Klemperer was placed in the Catholic St Vincent Hospital in Paderborn.
16 In a posthumously published response to Stephan Hermlin's attack on his *Modern French Prose* there is the following anecdote: 'During the First World War I was convalescing in a very Catholic hospital in Catholic Paderborn, I was invited by an urbane priest to make use of the library of the arch–episcopal seminary. That would be of little help to me, I said, I was concerned with the history of the French Enlightenment. I should come nevertheless, he advised me, and truly I found shelves and the best editions of all the anti-clerical literature of the Enlightenment. He observed my surprise and smiling, said: "We have to know our enemies, after all"'

(*Briefe an Hermlin 1946–84*, ed. by Silvia Schlenstedt, Berlin 1985).

17 Francois de Salignac de la Mothe-Fénelon (1651–1715), French theologist and prose writer; critic of Louis XIV's absolutism.

18 *The Good Woman of Sezuan*, play by Bertolt Brecht; written 1938–42, first performed 1943.

19 On 9 May 1957, in the West German Parliament, CDU politician Heinrich von Brentano (1904–64), West German Foreign Minister 1955–61, said: '. . . I am certainly of the opinion that the late poetry of Herr Brecht can only be compared with that of Horst Wessel.' – Horst Wessel, an ex-student, petty criminal and Nazi storm trooper was injured in a fight in a working-class area of Berlin and died of his wounds (1931). He was turned into a martyr by the Nazis and a song he had written, 'SA marschiert' became (in)famous as the 'Horst Wessel Lied'.

30 May

20 I.e. when the Klemperers were on the run after the bombing of Dresden.

18 June

21 In West Germany until at least the 1970s 'Middle Germany' (Mitteldeutschland) was the standard term for the GDR. (Since the Oder-Neisse Line was not officially recognised, the eastern German provinces which had been incorporated into Poland and the USSR in 1945 were described as 'East Germany'.)

23 June

22 On 23 June 1957 local elections were held in the GDR; once again a Unified List of the National Front was presented for approval or rejection.

1 July

23 Helmut Haress, Russian instructor at Halle University; in June 1957 he and several other doctoral students in Slavonic and Romance languages at Halle and Leipzig Universities were arrested; in 1958 he was sentenced to 20 months imprisonment for 'aiding and abetting treason'.

10 August

24 On 7–14 August 1957 a Soviet delegation led by Nikita S. Khrushchev and Anastas Mikoyan visited the GDR.

25 The establishment of a confederation of both German states, as an initial step towards re-unification was first proposed by Walter Ulbricht in an interview with *Neues Deutschland* on 31 December 1956; it was repeated by Otto Grotewohl in the Volkskammer on 27 July 1957.

26 The third elections to the West German Parliament to be held on 15 September 1957.

27 (Latin): From the deepest depths – paraphrase of the beginning of Psalm 130.

17 August

28 Nikolai Bulganin was not excluded from the Politburo and removed from his post as Prime Minister until 1958. On 4 July 1957 Malenkov, Molotov, Kaganovich and Shepilov were excluded from the leading Party bodies of the CPSU and removed from their government posts; they were accused of having opposed the Party line, particularly with respect to economic reforms and the policy of peaceful co-existence.

29 In fact Klemperer had to stop work on the second vol. of his *History of French Literature* after Jews were forbidden to use public libraries (see *I Shall Bear Witness*, 3 December 1938).

31 August

30 G. W. Pabst's 1931 film version of the Brecht–Weill musical play.

31 Friedrich Dürrenmatt (1921–90), Swiss dramatist, novelist, essayist. *The Judge and His Hangman* was first published in 1952.

20 September

32 (Russian): Peter the Great, after the Tsar (1672–1725).

6 October

33 Jean-Richard Bloch (1884–1947), French writer; participated in the 'Clarté' movement led by Henri Barbusse; co-founder, with Romain Rolland, of the periodical *L'europe*; in Soviet exile 1941–5.

34 Rudolf Besthorn (1909–84), Romance languages and literature scholar; lecturer in Greifswald 1953, professor 1964–75.

35 The article (24 August 1957) reviewed three of Victor Klemperer's works: his *History of French Literature in the 19th and 20th Centuries (1800–1925)*; his *Modern French Poetry* and the collection of essays *Before 33 – After 45*.

36 On 4 October 1957 the era of space travel was inaugurated with the launch by the USSR of the first man-made satellite 'Sputnik I'. (It weighed 83.6 kg and had a diameter of 0.58 metres.)

10 October

37 In July 1957 Walter Janka, the former director of the Aufbau publishing house, was sentenced to 5 years imprisonment for supposedly 'forming a counter-revolutionary group' at the publishing house and the weekly newspaper *Sonntag*. Klaus Gysi headed Aufbau 1957–66.

23 October

38 A fierce attack on Bloch as representative of a 'human' or 'ethical' Socialism.

39 On 15 October 1957 the GDR and Yugoslavia agreed to enter into diplomatic relations; West Germany thereupon for the first time put the Hallstein Doctrine into effect. This declared that any state entering into diplomatic relations with the GDR was committing an unfriendly act towards West Germany. It therefore broke off diplomatic relations with Yugoslavia.

6 November

40 One month after the launch of the first satellite, the USSR launched Sputnik II, a second, much larger craft (508 kg), into space, putting the first living being, the dog Laika, into orbit around the earth.

41 On 26 October 1957 Defence Minister Georgi K. Zhukov, who had become a full member of the Central Committee of the CPSU only a few months before, was replaced by Rodion Malinovski as Minister of Defence.

42 On 4 November 1957 the USSR withdrew from the UN Disarmament Commission and its subcommissions, after the Soviet proposal to set up a commission of all UN members had not met with approval.

43 I.e. the 40th anniversary of the Russian October Revolution, on 7 November 1957.

44 *Life of Galileo* (written 1938–9) by Bertolt Brecht; the 3rd version of the play was premièred by the Berliner Ensemble on 15 January 1957.

12 December

45 By way of an alteration of the Passport Law, adopted by the Volkskammer, 11 December 1957, it became possible to punish illegal departure from the GDR as 'flight from the

Republic', carrying a sentence of up to three years. A change of the penal code created the new criminal offences of treason, espionage and collection of information (all carrying heavy penalties).

13 December

46 I.e. the foreword to *Denkwürdigkeiten aus dem Leben des Herrn de Voltaire*, a translation of a volume of memoirs by Voltaire.
47 Gerhard Zwerenz (b. 1925), writer; studied philosophy with Bloch in Leipzig from 1952; journalism from 1956; escaped arrest by fleeing to West Berlin 1957. In an article 'Thoughts are free. Ernst Bloch and his opponents', in the *Telegraf* of 11 October 1957, Zwerenz summarised Bloch's philosophy and his opposition to Walter Ulbricht, the embodiment of Stalinist politics. Zwerenz went on to become a well-known writer, journalist and media personality in West Germany.

22 December

48 Molière's *The School for Wives*.
49 *La Garçonne*, French film based on the novel of the same name by Victor Margueritte (1922); Chaplin's film *A King in New York*, a satire of McCarthyism.
50 (French): European Meeting on the German Question.
51 Colloquium at the invitation of the Committee of French Resistance Fighters chaired by Senator J. Debu-Bridel.
52 Martin Niemöller (1892–1984), Protestant theologian (submarine commander First World War); pastor 1924; leading member of the Confessing Church (which resisted Nazi incorporation); imprisonment and concentration camp 1937. After 1945 held important posts in the Protestant Church. Was fiercely attacked in some quarters because of his assignment of guilt to the Protestant Church because of its attitude to Nazism and because of his critical position on nuclear arms.

1958

24 January

1 Alluding to the notion that an evil deed comes back on its perpetrator. Central motif of the Greek myths (or plays) about Atreus.
2 Johannes Heinz Horn (1909–58), philosopher; lecturer in logic University of Leipzig 1956; Deputy Director of the Institute of Philosophy and Secretary of the SED party group. Inaugurated the campaign against Bloch in spring 1957 with a lengthy report to the University Party officials. Bloch was forcibly retired later that year. Horn committed suicide 8 February 1958.

25 January

3 He read, among others, the stories 'Metamorphosis' and 'A Hunger Artist'.
4 *Jephta and his Daughters*, novel by Feuchtwanger first published 1957.

26 January

5 (Latin): Here and always and everywhere: between stools. Klemperer often used his own construction 'inter sedia' instead of the grammatically correct 'inter sedes'. (The description of himself as being 'between stools' is frequently repeated in the postwar diaries.)
6 *Fear and Loathing in the Third Reich* (1938), by Bertolt Brecht. A sequence of scenes examining varieties of behaviour under the dictatorship.

14 February

7 At the 35th meeting of the Central Committee of the SED, 3–6 February 1958, Fred Oelssner (until then the Party's chief ideologist) and Karl Schirdewan (1907–98), Secretary for Cadre Questions, were expelled from the Politburo for 'breaching the discipline of the Politburo' and 'fractionism'. Schirdewan and Ernst Wollweber (1898–1967), Minister of State Security July 1953–7, were also expelled from the Central Committee. The group had advocated a continuation of de-Stalinisation and a 'slowing down of the pace of Socialist construction'; a letter to the base organisations accused them of 'opportunism'.

8 *Amphitryon* 38 (1928), comedy by Jean Giraudoux.

15 February

9 *Der Müller von Sanssouci*, comedy by Peter Hacks (b. 1928), dramatist, poet, essayist, author of children's books; moved from West to East Germany in 1955.

27 February

10 Not to be confused with the thematically related and overlapping introduction to Voltaire's *Memoirs* on the relationship of Voltaire and Frederick II (or Great) of Prussia.

26 March

11 The Classicist Erich Reitzenstein, who went to West Germany in 1958, and the plant physiologist and biochemist Kurt Mothes (1900–83), professor in Halle 1950–67.

14 May

12 (Latin): An abbreviation (from Virgil's *Aeneid*, Book IV, line 265) of 'Exoriare aliquis nostris ex ossibus ultor' – May an avenger one day arise from my bones.

13 On 13 May 1958 French troops rebelled against the government in Paris; the leaders of the uprising demanded the appointment of General de Gaulle as head of government in order to maintain Algeria as part of France.

2 June

14 General Charles de Gaulle (1890–1970); after French defeat in 1940 the inspirational figure of the French resistance to Hitler; Prime Minister and Provisional President 1944–6. On 1 June 1958, thanks to the revolt of the army, entrusted by President Coty with forming a government. President December 1958.

15 On 28 May 1958 the Volkskammer approved the abolition of ration cards, to take effect from the following day; a uniform level of food prices was established and low wage earners were compensated for price rises with an increase in wages.

16 *Kuhle Wampe* (1932), film by Slatan Dudow and Bertolt Brecht about German workers during the Great Depression. Dudow, of Bulgarian origin, worked as a film-maker in East Germany from 1946.

23 June

17 Imre Nagy (1896–1953), Hungarian prime Minister 1953–5 and from 23 October 1956; after the suppression of the Hungarian Uprising in November 1956 he was abducted to Romania despite assurances of immunity. Brought back to Hungary in 1958 he was sentenced to death at a secret trial and executed on 16 June 1958 along with members of his 1956 government. The sentence was announced on 17 June 1958.

29 June

18 I.e. the anniversary of Eva Klemperer's death.

5 July
19 The 5th Party Congress of the SED in Berlin, 10–16 July 1958.
20 Rudolf Brummer, who had recently left the GDR for the West, was one of the contributors to the Festschrift for Klemperer's 75th birthday.

10 July
21 *Amphitryon* (1935), directed by Reinhold Schünzel; a musical comedy, now recognised as a classic, which used a classical setting to poke fun at the regimentation and ideology of Nazism. Schünzel left Germany shortly afterwards.

13 July
22 *The Mother. Life of the Revolutionary Pelagea Vlassova of Tver (after the novel of Maxim Gorki)*, play (1932) by Bertolt Brecht with the collaboration of Günther Weisenborn and Slatan Dudow, music by Hanns Eisler.

16 July
23 On 14 July members of the armed forces overthrew the monarchy in Baghdad and declared Iraq a republic. The Lebanese president, Shamoun, asked for American help and US marines landed the following day.

22 July
24 (French): superficial journalism.
25 Ralf Schröder (b. 1927), Slavonic studies scholar; assistant lecturer at Greifswald 1951, Leipzig 1953. Arrested June 1957; at the end of 1958 sentenced to 10 years imprisonment for advocating reforms ('treason'); released 1964. Editor at the Volk & Welt publishing house; edited and introduced numerous works of Russian-Soviet literature.
26 (Latin): revived.

2 August
27 The Buchenwald Memorial on the Ettersberg near Weimar.

17 August
28 *Welt und Wort* was a literary periodical published in Tübingen, West Germany, 1946–73.
29 I.e. a review of the first volume of the *History of French Literature in the 18th Century* and the two volumes of the *History of French Literature in the 19th and 20th Centuries*.

21 August
30 Georg Klemperer's wife was Maria, née Umber. His brother-in-law was Friedrich Umber (1871–1946), internist, director of the Berlin Westend Municipal Hospital.
31 Janet Klemperer.
32 I.e. Felix Klemperer's wife Elisabeth, née Goldschmidt, known as Betty.

31 August
33 'Schach von Wuthenow' (1883); story by Theodor Fontane.

10 September
34 On 23 August 1958 the People's Republic of China began shelling the islands of Quemoy and Matsu, held by the Nationalist Chinese but close to the mainland, to assert their claim. On 15 September negotiations between the USA and the People's Republic began, with the aim of achieving a peaceful solution to the conflict.

19 September

35 The sculptor Fritz Cremer (1906–93) had made the group of figures of the memorial which was finally unveiled on 14 September 1957.
36 The stelae displayed reliefs depicting the history of Buchenwald concentration camp.

25 September

37 The election to the GDR Volkskammer had been called for 16 November 1958.
38 Lion Feuchtwanger's novel *False Nero*, first published in 1936, and Thomas Mann's novel *Lotte in Weimar*, 1939.

28 September

39 On 28 September 1958 there was a plebiscite in France on the new constitution, which provided for greatly increased powers for the President; in metropolitan France 79.25% of voters approved the presidential regime of the 5th Republic.

7 October

40 Friedrich Wilhelm Brekenfeld, hygienist, professor at the HUB 1954–8, simultaneously section head at the Health Ministry.

24 October

41 Paul Wandel was GDR ambassador to China 1958–61.
42 Ludwig Turek (1898–1975) and Ludwig Grünberg (1891–1972) were writers of working-class background who had committed themselves as 'proletarian revolutionary writers' before 1933 and later became prominent in the GDR.

27 October

43 Johannes R. Becher died on 11 October 1958.
44 *Die Geschwister Oppermann* – The Oppermanns – second volume of Lion Feuchtwanger's 'Waiting Room' trilogy.

12 November

45 Erwin Silzer.

20 November

46 André Chenier (1762–94); considered the greatest French poet of the 18th century; executed in the Terror just two days before the fall of Robespierre (he was the hero of an opera by Umberto Giordano).

26 December

47 (French): he is my voice.
48 Two trials were held in Halle. Those sentenced had supposedly formed part of an oppositional group – a complete fiction. The trial was part of the ongoing effort to crush and discourage initiatives for democratic reform in the GDR. Those sentenced, including the writer Erich Loest, got prison sentences of between 10 and 20 years.

31 December–1 January

49 Afterword to a planned edition of Marivaux's novel *La vie de Marianne* (Pierre Charlet de Chamblain de Marivaux, 1688–1763).
50 (Latin): Behind the rider sits black death; paraphrase of Horace *Odes III*, Ode 1, line 40 – 'Behind the rider sits black sorrow'.

1959

11 January
1 The reference is to Feuchtwanger's novel *Erfolg* (Success), first published 1930.
2 Published in 1959 in an edition of Voltaire's novels.

19 February
3 Five students were arrested at the end of January/beginning of February 1959. There was a show trial with charges similar to those with which the Halle and Leipzig students were indicted, except that the Dresden students were also accused of 'preparations to carry out bomb attacks'; they likewise received prison sentences.

12 March
4 The International Romance Languages Congress 1959 was due to be held in Lisbon at the end of March/beginning of April.
5 The planned volume of 'Essays from 50 Years' was never published.

25 March
6 Hero of the novel *Les Misérables*, by Victor Hugo.

28 April
7 (Latin): Here begins the tragedy. On the night of 28/29 March 1959 Klemperer suffered a major heart attack in the Hotel Elysée, Brussels, as he and his wife were en route to Lisbon. He was allowed to travel back to Dresden on 1 April and on 2 April Dr Schmeiser ordered an ECG and two weeks rest in bed.
8 (Latin): There follow H's notes. – Hadwig Klemperer had circulated a letter to friends and relatives informing them of the journey to Brussels, the course of the attack and the return journey.

29 April
9 'Der Fall Deruga' (1917); a crime story by Ricarda Huch.
10 Feuchtwanger's novel *Jud Süss* was first published in 1925.
11 Klemperer had been invited to give the main speech at the Feuchtwanger commemoration of the Academy of Arts.

9 May
12 *Die hässliche Herzogin Margarete Maultasch*, first published 1923.

11 May
13 In his curriculum vitae etc., Klemperer's eldest brother, Georg, tended to conceal the fact that his father was a rabbi (and hence Jewish), as in his doctoral thesis, where he is described as a 'country cleric'.
14 A double anniversary was celebrated at the end of 1960: 250 years since the founding of the Charité Hospital and 150 years since the founding of Berlin University.

17 May
15 From 11 May to 20 June and 13 July to 5 August 1959 the foreign ministers of the Four Powers met in Geneva. The Federal Republic of Germany and the German Democratic Republic were represented by observer delegations of equal status. The conference was adjourned without tangible achievements; the Western powers presented the maintenance of the status quo in Berlin as a success.

21 May

16 (Italian): never again.

1 June

17 *Wir Wunderkinder* (1958), directed by Kurt Hoffmann from the novel by Hugo Hartung; lyrics and music by Günter Neumann and Franz Grothe.

18 *The Forty Days of Musa Dagh* (1933). The subject is the genocide against the Armenians living in the Ottoman Empire, which took place during the First World War.

26 October

19 I.e. a wheelchair.

28 October

20 Novels by Theodor Fontane.

CHRONOLOGY

1881
Victor Klemperer born in Landsberg on the Warthe (today Gorzow Wielkopolski in Poland) on 9 October. (Father: Rabbi Dr Wilhelm Klemperer; mother: Henriette Klemperer née Franke)

1884
The family moves to Bromberg (today Bydgoszcz in Poland)

1890
The family moves to Berlin (to 20 Albrechtstrasse, in the old centre of the city). His father becomes second preacher of the Berlin Reform Congregation

1893
Attends the French Grammar School in Berlin

1896
Attends the Friedrich-Werdersche Grammar School
Family moves to 26 Winterfeldtstrasse in the Schöneberg district of Berlin

1897
Begins a commercial apprenticeship in the fancy goods export company of Löwenstein & Hecht at 2 Alexandrinnenstrasse

1900–1902
Attends the Royal Grammar School in Landsberg/Warthe; Final Examination

1902–1905
Studies philosophy, Romance and German philology in Munich, Geneva, Paris and Berlin

1905–1912
Journalist and writer in Berlin

1906
Marries Eva Schlemmer (pianist and musicologist)

1912
Takes up his studies again in Munich

1913
Takes his doctorate with Franz Muncker
Second stay in Paris; research on Montesquieu for his habilitation thesis (qualification as university teacher)

1914
Habilitation under Karl Vossler

1914–1915
Assistant at the University of Naples (as a private – unsalaried – lecturer of the University of Munich)
Montesquieu, 2 vols.

1915
Volunteer (serves at the Front from November 1915 until March 1916)

1916–1918
Censor in the book Examination Office of the Press Section of the Military Government of Lithuania, first in Kowno then in Leipzig

1919
Associate professor at the University of Munich

1920–1935
Professor at the Technical High School, Dresden

1923
Moderne Französische Prosa (Modern French Prose)

1925–1931
Die französische Literatur von Napoleon bis zur Gegenwart (French Literature from Napoleon to the Present) 4 vols. (new edition in 1956 under the title *Geschichte der französischen Literatur im 19. und 20. Jahrhundert* – History of French Literature in the 19th and 20th Centuries)

1926
Romanische Sonderart. Geistesgeschichtliche Studien (Romance Particularity. Studies in Intellectual History)

1929
Idealistische Literaturgeschichte. Grundsätzliche und anwendende Studien (Idealist Literary History. Basic and Applied Studies)
Moderne Französische Lyrik (Modern French Poetry)

1933
Pierre Corneille

1935
'Retired from his duties' in accordance with the Law to Re-establish a Professional Civil Service

1945–1947
Professor at the Technical University, Dresden

1947
LTI – Notizbuch eines Philologen (LTI – Notebook of a Philologist)

1947–1948
Professor at the University of Greifswald

1948–1960
Professor at the University of Halle

1950–1958
Deputy of the Volkskammer (People's Chamber)

1951
Eva Klemperer dies on 8 July

1951–1954
Professor at the University of Berlin

1951
Honorary doctor of the Technical High School, Dresden

1952
Marries Hadwig Kirchner

1953
Member of the German Academy of Sciences in Berlin

1954
Geschichte der französischen Literatur im 18. Jahrhundert, Bd. I: Das Jahrhundert Voltaires
(History of French Literature in the 18th Century, vol. I: The Century of Voltaire)

1956
Vor 33/Nach 45. Gesammelte Aufsätze (Before '33/After '45. Collected Essays)

1960
Victor Klemperer dies in Dresden on 11 February

1966
Geschichte der französischen Literatur im 18. Jahrhundert, Bd. II: Das Jahrhundert Rousseaus
(History of French Literature in the 18th Century, vol. II: The Century of Rousseau)

1989
Curriculum vitae. Erinnerungen 1881–1918 (Curriculum Vitae. Memoirs)

1995
Ich will Zeugnis ablegen bis zum letzten. Tagebücher 1933–1945 (I Shall Bear Witness unto the Last. Diaries 1933–1945)

1996

Und so ist alles schwankend. Tagebücher Juni bis Dezember 1945 (And so Everything is in the Balance. Diaries June–December 1945)

Leben sammeln, nicht fragen wozu und warum. Tagebücher 1918–1932 (Collecting Life, not asking What For and Why)

1999

So sitze ich denn zwischen allen Stühlen. Tagebücher 1945–1959 (The Lesser Evil: Diaries 1945–1959)

INDEX